# PRACTICAL ENGLISH USAGE

Michael Swan

# PRACTICAL
# ENGLISH
# USAGE

*Third Edition*

OXFORD
UNIVERSITY PRESS

# OXFORD
UNIVERSITY PRESS

Great Clarendon Street, Oxford OX2 6DP

Oxford University Press is a department of the University of Oxford.
It furthers the University's objective of excellence in research, scholarship,
and education by publishing worldwide in

Oxford New York

Auckland Cape Town Dar es Salaam Hong Kong Karachi
Kuala Lumpur Madrid Melbourne Mexico City Nairobi
New Delhi Shanghai Taipei Toronto

With offices in

Argentina Austria Brazil Chile Czech Republic France Greece
Guatemala Hungary Italy Japan Poland Portugal Singapore
South Korea Switzerland Thailand Turkey Ukraine Vietnam

OXFORD and OXFORD ENGLISH are registered trade marks of
Oxford University Press in the UK and in certain other countries

Database right Oxford University Press (maker)

First published 2005

ISBN: 978 0 19 442099 0 (hardback)
2015 2014 2013
15 14 13 12

ISBN: 978 0 19 4420983 ( paperback)
2015 2014 2013
15 14

Printed in China

This book is printed on paper from certified and well-managed sources.

*Dedication*

To John Eckersley, who first encouraged my interest in this kind of thing.

# Acknowledgements

I am grateful to all the people who have helped me with the preparation of this third edition. A large number of teachers in different countries were kind enough to respond to an enquiry asking how they felt *Practical English Usage* could be improved: their feedback was extremely helpful, and I am very much in their debt. I am also greatly indebted to David Baker, whose comments and suggestions have added very significantly to the accuracy and clarity of the book, and to Hideo Hibino and Kenji Kashino, who have contributed valuable advice on specific problems. Many other teachers and students – too many to name – have taken the trouble to suggest ways in which particular entries could be improved; their input has benefited the book considerably. My use of the internet as a source of instances of authentic usage has been greatly facilitated by the kind assistance of Hiroaki Sato, of Senshu University, Japan, who made available his excellent software tool KwiconGugle. I must also reacknowledge my debt to Jonathan Blundell, Norman Coe, Michio Kawakami, Michael Macfarlane, Nigel Middlemiss, Keith Mitchell, Catherine Walter, Gareth Watkins, and the many other consultants and correspondents whose help and advice with the preparation of the first and second editions continue as an important contribution to the third.

Any pedagogic grammarian owes an enormous debt to the academic linguists on whose research he or she is parasitic. There is not enough space to mention all the scholars of the last hundred years or so on whose work I have drawn directly or indirectly, even if I had a complete record of my borrowings. But I must at least pay homage to two monumental reference works of the present generation: the *Comprehensive Grammar of the English Language*, by Quirk, Greenbaum, Leech and Svartvik (Longman 1985), and the *Cambridge Grammar of the English Language*, by Huddleston, Pullum and others (Cambridge University Press 2002). Their authoritative accounts of the facts of English structure and usage constitute an essential source of information for anyone writing pedagogic grammar materials today.

Finally, it is with particular pleasure that I express my gratitude, once again, to the editorial, design and production team at Oxford University Press, whose professional expertise is matched only by their concern to make an author's task as trouble-free as possible.

# Contents summary

# Introduction

## The purpose of this book

English, like all languages, is full of problems for the foreign learner. Some of these points are easy to explain – for instance, the formation of questions, the difference between *since* and *for*, the meaning of *after all*. Other problems are more tricky, and cause difficulty even for advanced students and teachers. How exactly is the present perfect used? When do we use past tenses to be polite? What are the differences between *at, on* and *in* with expressions of place? We can say *a chair leg* – why not *\*a cat leg*? When can we use the expression *do so*? When is *the* used with superlatives? Is *unless* the same as *if not*? What are the differences between *come* and *go*, between *each* and *every*, between *big, large* and *great*, between *fairly, quite, rather* and *pretty*? Is it correct to say *There's three more bottles in the fridge*? How do you actually say *3 × 4 = 12*? And so on, and so on.

*Practical English Usage* is a guide to problems of this kind. It deals with over 600 points which regularly cause difficulty to foreign students of English. It will be useful, for example, to a learner who is not sure how to use a particular structure, or who has made a mistake and wants to find out why it is wrong. It will also be helpful to a teacher who is looking for a clear explanation of a difficult language point. There is very full coverage of grammar, as well as explanations of a large number of common vocabulary problems. There are also some entries designed to clarify more general questions (e.g. formality, slang, the nature of standard English and dialects) which students and teachers may find themselves concerned with.

## Level

The book is intended for higher level students of English and for teachers. Being a reference book, it contains information at various levels, ranging from relatively simple points to quite advanced problems.

## Organisation

Problems are mostly explained in short separate entries: the book is more like a dictionary than a grammar in form. This makes it possible to give a clear complete treatment of each point, and enables the user to concentrate just on the question that he or she needs information about. Entries that deal with related topics (e.g. different uses of a tense) are grouped where this is useful, but can be read separately. In longer entries, basic information is generally given first, followed by more detailed explanations and discussions of less important points. Entries are arranged alphabetically by title and numbered in sequence. A comprehensive Index (pages 624–658) shows where each point can be found (see 'How to find things', page x).

## Approach and style

I have tried to make the presentation as practical as possible. Each entry contains an explanation of a problem, examples of correct usage, and (when this is useful) examples of typical mistakes. In some cases, an explanation may be somewhat different from that found in many learners' grammars; this is because the rules traditionally given for certain points (e.g. conditionals or indirect speech) are not always accurate or helpful. Explanations are, as far as possible, in simple everyday language. Where it has been necessary to use grammatical terminology, I have generally preferred to use traditional terms that are simple and easy to understand, except where this would be seriously misleading. Some of these terms (e.g. future tense) would be regarded as unsatisfactory by academic grammarians, but I am not writing for specialists. There is a dictionary of the terminology used in the book on pages xvii–xxv.

## The kind of English described

The explanations deal mainly with standard modern everyday British English, and are illustrated with realistic examples of current usage. Both explanations and examples have been thoroughly checked against large electronic databases ('corpora') of authentic spoken and written English. Stylistic differences (e.g. between formal and informal usage, or spoken and written language) are mentioned where this is appropriate. The few grammatical differences between British and American English are also described, and there is a good deal of information about other British-American differences, but the book is not intended as a systematic guide to American usage.

## Correctness

If people say that a form is not 'correct', they can mean several different things. They may for instance be referring to a sentence like *I have seen her yesterday, which normally only occurs in the English of foreigners. They may be thinking of a usage like less people (instead of fewer people), which is common in standard English but regarded as wrong by some people. Or they may be talking about forms like *ain't or 'double negatives', which are used in speech by many British and American people, but which do not occur in the standard dialects and are not usually written. This book is mainly concerned with the first kind of 'correctness': the differences between British or American English and 'foreign' English. However, there is also information about cases of divided usage in standard English, and about a few important dialect forms. (For a discussion of different kinds of English, see 308–309.)

## How important is correctness?

If someone makes too many mistakes in a foreign language, he or she can be difficult to understand, so a reasonable level of correctness is important. However, it is quite unnecessary to speak or write a language perfectly in order to communicate effectively (very few adults in fact achieve a perfect command of another language). Learners should aim to avoid serious mistakes (and a book like *Practical English Usage* will help considerably with this); but they should not become obsessed with correctness, or worry every time they make a mistake. Grammar is not the most important thing in the world!

## What this book does not do

*Practical English Usage* is not a complete guide to the English language. As the title suggests, its purpose is practical: to give learners and their teachers the most important information they need in order to deal with common language problems. Within this framework, the explanations are as complete and accurate as I can make them. However it is not always helpful or possible in a book of this kind to deal with all the details of a complex structural point; so readers may well find occasional exceptions to some of the grammatical rules given here. Equally, the book does not aim to replace a dictionary. While it gives information about common problems with the use of a number of words, it does not attempt to describe other meanings or uses of the words beside those points that are selected for attention.

## Other reference books

A book like this gives explanations of individual points of usage, but does not show how the separate points 'fit together'. Those who need a systematically organised account of the whole of English grammar should consult a book such as the *Oxford Learner's Grammar*, by John Eastwood (Oxford University Press), *A Student's Grammar of the English Language*, by Greenbaum and Quirk (Longman), or *Collins Cobuild English Grammar* (Collins). For a detailed treatment of English vocabulary, see the *Oxford Advanced Learner's Dictionary*, the *Cambridge Advanced Learner's Dictionary*, the *Longman Dictionary of Contemporary English*, the *Macmillan English Dictionary* or the *Collins Cobuild English Dictionary*.

## Changes in the third edition

English, like all languages, is changing, and British English is currently being quite strongly influenced by American English. Consequently, some usages which were unusual in standard British English a few decades ago have now become common – for example, the use of *like* as a conjunction (e.g. *like I do*), or the use of *Do you have . . .?* to ask about the immediate present (e.g. *Do you have a light?*). The third edition takes account of a number of changes of this kind, in order to give a fully up-to-date description of contemporary usage.

## How to find things

The best way to find information about a particular point is to look in the Index on pages 624–658. (The overview on pages xi–xvi is intended only to give a general picture of the topics covered in the book; it is not a complete guide to the contents.) Most points are indexed under several different names, so it is not difficult to locate the entry you need. For instance, if you want to know why we say *I'm not used to driving on the left* instead of *I'm not used to drive on the left*, you can find the number of the section where this is explained by looking in the index under 'used', 'be used', 'to' or '-ing forms'. (On the other hand, it would obviously not be helpful to look under 'drive': the rule is a general one about the use of *-ing* forms after *be used to*, not about the verb *drive* in particular.)

# Contents Overview

This overview gives a general picture of the topics covered in the book; it is not a complete guide to the contents. References are to entry numbers. To find information about a particular point, consult the Index on pages 624–658,

To find the answer to a specific question, see the Index ▶

To find the answer to a specific question, see the Index ▶

## other words and expressions

To find the answer to a specific question, see the Index ▶

# Language terminology

The following words and expressions are used in this book to talk about grammar and other aspects of language.

**abstract noun** (the opposite of a **concrete noun**) the name of something which we experience as an idea, not by seeing, touching etc. Examples: *doubt*; *height*; *geography*.

**active** An active verb form is one like *breaks, told, will help* (not like *is broken, was told, will be helped*, which are **passive** verb forms). The subject of an active verb is usually the person or thing that does the action, or that is responsible for what happens.

**adjective** a word like *green, hungry, impossible*, which is used when we describe people, things, events etc. Adjectives are used in connection with nouns and pronouns. Examples: *a **green apple**; **She's hungry**.*

**adverb** a word like *tomorrow, once, badly, there, also*, which is used to say, for example, when, where or how something happens. There are very many kinds of adverbs with different functions: see 22–27.

**adverb particle** a short adverb like *up, out, off*, often used as part of a phrasal verb (e.g. *clean **up**, look **out**, tell **off***).

**affirmative** an affirmative sentence is one that makes a positive statement – not a negative sentence or a question. Compare *I agree* (affirmative); *I don't agree* (negative).

**agent** In a passive sentence, the agent is the expression that says who or what an action is done by. Example: *This picture was probably painted by **a child**.*

**article** *A, an* and *the* are called 'articles'. *A/an* is called the 'indefinite article'; *the* is called the 'definite article'.

**aspect** Grammarians prefer to talk about progressive and perfective aspect, rather than progressive and perfect tense, since these forms express other ideas besides time (e.g. continuity, completion). However, in this book the term *tense* is often used to include aspect, for the sake of simplicity.

**attributive** Adjectives placed before nouns are in 'attributive position'. Examples: *a **green** shirt; my **noisy** son*. See also **predicative**.

**auxiliary verb** a verb like *be, have, do* which is used with another verb to make tenses, passive forms etc. Examples: *She **was** writing; Where **have** you put it?* See also **modal auxiliary verb**.

**clause** a part of a sentence which contains a subject and a verb, usually joined to the rest of a sentence by a conjunction. Example: *Mary said that **she was** tired.* (The word *clause* is also sometimes used for structures containing participles or infinitives with no subject or conjunction. Example: ***Not knowing what to do**, I telephoned Robin.*)

**cleft sentence** a sentence in which special emphasis is given to one part (e.g. the subject or the object) by using a structure with *it* or *what*. Examples: *It was you that caused the accident; What I need is a drink.*

**collective noun** a singular word for a group. Examples: *family; team.*

**comparative** the form of an adjective or adverb made with *-er* (e.g. *older, faster*); also the structure *more* + adjective/adverb, used in the same way (e.g. *more useful, more politely*).

**complement**   (1) a part of a sentence that gives more information about the subject (after *be, seem* and some other verbs), or, in some structures, about the object. Examples: *You're **the right person to help**; She looks **very kind**; They elected him **President**.*
(2) a structure or words needed after a noun, adjective, verb or preposition to complete its meaning. Examples: *the intention **to travel**; full **of water**; try **phoning**; down **the street**.*

**compound**   a compound noun, verb, adjective, preposition etc is one that is made of two or more parts. Examples: *bus driver; get on with; one-eyed.*

**concrete noun** (the opposite of an **abstract noun**)   the name of something which we can experience by seeing, touching etc. Examples: *cloud; petrol; raspberry.*

**conditional**   (1) a verb form made by using the auxiliary *would* (also *should* after *I* and *we*). Examples: *I would run; She would sing; We should think.*
(2) a clause or sentence containing *if* (or a word with a similar meaning), and perhaps containing a conditional verb form. Examples: *If you try you'll understand; I should be surprised if she knew; What would you have done if the train had been late?*

**conjunction**   a word like *and, but, although, because, when, if,* which can be used to join clauses together. Example: *I rang **because I was worried**.*

**consonant**   for example, the letters *b, c, d, f, g* and their usual sounds (see phonetic alphabet, page xxx). See also **vowel**.

**continuous**   the same as **progressive**.

**contraction**   a short form in which a subject and an auxiliary verb, or an auxiliary verb and the word *not*, are joined together into one word. Contractions are also made with non-auxiliary *be* and *have*. Examples: *I'm; who've; John'll; can't.*

**co-ordinate clause**   one of two or more main or subordinate clauses of equal 'value' that are connected. Examples: ***Shall I come to your place** or **would you like to come to mine**?; **It's cooler today** and **there's a bit of a wind**; she said **that it was late** and **that she was tired**.* See also **main clause, subordinate clause**.

**copular verb**   the same as **link verb**.

**countable noun**   a noun like *car, dog, idea,* which can have a plural form, and can be used with the indefinite article *a/an*. See also **uncountable noun**.

**declarative question**   a question which has the same grammatical form as a statement. Example: *That's your girlfriend?*

**definite article**   *the.*

**defining relative**   see **identifying relative**.

**demonstrative**   *this, these, that, those.*

**determiner**   one of a group of words that begin noun phrases. Determiners include *a/an, the, my, this, each, either, several, more, both, all.*

**direct object**   see **object**.

**direct speech**   speech reported 'directly', in the words used by the original speaker (more or less), without any changes of tense, pronouns etc. Example: *She looked at me and said '**This is my money**'.* See also **indirect speech**.

**discourse marker**   a word or expression which shows the connection between what is being said and the wider context. A discourse marker may, for example, connect a sentence with what comes before or after, or it may show the speaker's attitude to what he/she is saying. Examples: *on the other hand; frankly; as a matter of fact.*

**duration**   how long something lasts. The preposition *for* can be used with an expression of time to indicate duration.

**ellipsis**   leaving out words when their meaning can be understood from the context. Examples: *(It's a) Nice day, isn't it?*; *It was better than I expected (it would be)*.

**emphasis**   giving special importance to one part of a word or sentence (for example by pronouncing it more loudly; by writing it in capital letters; by using *do* in an affirmative clause; by using special word order).

**emphatic pronoun**   reflexive pronoun (*myself, yourself* etc) used to emphasise a noun or pronoun. Examples: *I'll tell him **myself**; I wouldn't sell this to the king **himself***. See also **reflexive pronoun**.

**ending**   something added to the end of a word, e.g. *-er, -ing, -ed*.

**first person**   see **person**.

**formal**   the style used when talking politely to strangers, on special occasions, in some literary writing, in business letters, etc. For example, *commence* is a more formal word than *start*.

**frequency**   Adverbs of frequency say how often something happens. Examples: *often; never; daily; occasionally*.

**fronting**   moving a part of a clause to the beginning in order to give it special emphasis. Example: ***Jack** I like, but **his wife** I can't stand*.

**full verb**   see **main verb**.

**future**   a verb form made with the auxiliary *shall/will* + infinitive without *to*. Examples; *I **shall arrive**; **Will** it **matter?***

**future perfect**   a verb form made with *shall/will* + *have* + past participle. Example: *I **will have finished** by lunchtime*.

**future progressive** (or **future continuous**)   a verb form made with *shall/will* + *be* + ...*ing*. Example: *I **will be needing** the car this evening*.

**gender**   the use of different grammatical forms to show the difference between masculine, feminine and neuter, or between human and non-human. Examples: *he; she; it; who; which*.

**gerund**   the form of a verb ending in *-ing*, used like a noun (for example, as the subject or object of a sentence). Examples: ***Smoking** is bad for you; I hate **getting** up early*. See also **present participle**.

**gradable**   *Pretty, hard* or *cold* are gradable adjectives: things can be more or less *pretty, hard* or *cold*. Adverbs of degree (like *rather, very*) can be used with gradable words. *Perfect* or *dead* are not gradable words: we do not usually say that something is *more* or *less perfect*, or *very dead*.

**grammar**   the rules that show how words are combined, arranged or changed to show certain kinds of meaning.

**hypothetical**   Some words and structures (e.g. modal verbs, *if*-clauses) are used for hypothetical situations – that is to say, situations which may not happen, or are imaginary. Example: *What would you do if you had six months free?*

**identifying** (or **defining**) **relative clause**   a relative clause which identifies a noun – which tells us which person or thing is being talked about. Example: *There's the woman **who tried to steal your cat**.* (The relative clause *who tried to steal your cat* identifies the woman – it tells us which woman is meant.) See also **non-identifying relative clause**.

**imperative**   the form of a verb used to give orders, make suggestions, etc. Examples: ***Bring** me a pen; **Have** a good holiday*.

**indefinite article**    *a/an.*

**indirect object**    see **object**.

**indirect speech**    a structure in which we report what somebody said by making it part of our own sentence (so that the tenses, word order, and pronouns and other words may be different from those used by the original speaker). Compare: *He said 'I'm tired'* (the original speaker's words are reported in direct speech) and *He said **that he was tired*** (the original speaker's words are reported in indirect speech).

**infinitive**    the 'base' form of a word (usually with *to*), used after another verb, after an adjective or noun, or as the subject or complement of a sentence. Examples: *I want **to go** home*; *It's easy **to sing***; *I've got a plan **to start** a business*; ***To err** is human, **to forgive** divine.*

**informal**    the style used in ordinary conversation, personal letters etc, when there is no special reason to speak politely or carefully. *I'll* is more informal than *I will*; *get* is used mostly in an informal style; *start* is a more informal word than *commence*.

**-ing form**    the form of a verb ending in *-ing*. Examples: *finding*; *keeping*; *running*. See also **gerund**, **present participle**.

**initial**    at the beginning. *Sometimes* is an adverb that can go in initial position in a sentence. Example: ***Sometimes** I wish I had a different job.*

**intensifying**    making stronger, more emphatic. *Very* and *terribly* are intensifying adverbs.

**interrogative**    Interrogative structures and words are used for asking questions. In an interrogative sentence, there is an auxiliary verb (or non-auxiliary *be*) before the subject (e.g. *Can you swim*?; *Are you ready*?). *What, who* and *where* are interrogative words.

**intonation**    the 'melody' of spoken language: the way the musical pitch of the voice rises and falls to show meaning, sentence structure or mood.

**intransitive**    An intransitive verb is one that cannot have an object or be used in the passive. Examples: *smile*; *fall*; *come*; *go*.

**inversion**    a structure in which an auxiliary or other verb comes before its subject. Examples: *Never **had she** seen such a mess*; *Here **comes John**.*

**irregular**    not following the normal rules. or not having the usual form. An irregular verb has a past tense and/or past participle that does not end in *-ed* (e.g. *swam, taken*); *children* is an irregular plural.

**link verb** (or **copular verb**)    *be, seem, feel* and other verbs which link a subject to a complement that describes it. Examples: *My mother **is** in Jersey*; *He **seems** unhappy*; *This **feels** soft.*

**main clause, subordinate clause**    Some sentences consist of a main clause and one or more subordinate clauses. A subordinate clause acts like a part of the main clause (e.g. like a subject, or an object, or an adverbial). Examples: ***Where she is** doesn't matter* (the subordinate clause *Where she is* is the subject of the main clause); *I told you **that I didn't care*** (the subordinate clause *that I didn't care* is the direct object in the main clause); *You'll find friends **wherever you go*** (the subordinate clause *wherever you go* acts like an adverb in the main clause: compare *You'll find friends **anywhere***).

**main verb** (or **full verb**)    A verb phrase often contains one or more auxiliary verbs together with a main verb. The main verb is the verb which expresses the central meaning; auxiliary verbs mostly add grammatical information (for instance they may show that a verb is progressive, future, perfect or passive). Examples: *is **going**; will **explain**; has **arrived**; would have been **forgotten**.*

**manner**    an adverb of manner describes how something happens. Examples: *well; suddenly; fast.*

**mid-position**    If an adverb is in mid-position in a sentence, it is with the verb. Example: *I have **never** been to Africa.*

**misrelated participle** (also called **hanging** or **dangling participle**)    a participle which appears to have a subject which is not its own. Example: ***Looking** out of the window, the mountains appeared very close.* (This seems to say that the mountains were looking out of the window.) The structure is usually avoided in careful writing because of the danger of misunderstanding.

**modal auxiliary verb**    one of the verbs *can, could, may, might, must, will, shall, would, should, ought.*

**modify**    An adjective is said to 'modify' the noun it is with: it adds to or defines its meaning. Examples: *a **fine** day; my **new** job.* An adverb can modify a verb (e.g. *run **fast***), an adjective (e.g. ***completely** ready*) or other words or expressions. In ***sports** car*, the first noun modifies the second.

**negative**    a negative sentence is one in which the word *not* is used with the verb. Example: *I **didn't** know.*

**nominal relative clause**    a relative clause (usually introduced by *what*) which acts as the subject, object or complement of a sentence. Example: *I gave him **what he needed**.*

**non-affirmative** (also called **non-assertive**)    The words *some, somebody, somewhere* etc are used most often in affirmative sentences. In other kinds of sentence they are often replaced by *any, anybody, anywhere* etc. Words like *any, anybody* etc are called 'non-affirmative' or non-assertive' forms. Other non-affirmative forms are *yet* and *ever.*

**non-identifying** (or **non-defining**) **relative clause**    a relative clause which does not identify the noun it refers to (because we already know which person or thing is meant). Example: *There's Hannah Smith, **who tried to steal my cat**.* (The relative clause, *who tried to steal my cat*, does not identify the person – she is already identified by the name *Hannah Smith*.) See also **identifying relative clause**.

**noun**    a word like *oil, memory, arm*, which can be used with an article. Nouns are most often the names of people or things. Personal names (e.g. *George*) and place names (e.g. *Birmingham*) are called 'proper nouns'; they are usually used without articles.

**noun phrase**    a group of words (e.g. article + adjective + noun) which acts as the subject, object or complement in a clause. Example: *the last bus.*

**number**    the way in which differences between singular and plural are shown grammatically. The differences between *house* and *houses, mouse* and *mice, this* and *these* are differences of number.

**object**    a noun phrase or pronoun that normally comes after the verb in an active clause. The direct object most often refers to a person or thing (or people or things) affected by the action of the verb. In the sentence *Take **the dog** for a walk*, *the dog* is the direct object. The indirect object usually refers to a person (or people) who receive(s) the direct object. In the sentence *Ann gave **me** a watch*, the indirect object is *me*, and the direct object is *a watch*. See also **subject**.

**participle**    see **present participle** and **past participle**.

**participle clause**    a clause-like structure which contains a participle, not a verb tense. Examples: ***Discouraged by his failure**, he resigned from his job*; ***Having a couple of hours to spare**, I went to see a film*.

**passive**    A passive verb form is made with *be* + past participle. Examples: *is broken*; *was told*; *will be helped* (but not *breaks, told, will help*, which are active verb forms). The subject of a passive verb form is usually the person or thing that is affected by the action of the verb. Compare: *They sent Lucas to prison for five years* (active) and *Lucas was sent to prison for five years* (passive). See also **active**.

**past participle**    a verb form like *broken, gone, stopped*, which can be used to form perfect tenses and passives, or as an adjective. (The meaning is not necessarily past, in spite of the name.)

**past perfect**    a verb form made with *had* + past participle. Examples: *I **had forgotten**; The children **had arrived**; She **had been working**; It **had been raining***. The first two examples are simple past perfect; the last two (with *had been* + . . .*ing*) are past perfect progressive (or continuous).

**past progressive (or continuous)**    a verb form made with *was/were* + . . .*ing*. Examples: *I **was going**; They **were stopping***.

**past simple**    see **simple past**.

**perfect**    a verb form made with the auxiliary *have* + past participle. Examples: *I **have forgotten**; She **had failed**; **having arrived**; to **have finished***.

**perfect conditional**    *should/would have* + past participle. Examples: *I **should/ would have agreed**; He **would have known***.

**perfect infinitive**    *(to) have* + past participle. Example: *to **have arrived***.

**person**    the way in which, in grammar, we show the difference between the person(s) speaking (*first person*), the person(s) spoken to (*second person*), and the person, people or thing(s) spoken about (*third person*). The differences between *I* and *you*, or between *am, are* and *is*, are differences of person.

**personal pronouns**    the words *I, me, you, he, him* etc.

**phrase**    two or more words that function together as a group. Examples: *dead tired; the silly old woman; would have been repaired; in the country*.

**phrasal verb**    a verb form that is made up of two parts: verb + adverb particle. Examples: *fill up; run over; take in*.

**plural**    grammatical form used to refer to more than one person or thing. Examples: *we; buses; children; are; many; these*. See also **singular**.

**possessive**    a form used to show possession and similar ideas. Examples: *John's; our; mine*.

**possessive pronoun**    *My, your, his, her* etc are possessive pronouns (they stand for 'the speaker's', 'the hearer's', 'that person's' etc). *Mine, yours, his, hers* etc are also possessive pronouns, for the same reason. *My, your* etc are used before nouns, so they are not only pronouns, but also determiners. (They are often called 'possessive adjectives', but this is not correct.) *Mine, yours* etc are used without following nouns.

**postmodifier**   a word that comes after the word which it modifies, e.g. *invited* in *The people **invited** all came late*. See also **premodifier**.

**predicative**   Adjectives placed after a verb like *be, seem, look* are in predicative position. Examples: *The house is **enormous**; She looks **happy***. See also **attributive**.

**prefix**   a form like *ex-, anti-* or *un-*, which can be added to the front of a word to give an additional or different meaning. Examples: ***ex**-wife, **anti**-British, **unhappy***. See also **suffix**.

**premodifier**   a word that comes before the word which it modifies, e.g. *invited* in *an **invited** audience*. See also **postmodifier**.

**preparatory subject, preparatory object**   When the subject of a sentence is an infinitive or a clause, we usually put it towards the end of the sentence and use the pronoun *it* as a preparatory subject. Example: ***It** is important **to get enough sleep***. *It* can also be used as a preparatory object in certain structures. Example: *He made **it** clear **that he disagreed***. *There* is used as a kind of preparatory subject in *there is . . .* and similar structures. Example: ***There** is somebody at the door*.

**preposition**   a word like *on, off, of, into*, normally followed by a noun or pronoun.

**prepositional verb**   a verb form that is made up of two parts: verb form + preposition. Examples: *insist on; care for; listen to*.

**present participle**   the form of a verb ending in *-ing*, used as an adjective, a verb or part of a verb. Examples: *a **crying** baby; **Opening** his newspaper, he started to read; She was **running***. (The meaning is not necessarily present, in spite of the name.) See also **gerund**.

**present perfect**   a verb form made with *have/has* + past participle. Examples: *I **have forgotten**; The children **have arrived**; I've **been working** all day; It has **been raining***. The first two examples are simple present perfect; the last two (with *have been* + *. . .ing*) are present perfect progressive (or present perfect continuous).

**present progressive** (or **continuous**)   a verb form made with *am/are/is* + *. . .ing*. Examples: *I **am going**; She **is staying** for two weeks*.

**present simple**   see **simple present**.

**progressive** (or **continuous**)   A verb form made with the auxiliary *be* + *. . .ing*. Examples: *to **be going**; We **were wondering**; I'll **be seeing** you*.

**progressive** (or **continuous**) **infinitive**   a form like *to **be going**; to **be waiting***.

**pronoun**   a word like *it, yourself, their*, which is used instead of a more precise noun or noun phrase (like *the cat, Peter's self, the family's*). The word *pronoun* can also be used for a determiner when this includes the meaning of a following noun which has been left out. Example: *I'll take **these***.

**proper noun** or **proper name**   a noun (most often with no article) which is the name of a particular person, place, organisation etc. Examples: *Andrew, Brazil; the European Union*.

**quantifier**   a determiner like *many, few, little, several*, which is used in a noun phrase to show how much or how many we are talking about.

**question tag**   an expression like *do you?* or *isn't it?*, consisting of an auxiliary verb (or non-auxiliary *be* or *have*) + pronoun subject, put on to the end of a sentence. Examples: *You don't eat meat, **do you**?; It's a nice day, **isn't it**?*

**reflexive pronoun**   *myself, yourself, himself* etc. Example: *I cut **myself** shaving this morning*. See also **emphatic pronoun**.

**regular**  following the normal rules or having the usual form. *Hoped* is a regular past tense; *cats* is a regular plural. See also **irregular**.

**relative clause**  a clause which modifies a noun, usually introduced by a relative pronoun like *who* or *which*. Example: *I like people **who** like me.* See also **identifying relative clause, non-identifying relative clause**.

**relative pronoun**  a pronoun used to connect a relative clause to its noun. *Who, whom, whose, which* and *that* can be used as relative pronouns, and sometimes also *when, where* and *why*. Examples: *There's the man **who** wants to buy my car; This is the room **which** needs painting; Do you remember the day **when** we met?*

**reply question**  a question (similar in structure to a question tag) used to reply to a statement, for instance to express interest. Example: *I've been invited to spend the weekend in London.~ **Have you**, dear?*

**second person**  see **person**.

**sentence**  a group of words that expresses a statement, command, question or exclamation. A sentence consists of one or more clauses, and usually has at least one subject and verb. In writing, it begins with a capital letter and ends with a full stop, question mark or exclamation mark.

**short answer**  an answer consisting of a subject and an auxiliary verb (or non-auxiliary *be* or *have*). Examples: *Has anybody phoned the police?~ **John has**.; Who's ready for more?~ **I am**.*

**simple past** (or **past simple**)  a past verb form that has no auxiliary verb in the affirmative. Examples: *I **stopped**; You **heard**; We **knew**.*

**simple present** (or **present simple**)  a present verb form that has no auxiliary verb in the affirmative. Examples: *He **goes** there often; I **know**; I **like** chocolate.*

**simple**  a verb form that is not progressive.

**singular**  a grammatical form used to talk about one person, thing, etc, or about an uncountable quantity or mass. Examples: *me; bus; water; is; much; this*. See also plural.

**slang**  a word, expression or special use of language found mainly in very informal speech, often in the usage of particular groups of people. Examples: *thick* (= stupid); *lose one's cool* (= get upset); *sparks* (= electrician).

**split infinitive**  a structure in which an adverb comes between *to* and the rest of the infinitive. Example: *to easily understand*. Some people consider split infinitives 'incorrect', but they are common in standard usage.

**standard**  A standard form of a language is the one that is most generally accepted for use in government, the law, business, education and literature. *I'm not* is standard English; *I ain't* is non-standard.

**statement**  a sentence which gives information; not a question. Examples: *I'm cold; Philip didn't come home last night.*

**stress**  the way in which one or more parts of a word, phrase or sentence are made to sound more important than the rest, by using a louder voice and/or higher pitch. In the word *particular*, the main stress is on the second syllable (*parTIcular*); in the sentence *Where's the new secretary?* there are three stresses (*WHERE'S the NEW SEcretary?*).

**strong form, weak form**  Certain words can be pronounced in two ways: slowly and carefully with the vowel that is written (strong form), or with a quicker pronunciation with the vowel /ə/ or /ɪ/ (weak form). Examples: *can* (/kæn/, /kən/), *was* (/wɒz/, /wəz/), *for* (/fɔː(r)/, /fə(r)/).

**subject**   a noun phrase or pronoun that normally comes before the verb in an affirmative clause. It often says (in an active clause) who or what does the action that the verb refers to. Examples: *Helen gave me a wonderful smile*; *Oil floats on water*. See also **object**.

**subjunctive**   a verb form (not very common in British English) used in certain structures. Examples: *If I **were** you . . .; It's important that he **be** informed immediately; We prefer that he **pay** in cash.*

**subordinate clause**   a clause which functions as part of another clause, for example as subject, object or adverbial in the main clause of a sentence. Examples: *I thought **that you understood**; **What I need** is a drink; I'll follow you **wherever you go***. See also **clause**, **main clause**.

**suffix**   a form like *-ology*, *-able* or *-ese*, which can be added to the end of a word to give an additional or different meaning. Examples: *climat**ology**; understand**able**; Chin**ese***. See also **prefix**.

**superlative**   the form of an adjective or adverb made with the suffix *-est* (e.g. *oldest, fastest*); also the structure *most* + adjective/adverb, used in the same way (e.g. *most intelligent, most politely*).

**swearword**   a taboo word used (usually with a change of meaning) to express strong emotion or emphasis. Example: *Fuck!*

**syllable**   The word *cat* has one syllable, *cattle* has two, *cataract* has three and *category* has four. A syllable normally has a vowel, and usually one or more consonants before and/or after it. Sometimes the consonant sounds *l*, *m* and *n* can act as syllables (for instance in the words *bottle* /'bɒtl/, *capitalism* /'kæpɪtəlɪzm/, *button* /'bʌtn/).

**taboo word**   a word (e.g. *fuck*) connected with a subject (such as sex) which is not talked about freely, so that some of its vocabulary is considered shocking. Taboo words are not used in formal speech or writing, and are avoided altogether by many people. See also **swearword**.

**tag**   a short phrase (e.g. pronoun subject + auxiliary verb) added on to the end of a sentence, especially in speech. Examples: *He likes to talk, **John does**; You can't swim, **can you**?; Very noisy, **those kids***. See also **question tag**.

**tense**   a verb form that shows the time of an action, event or state. Examples: *will go; is sitting; saw.*

**third person**   see **person**.

**transitive**   a transitive verb is one that can have an object. Examples: *eat (a meal); drive (a car); give (a present)*. See also **intransitive**.

**uncountable noun**   a noun which has no plural form and cannot normally be used with the article *a/an*. Examples: *mud; rudeness; furniture.*

**verb**   a word like *ask, wake, play, be, can*, which can be used with a subject to form the basis of a clause. In clauses, verbs often consist of an auxiliary verb + infinitive or participle (e.g. *will go; has spoken*). Most verbs refer to actions, events or states. See also **auxiliary verb**, **modal auxiliary verb**, **verb phrase**.

**verb phrase**   a verb that has more than one part. Example: *would have been forgotten.*

**vowel**   the letters *a, e, i, o, u* and their combinations, and their usual sounds (see phonetic alphabet, page xxx). See also **consonant**.

**weak form**   see **strong form**.

# *Don't say it!* 130 common mistakes

35 basic mistakes to avoid. Check in the sections to see why they're wrong.

| don't say/write | say/write | see section |
|---|---|---|
| Look – it rains. | Look – it's raining | 461-464 |
| It's often raining here. | It often rains here. | 461-464 |
| When I was 20 I was smoking. | When I was 20 I smoked. | 422 |
| I have seen Louis yesterday. | I saw Louis yesterday. | 456 |
| We're living here since April. | We've been living here since April. | 460 |
| I'll phone you when I will arrive. | I'll phone you when I arrive. | 212 |
| I'm not believing him. | I don't believe him. | 471 |
| I am born in Chicago. | I was born in Chicago. | 108 |
| My sister has 15 years. | My sister is 15 (years old). | 32 |
| I have cold in this house. | I am cold in this house. | 92 |
| I can to swim. | I can swim. | 121 |
| I must see the dentist yesterday. | I had to see the dentist yesterday. | 358 |
| I want go home. | I want to go home. | 613 |
| I came here for study English. | I came here to study English. | 289 |
| I drove there without to stop. | I drove there without stopping. | 298 |
| Where I can buy stamps? | Where can I buy stamps? | 480 |
| Is ready my new office? | Is my new office ready? | 480 |
| I'm no asleep. | I'm not asleep. | 382 |
| She looked, but she didn't see nothing. | ... she didn't see anything. / ... she saw nothing. | 370 |
| Where is station? | Where is the station? | 62 |
| My sister is photographer. | My sister is a photographer. | 62 |
| You speak a very good English. | You speak very good English. | 149 |
| The life is difficult. | Life is difficult. | 68 |
| I haven't got some free time today. | I haven't got any free time today. | 547 |
| Everybody were late. | Everybody was late. | 548 |
| It is more cold today. | It is colder today. | 137 |
| It's too much hot in this house. | It's too hot in this house. | 595 |
| The man which lives here is from Greece. | The man who lives here is from Greece. | 494 |
| The people in this town is very friendly. | The people in this town are very friendly. | 524 |
| She never listens me. | She never listens to me. | 449 |
| We went at the seaside on Sunday. | We went to the seaside on Sunday. | 80 |
| I like very much skiing. | I very much like skiing. / I like skiing very much. | 611 |
| This soup isn't enough hot. | This soup isn't hot enough. | 187 |
| I gave to her my address. | I gave her my address. | 610 |
| I have done a mistake. | I have made a mistake. | 160 |

## 35 mistakes that intermediate students often make. Check in the sections to see why they're wrong.

| don't say/write | say/write | see section |
|---|---|---|
| I promise I pay you tomorrow. | I promise I'll pay you tomorrow. | 217 |
| This is the first time I'm here. | ... the first time I've been here. | 591 |
| I've been here since three days. | ... for three days. | 208 |
| If I'll have time, I'll go home. | If I have time, ... | 257 |
| If I knew the price, I will tell you. | ... I would tell you. | 258 |
| He said me that he was Chinese. | He told me that he was Chinese. | 504 |
| She told me she has a headache. | She told me she had a headache. | 275 |
| There's the man that I work for him. | There's the man that I work for. | 494 |
| I've told you all what I know. | ... all (that) I know. | 494 |
| Although it was late, but she went out. | Although it was late, she went out. | 511 |
| You have better to see the doctor. | You had better see the doctor. | 230 |
| I use to play tennis at weekends. | I play tennis at weekends. | 604 |
| It can rain this evening. | It may/might/could rain ... | 345 |
| My parents wanted that I study. | My parents wanted me to study. | 283 |
| You must stop to smoke. | ... stop smoking. | 299 |
| I look forward to see you. | I look forward to seeing you. | 298 |
| I'm boring in the lessons. | I'm bored in the lessons. | 409 |
| He has much money. | He has a lot of / plenty of money. | 357 |
| Most of people agree with me. | Most people ... | 356 |
| I looked at me in the mirror. | I looked at myself ... | 493 |
| We waited during six hours. | ... for six hours. | 167 |
| I like eating chocolate milk. | ... milk chocolate. | 385 |
| Come here and look at that paper. | Come here and look at this paper. | 589 |
| We go there every Saturdays. | ... every Saturday. | 193 |
| Which is the biggest city of the world? | ... the biggest city in the world? | 139 |
| I'm thinking to change my job. | I'm thinking of changing my job. | 588 |
| Can you give me an information? | ... some information? | 148 |
| He's married with a doctor. | He's married to a doctor. | 449 |
| Can you mend this until Tuesday? | ... by Tuesday? | 602 |
| There's a hotel in front of our house. | ... opposite our house. | 402 |
| I like warm countries, as Spain. | ... warm countries, like Spain. | 326 |
| Please explain me what you want. | ... explain to me ... | 198 |
| When you come, take your bike. | ... bring your bike. | 112 |
| My brother has got a new work. | ... a new job. | 148 |
| He's Dutch, or better Belgian. | He's Dutch, or rather Belgian. | 157 |

Even advanced students make mistakes. Here are 35.
Check in the sections to see why they're wrong.

| don't say/write | say/write | see section |
|---|---|---|
| I'll ask you in case I need help. | I'll ask you if I need help. | 271 |
| I object to tell them my age. | I object to telling them my age. | 298 |
| I like the 60s music. | I like 60s music. / the music of the 60s. | 69 |
| ten thousand, a hundred and six | ten thousand, one hundred . . . | 389 |
| 'Who's that?' ~ 'He's John.' | . . . 'It's John.' | 428 |
| I don't like to be shouted. | I don't like to be shouted at. | 416 |
| It's ages since she's arrived. | It's ages since she arrived. | 522 |
| The police is looking for him. | The police are looking . . . | 524 |
| Prices are surely rising fast. | Prices are certainly rising fast. | 573 |
| I have big respect for her ideas. | . . . great respect . . . | 106 |
| I don't like nowadays fashions. | . . . today's/modern fashions. | 388 |
| She passed her exam, what surprised everybody. | . . . which surprised everybody. | 494 |
| I've good knowledge of German. | . . . a good knowledge of German. | 149 |
| Finally! Where have you been? | At last! . . . | 204 |
| I'll be home since 3 o' clock. | . . . from 3 o' clock. | 308 |
| We waited one and a half hour. | . . . one and a half hours. | 231 |
| It's time they go home. | It's time they went home. | 306 |
| I'll see you a few days later. | . . . in a few days. | 315 |
| All along the centuries, there have been wars. | All through the centuries . . . | 45 |
| I want a completely other colour. | . . . a completely different colour. | 54 |
| Let's go and have coffee to Marcel's. | . . . at Marcel's. | 80 |
| That's mine – I saw it at first! | . . . I saw it first! | 84 |
| Switzerland is among Germany, France, Austria and Italy. | . . . between Germany, France, Austria and Italy. | 105 |
| According to me, it's a bad film. | In my opinion / I think . . . | 8 |
| It was a too good party to miss. | . . . too good a party . . . | 14 |
| Whole Paris was celebrating. | The whole of Paris . . . | 40 |
| I nearly wish I'd stayed at home. | I almost wish . . . | 43 |
| One speaks Italian in my town. | We/They speak . . . | 396 |
| The girl wants an own room. | . . . her own room. | 405 |
| Couldn't you help me, please? | Could you . . .? / You couldn't . . ., could you? | 368 |
| I'll try to know when it starts. | I'll try to find out when it starts. | 313 |
| I love this so beautiful country. | . . . this country – it's so beautiful. | 538 |
| It's getting winter. | It's getting to be winter. | 223 |
| Our flat is decorated this week. | . . . is being decorated . . . | 412 |
| The Mont Blanc is 4808m high. | Mont Blanc is . . . | 70 |

Even *very* advanced students can make mistakes – nobody's perfect! Here are 25. Do you know why they're wrong? Check in the sections.

| don't say/write | say/write | see section |
|---|---|---|
| No doubt the world is getting warmer. | There is no doubt that the world is getting warmer. | 377 |
| I can't think of anybody whom to invite. | I can't think of anybody to invite. | 498 |
| My father, whom we hope will be out of hospital soon, ... | My father, who we hope ... | 498 |
| Would you follow me wherever I would go? | ... wherever I went? | 580 |
| We all have to live in the society. | ... in society. | 68 |
| The number of the unemployed is going up. | The number of unemployed ... | 70 |
| She was showing tiredness signs. | ... signs of tiredness. | 384 |
| She works the hardest when she's working for her family. | She works hardest ... | 141 |
| I'm thankful for your help. | I'm grateful ... | 582 |
| We talked about if it was ready. | ... about whether it was ready. | 453 |
| What live in those little holes? | What lives ... | 532 |
| Some people are interested, but the majority doesn't care. | ... the majority don't care. | 526 |
| It mustn't be the postman at the door. It's only 7 o' clock. | It can't be the postman ... | 359 |
| A third of the students is from abroad. | ... are from abroad. | 389 |
| Except Angie, everybody was there. | Except for Angie ... | 194 |
| I wish you felt / would feel better tomorrow. | I hope you feel ... | 630 |
| The train may be late, as it happened yesterday. | ... as happened yesterday. | 581 |
| When I wrote my letters, I did some gardening. | When I had written ... | 424 |
| When I had opened the door, the children ran in. | When I opened ... | 424 |
| Stefan can never return back to his country. | ... return to his country. / ... go back to his country. | 87 |
| Will you go and see me when I'm in hospital? | ... come and see me ... | 134 |
| May you go camping this summer? | Do you think you'll go ... | 339 |
| My cousin works for the NATO. | ... for NATO. | 2 |
| My wife will be angry unless I'm home by 7.00. | ... if I'm not home ... | 601 |
| We were poured water on. | We had water poured on us. / Water was poured on us. | 416 |

# Phonetic alphabet

It is necessary to use a special alphabet to show the pronunciation of English words, because the ordinary English alphabet does not have enough letters to represent all the sounds of the language. The following list contains all the letters of the phonetic alphabet used in this book, with examples of the words in which the sounds they refer to are found.

## Vowels and diphthongs (double vowels)

iː seat /siːt/, feel /fiːl/

ɪ sit /sɪt/, in /ɪn/

e set /set/, any /'enɪ:/

æ sat /sæt/, match /mætʃ/

ɑː march /mɑːtʃ/, after /'ɑːftə(r)/

ɒ pot /pɒt/, gone /gɒn/

ɔː port /pɔːt/, law /lɔː/

ʊ good /gʊd/, could /kʊd/

uː food /fuːd/, group /gruːp/

ʌ much /mʌtʃ/, front /frʌnt/

ɜː turn /tɜːn/, word /wɜːd/

ə away /ə'weɪ/, collect /kə'lekt/, until /ən'tɪl/

eɪ take /teɪk/, wait /weɪt/

aɪ mine /maɪn/, light /laɪt/

ɔɪ oil /ɔɪl/, boy /bɔɪ/

əʊ no /nəʊ/, open /'əʊpən/

aʊ house /haʊs/, now /naʊ/

ɪə hear /hɪə(r)/, deer /dɪə(r)/

eə air /eə(r)/, where /weə(r)/

ʊə tour /tʊə(r)/, endure /ɪn'djʊə(r)/

## Consonants

p pull /pʊl/, cup /kʌp/

b bull /bʊl/, rob /rɒb/

f ferry /'ferɪ:/, life /laɪf/

v veri /'verɪ:/, live /lɪv/

θ think /θɪŋk/, bath /bɑːθ/

ð then /ðen/, with /wɪð/

t take /teɪk/, set /set/

d day /deɪ/, red /red/

s sing /sɪŋ/, rice /raɪs/

z zoo /zuː/, days /deɪz/

ʃ show /ʃəʊ/, wish /wɪʃ/

ʒ pleasure /'pleʒə(r)/, occasion /ə'keɪʒən/

tʃ cheap /tʃiːp/, catch /kætʃ/

dʒ jail /dʒeɪl/, bridge /brɪdʒ/

k case /keɪs/, take /teɪk/

g go /gəʊ/, rug /rʌg/

m my /maɪ/, come /kʌm/

n no /nəʊ/, on /ɒn/

ŋ sing /sɪŋ/, finger /'fɪŋgə(r)/

l love /lʌv/, hole /həʊl/

r round /raʊnd/, carry /'kærɪ:/

w well /wel/

j young /jʌŋ/

h house /haʊs/

The sign (') shows stress (see 554).

# 1   abbreviated styles

Some styles of writing and speech have their own special grammar rules, often because of the need to save space or time.

## 1   advertisements and instructions

Small ads and instructions often leave out articles, subject or object pronouns, forms of *be* and prepositions.

> *Single man looking for flat Oxford area. Phone 806127 weekends.*
>
> *Job needed urgently. Will do anything legal. Call 312654.*
>
> *Pour mixture into large saucepan, heat until boiling, then add three pounds sugar and leave on low heat for 45 minutes.*

## 2   notes

Informal notes, to-do lists, diary entries etc often follow similar rules.

> *Gone to hairdresser. Back 12.30.*
>
> *Book tickets     phone Ann     see Joe 11.00     meeting Sue lunch*

The same style is common in postcards, short informal letters and emails (see 147).

> *Dear Gran*
>
> *Watching tennis on TV. A good book. Three meals a day. No washing-up. Clean sheets every day. Everything done for me. Yes, you've guessed – in hospital!!*
>
> *Only went to doctor for cold – landed up in hospital with pneumonia!! If you have time please tell the others – would love some letters to cheer me up. Hope to see you.*
>
> *Love, Pam*

## 3   commentaries

Commentaries on fast-moving events like football matches also have their own kind of grammar. Auxiliaries and other less important verbs are often left out.

> *Goal kick ... And the score still Spurs 3, Arsenal 1 ... that's Pearce ... Pearce to Coates ... good ball ... Sawyer running wide ... Billings takes it, through to Matthews, Matthews with a cross, oh, and Billings in beautifully, a good chance there – and it's a goal!*

## 4   titles, notices etc

Titles, labels, headings, notices and slogans usually consist of short phrases, not complete sentences. Articles are often left out, especially in the names of buildings and institutions.

> *ROYAL HOTEL*
>
> *INFORMATION OFFICE*
>
> *MORE MONEY FOR NURSES!*

## 5   headlines

News headlines have their own special grammar and vocabulary. For details, see 240.

> *RECORD DRUGS HAUL AT AIRPORT: SIX HELD*
>
> *FOUR DIE IN M6 BLAZE*

For other rules about leaving words out ('ellipsis'), see 177–182.

# 2 abbreviations and acronyms

## 1 punctuation

We usually write abbreviations without full stops in modern British English. Full stops (AmE 'periods') are normal in American English.

*Mr (AmE Mr.) = Mister (not usually written in full)*
*kg (AmE kg.) = kilogram     Ltd = limited (company)*

## 2 initial-letter abbreviations

Some abbreviations are made from the first letters of several words. This often happens with the names of organisations.

*the BBC = the British Broadcasting Corporation*

These abbreviations are most often stressed on the last letter.

*the BBC /ðə biː biː 'siː/     the USA /ðə juː es 'eɪ/*

If one of these abbreviations has an article (*a/an* or *the*), the form and pronunciation of the article depend on the pronunciation of the first letter of the abbreviation. Compare:

– *an EU country*
   *a US diplomat /ə juː . . ./ (NOT ~~an US~~ . . .)*
– *a BA degree*
   *an MP /ən em . . ./ (NOT ~~a MP~~)*
– *the USA /ðə juː . . ./ (NOT ~~ðiː juː~~ . . ./)*
   *the RSPCA /ðiː ɑːr . . ./ (NOT ~~ðə ɑːr~~ . . ./)*

## 3 acronyms

Some initial-letter abbreviations are pronounced like words. These are often called *acronyms*. Articles are usually dropped in acronyms.

*UNESCO /juːˈneskəʊ/ (NOT ~~the UNESCO~~) = the United Nations Educational, Scientific and Cultural Organisation*

Note that not all initial-letter abbreviations are pronounced as words.

*the CIA /siː aɪ 'eɪ/ (NOT /ˈsɪə/)     the IRA /aɪ ɑːr 'eɪ/ (NOT /ˈaɪrə/)*

## 4 plurals

An apostrophe (') is sometimes used before the *s* in the plurals of abbreviations.

*MP's, CD's* OR (more often) *MPs, CDs.*

For abbreviations used in text messages (e.g. *hope 2 c u* for *hope to see you*), see 147.
For a list of common abbreviations, see a good dictionary.

# 3 [be] able

We use *able* especially in the structure *be able* + **infinitive**. This often has the same meaning as *can* (see 122). There is a negative form *unable*.

*Some people **are able to** / **can** walk on their hands.*
*I **am unable to** / **can't** understand what she wants.*

*Can* is preferred in the sense of 'know how to', and in expressions like *can see, can hear* etc (see 125).

***Can** you knit?* (More natural than *Are you able to knit?*)

*I **can see** a ship.* (More natural than *I am able to see a ship.*)
*Be able* is used in cases (e.g. future, present perfect) where *can/could* is not
grammatically possible because it has no infinitive or participles (see 121.1d).
　　*One day scientists **will be able** to find a cure for cancer.*
　　　　(NOT ...~~will can find~~...)
　　*What **have** you **been able** to find out?* (NOT *What ~~have you could~~...?*)
　　*I **might be able** to help you.* (NOT *~~I might can~~...*)
*Able* is not often followed by passive infinitives.
　　*He **can't be understood.*** (More natural than *He's not able to be understood.*)
For differences between *could* and *was able*, see 122.5, 123.2.

# 4　about and on

Compare:
– *a book for children **about** Africa and its peoples*
　*a textbook **on** African history*
– *a conversation **about** money*
　*a lecture **on** economics*
We use *about* to talk about ordinary, more general kinds of communication.
*On* suggests that a book, talk etc is more serious, suitable for specialists.

# 5　about to

*About* + **infinitive** (with *to*) means 'going to very soon'; 'just going to'.
　　*Don't go out now – we're **about to** have lunch.*
　　*I was **about to** go to bed when the telephone rang.*
*Not about to* can mean 'unwilling to'.
　　*I'm **not about to** pay 100 dollars for that dress.*

# 6　above and over

## 1　'higher than': *above* or *over*

*Above* and *over* can both mean 'higher than'. *Above* is more common with this
meaning.
　　*The water came up **above/over** our knees.*
　　*Can you see the helicopter **above/over** the palace?*

## 2　'not directly over': *above*

We use *above* when one thing is not directly over another.
　　*We've got a little house **above** the lake.* (NOT ...~~over the lake.~~)

## 3　'covering': *over*

We prefer *over* when one thing covers and/or touches another.
　　*There is cloud **over** the South of England.*
　　*He put on a coat **over** his pyjamas.*
We use *over* or *across* (see 9) when one thing crosses another.
　　*The plane was flying **over/across** Denmark.*
　　*Electricity cables stretch **over/across** the fields.*　　　　　　▶

### 4 measurements: *above*

*Above* is used in measurements of temperature and height, and in other cases where we think of a vertical scale.

*The temperature is three degrees **above** zero.*
*The summit of Everest is about 8000 metres **above** sea level.*
*She's well **above** average in intelligence.*

### 5 ages, speeds, 'more than': *over*

We usually use *over*, not *above*, to talk about ages and speeds, and to mean 'more than'.

*You have to be **over** 18 to see this film.*
*The police said she was driving at **over** 110 mph.*
*There were **over** 100,000 people at the festival.*

### 6 books and papers

In a book or paper, *above* means 'written before'.

*The **above** rules and regulations apply to all students.*
*For prices and delivery charges, see **above**.*

See *over* means 'look on the next page'.

*There are cheap flights at weekends: see **over**.*

The difference between *below* and *under* is similar. See 100.
For other meanings of these words, see a good dictionary.

# 7 accept and agree

Before an infinitive, we usually use *agree*, not *accept*.

*I **agreed to meet** them here.* (More normal than *I accepted to meet ...*)

# 8 according to

*According to X* means 'in X's opinion', 'if what X says is true'.

*According to Harry, it's a good film.*
*The train gets in at 8.27, **according to the timetable**.*

We do not usually give our own opinions with *according to*. Compare:

*According to Ann, her boyfriend is brilliant.*
    (= If what Ann says is true, ...)
*In my opinion, Ann's boyfriend is an idiot.* (NOT ~~According to me,~~ ...)

# 9 across, over and through

### 1 on/to the other side of (line): *across* and *over*

*Across* and *over* can both be used to mean 'on or to the other side of a line, river, road, bridge etc'.

*His village is just **across/over** the border.*
*See if you can jump **across/over** the stream.*

## 2 high things: *over* preferred

We prefer *over* to say 'on/to the other side of something high'.
*Why are you climbing **over** the wall?* (NOT ...~~across the wall?~~)

## 3 flat areas: *across* preferred

We usually prefer *across* to say 'on/to the other side of a flat area or surface'.
*He walked right **across** the desert.*
*It took them six hours to row **across** the lake.*

## 4 the adverb *over (to)*

Note that the adverb *over* has a wider meaning than the preposition *over*. We often use *over (to)* for short journeys.
*I'm going **over to** John's.    Shall we drive **over** and see your mother?*

## 5 *across* and *through*

The difference between *across* and *through* is like the difference between *on* and *in*. *Through*, unlike *across*, is used for a movement in a three-dimensional space, with things on all sides. Compare:
– *We walked **across** the ice.* (We were **on** the ice.)
   *I walked **through** the wood.* (I was **in** the wood.)
– *We drove **across** the desert.*
   *We drove **through** several towns.*

For *over* and *above*, see 6.
For *across from* (AmE), see 402.1.
For other uses of these words, see a good dictionary.

# 10 active verb forms

## 1 future, present and past; simple, progressive and perfect

English verbs can refer to future, present or past time.
   future: *She **will see** you tomorrow.*
   present: *I'm **watching** you.*
   past: *Who **said** that?*
For each kind of time, there are three possibilities with most verbs: simple, progressive (*be* + *-ing*) and perfect (*have* + **past participle**).
   simple present: *I **start***
   present progressive: *I **am starting***
   present perfect: *I **have started***

## 2 verb forms ('tenses') and time

There is not a direct relationship between verb forms and time. For example, a past verb like *went* is not only used to talk about past events (e.g. *We **went** to Morocco last January*), but also about unreal or uncertain present or future events (e.g. *It would be better if we **went** home now*). And present verbs can be used to talk about the future (e.g. *I'm **seeing** Peter tomorrow*). Also, progressive and perfect forms express ideas that are not simply concerned with time – for example continuation, completion, present importance.    ▶

## 3 progressive forms

Progressive (or 'continuous') forms are used especially when we describe an event as going on or continuing (perhaps at a particular time, or up to a particular time). See 470–472 for more details.

*I can't talk to you now; I'm working.*
*When you phoned I was working in the garage.*
*I was tired because I had been working all day.*

## 4 perfect forms

Perfect forms are used, for example, when we want to suggest a connection between a past event and the present, or between an earlier and a later past event; or when we want to say that something is/was/will be completed by a particular time. See 427 for more details.

*I have worked with children before, so I know what to expect in my new job.*
*After I had worked with Jake for a few weeks, I felt I knew him pretty well.*
*I will have worked 10 hours by suppertime.*
Perfect progressive forms are also possible.

*I've been working all day.*

## 5 table of active verb forms

This is a list of all the active affirmative forms of an ordinary English verb, with their names, examples, and very brief descriptions of typical uses. For more information about the forms and their uses, see the entries for each one.

| NAME | CONSTRUCTION | EXAMPLE | TYPICAL USE |
|---|---|---|---|
| (simple) future | *will* + **infinitive** *I/we shall* also possible | *It will rain tomorrow.* | information about the future (see 212) |
| future progressive | *will be ...ing* *I/we shall* also possible | *This time tomorrow I'll be lying on the beach.* | continuing situation at a particular future time (see 220) |
| future perfect | *will have* + **past participle** *I/we shall* also possible | *I will have finished the repairs by this evening.* | completion by a particular future time (see 219) |
| future perfect progressive | *will have been ...ing* *I/we shall* also possible | *In June I will have been working here for ten years.* | continuity up to a particular future time (see 219) |
| simple present | same as infinitive, but -*s* on third person singular (e.g. *I/you/we/they* work; *he/she works*) | *It always rains in November.* | 'general' time; permanent situations (see 463) |

| NAME | CONSTRUCTION | EXAMPLE | TYPICAL USE |
|------|-------------|---------|-------------|
| present progressive | *am/are/is . . .ing* | *I can't talk to you now; I'm working.* | actions continuing at the moment of speaking (see 464) |
| present perfect | *have/has* + **past participle** | *I have worked with children before, so I know what to expect.* | past action with some present connection (see 455) |
| present perfect progressive | *have/has been . . .ing* | *It has been raining all day.* | continuation up to the present (see 458) |
| simple past | regular verbs: **infinitive + -(e)d** irregular verbs: various forms | *I worked all last weekend.* *I saw John yesterday.* | past events (see 421) |
| past progressive | *was/were . . .ing* | *I saw John when I was coming out of the supermarket.* | action continuing at a particular past time (see 422) |
| past perfect | *had* + **past participle** | *I couldn't get in because I had lost my keys.* | action before a particular past time (see 423) |
| past perfect progressive | *had been . . .ing* | *I was tired because I had been working all day.* | continuation up to a particular past time (see 425) |

For irregular past tenses and past participles, see 304.
For question forms, see 480. For negatives, see 367.
For the use of present forms to talk about the future, see 213–216.
For past verbs with present or future meanings, see 426.
For 'conditional' forms (*would* + **infinitive**), see 633 and 258–259.
For subjunctives (e.g. *. . . that she go*), see 567.
For passive verb forms, see 412.
For infinitives, see 280.        For imperatives, see 268.
For *-ing* forms, see 293.        For auxiliary verbs, see 85.
For verb forms constructed with modal auxiliary verbs, see 353.

# 11  actual(ly)

## 1  meaning and use

*Actual* means 'real'; *actually* means 'really' or 'in fact'.
They are used to make things clearer, more precise or more definite.
> *It's over 100 kilos. Let me look. Yes, the **actual** weight is 108 kilos.*
> *I've got a new job. **Actually**, they've made me sales manager.*
> *Did you enjoy your holiday? ~ Very much, **actually**.*

*Actual* and *actually* often introduce surprising or unexpected information.
> *It takes me an hour to drive to work, although the **actual** distance is only 20 miles.*

▶

page 7

> *She was so angry that she **actually** tore up the letter.*
> *How did you get on with my car? ~ Well, **actually**, I'm terribly sorry, I'm*
>     *afraid I had a crash.*
> *He's twelve, but he **actually** still believes in Father Christmas.*

They can be used to correct mistakes or misunderstandings.

> *The book says she died aged 47, but her **actual** age was 43.*
> *Hello, John. Nice to see you. ~ **Actually**, my name's Andy.*

*Actually* is more common in British than American English.

## 2 'false friends'

*Actual* and *actually* are 'false friends' for people who speak some languages. They do not mean the same as, for example, *actuel(lement)*, *aktuell*, or *attual(ment)e*. We express these ideas with *present, current, up to date; at this moment, now, at present*.

> *What's our **current** financial position?*
>     (NOT ... ~~our actual financial position?~~)
> *In 1900 the population of London was higher than it is **now**.*
>     (NOT ... ~~than it actually is.~~)

# 12 adjectives (1): normal position

## 1 two positions

Most adjectives can go in two main places in a sentence.

**a** with a noun, usually before it. This is called 'attributive position'.
> *The **new secretary** doesn't like me.*
> *He's going out with a **rich businesswoman**.*

In older English (see 392), it was quite common to put adjectives after nouns, especially in poetry and songs.
> *He came from his **palace grand**.*

In modern English, this only happens in a few cases (see 13).

For adjectives before personal pronouns (e.g. *Poor you!*), see 429.7.

**b** after *be, seem, look, become* and other 'link verbs' (see 328). This is called 'predicative position'.
> *That dress **is new**, isn't it?*
> *She **looks rich**.      I **feel unhappy**.*

## 2 adjectives used only before nouns

Some adjectives are used only (or mostly) before nouns. After verbs, other words must be used. Common examples:

*elder* and *eldest* Compare:
> *My **elder** sister is a pilot.      She's three years **older** than me.*

*live* /laɪv/ (meaning 'not dead') Compare:
> *a **live** fish      It's still **alive**.*

*old* (referring to relationships that have lasted a long time)
> *an **old** friend (not the same as a friend who is **old**)*

*little* (see 534) Compare:
> *a nice **little** house      The house is quite **small**.*

**intensifying (emphasising) adjectives**
>  *He's a **mere** child.* (BUT NOT ~~*That child is mere.*~~)
>  *It's **sheer** madness.* (BUT NOT ~~*That madness is sheer.*~~)
>  *You **bloody** fool!* (BUT NOT ~~*That fool is bloody.*~~)

## 3  adjectives used only after verbs

Some adjectives beginning with *a-*, and a few others, are used mainly after link verbs, especially *be*. Common examples: *afloat, afraid, alight, alike, alive, alone, asleep, awake*. Compare:

- *The baby's **asleep**.*          – *He was **afraid**.*
  *a **sleeping** baby* (NOT ~~*an asleep baby*~~)      *a **frightened** man*
- *The ship's still **afloat**.*
  *a **floating** leaf*

The adjectives *ill* (see 266) and *well* (see 617) are most common after verbs. Before nouns, many people prefer other words. Compare:

- *He's very **well**.*       – *You look **ill**.*
  *a **healthy/fit** man*      *Nurses take care of **sick** people.*

## 4  verb + object + adjective

Another possible position for adjectives is after the object, in the structure **verb + object + adjective**.
>  *I'll **get the car ready**.*
>  *Do I **make you happy**?*    *Let's **paint the kitchen yellow**.*

For the order of adjectives and other modifiers before nouns, see 15.
For *and* between adjectives, see 16.
For commas between adjectives, see 15.6.

# 13  adjectives (2): after nouns and pronouns

Adjectives come immediately after nouns in a few special cases.

## 1  fixed phrases

Adjectives come after nouns in some fixed phrases.

| | |
|---|---|
| *Secretary **General*** | *President **elect*** |
| *court **martial*** (= military court) | *God **Almighty**!* |
| *Poet **Laureate*** | *Attorney **General*** |

>  *The **Secretary General** of the United Nations has called for new peace talks.*

## 2  *available, possible* etc.

Some adjectives can be used after nouns in a similar way to relative clauses. This is common with adjectives ending in *-able/-ible*.
>  *Send all the **tickets available** / available tickets.*
>     (= ... tickets which are available.)
>  *It's the only **solution possible** / possible solution.*
Some adverbs can also be used like this.
>  *the woman **upstairs**     the people **outside***

▶

### 3  *present, proper*

Before a noun, *present* refers to time; after a noun it means 'here/there', 'not absent'. Compare:

*the **present members*** (= those who are members now)

*the **members present*** (= those who are/were at the meeting)

Before a noun, *proper* means 'real', 'genuine'. After a noun it refers to the central or main part of something. Compare:

*Snowdon's a **proper mountain**, not a hill.*

*After two days crossing the foothills, they reached the **mountain proper**.*

For the position and meaning of *opposite*, see 401.

### 4  expressions of measurement

Adjectives usually follow measurement nouns.

*two metres **high**     ten years **older**     two miles **long**     six feet **deep***

Exception: *worth* (e.g. ***worth** 100 euros*). See 632.

### 5  adjectives with complements

When an adjective has its own complement (e.g. *skilled in design*), the whole expression normally comes after a noun..

*We are looking for **people skilled in design**.* (NOT *. . . skilled in design people.*)

A relative clause is often more natural.

*We are looking for **people who are skilled in design**.*

In some cases an adjective can be put before a noun and its complement after it. This happens with *different, similar, the same, next, last, first, second* etc; comparatives and superlatives; and a few other adjectives like *difficult* and *easy*.

*a **different** life **from this one**          the **second** train **from this platform***

*the **next** house **to the Royal Hotel**          the **best** mother **in the world***

(OR *the house next to the Royal Hotel*)   *a **difficult** problem **to solve***

### 6  *something, everything* etc

Adjectives come after *something, everything, anything, nothing, somebody, anywhere* and similar words.

*Have you read **anything interesting** lately?*

*Let's go **somewhere quiet**.*

## 14  adjectives (3): position after **as, how, so, too**

After *as, how, so, too* and *this/that* meaning *so*, adjectives go before *a/an*. This structure is common in a formal style.

> *as/how/so/too/this/that* + adjective + *a/an* + noun

*I have **as good a voice** as you.*     *She is **too polite a person** to refuse.*

*How good a pianist** is he?*     *I couldn't afford **that big a car**.*

*It was **so warm a day** that I could hardly work.*

The structure is not possible without *a/an*.

*I like your country – it's so beautiful.* (NOT *I like your so beautiful country.*)

*Those girls are too kind to refuse.* (NOT *They are too kind girls to refuse.*)

For the structure with **adjective** + *as* in expressions like *tired as I was . . .*, see 71.

# 15 adjectives (4): order before nouns

When several adjectives come before a noun (or when nouns are used like adjectives before another noun), they are usually put in a more or less fixed order. For instance, we say *a fat old lady*, NOT ~~an old fat lady~~; *a small round black leather handbag*, NOT ~~a leather black round small handbag~~. Here are the most important rules.

## 1 description before classification: *an old political idea*

Words which describe come before words which classify (say what type of thing we are talking about).

|  | description | classification | noun | |
|---|---|---|---|---|
| an | old | political | idea | (NOT ~~a political old idea~~) |
| the | latest | educational | reform | (NOT ~~the educational latest reform~~) |
| a | green | wine | bottle | (NOT ~~a wine green bottle~~) |
|  | leather | dancing | shoes | (NOT ~~dancing leather shoes~~) |

## 2 opinion before description: *a wonderful old house*

Words which express opinions, attitudes and judgements usually come before words that simply describe. Examples are *lovely, definite, pure, absolute, extreme, perfect, wonderful, silly*.

|  | opinion | description | noun | |
|---|---|---|---|---|
| a | lovely | cool | drink | (NOT ~~a cool lovely drink~~) |
| a | wonderful | old | house | (NOT ~~an old wonderful house~~) |
|  | beautiful | green | mountains | (NOT ~~green beautiful mountains~~) |
| that | silly | fat | cat | (NOT ~~that fat silly cat~~) |

## 3 order of descriptive words

The order of descriptive words is not completely fixed. Words for origin and material usually come last. Words for size, age, shape and colour often come in that order.

|  | size | age | shape | colour | origin | material | noun |
|---|---|---|---|---|---|---|---|
| a | fat | old | | white | | | horse |
| a | big | | | grey | | woollen | sweater |
|  | | new | | | Italian | | boots |
| a | small | | round | black | | leather | handbag |
| an | enormous | | | brown | German | glass | mug |
| a | little | modern | square | | | brick | house |

## 4 numbers

Numbers usually go before adjectives.
   ***six large** eggs*     *the **second big** shock*
*First, next* and *last* most often go before *one, two, three* etc.
   *the **first three** days* (More common than *the three first days*)
   *my **last two** jobs*

▶

## 5   noun modifiers after adjectives

Note that noun modifiers (which often classify, or refer to material) usually follow adjectives.

*a big new **car** factory*      *enormous black **iron** gates*

## 6   commas

Before nouns, we generally use commas between adjectives (especially in longer sequences) which give similar kinds of information, for example in physical descriptions.

*a lovely, long, cool, refreshing drink*
*an expensive, ill-planned, wasteful project*

But commas can be dropped before short common adjectives.

*a tall(,) dark(,) handsome cowboy*

For *and* with adjectives, see 16. For commas with *and*, see 476.1.

# 16   adjectives (5): with **and**

When two or more adjectives (or other modifiers) come together, we sometimes put *and* before the last one and sometimes not. It depends partly on their position in the sentence.

## 1   after a verb

When adjectives come in predicative position (after *be*, *seem* and similar verbs – see 328), we usually put *and* before the last one.

*He was tall, dark **and** handsome.*
*You're like a winter's day: short, dark **and** dirty.*

In a very literary style, *and* is sometimes left out.

*My soul is exotic, mysterious, incomprehensible.*

## 2   before a noun

In attributive position (before a noun), *and* is less common.

*an **angry young** man* (NOT ~~an angry and young man~~)
*a **big beautiful** garden*

However, *and* is possible when the adjectives give similar kinds of information, especially when we are 'piling up' favourable or unfavourable descriptions.

*a **cruel (and) vicious** tyrant*      *a **warm (and) generous** personality*
*an **ill-planned, expensive (and) wasteful** project.*

*And* is necessary when two or more adjectives (or other modifiers) refer to different parts of something, or different types of thing.

*a **yellow and black** sports car*
*a **concrete and glass** factory*
***hot and cold** drinks* (= hot drinks and cold drinks)

We also use *and* when we say that something belongs to two or more different classes.

*It's a **social and political** problem.*      *She's a **musical and artistic** genius.*

## 3   *nice and ...*

In an informal style, the expression *nice and* is often used before another adjective or an adverb. It means something like 'pleasantly' or 'suitably'.

> *It's **nice and warm** in front of the fire.* (= pleasantly warm)
> *The work was **nice and easy**.*
> *Now just put your gun down **nice and slow**.*

For more information about *and*, see 52
For commas with adjectives, see 15.6.

# 17   adjectives (6): without nouns

We cannot usually leave out a noun after an adjective.

> *Poor **little boy**!* (NOT *Poor little!*)
> *The most **important thing** is to be happy.* (NOT *The most important is to be happy.*)

But there are some exceptions.

## 1   well-known groups

*The* + **adjective** is used to talk about certain well-known groups of people who are in a particular physical or social condition. Common expressions:

| | | | |
|---|---|---|---|
| *the blind* | *the handicapped* | *the old* | *the unemployed* |
| *the dead* | *the jobless* | *the poor* | *the young* |
| *the deaf* | *the mentally ill* | *the rich* | |

> *He's collecting money for **the blind**.*
> ***The unemployed** are losing hope.*

The meaning is usually general; occasionally a limited group is referred to.

> *After the accident, **the injured** were taken to hospital.*

These expressions are normally plural: *the dead* means 'all dead people' or 'the dead people', but not 'the dead person'.
Note that these expressions cannot be used with a possessive *'s*.

> *the problems of **the poor*** OR ***poor people's** problems*
>> (NOT *the poor's problems*)

Adjectives are normally only used in this way with *the* or a determiner like *many* or *more*.

> *This government doesn't care about **the poor**.* (NOT *... about poor.*)
> *There are **more unemployed** than ever before.*

However, adjectives without *the* are sometimes used in paired structures with *both ... and ...*

> *opportunities for **both rich and poor***

## 2   adjectives of nationality

A few adjectives of nationality ending in *-sh* or *-ch* (see 364.3) are used after *the* without nouns. They include *Irish, Welsh, English, British, Spanish, Dutch, French*.

> ***The Irish** are very proud of their sense of humour.*                    ▶

These expressions are plural; singular equivalents are for example
*an Irishwoman, a Welshman* (NOT *a Welsh*).
Where nouns exist, these are preferred to expressions with *the ...ish*:
we say *the Danes* or *the Turks* (NOT *the Danish* OR *the Turkish*).

## 3 singular examples

In a few formal fixed phrases, ***the* + adjective** can have a singular meaning.
These include *the accused, the undersigned, the deceased, the former* and
*the latter*.

> ***The accused** was released on bail.*
> *... Mr Gray and Mrs Cook; **the latter** is a well-known designer.*

## 4 abstract ideas

Adjectives are sometimes used after *the* to refer to general abstract ideas,
especially in philosophical writing. (Examples: *the beautiful, the supernatural,
the unreal*.) These expressions are singular.

> *She's interested in **the supernatural**.*

## 5 choices

We sometimes leave out a noun that has already been mentioned, or which
does not need to be mentioned, when thinking about a choice between two or
more different kinds of thing.

> *Have you got any bread? ~ Do you want **white** or **brown**?*
> *I'd like two large packets and one **small**.*

Colour adjectives can sometimes have a plural *-s* in this situation.

> *Wash **the reds** and **blues** separately.* (= red and blue clothes)

## 6 superlatives

Nouns are often left out after superlative adjectives.

> *I'm **the tallest** in my family.     We bought **the cheapest**.*

For other structures in which nouns can be left out, see 180.

# 18 adjectives (7): pronunciation of aged, naked etc

A few adjectives ending in *-ed* have a special pronunciation: the last syllable is
pronounced /ɪd/ instead of /d/ or /t/ (see 421.2).

| | |
|---|---|
| *aged* /ˈeɪdʒɪd/ (= very old) | *blessed* /ˈblesɪd/ |
| *beloved* /bɪˈlʌvɪd/ | *dogged* /ˈdɒɡɪd/ |
| *crooked* /ˈkrʊkɪd/ | *learned* /ˈlɜːnɪd/ |
| *cursed* /ˈkɜːsɪd/ | *sacred* /ˈseɪkrɪd/ |
| *naked* /ˈneɪkɪd/ | *wicked* /ˈwɪkɪd/ |
| *ragged* /ˈræɡɪd/ | *wretched* /ˈretʃɪd/ |
| *rugged* /ˈrʌɡɪd/ | *one/three/four-legged* /ˈleɡɪd/ |

Note that *aged* is pronounced /eɪdʒd/ when it means 'years old' (as in *He has a
daughter aged ten*), or when it is a verb.

# 19 adjectives (8): what can follow an adjective?

Many adjectives can be followed by 'complements' – words and expressions that 'complete' their meaning. Not all adjectives are followed by the same kind of complement. Some can be followed by **preposition + noun/-ing** (see 297).

*I'm **interested in cookery**.    I'm **interested in learning** to cook.*

Some can be followed by infinitives (see 284).

*You don't look **happy to see** me.    The soup is **ready to eat**.*

An infinitive may have its own subject, introduced by *for* (see 291).

*I'm **anxious for her to get** a good education.*

(= I'm anxious that she should get . . .)

Some adjectives can be followed by clauses (see 521, 567, 446–447).

*I'm **glad that you were able to come**.*

*It's **important that everybody should feel comfortable**.*

And many adjectives can have more than one kind of complement.

*I'm **pleased about** her promotion.    I'm **pleased to see** you here.*

*I'm **pleased that we seem to agree**.*

We rarely put **adjective + complement** before a noun (see 13.5).

*He's a **difficult** person **to understand**.*

(NOT *He's a difficult to understand person.*)

For the structures that are possible with a particular adjective, see a good dictionary.

# 20 adverb particles

## 1 adverb particles and prepositions

Words like *down, in, up* are not always prepositions. Compare:

- *I ran **down** the road.*          – *He's **in** his office.*
  *Please sit **down**.*                *You can go **in**.*
- *Something's climbing **up** my leg.*
  *She's not **up** yet.*

In the expressions *down the road, in his office* and *up my leg*, the words *down, in* and *up* are prepositions: they have objects (*the road, his office* and *my leg*). In *sit down, go in* and *She's not up*, the words *down, in* and *up* have no objects. They are adverbs, not prepositions.

Small adverbs like these are usually called 'adverb(ial) particles'. They include *above, about, across, ahead, along, (a)round, aside, away, back, before, behind, below, by, down, forward, in, home, near, off, on, out, over, past, through, under, up*. Many words of this kind can be used as both adverb particles and prepositions, but there are some exceptions: for example *back, away* (only adverb particles); *from, during* (only prepositions).

## 2 phrasal verbs

Adverb particles often join together with verbs to make two-word verbs, sometimes with completely new meanings (e.g. *break down, put off, work out, give up*). These are often called 'phrasal verbs'. For details of their use, see 599.

▶

## 3  adverb particles with *be*

Adverb particles are often used, rather like adjectives, as complements of the verb *be*.

*Why are all the lights on?*        *Hello! You're **back**!*
*The match will be **over** by 4.30.*

For inverted word order in sentences beginning with an adverb particle (e.g. *Out walked Sarah*), see 303.

# 21  adverb position (1): introduction

Different kinds of adverbs go in different positions in a clause. Here are some general rules; for more details, see 22–25.
Note: in the following explanations, the word *adverb* is generally used both for one-word adverbs like *here*, *often*, and for longer adverb phrases like *in this house*, *once every six weeks*.

## 1  verb and object: *She speaks English well*

We do not usually put adverbs between a verb and its object.

> adverb + verb + object

*I **often** get headaches.* (NOT *I get often headaches.*)

> verb + object + adverb

*She speaks English **well**.* (NOT *She speaks well English.*)
But an adverb particle like *on*, *off*, *out* can go between a verb and a noun object.

*Could you **switch off** the light?*

## 2  front, mid- and end position

There are three normal positions for adverbs:

a  front position (at the beginning of a clause)
   *Yesterday morning something very strange happened.*

b  mid-position (with the verb – for exact details see 24)
   *My brother **completely forgot** my birthday.*
   *I **have never understood** her.*

c  end position (at the end of a clause)
   *What are you doing **tomorrow**?*

## 3  what goes where?

**Connecting adverbs** (which join a clause to what came before) go in front position.
   ***However**, not everybody agreed.*
**Adverbs of indefinite frequency** (e.g. *always*, *often*) and **adverbs of certainty** usually go in mid-position.
   *My boss **often** travels to America.*
   *I've **definitely** decided to change my job.*

**Adverbs of manner** (how), place (where) and time (when) most often go in end position.

> *She brushed her hair **slowly**.*      *The children are playing **upstairs**.*
> *I phoned Alex **this morning**.*

**Time adverbs** can also go in front position.

> ***Tomorrow** I've got a meeting in Cardiff.*

For more details about the position of these and other kinds of adverb, see the next four sections.

# 22   adverb position (2): front position

Adverbs that usually go in front position: connecting adverbs (e.g. *then, next*); comment adverbs (e.g. *fortunately, surprisingly*); *maybe, perhaps*.
Adverbs that can go in front position: some adverbs of indefinite frequency (e.g. *sometimes*); adverbs of place; adverbs of time.

## 1   connecting adverbs: *then, next, ...*

These adverbs join a clause to what came before.
Examples: *then, next, besides, anyway, suddenly, however.*

> *I worked until five o'clock. **Then** I went home.*
> ***Next**, I want to say something about the future.*
> ***Suddenly** the door opened.*
> *Some of us want a new system. **However**, not everybody agrees.*

Other positions are possible.

> *I went home **then**.*      *Not everybody, **however**, agrees.*

## 2   comment adverbs: *fortunately, surprisingly, ...*

Adverbs which give the speaker's opinion of an action most often go in front position.

> ***Fortunately**, she has decided to help us.*      ***Stupidly**, I forgot my keys.*

Mid-position is also possible.

## 3   indefinite frequency: *usually, normally, ...*

*Usually, normally, often, frequently, sometimes* and *occasionally* can go in front position (but they are more common in mid-position – see 24.)

> ***Sometimes** I think I'd like to live somewhere else.*
> ***Usually** I get up early.*

*Always, ever, rarely, seldom* and *never* cannot normally go in front position.

> *I **always/never** get up early.* (NOT ~~Always/Never I get up early.~~)

However, *always* and *never* can begin imperative clauses.

> ***Always** look in the mirror before starting to drive.*
> ***Never** ask her about her marriage.*

## 4   certainty: *maybe, perhaps*

*Maybe* and *perhaps* usually come at the beginning of a clause.

> ***Maybe** I'm right and **maybe** I'm wrong.*
> ***Perhaps** her train is late.*

Other adverbs of certainty (e.g. *probably, definitely, certainly*) usually go in mid-position.

▶

## 5 place: *at the end of the garden, here, there*

Place adverbs most often go in end position, but front position is possible, especially in literary writing and if the adverb is not the main focus of the message. In this case the verb often comes before the subject (see 303).

*At the end of the garden stood a very tall tree.*
*On the grass sat an enormous frog.*    ***Down came** the rain.*

*Here* and *there* often begin clauses. Note the word order in *Here/There is, Here comes* and *There goes.*

***Here comes** your bus.* (NOT ~~Here your bus comes.~~)
***There's** Alice.*    ***There goes** our train!*

Pronoun subjects come directly after *here* and *there.*

***Here** it comes.* (NOT ~~Here comes it.~~)
***There** she is.* (NOT ~~There is she.~~)

## 6 time: *today, afterwards, in June, soon, every week*

Front position is common if the adverb is not the main focus of the message.

***Today** I'm going to London.*    ***In June** we went to Cornwall.*
***Afterwards** we sat round and talked.*    ***Soon** everything will be different.*

End-position is also common; *soon* can go in mid-position.
Time expressions beginning *every* can go in front position.

***Every week** she has a new hairstyle.*

But other expressions of definite frequency (e.g. *daily, weekly*) normally go in end position.

For *rarely, seldom, never, hardly* and *scarcely* in front position before **verb + subject** ('inversion'), see 302.7.

# 23 adverb position (3): end position

Adverbs of manner, place and time usually go in end position, often in that order. Adverbs of indefinite frequency (e.g. *occasionally*) sometimes go in end position.

## 1 adverbs of manner

Adverbs of manner say how something happens or is done.
Examples: *angrily, happily, fast, slowly, well, badly, nicely, noisily, quietly, hard, softly.*

*He drove off **angrily**.*    *She read the letter **slowly**.*
*You speak English **well**.*    *John works really **hard**.*

Adverbs in *-ly* can also go in mid-position if the adverb is not the main focus of the message.

*She **angrily** tore up the letter.*    *I **slowly** began to feel better again.*

**2** **adverbs of place**

Examples: *upstairs, around, here, to bed, in London, out of the window.*
  *The children are playing **upstairs**.*          *Come and sit **here**.*
  *Don't throw orange peel **out of the window**.*
  *She's sitting **at the end of the garden**.*
Front position is also possible, especially in literary writing and if the adverb is
not the main focus of the message (see 22.5).
  ***At the end of the garden** there was a very tall tree.*
Adverbs of direction (movement) come before adverbs of position.
  *The children are running **around upstairs**.*

**3** **adverbs of time and definite frequency**

Examples: *today, afterwards, in June, last year, finally, before, eventually,
already, soon, still, last, daily, weekly, every year.*
  *I'm going to London **today**.*          *What did you do **afterwards**?*
  *She has a new hairstyle **every week**.*
Front position is also common if the adverb is not the main focus of the
message.
  ***Today** I'm going to London.*     ***Every week** she has a new hairstyle.*
*Finally, eventually, already, soon* and *last* can also go in mid-position.

**4** **manner, place, time**

Most often, adverbs of manner, place and time go in that order.
  *Put the butter **in the fridge at once**.* (NOT *. . . ~~at once in the fridge.~~*)
  *Let's go **to bed early**.* (NOT *. . . ~~early to bed.~~*)
  *I worked **hard yesterday**.*
  *She sang **beautifully in the town hall last night**.*

**5** **adverbs of indefinite frequency: *usually, normally, often,
frequently, sometimes* and *occasionally*.**

These adverbs can go in end position if they are the main focus of the message
(but they are more common in mid-position – see 24).
  *I go there **occasionally**.*          *We see her **quite often**.*
  *I get very depressed **sometimes**.*

# 24 adverb position (4): mid-position

Adverbs that usually go in mid-position: adverbs of indefinite frequency
(e.g. *sometimes*), certainty (e.g. *probably*) and completeness (e.g. *almost*).
Adverbs that can go in mid-position: focusing adverbs (e.g. *just*), some adverbs
of manner (e.g. *angrily*), comment adverbs (e.g. *fortunately*).

**1** **What exactly is mid-position?**

Mid-position adverbs usually go before one-part verbs, after auxiliary verbs,
and after *am/are/is/was/were*.

before one-part verbs

  *I **always play** tennis on Saturdays.* (NOT *~~I play always tennis~~ . . .*)
  *It **certainly looks** like rain.*     *We **nearly won** the match.*          ▶

after auxiliary verbs

> *She **has never** written to me.* (NOT USUALLY *She never has written to me.*)
> *He **was definitely** trying to get into the house.*
> *The train **will probably** be late.*   *You **can almost** see the sea from here.*

after am/are/is/was/were

> *She **was always** kind to me.* (NOT USUALLY *She always was kind to me.*)
> *It **is probably** too late now.*   *I **am obviously** not welcome here.*

When there are two or more auxiliaries, the adverb usually goes after the first.

> *You **have definitely been** working too hard.*
> *She **would never have been** promoted if she hadn't changed jobs.*

When an auxiliary verb is used alone instead of a complete verb phrase (see 181), a mid-position adverb comes before it.

> *Are you working? ~ I **certainly am**.*
> *I don't trust politicians. I **never have**, and I **never will**.*

For some more advanced points, see paragraphs 8–11 below.

## 2 indefinite frequency (how often)

Examples: *always, ever, usually, normally, often, frequently, sometimes, occasionally, rarely, seldom, never.*

> *We **usually** go to Scotland in August.*
> *It **sometimes** gets very windy here.*   *I have **never** seen a whale.*
> *You can **always** come and stay with us if you want to.*
> *Have you **ever** played American football?*
> *My boss is **often** bad-tempered.*   *I'm **seldom** late for work.*
> *We have **never** been invited to one of their parties.*
> *She must **sometimes** have wanted to run away.*

*Usually, normally, often, frequently, sometimes* and *occasionally* can also go in front or end position (see 22–23).

> ***Sometimes** I think I'd like to live somewhere else.*
> *I see her **occasionally**.*

## 3 adverbs of certainty

Examples: *probably, certainly, definitely, clearly, obviously.*

> *He **probably** thinks you don't like him.*
> *It will **certainly** rain this evening.*   *There is **clearly** something wrong.*
> *I **definitely** feel better today.*   *The train has **obviously** been delayed.*

*Maybe* and *perhaps* usually come at the beginning of a clause (see 22).

> ***Maybe** I'm right and maybe I'm wrong.*
> ***Perhaps** her train is late.*

## 4 adverbs of completeness

Examples: *completely, practically, almost, nearly, quite, rather, partly, sort of, kind of, more or less, hardly, scarcely.*

> *I have **completely** forgotten your name.*   *The house is **partly** ready.*
> *Sally can **practically** read.*   *I **kind of** hope she wins.*
> *It was **almost** dark.*   *It **hardly** matters.*

Adverbs of completeness usually follow all auxiliary verbs.

> *I **will have completely** finished by next June.*
> (NOT ~~*I will completely have finished*~~ ...)
> *Do you think the repair **has been properly** done?*

## 5 comment adverbs

Adverbs which give the speaker's opinion of an action sometimes go in mid-position.

> *I **stupidly** forgot my keys.*    *She has **fortunately** decided to help us.*

## 6 focusing adverbs

These adverbs 'point to' one part of a clause.

Examples: *also* (see 46–47), *just* (see 307), *even* (see 189), *only* (see 398), *mainly, mostly, either* (see 175), *or, neither* (see 374), *nor* (see 374).

> *Your bicycle **just** needs some oil – that's all.*
> *She **neither** said 'Thank you' **nor** looked at me.*
> *He's been everywhere – he's **even** been to Antarctica.*
> *We're **only** going for two days.*
> *She's my teacher, but she's **also** my friend.*
> *The people at the meeting were **mainly** scientists.*

Some of these adverbs can also go in other places in a clause, directly before the words they modify. For details, see the entries on each adverb.

> ***Only you** could do a thing like that.*    *I feel **really** tired.*

## 7 adverbs of manner

These adverbs say how something happens or is done.

Examples: *angrily, happily, slowly, suddenly, noisily, quietly, softly.*

Adverbs of manner most often go in end position (see 23), but adverbs ending in *-ly* can often go in mid-position if the adverb is not the main focus of the message.

> *She **angrily** tore up the letter.*    *I **slowly** began to feel better again.*
> *We have **suddenly** decided to sell the house.*
> *This time next week I'll be **happily** working in my garden.*

Mid-position (after all auxiliary verbs) is especially common with passive verbs.

> *The driver **has been seriously injured**.*

## 8 mid-position (details): adverbs with negative verbs

In negative sentences, adverbs generally come before *not* if they emphasise the negative; otherwise they come after. Compare:

> *I **certainly do not** agree.*    *I **do not often** have headaches.*

Both positions are possible with some adverbs, often with a difference of meaning. Compare:

> *I **don't really** like her.* (mild dislike)
> *I **really don't** like her.* (strong dislike)

When adverbs come before *not*, they may also come before the first auxiliary verb; they always come before *do*.

> *I **probably will not** be there.* (OR *I **will probably not** be there.*)
> *He **probably does not** know.* (NOT ~~*He does probably not know.*~~)

Only one position is possible before a contracted negative.

> *I **probably won't** be there.*

▶

### 9 mid-position (details): adverbs with emphatic verbs

When we emphasise auxiliary verbs or *am/are/is/was/were*, we put most mid-position adverbs before them instead of after. Compare:
- *She **has certainly** made him angry.*     – *I'm **really** sorry.*
  *She **certainly** HAS made him angry!*     *I **really** AM sorry.*
- *Polite people **always say** thank-you.*
  ~ *Yes, well, I **always** DO say thank-you.*

### 10 mid-position (details): modal auxiliary verbs

When the first part of the verb phrase is a modal auxiliary (see 353), *used to* or *have to*, mid-position adverbs can come before or after the auxiliary.
  *They **sometimes must** be bored.* (OR *They **must sometimes** be bored.*)
  *She **could have easily** been killed.* (OR *She **could easily have** been killed.*)
  *We **always used to go** to the seaside in May.* (OR *We **used always to go** . . .*
    OR *We **used to always go** . . .*)

### 11 mid-position (details): American English

In American English (see 51), mid-position adverbs are often put before auxiliary verbs and *am/are/is/was/were*, even when the verb is not emphasised. Compare:
  *He **has probably** arrived by now.* (BrE normal)
  *He **probably has** arrived by now.* (AmE normal, BrE emphatic)
As an extreme example, here are four sentences in a journalistic style taken from an American newspaper article on crime in Britain. The most normal British equivalents are given in brackets.
  *'Britain **long has been** known as a land of law and order.'*
    (BrE *Britain **has long been** known . . .*)
  *'. . . but it **probably will** lead to a vote . . .'*
    (BrE *. . . but it **will probably** lead . . .*)
  *'. . . the Labor Party **often has** criticized police actions.'*
    (BrE *. . . the Labour Party **has often** criticised . . .*)
  *'. . . he **ultimately was** responsible for the treatment . . .'*
    (BrE *. . . he **was ultimately** responsible . . .*)

## 25 adverb position (5): emphasising adverbs

Examples: *very, extremely, terribly, just* (meaning 'exactly' or 'a short time'), *almost, really, right.*
These adverbs go directly before the words that they emphasise or 'point to'.
  *We all thought she sang **very well**.*
  *Everybody was **extremely annoyed** with Julian.*
  *I'm **terribly sorry** about last night.*
  *I'll see you in the pub **just before** eight o'clock.*
  *He threw the ball **almost over** the house.*
  *I'm **really tired** today.*
  *She walked **right past** me.*
*Almost* can also go in mid-position (see 24.4).

# 26  adverbs of manner and adjectives

## 1  adverbs of manner with verbs

Adverbs of manner say how something happens or is done.
Examples: *happily, terribly, fast, badly, well.*
These adverbs should not be confused with adjectives (*happy, terrible* etc). We
use adverbs, not adjectives, to modify verbs.

> verb + adverb

*She **danced happily** into the room.* (NOT *She danced happy* ...)
*She **sang badly**.* (NOT *She sang bad.*)
*I don't **remember** him very **well**.* (NOT ... *very good.*)

But note that adjective forms are sometimes used as adverbs in an informal
style, especially in American English (see 27).

*She talks **funny**.*

For the use of adjectives after link verbs like *look* or *seem*, see 328.

## 2  other uses

These adverbs can also modify adjectives, past participles, other adverbs and
adverbial phrases.

> adverb + adjective

*It's **terribly cold** today.* (NOT ... *terrible cold.*)

> adverb + past participle

*This steak is very **badly cooked**.* (NOT ... *bad cooked.*)

> adverb + adverb

*They're playing **unusually fast**.* (NOT ... *unusual fast.*)

> adverb + adverbial phrase

*He was **madly in love** with her.* (NOT ... *mad in love* ...)

For adjectives ending in *-ly*, see the next section.
For adverbs and adjectives with the same form, see the next section.
For the adjective *well*, see 617.
For the position of adverbs of manner, see 23.1.
For spelling rules, see 557.

# 27 adverbs or adjectives? confusing cases

## 1 adjectives ending in -ly

Some words ending in -ly are adjectives, and not normally adverbs. Common examples: *costly, cowardly, deadly, friendly, likely, lively, lonely, lovely, silly, ugly, unlikely.*

> *She gave me a **friendly** smile.*
> . *Her singing was **lovely**.*

There are no adverbs *friendly/friendlily, lovely/lovelily* etc.

> *She smiled **in a friendly way**.* (NOT ~~She smiled friendly.~~)
> *He **gave a silly laugh**.* (NOT ~~He laughed silly.~~)

*Daily, weekly, monthly, yearly, early* and *leisurely* are both adjectives and adverbs.

> *It's a **daily** paper.      It comes out **daily**.      an **early** train      I got up **early**.*

## 2 adjectives and adverbs with the same form; adverbs with two forms

Some adjectives and adverbs have the same form: for example, a *fast* car goes *fast*; if you do *hard* work, you work *hard*. In other cases, the adverb may have two forms (e.g. *late* and *lately*), one like the adjective and the other with *-ly*. There is usually a difference of meaning or use. Some examples follow; for more detailed information, check in a good dictionary.

**bloody** Some swearwords (see 575), including *bloody* (BrE), can be used both as adjectives and as adverbs.

> *You **bloody** fool. You didn't look where you were going. ~ I **bloody** did.*

**clean** The adverb *clean* means 'completely' before *forget* (informal) and some expressions of movement.

> *Sorry I didn't turn up – I **clean** forgot.*
> *The explosion blew the cooker **clean** through the wall.*

**dead** The adverb *dead* is used in certain expressions to mean 'exactly', 'completely' or 'very'. Examples: *dead ahead, dead certain, dead drunk, dead right, dead slow, dead straight, dead sure, dead tired.*
Note that *deadly* is an adjective, meaning 'fatal', 'causing death'. The adverb for this meaning is *fatally*. Compare:

> *Cyanide is a **deadly** poison.      She was **fatally** injured in the crash.*

**direct** *Direct* is often used informally as an adverb.

> *The plane goes **direct** from London to Houston without stopping.*
> *50% cheaper – order **direct** from the factory!*

**easy** *Easy* is used as an adverb in some informal expressions.

> *Go **easy**! (= Not too fast!)      Take it **easy**! (= Relax!)*
> ***Easy** come, **easy** go.      **Easier** said than done.*

**fair** *Fair* is used as an adverb after a verb in some expressions.

> *to play **fair**      to fight **fair**      to hit something **fair** and square*

For the adverb of degree *fairly*, see 199.

**fast** *Fast* can mean both 'quick' and 'quickly' (a *fast* car goes *fast*). *Fast* means 'completely' in the expression *fast asleep,* and it means 'tight', 'impossible to remove' in expressions like *hold fast, stick fast, fast colours.*

**fine** The adverb *fine* (= well) is used in some informal expressions.
*That suits me **fine**.     You're doing **fine**.*
The adverb *finely* is used to talk about small careful adjustments and similar ideas.
*a **finely** tuned engine     **finely** chopped onions* (= cut up very small)

**flat** *Flat* can be used as an adverb in a musical sense (*to sing **flat*** means 'to sing on a note that is too low'). In most other cases, the adverb is *flatly.*

**free** The adverb *free* (used after a verb) means 'without payment'; *freely* means 'without limit or restriction'. Compare:
*You can eat **free** in my restaurant whenever you like.*
*You can speak **freely** – I won't tell anyone what you say.*

**hard** The adverb *hard* means 'with a lot of force, energetically'.
*Hit it **hard**.     I trained really **hard** for the marathon.*
*Hardly* means 'almost not'.
*I've **hardly** got any clean clothes left.*
Compare:
*Ann works **hard**.     Her brother **hardly** works.*

For *hardly . . . when* in clauses of time, see 233.
For *hardly any, ever* etc, see 43.3.

**high** *High* refers to height; *highly* (rather formal) expresses an extreme degree (it often means 'very much'). Compare:
– *He can jump really **high**.*     – *It's **highly** amusing.*
  *Throw it as **high** as you can.*     *I can **highly** recommend it.*

**just** *Just* is an adverb with several meanings (see 307). There is also an adjective *just*, meaning 'in accordance with justice or the law'; the adverb is *justly.*
*He was **justly** punished for his crimes.*

**late** The adverb *late* has a similar meaning to the adjective *late; lately* means 'recently'. Compare:
*I hate arriving **late**.     I haven't been to the theatre much **lately**.*

**loud** *Loud* is often used informally as an adverb after a verb.
*Don't talk so **loud(ly)** – you'll wake the whole street.*

**low** *Low* is an adjective and adverb (*a **low** bridge, a **low** voice, bend **low***).

**most** *Most* is the superlative of *much,* and is used to form superlative adjectives and adverbs (see 137).
*Which part of the concert did you like **most**?*
*This is the **most** extraordinary day of my life.*
In a formal style, *most* can be used to mean 'very' (see 356.7).
*You're a **most** unusual person.*
*Mostly* means 'mainly', 'most often' or 'in most cases'.
*My friends are **mostly** non-smokers.*     ▶

**pretty** The informal adverb of degree *pretty* is similar to *rather* (see 199). *Prettily* means 'in a pretty way'. Compare:

>  *I'm getting **pretty** fed up.     Isn't your little girl dressed **prettily**?*

**quick** In an informal style, *quick* is often used instead of *quickly*, especially after verbs of movement.

>  *I'll get back as **quick(ly)** as I can.*

**real** In informal American English, *real* is often used instead of *really* before adjectives and adverbs.

>  *That was **real** nice.     He cooks **real** well.*

**right** *Right* with adverb phrases means 'just', 'exactly' or 'all the way'.

>  *She arrived **right** after breakfast.*
>  *The snowball hit me **right** on the nose.*
>  *Turn the gas **right** down.*

*Right* and *rightly* can both be used to mean 'correctly'. *Right* is only used after verbs, and is usually informal. Compare:

>  *I **rightly** assumed that Henry was not coming.     You guessed **right**.*
>  *It serves you **right**. ( ... rightly is not possible.)*

**sharp** *Sharp* can be used as an adverb to mean 'punctually'.

>  *Can you be there at six o'clock **sharp**?*

It also has a musical sense (*to sing **sharp*** means 'to sing on a note that is too high'), and is used in the expressions *turn **sharp** left* and *turn **sharp** right* (meaning 'with a big change of direction').
In other senses the adverb is *sharply*.

>  *She looked at him **sharply**.*
>  *I thought you spoke to her rather **sharply**.*

**short** *Short* is used as an adverb in the expressions *stop **short*** (= 'stop suddenly') and *cut **short*** (= 'interrupt'). *Shortly* means 'soon'; it can also describe an impatient way of speaking.

**slow** *Slow* is used as an adverb in road signs (e.g. SLOW – DANGEROUS BEND), and informally after *go* and some other verbs. Examples: *go **slow**, drive **slow**.*

**sound** *Sound* is used as an adverb in the expression ***sound** asleep*. In other cases, *soundly* is used (e.g. *She's sleeping **soundly***).

**straight** The adverb and the adjective are the same. A ***straight*** road goes ***straight*** from one place to another.

**sure** *Sure* is often used to mean 'certainly' in an informal style, especially in American English.

>  *Can I borrow your tennis racket? ~ **Sure**.*

*Surely (not)* is used to express opinions or surprise (see 573 for details).

>  ***Surely** house prices will stop rising soon!*
>  ***Surely** you're **not** going out in that old coat?*

**tight** After a verb, *tight* can be used instead of *tightly*, especially in an informal style. Typical expressions: *hold **tight**, packed **tight*** (compare ***tightly** packed*).

**well** *Well* is an adverb corresponding to the adjective *good* (*a **good** singer sings **well***). *Well* is also an adjective meaning 'in good health' (the opposite of *ill*).˙ For details, see 617.

**wide** The normal adverb is *wide*; *widely* suggests distance or separation. Compare:

>  The door was **wide** open.    She's travelled **widely**.
>  They have **widely** differing opinions.

Note also the expression **wide** awake (the opposite of *fast asleep*).

**wrong** *Wrong* can be used informally instead of *wrongly* after a verb. Compare:

>  I **wrongly** believed that you wanted to help me.
>  You guessed **wrong**.

## 3  comparatives and superlatives

Informal uses of adjective forms as adverbs are especially common with comparatives and superlatives.

>  Can you drive a bit **slower**?    Let's see who can do it **quickest**.

## 4  American English

In informal American English, many other adjective forms can also be used as adverbs of manner.

>  He looked at me real **strange**.    Think **positive**.

# 28  afraid

## 1  *afraid* and *fear*

In an informal style, *be afraid* is more common than *fear*.

>  Don't **be afraid**. (NOT *Don't fear*)    She's **afraid** that I might find out.
>  Are you **afraid** of the dark?        I'm not **afraid** to say what I think.

## 2  *I'm afraid* = 'I'm sorry'

*I'm afraid (that)* often means 'I'm sorry to tell you (that)'. It is used to introduce apologetic refusals and bad news.

>  **I'm afraid (that)** I can't help you.
>  **I'm afraid that** there's been an accident.

*I'm afraid so/not* are used as 'short answers'.

>  Can you lend me a pound? ~ **I'm afraid not**.
>  It's going to rain. ~ Yes, **I'm afraid so**.

## 3  not used before a noun

*Afraid* is one of the adjectives that are not usually used before a noun in 'attributive position' (see 12). Compare:

>  John's **afraid**.
>  John's a **frightened** man. (NOT *... an afraid man.*)

For information about *-ing* forms and infinitives after *afraid*, see 299.13.

# 29  after: adverb

## 1  *shortly after* etc.

*After* can be used in adverb phrases like *shortly after, long after, a few days after* etc.

> *We had oysters for supper. **Shortly after**, I began to feel ill.*

In more exact expressions of time, *later* is more common.

> *They started the job on the 16th and finished **three weeks later**.*

## 2  *after* not used alone

*After* is not normally used alone as an adverb. Instead, we use other expressions like *afterwards* (AmE also *afterward*), *then* or *after that*.

> *I'm going to do my exams, and **afterwards** I'm going to study medicine.*
> (NOT . . . ~~and after, I'm going~~ . . .)

# 30  after: conjunction

> *after* + clause, + clause
> clause + *after* + clause

## 1  use and position

The conjunction *after* joins one clause to another. *After* and its clause can come either before or after the other clause.

> ***After I left school**, I went to America.*
> *I went to America **after I left school**.*

(In both cases the speaker left school first and then went to America. In the second example, the *after*-clause is given more importance because it comes at the end. Note the comma in the first structure.)

> ***After he did military service**, he went to university.*
> (He did military service first.)
> *He did military service **after he went to university**.*
> (He went to university first.)

## 2  present with future meaning

We use *after* with a present tense to talk about the future (see 580).

> *I'll telephone you **after I arrive**.* (NOT . . . ~~after I will arrive.~~)

## 3  perfect tenses

In clauses with *after*, we often use present and past perfect tenses to show that one thing is completed before another starts.

> *I'll telephone you **after I've seen Jake**.*
> ***After I had finished school**, I went to America.*

## 4  *after . . . ing*

In a formal style, we often use the structure *after + -ing*.

> ***After completing this form**, give it to the secretary.*

*After having* + past participle is also possible when talking about the past.

> *He wrote his first book **after returning / having returned** from Mongolia.*

## 31 after all

### 1 two meanings

*After all* can mean 'in spite of what was said before' or 'contrary to what was expected'. Position: usually at the end of a clause.

> *I'm sorry. I know I said I would help you, but I can't **after all**.*
> *I expected to fail the exam, but I passed **after all**.*

Another meaning is 'we mustn't forget that . . .', introducing an argument or reason which may have been forgotten. Position: at the beginning or end of a clause.

> *Of course you're tired. **After all**, you were up all night.*
> *Let's finish the cake. Somebody's got to eat it, **after all**.*

### 2 not used for 'finally'

*After all* does not mean 'finally', 'at last', 'in the end'.

> *After the theatre we had supper and went to a nightclub; then we **finally** went home.* (NOT *. . . after all we went home.*)

## 32 age

### 1 use of *be*

We most often talk about people's ages with *be* + number

> *He **is** thirty.* (NOT *He has thirty.*)

or *be* + number + *years old* (more formal: *. . . of age*).

> *He **is** thirty years old / of age.* (NOT *. . . thirty years.*)

We ask *How old are you?*, not normally *What is your age?*

### 2 *be* + . . . *age*

Note the structure *be* + . . . *age* (without a preposition).

> *When I **was your age** I was working.* (NOT *When I was at your age . . .*)
> *The two boys **are the same age**.*     *She's **the same age** as me.*

### 3 prepositions

In other structures, *at* is common before *age*.

> *He could read **at the age** of three.* (NOT *. . . in the age . . .*)
> ***At your age** I already had a job.*

## 33 ago

### 1 word order: *six weeks ago*

*Ago* follows an expression of time.

> *I met her **six weeks ago**.* (NOT *. . . ago six weeks.*)     *a long **time ago***

### 2 tenses

An expression with *ago* refers to a finished time, and is normally used with a past tense, not a present perfect (see 455.5).

> *She **phoned** a few minutes ago.* (NOT *She has phoned . . .*)
> *Where's Mike? ~ He **was working** outside ten minutes ago.*     ▶

### 3 the difference between *ago* and *for*

*Ago* says how long before the present something happened; *for* (with a past tense) says how long it lasted. Compare:

> *He died **three years ago**.* (= three years before now)
> (NOT *He died for three years.* OR *...for three years ago.*)
> *He was ill **for three years** before he died.* (= His illness lasted three years.)

### 4 *ago* and *before* with time expressions: counting back

We use *ago* with a past tense and a time expression to 'count back' from the present; to say how long before now something happened.

We can use *before* in the same way (with a past perfect tense) to count back from a past moment (see also 96). Compare:

> *I met that woman in Scotland **three years ago**.*
> (NOT *...three years before / before three years.*)
> *When we got talking, I found out that I had been at school with her husband **ten years before**.* (NOT *...ten years ago.*)

---

**ago** and **before**

*I met her three years ago. I had been at school with her husband ten years before.*

```
          ten years before          three years ago

PAST |  |  |  |  |  |  |  |  |  |  |  |  |  |  |  | NOW
```

---

For other uses of *before*, see 97–98.

## 34 alike

The adjective *alike* means 'like each other'. Compare:

> *The two boys are **alike** in looks, but not in personality.*
> *He's **like** his brother.* (NOT *He's alike his brother.*)

*Alike* is not often used before a noun (see 12). Compare:

> *His two daughters are very much **alike**.*
> *He's got two very **similar-looking** daughters.* (NOT *...alike daughters.*)

## 35 all (1): introduction

### 1 three or more items

*All* refers to three or more items. Compare:

> *I'll take **all** three shirts, please.*
> *I'll take **both** shirts.* (NOT *... all two shirts.*)

## 2   *all (of)* with nouns and pronouns

*All* modifies nouns or pronouns.

>*All (of) the people were singing.*     *I haven't read **all of it**.*
>*Give my love to **them all**.*

See 36 for details of word order, and the use of *all of*.

## 3   with the subject or the verb

When *all* modifies the subject, it can go either with the subject or with the verb.

>***All the people** were singing.*     *The people **were all singing**.*

For more examples, see 36–37.

## 4   *all* without a noun

*All* can sometimes be used without a noun to mean 'everything' but only in certain structures (see 38).

>***All** that matters is to be happy.*     *That's **all**.*

## 5   *all* with adjectives, adverbs etc

*All* can be used to emphasise some adjectives, prepositions and adverbs.

>*You're **all wet**.*                       *She **walked all round** the town.*
>*I was **all alone**.*                       *Tell me **all about** your holiday.*
>*It's **all because of** you.*             *I looked **all round**, but I couldn't*
>                                             *see anything.*

*All, both* and *half* follow similar grammar rules. For *both*, see 110; for *half*, see 231.

# 36   all (2): **all (of)** with nouns and pronouns

## 1   *all* and *all of*

*All (of)* can modify nouns and pronouns.
Before a noun with a determiner (for example *the, my, this*), *all* and *all of* are both possible. *All* is more common than *all of*.

>*She's eaten **all (of) the cake**.*     ***All (of) my friends** like riding.*

Before a noun with no determiner, we do not normally use *of*.

>***All children** can be difficult.* (NOT ~~*All of children*~~ . . .)

## 2   *all of* + personal pronoun

With personal pronouns, we use *all of* + *us/you/them*.
*All of us/you/them* can be a subject or object.

>***All of us** can come tomorrow.* (NOT ~~*All we*~~ . . .)
>*She's invited **all of you**.*     *Mary sent **all of them** her love.*

## 3   pronoun + *all*

We can put *all* after pronouns used as objects.

>*She's invited **you all**.*     *Mary sent her love to **them all**.*
>*I've made **us all** something to eat.*

▶

This does not happen with complement pronouns (after *be*) or in short answers.

> *I think that's **all of them**.* (NOT *~~I think that's them all~~.*)
> *Who did she invite? ~**All of us**.* (NOT *~~Us all~~.*)

*All* can follow a subject pronoun (e.g. *They **all** went home*), but in this case it belongs grammatically with the verb (see 37) and may be separated from the pronoun (e.g. *They have **all** gone home*).

For the American plural pronoun *you all*, see 429.8.

## 4  types of noun

*All* is used mostly before uncountable and plural nouns.

> *all the **water**       all my **friends***

However, *all* can be used before some singular countable nouns referring to things that can naturally be divided into parts.

> *all that **week**       all my **family**       all the **way***

We can also use *all (of)* before proper nouns (e.g. the names of places or writers).

> ***All (of) London** knew about her affairs.       I've read **all (of) Shakespeare**.*

With other singular countable nouns, it is more natural to use *whole* (e.g. *the whole story*). For details, see 40.

## 5  leaving out *the*

After *all*, we sometimes leave out *the* before numbers.

> *all (the) **three** brothers*

And we usually leave out *the* in *all day*, *all night*, *all week*, *all year*, *all winter* and *all summer*.

> *She stayed here **all day**.* (NOT *. . . ~~all the day~~*).

## 6  *not all . . .*

It is not very common to use ***all** + noun* as the subject of a negative verb (e.g. *All Americans don't like hamburgers*). We more often use ***not all** + noun + **affirmative verb**.

> ***Not all** Americans like hamburgers.*

Note the difference between *not all* and *no*. Compare:

> ***Not all** birds can fly.*
> ***No** birds can play chess.*

# 37  all (3): with the verb

When *all* refers to the subject of a clause, it can go with the verb, in 'mid-position' (for details of word order, see 24).

> *We **can all** swim.*                *Those apples **were all** bad.*
> *The guests **have all arrived**.*    *My family **all work** in education.*

Note that these meanings can also be expressed by using *all (of)* with the subject (see 36).

> ***All of us** can swim.*    ***All (of) the guests** have arrived.*

# 38 all (4): all, everybody/everyone and everything

## 1 *all* and *everybody/everyone*

We do not normally use *all* without a noun to mean 'everybody'. Compare:
*All the people* stood up.
*Everybody/Everyone* stood up. (NOT ~~All stood up.~~)

## 2 *all* and *everything*

*All* can mean 'everything', but usually only in the structure *all* + **relative clause** (*all that . . .*). Compare:
– *All (that) I have* is yours. (NOT ~~All what I have~~ . . .)
  *Everything is yours.* (NOT ~~All is yours.~~)
– *She lost **all (that) she owned.***
  *She lost everything.* (NOT ~~She lost all.~~)
This structure often has a rather negative meaning, expressing ideas like 'nothing more' or 'the only thing(s)'.
  *This is **all I've got.*** *All I want* is a place to sit down.
  ***All that happened** was that he went to sleep.*
Note also *That's all* (= It's finished; There's no more).

## 3 older English

In older English, *all* could be used alone to mean 'everybody' or 'everything' (e.g. *Tell me all*; *All is lost*; *All are dead*). This only happens regularly in modern English in dramatic contexts like newspaper headlines (e.g. *SPY TELLS ALL*).

# 39 all and every

*All* and *every* can both be used to talk about people or things in general, or about all the members of a group. There is little difference of meaning; *every* often suggests 'without exception'. The two words are used in different structures.

## 1 *every* with singular nouns; *all* with plurals

*Every* is used with a singular noun. To give the same meaning, *all* is used with a plural noun. Compare:
– *Every child* needs love. (NOT ~~All child needs love.~~)
  *All children* need love.
– *Every light* was out.
  *All (of) the lights* were out.

## 2 *every* not used with determiners

We can use *all (of)*, but not normally *every*, with certain determiners (articles, possessives or demonstratives). Compare:
– *All (of) the plates* were broken.
  *Every plate* was broken. (NOT ~~Every the plate / The every plate~~ . . .)
– *I've written to all (of) my friends.*
  *I've written to **every friend I have.*** (NOT . . . ~~every my friend / my every friend.~~)

▶

## 3 *all* with uncountables

We can use *all*, but not *every*, with uncountable nouns.
> *I like **all music**.* (NOT ... *every music.*)

## 4 *all day* and *every day* etc

Note the difference between *all day/week* etc and *every day/week* etc.
> *She was here **all day**.* (= from morning to night)
> *She was here **every day**.* (Monday, Tuesday, Wednesday, ...)

For the difference between *every* and *each*, see 170.

# 40 all and whole

## 1 pronunciation

all /ɔːl/ whole /həʊl/

## 2 word order

*All (of)* and *whole* can both be used with singular nouns to mean 'complete', 'every part of'. The word order is different.

> *all (of)* + determiner + noun
> determiner + *whole* + noun

– *Julie spent **all (of)** the summer at home.*    – *all (of)* my life
   *Julie spent **the whole** summer at home.*    *my whole* life

## 3 indefinite reference

*All* is not generally used before indefinite articles.
> *She's eaten **a whole loaf**.* (NOT ... *all a loaf.*)

## 4 uncountable nouns

With most uncountable nouns we prefer *all (of)*.
> *I've drunk **all (of)** the milk.* (NOT ... *the whole milk.*)

## 5 *the whole of*

Instead of *whole* we can generally use *the whole of*.
> *Julie spent **the whole of** the summer at home.*
> ***the whole of** my life*

Before proper nouns (names) and pronouns we always use *the whole of*, not *whole*. *All (of)* is also possible.
> ***The whole of** / **All of** Venice was under water.* (NOT *Whole Venice* ...)
> *I've just read **the whole of** / **all of** 'War and Peace'.*
> *I've read **the whole of** / **all of** it.*

## 6 plural nouns

With plural nouns, *all* and *whole* have different meanings. *All* is like *every*; *whole* means 'complete', 'entire'. Compare:
> ***All Indian tribes** suffered from white settlement in America.* (= Every Indian tribe suffered ...)
> ***Whole Indian tribes** were killed off.* (= Complete tribes were killed off; nobody was left alive in these tribes.)

# 41  all right and alright

The standard spelling is *all right*. *Alright* is common, but some people consider it incorrect.

# 42  allow, permit and let

## 1  *allow* and *permit*

These words have similar meanings and uses. *Permit* is more formal. Both words can be followed by **object + infinitive**.

*We do not **allow/permit people to smoke** in the kitchen.*

When there is no personal object, an *-ing* form is used.

*We do not **allow/permit smoking** in the kitchen.*

Passive structures are common; personal subjects and gerund (*-ing* form) subjects are both possible.

***People are not allowed/permitted** to smoke in the kitchen.*

***Smoking is not allowed/permitted** in the kitchen.*

The passive structure with *it* is only possible with *permit*.

***It is not permitted** to smoke in the kitchen.* (BUT NOT ~~It is not allowed to smoke...~~)

*Allow*, but not *permit*, can be used with adverb particles.

*She wouldn't **allow** me **in**.*   *Mary isn't **allowed out** at night.*

## 2  *let*

*Let* is the least formal of these three words, and is followed by **object + infinitive** without *to*. Compare:

*Please **allow me to buy** you a drink.* (polite and formal)

***Let me buy** you a drink.* (friendly and informal)

*Let* is not usually used in the passive.

*I **wasn't allowed** to pay for the drinks.* (NOT ~~I wasn't let...~~)

*Let* can be used with adverb particles; passives are possible in this case.

*She wouldn't **let** me **in**.*   *I've been **let down**.*

For more about *let*, see 322–323.

# 43  almost and nearly; practically

## 1  progress, measurement and counting

*Almost* and *nearly* can both express ideas connected with progress, measurement or counting. *Nearly* is less common in American English.

*I've **almost/nearly** finished.*

*There were **almost/nearly** a thousand people there.*

Sometimes *almost* is a little 'nearer' than *nearly*. Compare:

*It's **nearly** ten o'clock.* (= perhaps 9.45)

*It's **almost** ten o'clock.* (= perhaps 9.57)

*Very* and *pretty* can be used with *nearly* but not *almost*.

*I've **very/pretty nearly** finished.* (NOT ... ~~very almost~~...)

▶

## 2 other meanings

We can use *almost* to mean 'similar to, but not exactly the same', and to make statements less definite. *Nearly* is not used like this.

>*Jake is **almost** like a father to me.*
>*Our cat understands everything – he's **almost** human.* (NOT ... ~~he's nearly human.~~)
>*My aunt's got a strange accent. She **almost** sounds foreign.* (NOT ... ~~She nearly sounds foreign.~~)
>*I **almost** wish I'd stayed at home.* (NOT ~~I nearly wish~~ ...)

## 3 never, nobody, nothing etc

We do not usually use *nearly* before negative pronouns or adverbs like *never, nobody, nothing*. Instead, we use *almost*, or we use *hardly* with *ever, anybody, anything* etc.

>*She's **almost never** / **hardly ever** at home.* (NOT ... ~~nearly never~~ ...)
>*Almost nobody / hardly anybody was there.*

## 4 everybody, everything, anybody, anything etc

We also prefer *almost* before *everybody/-one/-thing/-where*, and *almost* is much more common than *nearly* before *anybody/-one/-thing/-where*.

>*She likes **almost everybody**.*       *Almost anybody can do this job.*
>*He's been **almost everywhere**.*       *He eats **almost anything**.*

## 5 practically

*Practically* can be used in the same way as *almost*.

>*I've **practically** finished.*       *Jake is **practically** like a father to me.*
>*She's **practically** never at home.*

# 44 alone, lonely, lonesome and lone

*Alone* means 'without others around'. *Lonely* (and informal AmE *lonesome*) means 'alone and unhappy because of it'. Compare:

>*I like to be **alone** for short periods.*
>*But after a few days I start getting **lonely/lonesome**.*

*Alone* can be emphasised by *all*.

>*After her husband died, she was **all alone**.*

*Alone* is not used before a noun (see 12.3). *Lone* and *solitary* can be used instead; *lone* is rather literary.

>*The only green thing was a **lone/solitary pine tree**.*

# 45 along

The preposition *along* is used with nouns like *road, river, corridor, line*: words that refer to things with a long thin shape.

>*I saw her running **along the road**.*
>*His office is **along the corridor**.*

To talk about periods or activities, we prefer *through*.
> ***through the centuries*** (NOT ~~*along the centuries*~~)
> *all **through the journey*** (NOT ~~*all along the journey*~~)
> *right **through the meal***

Note the special use of *along* as an adverb particle in expressions like *Come along* (= Come with me) or *walking along* (= walking on one's way).

# 46 also, as well and too

## 1 position

*Also, as well* and *too* have similar meanings, but they do not go in the same position in clauses. *Also* usually goes with the verb, in mid-position (see 24); *as well* and *too* usually go at the end of a clause. *As well* is less common in AmE.
> *She not only sings; she **also** plays the piano.*
> *She not only sings; she plays the piano **as well**.*
> *She not only sings; she plays the piano **too**.*

*As well* and *too* do not go at the beginning of a clause. *Also* can go at the beginning of a clause to give more importance to a new piece of information.
> *It's a nice house, but it's very small. **Also**, it needs a lot of repairs.*

## 2 reference

These words can refer to different parts of a clause, depending on the meaning. Consider the sentence *We work on Saturdays as well*. This can mean three different things:
a (Other people work on Saturdays, and) we work on Saturdays as well.
b (We do other things on Saturdays, and) we work on Saturdays as well.
c (We work on other days, and) we work on Saturdays as well.
When we speak, we show the exact meaning by stressing the word or expression that *also / as well / too* refers to.

## 3 imperatives and short answers

*As well* and *too* are used in imperatives and short answers, but not usually *also*.
> *Give me some bread **as well**, please.* (More natural than *Also give me . . .*)
> *She's nice. ~ Her sister is **as well**.* (More natural than *Her sister is also.*)
> *I've got a headache. ~ I have **too**.* (More natural than *I also have.*)

In very informal speech, we often use *Me too* as a short answer.
> *I'm going home. ~ **Me too**.*

More formal equivalents are *So am I* (see 541) or *I am too*, BUT NOT ~~*I also*~~.

## 4 *too* in a formal style

In a formal or literary style, *too* can be placed directly after the subject.
> *I, **too**, have experienced despair.*

For *also, as well, too* and *either* in negative clauses, see 47.
For *also* and *even*, see 189.3.
For *as well as*, see 78.

# 47 also, as well, too and either in negative clauses

## 1 negative + negative: *either*

After mentioning a negative idea or fact, we can add another negative point by using *not . . . either.*

> Peter **isn't** here today. John **isn't** here **either**. (NOT ~~John isn't here neither.~~)

*Also, as well* and *too* are not normally used with *not* in this way.

> You **can't** have an apple, and you **can't** have an orange **either**.
> (NOT . . . ~~and you can't have an orange also / as well / too.~~)

## 2 affirmative + negative: *also / as well / too*

After mentioning an affirmative (non-negative) fact or idea, we can add a negative point by using *not . . . also, not . . . as well* or *not . . . too.*

> You **can** have an apple, but you **can't** have an orange **too**.
> He **drinks** too much, but at least he **doesn't smoke as well**.

# 48 alternate(ly) and alternative(ly)

*Alternate(ly)* means 'every second', 'first one and then the other', 'in turns'.

> We spend **alternate** weekends at our country cottage.
> I'm **alternately** happy and depressed.

*Alternative(ly)* is similar to 'different', 'instead', 'on the other hand'.

> Janet's not free on the 27th. We'll have to find an **alternative** date.
> You could go by air, or **alternatively** you could drive there.

# 49 although, though, but and however: contrast

## 1 *although* and *though*: conjunctions

Both these words can be used as conjunctions, with the same meaning. In informal speech, *though* is more common. They introduce an idea ('A') with which the main clause ('B') is in contrast. When we say '(Al)though A, B', there is something unexpected or surprising about 'B'.

> *(Al)***though** (A) I don't like him, (B) I agree that he's a good manager.
> (B) I'd quite like to go out, *(al)***though** (A) it is a bit late.

## 2 *but* and *however*

We can give the same meaning by putting *but* or *however* with the contrasting, 'unexpected' clause ('B').

> (A) I don't like him, **but** (B) I agree that he's a good manager.
> (A) I don't like him. **However**, (B) I agree that he's a good manager.
> (A) It is a bit late, **but** (B) I'd quite like to go out.
> (A) It is a bit late; **however**, (B) I'd quite like to go out.

## 3 *but* and *however*: the difference

*But* is a conjunction: it joins two clauses, and comes at the beginning of the second. *However* is an adverb: it does not connect its sentence grammatically to the one before. This is why it comes after a full stop or a semi-colon in the above examples.

*However* can go in various positions. It is normally separated from its sentence by one or two commas, depending on its position.

> **However**, *the police did not believe him.*
> *The police,* **however**, *did not believe him.*
> *The police did not believe him,* **however**.

### 4 *though* used as an adverb

We can use *though* as an adverb (often at the end of a sentence), to mean 'however'.

> *Nice day.* ~ *Yes. Bit cold,* **though**.
> *The strongest argument,* **though**, *is economic and not political.*

For *as though*, see 74.
For sentences like *Cold though it was, I went out*, see 71.

## 50 altogether and all together

*Altogether* means 'completely' or 'considering everything'.

> *My new house isn't* **altogether** *finished.*
> **Altogether**, *she decided, marriage was a bit of a mistake.*

*Altogether* can also be used to give totals.

> *That's £4.38* **altogether**.

*All together* usually means 'everybody/everything together'.

> *Come on, everybody sing.* **All together** *now* . . .
> *They* **all** *went to the cinema* **together**.

## 51 American and British English

These two varieties of English are very similar. There are a few differences of grammar and spelling, and rather more differences of vocabulary and idiom. Modern British English is heavily influenced by American English, so some contrasts are disappearing. Pronunciation is sometimes very different, but most American and British speakers can understand each other easily.

### 1 grammar

Here are examples of the most important differences. In many cases, two different forms are possible in one variety of English, while only one of the forms is possible or normal in the other variety.

| American English | British English |
|---|---|
| *He* **just went** *home.* | *He's* **just gone** *home.* (See 307.2) |
| (OR *He's* **just gone** *home.*) | |
| *I've never really* **gotten** *to know her.* | *I've never really* **got** *to know her.* (See 223.7.) |
| *I* **(can)** **see** *a car coming.* | *I* **can see** *a car coming.* (See 125.1.) |

▶

| American English | British English |
|---|---|
| *Her feet were sore because her shoes fit/fitted badly.* | *Her feet were sore because her shoes fitted badly.* (See 304.3.) |
| *It's important that he be told.* | *It's important that he should be told.* (See 567.) |
| *Will you buy it? ~ I may.* | *... I may (do).* (See 161.) |
| *The committee meets tomorrow.* | *The committee meet/meets tomorrow.* (See 526.1.) |
| (on the phone) *Hello, is this Susan?* | *Hello, is that Susan?* (See 589.5.) |
| *It looks like it's going to rain.* | *It looks as if / like it's going to rain.* (See 74.3.) |
| *He looked at me real strange.* (very informal) OR *He looked at me really strangely.* | *He looked at me really strangely.* (See 27.) |
| *He probably has arrived by now.* OR *He has probably arrived ...* | *He has probably arrived by now.* (see 24.11.) |

Besides *get* and *fit*, some other irregular verbs have different forms in British and American English. For details, see 304.3.

For the Southern US second person plural pronoun *you all*, see 429.8.

## 2   vocabulary

There are very many differences. Sometimes the same word has different meanings (BrE *mad* = crazy; AmE *mad* = angry). And very often, different words are used for the same idea (BrE *lorry* = AmE *truck*). Here are a few examples, with very brief information about the words and their meanings. (A larger list with more complete information, can be found in *The British/ American Dictionary* by Norman Moss, published by Hutchinson. This is unfortunately now out of print, but may be obtainable in libraries. A more recently published guide to British-American differences is: *Mighty Fine Words and Smashing Expressions – Making Sense of Transatlantic English*, edited by Orin Hargraves, Oxford University Press.)

| American English | British English |
|---|---|
| airplane | aeroplane |
| anyplace, anywhere | anywhere |
| apartment | flat, apartment |
| area code | dialling code (*phone*) |
| attorney, lawyer | barrister, solicitor, lawyer |
| busy | engaged (*phone*) |
| call collect | reverse the charges (*phone*) |
| can | tin, can |
| candy | sweets |
| check/bill | bill (*in a restaurant*) |
| coin-purse | purse |
| cookie, cracker | biscuit |
| corn | sweet corn, maize |
| crib | cot |

| American English | British English |
|---|---|
| crazy | mad |
| crosswalk | pedestrian/zebra crossing |
| cuffs | turn-ups (*on trousers*) |
| diaper | nappy |
| doctor's office | doctor's surgery |
| dumb, stupid | stupid |
| elevator | lift |
| eraser | rubber, eraser |
| fall, autumn | autumn |
| faucet, tap | tap (*indoors*) |
| first floor, second floor etc | ground floor, first floor etc |
| flashlight | torch |
| flat (tire) | flat tyre, puncture |
| french fries | chips |
| garbage, trash | rubbish |
| garbage can, trashcan | dustbin, rubbish bin |
| gas(oline) | petrol |
| gear shift | gear lever (*on a car*) |
| highway, freeway | main road, motorway |
| hood | bonnet (*on a car*) |
| intersection | crossroads |
| mad | angry |
| mean | nasty |
| movie, film | film |
| one-way (ticket) | single (ticket) |
| pants, trousers | trousers |
| parking lot | car park |
| pavement | road surface |
| pitcher | jug |
| pocketbook, purse, handbag | handbag |
| (potato) chips | crisps |
| railroad | railway |
| raise | rise (*in salary*) |
| rest room, bathroom | (public) toilet |
| resumé | CV |
| round trip | return (journey/ticket) |
| schedule, timetable | timetable |
| sidewalk | pavement |
| sneakers | trainers (= *sports shoes*) |
| spigot, faucet | tap (*outdoors*) |
| stand in line | queue |
| stingy | mean (*opposite of 'generous'*) |
| store, shop | shop |
| subway | underground |
| truck | van, lorry |
| trunk | boot (*of a car*) |
| two weeks | fortnight, two weeks |
| vacation | holiday(s) |
| windshield | windscreen (*on a car*) |

▶

| American English | British English |
|---|---|
| zee | zed (*the name of the letter 'z'*) |
| zipper | zip |

**Expressions with prepositions and particles**

| American English | British English |
|---|---|
| check something (**out**) | **check** something |
| different **from/than** | different **from/to** (see 155) |
| do something **over/again** | do something **again** |
| **in** a course | **on** a course |
| live **on** X street | live **in** X street |
| look **around** the church | look **(a)round** the church (see 60) |
| **meet** somebody (*by chance*) /<br>**meet with** somebody<br>(*planned*) | **meet** somebody |
| Monday **through/to** Friday | Monday **to** Friday |
| **on** a team | **in** a team |
| **on** the weekend | **at** the weekend |
| ten **after/past** four (*time*) | ten **past** four |
| ten **to/of/before/till** four | ten **to** four |

## 3 spelling

A number of words end in *-or* in American English and *-our* in British English (e.g. *color/colour*). Some words end in *-er* in American English and *-re* in British English (e.g. *center/centre*). Many verbs which end in *-ize* in American English (e.g. *realize*) can be spelt in British English with *-ize* or *-ise* (see 558). Some of the commonest words with different forms are:

| American English | British English |
|---|---|
| aluminum | aluminium |
| analyze | analyse |
| catalog(ue) | catalogue |
| center | centre |
| check | cheque (*paid by a bank*) |
| color | colour |
| defense | defence |
| enroll | enrol |
| fulfill | fulfil |
| honor | honour |
| jewelry | jewellery |
| labor | labour |
| liter | litre |
| meter (*measure*) | metre |
| neighbor | neighbour |
| organize | organise/organize |
| pajamas | pyjamas |
| paralyze | paralyse |
| practice, practise | practise (*verb*) |
| program | programme |
| realize | realise/realize |

| American English | British English |
|---|---|
| skillful | skilful |
| theater/theatre | theatre |
| tire | tyre (*on a wheel*) |
| trave(l)ler | traveller (see 562) |
| whiskey | (Scotch) whisky, (Irish) whiskey |

## 4  pronunciation

There are, of course, many different regional accents in both Britain and America. The most important general differences between American and British speech are as follows:

**a**  Certain vowels are nasal (pronounced through the nose and mouth at the same time) in some varieties of American English, but not in most British accents.

**b**  British English has one more vowel than American English. This is the rounded short o (/ɒ/) used in words like *cot, dog, got, gone, off, stop, lost*. In American English these words are pronounced either with /ɑː/, like the first vowel in *father*, or with /ɔː/, like the vowel in *caught*. (This vowel is also pronounced rather differently in British and American English.)

**c**  Some words written with *a* + **consonant** (e.g. *fast, after*) have different pronunciations: with /ɑː/ in standard southern British English, and with /æ/ in American and some other varieties of English.

**d**  The vowel in *home, go, open* is pronounced /əʊ/ in standard southern British English, and /oʊ/ in American English. The two vowels sound very different.

**e**  In standard southern British English, *r* is only pronounced before a vowel sound. In most kinds of American English, (and most other British varieties) *r* is pronounced in all positions where it is written in a word, and it changes the quality of a vowel that comes before it. So words like *car, turn, offer* sound very different in British and American speech.

**f**  In many varieties of American English, *t* and *d* both have a very light voiced pronunciation (/d/) between vowels – so *writer* and *rider*, for example, can sound the same. In British English they are quite different: /ˈraɪtə(r)/ and /ˈraɪdə(r)/.

**g**  Some words which are pronounced with /uː/ in most varieties of American English have /juː/ in British English. These are words in which *th, d, t* or *n* (and sometimes *s* or *l*) are followed by *u* or *ew* in writing.

| | | |
|---|---|---|
| *enthusiastic* | AmE /ɪnˌθuːziˈæstɪk/ | BrE /ɪnˌθjuːziˈæstɪk/ |
| *duty* | AmE /ˈduːti/ | BrE /ˈdjuːti/ |
| *tune* | AmE /tuːn/ | BrE /tjuːn/ |
| *new* | AmE /nuː/ | BrE /njuː/ |
| *illuminate* | AmE /ɪˈluːmɪneɪt/ | BrE /ɪˈljuːmɪneɪt/ |

▶

**h** Words ending in unstressed *-ile* (e.g. *fertile, reptile, missile, senile*) are pronounced with /aɪl/ in British English; some are pronounced with /l/ in American English.
*fertile*   AmE /ˈfɜːrtl/ (rhyming with *turtle*)
            BrE /ˈfɜːtaɪl/ (rhyming with *her tile*)

**i** Some long words ending in *-ary*, *-ery* or *-ory* are pronounced differently, with one more syllable in American English.
*secretary*   AmE /ˈsekrəteri/   BrE /ˈsekrətri/

**j** *Borough* and *thorough* are pronounced differently.
AmE /ˈbʌroʊ, ˈθʌroʊ/
BrE /ˈbʌrə, ˈθʌrə/

**k** Words borrowed from French are often stressed differently, especially if their pronunciation ends with a vowel sound. The final vowel is usually stressed in American English but not in British English.
*paté*   AmE /pæˈteɪ/   BrE /ˈpæteɪ/
*ballet*   AmE /bæˈleɪ/   BrE /ˈbæleɪ/

## 52   and

### 1   use

When we join two or more grammatically similar expressions, we usually put *and* before the last.
> *bread **and** cheese*
> *We drank, talked **and** danced.*
> *I wrote the letters, Peter addressed them, George bought the stamps **and** Alice posted them.*

*And* is sometimes left out in a very literary or poetic style, but this is unusual.
> *My dreams are full of darkness, despair, death.*

### 2   fixed expressions

Some common expressions with *and* have a fixed order which cannot be changed. The shortest expression often comes first.
> *bread and butter* (NOT ~~butter and bread~~)
> *hands and knees* (NOT ~~knees and hands~~)
> *young and pretty*      *thunder and lightning*
> *black and white*      *cup and saucer*      *knife and fork*

Note: *and* is usually pronounced /ənd/, not /ænd/ (see 616).

For *and* with adjectives, see 16.
For rules about the use of commas, see 476.
For ellipsis after *and*, in expressions like *a knife and (a) fork, the bread and (the) butter*, see 178.
For singular and plural verbs after subjects with *and*, see 527.5.
For *and* after *try, wait, go, come* etc, see 53.
For *both . . . and*, see 111.

# 53 **and** after **try, wait, go** etc

## 1 *try / be sure / wait and ...*

We often use *and ...* instead of *to* after *try / be sure.* This is informal.
> **Try and** *eat something – you'll feel better if you do.*
> **I'll try and** *phone you tomorrow morning.*
> **Be sure and** *ask Uncle Joe about his garden.*

Note also the common expression *Wait and see.*
> *What's for lunch? ~* **Wait and see.**

We only use this structure with the simple base forms *try / be sure / wait.* It is not possible, for example, with *tries, trying, was sure* or *waited.* Compare:
> **Try and** *eat something.*
> **I tried to** *eat something.* (NOT *I tried and ate something.*)
> *We* **waited to see** *what would happen.* (NOT *We waited and saw ...*)

## 2 *come/go/etc and ...*

*Come and ..., go and ..., run and ..., hurry up and ..., stay and ...* are often used informally.
> **Come and** *have a drink.*
> **Stay and** *have dinner.*     **Hurry up and** *open the door.*

With these verbs, the structure is not only used with the base form.
> *He often* **comes and spends** *the evening with us.*
> *She* **stayed and played** *with the children.*     *She thought of* **going and getting** *him.*

## 3 **American English**

In informal American English, *and* is sometimes dropped after the base forms *go* and *come.*
> *Let's* **go see** *if Anne's home.*
> **Go jump** *in the river.*     **Come sit** *on my lap.*

# 54 **another** and **other(s)**

## 1 **spelling of** *another*

*Another* is one word.
> *He's bought* **another** *car.* (NOT *... an other car.*)

## 2 **'additional, extra'**

*Another* can mean 'an additional, extra'. It is used with singular countable nouns.
> *Could I have* **another piece** *of bread?*

*Another* can be used without a noun, or with *one,* if the meaning is clear from what has come before.
> *Those cakes are wonderful. Could I have* **another (one)?**

With uncountable and plural nouns, we normally use *more,* not *other,* with this meaning.
> *Would you like some* **more meat?** (NOT *... other meat?*)     ▶

*Would you like some **more peas**?* (NOT . . . ~~other peas?~~)
However, we can use *another* before a plural noun in expressions with *few* or a number.
> *I'm staying for **another few weeks**.*     *We need **another three chairs**.*
For other cases where *a(n)* is followed by a plural, see 532.6.

### 3 'alternative'

*(An)other* can also mean '(an) alternative', 'besides / instead of this/these'.
> *I think we should paint it **another** colour.*
> *Have you got any **other** cakes, or are these the only ones?*
*Other people* often means 'people besides oneself'.
> *Why don't you think more about **other people**?*

### 4 *other* and *others*

When *other* is used with a noun it has no plural form.
> *Where are the **other** photos?* (NOT . . . ~~the others photos?~~)
But used alone, without a noun, it can have a plural form.
> *I've got one lot of photos. Where are the **others**?*
> *These are too small. Have you got any **others**?*
Normally, *other(s)* is only used alone if it refers to a noun that has been mentioned before. An exception is the common plural use of *(the) others* to mean *(the) other people*.
> *He never thinks of **others**.*     *Jake's arrived – I must tell **the others**.*
> BUT NOT ~~On the phone, one cannot see the other~~ OR ~~He never listens to another~~.

### 5 not used like an adjective

*Other* is a determiner or pronoun; it is not used exactly like an adjective. So it cannot normally have an adverb before it, or be used after a link verb.
> *I'd prefer a **completely different** colour.* (NOT . . . ~~a completely other colour.~~)
> *You **look different** with a beard.* (NOT ~~You look other~~ . . .)

For *one another*, see 171.

# 55 any

### 1 meaning

*Any* is a determiner (see 154). It generally suggests an indefinite amount or number, and is used when it is not important to say how much/many we are thinking of. Because of its 'open', non-specific meaning, *any* is often used in questions and negative clauses, and in other cases where there is an idea of doubt or negation.
> *Have you got **any** biscuits?*
> *We didn't have **any** problems going through customs.*
> *You never give me **any** help.*
> *The noise of the party stopped me getting **any** sleep.*
> *I suddenly realised I'd come out without **any** money.Any is common after if.*
> *If you find **any** blackberries, keep some for me.*
Sometimes *any* means 'if there is/are any' or 'whatever there is/are'.

*Any fog will clear by noon.* (= If there is any fog, it will clear by noon.)
*Perhaps you could correct **any** mistakes I've made.*

*Any* can be used to emphasise the idea of open choice: 'it doesn't matter who/what/which'.

*You can borrow **any** book you like.*

For details of this use, see paragraph 5 below.

## 2   any and *some*

*Any* often contrasts with *some*, which is most common in affirmative clauses. Compare:

*I need **some** razor blades.*          *Have you got **any** razor blades?*
*Sorry, I haven't got **any** razor blades.*

For details of the difference, see 547.

## 3   any and *not any*

*Any* alone does not have a negative meaning. It is only negative when used with *not*.

*She's unhappy because she hasn't got **any** friends.* (NOT ... ~~because she has got any friends.~~)

*No* (see 376) means the same as *not any*, but is more emphatic.

*She's got **no** friends.*

*Not any* cannot begin a sentence; *no* is used instead.

***No** cigarette is harmless.* (NOT ~~Not any cigarette~~...)
***No** tourists came to the town that year.*

We do not usually use *not any* with singular countable nouns.

*She hasn't got **a job**.* (NOT ~~She hasn't got any job.~~)

## 4   nouns with and without *any*

With an uncountable or plural noun, *any* usually suggests the idea of an indefinite amount or indefinite number. Compare:

– *Is there **any** water in that can?*
  *Is there **water** on the moon?* (The interest is in the existence of water, not its amount.)
– *Dad hasn't got **any** hair.* (He has lost the amount he had.)
  *Birds have feathers, not **hair**.* (No idea of amount.)
– *None of her children have got **any** sense.* (Not even a small amount.)
  *Ann looks like her mother, but she hasn't got **blue eyes**.* (NOT... ~~she hasn't got any blue eyes~~ – people have a definite number of eyes: two.)

## 5   any = 'it doesn't matter who/which/what'

*Any* can be used to emphasise the idea of free choice, with the meaning of 'it doesn't matter who/which/what'. With this meaning, *any* is common in affirmative clauses as well as questions and negatives, and is often used with singular countable nouns as well as uncountables and plurals. In speech, it is stressed.

*Ask **any** doctor – they'll all tell you that alcohol is a poison.*
*She goes out with **any** boy who asks her.*
*When shall I come? ~ **Any** time.*

We can use *just any* if necessary to make the meaning clear.          ▶

*I don't do just any work – I choose jobs that interest me.*
  (*I don't do any work* ... could be misunderstood.)
Note that we use *either* (see 174), not *any*, to talk about a choice between two alternatives.
  *I can write with either hand.* (NOT ... ~~any hand.~~)

## 6 at all

*At all* (see 83) is often used to emphasise the meaning of *(not) any*.
  *I'll do any job at all – even road-sweeping.*
  *She doesn't speak any English at all.*

## 7 any and any of

Before a determiner (definite article, demonstrative or possessive word) or a pronoun, we use *any of* (see 154.4) Compare:
  – *I didn't go to any lectures last term.* (NOT ... ~~any of lectures~~ ...)
    *I wasn't interested in any of the lectures.* (NOT ... ~~any the lectures.~~)
  – *Do any books here belong to you?*
    *Do any of these books belong to you?*
  – *I don't think any staff want to work tomorrow.*
    *I don't think any of us want to work tomorrow.*
Note that when *any of* is followed by a plural subject, the verb can be singular or plural. A singular verb is more common in a formal style.
  *If any of your friends is/are interested, let me know.*

## 8 without a noun

A noun can be dropped after *any*, if the meaning is clear.
  *Did you get the oil?* ~ *No, there wasn't any left.*
Instead of *not any* without a noun, *none* (see 376) can be used. This is often more emphatic.
  *There was none left.*
We don't use *any* or *not any* alone as answers.
  *What day shall I come?* ~ *Any day.* (NOT ~~Any.~~)
  *How much money have you got?* ~ *None.* (NOT ~~Not any.~~)

## 9 compounds

Many of the rules given above also apply to the compounds *anybody, anyone, anything* and *anywhere*. For more information about these, see 548.

For the use of *any* and *no* as adverbs, see 57.
For *any ... but*, see 116.
For *any* and *every*, see 56.

# 56 any and every

*Any* and *every* can both be used to talk in general about all the members of a class or group.
  *Any/Every child can learn to swim.*
The meaning is not quite the same. *Any* looks at things one at a time: it means 'whichever one you choose', 'this or that or the other'. *Every* looks at things together: its meaning is closer to 'all', 'this and that and the other'. Compare:

*Which newspaper would you like?* ~ *It doesn't matter. **Any** one.* (= one or another or another) (NOT . . . ~~Every one.~~)
*On the stand there were newspapers and magazines of **every** kind.* (= one and another and another) (NOT . . . ~~magazines of any kind.~~)

For more information about *any*, see 55.
For *every*, see 193.

# 57 **any** and **no**: adverbs

## 1 *any* and *no* with comparatives

*Any* can modify comparatives. This happens mostly in questions and negative sentences, and after *if* (see also 381).
   *Can you go **any faster**?*
   *You don't look **any older** than your daughter.* (= You don't look at all older . . .)
   *If I were **any younger**, I'd fall in love with you.*
*No* can also be used in this way (but not *some*).
   *I'm afraid the weather's **no better** than yesterday.*

## 2 *any/no different*

We can also use *any* and *no* with *different*.
   *This school isn't **any different** from the last one.*
   *Is John any better?* ~ **No different**. *Still very ill.*

## 3 *any/no good; any/no use*

Note the expressions *any good/use* and *no good/use*.
   *Was the film **any good**?*     *This watch is **no use**. It keeps stopping.*

# 58 **appear**

## 1 link verb: 'seem'

*Appear* can be a link verb (see 328), used to say how things look or seem. It is used in similar ways to *seem* (see 507 for details), but is less frequent, especially in an informal style.
With this meaning, *appear* is followed by adjectives, not adverbs. We can use *appear* or *appear to be*.
   *He **appears (to be)** very **angry** today.* (NOT *He appears very angrily today.*)
Before nouns we generally use *appear to be*.
   *It **appears to be** some kind of bomb.*
   *The boys on the bus **appeared to be** students.*
Structures with preparatory *there* (see 587) or *it* (see 446) are possible.
   **There** *appears to be a problem with the oil pressure.*
   **It** *appears that we may be mistaken.*

## 2 *appear* and *seem*: differences

*Seem* can be used to talk both about objective facts and about subjective impressions and feelings (see 507 for examples). *Appear* is mostly used to talk about objective facts. Compare:

▶

The baby *seems/appears (to be)* hungry.
She doesn't want to go on studying. It *seems* a pity. (NOT ~~It appears a pity.~~)
*Seem* is often used with *like*. This is not normal with *appear*.
It *seemed like* a good idea. (More natural than *It appeared like a good idea.*)
*Seem* can be used in a special structure with *can't* (see 507.4). This is not
possible with *appear*.
I *can't seem* to make him understand. (BUT NOT ~~I can't appear to make him~~
~~understand.~~)

### 3  'come into sight'

*Appear* can also mean 'come into sight' or 'arrive'. In this case it can be
modified by an adverb.
She *suddenly appeared* in the doorway.

For structures with *look*, see 331.

## 59  arise and rise

*Arise* means 'begin', 'appear', 'occur', 'come to one's notice'. It is used mostly
with abstract nouns as subjects.
A discussion *arose* about the best way to pay.
I'm afraid a difficulty has *arisen*.
*Rise* usually means 'get higher', 'come/go up'.
Prices keep *rising*. What time does the sun *rise*?
My hopes are *rising*.
Note that we usually say that people *get up* in the morning. *Rise* is only used
with this meaning in a very formal style.
*Arise* and *rise* are irregular verbs.
*(a)rise – (a)rose – (a)risen*

For the difference between *rise* and *raise*, see 304.2.

## 60  (a)round and about

### 1  circular movement etc: *(a)round*

We use both *round* and *around* (AmE usually *around*) for movement or
position in a circle or a curve.
She walked *(a)round* the car and looked at the wheels.
I'd like to travel *(a)round* the world.
Where do you live? ~ Just *(a)round* the corner.

### 2  touring; distribution: *round*

We also use *round* or *around* (AmE usually *around*) to talk about going to all
(or most) parts of a place, or giving things to everybody in a group.
We walked *(a)round* the old part of the town.
Can I look *(a)round*? Could you pass the cups *(a)round*, please?

## 3 indefinite movement and position

We use *around* or *about* (AmE usually *around*) to refer to movements or positions that are not very clear or definite: 'here and there', 'in lots of places', 'in different parts of', 'somewhere in' and similar ideas.

*The children were running **around/about** everywhere.*
*Stop standing **around/about** and do some work.*
*Where's John? ~ Somewhere **around/about**.*
*I like doing odd jobs **around/about** the house.*

We also use these words in some common expressions to talk about time-wasting or silly activity.

*Stop **fooling around/about**. We're late.*

## 4 approximately: *about*

*About* (less often *around*) can mean 'approximately', 'not exactly'.

*There were **about/around** fifty people there.*
*What time shall I come? ~ **About/Around** eight.*

For other uses of these words, see a good dictionary.

# 61 articles (1): introduction

## 1 What are articles?

Articles are small words that are often used at the beginning of noun phrases. There are two: *the* (the 'definite article') and *a/an* (the 'indefinite article'). They belong to a group of words called 'determiners' (see 154).

## 2 What are articles used for?

Articles can show whether we are talking about things that are known both to the speaker/writer and to the listener/reader ('definite'), or that are not known to them both ('indefinite').

## 3 How much do articles matter?

The correct use of the articles is one of the most difficult points in English grammar. Fortunately, most article mistakes do not matter too much. Even if we leave all the articles out of a sentence, it can usually be understood.

*Please can you lend me pound of butter till end of week?*

However, it is better to use the articles correctly if possible. Sections 62–70 give the most important rules and exceptions.

## 4 speakers of Western European languages

Most languages of Western European origin, and one or two others, have article systems quite like English. However, there are some differences in the way articles are used in English and these other languages. The most important differences are explained in Section 63. Students should read this first if they speak one of the following languages perfectly or very well: French, German, Dutch, Danish, Swedish, Norwegian, Icelandic, Spanish, Catalan, Italian, Portuguese, Greek, Romanian. There is more detailed information on difficult points in Sections 64–70.

▶

## 5   speakers of other languages

If a student's language is one (e.g. Russian or Japanese) that is not listed in paragraph 4, he or she may have more difficulty with the correct use of articles. The most important rules are explained in Section 62, and students should read this first. There is more detailed information on difficult points in Sections 64–70.

# 62   articles (2): basic information (A)

(This Section is for students who speak languages (e.g. Russian or Japanese) that do not have articles like English *a/an* and *the*. Students who speak languages which have articles (e.g. German or Portuguese) should read Section 63.)

## 1   two basic rules

- To say 'You know which I mean', we put *the* before a noun.
  *I've been to the doctor.* (You know which one: my doctor.)
  *Have you fed the dogs?* (You know which ones I mean.)
  *Could you pass the salt?* (You can see the salt that I want.)
- When we can't say 'You know which I mean', we:
  – put *a/an* before a singular countable noun (see 65).
  *There's a rat in the kitchen!*   *I need an envelope.*
  – put no article with a plural or uncountable noun.
  *She's afraid of rats.*   *I need help.*

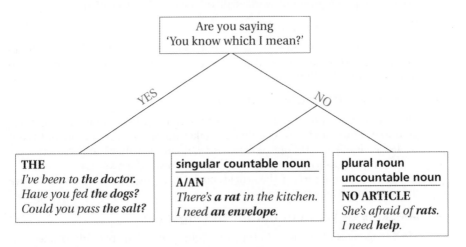

## 2   four common mistakes to avoid

- Don't use *a/an* with plural or uncountable nouns.
  *John collects stamps.* (NOT ... ~~a stamps.~~)
  *Our garden needs water.* (NOT ... ~~a water.~~)

- Don't use *the* to talk about things in general. *The* does not mean 'all'. (For exceptions, see 68.2.)

  **Elephants** *can swim very well.* (NOT ~~The elephants can swim~~ ...)

  **Petrol** *is expensive.* (NOT ~~The petrol~~ ...)

- Don't use articles together with *my*, *this*, or other determiners.

  **my work** (NOT ~~the my work~~)

  **this problem** (NOT ~~the this problem~~)

  **a friend** *of mine* (NOT ~~a my friend~~)

- Don't use singular countable nouns alone, without an article or other determiner. We can say *a cat*, *the cat*, *my cat*, *this cat*, *any cat*, *either cat* or *every cat*, but not just *cat*. (For exceptions, see 70.)

  *Give it to* **the cat**. (NOT ~~Give it to cat.~~)

  *Annie is* **a doctor**. (NOT ~~Annie is doctor.~~)

For more detailed information about articles, see the following sections.

# 63 articles (3): basic information (B)

(This Section is for students who speak a language that has articles: e.g. French, German, Swedish, Norwegian, Spanish, Italian, Greek. If you speak a language without articles – for example Russian or Japanese – read Section 62.)

Articles are often used in similar ways in English and other languages, but there are some differences. The most important are as follows.

## 1 talking in general

In English, when we are talking about people or things in general, we do not usually use *the* with uncountable or plural nouns.

**Life** *is complicated.* (NOT ~~The life is complicated.~~)

*My sister loves* **horses**. (NOT ... ~~the horses.~~)

## 2 talking about jobs, types etc

In English, we normally put *a/an* with a singular noun that is used for classifying – saying what job somebody has, what class, group or type somebody or something belongs to, what we use something for, etc.

*She's* **a dentist**. (NOT ~~She's dentist.~~)

*I'm looking forward to being* **a grandmother**.

*I used my shoe as* **a hammer**.

For more detailed information about articles, see the following Sections.

# 64 articles (4): more about the

## 1 *the* = 'you know which one(s)'

*The* usually means something like 'you know which I mean'. We use *the* before a noun (singular, plural or uncountable) when our listener/reader knows (or can easily see) which particular person(s), thing(s) etc we are talking about. Compare:

- *I'm going to* **the post office**. (The listener knows which: the usual one.)

  *Is there* **a post office** *near here?* (Any post office.)

- *I didn't like* **the film**. (The one that the speaker and listener saw.)

  *Let's go and see* **a film**. (The speaker doesn't say which one.) ▶

- *She arrived on **the 8.15 train**.* (The speaker says which train.)
  *She arrived in **an old taxi**.* (The speaker doesn't say which taxi.)
- *Did you wash **the clothes**?* (The listener knows which clothes.)
  *I need to buy **clothes**.* (The listener does not know which clothes.)
- *What did you do with **the coffee** I bought?* (The speaker says which coffee.)
  *I don't drink **coffee**.* (Any coffee.)

Our listener/reader may know which one(s) we mean because:

a we have mentioned it/them before
  *She's got two children: a boy and a girl. **The boy**'s fourteen and **the girl**'s eight.*
  *So what did you do then? ~ Gave **the money** straight back to **the policeman**.* (The listener has already heard about the money and the policeman.)

b we say which one(s) we mean
  *Who are **the girls over there** with John?*
  *Tell Pat **the story about John and Susie**.     I'll try **the green shirt**.*

c it is clear from the situation which one(s) we mean
  *Could you close **the door**?* (Only one door is open.)
  *Ann's in **the kitchen**.        Could you feed **the dogs**?*
  *Did you enjoy **the party**?     What's **the time**?*

## 2   *the* = 'the only one(s) around'

The listener may know which one we mean because there is no choice – there is only one (e.g. *the sun, the moon, the earth, the world, the universe, the future*) or there is only one in our part of the world (e.g. *the government*).
  *I haven't seen **the sun** for days.       Do you trust **the government**?*
  *People used to think **the earth** was flat.*

## 3   superlatives

We usually use *the* with superlatives (see 141.6) because there is normally only one best, biggest etc individual or group (so it is clear which one(s) we are talking about). For the same reason, we usually use *the* with *first, next, last, same* and *only*.
  *I'm **the oldest** in my family.       Can I have **the next** pancake?*
  *We went to **the same** school.*

## 4   *the* meaning 'the well-known'

After a name, an identifying expression with *the* is often used to make it clear that the person referred to is 'the well-known one'.
  *She married Richard Burton, **the actor**.*
  *I'd like you to meet Cathy Parker, **the novelist**.*

## 5   possessives and demonstratives

We do not use *the* with possessives or demonstratives.
  *This is **my uncle**.* (NOT *... ~~the my uncle.~~*)
  *Is that **Mary's car**?* (NOT *... ~~the Mary's car?~~*)
  *I like **this beer**.* (NOT *... ~~the this beer.~~*)

## 6   proper nouns (names)

We do not usually use *the* with singular proper nouns (there are some exceptions – see 70.17–18).

   *Mary lives in Switzerland.* (NOT ~~The Mary lives in the Switzerland.~~)
But note the use of *the* (pronounced /ðiː/) with a person's name to mean 'the well-known'.

   *My name's James Bond.* ~ *What, not the James Bond?*

## 7   things in general

We usually use no article, not *the*, to talk about things in general – *the* does not mean 'all'. (For details and exceptions, see 68.)

   *Books are expensive.* (NOT ~~The books are expensive.~~)
   *Life is hard.* (NOT ~~The life is hard.~~)

## 8   pronunciation

*The* is normally pronounced /ðiː/ before a vowel and /ðə/ before a consonant. Compare:

   *the ice* /ðiː aɪs/        *the snow* /ðə snəʊ/
The choice between /ðiː/ and /ðə/ depends on pronunciation, not spelling. We pronounce /ðiː/ before a vowel sound, even if it is written as a consonant.

   *the hour* /ðiː 'aʊə(r)/        *the MP* /ðiː em 'piː/
And we pronounce /ðə/ before a consonant sound, even if it is written as a vowel.

   *the **u**niversity* /ðə juːnɪ'vɜːsəti/
   *the **o**ne-pound coin* /ðə 'wʌn 'paʊnd 'kɔɪn/
We sometimes pronounce a stressed /ðiː/ before a hesitation, or when we want to stress the following word, even if it begins with a consonant.

   *He's the* /ðiː/ *– just a moment – deputy assistant vice-president.*
   *I've found the* /ðiː/ *present for Angela!*

For *the town, the country, the sea, the mountains*, etc, see 69.4.
For *on the bus, at the hairdresser*, etc, see 69.5.
For other advanced points, see 69.

# 65   articles (5): more about a/an

## 1   countable and uncountable nouns

Countable nouns are the names of separate objects, people, ideas etc which we can count.

   *a cat – three cats*
   *a secretary – four secretaries*
   *a plan – two plans*
Uncountable nouns are the names of materials, liquids and other things which we do not usually see as separate objects.

   *wool* (BUT NOT ~~a wool, two wools~~)
   *water* (BUT NOT ~~a water, three waters~~)
   *weather* (BUT NOT ~~a weather, four weathers~~)
   *energy* (BUT NOT ~~an energy, several energies~~)

For more detailed information, see 148–149.                              ▶

## 2   *a/an* with singular countable nouns

We normally use *a/an* only with singular countable nouns.
**a secretary      an office**
BUT NOT ~~a salt~~ OR ~~an offices~~

For expressions like *a good two hours*, see 532.6.

## 3   uses of *a/an*

*A/an* does not add much to the meaning of a noun – it is like a weak form of 'one'. It has several common uses.

### a   one person or thing

We can use *a/an* when we talk about one person or thing.
*There's **a police car** outside.*
*My brother's married to **a doctor**.     Andy lives in **an old house**.*

### b   any one member of a class.

We can use *a/an* when we talk about **any one member** of a class.
***A doctor** must like people.* (= any doctor)
*I would like to live in **an old house**.* (= any old house)

### c   classifying and defining

We can use *a/an* when we classify or define people and things – when we say what they are, what job they do, or what they are used for.
*She's **a doctor**.*
*I'm looking forward to being **a grandmother**.*
*A glider is **a plane** with no engine.*
*Don't use your plate as **an ashtray**.*

### d   descriptions

*A/an* is common before nouns that are used in descriptions.
*She's **a nice person**.          That was **a lovely evening**.*
*He's got **a friendly face**.      It's **an extremely hot day**.*

## 4   when *a/an* cannot be left out

We do not normally leave out *a/an* in negative expressions, after prepositions or after fractions.
*Lend me your pen. ~ I haven't got **a pen**.* (NOT ~~I haven't got pen.~~)
*You mustn't go out without **a coat**.* (NOT *. . .* ~~without coat.~~)
*three-quarters of **a pound*** (NOT ~~three-quarters of pound~~)
And we do not leave out *a/an* when we say what jobs people have, or how things are used (see above).
*She's **an engineer**.* (NOT ~~She's engineer.~~)
*I used my shoe as **a hammer**.* (NOT *. . .* ~~as hammer.~~)

## 5   when *a/an* is not used: adjectives alone; possessives

*A/an* cannot normally be used with an adjective alone (without a noun). Compare:
*It's **a good car**.      It's **good**.* (NOT ~~It's a good.~~)

*A/an* cannot be used together with a possessive. Instead, we can use the structure *a . . . of mine/yours* etc (see 443).
>He's ***a friend of mine***. (NOT ~~He's a my friend.~~)

## 6 a/an and *the*

Instead of *a/an*, we use *the* when we want to say 'You and I both know which one I mean'. Compare:
>She lives in ***a big house***. (The hearer doesn't know which one.)
>She lives in ***the big house*** *over there*. (The hearer knows which one.)

For details, see 64.

## 7 *a* and *an*: the difference

We do not normally pronounce the sound /ə/ before a vowel. So before a vowel, the article *a* (/ə/) changes to *an*. Compare:
>*a rabbit*          *a lemon*          *an elephant*          *an orange*

The choice between *a* and *an* depends on pronunciation, not spelling. We use *an* before a vowel sound, even if it is written as a consonant.
>*an hour* /ən 'aʊər/    *an MP* /ən em 'piː/

And we use *a* before a consonant sound, even if it is written as a vowel.
>*a university* /ə juːnɪ'vɜːsəti/    *a one-pound coin* /ə 'wʌn . . ./

Some people say *an*, not *a*, before words beginning with *h* if the first syllable is unstressed.
>*an hotel* (*a hotel* is more common)
>*an historic occasion* (*a historic . . .* is more common)
>(BUT NOT ~~an housewife~~ – the first syllable is stressed.)

*A* is sometimes pronounced /eɪ/ before a hesitation, when we want to emphasise the following word, or when we want to make a contrast with *the*.
>*I think I'll have a* /eɪ/ *– chocolate ice cream.*
>*It's a* /eɪ/ *reason – it's not the only reason.*

# 66  articles (6): no article with plural and uncountable nouns

## 1  *a/an* not used

Plural and uncountable nouns (e.g. *cats, wool* – see 65.1) cannot normally be used with *a/an* (because *a/an* has a similar meaning to 'one'). Instead, we most often use no article.
>There were ***cats*** *in every room.* (NOT *. . .* ~~a cats~~ *. . .*)
>Doctors generally work long ***hours***.          He's got very big ***ears***.
>Her coat is made of pure ***wool***.
>What's that? ~ I think it's ***pepper***.

## 2  confusing nouns

Some nouns that are countable in some other languages are uncountable in English (see 148.3 for a list).
>I need ***information*** and ***advice***. (NOT *. . .* ~~an information and an advice~~)
>You've made very good ***progress***. (NOT *. . .* ~~a very good progress.~~)

▶

And note that we never use *a/an* with *weather* or *English*.
> *We're having terrible **weather**.* (NOT . . . ~~a terrible weather.~~)
> *She speaks very good **English**.* (NOT . . . ~~a very good English.~~)

### 3  *some* and *any*

Instead of no article, we can sometimes use *some* or *any*.
> *We met **some** nice French girls on holiday.*
> *Have you got **any** matches?*
For details, see 67.

### 4  *the*

Instead of no article, we use *the* when we want to say 'You and I both know which I mean' (see 64). Compare:
> – *I'm working with **children**.* (The hearer doesn't know which ones.)
>   *How are **the children**?* (= the hearer's children)
> – *We need **salt**.* (= any salt)
>   *Could you pass **the salt**?* (The hearer can see the salt that is wanted.)
But we usually use no article, not *the*, to talk about people, things etc in general (see 68).
> *Are **dogs** more intelligent than cats?* (NOT . . . ~~the dogs~~ . . . ~~the cats~~)
> *Everybody likes **music**.* (NOT . . . ~~the music.~~)

For expressions like *a coffee, a knowledge of Spanish*, see 148.4, 6.

# 67  articles (7): the difference between some/any and no article

### 1  use with uncountable and plural nouns

Uncountable and plural nouns can often be used either with *some/any* or with **no article**. There is not always a great difference of meaning.
> *We need **(some) cheese**.*     *I didn't buy **(any) eggs**.*
*Some* is used especially in affirmative sentences; *any* is more common in questions and negatives (for details, see 547).

### 2  *some/any* or no article?

We prefer *some/any* when we are thinking about limited but rather indefinite numbers or quantities – when we don't know, care or say exactly how much/many. We prefer **no article** when we are thinking about unlimited numbers or quantities, or not thinking about numbers/quantities at all. Compare:
> – *We've planted **some roses** in the garden.* (A limited number; the speaker doesn't say how many.)
>   *I like **roses**.* (No idea of number.)
> – *We got talking to **some students**.* (A limited number.)
>   *Our next-door neighbours are **students**.* (The main idea is classification, not number.)
> – *I've just bought **some books** on computing.* (A limited number.)
>   *There were **books** on the desk, on the floor, on the chairs, . . .* (A large number.)

- *Would you like **some** more rice?* (An indefinite amount – as much as the listener wants.)
   *We need **rice**, sugar, eggs, butter, beer, and toilet paper.* (The speaker is thinking just of the things that need to be bought, not of the amounts.)
- *Is there **any water** in the fridge?* (The speaker wants a limited amount.)
   *Is there **water** on the moon?* (The interest is in the existence of water, not the amount.)
- *This engine hardly uses **any** petrol.* (The interest is in the amount.)
   *This engine doesn't use **petrol**.* (The interest is in the type of fuel, not the amount.)

We do not use *some/any* when it is clear exactly how much/many we are talking about. Compare:
- *You've got **some great books**.*
   *You've got **pretty toes**.* (A definite number – ten. *You've got some pretty toes* would suggest that the speaker is not making it clear how many – perhaps six or seven!)

For details of the difference between *some* and *any*, see 547.
For full details of the uses of *some*, see 546; for *any*, see 55.

# 68 articles (8): talking in general

## 1 *the* does not mean 'all'

We do not use *the* with uncountable or plural nouns to talk about things in general – to talk about all books, all people or all life, for example. *The* does not mean 'all'. Instead, we use **no article**. Compare:
- *Move **the books** off that chair and sit down.* (= particular books)
   ***Books** are expensive.* (NOT ~~The books are expensive.~~)
- *I'm studying **the life** of Beethoven.* (= one particular life)
   ***Life** is complicated.* (NOT ~~The life...~~ )
- *Where's **the cheese**? ~ I ate it.*      – *Why has **the light** gone out?*
   *I love **cheese**.*                   *Nothing can travel faster than **light**.*
- *I've joined **the** local Dramatic **Society**.*
   *It's not always easy to fit in with **society**.*
- *I never really understood **the nature** of my father's work.*
   *She's very interested in **nature**, especially animals and birds.*
- *Write your name in **the space** at the bottom of the page.*
   *Would you like to travel into **space**?*

Note that *most* (meaning 'the majority of') is used without *the*.
   ***Most** birds can fly.* (NOT ~~The most...~~)
   ***Most** of the children got very tired.* (NOT ~~The most...~~)

## 2 generalisations with singular countable nouns

Sometimes we talk about things in general by using *the* with a singular countable noun.
   *Schools should concentrate more on **the child** and less on exams.*
This is common with the names of scientific instruments and inventions, and musical instruments.
   *Life would be quieter without **the telephone**.*
   ***The violin** is more difficult than **the piano**.*

▶

We can also generalise by talking about one example of a class, using *a/an* (meaning 'any') with a singular countable noun.

> *A **baby deer** can stand as soon as it's born.*
> *A **child** needs plenty of love.*

Note that we cannot use *a/an* in this way when we are generalising about all of the members of a group together.

> *The tiger is in danger of becoming extinct.* (NOT *A tiger is in danger of becoming extinct.* The sentence is about the whole tiger family, not about individuals.)
> *Do you like **horses**?* (NOT *Do you like a horse?*)

For the use of *the* + **adjective** to generalise about groups (e.g. *the old, the blind*) see 17.

# 69 articles (9): the (difficult cases)

It is sometimes difficult to know whether or not to use *the*. For example, we use no article to **generalise** with uncountable and plural words (see 68); but we use *the* to show that the listener/reader **knows which** people or things we are talking about (see 64). Sometimes both these meanings come together, and it is difficult to know which form is correct. The grammatical distinctions in this area are not very clear; often the same idea can be expressed both with *the* and with no article. The following notes may help.

## 1 groups: *nurses* or *the nurses*; *railways* or *the railways*?

When we generalise about **members** of a group, we usually use no article. But if we talk about the group **as a whole** – as if it was a well-known unit – we are more likely to use *the*. Compare:

- *Nurses mostly work very hard.*            – *Stars vary greatly in size.*
  *The nurses have never gone on strike.*      *The stars are really bright tonight.*
- *Farmers often vote Conservative.*
  *What has this government done for **the farmers**?*
- *It's difficult for **railways** to make a profit.* (any railways)
  *The railways are getting more and more unreliable.* (our well-known railways)

This often happens when we talk about nationalities. Compare:

> *New Zealanders don't like to be mistaken for **Australians**.*
> *The Australians suffered heavy losses in the First World War.*

## 2 *French painters; the Impressionists*

We are more likely to use *the* if we are talking about a 'closed' group or class with a relatively definite, limited number of members. Compare:

- *French painters* (a large, indefinite group)
  *the Impressionists* (a particular artistic movement; we know more or less who belonged to the group)
- *19th-century poets*
  *the Romantic poets* (Shelley, Keats, Byron, Wordsworth and a few others)
- *British comprehensive schools*
  *the British 'Public Schools'* (a limited group of expensive high-prestige schools)

Specialists are likely to use *the* for groups or classes that they study or know about. Compare:

>  *Metals are mostly shiny.*
>  *Next term we're going to study the metals in detail.*

## 3  *1960s music; the music of the 1960s*

Some expressions are 'half-general' – in the middle between general and particular. If we talk about *1960s music, eighteenth-century history* or *poverty in Britain,* we are not talking about all music, history or poverty, but these are still rather general ideas (compared *with the music we heard last night, the history I did at school* or *the poverty I grew up in*). In these 'half-general' expressions, we usually use no article. However, *the* is often used when the noun is followed by a limiting, defining phrase, especially one with *of.* Compare:

– *1960s music*  – *African butterflies*
  *the music of the 1960s*  *the butterflies of Africa*

## 4  **physical environment: *the town, the sea***

*The* is used with a number of rather general expressions referring to our physical environment – the world around us and its climate. *The* suggests that everybody is familiar with what we are talking about. Examples are:
*the town, the country, the mountains, the sea, the seaside, the wind, the rain, the weather, the sunshine, the night.*

>  *My wife likes the seaside, but I prefer the mountains.*
>  *British people talk about the weather a lot.*
>  *I love listening to the wind.*

But note that no article is used with *nature, society* or *space* when these have a 'general' meaning (see 68).

## 5  **on the bus; at the hairdresser**

We use *the* (with a singular countable noun) when we talk about some kinds of thing that are part of everybody's lives, like 'the bus' or 'the hairdresser'. In this case *the bus*, for example, does not mean 'one bus that you know about'; we use *the* to suggest that taking a bus is a common experience that we all share.

>  *I have some of my best ideas when I'm on the bus.*
>  *Most of my friends go to the hairdresser two or three times a month.*
>  *Do you sing in the bath?*
>  *I've stopped reading the newspaper because it's too depressing.*

For similar expressions with no article (e.g. *in bed, in hospital*), see 70.1.

## 6  **She kicked him on the knee; He sat at the side**

We sometimes use *the* even when it is not exactly clear which of several particular persons or things we are talking about. This can happen when there are several similar possibilities, and it is unnecessary to be more definite.

>  *Lying by the side of the road we saw the wheel of a car.*
>      (NOT ... ~~a wheel of a car.~~)
>  *John Perkins is the son of a rich banker.* (who may have more than one son)
>  *She kicked him on the knee.*  ▶

*The* is often used like this with *side* and *wrong*.
> *I usually sit at **the side** in church.*      *He's **the wrong** man for me.*
> (on the phone) *I'm sorry. You've got **a/the wrong** number.*

# 70 articles (10): special rules and exceptions

## 1 common expressions without articles

In some common fixed expressions to do with place, time and movement, normally countable nouns are treated as uncountables, without articles. Examples are:

> *to/at/in/from school/university/college*
> *to/at/in/into/from church*      *to/in/into/out of bed/prison*
> *to/in/into/out of hospital* (BrE)      *to/at/from work*
> *to/at sea*      *to/in/from town*
> *at/from home*      *leave home*
> *leave/start/enter school/university/college*
> *by day*      *at night*
> *by car/bus/bicycle/plane/train/tube/boat*      *on foot*
> *by radio/phone/letter/mail*

With place nouns, expressions with or without articles may have different meanings. Compare:

– *I met her **at college**.* (when we were students)
  *I'll meet you **at the college**.* (The college is just a meeting place.)
– *Jane's **in hospital**.* (as a patient)
  *I left my coat **in the hospital** when I was visiting Jane.*
– *Who smokes **in class**?* (= ... in the classroom?)
  *Who **in the class** smokes?* (= Who is a smoker ...?)

In American English, *university* and *hospital* are not used without articles.
> *She was unhappy **at the university**.*
> *Say that again and I'll put you **in the hospital**.*

## 2 double expressions

Articles are often dropped in double expressions, particularly with prepositions.

> *with knife and fork*      *on land and sea*      *day after day*
> *with hat and coat*        *arm in arm*           *husband and wife*
> *from top to bottom*       *inch by inch*

For cases like *the bread and (the) butter*, see 178.

## 3 possessive 's

Nouns lose their articles after possessive *'s*.

> ***the coat** that belongs to John* = *John's **coat*** (NOT ~~John's the coat~~ OR ~~the John's coat~~)
> ***the economic problems** of America* = *America's **economic problems*** (NOT ~~the America's economic problems~~)

But the possessive noun itself may have an article.
> ***the wife** of **the boss*** = ***the boss's** wife*

## 4 noun modifiers

When a noun modifies another noun, the first noun's article is dropped.
*lessons in how to play **the guitar** = **guitar** lessons*
*a spot on **the sun** = a **sunspot***

## 5 *both* and *all*

We often leave out *the* after *both*.
***Both (the)** children are good at maths.*
And we often leave out *the* between *all* and a number.
***All (the) three** brothers were arrested.*
We usually leave out *the* after *all* in *all day, all night, all week, all year, all winter* and *all summer*.
*He's been away **all week**.    I haven't seen her **all day**.*

## 6 *kind of* etc

We usually leave out *a/an* after *kind of, sort of, type of* and similar expressions (see 551).
*What **kind of (a) person** is she?*
*Have you got a cheaper **sort of radio**?*
*They've developed a new **variety of sheep**.*

## 7 *amount* and *number*

*The* is dropped after *the amount/number of*.
*I was surprised at **the amount of money** collected. (*NOT ...~~of the money~~*)*
*The **number of unemployed** is rising steadily.*

## 8 *man* and *woman*

Unlike other singular countable nouns, *man* and *woman* can be used in a general sense without articles.
***Man** and **woman** were created equal.*
But we more often use *a woman* and *a man*, or *men* and *women*.
*A **woman** without a **man** is like a fish without a bicycle. (old feminist joke)*
***Men** and **women** have similar abilities and needs.*
*Man* is also commonly used to mean 'the human race', though many people regard this usage as sexist and prefer to avoid it (see 222.6).
*How did **Man** first discover fire?*

## 9 days, months and seasons

We drop *the* when we mean 'the day/month before or after this one'.
*Where were you **last Saturday**?    See you on **Thursday**.*
*I was away in **April**.                We're moving **next September**.*
To talk about the seasons in general, we can say *spring* or *the spring, summer* or *the summer*, etc. There is little difference.
*Rome is lovely in **(the) spring**.    I like **(the) winter** best.*
When we are talking about particular springs, summers etc, we are more likely to use *the*.
*I worked very hard in **the summer** that year.*    ▶

## 10   musical instruments

We often use *the* + **singular** when we talk about musical instruments in general, or about playing musical instruments.
> *The violin is really difficult.*       *Who's that on the piano?*
But *the* is often dropped when talking about jazz or pop, and sometimes when talking about classical music.
> *This recording was made with Miles Davis on trumpet.*
> *She studied oboe and saxophone at the Royal Academy of Music.*

## 11   (the) radio, (the) cinema, (the) theatre and television

When we talk about our use of these forms of entertainment, we generally say *the radio, the cinema, the theatre*, but *television* or *TV*.
> *I always listen to the radio while I'm driving.*
> *It was a great treat to go to the cinema or the theatre when I was a child.*
> *What's on TV?*
*The* is often dropped in all four cases when we talk about these institutions as art forms or professions.
> *Cinema is different from theatre in several ways.*
> *He's worked in radio and television all his life.*

## 12   jobs and positions

*The* is not used in titles like *Queen Elizabeth, President Lincoln*. Compare:
> *Queen Elizabeth had dinner with President Kennedy.*
> *The Queen had dinner with the President.*
And *the* is not usually used in the complement of a sentence, when we say that somebody has or gains a unique position (the only one in the organisation). Compare:
> – *They appointed him Head Librarian.*   – *He was elected President in 1879.*
> *Where's the librarian?*                       *I want to see the President.*

## 13   exclamations

We use *a/an* with singular countable nouns in exclamations after *What*.
> *What a lovely dress!* (NOT ~~What lovely dress!~~)
Note that *a/an* cannot be used in exclamations with uncountable nouns.
> *What nonsense!* (NOT ~~What a nonsense!~~)
> *What luck!*

## 14   illnesses

The names of illnesses and pains are usually uncountable, with no article, in standard British English (for more details, see 148.7).
> *Have you had appendicitis?*     *I've got toothache again.*
*A/an* is used in a few cases such as *a cold, a headache*.
> *I've got a horrible cold.*       *Have you got a headache?*
*The* can be used informally with a few common illnesses.
> *I think I've got (the) flu.*     *She's never had (the) measles.*
American usage is different in some cases.
> *I've got a toothache / an earache / a backache / a stomachache.* (BrE *I've got toothache/earache* etc)

## 15 parts of the body etc

When talking about parts of someone's body, or about their possessions, we usually use possessives, not *the*.

> *Katy broke **her arm** climbing.* (NOT ~~Katy broke the arm climbing.~~)
> *He stood in the doorway, **his coat** over **his arm**.* (NOT *...~~the coat over the arm.~~*)

But *the* is common after prepositions, especially when we are talking about blows, pains and other things that often happen to parts of people's bodies.

> *She hit him **in the stomach**.*     *He was shot **in the leg**.*
> *Can't you look me **in the eye**?*

## 16 measurements

Note the use of *the* in measuring expressions beginning with *by*.

> *Do you sell eggs **by the kilo** or **by the dozen**?*
> *He sits watching TV **by the hour**.*     *Can I pay **by the month**?*

*A/an* is used to relate one measuring unit to another.

> *sixty pence **a** kilo*     *thirty miles **an** hour*     *twice **a** week*

## 17 place names

We use *the* with these kinds of place names:
- seas (***the** Atlantic*)
- mountain groups (***the** Himalayas*)
- island groups (***the** West Indies*)
- rivers (***the** Rhine*)
- deserts (***the** Sahara*)
- most hotels (***the** Grand Hotel*)
- most cinemas and theatres (***the** Odeon*; ***the** Playhouse*)
- most museums and art galleries (***the** British Museum*; ***the** Frick*)

We usually use **no article** with:
- continents, countries, states, counties, departments etc (*Africa, Brazil, Texas, Berkshire, Westphalia*)
- towns (*Oxford*)
- streets (*New Street, Willow Road*)
- lakes (*Lake Michigan*)

Exceptions: places whose name is (or contains) a common noun like *republic, state, union* (e.g. **the** *People's Republic of China,* **the** *United Kingdom,* **the** *United States*).

Note also **the** *Netherlands*, and its seat of government **The** *Hague*.

*The* is unusual in the titles of the principal public buildings and organisations of a town, when the title begins with the town name.

> *Oxford University* (NOT ~~the Oxford University~~)
> *Hull Station* (NOT ~~the Hull Station~~)
> *Salisbury Cathedral*     *Manchester City Council*
> *Birmingham Airport*     *Cheltenham Football Club*

With the names of less important institutions, usage varies.

> *(**The**) East Oxford Community Centre.*     *(**The**) Newbury School of English.*

Names of single mountains vary. Most have no article.

> *Everest     Kilimanjaro     Snowdon     Table Mountain*

But definite articles are usually translated in the English versions of European mountain names, except those beginning *Le Mont*.     ▶

*The Meije* (= *La Meije*)    *The Matterhorn* (= *Das Matterhorn*)
BUT *Mont Blanc* (NOT ~~the Mont Blanc~~)

## 18   newspapers and magazines

The names of newspapers usually have *the*.
  *The Times*    *The Washington Post*
The names of magazines do not always have *the*.
  *New Scientist*

## 19   abbreviated styles

We usually leave out articles in abbreviated styles (see 1).

| | |
|---|---|
| **newspaper headlines** | *MAN KILLED ON MOUNTAIN* |
| **headings** | *Introduction*    *Chapter 2*    *Section B* |
| **picture captions** | *Mother and child* |
| **notices, posters etc** | *SUPER CINEMA, RITZ HOTEL* |
| **instructions** | *Open packet at other end.* |
| **numbering and** | *Go through door A.* |
| **labelling** | *Control to Car 27: can you hear me?* |
| | *Turn to page 26.* (NOT *... ~~the page 26.~~*) |
| **dictionary entries** | *palm inner surface of hand ...* |
| **lists** | *take car to garage; pay phone bill; ...* |
| **notes** | *J thinks company needs new office* |

For articles with abbreviations (*NATO*, *the USA*), see 2.2–3.
For *the* in double comparatives (*the more, the better*), see 139.5.
For *a* with *few* and *little*, see 329.
For *a* with *hundred, thousand* etc, see 389.11.
For *the blind* etc, see 17.1.
For *the Japanese* etc, see 17.2.
For *next* and *the next*, see 375; for *last* and *the last*, see 314.
For *the* instead of *enough*, see 187.8.
For *another two days, a good three weeks* etc, see 532.6.

# 71   as and **though**: special word order

## adjective/adverb/noun + *as* + clause

*As* and *though* can be used in a special structure after an adjective, adverb or
noun. In this case they both mean 'although', and suggest an emphatic
contrast. (In AmE only *as* is normally used like this; *though* is unusual.)
  *Cold as/though it was, we went out.* (= Although it was very cold, ...)
  *Bravely as/though they fought, they had no chance of winning.*
  *Much as/though I respect your point of view, I can't agree.*
  *Strange though it may seem, I don't like watching cricket.*
  *Scot though she was, she supported the English team.*
Occasionally *as* can be used in this structure to mean 'because'.
  *Tired as she was, I decided not to disturb her.*
In American English, *as ... as* is common.
  *As cold as it was, we went out.*

For the word order in structures like *I did as good a job as I could*, see 14.

# 72  as, because, since and for

All four of these words can be used to refer to the reason for something. (For *as*, *since* and *for* referring to time, see 73, 208 and 522.) They are not used in the same way.

## 1  *as* and *since*

*As* and *since* are used when the reason is already known to the listener/reader, or when it is not the most important part of the sentence. *As*- and *since*-clauses often come at the beginning of sentences.

**As it's raining again,** *we'll have to stay at home.*
**Since he had not paid his bill,** *his electricity was cut off.*

*As*- and *since*-clauses are relatively formal; in an informal style, the same ideas are often expressed with *so*.

*It's raining again,* **so** *we'll have to stay at home.*

## 2  *because*

*Because* puts more emphasis on the reason, and most often introduces new information which is not known to the listener/reader.

**Because** *I was ill for six months, I lost my job.*

When the reason is the most important part of the sentence, the *because*-clause usually comes at the end. It can also stand alone. *Since* and *as* cannot be used like this.

*Why am I leaving? I'm leaving* **because** *I'm fed up!*
(NOT ... ~~I'm leaving as/since I'm fed up!~~)
*Why are you laughing?* ~ **Because** *you look so funny.*

A *because*-clause can be used to say how one knows something.

*You didn't tell me the truth,* **because** *I found the money in your room.*
(= ... I know because I found ...)

For more information about *because*, see 94.

## 3  *for*

*For* introduces new information, but suggests that the reason is given as an afterthought. A *for*-clause could almost be in brackets. *For*-clauses never come at the beginning of sentences, and cannot stand alone. *For*, used in this sense, is most common in a formal written style.

*I decided to stop and have lunch –* **for** *I was feeling hungry.*

# 73  as, when and while: simultaneous events

To talk about actions or situations that take place at the same time, we can use *as*, *when* or *while*. There are some differences.

## 1  'backgrounds': *as, when* or *while*

We can use all three words to introduce a longer 'background' action or situation, which is/was going on when something else happens/happened.

**As I was walking down the street** *I saw Joe driving a Porsche.*
*The telephone always rings* **when you are having a bath**.
**While they were playing cards**, *somebody broke into the house.*          ▶

*As-*, *when-* and *while-*clauses can go at the beginning or end of sentences, but *as*-clauses usually introduce less important information, and most often go at the beginning.

A progressive tense is usually used for the longer 'background' action or situation (*was walking; are having; were playing*). But *as* and *while* can be used with a simple tense, especially with a 'state' verb like *sit, lie,* or *grow.*

> *As I sat reading the paper, the door burst open.*

## 2 simultaneous long actions: *while; as*

We usually use *while* to say that two longer actions or situations go/went on at the same time. We can use progressive or simple tenses.

> *While you were reading the paper, I was working.*
> *John cooked supper while I watched TV.*

*As* is used (with simple tenses) to talk about two situations which develop or change together.

> *As I get older I get more optimistic.*

We prefer *when* to refer to ages and periods of life.

> *When I was a child we lived in London.* (NOT ~~As/While I was a child~~ ...)
> *His parents died when he was twelve.* (NOT ... ~~while he was twelve.~~)

## 3 simultaneous short actions: *(just) as; (just) when*

We usually use *(just) as* to say that two short actions or events happen/ happened at the same time.

> *As I opened my eyes I heard a strange voice.*
> *Mary always arrives just as I start work.*

*(Just) when* is also possible.

> *I thought of it just when you opened your mouth.*

## 4 reduced clauses with *when* and *while*

It is often possible to leave out **subject + be** after *when* (especially when it means 'whenever'), and after *while.* This is rather formal.

> *Don't forget to signal when turning right.*
> (= ... when you are turning right.)
> *Climb when ready.*
> (= ... when you are ready.)
> *While in Germany, he got to know a family of musicians.*
> (= While he was ...)

Note that *as* is usually pronounced /əz/ (see 616).
For other uses of *as, when* and *while,* see the Index.

# 74 as if and as though; like

## 1 meaning

*As if* and *as though* are both used to say what a situation seems like. They can refer to something that we think may be true.

> *It looks as if/though it's going to rain.*
> *It sounds as if/though John's going to change his job.*

They can also be used to talk about things which we know are not true.
*I feel **as if/though** I'm dying.*
*She was acting **as if/though** she was in charge.*

## 2 tenses

When we talk about things which we know are not true, we can use a past tense with a present meaning after *as if/though*. This emphasises the meaning of unreality. Compare:
– *She looks **as if** she **is** rich.* (Perhaps she is.)
  *He talks **as if** he **was** rich.* (But he is definitely not.)
– *You look **as though** you **know** each other.*
  *Why is he looking at me **as though** he **knew** me? I've never seen him before.*
In a formal style, *were* can be used instead of *was* in an 'unreal' comparison. This is common in American English.
*He talks **as if** he **were** rich.*

## 3 *like* meaning 'as if/though'

*Like* is often used in the same way as *as if/though*, especially in an informal style. This used to be typically AmE, but it is now common in BrE.
*It seems **like** it's going to rain.*
*He sat there smiling **like** it was his birthday.*

For the difference between *like* and *as*, see 326.

# 75 as long as

## 1 tenses

After *as long as*, we use a present tense to express a future idea.
*I'll remember that day **as long as** I live.* (NOT . . . ~~as long as I will live.~~)

For other conjunctions which are used in this way, see 580.

## 2 conditions

*As/so long as* is often used to state conditions.
*You can take my car **as/so long as** you drive carefully.*
    (= . . . on condition that you drive carefully.)

## 3 emphatic use

Before a number, *as long as* can be used to suggest great length.
*These meetings can last **as long as** four hours.*

For a similar use of *as much/many as*, see 136.6.

# 76 as such

*Not . . . as such* is used to say that something is not exactly what has been suggested.
*So you went to Japan on holiday? ~ Well, **not** a holiday **as such** – I went on business. But I managed quite a lot of sightseeing.*
*I'm **not** a teacher **as such**, but I've taught English to some of my friends.*  ▶

# 77 as usual

Note that in this expression we use the adjective *usual*, not the adverb *usually*.
*The train's late, as usual.* (NOT ... ~~as usually.~~)

# 78 as well as

## 1 meaning

*As well as* has a similar meaning to 'not only ... but also'.
*She's got a goat, as well as five cats and three dogs.*
*He's clever as well as nice.* (= He's not only nice, but also clever.)
*She works in television as well as writing children's books.*
When some information is already known to the listener/reader, we put this with *as well as*.
*As well as birds, some mammals can fly.* (NOT ~~Birds can fly, as well as some mammals.~~)
*They speak French in parts of Italy as well as France.* (NOT ~~They speak French in France as well as parts of Italy.~~)

## 2 verbs after *as well as*

When we put a verb after *as well as*, we most often use the *-ing* form.
*Smoking is dangerous, as well as making you smell bad.* (NOT ... ~~as well as it makes you smell bad.~~)
*As well as breaking his leg, he hurt his arm.* (NOT ... ~~as well as he broke his leg, ...~~)
After an infinitive in the main clause, an infinitive without *to* is possible.
*I have to feed the animals as well as look after the children.*
Note the difference between:
*She sings as well as playing the piano.*
    (= She not only plays, but also sings.)
*She sings as well as she plays the piano.*
    (= Her singing is as good as her playing.)

For *as well*, *also* and *too*, see 46–47.

# 79 ask

## 1 *ask* and *ask for*

*Ask for*: ask somebody to give something
*Ask* without *for*: ask somebody to tell something.

Compare:
– *Don't ask me for money.* (NOT ~~Don't ask me money.~~)
 *Don't ask me my name.*
    (More common than *Don't ask me for my name.*)
– *Ask for the menu.*
 *Ask the price.*

*Ask* is sometimes used without *for* when talking about asking for sums of money, especially in connection with buying, selling and renting.
> *They're **asking £500** a month rent.*
> *How much is the car? ~ I'm **asking fifteen hundred**.*

Note also the expressions *ask a lot of somebody, ask too much of somebody, ask a favour of somebody* and *ask (for) permission*.

## 2 infinitive structures

We can use infinitive structures after *ask* (see 282–283).

> *ask* + infinitive

> *I **asked to go** home.* (= I asked permission to go home.)

> *ask* + object + infinitive

> *I **asked John to go** home.* (= I told John I would like him to go home.)

> *ask* + *for* + object + infinitive

> *I **asked for the children to have** extra milk.*
> *I **asked for the parcel to be sent** to my home address.*

Note the difference between these two sentences:
> *I **asked John to go** home.* (I wanted John to go home.)
> *I **asked John if I could go** home.* (I wanted to go home myself.)

# 80 at/in and to

## 1 the difference

*At* and *in* are generally used for position (for the difference, see 81); *to* is used for movement or direction. Compare:
- *He works **at** the market.*     – *My father lives **in** Canada.*
  *He gets **to** the market by bike.*     *I go **to** Canada to see him whenever I can.*

## 2 expressions of purpose

If we mention the purpose of a movement before we mention the destination, we usually use *at/in* before the place. Compare:
- *Let's go **to** Marcel's for coffee.*
  *Let's go and have coffee **at** Marcel's.* (NOT *Let's go and have coffee to Marcel's.*)
- *I went **to** Canada to see my father.*
  *I went to see my father **in** Canada.* (NOT *I went to see my father to Canada.*)

## 3 targets

After some verbs, *at* is used with the 'target' of a perception or non-verbal communication. Common examples are *look, smile, wave, frown*.
> *Why are you **looking at** her like that?*
> *Because she **smiled at** me.*

*At* is also used after some verbs referring to attacks or aggressive behaviour. Common examples are *shoot, laugh, throw, shout* and *point*.
> *It's a strange feeling to have somebody **shoot at** you.*
> *If you can't **laugh at** yourself, who can you **laugh at**?*
> *Stop **throwing** stones **at** the cat, darling.*
> *You don't need to **shout at** me.*
> *In my dream, everybody was **pointing at** me and laughing.*     ▶

*Throw to, shout to* and *point to* are used when there is no idea of attack.
> *Please do not **throw** food **to** the animals.*
> *Could you **shout to** Phil and tell him it's breakfast time?*
> *'The train's late again,' she said, **pointing to** the timetable.*

*Arrive* is generally followed by *at* or *in*; never by *to*.
> *We should **arrive at** Pat's in time for lunch.* (NOT ... ~~arrive to Pat's~~ ...)
> *When did you **arrive in** New Zealand?* (NOT ... ~~to New Zealand?~~)

For *in* and *into*, see 269.

## 81 at, on and in: place

### 1 at

*At* is used to talk about position at a point.
> *It's very hot **at** the centre of the earth.*
> *Turn right **at** the next corner.*

Sometimes we use *at* with a larger place, if we just think of this as a point: a stage on a journey or a meeting place, for example. Compare:
> – *The plane stops for an hour **at** Frankfurt.* (a point on a journey)
> *She lives **in** Frankfurt.* (somebody's home)
> – *Let's meet **at** the club.* (a meeting point)
> *It was warm and comfortable **in** the club.* (a place to spend time)

We very often use *at* before the name of a building, when we are thinking not of the building itself but of the activity that happens there.
> *There's a good film **at** the cinema in Market Street.*
> *Eat **at** the Steak House – best food in town.*
> *Sorry I didn't phone last night – I was **at** the theatre.*

*At* is particularly common with proper names used for buildings or organisations. Compare:
> – *I first met your father **at/in** Harrods.*
> *I first met your father **in** a shop.*
> – *She works **at** Legal and General Insurance.*
> *She works **in** a big insurance company.*

*At* is used to say where people study.
> *He's **at** the London School of Economics.*

We use *at* with the name of a city to talk about the city's university. Compare:
> *He's a student **at** Oxford.*    *He lives **in** Cambridge.*

*At* is also used before the names of group activities.
> *at a party     at a meeting     at a concert*
> *at a lecture     at the match*

### 2 on

*On* is used to talk about position on a line (for example a road or a river).
> *His house is **on** the way from Aberdeen to Dundee.*
> *Stratford is **on** the river Avon.*

But *in* is used for the position of things which form part of the line.
> *There's a misprint **in** line 6 on page 22.*
> *Who's the good-looking boy **in** the sixth row?*

*On* is used for position on a surface.
> *Hurry up – supper's **on the table!***
> *That picture would look better **on the other wall**.*
> *There's a big spider **on the ceiling**.*

*On* can mean 'attached to'.
> *Why do you wear that ring **on** your first finger?*
> *There aren't many apples **on** the tree this year.*

*On* is also used for position by a lake or sea.
> *Bowness is **on Lake Windermere**.*
> *Southend-**on-Sea***

## 3  in

*In* is used for position inside large areas, and in three-dimensional space (when something is surrounded on all sides).

> *I don't think he's **in his office**.*  *Let's go for a walk **in the woods**.*
> *She grew up **in Swaziland**.*  *I last saw her **in the car park**.*
> *He lived **in the desert** for three years.*

## 4  public transport

We use *on* (and *off*) to talk about travel using public transport (buses, trains, planes and boats), as well as (motor)cycles and horses.
> *There's no room **on the bus**; let's get **off** again.*
> *He's arriving **on the 3.15 train**.* (NOT *. . . ~~in/with the 3.15 train.~~*)
> *We're booked **on flight 604**.*
> *It took five days to cross the Atlantic **on the Queen Elizabeth**.*
> *I'll go down to the shop **on my bike**.*

But we use *in* and *out (of)* to talk about cars and small private planes and boats.
> *She came **in a taxi**.*
> *He fell into the river when he was getting **out of his canoe**.*

## 5  arrive

We generally use *at* (not *to*) after *arrive*; *in* is used before very large places.
> *He **arrives at** the airport at 15.30.* (NOT *He ~~arrives to the airport~~ . . .*)
> *What time do we **arrive in** New York?*

## 6  addresses

We generally use *at* to talk about addresses.
> *Are you still **at the same address**?*
> *She lives **at 73 Albert Street**.*

We use *in* (AmE *on*) if we just give the name of the street.
> *She lives **in Albert Street**.*

We use *on* for the number of the floor.
> *She lives in a flat **on the third floor**.*

*At* can be used with a possessive to mean 'at somebody's house or shop'.
> *Where's Jane? ~ She's round **at Pat's**.*
> *You're always **at the hairdresser's**.*

▶

### 7 special expressions

Note these expressions:

> *in/at* church **at** home/work *in/at* school/college **in** *a picture*
> **in** *the sky* **in** *the rain* **in** *a tent* **in** *a hat*
> *The map is* **on page 32**. (BUT *I opened the book* **at page 32**.)
> **in** *bed / (the) hospital / prison* **on** *a farm* *working* **on** *the railway*

Note that *at* is usually pronounced /ət/, not /æt/ (see 616).
For the difference between *at/in* and *to*, see 80.
For *smile at, shoot at* etc, see 80.3.

## 82 at, on and in: time

> *at* + clock time         *at* + weekend, public holiday
> *in* + part of day        *in* + longer period
> *on* + particular day

### 1 clock times: *at*

> *I usually get up* **at six o'clock**.
> *I'll meet you* **at 4.15**.          *Phone me* **at lunch time**.

*At* is usually left out before *what time* in an informal style (see paragraph 7).
> **What time** *does your train leave?*

### 2 parts of the day: *in*

> *I work best* **in the morning**.    *three o'clock* **in the afternoon**
> *We usually go out* **in the evening**.

Note the difference between *in the night* (mostly used to mean 'during one particular night') and *at night* (= during any night). Compare:
> *I had to get up* **in the night**.
> *I often work* **at night**.

In an informal style, we sometimes use plurals (*days* etc) with no preposition.
> *Would you rather work* **days** *or* **nights**?

We use *on* if we say which morning/afternoon etc we are talking about, or if we describe the morning/afternoon etc.
> *See you* **on Monday morning**.
> *We met* **on a cold afternoon** *in early spring*.

### 3 days: *on*

> *I'll ring you* **on Tuesday**.       *My birthday's* **on March 21st**.
> *They're having a party* **on Christmas Day**.

In an informal style we sometimes leave out *on*.
> *I'm seeing her* **Sunday morning**.

We use plurals (*Sundays, Mondays* etc) to talk about repeated actions.
> *We usually go and see Granny* **on Sundays**.

## 4 public holidays and weekends: *at*

We use *at* to talk about the whole of the holidays at Christmas, New Year, Easter and Thanksgiving (AmE).

*We're having the roof repaired **at Easter**.*

But we use *on* to talk about one day of the holiday.

*Come and see us **on Christmas Day**.*

*What are you doing **on Easter Monday**?*

British people say *at the weekend*; Americans use *on*.

*What did you do **at the weekend**?*

## 5 longer periods: *in*

*It happened **in the week** after Christmas.*

*I was born **in March**.*

*Our house was built **in the 15th century**.*

*Kent is beautiful **in spring**.*

*He died **in 1616**.*

## 6 other uses of *in*

*In* can also be used to say how soon something will happen, and to say how long something takes to happen.

*Ask me again **in three or four days**.*

*I can run 200 metres **in about 30 seconds**.*

The expression *in ...'s time* is used to say how soon something will happen, not how long something takes. Compare:

*I'll see you again **in a month's time**.*   *It'll be ready **in three weeks' time**.*

*He wrote the book **in a month**.* (NOT *...~~in a month's time~~.*)

In American English, *in* can be used in negative sentences, like *for*, to talk about periods up to the present.

*I haven't seen her **in years**.*

## 7 expressions with no preposition

*At/on/in* are not normally used in expressions of time before *next*, *last*, *this*, *that* (sometimes), *one*, *any* (in an informal style), *each*, *every*, *some*, *all*.

*See you **next week**.*   *Come **any time**.*

*Are you free **this morning**?*   *I didn't feel very well **that week**.*

*I'm at home **every evening**.*   *Let's meet **one day**.*

*We stayed **all day**.*

These prepositions are not normally used, either, before *yesterday*, *the day before yesterday*, *tomorrow* or *the day after tomorrow*.

*What are you doing **the day after tomorrow**?*

And prepositions are usually dropped in questions beginning **What/Which +
expression of time**, and in answers which only contain an expression of time.

***What day** is the meeting?*

***Which week** did you say you're on holiday?*

***What time** are you leaving? ~ **Eight o'clock**.*

Note that *at* is usually pronounced /ət/, not /æt/ (see 616).
For the difference between *in* and *during*, see 168.

# 83 at all

## 1 *at all* with a negative

We often use *at all* to emphasise a negative idea.

> *I didn't understand anything **at all**.* (= I didn't understand even a little.)
> *She was hardly frightened **at all**.*

## 2 questions etc

*At all* can also be used in questions, and with 'non-affirmative' words like *if, ever* and *any*.

> *Do you play poker **at all**?* (= ... even a little?)
> *He'll come before supper if he comes **at all**.*
> *You can come whenever you like – any time **at all**.*

## 3 *Not at all*

The expression *Not at all* is used (especially in British English) as a rather formal answer to *Thank you* (see 545.19) and to *Do you mind if...?* (see 351).

# 84 at first and first

We use *at first* to talk about the beginning of a situation, to make a contrast with something different that happens/happened later. *At first ...* is often followed by *but*.

> *At **first** they were very happy, but then things started going wrong.*
> *The work was hard **at first**, but I got used to it.*

In other cases, we usually prefer *first*.

> *That's mine – I saw it **first**!* (NOT ... ~~I saw it at first.~~)
> *We lived there when we were **first** married.* (= ... in the early days of our marriage.) (NOT ... ~~when we were at first married.~~)
> *First, I want to talk about the history of the problem; then I'll outline the situation today; and then we'll discuss possible solutions.* (NOT ~~At first, I want to talk~~ ...)

Note that *at last* is not the opposite of *at first* – see 204.
For *first(ly)* as a discourse marker, see also 157.10.

# 85 auxiliary verbs

## 1 the need for auxiliary verbs

In English sentences, a lot of important meanings are expressed by the verb phrase – for example questioning, negation, time, completion, continuation, repetition, willingness, possibility, obligation. But English verbs do not have many different forms: the maximum (except for *be*) is five (e.g. *see, sees, seeing, saw, seen*). So to express all these meanings, 'auxiliary' (or 'helping') verbs are added to other verbs. There are two groups.

## 2 *be, do* and *have*

*Be* is added to other verbs to make progressive and passive forms.
*Is it raining?    She **was** imprisoned for three years.*
*Do* is used to make questions, negatives and emphatic forms of non-auxiliary verbs.
***Do** you smoke?    It **didn't** matter.    **Do** come in.*
*Have* is used to make perfect forms.
*What **have** you done?        I realised that I **hadn't** turned the lights off.*
See the Index for details of entries on these forms and their uses, and on non-auxiliary uses of *be, do* and *have*.

## 3 modal auxiliary verbs

The verbs *will, shall, would, should, can, could, may, might, must* and *ought* are usually called 'modal auxiliary verbs'. They are used with other verbs to add various meanings, mostly to do with certainty or obligation.
*She **may** be on holiday.*
*You **must** write to Uncle Arthur.*
For details, see 353–354 and the entries for each verb.

## 4 other verb + verb structures

Other verbs (e.g. *seem*) which are used in **verb + verb** structures are not usually called 'auxiliary verbs'. One important difference is grammatical. In auxiliary verb structures, questions and negatives are made without *do*; in other **verb + verb** structures the auxiliary *do* has to be added to the first verb. Compare:
– *She ought to understand.*      – *He is swimming.*
  ***Ought she** to understand?*      *He **is not** swimming*
– *She seems to understand.*      – *He likes swimming.*
  ***Does she seem** to understand?*    *He **doesn't like** swimming.*

# 86  (a)wake and (a)waken

## 1 use

*Wake* is the most common of these four verbs. It can mean 'stop sleeping' or 'make (somebody else) stop sleeping'. It is often followed by *up*, especially when it means 'stop sleeping'.
*I **woke up** three times in the night.*
***Wake up**! It's time to go to work.* (NOT ~~Wake!~~...)
*Could you **wake** me **(up)** at half past six?*
*Waken* is a more literary alternative to *wake (up)*.
*The princess **did** not **waken** for a hundred years.*
*Then the prince **wakened** her with a kiss.*
*Awake* and *awaken* are also rather literary words. They can be used to mean 'wake (up)', but are more often used figuratively, to talk not about waking from sleep, but about the waking of emotions, understanding etc.
*I slowly **awoke** to the danger that threatened me.*
*At first I paid little attention, but slowly my interest **awoke**.*
*The smell of her perfume **awakened** the gipsy's desire.*                    ▶

## 2   *awake* and *asleep* (adjectives)

In informal British English the adjectives *awake* and *asleep* are more common in predicative position (after *be*) than the verb forms *waking* and *sleeping*.

> *Is the baby **awake** yet?*          *You were **asleep** at ten o'clock.*

# 87   **back** and **again**

*Back* and *again* can be used with similar meanings, but there are some differences.

### 1   *back* with a verb

With a verb, we use *back* to suggest a return to an earlier situation, a movement in the opposite direction to an earlier movement, and similar ideas. *Again* is not normally used in this way with a verb.

> *Give me my watch **back**.* (NOT ~~Give me my watch again.~~)
> *I'm taking this meat **back** to the shop.* (NOT ~~I'm taking this meat to the shop again.~~)

### 2   *again* with a verb

With a verb, *again* usually suggests repetition. Compare:
- *That was lovely. Can you play it **again**?*
  *When I've recorded your voice I'll play it **back**.*
- *Eric was really bad-mannered. I'm never going to invite him **again**.*
  *She comes to our parties but she never invites us **back**.*
- *I don't think he got your letter. You'd better write **again**.*
  *If I write to you, will you write **back**?*

Note the difference between *sell back* (to the same person) and *sell again*.

> *The bike you sold me is too small. Can I **sell** it **back** to you?*
> *If we buy this house and then have to move somewhere else, how easy will it be to **sell** it **again**?*

### 3   cases when *back* is not used

When the verb itself already expresses the idea of 'return to an earlier situation' or 'movement in the opposite direction', *back* is not generally used.

> *Stefan can never **return** to his country.* (More natural than *Stefan can never return back . . .*)
> *Who opened the window? Could you **close** it, please?* (NOT *. . . ~~close it back~~ . . .*)

However, *again* can be used to emphasise the idea of 'return'.

> *Stefan can never **return** to his country **again**.*
> *Who opened the window? Could you **close** it **again**, please?*

### 4   adverb particles etc

With adverb particles and prepositional phrases, we can use both *back* and *again* to suggest 'return to an earlier situation' etc.

> *I stood up, and then I sat (**back**) **down** (**again**).*
> *He tasted the apple and spat it (**back**) **out** (**again**).*
> *Go (**back**) **to sleep** (**again**).*
> *I'll be (**back**) **in the office** (**again**) on Monday.*

### 5   *ring/call back*

Note that *ring back* (BrE only) and *call back* can be used to mean both 'return a phone call' and 'repeat a phone call'.

> *She's not here just now.* ~ *Ask her to **ring me back**.* (= return my call)
> *I haven't got time to talk now.* ~ *OK, I'll **ring back** later.* (= ring again)

### 6   **word order**

*Back* is an adverb particle (see 20), and can usually go between a verb and its object, unless this is a pronoun (see 599.4). *Again* cannot.

> *Take **back your money** – I don't want it.* (OR *Take **your money back** ...*)
> *Count **the money again**, please.* (NOT *Count again the money ...*)

For other uses of *back* and *again*, see a good dictionary.

## 88   bath and bathe

### 1   *bath*

Pronunciation:   *bath* /bɑːθ/   *bathing* /'bɑːθɪŋ/   *bathed* /bɑːθt/

This verb is not used in American English.
It can have an object.

> *It's your turn to **bath** the baby.*

And it can be used to mean 'bath oneself'.

> *I don't think he **baths** very often.*

This use is rather formal; people more often say *have/take a bath*.

> *I'm feeling hot and sticky; I think I'll **have a bath**.*

### 2   *bathe*

Pronunciation:   *bathe* /beɪð/   *bathing* /'beɪðɪŋ/   *bathed* /beɪðd/

*Bathe* is the American equivalent of *bath*. (*Take a bath* is also common.)

> *It's your turn to **bathe** the baby.* (AmE)
> *I always **bathe** before I go to bed.* (AmE) (OR ... *take a bath*)

*Bathe* can also be used (in both British and American English) to talk about putting water on a part of the body that hurts (for instance sore eyes).

> *Your eyes are very red – you ought to **bathe** them.*

And *bathe* can be used (in British English only) to mean 'swim for pleasure'.

> NO BATHING FROM THIS BEACH

This use is rather formal; people more often say *have a swim, go for a swim, go swimming* or just *swim*.

> *Let's **go for a swim** in the river.*

## 89   be: progressive forms

> *I am being / you are being* etc + adjective/noun

We can use this structure to talk about actions and behaviour, but not usually to talk about feelings. Compare:

– *You're **being** stupid.* (= You're doing stupid things.)
> *I **was being** very careful.* (= I was doing something carefully.)

▶

*Who's **being** a silly baby, then?*
– *I'm happy just now.* (NOT ~~I'm being happy just now~~.)
    *I **was** depressed when you phoned.* (NOT ~~I was being depressed~~...)
Note the difference between *He's being sick* (BrE = He's vomiting – bringing food up from the stomach) and *He's sick* (= He's ill).

For the use of *am being* etc in passive verb forms, see 412.2.

# 90 be with auxiliary do

Normally, *be* is used without the auxiliary *do.*
    *I'm **not** often sick.* (NOT ~~I don't often be sick~~.)
But *do* is used to make negative imperative sentences with *be* (when we tell somebody not to do something).
    ***Don't be** silly!*        ***Don't be** such a nuisance!*
And *do be* can begin emphatic imperatives.
    ***Do be** careful!*        ***Do be** quiet, for God's sake!*
In an informal style, people sometimes use *do* with *be* in one or two other structures which have a similar meaning to imperative sentences.
    *Why **don't** you **be** a good boy and sit down?*
    *If you **don't be** quiet you'll go straight to bed.*

For other auxiliary uses of *do*, see 159.

# 91 be + infinitive: I am to ..., you are to ... etc

## 1 plans and arrangements: *He is to visit Nigeria*

We use this structure in a formal style to talk about official and other plans and arrangements.
    *The President **is to visit** Nigeria next month.*
    *We **are to get** a 10 per cent wage rise in June.*
    *I felt nervous because I **was** soon **to leave** home for the first time.*
A perfect infinitive can be used to show that a planned event did not happen.
    *I **was to have started** work last week, but I changed my mind.*

## 2 'fate': *We were to meet again*

Another use is to talk about things which are/were 'hidden in the future', fated to happen.
    *I thought we were saying goodbye for ever. But we **were to meet** again, many years later, under very strange circumstances.*

## 3 pre-conditions: *If we are to get there in time ...*

The structure is common in *if*-clauses, when the main clause expresses a pre-condition – something that must happen first if something else is to happen.
    *If we **are to get** there by lunchtime we had better hurry.*
    *He knew he would have to work hard if he **was to pass** his exam.*

## 4 orders: *You are to do your homework*

The structure is used to give orders, often by parents speaking to children.
> You **are to do** your homework before you watch TV.
> She can go to the party, but she's **not to be** back late.

## 5 *be* + passive infinitive: *It is not to be removed*

*Be* + **passive infinitive** is often used in notices and instructions.

> *am/are/is (not) to be* + past participle

> This cover is **not to be removed**.

Sometimes only the passive infinitive is used.
> **To be taken** three times a day after meals. (on a medicine bottle)

Some other common expressions with *be* + **passive infinitive**:
> There's **nothing to be done**.      She was **nowhere to be found**.
> I looked out of the window, but there was **nothing to be seen**.

## 6 tenses

Note that this structure exists only in present and past tenses. We cannot say
that somebody ~~has been to go~~ somewhere, or ~~will/must be to go~~ somewhere.
Participle structures (~~being to go~~) are not possible either.

For other ways of talking about the future, see 211–221.

# 92 be and have

## 1 physical conditions: hunger, thirst etc

To talk about experiencing hunger, thirst, heat, cold and certain other
common physical conditions, we normally use *be* (or *feel*) + **adjective**,
not *have* + **noun**. Note the following expressions:
> be hungry (NOT ~~have hunger~~)      be thirsty      be warm
> be hot      be cold      be sleepy      be afraid

Note also:
> be right      be wrong      be lucky

## 2 age, height, weight, size and colour

*Be* is also used to talk about age, height, length, weight, size, shape and colour.
> I'm nearly thirty. (NOT ~~I have nearly thirty~~.)
> She **is** nearly my age.      He **is** six feet tall.
> I wish I **was** ten kilos lighter.      What size **are** your shoes?
> The room **is** ten metres long.      What colour **are** his eyes?
> She **is** the same height as her father.

*Be heavy* is not usually used in measuring expressions.
> It **weighs** 37 kilos. (NOT ~~It's 37 kilos heavy~~.)

For *have* in expressions like *have a bath, have a drink, have a walk*, see 236.

## 93 **beat** and **win**

You can *win* (in) a game, a race, a battle, an argument etc, and you can *win* a prize, money etc. You can *beat* a person that you are playing/arguing/fighting etc against. Compare:

> My girlfriend usually **wins** when we play poker.
> My girlfriend **beat** me at poker the first time we played. (NOT *My girlfriend* *won me at poker* ...)

Both verbs are irregular:

> *beat – beat – beaten*          *win – won – won*

## 94 **because**

### 1 *because* and *because of*

*Because* is a conjunction. It is used at the beginning of a clause, before a subject and verb. *Because of* is a two-word preposition, used before a noun or a pronoun. Compare:

> – We were late **because it rained**. (NOT ... *because of it rained.*)
> We were late **because of the rain**. (NOT ... *because the rain.*)
> – I'm happy **because I met you**.
> I'm happy **because of you**.

### 2 position of *because*-clauses

*Because* and its clause can go after or before the main clause.

> I finished early **because I worked fast**.
> **Because I worked fast**, I finished early.

*Because*-clauses can sometimes stand alone, especially as answers or after hesitations.

> Why are you crying? ~ **Because John and I have had a row**.
> I don't think I'll go to the party ... **Because I'm feeling a bit tired**.

### 3 *just because ... (it) doesn't mean ...*

This is quite a common structure in informal speech.

> **Just because** you're older than me **(it) doesn't mean** you can do what you like.
> **Just because** I'm your brother **(it) doesn't mean** you can keep asking me for money.

For *because* after *reason*, see 492.
For the differences between *because, as, since* and *for*, see 72.

## 95 **been** meaning 'come' or 'gone'

*Been* is often used as a past participle of *come* and *go*.

> Granny has **been** to see us twice since Christmas.
> I haven't **been** to the theatre for ages.
> Have you ever **been** to Northern Ireland?

Note that *been* is only used for completed visits. Compare:
- *The postman's already **been**.* (He has come and gone away again.)
  *Jane's **come**, so we can start work.* (She has come and is still here.)
- *I've **been** to London three times this week.*
  *Where's Lucy? ~ She's **gone** to London.*

For *be gone*, see 229.

## 96 before: adverb

### 1 'at any time before now/then'

We can use *before* to mean 'at any time before now'. In British English, a present perfect tense is normally used.
*I think **I've seen** this film **before**.*      **Have** you ever **been** here **before**?
*Before* can also mean 'at any time before then – before the past moment that we are talking about'. In this case a past perfect tense is used.
*She realised that she **had seen** him **before**.*

### 2 counting back from a past time: *eight years before*

We also use *before* after a time expression to 'count back' from a past moment – to say how much earlier something else had happened. A past perfect tense is normally used.
*When I went back to the town that I **had left eight years before**, everything was different.* (NOT ...~~that I had left before eight years~~...)
To count back from the present, we use *ago*, not *before* (see also 33).
*I left school **four years ago**.* (NOT ...~~four years before / before four years~~)

### 3 *before*, *before that* and *first*

*Before* is not generally used alone to mean 'first' or 'before that happens'. Instead we use *first* or *before that*.
*I want to get married one day. But **before that** / **first**, I want to travel.*
(NOT ...~~But before, I want to travel.~~)

For the difference between *before* and *ever*, see 191.
For *before* as a conjunction and preposition, see 97–98.

## 97 before: conjunction

> *before* + clause, + clause
> clause + *before* + clause

### 1 position of *before*-clause

*Before* can join one clause to another. Compare:
***Before I have breakfast**, I spend half an hour doing physical exercises.*
*I prefer to do my exercises **before I have breakfast**.*
(In both sentences, the speaker does exercises first and then has breakfast. In the second example, the *before*-clause is given more importance because it comes at the end. Note the comma in the first example.)
***Before he did military service**, he went to university.*
    (He went to university first.)

▶

*He did military service **before he went to university**.*
(He did military service first.)

## 2 present tense with future meaning

With *before*, we use a present tense if the meaning is future (see 580).
*I'll telephone you **before I come**.* (NOT ... ~~before I will come.~~)

## 3 perfect tenses

In clauses with *before*, we often use present perfect and past perfect tenses to emphasise the idea of completion.
*You can't go home **before I've signed** the letters.* (= ... before the moment when I have completed the letters.)
*He went out **before I had finished** my sentence.* (= ... before the moment when I had completed my sentence.)
(Note that in sentences like the last, a past perfect tense can refer to a time *later* than the action of the main verb. This is unusual.)

## 4 before things that don't happen

We sometimes use *before* to talk about things that don't happen (because something stops them).
*We'd better get out of here **before your father catches us**.*
*She left **before I could ask** for her phone number.*

## 5 *before ...ing*

In a formal style, we often use the structure *before ...ing*.
*Please put out all lights **before leaving the office**.*
***Before beginning the book**, she spent five years on research.*

For *before* as an adverb and preposition, see 96, 98.

# 98 before (preposition) and in front of

*before*: time
*in front of*: place

Compare:
*I must move my car **before nine o'clock**.*
*It's parked **in front of the post office**.* (NOT ... ~~before the post office.~~)

*Before* is normally used to refer to time. However, it can refer to place:
**a** to talk about order in queues, lists, documents etc
*Do you mind? I was **before / in front of you**!*
*Her name comes **before mine** in the alphabet.*
*We use 'a' **before a consonant** and 'the' **before a vowel**.*

**b** to mean 'in the presence of (somebody important)'
*I came up **before the magistrates** for dangerous driving last week.*

**c** in the expressions *right before one's eyes, before one's very eyes*.

For the difference between *in front of* and *facing/opposite*, see 402.
For *before* as an adverb and conjunction, see 96–97.
For *by* meaning 'at/on or before', see 117.

## 99  begin and start

### 1  meaning; formality

*Begin* and *start* can both be used with the same meaning.
  *I began/started teaching when I was 24.*
  *If Sheila doesn't come soon, let's begin/start without her.*
We generally prefer *begin* when we are using a more formal style. Compare:
  *We will begin the meeting with a message from the President.*
  *Damn! It's starting to rain.*

### 2  cases where *begin* is not possible

*Start* (but not *begin*) is used to mean:

**a** 'start a journey'
  *I think we ought to start at six, while the roads are empty.*

**b** 'start working' (for machines)
  *The car won't start.*

**c** 'make something start'
  *How do you start the washing machine?*
  *The President's wife fired the gun to start the race.*

For infinitives and *-ing* forms after *begin* and *start*, see 299.10.

## 100  below, under, underneath, beneath

### 1  'lower than': *below* or *under*

The prepositions *below* and *under* can both mean 'lower than'.
  *Look in the cupboard below/under the sink.*

### 2  not directly under: *below*

We prefer *below* when one thing is not directly under another.
  *The climbers stopped 300m below the top of the mountain.*
  *A moment later the sun had disappeared below the horizon.*

### 3  covered: *under*

We prefer *under* when something is covered or hidden by what is over it, and
when things are touching.
  *I think the cat's under the bed.*
  *What are you wearing under your sweater?*
  *The whole village is under water.* (NOT *... below water.*)

### 4  measurements: *below*

*Below* is used in measurements of temperature and height, and in other cases
where we think of a vertical scale.
  *The temperature is three degrees below zero.*
  *Parts of Holland are below sea level.*
  *The plane came down below the clouds.*
  *She's well below average in intelligence.*                    ▶

## 5 'less than': *under*

We usually use *under*, not *below*, to mean 'less than' or 'younger than'.
> *There were **under** twenty people at the lecture.*
> *You can't see this film if you're **under** 18.*

## 6 *underneath*

*Underneath* is sometimes used as a preposition instead of *under*, but only for physical position. Compare:
> *There's a mouse **under(neath)** the piano.*
> *He's still **under** 18.* (NOT ... ~~underneath 18.~~)

## 7 *beneath*

*Beneath* is used mostly in a rather literary style.
> *The ship sank slowly **beneath** the waves.*

It is common before abstract nouns in some fixed expressions.
> *He acts as if I was **beneath his notice**.* (= not worth considering)
> *Her behaviour is **beneath contempt**.* (= really disgraceful)

## 8 adverbs

*Below* can be used as an adverb.
> *We looked over the cliff at the waves crashing on the rocks **below**.*

*Under* can be used as an adverb particle (see 20) with some verbs.
> *A lot of businesses are **going under** because of the economic crisis.*

In other cases we prefer *underneath* for adverbial use.
> *I can't take my sweater off – I haven't got anything on **underneath**.*
> (NOT ... ~~anything on under.~~)

In a book or a paper, *see below* means 'look at something written later'.

The difference between *above* and *over* is similar to the difference between *below* and *under*. See 6 for details.

# 101 beside and besides

*Beside* is a preposition meaning 'at the side of', 'by', 'next to'.
> *Who's the big guy sitting **beside** Jane?*

*Besides* can be used like *as well as* (see 78), when we add new information to what is already known.
> ***Besides** literature, we have to study history and philosophy.*
> *Who was at the party **besides** Jack and the Bensons?*

*Besides* can also be used as a discourse marker (see 157.11) meaning 'also', 'as well', 'in any case'. It is often used to add a stronger, more conclusive argument to what has gone before. In this case, *besides* usually goes at the beginning of a clause.
> *I don't like those shoes; **besides**, they're too expensive.*
> *It's too late to go out now. **Besides**, it's starting to rain.*

## 102 besides, except and apart from

These expressions are sometimes confused.
*Besides* usually adds: it is like saying *with*, or *plus* (+).
> **Besides** *the violin, he plays the piano and the flute.* (He plays three instruments.)

*Except* subtracts: it is like saying *without*, or *minus* (-).
> *I like all musical instruments* **except** *the violin.*

*Apart from* can be used in both senses.
> **Apart from the violin**, *he plays the piano and the flute.* (= **Besides** the violin . . .)

> *I like all musical instruments* **apart from** *the violin.*(= . . . **except** the violin.)

After *no, nobody, nothing* and similar negative words, the three expressions can all have the same meaning.
> *He has* **nothing besides** / **except** / **apart from** *his salary.* (= He only has his salary.)

For the use of *besides* as an adverbial discourse marker, see 157.11.   For *beside*, see 101.
For *except* and *except for*, see 194.

## 103 bet

### 1 use

*I bet (you)* can be used in an informal style to mean 'I think it's probable that'. *That* is usually dropped.
> **I bet (you)** *she's not at home.*
> (More natural than *I bet (you) that she's not at home.*)

*I'll bet . . .* is also possible.
> *I'll* **bet** *you she's not at home.*

### 2 tenses

After *I bet (you)*, we often use a present tense to refer to the future.
> *I bet (you) they* **don't come** *this evening.* (OR *I bet (you) they won't come . . .*)
> *I bet (you) the Conservatives* **(will) lose**.

### 3 two objects

When *bet* is used to talk about real bets, it can be followed by two objects: the person with whom the bet is made, and the money or thing that is bet.
> *I bet* **you £5** *it doesn't rain this week.*
> *My father bet* **my mother dinner** *at the Ritz that she would marry him. He won, but she never bought him the dinner.*

*Bet* is irregular (*bet – bet – bet*).

## 104 better

### 1 'recovered'

When *better* means 'recovered from an illness', it can be used with *completely* or *quite* (unlike other comparative adjectives).
> *Don't start work again until you're* **quite better**.   ▶

## 2 correcting mistakes

We do not normally use *better* to correct mistakes.
> *She's gone to Hungary – or **rather**, Poland.* (NOT ... ~~or better, Poland.~~)

For the structure *had better*, see 230.

# 105 between and among

## 1 *between* two

We say that something is *between* two people, things, or groups of things.
> *She was standing **between** Alice and Mary.*
> *a long valley **between** high mountains*

*Between* is often used to talk about distances or intervals.
> *We need **two metres between** the windows.*
> *I'll be at the office **between nine and eleven**.*

*Between* is common before *each*.
> *There seems to be less and less time **between each** birthday.*

## 2 *between* or *among* more than two

We usually say that somebody or something is *between* several clearly separate people or things. We prefer *among* when somebody or something is in a group, a crowd or a mass of people or things which we do not see separately.
Compare:
– *Our house is **between the woods, the river and the village**.*
  *His house is hidden **among the trees**.*
– *I saw something **between the wheels** of the car.*
  *Your letter is somewhere **among all these papers**.*

*Among* is normal before a singular (uncountable) noun.
> *They found an envelope full of money **among all the rubbish**.*

## 3 dividing and sharing; *difference*

We can talk about *dividing* or *sharing* things *between* or *among* more than two people or groups.
> *He **divided** all his money **between/among** his children and grandchildren.*
> *We **shared** the work **between/among** the five of us.*

We normally use *between* after *difference*.
> *There are enormous **differences between** languages.*
> *What's the **difference between** 'between' and 'among'?*

## 4 'one of' etc

*Among* can mean 'one of', 'some of' or 'included in'.
> ***Among** the first to arrive was the ambassador.*
> *He has a number of criminals **among** his friends.*

# 106  big, large and great

## 1  concrete nouns: usually *big* or *large*

With concrete nouns – the names of things you can see, touch etc – we mostly use *big* and *large*. *Big* is most common in an informal style.

> Get your **big** feet off my flowers.
> She is a small woman, but she has very **large** feet.
> It was a **large** house, situated near the river.

## 2  *great* with concrete nouns

*Great* is not normally used simply to talk about physical size. In an informal style, it is often used with concrete nouns to mean 'wonderful'.

> I've just got a **great** new flat.

And it can also be used with meanings like 'large and impressive'.

> **Great** clouds of smoke rose above the burning cathedral.

Another meaning is 'famous' or 'important'.

> Do you think Napoleon was really a **great** man?

## 3  abstract nouns: usually *great*

*Great* is common with abstract nouns – the names of things you cannot see, touch etc.

> I have **great respect** for her ideas. (NOT ~~big/large respect~~)
> His behaviour caused **great annoyance**. (NOT ~~big/large annoyance~~)
> You are making a **great mistake**.
> Her work showed a **great improvement** last year.

*Big* can be used with countable abstract nouns in an informal style.

> You're making **a big mistake**.
> **Big bargains** for weekend shoppers!

*Large* is used with countable abstract nouns referring to quantities, amounts and proportions.

> We're thinking of giving your firm a very **large order**.
> There was a **large error** in the accounts.
> She spent **large sums** on entertaining.
> He wrote a **large part** of the book while he was in hospital.

*Big* and *large* are not generally used with uncountable nouns – but note the fixed expressions *big business, big trouble*.

## 4  *large* and *wide*

*Large* is a 'false friend' for speakers of some languages. It does not mean 'wide'.

> The river is 100 metres **wide**. (NOT ... ~~100 metres large.~~)

For *wide* and *broad*, see 115.

# 107  [a] bit

## 1  use

*A bit* is often used as an adverb with the same meaning as *a little* (see 329).

> She's **a bit** old to play with dolls, isn't she? ▶

*Can you drive **a bit** slower?    Wait **a bit**.*
Note that when *a bit* and *a little* are used with non-comparative adjectives, the meaning is usually negative or critical.
*a bit **tired**    a bit **expensive**    a little (too) **old***
(BUT NOT *a bit kind, a little interesting*)

## 2  *a bit of a*

*A bit of a* can be used before some nouns in an informal style. The meaning is similar to *rather a* (see 490).
*He's **a bit of a** fool, if you ask me.    I've got **a bit of a** problem.*

## 3  *not a bit*

The informal expression *not a bit* means 'not at all'.
*I'm **not a bit** tired.    Do you mind if I put some music on? ~ **Not a bit**.*

For *a bit* with comparative adjectives and adverbs, see 140.

# 108  born and **borne**

## 1  *be born*

To talk about coming into the world at birth, we use the passive expression *to be born*.
*Hundreds of children **are born** deaf every year.*
To give a place or date of birth, we use the simple past: *was/were born*.
*I **was born** in 1936.* (NOT *I am born in 1936.*)
*My parents **were born** in Scotland.*

## 2  the verb *bear*

The verb *bear* (*bore, borne*) is used to talk about accepting or tolerating difficult experiences. It is most common in the expression *can't bear* (= hate, can't stand).
*I **can't bear** her voice.*
In a very formal style, *bear* can be used with other meanings, including 'give birth to' and 'carry'.
*She **bore** six children in seven years.* (More normal: *She had six children . . .*)
*The king's body was **borne** away to the cathedral.*

# 109  borrow and **lend**

**Borrowing** is **taking** (for a time).
*Can I **borrow** your bicycle?* (NOT *Can I lend your bicycle?*)
You borrow something **from** somebody.
*I **borrowed** a pound **from** my brother.* (NOT *I borrowed my brother a pound.*)
**Lending** (AmE also *loaning*) is **giving** (for a time). You lend something **to** somebody, or **lend somebody** something.
*I **lent** my coat **to** Steve, and I never saw it again.*
***Lend** me your comb for a minute, will you?* (NOT *Borrow me your . . .*)

For *lend* in passive structures, see 415.

# 110 both

## 1 meaning

*Both* means 'each of two'.
> **Both** my parents were born in Scotland.

We do not normally use *both* when the meaning is not 'each'.
> **My two** brothers carried the piano upstairs. (More natural than *Both my brothers carried the piano upstairs* – they didn't each carry it separately.)

## 2 both and both of

Before a noun with a determiner (e.g. *the, my, these*), *both* and *both of* are both possible.
> She's eaten **both (of) the** chops.     **Both (of) these** oranges are bad.
> He lost **both (of) his** parents when he was a child.

We often drop *the* or a possessive after *both*; *of* is not used in this case.
> She's eaten **both chops**. (NOT *. . . both of chops*)
> He lost **both parents** when he was a child.

## 3 the not used before both

Note that we do not put *the* before *both*.
> **both (the)** children (NOT *the both children*)

## 4 personal pronouns: both of

With personal pronouns, we use **both of** + *us/you/them*. *Both of us/you/them* can be a subject or object.
> **Both of them** can come tomorrow.
> She's invited **both of us**.     Mary sends **both of you** her love.

We can put *both* after pronouns used as objects.
> She's invited **us both**.     Mary sends **you both** her love.

But this structure is not used in complements (after *be*) or in short answers.
> Who broke the window – Sarah or Alice? ~ It was **both of them**.
> (NOT *. . . them both.*)
> Who did she invite? ~ **Both of us**. (NOT *Us both.*)

## 5 both with a verb

When *both* refers to the subject of a clause, it can go with the verb, in 'mid-position' (for details of word order, see 24).
> We **can both swim**.     Those oranges **were both** bad.
> The children **have both gone** to bed.     My sisters **both work** in education.

Note that these meanings can also be expressed by using *both (of)* with a subject (see above).
> **Both of us** can swim.     **Both (of) the children** have gone to bed.

## 6 negative structures

Instead of *both . . . not*, we normally use *neither* (see 372).
> **Neither of them** is here. (NOT *Both of them are not here.*)

# 111 both . . . and

We often balance this structure, so that the same kind of words or expressions follow *both* and *and*.

>She's **both** *pretty* **and** *clever*. (adjectives)
>I spoke to **both** *the Director* **and** *her secretary*. (nouns)
>She **both** *dances* **and** *sings*. (verbs)

However, unbalanced sentences with *both . . . and* are common. Some people prefer to avoid them.

>She **both** *dances* **and** *she sings*. (*both* + verb; *and* + clause)
>I **both** *play the piano* **and** *the violin.*

*Both* cannot begin a complete clause in this structure.

>You can **both** *borrow the flat* **and** *(you can) use our car.* (BUT NOT ~~Both you can borrow the flat and you can use the car.~~)

See also *either . . . or* (175), *neither . . . nor* (373) and *not only . . . but also* (383).

# 112 bring and take

## 1 speaker's/hearer's position

We use *bring* for movements to the place where the speaker or hearer is, but we use *take* for movements to other places. Compare:

- *This is a nice restaurant. Thanks for **bringing** me here.* (NOT . . . ~~thanks for taking me here.~~)
  *Let's have another drink, and then I'll **take** you home.* (NOT . . . ~~and then I'll bring you home.~~)
- (on the phone) *Can we come over on Sunday? We'll **bring** a picnic.*
  *Let's go and see Aunt May on Sunday. We can **take** a picnic.*

## 2 speaker's/hearer's past or future position

We can also use *bring* for a movement to a place where the speaker or hearer already was or will be. Compare:

- *Where's that report? ~ I **brought** it to you when you were in Mr Allen's office. Don't you remember?*
  *I **took** the papers to John's office.*
- *I'll arrive at the hotel at six o'clock. Can you **bring** the car at six-thirty?*
  *Can you **take** the car to the garage tomorrow? I won't have time.* (NOT ~~Can you bring the car to the garage tomorrow? . . .~~)

## 3 joining a movement

*Bring (with)* can be used to talk about joining a movement of the speaker's/hearer's, even if *take* is used for the movement itself.

>I'm **taking** the kids to the cinema tonight. Would you like to come with us and **bring** Susie?

## 4 somebody else's position

Sometimes when we are talking about somebody else (not the speaker or hearer), that person can become the centre of our attention. In that case, we use *bring* for movements to the place where he/she is (or was or will be). This often happens in stories.

> *He heard nothing for months. Then one day his brother **brought** him a letter.*

### 5 American English

Americans often use *bring* where British English has *take*.

> *Let's go and see Aunt May on Sunday. We can **bring** a picnic.*

The difference between *come* and *go* is similar. See 134.

For other uses of *take*, see 576.

## 113 bring up and educate

*Bring up* and the noun *upbringing* are mostly used for the moral and social training that children receive at home. *Educate* and *education* are used for the intellectual and cultural training that people get at school and university.

> *Lucy was **brought up** by her aunt and **educated** at the local school.*
> *Their kids are very badly **brought up** – always screaming and fighting.*
> (NOT *Their kids are very badly educated*. . .)
> *Which is better: a good **upbringing** and a bad **education**, or the opposite?*

## 114 Britain, the United Kingdom, the British Isles and England

*(Great) Britain* is normally used to mean the island which includes England, Scotland and Wales; *British* is used for the people of these three countries. Great Britain and Northern Ireland together are called *the United Kingdom*; some people also use *Britain* in this wider sense.

*The British Isles* is a geographical, not a political term. It is the name for England, Scotland, Wales, the whole of Ireland (which includes both Northern Ireland and the Republic of Ireland, also called 'Eire'), and the smaller islands round about.

Note that *England* is only one part of Britain. Scotland and Wales are not in England, and Scottish and Welsh people do not like to be called 'English'.

A very informal word for a British person is *Brit*. *Briton* is used mainly in news reports and newspaper headlines (e.g. *THREE BRITONS DIE IN AIR CRASH*), and to refer to the ancient inhabitants of Britain.

## 115 broad and wide

### 1 physical distance

To talk about the physical distance from one side of something to the other, we more often use *wide*.

> *We live in a very **wide** street.*     *The car's too **wide** for the garage.*

*Broad* can also be used in this physical sense, especially in more formal descriptions.

> *Across the **broad** valley, the mountains rose blue and mysterious.*
> *She wore a simple green dress with a **broad** black belt.*     ▶

Note also: **broad** *shoulders; a* **broad** *back;* **wide** *eyes; a* **wide** *mouth.*
*Wide* is used in expressions of measurement: note the word order.
*The river is about* **half a mile wide.** (NOT *. . . wide half a mile.*)

## 2 abstract meanings

Both words can express more abstract meanings. Common expressions:
> **broad** *agreement* (= agreement on most important points)
> **broad**-*minded* (= tolerant)      **broad** *daylight* (= full, bright daylight)
> *a* **wide** *variety/range* (of opinions etc)

For other common expressions with *broad* and *wide,* see a good dictionary.

# 116 but meaning 'except'

## 1 use

We use *but* to mean 'except' after *all, none, every, any, no* (and *everything, everybody, nothing, nobody, anywhere* etc).
> *He eats* **nothing but** *hamburgers.*      **Everybody's** *here* **but** *George.*
> *I've finished* **all** *the jobs* **but** *one.*

Note the expressions *next but one, last but two* etc (mainly BrE).
> *Jackie lives* **next** *door* **but one.** (= two houses from me)
> *I was* **last but two** *in the race yesterday.*

*But for* expresses the idea 'if something had not existed/happened'.
> *I would have been in real trouble* **but for** *your help.*
> **But for** *the storm, I would have been home before eight.*

Note also the structure *who/what should . . . but* (used to talk about surprising appearances, meetings etc).
> *I walked out of the station, and* **who should** *I see* **but** *old Beryl?*
> *I looked under the bed, and* **what should** *I find* **but** *the keys I lost last week?*

## 2 pronouns after *but*

After *but,* we usually use object pronouns (*me, him* etc). Subject pronouns (*I, he* etc) are possible in a more formal style before a verb.
> *Nobody* **but her** *would do a thing like that.*
> (More formal: *Nobody but she . . .*)

## 3 verbs after *but*

The verb form after *but* usually depends on what came before. Infinitives are normally without *to.*
> *She's not interested in anything* **but skiing.** (*interested in . . . skiing*)
> *That child does nothing* **but watch** *TV.* (*does . . . watch*)

*Cannot (help) but* + **infinitive without** *to* is sometimes used with the meaning of 'can't help . . .ing' (see 126). *Cannot but . . .* is very formal; *cannot help but . . .* is especially common in American English.
> *One* **cannot (help) but admire** *his courage.* (= One has to admire . . .)
> *I* **can't help but wonder** *what's going to happen to us all.*

Infinitives with *to* are used after *no alternative/choice/option but.*
> *The train was cancelled, so I had* **no alternative but to take** *a taxi.*

**4**  *but* meaning 'only'

In older English, *but* was used to mean 'only', but this is now very unusual.
*She is **but** a child.*

Note: *but* is usually pronounced /bət/, not /bʌt/ (see 616).
For *except*, see 194.
For *but* as a conjunction and ellipsis after *but*, see 178.

# 117  by: time

**1**  not later than

*By* can mean 'not later than'.
*I'll be home **by** five o'clock.* (= at or before five)
*Can I borrow your car?* ~ *Yes, but I must have it back **by** tonight.* (= tonight or before)
*By* can also suggest the idea of 'progress up to a particular time'.
***By** the end of the meal, everybody was drunk.*
Before a verb, we use *by the time (that)*.
*I'll be in bed **by the time** you get home.*
***By the time that** the guards realised what was happening, the gang were already inside the bank.*

For the difference between *by* and *until*, see 602.6.

**2**  other meanings

*By* can also be used to talk about time in the rather literary expressions *by day* and *by night* (= during the day/night).
*He worked **by night** and slept **by day**.*
Note also *day by day, hour by hour* etc.
*The situation is getting more serious **day by day**.* (= ... each day.)
And one can pay *by the hour, by the day* etc.
*In this job we're paid **by the hour**.*
*You can hire a bicycle **by the day** or **by the week**.*

# 118  by and near

*By* means 'just at the side of'; something that is *by* you may be closer than something that is *near* you. Compare:
*We live **near the sea**.* (perhaps five kilometres away)
*We live **by the sea**.* (We can see it.)

# 119  by (method, agent) and with (tools etc)

**1**  the difference

*By* and *with* can both be used to say how somebody does something, but there is an important difference.
We use *by* to talk about an action – what we **do** to get a result. We use *with* to talk about a tool or other object – what we **use** to get a result. Compare:  ▶

– *I killed the spider* **by hitting it.** (Note the *-ing* form after **by.**)
  *I killed the spider* **with a shoe.** (NOT ...~~by a shoe.~~)
– *I got where I am* **by hard work.** ~ *No you didn't. You got there* **with your wife's money.**

*Without* is the opposite of both *by* and *with* in these cases. Compare:
– *I got her to listen* **by shouting.**
  *It's difficult to get her to listen* **without shouting.**
– *We'll have to get it out* **with a screwdriver.**
  *We can't get it out* **without a screwdriver.**

*By* is also used to refer to means of transport (*by bus, by train* etc). See 70.1.

### 2 passive clauses

In passive clauses, *by* introduces the agent – the person or thing that does the action (see 413).

> *I was interviewed* **by three directors.**
> *My car was damaged* **by a falling branch.**

We generally prefer *with* to refer to a tool or instrument used by somebody. Compare:

> *He was killed* **by a heavy stone.** (This could mean 'A stone fell and killed him'.)
> *He was killed* **with a heavy stone.** (This means 'Somebody used a stone to kill him'.)

## 120 call

*Call* (with no object) can mean both 'telephone' and 'visit'. This sometimes causes confusion.

> *Alice* **called** *this morning.* ~ *You mean she came round or she phoned?*

## 121 can and could (1): introduction

### 1 grammar

*Can* and *could* are modal auxiliary verbs (see 353–354).

a  There is no *-s* in the third person singular.
   *She* **can** *swim very well.* (NOT *She* ~~cans~~...)

b  Questions and negatives are made without *do*.
   **Can** *you swim?* (NOT ~~Do you can swim?~~)
   *I* **couldn't** *understand her.* (NOT ~~I didn't could~~...)

c  After *can* and *could*, we use the infinitive of other verbs, without *to*.
   *I can* **speak** *a little Arabic.* (NOT ~~I can to speak~~...)
   *Do you think she can still* **be working?** *It's very late.*

d  *Can* and *could* have no infinitives or participles (~~to can, canning, I have could~~ do not exist). When necessary, we use other words, for example forms of *be able* (see 3) or *be allowed* (see 42).
   *I'd like to* **be able** *to stay here.* (NOT ...~~to can stay~~...)
   *You'll* **be able** *to walk soon.* (NOT ~~You'll can~~...)

*I've always **been able** to play games well.* (NOT ~~I've always could~~ ...)
*She's always **been allowed** to do what she liked.*

e *Could* is sometimes used as the past of *can*.
  *When I was younger I **could** play tennis very well.*
However, it can also be used as a less definite or conditional form of *can*,
referring to the present or future (see 122.6, 124.1,4–6).
  ***Could** I ask you something?* (More polite than *Can I ...?*)
  *What shall we do this evening? ~ We **could** go and see a film.*
  *I **could** get a better job if I spoke French.* (= I would be able to ...)

f Certain past ideas can be expressed by *can* or *could* followed by a perfect
  infinitive (***have** + **past participle***). For details, see 122.7, 123.5 and 124.7.
  *I don't know where she **can have gone**.*
  *That was dangerous – he **could have killed** somebody.*

g *Can* has two pronunciations: a strong form /kæn/ and a weak form /kən/.
  *Could* has a strong form /kʊd/ and a weak form /kəd/. The weak
  pronunciation is used in most cases. For more details of strong and weak
  pronunciations, see 616.

h Contracted negative forms (see 143) are *can't* (pronounced /kɑːnt/ in standard
  British English and /kænt/ in standard American English) and *couldn't*
  (/ˈkʊdnt/). *Cannot* is usually written as one word in British English.

## 2 meanings

*Can* and *could* are both used to talk about ability, to ask for and give
permission, and to make requests and offers.
  ***Can** you speak French?* (ability)
  *You **can** stop work early today.* (permission)
  ***Could** I have some more tea?* (request)
  ***Can** I help you?* (offer)
*Could* is also used to talk about the chances that something will happen, or is
happening. *Can* is not used in this way.
  *It **could** rain this afternoon.* (NOT ~~It can rain this afternoon.~~)
*Can't* is not only used to talk about ability or permission; it can also express
negative certainty (see 359.2).
  *It **can't** be true.* (= It is not possible that it is true.)
With *see*, *hear* and some other verbs, *can* is used to give a kind of present
progressive meaning.
  *I **can hear** the sea.* (NOT ~~I am hearing the sea.~~)
*May* and *might* are often used in similar ways to *can* and *could*. For the main
differences, see 345.

# 122 can and could (2): ability

## 1 knowledge, skill, strength etc: *I can read Italian*

We use *can* to say what people and things are able (or unable) to do because of
their knowledge, skill, strength, nature, design etc.
  *I **can** read Italian, but I **can't** speak it.*    *These roses **can** grow anywhere.*
  *Dogs **can't** climb trees.*                         ***Can** gases freeze?*                   ▶

*Henry **can** lift 100 kilos.*       *My car **can** do 180kph.*

Be able to (see 3) is used with similar meanings, especially when we are talking about people's ability.

*Henry **is able to** lift 100 kilos.*

## 2 common or typical

We often use *can* to say what is common or typical.

*Scotland **can** be very warm in September.*
*Ann **can** really get on your nerves sometimes.*

## 3 possible in the situation: *We can go to Paris*

We also use *can* to say what we are able (or unable) to do because of the circumstances that we are in – what is possible in the situation.

*We **can** go to Paris this weekend, because I don't have to work.*
*I **can't** come out this evening: I have to see my brother.*
*There are three possibilities: we **can** go to the police, we **can** talk to a lawyer, or we **can** forget all about it.*
*What shall we do? ~ We **can** try asking Lucy for help.*
*Anybody who wants to **can** join the club.*

## 4 past: *She could read when she was four*

We use *could* to talk about the past.

*She **could** read when she was four.*
*My grandmother **could** sing like an angel.*
*My last car **could** do 200kph.*
*In those days everybody **could** find a job.*
*It **could** be quite frightening if you were alone in our big old house.*

Was able to is also possible, especially to talk about people's ability.

*She **was able to** read when she was four.*

## 5 past: *could* is not always possible

We use *could* for 'general ability' – for example to say that somebody could do something at any time, whenever he/she wanted.

*When I was younger, I **could** run 10km in under 40 minutes.*

We do not normally use *could* to say that somebody did something on one occasion. Instead, we use other expressions.

*I **managed to** run 10km yesterday in under an hour.* (NOT ~~I could run 10km yesterday~~ . . .)
*How many eggs **were** you **able to** get?* (NOT . . . ~~could you get?~~)
*After six hours' climbing, we **succeeded in** getting to the top of the mountain.* (NOT . . . ~~we could get to the top~~ . . .)
*I **found** a really nice dress in the sale.* (NOT ~~I could find~~ . . .)

However, we use *couldn't* to say that something did not happen on one occasion.

*I managed to find the street, but I **couldn't** find her house.*

## 6 other uses of *could*

*Could* is not only past: we also use it as a 'softer', less definite form of *can*.

*What shall we do tomorrow? ~ Well, we **could** go fishing.*
*When you're in Spain, you **could** go and see Alex.*

*Could* can mean 'would be able to'.

*You **could** get a better job if you spoke a foreign language.*
*Could* is used in past indirect speech, when *can* was used in direct speech.
*   **Can** *you help me?* ~ *What did you say?* ~ *I asked if you **could** help me.*

## 7 could have ...

We use a special structure to talk about unrealised past ability or opportunities
– to say that somebody was able to do something, but did not try to do it; or
that something was possible, but did not happen.

> could have + past participle

*I **could have married** anybody I wanted to.*
*I was so angry I **could have killed** her!*
*Why did you jump out of the window? You **could have hurt** yourself.*
*I **could have won** the race if I hadn't fallen.*

This structure can be used to criticise people for not doing things.

*You **could have helped** me – why did you just sit and watch?*

Negative sentences suggest that somebody would not have been able to do
something even if they had wanted or tried to.

*I **couldn't have won**, so I didn't go in for the race.*
*I **couldn't have enjoyed** myself more – it was a perfect day.*

The structure is sometimes used to talk about past events which are not
certain to have happened (like *may/might have* – see 339.7).

*Who sent those flowers?* ~ *I'm not sure. It **could have been** your mother.*

## 8 chances: *Will it happen? / Is it happening?* Can not used

We do not use *can* to talk about the chances (probability) that something will
actually happen, or is actually happening. Instead, we use *may* (see 339).

*We **may** go camping this summer.* (NOT *We ~~can go~~...*)
*There **may** be a strike next week.* (NOT *There ~~can be~~...*)
*Where's Sarah?* ~ *She **may** be with Joe.* (NOT *She ~~can be~~...*)
*Some of these desserts **may** contain alcohol.* (NOT *...~~can contain~~...*)

However, *could* is possible in this sense.

*It **could** rain later this evening, perhaps.* (BUT NOT *It ~~can rain later~~...*)
*I **could** possibly have a new job soon.* (BUT NOT *I ~~can possibly have~~...*)

For a comparison between *can*, *could*, *may* and *might*, see 345.
For *can't* used to express certainty (e.g. *It can't be true*), see 359.2.

# 123 can and could (3): ability (advanced points)

## 1 future: *can* or *will be able*

We use *can* to talk about future actions which we will be able to do because of
present ability, present circumstances, present decisions etc.

*She **can** win the race tomorrow if she really tries.*
*I've bought the tent, so we **can** go camping next weekend if we want to.*
*I haven't got time today, but I **can** see you tomorrow.*
***Can** you come to a party on Saturday?*

In other cases we prefer other structures, for example *will be able to*.

*I'll **be able** to speak French at the end of this course.*
(NOT *I ~~can speak French~~...*)

▶

*One day people **will be able** to go to the moon on holiday.*
(OR *it will be possible to go . . .*)

## 2 *could* in the past

Could is not normally used to say that somebody did something on one
occasion in the past (see 122.5).

*I **managed to** buy a really nice coat yesterday.* (NOT ~~I could buy a really nice~~
~~coat yesterday.~~)

However, *could* can refer to one occasion with certain verbs: *see, hear, taste,
feel, smell, understand, remember* and *guess* (see 125).

*I **could smell** something burning.     I **could understand** everything she said.*

And we can use *could* to talk about one occasion with words like *hardly* or
*only*, that have a negative sense.

*She **could hardly** believe her eyes.          I **could only** get six eggs.*

*Could* can also sometimes refer to one occasion in subordinate clauses.

*I'm so glad that you **could** come.*

## 3 languages and instruments: *She speaks Greek*

We often leave out *can* when we are talking about the ability to speak
languages or to play instruments.

*She **speaks** Greek. / She **can speak** Greek.*
*Do/Can you **play** the piano?*

## 4 *can/could always*

*Can/could always* can mean 'can/could . . . if there is nothing better'.

*I don't know what to get Mark for his birthday. ~ Well, you **can always** give
him a book token.*
*What are we going to eat? ~ We **could always** warm up that soup.*

## 5 *could have . . .* for present situations

Could have + past participle can refer to present situations which were
possible but have not been realised.

*He **could have been** Prime Minister now if he hadn't decided to leave politics.*
*We **could have spent** today at the seaside, but we thought it was going to
rain, so we decided not to.*

# 124  can and could (4):
# interpersonal uses (permission, requests etc)

## 1 asking for and giving permission: *Can I . . .?*

We use *can* to ask for and give permission.

*Can I ask you something? ~ Yes, of course you **can**.*
*You **can** go now if you want to.*

Can't is used to refuse permission (often with other words to soften the
refusal).

*Can I have some more cake? ~ No, I'm afraid you **can't**.*

We also use *could* to ask for permission; it is more polite or formal than *can*. We do not use *could* to give or refuse permission (it suggests respect, so is more natural in asking for permission than in giving it).

> *Could I ask you something?* ~ *Yes, of course you can.* (NOT . . . ~~of course you could.~~)

*May* and *might* are also used to ask and give permission (see 340). They are more formal than *can/could*. Some people consider them more 'correct', but in fact *can* and *could* are normally preferred in informal educated usage.

## 2 talking about permission: *Can everybody park here?*

*Can* and *could* are also used to talk about permission that has already been given or refused, and about things that are (not) allowed by rules and laws. (Note that *may* is not normally used to talk about rules and laws – see 340.3.)

> *She said I **could** come as often as I liked.*
> *Can everybody park here?* (NOT ~~May everybody park here?~~)

## 3 past: *could* is not always possible

In talking about the past, we use *could* to say that somebody had permission to do something at any time ('general permission'), but we do not use *could* to talk about permission for one particular action in the past. Compare:

> *When I was a child, I **could** watch TV whenever I wanted to.*
> *Yesterday evening, Peter **was allowed** to watch TV for an hour.* (NOT . . . ~~Peter could watch TV for an hour.~~)

But *could not* can be used to talk about one particular action.

> *Peter **couldn't** watch TV yesterday because he was naughty.*

(The difference between *could* and *was/were allowed* is similar to the difference between *could* and *was/were able* – see 122.5.)

## 4 could = 'would be allowed'

*Could* has a conditional use (= would be allowed).

> *He **could** borrow my car if he asked.*

*Could have* + **past participle** means 'would have been allowed'.

> *I **could have** kissed her if I'd wanted to.*

## 5 offers

We often use *can* when we offer to do things for people.

> *Can I carry your bag?* ( = Would you like me to . . .) ~ *Oh, thank you.*
> *I **can** baby-sit for you this evening if you like.* ~ *No, it's all right, thanks.*

*Could* is possible if we want an offer to sound less definite.

> *I **could** mend your bicycle for you, if that would help.*

## 6 requests, orders and suggestions

We can use *can* and *could* to ask or tell people to do things. *Could* is more polite, more formal or less definite, and is often used for making suggestions.

> *Can you put the children to bed?*
> *Could you lend me five pounds until tomorrow?*
> *Do you think you **could** help me for a few minutes?*
> *When you've finished the washing-up you **can** clean the kitchen. Then you **could** iron the clothes, if you like.*
> *If you haven't got anything to do you **could** sort out your photos.* ▶

## 7  criticisms

*Could* can be used to criticise people for not doing things.
>  You **could** ask before you borrow my car.

*Could have* + **past participle** is used for criticisms about the past.
>  You **could have told** me you were getting married.

For the use of *might* in similar cases, see 344.

## 8  indirect speech

*Could* is used in past indirect speech, when *can* was used in direct speech.
>  **Can** you give me a hand? ~ What? ~ I asked if you **could** give me a hand.

# 125  can and could (5): with see, hear, etc

## 1  *see, hear, feel, smell, taste*

When these verbs refer to perception (receiving information through the eyes, ears etc), we do not normally use progressive forms. To talk about seeing, hearing etc at a particular moment, we often use *can see, can hear* etc (especially in British English).
>  I **can see** Susan coming. (NOT ~~I'm seeing~~...)
>  **Can** you **hear** somebody coming up the stairs?
>  What did you put in the stew? I **can taste** something funny.
>  Suddenly she realised she **could smell** something burning.

In American English, *I see/hear* etc are common in this sense.

## 2  *guess, tell*

*Can* and *could* are often used with *guess* and with *tell* (meaning *see, know*). *Can/could* are not normally used with *know* in the sense of 'find out' (see 313.5).
>  I **could guess** what she wanted.
>  You **can tell** he's Irish from his accent. (NOT ~~You can know~~...)

## 3  *understand, follow, remember*

*Can/could* is often used with these verbs too. It does not always add very much to the meaning.
>  I **can't/don't understand** what she's talking about.
>  Do/**Can** you **follow** what he's saying?
>  I (**can**) **remember** your grandfather.

# 126  can't help

If you say that you *cannot/can't help* doing something, you mean that you can't stop yourself, even if you don't want to do it.
>  She's a selfish woman, but somehow you **can't help** liking her.
>  Excuse me – I **couldn't help** overhearing what you said.
>  Sorry I broke the cup – I **couldn't help** it.

*Can't help* can be followed by *but* + **infinitive without *to*** (see 116.3), with the same meaning as *can't help ...ing*. This is common in American English.
>  I **can't help but wonder** what I should do next.

# 127 care: take care (of), care (about) and care for

## 1 take care of

*Take care of* normally means 'look after' or 'take responsibility for'.
> *Nurses **take care of** people in hospital.*
> *It's no good giving Peter a rabbit: he's too young to **take care of** it properly.*
> *Ms Savage **takes care of** marketing, and I'm responsible for production.*

*Take care* (without a preposition) means 'be careful'. Some people use it as a formula when saying goodbye.
> ***Take care** when you're crossing the road, children.*
> *Bye, Ruth. ~ Bye, Mike. **Take care**.*

## 2 care (about)

*Care (about)* is used to say whether you feel something is important to you. This is very common in negative sentences. *About* is used before an object, but is usually left out before a conjunction.
> *Most people **care about** other people's opinions.*
>    (NOT . . . ~~take care of / care for other people's opinions~~)
> *I don't **care whether** it rains – I'm happy.*
> *I'll never speak to you again. ~ I don't **care**.*
> *Your mother's upset with you. ~ I couldn't **care** less.* (= I don't care at all.)

## 3 care for

*Care for* can be used to mean 'look after'.
> *He spent years **caring for** his sick mother.*

Another meaning is 'like' or 'be fond of', but this is not very common in modern English.
> *I don't much **care for** strawberries.*

# 128 changes: become, get, go, grow, etc

*Become, get, go, come, grow* and *turn* can all be used with similar meanings to talk about changes. The differences between them are complicated – they depend partly on grammar, partly on meaning and partly on fixed usage.

## 1 become dark, become a pilot etc

*Become* can be used before adjectives and noun phrases.
> *It was **becoming very dark**.*
> *What do you have to do to **become a pilot**?*

*Become* is not usually used to talk about single deliberate actions.
> *Please **get ready** now.* (NOT *Please ~~become ready now~~.*)

## 2 get dark, younger etc

*Get* (informal) is very common before adjectives (without nouns).
> *It was **getting very dark**.* (informal)
> *You **get younger** every day.* (informal)

*Get* can also be used before past participles like *lost, broken, dressed, married*.
> *They **got married** in 1986, and **got divorced** two years later.* ▶

We generally use *go*, not *get*, to talk about changes of colour and some changes for the worse (like *go mad*) – see paragraph 4 below.
*Get* is not normally used before nouns to talk about changes.
> I **became a grandfather** last week. (NOT ~~I got a grandfather~~...)

For *get used to*, see 605.

## 3 get + infinitive

We can sometimes use *get* with an infinitive to talk about a gradual change.
> After a few weeks I **got to like** the job better.
> She's nice when you **get to know** her.

## 4 go red, go mad etc

*Go* can be used before adjectives to talk about change, especially in an informal style. This is common in two cases.

### a colours

*Go* (and not *get*) is used to talk about changes of colour.
> Leaves **go brown** in autumn. (NOT ~~Leaves get brown~~...)
> She **went white** with anger.
> Suddenly everything **went black** and I lost consciousness.

Other examples: *go blue with cold / red with embarrassment / green with envy.*
*Turn* can also be used in these cases (see below), and so can *grow* when the change is gradual. *Go* is more informal than *turn* and *grow*.

### b changes for the worse

*Go* (not usually *get*) is used before adjectives in some expressions that refer to changes for the worse. People **go mad** (BrE), *crazy, deaf, blind, grey* or *bald*; horses **go lame**; machines **go wrong**; iron **goes rusty**; meat, fish or vegetables **go bad**; cheese **goes mouldy**; milk **goes off** or *sour*; bread **goes stale**; beer, lemonade, musical instruments and car tyres **go flat**.
> He **went bald** in his twenties.     The car keeps **going wrong**.

Note that we use *get*, not *go*, with *old, tired* and *ill*.

## 5 come true etc

*Come* is used in a few fixed expressions to talk about things finishing up all right. The most common are *come true* and *come right*.
> I'll make all your dreams **come true**.
> Trust me – it will all **come right** in the end.

*Come* + **infinitive** can be used to talk about changes in mental state or attitude.
> I slowly **came to realise** that she knew what she was doing.
> You will **come to regret** your decision.

## 6 grow old etc

*Grow* is used before adjectives especially to talk about slow and gradual changes. It is more formal than *get* or *go*, and a little old-fashioned or literary.
> Without noticing it he **grew old**.
> When they **grew rich** they began to drop their old friends.
> As the weather **grows colder**, my thoughts turn to holidays in the sun.

*Grow* + **infinitive** can be used (like *come* + **infinitive**) to talk about changes in attitude, especially if these are gradual.

> *He **grew to accept** his stepmother, but he never **grew to love** her.*

## 7 turn red etc

*Turn* is used mostly for visible or striking changes of state. It is common before colour words (and is not so informal as *go*).

> *She **turned bright red** and ran out of the room.*
> *He **turns nasty** after he's had a couple of drinks.*

We can use *turn* before numbers to talk about important changes of age.

> *I **turned fifty** last week. It's all downhill from now on.*

*Turn into* is used before nouns.

> *He's a lovely man, but when he gets jealous he **turns into a monster**.*
> *A girl has to kiss a lot of frogs before one of them **turns into a prince**.*

*Turn to* and *turn into* can both be used before the names of materials.

> *Everything that King Midas touched **turned (in)to gold**.*
> *They stood there as if they had been **turned (in)to stone**.*

To talk about a change of occupation, religion, politics etc, we sometimes use *turn* with a noun (with no preposition or article) or an adjective.

> *He worked in a bank for thirty years before **turning painter**.*
> *Towards the end of the war he **turned traitor**.*
> *At the end of her life she **turned Catholic**.*

*Turn (in)to* can also be used to talk about changing one thing into another.

> *In the Greek legend, Circe **turned men into pigs**.*

## 8 fall ill etc

*Fall* is used to mean 'become' in *fall ill*, *fall asleep* and *fall in love*.

## 9 verbs related to adjectives: *thicken, brighten* etc

A number of verbs which are related to adjectives have meanings like 'get more ...' or 'make more ...'. Many of them end in *-en*. Examples:

> *The fog **thickened**.*  *They're **widening** the road here.*
> *The weather's beginning to **brighten** up.*  *His eyes **narrowed**.*
> *Could you **shorten** the sleeves on this jacket?*

## 10 no change: *stay, keep, remain*

To talk about things not changing, we can use *stay, keep* or *remain* before adjectives. *Remain* is more formal.

> *How do you manage to **stay young** and fit?*  *Keep calm.*
> *I hope you will always **remain so charming**.*

*Stay* and *remain* are also sometimes used before noun phrases.

> *Promise me you will always **stay/remain my little boy**.*

*Keep* can be used before *-ing* forms.

> *Keep smiling whatever happens.*

For other uses of the words discussed in this section, see a good dictionary.

# 129 city and town

Most people simply use *city* to talk about large and important towns –
examples in the UK are Belfast, Cardiff, Edinburgh, Glasgow, Manchester,
Liverpool and London.
*City* can be used in a more exact way to talk about a town that has been given a
special status by the king or queen (in Britain) or by the state (in some other
English-speaking countries).

# 130 cleft sentences (1): What I need is a holiday

We can emphasise particular words and expressions by putting everything into
a kind of relative clause except the words we want to emphasise: this makes
them stand out. These structures are called 'cleft sentences' by grammarians
(*cleft* means 'divided'). They are useful in writing (because we cannot use
intonation for emphasis in written language), but they are also common in
speech.

## 1 *Mary is the person who ...; What I need is ...*

The words to be emphasised are joined to the relative clause by *is/was* and an
expression like *the person who*, or *what* (= the thing that).
We can put the words to be emphasised first or last in the sentence. Compare:
– *MARY kept a pig in the garden shed.*
  *Mary was **the person who** kept a pig in the garden shed.*
  ***The person who** kept a pig in the garden shed was Mary.*
– *Mary kept A PIG in the garden shed.*
  *A pig was **what** Mary kept in the garden shed.*
  ***What** Mary kept in the garden shed was a pig.*
– *Phil is THE SECRETARY.*
  *The secretary is **what** Phil is.*
  ***What** Phil is is the secretary.*
Instead of *the person* or *what*, we can use less general expressions.
  *You're **the woman (that)** I'll always love best.*
  *Casablanca is **a film (that)** I watch again and again.*
A *what*-clause is normally considered to be singular; if it begins a cleft
sentence it is followed by *is/was*. But a plural verb is sometimes possible
before a plural noun in an informal style.
  *What we want **is/are** some of those cakes.*

For more information about *what*-clauses, see 497.

## 2 *the place where ...; the day when ...; the reason why ...*

We can use these expressions to emphasise a place, time or reason.
– *Mary kept a pig IN THE GARDEN SHED.*
  *The garden shed was **the place where** Mary kept a pig.*
  ***The place where** Mary kept a pig was the garden shed.*

– *Jake went to London ON TUESDAY to see Colin.*
  *Tuesday was **the day when/that** Jake went to London to see Colin.*
  ***The day when** Jake went to London to see Colin was Tuesday.*
– *Jake went to London on Tuesday TO SEE COLIN.*
  *To see Colin was **the reason why** Jake went to London on Tuesday.*
  ***The reason why** Jake went to London on Tuesday was to see Colin.*
*The place, the day* or *the reason* can be dropped in an informal style, especially in the middle of a sentence.
  *Spain's **where** we're going this year.*
  ***Why** I'm here is to talk about my plans.* (More formal: *The reason why I'm here is ...*)

## 3 emphasising verbs: *What he did was ...*

When we want to emphasise a verb (or an expression beginning with a verb), we have to use a more complicated structure with *what ... do*. Infinitives with and without *to* are possible.
– *He SCREAMED.*
  ***What** he **did** was (to) scream.*
– *She WRITES SCIENCE FICTION.*
  ***What** she **does** is (to) write science fiction.*
Instead of an infinitive, we often use **subject + verb** in an informal style.
  *What she does is, **she writes** science fiction.*
  *What I'll do is, **I'll phone** John and ask his advice.*

## 4 emphasising a whole sentence

A whole sentence can be given extra emphasis by using a cleft structure with *what* and the verb *happen*. Compare:
  *The car broke down.*
  ***What happened** was (that) the car broke down.*

## 5 other structures

*All (that)*, and expressions with *thing*, can be used in cleft sentences.
  ***All** I want is a home somewhere.*      ***All** you need is love.*
  ***All** (that) I did was (to) touch the window, and it broke.*
  ***The only thing** I remember is a terrible pain in my head.*
  ***The first thing** was to make some coffee.*
  *My first journey abroad is **something** I shall never forget.*
Time expressions can be emphasised with *It was not until ...* and *It was only when ....*
  ***It was not until** I met you that I knew real happiness.*
  ***It was only when** I read her letter that I realised what was happening.*
At the beginning of a cleft sentence, *this* and *that* often replace emphasised *here* and *there*. Compare:
– *You pay here.*                        – *We live there.*
  ***This** is where you pay.*              ***That's** where we live.*
  (OR *Here is where you pay.*)           (OR *There's where we live.*)

For more about question-word clauses, see 485.
For more general information about sentence structure and the arrangement of information in sentences, see 512.

# 131 cleft sentences (2): **it was my secretary who ...**

## 1 preparatory *it*

We can use preparatory *it* (see 446) in cleft sentences. The words to be emphasised are usually joined to the relative clause by *that*.
Compare:

> *My secretary sent the bill to Mr Harding yesterday.*
> ***It was my secretary that*** *sent the bill to Mr Harding yesterday.*
> (not somebody else)
> ***It was the bill that*** *my secretary sent to Mr Harding yesterday.*
> (not something else)
> ***It was Mr Harding that*** *my secretary sent the bill to yesterday.*
> (not to somebody else)
> ***It was yesterday that*** *my secretary sent the bill to Mr Harding.*
> (not another day)

Negative structures are also possible.

> ***It wasn't my husband that*** *sent the bill ...*

*Who* is possible instead of *that* when a personal subject is emphasised.

> *It was my secretary **who** sent ...*

When a plural subject is emphasised, the verb is plural.

> *It was the students that **were** angry ...* (NOT *... that was angry ...*)

The verb cannot be emphasised with this structure: we cannot say

> *It was sent that my secretary the bill ....*

## 2 *It is I who ... ; It is me that ...*

When an emphasised subject is a pronoun, there are two possibilities.
Compare:

> – *It is **I who am** responsible.* (formal)
> *It's **me that's/who's** responsible.* (informal)
> – *It is **you who are** in the wrong.* (formal)
> *It's **you that's** in the wrong.* (informal)

To avoid being either too formal or too informal in this case, we could say, for example,

> *I'm the person / the one who's responsible.*

# 132 close and shut

## 1 use

*Close* /kləʊz/ and *shut* can often be used with the same meaning.

> *Open your mouth and **close/shut** your eyes.*
> *I can't **close/shut** the window. Can you help me?*
> *The shop **closes/shuts** at five o'clock.*

You can *shut*, but not *close*, somebody/something in or out of a place.

> *I **shut** the letters in my desk drawer and locked it.* (NOT *I closed the letters ...*)
> *She **shut** him out of the house.*

## 2 past participles

The past participles *closed* and *shut* can be used as adjectives.
> *The post office is **closed**/**shut** on Saturday afternoon.*
*Shut* is not usually used before a noun.
> *a **closed** door* (NOT ~~a shut door~~)  *closed eyes* (NOT ~~shut eyes~~)

## 3 cases where *close* is preferred

We prefer *close* for slow movements (like flowers closing at night), and *close* is more common in a formal style.
> *As we watched, he **closed** his eyes for the last time.*
Compare:
> ***Close** your mouth, please.* (dentist to patient)
> ***Shut** your mouth!* (a rude way of saying 'Be quiet!')
We *close* roads, railways etc (channels of communication). And we *close* (= end) letters, bank accounts, meetings etc.

# 133 cloth and clothes

*Cloth* (pronounced /klɒθ/) is material made from wool, cotton etc, used for making clothes, curtains, soft furnishings and so on. (In informal English, it is more common to say *material* or *fabric*.)
> *His suits were made of the most expensive **cloth**.*
A *cloth* is a piece of material used for cleaning, covering things etc.
> *Could you pass me a **cloth**? I've spilt some milk on the floor.*
*Clothes* (pronounced /kləʊðz/) are things you wear: skirt, trousers etc. *Clothes* has no singular; instead of ~~a clothe~~, we say *something to wear* or *an article* / *a piece of clothing*.
> *I must buy some new **clothes**; I haven't got anything to wear.*

# 134 come and go

## 1 speaker's/hearer's position

We use *come* for movements to the place where the speaker or hearer is.
> *Maria, would you **come** here, please?* ~ *I'm **coming**.* (NOT ... ~~I'm going.~~)
> *When did you **come** to live here?*
> (on the phone): *Can I **come** and see you?*
We use *go* for movements to other places.
> *I want to **go** and live in Greece.*  *Let's **go** and see Peter and Diane.*
> *In 1577, he **went** to study in Rome.*

## 2 speaker's/hearer's past or future position

We can use *come* for a movement to a place where the speaker or hearer already was or will be at the time of the movement. Compare: ▶

– *What time did I **come** to see you in the office yesterday?*
*I **went** to John's office yesterday, but he wasn't in.*
– *Will you **come** and visit me in hospital when I have my operation?*
*He's **going** into hospital next week.*
– *Susan can't **come** to your birthday party.*
*She's **going** to see her mother.*

### 3 joining a movement

*Come (with)* can be used to talk about joining a movement of the speaker's/ hearer's, even if *go* is used for the movement itself.
*We're **going** to the cinema tonight. Would you like to **come** with us?*

### 4 somebody else's position

Sometimes when we are talking about somebody else (not the speaker or hearer), that person can become the centre of our attention. In that case, we use *come* for movements to the place where he/she is (or was or will be). This often happens in stories.
*He waited till four o'clock, but she didn't **come**.*

### 5 *come to; come from*

*Come to* can mean *arrive at*.
*Carry straight on till you **come to** a crossroads.*
*Come from* is used (in the present) to say where people's homes are or were.
*She **comes from** Scotland, but her mother's Welsh.*
*Originally I **come from** Hungary, but I've lived here for twenty years.*
(NOT *Originally I came from Hungary* . . .)
The difference between *bring* and *take* is similar. See 112.

For *come/go and* . . ., see 53.
For *come/go* . . .*ing*, see 228.     For *been = come/gone*, see 95.

## 135 comparison (1): structures

Various words and structures can be used for comparing.

### 1 similarity and identity: *as, like, so do I, too, the same*, etc

If we want to say that people, things, actions or events are similar, we can use *as* or *like* (see 326); *so/neither do I* and similar structures (see 541); or adverbs such as *too, also* and *as well* (see 46). To say that they are identical, we can use *the same (as)* (see 503).
*He liked working with horses, **as** his father did.*
*Your sister looks just **like** you.      The papers were late and the post was **too**.*
*She likes music, and **so do I**.      His eyes are just **the same** colour **as** mine.*

### 2 equality: *as . . . as*

To say that people, things etc are equal in a particular way, we often use the structure *as (much/many) . . . as* (see 136).
*My hands were **as** cold **as** ice.      I earn **as much** money **as** you.*

**3  inequality: *more ... than; older ... than; most, oldest,* etc**

To say that people, things etc are unequal in a particular way, we can use
comparative adjectives and adverbs, or ***more* + adjective/adverb** (see 137–141).
  *He's much **older** than her.*          *The baby's **more attractive** than you.*
To say which one of a group is outstanding in a particular way, we can use a
superlative or ***most* + adjective/adverb** (see 137–141).
  *You're the **laziest** and **most annoying** person in the whole office.*

**4  inequality: *less, least; not so/as ... as***

We can also talk about inequality by looking at the 'lower' end of the scale.
One possibility is to use *less (than)* (see 320) or *least* (see 318).
  *The baby's **less** ugly than you.*
  *I want to spend the **least** possible time working.*
In informal usage, we more often use *not so ... as* or *not as ... as* (see 136).
  *The baby's **not so** ugly **as** you.*

# 136  comparison (2): as ... as; as much/many as

**1  use**

We use *as ... as* to say that people or things are equal in some way.
  *She's **as** tall **as** her brother.*          *Is it **as** good **as** you expected?*
  *She speaks French **as** well **as** the rest of us.*

**2  negative structures**

After *not*, we can use *so ... as* instead of *as ... as*.
  *He's **not as/so** friendly **as** she is.* (more informal than *He's **less** friendly ...*)

**3  *as ... as* + adjective/adverb**

Note the structure ***as ... as* + adjective/adverb**.
  *Please get here **as** soon **as** possible.*
  *I'll spend **as** much **as** necessary.*    *You're **as** beautiful **as** ever.*

**4  pronouns after *as***

In an informal style we can use object pronouns (*me, him* etc) after *as*.
  *She doesn't sing **as** well **as** me.*
In a formal style, we prefer **subject + verb** after *as*.
  *She doesn't sing **as** well **as** I do.*
A subject form without a verb (e.g. *as well as he*) is unusual in this structure in
modern English.

**5  *as much/many ... as***

We can use *as much/many ... as* to talk about quantity.
  *I haven't got **as much** money **as** I thought.*
  *We need **as many** people **as** possible.*
*As much/many* can be used without following nouns.
  *I ate **as much as** I could.*    *She didn't catch **as many as** she'd hoped.*
And *as much ...* can be used as an adverb.
  *You ought to rest **as much as** possible.*

▶

**6   emphatic use: *as much as 80kg***

*As much/many as* can be used before a number to mean 'the large amount/ quantity'.

> *Some of these fish can weigh **as much as 80kg**.*
> *There are sometimes **as many as 40** students in the classes.*

*As little/few* can be used to mean 'the small amount/quantity'.

> *You can fly to Paris for **as little as 20** euros.*

**7   half as ... as etc**

*Half, twice, three times* etc can be used before *as ... as*.

> *You're not **half as** clever **as** you think you are.*
> *I'm not going out with a man who's **twice as** old **as** me.*
> *It took **three times as** long **as** I expected.* (OR *... **three times longer** than I*
>    *expected* – see 141.3)

**8   modification**

Before *as ... as* we can use *(not) nearly, almost, just, nothing like, every bit, exactly, not quite*.

> *It's **not nearly as** cold as yesterday.*        *He's **just as** strong as ever.*
> *You're **nothing like as** bad-tempered as you used to be.*
> *She's **every bit as** beautiful as her sister.*
> *I'm **not quite as** tired as I was last week.*

**9   infinitives**

Where *as ... as* is used with two infinitives, the second is often without *to*.

> *It's as easy to do it right as **(to) do** it wrong.*

**10   tenses**

In *as ... as*-clauses (and other kinds of *as*-clauses), a present tense is often used to refer to the future, and a past tense can have a conditional meaning (see 580).

> *We'll get there as soon as you **do/will**.*
> *If you married me, I'd give you as much freedom as you **wanted**.*

**11   leaving out the second part**

The second part of the *as ... as* or *so ... as* structure can be left out when the meaning is clear from what comes before.

> *The train takes 40 minutes. By car it'll take you twice **as long**.*
> *I used to think he was clever. Now I'm not **so sure**.*

In cases like this, *not so* is much more common than *not as*.

**12   traditional expressions**

We use the structure *as ... as ...* in a lot of traditional comparative expressions.

> ***as** cold **as** ice*        ***as** hard **as** nails*
> ***as** black **as** night*     ***as** ... **as** hell*

The first *as* can be dropped in these expressions in an informal style.

> *She's **hard as nails**.*
> *I'm tired **as hell** of listening to your problems.*

Note that *as* is usually pronounced /əz/ (see 616).
For *as long as*, see 75. For *as well as*, see 78.
For the word order in sentences like *She's as good a dancer as her brother*, see 14.
For *as* replacing subject or object (e.g. *as many people as want it*), see 581.
For other comparative structures, see 137–141.

# 137 comparison (3):
## comparative and superlative adjectives

One-syllable adjectives normally have comparatives and superlatives ending in *-er*, *-est*. Some two-syllable adjectives are similar; others have *more* and *most*. Longer adjectives have *more* and *most*.

### 1 one-syllable adjectives (regular comparison)

| Adjective | Comparative | Superlative | |
|---|---|---|---|
| old | older | oldest | Most adjectives: |
| tall | taller | tallest | + *-er*, *-est*. |
| cheap | cheaper | cheapest | |
| late | later | latest | Adjectives ending in *-e*: |
| nice | nicer | nicest | + *-r*, *-st*. |
| fat | fatter | fattest | |
| big | bigger | biggest | One vowel + one consonant: |
| thin | thinner | thinnest | double consonant. |

Note the pronunciation of:
*younger* /'jʌŋgə(r)/ *youngest* /'jʌŋgɪst/
*longer* /'lɒŋgə(r)/ *longest* /'lɒŋgɪst/
*stronger* /'strɒŋgə(r)/ *strongest* /'strɒŋgɪst/

### 2 irregular comparison

| Adjective | Comparative | Superlative |
|---|---|---|
| good | better | best |
| bad | worse | worst |
| ill | worse | |
| far | farther/further (see 201) | farthest/furthest |
| old | older/elder (see 176) | oldest/eldest |

▶

The determiners *little* and *much/many* have irregular comparatives and superlatives:

*little* (see 329)    *less* (see 320)    *least* (see 318)
*much/many* (see 357)    *more* (see 355)    *most* (see 356)

*Few* has two possible comparatives and superlatives: *fewer/less* and *fewest/least*. See 320, 318.

### 3 two-syllable adjectives

Adjectives ending in *-y* have *-ier* and *-iest*.

*happy*    *happier*    *happiest*
*easy*    *easier*    *easiest*

Some other two-syllable adjectives can have *-er* and *-est*, especially adjectives ending in an unstressed vowel, /l/ or /ə(r)/.

*narrow*    *narrower*    *narrowest*
*simple*    *simpler*    *simplest*
*clever*    *cleverer*    *cleverest*
*quiet*    *quieter*    *quietest*

With many two-syllable adjectives (e.g. *polite*, *common*), *-er/-est* and *more/most* are both possible. With others (including adjectives ending in *-ing*, *-ed*, *-ful* and *-less*), only *more/most* is possible. In general, the structure with *more/most* is becoming more common. To find out the normal comparative and superlative for a particular two-syllable adjective, check in a good dictionary.

### 4 longer adjectives

Adjectives of three or more syllables have *more* and *most*.

*intelligent*    *more intelligent*    *most intelligent*
*practical*    *more practical*    *most practical*
*beautiful*    *more beautiful*    *most beautiful*

Words like *unhappy* (the opposites of two-syllable adjectives ending in *-y*) are an exception: they can have forms in *-er* and *-est*.

*unhappy*    *unhappier / more unhappy*    *unhappiest / most unhappy*
*untidy*    *untidier / more untidy*    *untidiest / most untidy*

Some compound adjectives like *good-looking* or *well-known* have two possible comparatives and superlatives.

*good-looking*    *better-looking*    *best-looking*
    OR *more good-looking*    *most good-looking*
*well-known*    *better-known*    *best-known*
    OR *more well-known*    *most well-known*

### 5 *more, most* with short adjectives

Sometimes *more/most* are used with adjectives that normally have *-er/-est*. This can happen, for example, when a comparative is not followed immediately by *than*; forms with *-er* are also possible.

*The road's getting **more and more steep**. (*OR *. . . **steeper and steeper**.)

When we compare two descriptions (saying that one is more suitable or accurate than another), we use *more*; comparatives with *-er* are not possible.

*He's **more lazy** than stupid. (*NOT *He's lazier than stupid.*)

In a rather formal style, *most* can be used with adjectives expressing approval and disapproval (including one-syllable adjectives) to mean 'very'.

*Thank you very much indeed. That is **most kind** of you.* (NOT ... ~~That is kindest of you.~~)

*Real, right, wrong* and *like* always have *more* and *most*.

*She's **more like** her mother than her father.* (NOT ... ~~liker her mother~~...)

For information about how to use comparatives and superlatives, see 139, 141.
For modification of comparatives and superlatives (e.g. *much older, far the best*), see 140.

# 138 comparison (4):
## comparative and superlative adverbs

Most comparative and superlative adverbs are made with *more* and *most*.

*Could you talk **more quietly**?* (NOT ... ~~quietlier~~)

Adverbs that have the same form as adjectives (see 27), and a few others, have comparatives and superlatives with *-er* and *-est*. The most common are: *fast, early, late, hard, long, near, high, low, soon, well* (*better, best*), *badly* (*worse, worst*), and in informal English *easy, slow, loud* and *quick*.

*Can't you drive any **faster**?*      *Can you come **earlier**?*

*Talk **louder**.* (informal)

*We've all got terrible voices, but I sing **worst** of all.*

Note also the irregular comparatives and superlatives of *far* (*farther/further, farthest/furthest,* see 201), *much* (*more, most,* see 355 and 356), *little* (*less, least,* see 320 and 318).

For the use of comparatives and superlatives, see the following sections.

# 139 comparison (5):
## using comparatives and superlatives

### 1 than

After comparatives we use *than*, not *that* or *as*.

*Today's hotter **than** yesterday.* (NOT ... ~~hotter that~~... OR ... ~~hotter as~~...)

### 2 the difference between comparatives and superlatives

We use a comparative to compare one person, thing, action, event or group with another person, thing etc. We use a superlative to compare somebody/something with the whole group that he/she/it belongs to.
Compare:

– *Mary's **taller** than her three sisters.*
  *Mary's **the tallest** of the four girls.* (NOT ... ~~the taller~~...)
– *Your accent is **worse** than mine.*
  *Your accent is **the worst** in the class.* (NOT ... ~~the worse~~...)
– *He plays **better** than everybody else in the team.*
  *He's **the best** in the team.*

▶

## 3   groups with two members

When a group only has two members, we sometimes use a comparative instead of a superlative.

*I like Betty and Maud, but I think Maud's **the nicer/nicest** of the two.*
*I'll give you **the bigger/biggest** steak: I'm not very hungry.*

Some people feel that a superlative is incorrect in this case.

## 4   double comparatives: *fatter and fatter; more and more slowly*

We can use double comparatives to say that something is changing.

*I'm getting **fatter and fatter**.*
*We're going **more and more slowly**. (NOT . . . ~~more slowly and more slowly.~~)*

## 5   *the . . . the . . .*

We can use comparatives with *the . . . the . . .* to say that things change or vary together.

Word order (in both clauses):

> *the* + comparative expression + subject + verb

*The older I get, the happier I am. (NOT ~~Older I get, more I am happy.~~)*
*The more dangerous it is, the more I like it.*
     *(NOT ~~The more it is dangerous,~~ . . .)*
*The more I study, the less I learn.*

*More* can be used with a noun in this structure.

*The more money he makes, the more useless things he buys.*

In longer structures, *that* is sometimes used before the first verb.

*The more information **that** comes in, the more confused the picture is.*

A short form of this structure is used in the expression *The more the merrier*, and in sentences ending *the better*.

*How do you like your coffee? ~ **The stronger the better**.*

Note that in this structure, the word *the* is not really the definite article – it was originally a form of the demonstrative pronoun, meaning 'by that much'.

## 6   *than me; than I (am)*

In an informal style, object pronouns (*me* etc) are used after *than*. In a more formal style, subject pronouns (*I* etc) are used (usually with verbs).

*She's older than **me**. (informal)*          *She is older than **I** (am). (formal)*

## 7   *the happiest man in the world*

After superlatives, we do not usually use *of* with a singular word referring to a place or group.

*I'm the **happiest** man **in** the world. (NOT . . . ~~of the world.~~)*
*She's the **fastest** player **in** the team. (NOT . . . ~~of the team.~~)*

But *of* can be used before plurals, and before *lot*.

*She's the fastest player **of them all**.*          *He's the best **of the lot**.*

Note also the structure with possessive *'s*.

*He thinks he's **the world's strongest** man.*

## 8  *than anybody; the best ... ever*

'Non-affirmative' words like *ever, yet* and *any* (see 381) often follow comparatives and superlatives.

> *You're **more stubborn** than **anybody** I know.*
> *It's the **best** book I've **ever** read.*   *This is my **hardest** job **yet**.*

For the formation of comparatives and superlatives, see 137.
For tenses after *than*, see 580.
For the *first/second/best* etc + present/past perfect, see 591.

# 140  comparison (6): much, far etc with comparatives and superlatives

## 1  *much, far* etc with comparatives

We cannot use *very* with comparatives. Instead, we use, for example, *much, far, very much, a lot* (informal), *lots* (informal), *any* and *no* (see 57), *rather, a little, a bit* (informal), and *even*.

> *My boyfriend is **much/far older** than me.* (NOT ... *very older than me.*)
> *Russian is **much/far more difficult** than Spanish.*
> ***very much** nicer*         ***rather** more quickly*
> ***a bit** more sensible* (informal)   *She looks **no older** than her daughter.*
> ***a lot** happier* (informal)     ***a little** less expensive*
> *Is your mother **any better**?*    *Your cooking is **even worse** than Harry's.*

*Quite* cannot be used with comparatives except in the expression *quite better*, meaning 'recovered from an illness' (see 104.1). *Any, no, a bit* and *a lot* are not normally used to modify comparatives before nouns.

> *There are **much/far nicer shops** in the town centre.* (BUT NOT ... *a bit nicer shops* ...)

## 2  *many more/less/fewer*

When *more* (see 355) modifies a plural noun, it is modified by *many* instead of *much*. Compare:

> *much / far / a lot* etc *more money*
> *many / far / a lot* etc ***more opportunities***

*Many* is sometimes used to modify *less* (before a plural noun) and *fewer*, but this is unusual; *far, a lot* etc are more common.

> ***far less** words* (more common than *many less words*)
> ***a lot fewer** accidents* (more common than *many fewer accidents*)

## 3  *much, by far, quite* etc with superlatives

Superlatives can be modified by *much* and *by far*, and by other adverbs of degree such as *quite* (meaning 'absolutely'), *almost, practically, nearly* and *easily*.

> *He's **much the most imaginative** of them all.*
> *She's **by far the oldest**.*
> *We're walking **by far the slowest**.*
> *He's **quite the most stupid** man I've ever met.*
> *I'm **nearly the oldest** in the firm.*
> *This is **easily the worst** party I've been to this year.*

▶

## 4 *very* with superlatives

Note the special use of *very* to emphasise superlatives and *first*, *next* and *last*.
> *Bring out your **very best** wine – Michael's coming to dinner.*
> *You're the **very first** person I've spoken to today.*
> *This is your **very last** chance.*

For modification of *too*, see 595.3.

# 141 comparison (7): advanced points

## 1 comparative meaning 'relatively', 'more than average'

Comparatives can suggest ideas like 'relatively', 'more than average'. Used like
this, comparatives make a less clear and narrow selection than superlatives.
Compare:
> *There are two classes – one for the **cleverer** students and one for the **slower**
> learners.*
> *The **cleverest** students were two girls from York.*

Comparatives are often used in advertising to make things sound less definite.
> ***less expensive** clothes for the **fuller** figure*
> (Compare *cheap clothes for fat people*)

## 2 *all/any/none the* + comparative

*All the* + comparative suggests the idea of 'even more ...'.
> *I feel **all the better** for that swim.*
> *Her accident made it **all the more important** to get home fast.*

*Any* and *none* can be used in similar structures.
> *He didn't seem to be **any the worse** for his experience.*
> *He explained it all carefully, but I was still **none the wiser**.*

Note that this structure is used mainly to express abstract ideas. We would not
say, for example, *Those pills have made him all the slimmer.*
In this structure, *the* was originally a demonstrative, meaning 'by that'.

## 3 *three times ...er* etc

Instead of *three/four* etc *times as much* (see 136.7), we can use ***three/four*** etc
***times*** + comparative.
> *She can walk **three times faster** than you.*
> *It was **ten times more difficult** than I expected.*

Note that *twice* and *half* are not possible in this structure.
> *She's **twice as lively** as her sister.* (NOT ... ~~twice livelier~~ ...)

## 4 words left out after *than*

*Than* often replaces a subject or object pronoun or an adverbial expression,
rather like a relative pronoun or adverb (see 581).
> *She spent more money **than was sensible**.* (NOT ... ~~than it was sensible.~~)
> *There were more people **than we had expected**.* (NOT ... ~~than we had
> expected them.~~)
> *I love you more **than she does**.* (NOT ... ~~than how much she does.~~)
(In some English dialects, the above sentences would be constructed with
*than what*.)

## 5   *the youngest person to ...*

After a superlative, an infinitive can mean the same as a relative clause.
> *She's the **youngest** person ever **to swim** the Channel.* (= . . . the youngest
> person who has ever swum . . .)

This structure is also common after *first, last* and *next.*
> *Who was the **first** woman **to climb** Everest?*
> *The **next to speak** was Mrs Fenshaw.*

Note that this structure is only possible in cases where the noun with the
superlative (or *first* etc) has a subject relationship with the following verb. In
other cases, infinitives cannot be used.
> *Is this the first time that you have stayed here?* (NOT . . . ~~the first time for you~~
> ~~to stay here~~: *time* is not the subject of *stay.*)

## 6   *the* with superlatives

Nouns with superlative adjectives normally have the article *the.*
> *It's **the best book** I've ever read.*

After link verbs, superlative adjectives also usually have *the,* though it is
sometimes dropped in an informal style.
> *I'm **the greatest**.*          *Which of the boys is **(the) strongest?***
> *This dictionary is **(the) best**.*

*The* cannot be dropped when a superlative is used with a defining expression.
> *This dictionary is **the best I could find**.* (NOT ~~This dictionary is best I could~~
> ~~find.~~)

However, we do not use *the* with superlatives when we compare the same
person or thing in different situations. Compare:
– *Of all my friends, he's **(the) nicest**.* (comparing different people)
  *He's **nicest** when he's with children.* (NOT ~~He's the nicest when~~ . . .: we're
  comparing the same person in different situations.)
– *She works **(the) hardest** in the family; her husband doesn't know what work
  is.* (A woman is being compared with a man – *the* is possible.)
  *She works hardest when she's doing something for her family.*
  (NOT ~~She works the hardest when~~ . . .: – a woman's work is being
  compared in different situations.)

*The* is sometimes dropped before superlative adverbs in an informal style.
> *Who can run **(the) fastest?***

For tenses after *than,* see 580.

# 142   continual(ly) and continuous(ly)

*Continual(ly)* is generally used for things that happen repeatedly, often
annoyingly.
> *I can't work with these **continual** interruptions.*
> *She's **continually** taking days off.*

*Continuous(ly)* is used for things that continue without stopping.
> *There has been **continuous** fighting on the border for the last 48 hours.*
> *I've been working almost **continuously** since yesterday evening.*

# 143 contractions

## 1 general rules

Forms like *I've*, *don't* are called 'contractions'. There are two kinds.

> noun/pronoun etc + (auxiliary) verb

| | |
|---|---|
| *I'm* tired. | My *father's* not very well. |
| Do you know when *you'll* arrive? | *Where's* the station? |
| *I've* no idea. | *There's* a problem. |
| *She'd* like to talk to you. | *Somebody's* coming. |
| *Here's* our bus. | |

> (auxiliary) verb + *not*

| | |
|---|---|
| They **aren't** ready. | I **haven't** seen him for ages. |
| You **won't** be late, will you? | **Can't** you swim? |

Contractions are formed with auxiliary verbs, and also with *be* and sometimes *have* when these are not auxiliary verbs.

The short form *'s* (= *is*/*has*) can be written after nouns (including proper names), question words, *here* and *now* as well as pronouns and unstressed *there*. The short forms *'ll*, *'d* and *'re* are commonly written after pronouns and unstressed *there*, but in other cases we more often write the full forms (especially in British English), even if the words would be contracted in pronunciation.

*'Your **mother will** (/'mʌðərl/) be surprised', she said.*

*I wondered **what had** (/'wɒtəd/) happened.*

Contractions are not usually written with double subjects.

**John and I have** *decided to split up.* (NOT ~~John and I've decided~~ ...)

The apostrophe (') goes in the same place as the letters that we leave out: *has not* = **hasn't** (NOT ~~ha'snt~~). But note that *shan't* (BrE = *shall not*) and *won't* (= *will not*) only have one apostrophe each.

Contractions are common and correct in informal writing: they represent the pronunciation of informal speech. They are not generally used in a formal style.

## 2 alternative contractions

Some negative expressions can have two possible contractions. For *she had not* we can say *she'd not* or *she hadn't*; for *he will not* we can say *he'll not* or *he won't*. The two negative forms of *be* (e.g. *she isn't* and *she's not*) are both common in British English; American English prefers the forms with *not* (e.g. *she's not*). With other verbs, forms with *n't* (e.g. *she hadn't*) are more common in most cases in standard southern British English; they are the only forms normally used in AmE. (Forms with *not* – e.g. *she'd not* – tend to be more common in northern and Scottish English.)

Double contractions are not normally written: ~~she'sn't~~ is impossible.

## 3 position

Contractions in the first group (**noun / pronoun / question word + auxiliary verb**) do not normally come at the ends of clauses.

– *I'm late.*
Yes, *you are*. (NOT ~~Yes, you're.~~)

– *I've forgotten.*
Yes, *you have*. (NOT ~~Yes, you've.~~)

Negative contractions can come at the ends of clauses.
*They really **aren't**.*     *No, I **haven't**.*

## 4  list of contractions

| Contraction | Pronunciation | Meaning |
|---|---|---|
| *I'm* | /aɪm/ | I am |
| *I've* | /aɪv/ | I have |
| *I'll* | /aɪl/ | I will |
| *I'd* | /aɪd/ | I had/would |
| *you're* | /jɔː(r)/ | you are |
| *you've* | /juːv/ | you have |
| *you'll* | /juːl/ | you will |
| *you'd* | /juːd/ | you had/would |
| *he's* | /hiːz/ | he is/has |
| *he'll* | /hiːl, hɪl/ | he will |
| *he'd* | /hiːd/ | he had/would |
| *she's* | /ʃiːz/ | she is/has |
| *she'll* | /ʃiːl, ʃɪl/ | she will |
| *she'd* | /ʃiːd/ | she had/would |
| *it's* | /ɪts/ | it is/has |
| *it'd* (uncommon) | /ˈɪtəd/ | it had/would |
| *we're* | /wɪə(r)/ | we are |
| *we've* | /wiːv/ | we have |
| *we'll* | /wiːl, wɪl/ | we will |
| *we'd* | /wiːd/ | we had/would |
| *they're* | /ðeə(r)/ | they are |
| *they've* | /ðeɪv/ | they have |
| *they'll* | /ðeɪl, ðel/ | they will |
| *they'd* | /ðeɪd/ | they had/would |
| *there's* | /ðəz/ | there is/has |
| *there'll* | /ðəl/ | there will |
| *there'd* | /ðəd/ | there had/would |
| *aren't* | /ɑːnt/ | are not |
| *can't* | /kɑːnt/ | cannot |
| *couldn't* | /ˈkʊdnt/ | could not |
| *daren't* | /deənt/ | dare not |
| *didn't* | /ˈdɪdnt/ | did not |
| *doesn't* | /ˈdʌznt/ | does not |
| *don't* | /dəʊnt/ | do not |
| *hadn't* | /ˈhædnt/ | had not |
| *hasn't* | /ˈhæznt/ | has not |
| *haven't* | /ˈhævnt/ | have not |
| *isn't* | /ˈɪznt/ | is not |
| *mightn't* | /ˈmaɪtnt/ | might not |
| *mustn't* | /ˈmʌsnt/ | must not |
| *needn't* | /ˈniːdnt/ | need not |
| *oughtn't* | /ˈɔːtnt/ | ought not |

▶

| Contraction | Pronunciation | Meaning |
|---|---|---|
| *shan't* | /ʃɑːnt/ | shall not |
| *shouldn't* | /ˈʃʊdnt/ | should not |
| *usedn't* | /ˈjuːsnt/ | used not |
| *wasn't* | /ˈwɒznt/ | was not |
| *weren't* | /wɜːnt/ | were not |
| *won't* | /wəʊnt/ | will not |
| *wouldn't* | /ˈwʊdnt/ | would not |

Notes
1. Do not confuse *it's* (= *it is/has*) and *its* (possessive).
2. *Am not* is only normally contracted in questions to *aren't* (BrE) (/ɑːnt/).
      *I'm late, aren't I?*
3. Note the difference in pronunciation of *can't* in British English (/kɑːnt/) and American English (/kænt/).
4. *Daren't, shan't* and *usedn't* are not often used in American English.
5. In non-standard English, *ain't* (pronounced /eɪnt/ or /ent/) is used as a contraction of *am not, are not, is not, have not* and *has not*.
      *I ain't going to tell him.*
      *Don't talk to me like that – you ain't my boss.*
      *It's raining. ~ No it ain't.*
      *I ain't got no more cigarettes.*
      *Bill ain't been here for days.*
6. For the contraction *let's*, see 323.
7. *May not* is not normally contracted: *mayn't* is very rare.

# 144 contrary

## 1 *on the contrary* and *on the other hand*

*On the contrary* is used to contradict – to say that what has been said or suggested is not true. If we want to give the other side of a question, we use *on the other hand*, not *on the contrary*. Compare:
– *I suppose the job was boring? ~ **On the contrary**, it was really exciting.*
   *The job was boring, but **on the other hand** it was well paid.* (NOT . . . ~~on the contrary, it was well paid.~~)
– *He did not make things easy for his parents. **On the contrary**, he did everything he could to annoy and worry them.*
   *He did not make things easy for his parents. **On the other hand**, he could often be wonderfully sweet and loving.*

## 2 *contrary* and *opposite*

We use *opposite* (see 401), not *contrary*, to talk about contrasting words.
   *'Short' is the **opposite** of 'tall', and also of 'long'.*
      (NOT . . . ~~the contrary of 'tall'~~ . . .)

# 145 control

*Control* is a 'false friend' for people who speak some languages. It generally means *manage, direct,* not *check* or *inspect.* Compare:
- *The crowd was too big for the police to* **control**. (= ... to keep in order.)
  *The police were* **checking** *everybody's papers.* (NOT ...~~controlling everybody's papers.~~)
- *I found the car difficult to* **control** *at high speeds.*
  *I took the car to the garage and asked them to* **have a look** *at the steering.*
  (NOT ...~~to control the steering.~~)

However, the noun *control* is used with the meaning of 'inspection point' in expressions like *passport/customs control.*

# 146 correspondence (1): letters

Each culture has its own way of organising a letter and arranging it on a page. English-speaking people generally observe the following rules.

1   Put your own address at the top on the right. Addresses generally follow the rule of 'smallest first': house number, then street, then town. Postcode and telephone number / fax number / email address come last. Don't put your name with the address.

2   Put the date directly under the address. A common way to write the date is to put the number of the day, followed by the month and year (e.g. *17 May 2005*). For other ways (and differences between British and American customs) see 152.

3   In formal letters and business letters, put the name and address of the person you are writing to on the left side of the page, starting on the same level as the date or slightly below.

4   Different styles are common in formal letters on paper which has the address ready-printed at the top of the page. For example, the date may be put on the left, and the address of the person written to may come at the end of the letter or of the first page.

5   Begin the letter (*Dear X*) on the left. Common ways of addressing people are:
    - by first name (informal): *Dear Penny*
    - by title and surname (more formal): *Dear Ms Hopkins*
    - *Dear Sir(s), Dear Sir or Madam, Dear Madam* (especially to somebody whose name is not known)
    Some people like to use the first name and surname (*Dear Penny Hopkins*) when writing to strangers or people that they do not know well.
    Do not use a title like *Mr* together with a first name (NOT ~~Dear Mr James Carter~~).

▶

6 After 'Dear X', put a comma or nothing at all, not an exclamation mark (!). **Either** leave an empty line after 'Dear X' and start again on the left, **or** start again on the next line, a few spaces from the left. Do the same for each new paragraph. (The first method is now the most common in Britain.)

7 Letters which begin *Dear Sir(s)* or *Dear Madam* usually finish *Yours faithfully* in British English. Formal letters which begin with the person's name (e.g. *Dear Miss Hawkins, Dear Peter Lewis*) usually finish *Yours sincerely*. Common American endings are *Sincerely yours* or *Sincerely*. Informal letters may finish, for example, *Yours, See you* or *Love*. (*Love* is not usually used by one man to another.) In formal letters, many people put a closing formula before *Yours* . . ., especially when writing to people they know: common expressions are *With best wishes* and *With kind regards*.

8 Sign with your first name (informal) or your full name (formal), but without writing any title (*Mr/Ms/Dr* etc). Ways of writing one's full name: *Alan Forbes, A Forbes, A J Forbes*.
In a formal typewritten letter, add your full typewritten name after your handwritten signature. Friendly business letters are often signed with the first name only above the full typewritten name:

> *Yours sincerely*
> Alan
>
> *Alan Forbes*

9 In informal letters, afterthoughts that are added after the signature are usually introduced by *P S* (Latin *post scriptum* = written afterwards).

10 On the envelope, put the first name before the surname. People usually write a title (*Mr, Mrs* etc) before the name. You can write the first name in full (*Mrs Angela Brookes*), or you can write one or more initials (*Mrs A E Brookes*). It was once common to put the abbreviated title *Esq* (= *Esquire*) after a man's name; this is now very unusual.

11 British people now usually write abbreviated titles, initials, addresses, dates, and opening and closing formulae without commas or full stops.

12 American usage is different from British in some ways:
- Commas are sometimes used at the ends of lines in addresses; full stops may be used at the ends of addresses; full stops are used after abbreviated titles. After the opening salutation, Americans may put a colon, especially in business letters (*Dear Mr. Hawkes:*), or a comma.
- *Gentlemen* is used instead of *Dear Sirs.*
- Dates are written differently (month before day) – see 152.
- *Yours faithfully* is not used; common endings are *Sincerely, Sincerely yours* or *Yours truly*, followed by a comma.
- Americans are often addressed (and sign their names) with the first name in full, followed by the initial of a middle name (*Alan J. Parker*). This is less usual in Britain.

13   Letters to strangers often begin with an explanation of the reason for writing.
*Dear X*
*I am writing to ask ...*
One does not normally begin a letter to a stranger with an enquiry about
health. (NOT ~~*Dear X, How are you getting on?*~~)

For more information about names and titles, see 363.
For more information about the use of commas and full stops, see 476, 473.
For more information about paragraphing, see 406.

### Examples of letters and envelopes
### Formal

14 Plowden Road
Torquay
Devon
TQ6 1RS
Tel 0742 06538

The Secretary                         16 June 2005
Hall School of Design
39 Beaumont Street
London
W4 4LJ

Dear Sir or Madam

I should be grateful if you would send me information
about the regulations for admission to the Hall School
of Design. Could you also tell me whether the School
arranges accommodation for students?

Yours faithfully

*Keith Parker*

Keith Parker

---

The Secretary
Hall School of Design
39 Beaumont Street
London
W4 4LJ

▶

Informal

22 Green Street
London
W1B 6DH
Phone 071 066 429

19 March

Dear Keith and Ann

Thanks a lot for a great weekend. We really enjoyed ourselves.

Bill and I were talking about the holidays. We thought it might be nice to go camping in Scotland for a couple of weeks. Are you interested? Let me know if you are, and we can talk about dates etc.

See you soon, I hope. Thanks again.

Love
Cathy

P S Did I leave a pair of jeans behind in the bedroom? If so, do you think you could send them on?

Keith and Ann Sharp
14 West Way House
Bothey Road
Oxford
OX3 5JP

# 147 correspondence (2): emails and text messages

## 1 formal emails: style and layout

Formal emails are similar in style to letters on paper. The writer's postal address and phone/fax number, if they are included, follow the signature.

## 2   informal emails

Personal emails are usually much more informal in style than letters on paper. Instead of 'Dear X', they often begin for example 'X', 'Hi, X', 'Hello, X'; or with no salutation at all.

## 3   addresses

email addresses are read as follows:

| | |
|---|---|
| j.harris@funbiz.co.uk | 'j dot harris at funbiz dot co dot u k' |
| mary@log-farm.com | 'mary at log dash farm dot com' |
| the_rabbit@coolmail.gr | 'the underline rabbit at coolmail dot g r' |

Note also the names of symbols in 'urls' (internet addresses):
/ 'forward slash'          \ 'backslash'          : 'colon'

*Example of an informal email*

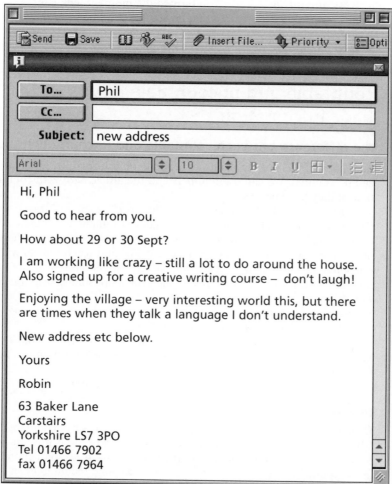

## 4 txt msgs (text messages)

Text messages (sent for example by mobile phone) use a large number of abbreviations to save time and space. Words are shortened, often by leaving out vowels. Letters and numbers are used instead of words (or parts of words) that sound the same. Initial letters only are used for some common expressions. Some typical examples:

| | |
|---|---|
| *c u l8r* | See you later. |
| *r u cumin 2day?* | Are you coming today? |
| *tx 4 a gr8 party* | Thanks for a great party. |
| *just 2 let u no* | Just to let you know. |
| *wil u b hr Thu eve?* | Will you be here Thursday evening? |
| *RUOK?* | Are you OK? |
| *got ur msg* | Got your message. |
| *wil b @ bbq @ 9* | Will be at barbecue at 9. |
| *2 bsy atm, tlk l8r* | Too busy at the moment, talk later. |
| *if Uv tym, send pix o kids* | If you have time, send pictures of kids. |
| *need mo infmtn* | Need more information. |

# 148 countable and uncountable nouns (1): basic information

## 1 the difference between countable and uncountable nouns

Countable nouns are the names of separate objects, people, ideas etc which can be counted. We can use numbers and the article *a/an* with countable nouns; they have plurals.

> *a cat*      *a newspaper*      *three cats*      *two newspapers*

Uncountable (or 'mass') nouns are the names of materials, liquids, abstract qualities, collections and other things which we see as masses without clear boundaries, and not as separate objects. We cannot use numbers with uncountable nouns, and most are singular with no plurals. We do not normally use *a/an* with uncountable nouns, though there are some exceptions (see 149.4).

> *water* (NOT ~~a water, two waters~~)      *wool* (NOT ~~a wool, two wools~~)
> *weather* (NOT ~~a weather, two weathers~~)

Some determiners (see 154) can only be used with countable nouns (e.g. *many, few*); others can only be used with uncountables (e.g. *much, little*). Compare:

> *How **many hours** do you work?*      *How **much money** do you earn?*

## 2 problems

Usually it is easy to see whether a noun is countable or uncountable. Obviously *house* is normally a countable noun, and *sand* is not. But it is not always so clear: compare *a journey* (countable) and *travel* (uncountable); *a glass* (countable) and *glass* (uncountable); *vegetables* (countable) and *fruit* (uncountable). The following rules will help, but to know exactly how a particular noun can be used, it is necessary to check in a good dictionary.

## 3  *travel* and *a journey; a piece of advice*

*Travel* and *journey* have very similar meanings, but *travel* is normally uncountable (it means 'travelling in general', and we do not talk about 'a travel'), while *journey* is countable (*a journey* is one particular movement from one place to another) and can have a plural: *journeys.*

I like **travel**, but it's often tiring.          Did you have **a** good **journey?**

Often we can make an uncountable word countable by putting 'a piece of' or a similar expression in front of it.

He never listens to **advice**.          Can I give you **a piece of advice?**

Here are some other examples of general/particular pairs. (Note that some words that are uncountable in English have countable equivalents in other languages.)

| Uncountable | Countable |
|---|---|
| *accommodation* | *a place to live* (NOT ~~an accommodation~~) |
| *baggage* | *a piece/item of baggage; a case/trunk/bag* |
| *bread* | *a piece/loaf of bread; a loaf; a roll* |
| *chess* | *a game of chess* |
| *chewing gum* | *a piece of chewing gum* (NOT ~~a chewing gum~~) |
| *equipment* | *a piece of equipment; a tool etc* |
| *furniture* | *a piece/article of furniture; a table, chair etc* |
| *information* | *a piece of information* |
| *knowledge* | *a fact* |
| *lightning* | *a flash of lightning* |
| *luck* | *a piece/bit/stroke of luck* |
| *luggage* | *a piece/item of luggage; a case/trunk/bag* |
| *money* | *a note; a coin; a sum* |
| *news* | *a piece of news* |
| *permission* | – |
| *poetry* | *a poem* |
| *progress* | *a step forward; an advance* |
| *publicity* | *an advertisement* |
| *research* | *a piece of research; an experiment* |
| *rubbish* | *a piece of rubbish* |
| *slang* | *a slang word/expression* |
| *thunder* | *a clap of thunder* |
| *traffic* | *cars etc* |
| *vocabulary* | *a word/expression* |
| *work* | *a job; a piece of work* |

Note that when uncountable English words are borrowed by other languages, they may change into countable words with different meanings (for example *parking* means the activity of parking in general, but French *un parking* means 'a car park').

## 4  materials: *glass, paper* etc

Words for materials are uncountable, but we can often use the same word as a countable noun to refer to something made of the material. Compare:

▶

– *I'd like some typing **paper**.*
*I'm going out to buy **a paper*** (= a newspaper)
– *The window's made of unbreakable **glass**.*
*Would you like **a glass** of water?*
Nouns for materials, liquids etc can be countable when they are used to talk about different types.
*Not all washing **powders** are kind to your hands.*
*We have a selection of fine **wines** at very good prices.*
The same thing happens when we talk about ordering drinks. Compare:
*Have you got **any coffee**?*
*Could I have **two coffees**?* (= cups of coffee)

## 5  fruit, rice, wheat, spaghetti, hair; vegetables, peas, grapes, oats

Many things (e.g. *rice, grapes*) can be seen either as a collection of separate elements or as a mass. Some names for things of this kind are uncountable, while others are countable (usually plural).
Uncountable: *fruit, rice, spaghetti, macaroni* (and other pasta foods), *sugar, salt, corn, wheat, barley, rye, maize.*
Countable: *vegetable(s), bean(s), pea(s), grape(s), oats, lentil(s).*
**Fruit is** *very expensive, but **vegetables are** cheap.*
**Wheat is** *used to make bread; **oats are** used to make porridge.*
**Is the spaghetti** *ready?*        *These **grapes are** sour.*
*Hair* is normally uncountable in English.
*His **hair is** black.*
But one strand of hair is *a hair* (countable).
*So why has he got **two** blonde **hairs** on his jacket?*
For words that are used to talk about one 'piece' of uncountable collections (e.g. *a grain of corn, a blade of grass*), see 430.

## 6  abstract nouns: time, life, experience etc

Many abstract nouns can have both uncountable and countable uses, often corresponding to more 'general' and more 'particular' meanings. Compare:
– *Don't hurry – there's plenty of **time**.*
*Have **a** good **time**.*
*There are **times** when I just want to stop work.*
– **Life** *is complicated.*
*He's had **a** really difficult **life**.*
– *She hasn't got enough **experience** for the job.*
*I had some strange **experiences** last week.*
– *It's hard to feel **pity** for people like that.*
*It's **a pity** it's raining.*
– *Your plan needs more **thought**.*
*I had some frightening **thoughts** in the night.*
– *I need to practise **conversation**.*
*Jane and I had **a** very interesting **conversation**.*

See 149.2 for more details.
For more about *time*, see 593; for *life*, see 324.

## 7   illnesses

The names of illnesses are usually singular uncountable in English, including those ending in *-s*.
> *If you've already had **measles**, you can't get **it** again.*
> *There's a lot of **flu** around at the moment.*

The words for some minor ailments are countable: e.g. *a cold, a sore throat, a headache*. However, *toothache, earache, stomach-ache* and *backache* are usually uncountable in British English. In American English, these words are generally countable if they refer to particular attacks of pain. Compare:
> *I've got **toothache**.* (BrE)          *I have **a toothache**.* (AmE)

For *the* with *measles, flu* etc, see 70.14.
For more information on the use of articles with countable and uncountable nouns, see 65.

# 149   countable and uncountable nouns (2): advanced points

## 1   *20 square metres of wall*

Singular countable nouns are sometimes used as uncountables (e.g. with *much, enough, plenty of* or *a lot of*) in order to express the idea of amount.
> *There's enough paint for 20 square metres of **wall**.*
> *I've got **too much nose** and **not enough chin**.*
> *If you buy one of these you get **plenty of car** for your money.*

## 2   *not much difference*

Some countable abstract nouns can be used uncountably after *little, much* and other determiners. Common examples are *difference, point, reason, idea, change, difficulty, chance* and *question*.
> *There's **not much difference** between 'begin' and 'start'.*
> *I don't see **much point** in arguing about it.*
> *We have **little reason** to expect prices to fall.*
> *I haven't got **much idea** of her plans.*
> *There isn't **any change** in his condition.*
> *They experienced **little difficulty** in stealing the painting.*
> *Do you think we have **much chance** of catching the train?*
> *There's **some question** of our getting a new Managing Director.*

Note the expression *have difficulty (in) ...ing*.
> *I have difficulty (in) remembering faces.* (NOT ~~I have difficulties~~...)

## 3   *in all weathers; on your travels*

A few uncountable nouns have plural uses in fixed expressions.
> *He goes running **in all weathers**.*
> *Did you meet anybody exciting **on your travels**?*
> ***Gulliver's Travels** (novel by Jonathan Swift)*                                         ▶

## 4 *a/an* with uncountable nouns

With certain uncountable nouns – especially nouns referring to human emotions and mental activity – we often use *a/an* when we are limiting their meaning in some way.

> *We need a secretary with **a first-class knowledge** of German.* (NOT ...~~with first-class knowledge of German.~~)
> *She has always had **a deep distrust** of strangers.*
> *That child shows **a surprising understanding** of adult behaviour.*
> *My parents wanted me to have **a good education**.* (NOT ...~~to have good education.~~)
> *You've been **a great help**.*
> *I need **a good sleep**.*

Note that these nouns cannot normally be used in the plural, and that most uncountable nouns cannot be used with *a/an* at all, even when they have an adjective.

> *My father enjoys **very good health**.* (NOT ...~~a very good health.~~)
> *We're having **terrible weather**.* (NOT ...~~a terrible weather.~~)
> *He speaks **excellent English**.* (NOT ...~~an excellent English.~~)
> *It's **interesting work**.* (NOT ...~~an interesting work.~~)

## 5 plural uncountables

Some uncountable nouns are plural. They have no singular forms with the same meaning, and cannot normally be used with numbers.

> *I've bought the **groceries**.* (BUT NOT ...~~a grocery.~~ OR ...~~three groceries.~~)
> *The Dover **customs** have found a large shipment of cocaine.* (BUT NOT ~~The Dover custom has~~...)
> *Many **thanks** for your help.* (BUT NOT ~~Much thank~~...)

For details, see 524.7.

# 150 country

## 1 countable use

*Country* (countable) = 'nation', 'land'.

> *Scotland is a cold **country**.*
> *France is the **country** I know best.*
> *How many **countries** are there in Europe?*

## 2 uncountable use

*Country* (uncountable) = 'open land without many buildings'.

> *I like wild **country** best.*

With this meaning, we cannot say *a country* or *countries*.

> *My parents live in nice **country** near Belfast.* (NOT ...~~in a nice country~~...)

The expression *the country* (the opposite of *the town*) is very common.

> *We live in **the country** just outside Manchester.*
> *Would you rather live in the town or **the country**?*

For information about countable and uncountable nouns, see 148–149.

# 151 dare

## 1 uncommon

In modern English, *dare* is not a very common verb. In an informal style, people generally use other expressions.

*He's not afraid to say what he thinks.*

## 2 negative use; *daren't*

*Dare* is, however, quite often used in negative sentences. It can be followed by an infinitive with or without *to*.

*She **doesn't dare (to) go** out at night.*
*The old lady **didn't dare (to) open** the door.*

A special negative form *daren't* (+ infinitive without *to*) is common in British English.

*I **daren't look**.*

The third person singular is also *daren't*, without *-s*.

*She **daren't** tell him what she thinks.*

## 3 special expressions

*Don't you dare!* is sometimes used to discourage people from doing unwanted things.

*Mummy, can I draw a picture on the wall? ~ **Don't you dare**!*

*How dare you?* is sometimes used as an indignant exclamation.

***How dare you?** Take your hands off me at once!*

And *I dare say* (sometimes written *I daresay*) is used to mean 'I think probably', 'I suppose'.

*I **dare say** it'll rain soon.*          *I **daresay** you're ready for a drink.*

Children use the expression *I **dare you** + **infinitive** to challenge each other to do frightening things.

*I **dare you to run** across the road with your eyes shut.*

# 152 dates

## 1 writing

In Britain, the commonest way to write the day's date is as follows. Note that the names of months always begin with capital letters (see 556).

*30 March 2004      27 July 2003*

The last two letters of the number word are sometimes added (e.g. *1st, 2nd, 3rd, 6th*). Some people write a comma before the year, but this is no longer very common in Britain except when the date comes inside a sentence.

*30th March(,) 2004*

*He was born in Hawick on 14 December, 1942.*

The date may be written entirely in figures.

*30/3/04      30-3-04      30.3.04*

In the USA it is common to write the month first and to put a comma before the year.

*March 30, 2004*

▶

All-figure dates are written differently in Britain and America, since British people put the day first while Americans generally start with the month. So for example, *6.4.02* means '6 April 2002' in Britain, but 'June 4, 2002' in the USA. The longer names of the months are often abbreviated as follows:

*Jan     Feb     Mar     Apr     Aug     Sept     Oct     Nov     Dec*

The names of decades (e.g. *the nineteen sixties*) can be written like this: *the 1960s.*

For the position of dates in letters, see 146.
For full stops in abbreviations, see 2.

## 2  speaking

30 March 1993 = 'March the thirtieth, nineteen ninety-three' (AmE also 'March thirtieth . . .') or 'the thirtieth of March, nineteen ninety-three'

1200 = 'twelve hundred'
1305 = 'thirteen hundred and five' or 'thirteen O (/əʊ/) five'
1498 = 'fourteen (hundred and) ninety-eight'
1910 = 'nineteen (hundred and) ten'
1946 = 'nineteen (hundred and) forty-six'
2000 = 'two thousand'
2005 = 'two thousand and five'

To announce the date, *It's* is used.
  *It's April the first.*
To ask about dates, we can say for instance:
  *What's the date (today)?        What date is it?*
  *What date is your birthday?*

## 3  BC and AD

To distinguish between dates before and after the birth of Christ, we use the abbreviations *BC* (= Before Christ) and *AD* (= Anno Domini – Latin for 'in the year of the Lord'). *BC* follows the date; *AD* can come before or after it.
  *Julius Caesar first came to Britain in **55 BC**.*
  *The emperor Trajan was born in **AD 53** / **53 AD**.*

# 153  dead, died and death

*Dead* is an adjective.
  *a **dead** man        Mrs McGinty is **dead**.*
  *That idea has been **dead** for years.*
*Died* is the past tense and past participle of the verb *die*.
  *Shakespeare **died** in 1616.* (NOT *Shakespeare dead* . . .)
  *She **died** in a car crash.* (NOT *She is dead in* . . .)
  *So far 50 people have **died** in the fighting.*
Note the spelling of the present participle *dying* (see 561).
*Death* is a noun meaning 'the end of life'.
  *After his **death** his wife went to live in Canada.*

For expressions like *the dead* (= dead people), see 17.

# 154 determiners: the, my, some, several etc

## 1 What are determiners?

Determiners are words like *the, a, my, this, some, either, every, enough, several*. Determiners come at the beginning of noun phrases, but they are not adjectives.

| | | |
|---|---|---|
| *the moon* | *this house* | *every week* |
| *a nice day* | *some problems* | *enough trouble* |
| *my fat old cat* | *either arm* | *several young students* |

There are two main groups of determiners.

## 2 Group A determiners: *the, my, this, ...*

These help to identify things – to say whether they are known or unknown to the hearer, which one(s) the speaker is talking about, whether the speaker is thinking of particular examples or speaking in general, etc. There are three kinds:

**articles:** *a/an, the* (see 61–70)

**possessives:** *my, your, his, her, its, our, your, their, one's, whose* (see 441, 626)

**demonstratives:** *this, these, that, those* (see 589)

We cannot put two Group A determiners together. We can say *a friend, my friend* or *this friend*, but not *the my friend, the this friend, this my friend* or *my this friend*. To put a possessive together with *a/an* or a demonstrative, we can use the structure *a/this ... of mine/yours* etc (see 443).

*She's a friend of mine.* (NOT ~~She's a my friend.~~)

Nouns with possessive *'s* (see 439–440) can be used like determiners (e.g. *Britain's weather*).

## 3 Group B determiners: *some, each, much, enough* etc

Most of these are 'quantifiers': they say how much or how many we are talking about. The most important are:

> *some, any, no*
> *each, every, either, neither*
> *much, many, more, most; (a) little, less, least; (a) few, fewer, fewest; enough;
>     several*
> *all, both, half*
> *what, whatever, which, whichever*

Some Group B determiners are used with singular nouns (e.g. *each*), some with plurals (e.g. *many*), some with uncountables (e.g. *much*), and some with more than one kind of noun (e.g. *which*).

We can put two Group B determiners together if the combination makes sense.

> *We meet **every few** days.*      *Have you got **any more** coffee?*

For details of the use of Group B determiners, look up the sections on particular words.

▶

## 4 Group B + Group A: *some of the people*

Group B determiners can be used directly before nouns, without *of.*
>*Have you got **any** sugar?* (NOT ...~~any of sugar.~~)
>***Most** people agree with me.* (NOT ~~Most of people~~ ...)

But if we want to put a Group B determiner before a noun which has a Group A determiner (article, possessive or demonstrative), we have to use *of.* Compare:

| | |
|---|---|
| – *some people*<br>*some **of the** people* | – ***enough** remarks*<br>***enough of those** remarks* |
| – *which friends*<br>*which **of your** friends* | – ***neither** door*<br>***neither of these** doors* |
| – *each child*<br>*each **of my** children* | – ***most** shops*<br>***most of the** shops* |

A **Group B determiner** + *of* can be used directly before a noun in a few cases. This happens with proper nouns such as place names, and sometimes with uncountable nouns that refer to the whole of a subject or activity.
>***Most of** Wales was without electricity last night.*
>***Much of** philosophy is concerned with questions that have no answers.*

## 5 Group B + of + pronoun: *most of us*

Group B determiners are used with *of* before pronouns.
>*neither **of them***        *which **of us***        *most **of you***

## 6 *no* and *none*; *every* and *every one*

*No* and *every* are not used before *of*; instead we use *none* and *every one.* Compare:

| | |
|---|---|
| – ***no** friends*<br>***none of my** friends* | – ***every** blouse*<br>***every one of these** blouses* |

## 7 *all (of), both (of), half (of)*

We can leave out *of* after *all, both* and *half* when they are followed by nouns (but not when they are followed by pronouns).
>***all (of)** his ideas*        ***half (of)** her income*
>***both (of)** my parents*        *but **all of** us* (NOT ~~all us~~)

Note that when *each, every, either* and *neither* are used directly before nouns without *of,* the nouns are singular. Compare:

| | |
|---|---|
| – *each **tree*** | – *neither **partner*** |
| *each of the **trees*** | *neither of the **partners*** |

## 8 Group A + Group B: *his many friends*

Certain Group B determiners can be used after Group A determiners. They are *many, most, little, least* and *few.*
>*his **many** friends*    *these **few** poems*    *the **least** time*
>*the **most** money*    *a **little** time*    *a **few** questions*

For the difference between *little* and *a little,* and between *few* and *a few,* see 329.

## 9 other determiners: *other, such, what, only,* numbers

There are a few other determiners that do not fit into Groups A and B. They are *other, such, what* (in exclamations), *only* and numbers. *Other, only* and numbers come after Group A determiners (*another* is written as one word); *such* and *what* come before the article *a/an*.

    **my other** *sister*              **such a** *nice day*
    **the only** *possibility*         **the three** *bears*
                                 **what a** *pity*

*Other* and *such* can also come after some Group B determiners.

    **many other** *problems*         **most such** *requests*

## 10 determiners without nouns; *I haven't read any*

Nouns are often dropped after determiners if the meaning is clear.

    *Do you know Orwell's books? ~ I haven't read **any**.*
    *Have we got any tomatoes? ~ A **few**.*
    *Which chair do you want? ~ **This** will do.*

Determiners are sometimes used without nouns to refer to people in general. This is formal and generally rather old-fashioned.

    ***Many*** *are called but **few** are chosen.* (The Bible)
    ***Some*** *say one thing, some say another.*
    *OPEN MEETING: ALL (ARE) WELCOME.*

Possessives (except *whose* and *his*) have different forms when they are used without nouns: *mine, yours, hers, ours, theirs* (see 442). Compare:

    *That's **my** coat*                 *That's **mine**.*

*Its* and *one's* are not used without nouns. (See 442)

For *others* meaning 'other people', see 54.4. For *all* meaning *everything*, see 38.2.
For expressions like *a lot of, a heap of, the majority of,* see 333.
For more information about particular determiners, consult the entries for the individual words (see Index).

# 155 different

## 1 modifiers: *any different* etc

*Different* is a little like a comparative: unlike most adjectives, it can be modified by *any* and *no, (a) little* and *not much.*

    *I hadn't seen her for years, but she wasn't **any** different.*
    *How's the patient, doctor? ~ **No** different.*
    *His ideas are **little** different from those of his friends.*
    *The new school isn't **much** different from the old one.*

*Quite different* means 'completely different' (see 489.3).

    *I thought you'd be like your sister, but you're **quite different**.*

Unlike comparatives, *different* can also be modified by *very*.

    *She's **very** different from her sister.*

## 2 prepositions: *different from/to*

*From* is generally used after *different*; many British people also use *to*. In American English, *than* is common.

    *American football is very different **from/to** soccer.*
        (AmE ... *different **from/than** soccer.*)

Before a clause, *different than* is also possible in British English.

    *The job's different **than I expected**.*
        (OR ... *different **from/to** what I expected.*)

For the difference between *different* and *other*, see 54.5.

# 156 **direct speech**: reporting verbs and word order

## 1 **informal spoken reports: *said, thought***

When we repeat people's words or thoughts, we normally use *say* or *think*. They can go before sentences or at other natural breaks (e.g. between clauses or after discourse markers).

> *So I **said** 'What are you doing in our bedroom?' 'I'm sorry', he **said**, 'I thought it was my room.' Well, I **thought**, that's funny, he's got my handbag open. 'If that's the case,' I **said**, 'what are you doing with my handbag?'*

## 2 **literary direct speech: *ask, exclaim, suggest . . .***

In novels, short stories etc, a much wider variety of reporting verbs are used: for example *ask, exclaim, suggest, reply, cry, reflect, suppose, grunt, snarl, hiss, whisper*. And reporting verbs are often put before their subjects ('inversion' – see 303).

> *'Is this Mr Rochester's house?' **asked Emma**.*
> *'Great Heavens!' **cried Celia**. 'Is there no end to your wickedness? I implore you – leave me alone!' 'Never,' **hissed the Duke** . . .*

Inversion is not normal with pronoun subjects.

> *'You monster!' **she screamed**.* (NOT *. . . ~~screamed she~~.*)

In literary writing, reporting expressions often interrupt the normal flow of the sentences quoted.

> *'Your information,' **I replied**, 'is out of date.'*

# 157 **discourse markers**

*Discourse* means 'pieces of language longer than a sentence'. Some words and expressions are used to show how discourse is constructed. They can show the connection between what a speaker is saying and what has already been said or what is going to be said; they can help to make clear the structure of what is being said; they can indicate what speakers think about what they are saying or what others have said. There are a very large number of these 'discourse markers', and it is impossible to give a complete list in a few pages. Here are a few of the most common examples. Some of these words and expressions have more than one use; for more information, look in a good dictionary. Some discourse markers are used mostly in informal speech or writing; others are more common in a formal style. Note that a discourse marker usually comes at the beginning of a clause.

## 1 **focusing and linking**

> □ *with reference to; talking/speaking of/about; regarding; as regards; as far as . . . is concerned; as for*

These expressions focus attention on what is going to be said, by announcing the subject in advance. Some of them also make a link with previous discourse, by referring back to what was said before.

*With reference to* is a very formal expression used mainly at the beginning of business letters.

> ***With reference to** your letter of 17 March, I am pleased to inform you . . .*

*Speaking/talking of/about* ... is used to make a link with what has just been said. It can help a speaker to change the subject.

> *I saw Max and Lucy today. You know, she – ~ **Talking of** Max, did you know he's going to Australia?*

*Regarding* can come at the beginning of a piece of discourse.

> *Hello, John. Now look, **regarding** those sales figures – I really don't think ...*

*As regards* and *as far as* ... *is concerned* usually announce a change of subject by the speaker/writer.

> *... there are no problems about production. Now **as regards** marketing ...*
> *... about production. **As far as** marketing **is concerned**, I think ...*

People sometimes leave out *is concerned* after *as far as* ... This is usually considered incorrect.

> ***As far as** the new development plan, I think we ought to be very careful.*

*As for* often suggests lack of interest or dislike.

> *I've invited Andy and Bob. **As for** Stephen, I never want to see him again.*

## 2 balancing contrasting points

☐  *on the one hand* (formal), *on the other hand; while; whereas*

These expressions are used to balance two facts or ideas that contrast, but do not contradict each other.

> *Arranged marriages are common in many Middle Eastern countries. In the West, **on the other hand**, they are unusual.*
> ***On the one hand**, we need to reduce costs. **On the other hand**, investment ...*
> *I like the mountains, **while/whereas** my wife prefers the seaside.*

*While* and *whereas* can be put before the first of the contrasting points.

> ***While/Whereas** some languages have 30 or more different vowel sounds, others have five or less.*

For a comparison of *on the other hand* and *on the contrary*, see 144.

## 3 emphasising a contrast

☐  *however; nevertheless; nonetheless; mind you; still; yet; in spite of this/that; despite this/that*

*However, nevertheless* and *nonetheless* emphasise the fact that the second point contrasts with the first. *Nevertheless* is very formal.

> *Britain came last in the World Children's Games. **However**, we did have one success, with Annie Smith's world record in the sack race.*
> *It was an oppressive dictatorship, but **nevertheless** it ensured stability.*

*Mind you* (less formal) and *still* introduce the contrasting point as an afterthought.

> *I don't like the job much. **Mind you / Still**, the money's OK.*

*Yet, still, in spite of this/that* and *despite this/that* (more formal) can be used to suggest that something is surprising, in view of what was said before.

> *He says he's a socialist, and **yet** he owns three houses and drives a Rolls.*
> *The train was an hour late. **In spite of this**, I managed to get to the meeting in time.* (OR *... I **still** managed to get ...*)  ▶

## 4   similarity

□   *similarly; in the same way; just as*

These are most common in a formal style.

> *The roads are usually very crowded at the beginning of the holiday season.*
> ***Similarly**, there are often serious traffic jams at the end of the holidays.*
> *James Carter did everything he could to educate his children. **In the same***
> ***way**, they in turn put a high value on their own children's education.*
> ***Just as** the Greeks looked down on the Romans, the Romans looked down on*
> *their uncivilised neighbours.*

## 5   concession and counter-argument

□   concession: *it is true; certainly; of course; granted; if; may;* stressed
auxiliaries.

□   counter-argument: *however; even so; but; nevertheless; nonetheless; all
the same; still*

These expressions are used in a three-part structure: (1) there is discussion of
facts that point in a certain direction; (2) it is agreed (the concession) that a
particular contradictory fact points the other way; (3) but the speaker/writer
dismisses this and returns to the original direction of argument.

> *. . . cannot agree with colonialism. **It is true** that the British **may** have done*
> *some good in India. **Even so**, colonialism is basically evil.*
> *. . . incapable of lasting relationships with women. **Certainly**, several women*
> *loved him, and he was married twice. **All the same**, the women closest to*
> *him were invariably deeply unhappy.*
> *Very few people understood Einstein's theory. **Of course**, everybody had heard*
> *of him, and a fair number of people knew the word 'relativity'. **But** hardly*
> *anybody could tell you what he had actually said.*
> *I'm not impressed by her work. **Granted**, she writes like an angel. **But** she*
> *doesn't write about anything of any interest.*
> *It was a successful party. The Scottish cousins, **if** a little surprised by the*
> *family's behaviour, were **nonetheless** impressed by the friendly welcome*
> *they received.*
> *I'm glad to have a place of my own. **It's true** it's a bit small, and it's a long*
> *way from the centre, and it does need a lot of repairs done. **Still**, it's home.*

For other uses of *still*, see 566.        For other uses of *of course*, see 390.

## 6   contradicting

□   *on the contrary; quite the opposite*

These expressions can contradict a suggestion made by another speaker.

> *Interesting lecture? ~ **On the contrary / Quite the opposite**, it was a complete*
> *waste of time.*

They can also be used when a speaker/writer strengthens a negative statement
which he/she has just made.

> *She did not allow the accident to discourage her. **On the contrary / Quite the***
> ***opposite**, she began to work twice as hard.*

For a comparison of *on the contrary* and *on the other hand*, see 144.

## 7  dismissal of previous discourse

☐  *at least; anyway; anyhow; at any rate; in any case*

*At least* can suggest that one thing is certain or all right, even if everything else is unsatisfactory.

> *The car's completely smashed up – I don't know what we're going to do.*
> ***At least** nobody was hurt.*

The other four expressions are used (mostly informally) to mean 'What was said before doesn't matter – the main point is as follows'.

> *I'm not sure what time I'll arrive, maybe seven or eight. **Anyway** / **Anyhow** /*
> ***At any rate** / **In any case**, I'll certainly be there before eight thirty.*

Note that *anyway* is not the same as *in any way*, which means 'by any method'.

> *Can I help you **in any way**?*

## 8  change of subject

☐  *by the way; incidentally; right; all right; now; OK*

*By the way* and *incidentally* are used to introduce something one has just thought of that is not directly part of the conversation.

> *I was talking to Phil yesterday. Oh, **by the way**, he sends you his regards.*
> *Well, he thinks . . .*
> *Janet wants to talk to you about advertising. **Incidentally**, she's lost a lot of*
> *weight. Anyway, it seems the budget . . .*

These two expressions are sometimes used to change the subject completely.

> *Freddy's had another crash. ~ Oh, yes? Poor old chap. **By the way**, have you*
> *heard from Joan recently?*
> *Lovely sunset. ~ Yes, isn't it? Oh, **incidentally**, what happened to that bike I*
> *lent you?*

*(All) right, now* and *OK* are often used informally by teachers, lecturers and people giving instructions, to indicate that a new section of the discourse is starting.

> *Any questions? **Right**, let's have a word about tomorrow's arrangements.*
> ***Now**, I'd like to say something about the exam . . .*
> *Is that all clear? **OK**, now has anybody ever wondered why it's impossible to*
> *tickle yourself? . . .*

## 9  return to previous subject

☐  *to return to the previous point* (formal); *as I was saying* (informal)

These expressions are used to return to an earlier subject after an interruption or a brief change of subject.

> *. . . especially in France. **To return to the previous point**, non-European*
> *historians . . .*
> *. . . on the roof – Jeremy, put the cat down, please. **As I was saying**, if Jack gets*
> *up on the roof and looks at the tiles . . .*

## 10  structuring

☐  *first(ly), first of all, second(ly), third(ly)* etc; *lastly; finally; to begin with; to start with; in the first/second/third place; for one thing* (informal); *for another thing* (informal)

▶

We use these to show the structure of what we are saying.
> *First(ly), we need somewhere to live. Second(ly), we need to find work.*
> *There are three reasons why I don't want to dance with you. To start with,*
>   *my feet hurt. For another thing, you can't dance. And lastly, . . .*

*Firstly, secondly* etc are more formal than *first, second* etc.

For *at first*, see 84.       For *at last*, see 204.

## 11  adding

☐   *moreover* (very formal); *furthermore* (formal); *in addition*; *as well as that*;
*on top of that* (informal); *another thing is* (informal); *what is more*; *also*;
*besides*; *in any case*

These expressions introduce additional information or arguments.
> *The Prime Minister is unwilling to admit that he can ever be mistaken.*
>   ***Moreover,** he is totally incapable . . .*
> *The peasants are desperately short of food. **Furthermore** / **In addition,** they*
>   *urgently need doctors and medical supplies.*
> *She borrowed my bike and never gave it back. And **as well as that** / **on top of***
>   ***that** / **what is more,** she broke the lawnmower and then pretended she*
>   *hadn't.*
> *If Janet and Pete come and stay, where's Mary going to sleep? **Another thing***
>   ***is,** we can't go away next weekend if they're here.*
> *Her father was out of work. **Also,** her mother was in poor health.*

*Besides* and *in any case* can add an extra, more conclusive fact or argument.
> *What are you trying to get a job as a secretary for? You'd never manage to*
>   *work eight hours a day. **Besides** / **In any case,** you can't type.*

## 12  generalising

☐   *on the whole*; *in general*; *in all/most/many/some cases*; *broadly speaking*;
*by and large*; *to a great extent*; *to some extent*; *apart from . . .*; *except for . . .*.

These expressions say how far the speaker/writer thinks a generalisation is
true.
> ***On the whole,** I had a happy childhood.*
> ***In general,** we are satisfied with the work.*
> ***In most cases,** people will be nice to you if you are nice to them.*
> ***Broadly speaking,** teachers are overworked and underpaid.*
> ***By and large,** this is a pleasant place to live.*
> ***To a great extent,** a person's character is formed by the age of eight.*

*Apart from* and *except for* (see 102) introduce exceptions to generalisations.
> ***Apart from** the soup, I thought the meal was excellent.*
> ***Except for** Sally, they all seemed pretty sensible.*

## 13  giving examples

☐   *for instance*; *for example*; *e.g.*; *in particular*

These expressions introduce particular examples to illustrate what has been
said.
> *People often behave strangely when they're abroad. Take Mrs Ellis, **for***
>   ***example** / **for instance,** . . .*

In writing, the abbreviation *e.g.* (Latin *exempli gratia*), pronounced /iː ˈdʒiː/, is often used to mean 'for example'.

*Some common minerals, **e.g.** silica or olivine, . . .*

*In particular* focuses on a special example.

*We are not at all happy with the work you did on the new kitchen. **In particular**, we consider that the quality of wood used . . .*

## 14 logical consequence

□   *therefore* (formal); *as a result* (formal); *consequently* (formal); *so*; *then*

These expressions show that what is said follows logically from what was said before.

*She was **therefore** unable to avoid an unwelcome marriage.*
*So she had to get married to a man she didn't like.*
*The last bus has gone. ~ **Then** we're going to have to walk.*

*Therefore* is used in logical, mathematical and scientific proofs.

***Therefore** 2x - 15 = 17y + 6.*

*So* is often used as a general-purpose connector, rather like *and*, in speech.

*So anyway, this man came up to me and said 'Have you got a light?'*
*So I told him no, I hadn't. So he looked at me and . . .*

For the difference between *so* and *then*, see 537.

## 15 making things clear; giving details

□   *I mean*; *actually*; *that is to say*; *in other words*

We use *I mean* (see 348) when we make things clearer or give more details.

*It was a terrible evening. **I mean**, they all sat round and talked politics.*

*Actually* (see 11) can introduce details, especially when these are unexpected.

*Tommy's really stupid. He **actually** still believes in Father Christmas.*

*That is to say* and *in other words* are used when the speaker/writer says something again in another way.

*We cannot continue with the deal on this basis. **That is to say** / **In other words**, unless you can bring down the price we shall have to cancel the order.*

## 16 softening and correcting

□   *I think*; *I feel*; *I reckon* (informal); *I guess* (informal); *in my view/opinion* (formal); *apparently*; *so to speak*; *more or less*; *sort of* (informal); *kind of* (informal); *well*; *really*; *that is to say*; *at least*; *I'm afraid*; *I suppose*; *or rather*; *actually*; *I mean*

*I think/feel/reckon/guess* and *in my view/opinion* are used to make opinions and statements sound less dogmatic – they suggest that the speaker is just giving a personal opinion, with which other people may disagree.

*I think you ought to try again.*
*I really feel she's making a mistake.*
*I reckon/guess she just doesn't respect you, Bill.*
*In my view/opinion, it would be better to wait until July.*

*Apparently* can be used to say that the speaker has got his/her information from somebody else (and perhaps does not guarantee that it is true).

*Have you heard? **Apparently** Susie's pregnant again.*

▶

*So to speak, more or less* and *sort/kind of* (see 551) are used to show that one is not speaking very exactly, or to soften something which might upset other people. *Well* and *really* can also be used to soften.

*I **sort of** think we ought to start going home, perhaps, **really**.*

*I **kind of** think it's **more or less** a crime.*

*Do you like it? ~ **Well**, yes, it's all right.*

*That is to say* and *at least* can be used to 'back down' from something too strong or definite that one has said.

*I'm not working for you again. Well, **that's to say**, not unless you put my wages up.*

*Ghosts don't exist. **At least**, I've never seen one.*

*I'm afraid* (see 28.2) is apologetic: it can introduce a polite refusal, or bad news.

*I'm afraid I can't help you.*      *I'm afraid I forgot to buy the stamps.*

*I suppose* can be used to enquire politely about something (respectfully inviting an affirmative answer).

*I **suppose** you're very busy just at the moment?*

It can also be used to suggest unwilling agreement.

*Can you help me for a minute? ~ I **suppose** so.*

*Actually* (see 11) can correct misunderstandings.

*Hello, John. ~ **Actually**, my name's Andy.*

*Well* can soften corrections, suggesting 'That's nearly right'.

*You live in Oxford, don't you? ~ **Well**, near Oxford.*

*Or rather* is used to correct oneself.

*I'm seeing him in May – **or rather** early June.*

*I mean* (see 348) can be used to correct oneself or to soften.

*Let's meet next Monday – I **mean** Tuesday.*

*She's not very nice. I **mean**, I know some people like her, but . . .*

## 17  gaining time

□  *let me see; let's see; well; you know; I don't know; I mean; kind of; sort of*

Expressions of this kind (often called 'fillers') give the speaker time to think.

*How much are you selling it for? ~ Well, **let me see** . . .*

*Why did you do that? ~ Oh, **well, you know, I don't know**, really, **I mean**, it just **sort of** seemed a good idea.*

## 18  showing one's attitude to what one is saying

□  *honestly; frankly; no doubt*

*Honestly* can be used to claim that one is speaking sincerely.

***Honestly**, I never said a word to him about the money.*

Both *honestly* and *frankly* can introduce critical remarks.

***Honestly**, John, why do you have to be so rude?*

*What do you think of my hair? ~ **Frankly**, dear, it's a disaster.*

*No doubt* (see 377) suggests that the speaker/writer thinks something is probable, but does not know for certain himself/herself.

***No doubt** the Romans enjoyed telling jokes, just like us.*

## 19   persuading

□   *after all; look; look here*

*After all* (see 31) suggests 'this is a strong argument that you haven't taken into consideration'. *Look* is more strongly persuasive.

> *I think we should let her go on holiday alone.* **After all**, *she is fifteen – she's not a child any more.*
> *You can't go there tomorrow.* **Look**, *the trains aren't running.*

*Look here* is an angry exclamation meaning 'You can't say/do that!'

> **Look here**! *What are you doing with my suitcase?*

*No doubt* can be used to persuade people politely to do things.

> **No doubt** *you'll be paying your rent soon?*

## 20   referring to the other person's expectations

□   *actually* (especially BrE); *in fact; as a matter of fact; to tell the truth; well*

These expressions are used when we show whether somebody's expectations have been fulfilled or not. *Actually* (see 11) can be used to say that somebody 'guessed right'.

> *Did you enjoy your holiday?* ~ *Very much,* **actually**.

*Actually, in fact* and *as a matter of fact* can introduce additional surprising or unexpected information.

> *The weather was awful.* **Actually**, *the campsite got flooded and we had to come home.*
> *Was the concert nice?* ~ *Yes,* **as a matter of fact** *it was terrific.*
> *Did you meet the Minister?* ~ *Yes.* **In fact**, *he asked us to lunch.*

*Actually, in fact, as a matter of fact* and *to tell the truth* can be used to say that the hearer's expectations were not fulfilled.

> *How was the holiday?* ~ *Well,* **actually**, *we didn't go.*
> *Where are the carrots?* ~ *Well,* **in fact** / **to tell the truth**, *I forgot to buy them.*
> *I hope you passed the exam.* ~ *No,* **as a matter of fact**, *I didn't.*

After a new subject has been announced, *well* can suggest that something new or surprising is going to be said about it.

> *What did you think of her boyfriend?* ~ **Well**, *I was a bit surprised* . . .
> *You know that new house?* **Well**, *you'll never guess who's bought it.*

## 21   summing up

□   *in conclusion; to sum up; briefly; in short*

These expressions are most common in a formal style.

> . . . **In conclusion**, *then, we can see that Britain's economic problems were mainly due to lack of industrial investment.*
> **To sum up**: *most of the committee members supported the idea but a few were against it.*
> *He's lazy, he's ignorant and he's stupid.* **In short**, *he's useless.*

# 158 **do** (1): introduction

*Do* has three main uses.

## 1 auxiliary verb

The auxiliary *do* is used to form the questions and negatives of other verbs, as well as emphatic and shortened forms. For details, see 159.

> **Did** *you remember to post my letters?*
> *This* **doesn't** *taste very nice.*      *I* **do** *like your earrings.*
> *John eats too much.* ~ *He certainly* **does**.

## 2 general-purpose verb

*Do* is also an ordinary (non-auxiliary) verb. It can refer to almost any kind of activity, and is used when it is not necessary or not possible to be more precise. For details, and the difference between *do* and *make*, see 160.

> *What are you* **doing**?      *Don't just stand there.* **Do** *something.*
> *I've finished the phone calls, and I'll* **do** *the letters tomorrow.*

## 3 substitute verb

In British English, *do* can be used alone as a substitute for a main verb after an auxiliary. For details, see 161.

> *Do you think Phil will come?* ~ *He might* **do**. (AmE *He might.*)

*Do so/it/that* can be used as a substitute expression when we want to avoid repeating another verb and what follows. For details, see 162.

> *I need to take a rest, and I shall* **do so** *as soon as I can find time.*
> *He told me to open the door. I* **did it** *as quietly as I could.*

## 4 combined forms

Auxiliary *do* and non-auxiliary *do* can occur together.

> **Do** *you* **do** *much gardening?*      *How* **do** *you* **do**?
> *The company* **didn't do** *very well last year.*

# 159 **do** (2): auxiliary verb

The auxiliary verb *do* is followed by infinitives without *to*. It has several uses.

## 1 questions

We use *do* to make questions with ordinary verbs, but not with other auxiliary verbs (see 480). Compare:

> **Do** *you like football?* (NOT ~~Like you football?~~)
> *Can you play football?* (NOT ~~Do you can play football?~~)

The auxiliary *do* can make questions with the ordinary verb *do*.

> *What* **do** *you* **do** *in the evenings?*

## 2 negatives

We use *do* to make negative clauses with ordinary verbs (including the ordinary verb *do*), but not with other auxiliary verbs (see 367).

> *I **don't** like football.* (NOT ~~I like not football.~~)
> ***Don't** go.*      *I **don't do** much in the evenings.*
> BUT *I can't play football.* (NOT ~~I don't can play football.~~)

## 3 emphasis

We can use *do* in an affirmative clause for emphasis (see 184).

> ***Do** sit down.*      *You **do** look nice today!*
> *She thinks I don't love her, but I **do** love her.*
> *I don't do much sport now, but I **did** play football when I was younger.*

## 4 inversion

*Do* is used in some inversion (verb before subject) structures (see 302).

> *At no time **did** he lose his self-control.*

## 5 ellipsis

In cases where an auxiliary is used instead of a whole verb phrase (see 181), *do* is common in affirmative clauses as well as questions and negatives.

> *She doesn't like dancing, but I **do**.* (= ... but I like dancing.)
> *You saw Alan, **didn't** you?*
> *That meat smells funny. ~ Yes, it **does**, **doesn't** it?*
> *Ann thinks there's something wrong with Bill, and so **do** I.*

For *do* with *be*, see 90.
For weak pronunciations of *do* and *does*, see 616.
For *do* in short answers, see 517.

# 160 do (3): general-purpose verb; do and make

The general-purpose verb *do* has several uses, and can sometimes be confused with *make*.

## 1 *do* for indefinite activities

We use *do* when we do not say exactly what activity we are talking about – for example with words like *thing, something, nothing, anything, what.*

> *Then he **did** a very strange **thing**.* (NOT ~~Then he made a very strange thing.~~)
> ***Do** something!*
> *I like **doing nothing**.* (NOT ... ~~making nothing.~~)
> ***What** shall we **do**?*

## 2 *do* for work

We use *do* when we talk about work and jobs.

> *I'm not going to **do** any work today.*      *Could you **do** the shopping for me?*
> *It's time to **do** the accounts.*      *I wouldn't like to **do** your job.*
> *I **did** (= studied) French and German at school.*
> *Has Ben **done** his homework?*
> *Could you **do** the ironing first, and then **do** the windows if you've got time?*

▶

### 3 *do ...ing*

We use *do* in the informal structure *do ...ing*, to talk about activities that take a certain time, or are repeated (for example jobs and hobbies). There is usually a determiner (e.g. *the, my, some, much*) before the *-ing* form.

*During the holidays I'm going to* **do some walking** *and* **a lot of reading***.*

*Let your fingers* **do the walking***.* (advertisement for telephone shopping)

Note that the verb after *do* cannot have an object in this structure.

*I'm going to* **watch some TV***.* (NOT ~~I'm going to do some watching TV.~~)

But *do* can be used with a compound noun that includes **verb + object**.

*I want to* **do some bird-watching** *this weekend.*

*It's time I* **did some letter-writing***.*

### 4 *make* for constructing, creating etc

We often use *make* to talk about constructing, building, creating etc.

*I've just* **made a cake***.*          *Let's* **make a plan***.*

*My father and I once* **made** *a boat.*

### 5 *do* instead of *make*

We sometimes use *do* in place of *make*, to sound casual about a creative activity – as if we are not claiming to produce any very special results.

*What shall we eat?* ~ *Well, I could* **do** *an omelette.*

### 6 common fixed expressions

*do* *good, harm, business, one's best, a favour, sport, exercise, one's hair, one's teeth, one's duty, 50 mph*

*make* *a journey, an offer, arrangements, a suggestion, a decision, an attempt, an effort, an excuse, an exception, a mistake, a noise, a phone call, money, a profit, a fortune, love, peace, war, a bed, a fire, progress*

Note that we say **make** *a bed*, but we often talk about **doing** *the bed(s)* as part of housework. Compare:

*He's old enough to* **make his own bed** *now.*

*I'll start on the vegetables as soon as I've* **done the beds***.*

We use *take*, not *make*, in *take a photo*, and *have*, not *make*, in *have an (interesting) experience*.

For information about sentence structures with *make*, see 335.

## 161 **do** (4): substitute verb

### auxiliary verb + *do*

In British English (but not American), *do* can be used alone as a substitute verb after an auxiliary verb.

*Come and stay with us.* ~ *I may (***do***), if I have the time.* (AmE *I may, if ...* OR *I may come, if ...*)

*He's supposed to have locked the safe.* ~ *He has (***done***).* (AmE *He has.* OR *He has locked it.*)

*I found myself thinking of her as I had never* **done** *before.*

*He didn't pass his exam, but he could have (***done***) if he'd tried harder.*

*He smokes more than he used to (***do***).*

Progressive forms are possible, but not very common.
*You should be getting dressed. ~ I am (doing).*
Note that the auxiliary verb is stressed in this structure.
*Close the door. ~ I HAVE done.* (NOT *...I have ~~DONE~~.*)

For auxiliary verbs used instead of complete verb phrases, see 181.

# 162   do so/it/that

## 1   *do so*

The expression *do so* can be used to avoid repeating a verb and its object or complement. It is usually rather formal.
*Put the car away, please. ~ I've already done so.*
*Eventually she divorced Stephen. It was a pity she had not done so earlier.*
*He told me to get out, and I did so as quietly as possible.*

## 2   *do so* and *do it/that*

*Do it* and *do that* can be used instead of *do so*.
*I promised to get the tickets, and I will do so/it as soon as possible.*
*She rode a camel: she had never done so/that before.*
We use *do so* mainly to refer to the same action, with the same subject, that was mentioned before. In other cases we prefer *do it/that* or *do* alone.
*I haven't got time to get the tickets. Who's going to do it?* (NOT *...~~Who's going to do so?~~*)
*I rode a camel in Morocco. ~ I'd love to do that.* (NOT *...~~to do so.~~*)
*I always eat peas with honey. My wife never does.* (NOT *...~~My wife never does so.~~*)

## 3   *do so/it/that*: deliberate actions

*Do so/it/that* are mainly used to refer to deliberate dynamic actions. We do not usually use these expressions to replace verbs like *fall, lose, like, remember, think, own*, which refer to involuntary actions or states.
*I like the saxophone, and I always have (done).*
    (NOT *... ~~and I have always done so/it/that.~~*)
*She lost her money. I wasn't surprised that she did.*
    (NOT *... ~~that she did so/it/that.~~*)
*I think Jake's wrong. I did when he first spoke to me.*
    (NOT *... ~~I did so/it/that when~~ ...*)

## 4   other verbs

Note that *so, it* and *that* are not normally used in this way after auxiliary verbs. It is not possible in standard English to say *I can so, She was it* or *I have that*.

For *so I am, so it is* etc, see 541.2.
For *so do I, so am I* etc, see 541.1.
For *so* with *say* and *tell*, see 540.
For *so* with *think, believe, hope* and similar verbs, see 539.
For auxiliary *do* as substitute for a whole verb phrase, see 181.
For differences between *it* and *that*, see 590.

# 163 doubt

Clauses after the verb *doubt* can be introduced by *whether, if* or *that.*
> Economists **doubt whether** interest rates will fall in the near future.
> I **doubt if** she'll come this evening.
> The directors **doubt that** new machinery is really necessary.

In an informal style, people sometimes use no conjunction.
> I **doubt we'll** have enough money for a holiday.

After negative forms of *doubt,* we normally use *that* or no conjunction.
> I **don't doubt (that)** there will be more problems.

For *no doubt* meaning 'probably', see 377.

# 164 dress

## 1 noun

The countable noun *dress* means an article of women's clothing (it goes from the shoulders to below the hips).
> This is the first time I've seen you wearing **a dress.**

There is also an uncountable noun *dress* (not used with the article *a/an*). It means 'clothing', 'clothes'. It is not very common in modern English, and is used mostly to talk about special kinds of clothing (for example *national dress, evening dress, battledress*).
> He looks good in evening **dress.** (NOT ... *in an evening dress.*)

## 2 verb: putting clothes on

The verb *dress* can be used to talk about putting clothes on oneself or somebody else. *Undress* is used for taking clothes off.
> It only takes me five minutes to **dress** in the morning.
> Could you **dress** the children for me?
> I'm going to **undress** in front of the fire.

In informal English, we use *get dressed/undressed* to talk about dressing or undressing oneself.
> Get **dressed** and come downstairs at once!

*Put on* and *take off* are generally used when clothes are mentioned.
> I **put on** a sweater, but it was so warm that I had to **take it off** again.
> Can you **take** John's boots **off** for him?

## 3 verb: wearing clothes

To say what somebody is/was wearing on a particular occasion, we can use the form *be dressed in* (note the preposition).
> I didn't recognise him because he **was dressed in** a dark suit.
> (NOT ... *dressed with* ... OR ... *dressing in* ...)
> She **was dressed in** orange pyjamas.

*Be wearing* and *have on* (especially AmE) are also very common.
> She **was wearing** orange pyjamas.
> She **had on** orange pajamas. (AmE)

The active form *dress (in)* can be used to give the idea of repetition or habit.
> She always **dresses in** green.     He **dresses** well.

Note also the expression *well dressed.*

## 165 drown

Both active and passive forms of *drown* are common when we talk about accidental drowning.

> *He (was) **drowned** while trying to swim across a river.*

## 166 due to and owing to

*Due to* and *owing to* are similar to 'because of'. *Due to* is more common than *owing to*.

Phrases beginning *due/owing to* are often separated from the rest of their sentence by a comma.

> ***Due/Owing to** the bad weather(,) the match was cancelled.*
>
> *We have had to postpone the meeting(,) **due/owing to** the strike.*

Some people believe it is incorrect to use *due to* at the beginning of a clause in this way, but the structure is common in educated usage.

*Due to* can also follow the verb *be*. *Owing to* is not usually used like this.

> *His success was **due to** his mother.* (NOT ... ~~was owing to his mother.~~)

## 167 during and for

*During* is used to say **when** something happens; *for* is used to say **how long** it lasts. Compare:

– *My father was in hospital **during the summer**.*
  *My father was in hospital **for six weeks**.* (NOT ... ~~during six weeks.~~)
– *It rained **during the night for two or three hours**.*
  *I'll call in and see you **for a few minutes during the afternoon**.*

For *during* and *in*, see 168.
For *for*, *since*, *in* and *from*, see 208.

## 168 during and in

We use both *during* and *in* to say that something happens inside a particular period of time.

> *We'll be on holiday **during/in** August.*     *I woke up **during/in** the night.*

We use *during* to stress that we are talking about the whole of the period.

> *The shop's closed **during the whole** of August.* (NOT ... ~~in the whole of August.~~)

And we use *during* when we are talking about an event, activity or experience (not a period of time).

> *He had some strange experiences **during his military service**.* (NOT ... ~~in his military service.~~)
>
> *I'll try to phone you **during the meeting**.* (NOT ... ~~in the meeting.~~)
>
> *I met them **during my stay in China**.*

# 169 each

## 1 *each* + singular

*Each* is a determiner (see 154). We use it before a singular noun.
> *I enjoy **each moment**.* (NOT ... ~~each moments.~~)

A following verb is also singular.
> *Each new day **is** different.* (NOT ... ~~are different.~~)

## 2 *each of*

We use *each of* before a plural pronoun, or before a determiner (for example *the, my, these* – see 154) with a plural noun.
> ***Each of us** sees the world differently.*
> *I write to **each of my children** once a week.*

A following verb is normally singular.
> *Each of them **has** problems.*

## 3 pronouns

When a pronoun or possessive is used later in a clause to refer back to ***each (of)* + noun/pronoun**, the later word can be singular (more formal) or plural (less formal).
> *Each girl wore what **she** liked best.* (more formal)
> *Each student wore what **they** liked best.* (less formal)
> *Each of them explained it in **his/her/their** own way.*

## 4 position with object

*Each* can follow an object (direct or indirect), but does not normally come at the end of a clause.
> *She kissed **them each** on the forehead.* (BUT NOT ~~She kissed them each.~~)
> *I want **them each** to make their own decision.*
> *I sent **the secretaries each** a Christmas card.*

However, *each* can come at the end of a clause in expressions referring to amounts and quantities.
> *They cost **£3.50 each**.*　　　*I bought the girls **two ice-creams each**.*

## 5 without a noun

We can drop a noun after *each*, if the meaning is clear. However, *each one* or *each of them* is more common in an informal style.
> *I've got five brothers, and **each (one/of them)** is different.*

## 6 with the verb

When *each* refers to the subject, it can also go with a verb in mid-position, like some adverbs (for details of word order, see 24). In this case plural nouns, pronouns and verbs are used.
> *They **have each been** told.*
> *We **can each apply** for our own membership card.*
> *You **are each right** in a different way.*
> *The plans **each have** certain advantages and disadvantages.*

For the difference between *each* and *every*, see 170.

# 170 **each** and **every**: the difference

## 1 *each* with two or more; *every* with three or more

*Each* and *every* are both normally used with singular nouns. *Each* can be used to talk about two or more people or things; *every* is normally used to talk about three or more.

*The business makes less money **each/every year**.* (NOT . . . ~~each/every years.~~)
*She had a child holding on to **each hand**.* (NOT . . . ~~every hand.~~)

For expressions like *every two years, every three steps*, see 532.8.

## 2 meaning

*Each* and *every* can often be used without much difference of meaning.
*You look more beautiful **each/every** time I see you.*
But we prefer *each* when we are thinking of people or things separately, one at a time. And *every* is more common when we are thinking of people or things together, in a group. (*Every* is closer to *all*.) So we are more likely to say:
***Each person** in turn went to see the doctor.*
but
***Every patient** came from the same small village.*

## 3 structures

We do not use *each* with words and expressions like *almost, practically, nearly* or *without exception*, which stress the idea of a whole group.
*She's lost nearly **every friend** she had.* (NOT . . . ~~nearly each friend~~ . . .)
*Each* can be used in some structures where *every* is impossible.
*They **each** said what they thought.* (BUT NOT ~~They every~~ . . .)
***Each of them** spoke for five minutes.* (BUT NOT ~~Every of them~~ . . .)

For more details, see 169 (*each*) and 193 (*every*).

# 171 **each other** and **one another**

## 1 no difference

*Each other* and *one another* mean the same.
*Ann and I write to **each other** / **one another** every week.*
*Each other* is more common than *one another*, especially in an informal style.

## 2 not used as subject

*Each other* and *one another* are not normally used as subjects (though this occasionally happens in subordinate clauses in very informal speech).
*They **each** listened carefully to what **the other** said.* (NOT USUALLY *They listened carefully to what each other said.*)

## 3 *each other's* / *one another's*

Both expressions have possessive forms.
*They'll sit for hours looking into **each other's** / **one another's** eyes.*    ▶

**4** *-selves* and *each other / one another*

Note the difference between *-selves* and *each other / one another*. Compare:
> *John and Mary are strange: they talk to **themselves** a lot.* (John talks to John; Mary talks to Mary.)
> *Susan and Peter talk to **each other** on the phone every day.* (Susan talks to Peter; Peter talks to Susan.)

**5** words used without *each other / one another*

We do not normally use *each other / one another* after words like *meet* or *marry*, where the verb itself makes the meaning clear.
> *They met in 1992 and **married** in 1994.*

## 172 east and eastern, north and northern etc

**1** adjectives: the difference

We often prefer *eastern, northern* etc when we are talking about vague, indefinite or larger areas, and *east, north* etc for more clearly defined places (e.g. the names of countries or states). Compare:

– *the **northern** part of the country*     – *southern Africa* (an area)
*the **north** side of the house*         *South Africa* (a country)
– *the **southern** counties of Britain*   – *the **northern** United States*
*the **south** coast*                      *North Carolina*

However, place names do not always follow this rule. Note the following:
> **Northern** Ireland     **North/East/West** Africa     **North/South** America
> **East/South** etc Asia BUT: **Western/Eastern** etc Europe
> **South** Australia BUT: **Western** Australia; the **Northern** Territory
> the **North/South** Atlantic/Pacific
> the **Northern/Southern** hemisphere

**2** 'belonging to'

We use *eastern, northern* etc to mean 'belonging to' or 'typical of'.
> *a **southern** accent*         *a group of **northern** poets*

**3** capital letters

Capital letters are used at the beginning of *East, Eastern, North, Northern* etc when these come in official or well-established place names.
> *North Carolina*        *Western Australia*        *the Far East*
> *unemployment in the North* (place name meaning 'the North of England')

In other cases, adjectives, nouns and adverbs begin with small letters.
> *We spent the winter in **southern** California.*
> *I live in **north** London.*       *There's a strong **north** wind.*
> *The sun rises in the **east**.*     *By sunrise we were driving **south**.*

**4** prepositions

Note the difference between *in the east* etc *of . . .* and *to the east* etc *of . . .*
> *I live **in the east of** Scotland.*
> *Denmark is about 500 km **to the east of** Scotland.*

# 173 efficient and effective

If somebody/something is *efficient*, he/she/it works in a well-organised way without wasting time or energy.

> *He's not very **efficient**: he keeps filing letters in the wrong place, he works very*
>     *slowly, and he keeps forgetting things.*
> *The postal service is even less **efficient** than the telephone system.*

If something is *effective*, it has the right effect: it solves a problem or gets a result.

> *My headache's much better. Those tablets really are **effective**.*
> *I think a wide black belt would look very **effective** with that dress.*

# 174 either: determiner

## 1 *either* + singular

We use *either* with a singular noun to mean 'one or the other' of two.

> *Come on Tuesday or Thursday. **Either day** is OK.* (NOT *Either days* ...)
> *She didn't get on with **either parent**.* (NOT *... either parents*)

## 2 *either of*

We use *either of* before a determiner (for example *the, my, these* – see 154) or a pronoun. A following noun is plural.

> *You can use **either of the bathrooms**.*
> *I don't like **either of my maths teachers**.*
> *I don't like **either of them**.*

A verb after *either of* is more often singular, but it can sometimes be plural in an informal style.

> *Either of the children **is** perfectly capable of looking after the baby.*
> *She just doesn't care what either of her parents **say(s)**.*

## 3 without a noun

We can use *either* alone if the meaning is clear.

> *Would you like tea or coffee?* ~ *I don't mind. **Either**.*

## 4 pronouns

When a pronoun is used later in a clause to refer back to ***either* + noun/ pronoun**, the later pronoun can be singular (more formal) or plural (more informal).

> *If either of the boys phones, tell **him/them** I'll be in this evening.*

## 5 *either side/end*

In these expressions, *either* sometimes means 'each'.

> *There are roses on **either side** of the door.*

## 6 pronunciation

*Either* is pronounced /ˈaɪðə(r)/ or /ˈiːðə(r)/ (in American English usually /ˈiːðər/).

For *either ... or*, see 175.
For *not ... either, neither* and *nor*, see 374.

## 175 either . . . or

We use *either . . . or* to talk about a choice between two possibilities (and sometimes more than two).

*I don't speak **either** French **or** German.*

*You can **either** come with me now **or** walk home.*

*If you want ice-cream there's **either** raspberry, lemon **or** vanilla.*

We often balance this structure, so that the same kind of words or expressions follow *either* and *or*.

*You can have **either** tea **or** coffee.* (nouns)

*He's **either** in London **or** in New York.* (prepositional expressions)

***Either** you'll leave this house **or** I'll call the police.* (clauses)

However, unbalanced sentences with *either . . . or* are common. Some people prefer to avoid them.

*You can **either** have tea **or** coffee.*

*He's **either** in London **or** New York.*

*You'll **either** leave this house **or** I'll call the police.*

For *either* as a determiner, see 174.
For pronunciation, see 174.5.
For *not . . . either, neither* and *nor*, see 374.

## 176 elder and eldest

*Elder* and *eldest* can be used instead of *older* and *oldest* to talk about the order of birth of the members of a family. They are only used attributively (before nouns). Compare:

- *My **elder**/older brother has just got married.*

  *He's three years **older** than me.* (NOT . . . *elder than me.*)

- *His **eldest**/oldest daughter is a medical student.*

  *She's the **oldest** student in her year.*

*Elder brother/sister* are used when a person has only one brother/sister who is older; *eldest* is used when there are more. An *elder son/daughter* is the older of two; an *eldest son/daughter* is the oldest of two or more.

## 177 ellipsis (1): introduction

We often leave out words to avoid repetition, or in other cases when the meaning can be understood without them. This is called 'ellipsis'.

### 1 replies

In replies we usually avoid repeating information that has just been given.

*What time are you coming? ~ **About ten**.* (More natural than *I'm coming about ten.*)

*Who said that? ~ **John**.* (More natural than *John said that.*)

*How many chairs do you need? ~ **Three**.* (More natural than *I need three chairs.*)

*She's out this evening? ~ Yes, **working**.* (More natural than *Yes, she's working this evening.*)

## 2 structures with *and, but* and *or*

Repeated words are often dropped in co-ordinate structures (see 178).
*a knife **and fork** (= a knife and a fork)*
*She was poor **but honest**. (= . . . but she was honest.)*

## 3 at the beginning of a sentence

In informal speech, unstressed words are often dropped at the beginning of a sentence, if the meaning is clear. For details, see 179.
***Seen** Lucy? (= Have you seen Lucy?)*
***Doesn't** know what she's talking about. (= She doesn't . . .)*

## 4 at the end of a noun phrase

It is sometimes possible to drop nouns after adjectives, noun modifiers and/or determiners. For details, see 180.
*Do you want large eggs? ~ No, I'll have **small**. (= . . . small eggs.)*
*My car isn't working. I'll have to use **Mary's**. (= . . . Mary's car.)*
*We're going to hear the **London Philharmonic** tonight. (= . . . the London Philharmonic Orchestra.)*
*Which shoes are you going to wear? ~ **These**. (= These shoes.)*

## 5 at the end of a verb phrase

Auxiliary verbs are often used alone instead of full verbs. For details, see 181.
*I haven't paid. ~ I **haven't** either. (= . . . I haven't paid either.)*
*She said she'd phone, but she **didn't**. (= . . . didn't phone.)*
This type of ellipsis can include words that follow the verb phrase.
*I was planning to go to Paris next week, but I **can't**.*
*(= . . . I can't go to Paris next week.)*
The same structures are possible with non-auxiliary *be* and *have*.
*I thought she would be angry, and she **was**.*
*He says he hasn't any friends, but I know he **has**.*

## 6 infinitives

We can use *to* instead of repeating a whole infinitive. For details, see 182.
*Are you and Gillian getting married? ~ We hope **to**.*
*(= We hope to get married.)*
*I don't dance much now, but I used **to** a lot.*
Sometimes a whole infinitive, including *to*, is left out.
*Come when you **want**. (= . . . when you want to come.)*
*Have a good time. ~ I'll **try**. (= I'll try to have a good time.)*

## 7 comparative structures with *as* and *than*

We can leave out words after *as* and *than*, if the meaning is clear.
*The weather isn't as good **as last year**. (= . . . as it was last year.)*
*I found more blackberries **than you**. (= . . . than you found.)*

For missing subject or object after *as* and *than* (e.g. *as was expected*), see 581.  ▶

8  **question-word clauses**

Clauses can be dropped after question words.
>  *Somebody's been stealing our flowers, but I don't know **who**.*
>  (= ... I don't know who's been stealing our flowers.)
>  *Become a successful writer. This book shows you **how**.*

9  ***that* and relative pronouns**

In an informal style, the conjunction *that* is often dropped (see 584); object relative pronouns can also be dropped (see 495.4).
>  *I knew **(that)** she didn't want to help me.*
>  *This is the restaurant **(which)** I was talking about.*

10  **reduced relative structures: *the tickets available* etc**

We can sometimes leave out a relative pronoun and the verb *be* before participles or adjectives such as *available, possible*. For details, see 498.10.
>  *Who's the girl **dancing** with your brother?* (= ... who is dancing ...)
>  *Please let me have all the tickets **available**.* (= ... that are available.)

11  ***be* after conjunctions**

Subject pronouns with forms of *be* can be left out after certain conjunctions, especially in a formal style.
>  *Start **when ready**.* (= ... when you are ready.)
>  ***Though intelligent**, he was very poorly educated.*
>  (= Though he was intelligent ...)
>  ***When ordering**, please send £1.50 for postage and packing.*
>  *Phone me **if (it is) necessary**.*  *He had a small heart attack **while asleep**.*
>  *I'm enclosing my cheque for £50, **as agreed**.*  *Leave in oven **until cooked**.*

12  **prepositions**

In an informal style, prepositions can be dropped in a few time expressions (see 451).
>  *See you **(on)** Monday night.*
>  *We're staying here **(for)** another three months.*
>  *What time shall I come?* (More natural than *At what time ...?*)

For cases like *We need a place to live **(in)***, see 431.

13  **pronouns after prepositions**

In British English, pronoun objects can sometimes be dropped after prepositions. This happens, for example, when *have* or *with* are used in descriptive structures.
>  *My socks have got holes **in** (them).*
>  *I'd like a piece of toast with butter **on** (it).*

14  **abbreviated styles**

In certain styles, many or all non-essential words can be dropped. For details, see 1.
>  *Take 500g butter and place in small saucepan.*
>  *Single man looking for flat Oxford area.*
>  WOMAN WALKS ON MOON

# 178 ellipsis (2): with **and, but** and **or**

## 1 various kinds of word left out

When expressions are joined by *and, but* or *or,* we often leave out repeated words or phrases of various kinds.

*a knife **and** (a) fork*          *antique (furniture) **or** modern furniture*

*these men **and** (these) women*          *in France, (in) Germany **or** (in) Spain*

*ripe apples **and** (ripe) pears*          *She can read, **but** (she) can't write.*

*The Minister likes golf **but** (the Minister) hates fishing.*

*We drove (across America), rode (across America), flew (across America) **and** walked across America.*

*She was poor **but** (she was) honest.*

*The food (is ready) **and** the drinks are ready.*

*Phil (washed the dishes) **and** Sally washed the dishes.*

We can sometimes drop a verb that is repeated in a different form.

*I have always **paid** my bills and I always will (**pay** ...).*

## 2 word order

Note that when two verbs, objects etc are the same, it is not always the second that is left out. We may have to leave out the first to avoid confusion, or to produce a simpler word order and sentence structure.

*Cats (catch mice) and dogs catch mice.* (NOT ~~Cats catch mice and dogs.~~)

*I can (go) and will go.*

In informal speech and writing, ellipsis does not usually interrupt the normal word order of a clause or sentence. Sentences like the following are typical of a more formal style.

*Peter planned and Jane paid for the holiday.* (Less formal: *Peter planned the holiday and Jane paid for it.*)

*Kevin likes dancing and Annie athletics.* (Less formal: *Kevin likes dancing and Annie likes athletics.*)

*The children will carry the small boxes and the adults the large ones.*

*Jane went to Greece and Alice to Rome.*

*You seem, and she certainly is, ill.*

## 3 other conjunctions

Ellipsis is not normally possible after other conjunctions besides *and, but* and *or.*

*She didn't know where she was **when** she woke up.* (NOT *... ~~when woke up.~~*)

However, ellipsis of subject pronouns with forms of *be* is possible in some cases (e.g. *if possible, when arriving*). See 261.6, 73.4, 411.6.

## 4 *(and) then*

In an informal style, ellipsis is sometimes possible after *then,* even if *and* is dropped.

*Peter started first, (and) **then** Colin (started).*

For singular or plural verbs after expressions with *and* or *or,* see 532.2.
For singular and plural verbs with *neither ... nor,* see 373.

# 179 ellipsis (3): at the beginning of a sentence

### 1 words that can be left out

In informal spoken English we often leave out unstressed words at the beginning of a sentence if the meaning is clear without them. Words that can be left out include articles (*the, a/an*), possessives (*my, your* etc), personal pronouns (*I, you* etc), auxiliary verbs (*am, have* etc) and the preparatory subject *there*.

> *Car's running badly.* (= The car's . . .)
> *Wife's on holiday.* (= My wife's . . .)
> *Couldn't understand a word.* (= I couldn't . . .)
> *Must dash.* (= I must dash.)
> *Won't work, you know.* (= It won't work . . .)
> *Seen Joe?* (= Have you seen Joe?)
> *Keeping well, I hope?* (= You're keeping well . . .)
> *Nobody at home.* (= There's nobody at home.)
> *Careful what you say.* (= Be careful . . .)
> *Be four pounds fifty.* (= That'll be . . .)

This structure is common in advertisements. Two real examples:

> *Thinking of postgraduate study? Call for a place now.* (= Are you thinking . . .?)
> *Speak a foreign language? Speak it better.* (= Do you speak . . .?)

### 2 unstressed forms of *be, will, would, have*

We do not usually drop words so as to begin sentences with unstressed forms of *be, will, would* or auxiliary *have* (though this sometimes happens in postcards, diary entries and other kinds of very informal writing).

> *I'm coming tomorrow.* OR *Coming tomorrow.* (BUT NOT ~~*Am coming tomorrow*~~. *Am* is not stressed.)
> *I'll see you soon.* OR *See you soon.* (BUT NOT ~~*Will see you soon*~~. *Will* is not stressed.)
> *Haven't seen him.* (BUT NOT ~~*Have seen him*~~. *Have* is not stressed.)

### 3 before pronouns: *You ready?*

Auxiliary verbs can be left out before personal pronouns except *I* and *it*.

> *You ready?* (= Are you ready?)
> *She want something?* (= Does she want something?)
> (BUT NOT ~~*I late? It raining?*~~)

### 4 *Dutch, aren't you?*

Ellipsis is very common in sentences that have some sort of tag (see 487–488, 514) on the end, especially in British English.

> *Can't swim, **myself**.*    *Like a cigar, **I do**.*    *Dutch, **aren't you**?*
> *Getting in your way, **am I**?*    *Going on holiday, **your kids**?*

# 180 ellipsis (4): in noun phrases

## 1 ellipsis after adjectives: *boiled, please*

A repeated noun can sometimes be dropped after an adjective, if the meaning is clear, especially when one is talking about common kinds of choice.

*What kind of potatoes would you like? ~ **Boiled** (potatoes), please.*
*We haven't got any large eggs. Only **small** (eggs).*

This often happens after superlatives.

*I think I'll buy the **cheapest**.*

Note that nouns are not normally dropped in other situations.

*Poor little **boy**!* (NOT *Poor little!*)
*The most important **thing** is to keep calm.* (NOT *The most important is to . . .*)

For other structures in which adjectives are used without nouns, see 17.

## 2 ellipsis after *this*, numbers, possessives etc

Nouns can also be dropped after most determiners (see 154), if the meaning is clear.

*This is Helen's coat, and **that** (coat) is mine.*

This also happens after numbers, nouns with possessive *'s*, *own* and *(an)other*.

*I'm not sure how many packets I need, but I'll take **two** (packets) to start with.*
*Our train's the **second** (train) from this platform.*
*You take Pete's car, and I'll take **Susie's** (car).*
*Can I borrow your pen? ~ No, find your **own** (pen).*
*That beer went down fast. ~ Have **another** (beer).*

## 3 well-known names

The last words of well-known names are often dropped.

*She's playing the **Beethoven** with the **London Philharmonic** tomorrow night.* (= . . . the Beethoven violin concerto with the London Philharmonic Orchestra . . .)
*He's staying at the **Hilton**.* (= . . . the Hilton Hotel.)
*We're going to see 'Hamlet' at the **Mermaid**.* (= . . . the Mermaid Theatre.)

When we talk about people's houses and shops, the words *house* and *shop* are often dropped (see 439.4).

*We spent the weekend at **John and Mary's**.*
*Could you pick up some chops from the **butcher's**?*

# 181 ellipsis (5): after auxiliary verbs

## 1 auxiliary instead of complete verb phrase

We can avoid repetition by using an auxiliary verb instead of a complete verb phrase, if the meaning is clear. The auxiliary verb usually has a 'strong' pronunciation (see 616), and contractions (see 143) are not normally used except in negatives.

▶

*Get up. ~ I **am** /æm/.* (= I am getting up.)
*He said he'd write, but he **hasn't**.* (= . . . hasn't written.)
*I'll come and see you when I **can**.* (= . . . can come and see you.)
*Shall I tell him what I think? ~ I **wouldn't** if I were you.*

*Do* can be used before ellipsis if there is no other auxiliary to repeat.

*I may come to London. I'll phone you if I **do**.*
*He said he would arrive before seven, and he **did**.*

Other words, as well as the rest of the verb phrase, can be left out after the auxiliary.

*I can't see you today, but I **can** tomorrow.* (= . . . I can see you . . .)
*I've forgotten the address. ~ I **have** too.*
*You're not trying very hard. ~ I **am**.*
*You wouldn't have won if I hadn't helped you. ~ Yes, I **would**.*

This also happens after non-auxiliary *be* and *have*.

*I'm tired. ~ I **am** too.*          *Who's the driver? ~ I **am**.*
*Who has a dictionary? ~ I **have**.*

## 2   short answers etc: *Yes, I have.*

Ellipsis is used regularly in short answers (see 517), reply questions (see 484) and question tags (see 487-488).

*Have you finished? ~ Yes, I **have**.*
*I can whistle through my fingers. ~ **Can** you, dear?*
*You don't want to buy a car, **do** you?*

## 3   *so am I* etc

Ellipsis also happens after *so* (see 541), *neither* and *nor* (see 374). Note the word order.

*I've forgotten the address. ~ So **have** I.*
*She doesn't like olives, and neither **do** I.*

## 4   ellipsis before complete form

Ellipsis normally happens when an expression is used for a second time, after the complete form has already been used once (see above examples).
However, it can sometimes happen the other way round. This is common in sentences beginning with *if*.

*If you **can**, send me a postcard when you arrive.*
*If you **could**, I'd like you to help me this evening.*
*If you **prefer**, we can go tomorrow instead.*

## 5   more than one auxiliary

When there is more than one auxiliary, ellipsis usually happens after the first.

*You wouldn't have enjoyed the film. ~ Yes, I **would**.* (= . . . I would have enjoyed the film.)

However, more auxiliaries can be included. The first is stressed.

*Could you have been dreaming? ~ I suppose I **could** / COULD have / COULD have been.*

We often include a second auxiliary verb if it has not appeared before in the same form.

*I think Mary should **be** told. ~ She **has been**.* (More natural than . . . *She has*.)

And we normally include a second auxiliary verb after a change of modal auxiliary.

*Mary **should** be told. ~ She **must** be.* (More natural than ... *She must.*)

## 6 substitution with *do*

In British English, a main verb that is left out after an auxiliary can be replaced by *do*. For details, see 161.

*Do you think he'll phone? ~ He might **do**.* (AmE ... *He might.*)

For *do so*, see 162.

# 182 ellipsis (6): infinitives

## 1 *to* used instead of whole infinitive

We can use *to* instead of the whole infinitive of a repeated verb (and following words), if the meaning is clear.

*Are you and Gillian getting married? ~ We hope **to**.*
*Let's go for a walk. ~ I don't want **to**.*
*I don't dance much now, but I used **to** a lot.*
*Sorry I shouted at you. I didn't mean **to**.*
*Somebody ought to clean up the bathroom. ~ I'll ask John **to**.*

*Be* and *have* (used for possession) are not usually dropped.

*There are more flowers than there used **to be**.* (NOT ... ~~than there used to.~~)
*She hasn't been promoted yet, but she ought **to be**.* (NOT ... ~~but she ought to.~~)
*You've got more freckles than you used **to have**.* (NOT ~~You've got more freckles than you used to.~~)

## 2 ellipsis of whole infinitive

In some cases the whole infinitive can be left out. This happens after nouns and adjectives.

*He'll never leave home; he hasn't got the **courage** (to).*
*You can't force him to leave home if he's not **ready** (to).*

It also happens after verbs which can stand alone without a following infinitive.

*Can you start the car? ~ I'll **try** (to).*

## 3 *(would) like, want* etc

We cannot usually leave out *to* after *would like/love/hate/prefer, want* and *choose*.

*Are you interested in going to University? ~ I'd **like to**.* (NOT ... ~~I'd like.~~)
*My parents encouraged me to study art, but I didn't **want to**.* (NOT ... ~~I didn't want.~~)

However, *to* is often dropped after *want*, and almost always after *like*, when these are used after certain conjunctions – for instance *when, if, what, as*.

*Come **when** you **want** (to).*
*I'll do **what** I **like**.*          *Stay as long **as** you **like**.*

# 183 else

## 1 use

We use *else* to mean 'other' after:
*somebody, someone, something, somewhere; anybody, everybody, nobody* etc;
question words; *whatever, whenever* etc; *little, much.*
> *Would you like **anything else**?*
> *I'm sorry. I mistook you for **somebody else**.*
> ***Where else** did you go besides Madrid?*
> ***Whatever else** he may be, he's not a mathematician.*
> *We know when Shakespeare was born and when he died, but we don't know*
> *  **much else** about his life.*

In a formal style, *else* is sometimes used after *all*.
> *When **all else** fails, read the instructions.*

## 2 word order

Note that *else* comes immediately after the word it modifies.
> ***What else** would you like?* (NOT ~~What would you like else?~~)

## 3 else's

*Else* has a possessive *else's*.
> *You're wearing somebody **else's** coat.*

## 4 singular only

There is no plural structure with *else*.
> *I didn't see **any other** people.* (NOT ... ~~any else people.~~)

## 5 or else

*Or else* means 'otherwise', 'if not'.
> *Let's go, **or else** we'll miss the train.*

*Or else* is sometimes used with no continuation, as a threat.
> *You'd better stop hitting my little brother, **or else**!*

## 6 elsewhere

This is a formal word for *somewhere else*.
> *If you are not satisfied with my hospitality, go **elsewhere**.*

# 184 emphasis

## 1 emotive and contrastive emphasis

We often emphasise ('strengthen') a particular word or expression. There are
two main reasons for this. We may wish to show that we feel strongly about
what we are saying ('emotive emphasis').
> *You **do** look nice today!*
> *Your hair looks **so** good like that.*

Or we may wish to show a contrast between, for example, true and false, or present and past, or a rule and an exception ('contrastive emphasis').

*Why weren't you at the meeting?* ~ *I was at the meeting.*

*I don't do much sport now, but I did play football when I was younger.*

*I don't see my family much, but I do visit my mother occasionally.*

We can also use emphasis to show that something expected actually happened.

*I thought I'd pass the exam, and I did pass.*

## 2  pronunciation: stress

In speech, we can give words extra stress – make them sound 'stronger' – by pronouncing them louder and with a higher intonation (see 554). We may also make the vowel longer, and pause before a stressed word. Stress is reflected in printing by using *italics* or **bold type**, and in writing by using CAPITAL LETTERS or by underlining.

This is the *last* opportunity.

He lived in **France**, not Spain.

Mary, I'm IN LOVE! Please don't tell anybody!

Changes in stress can affect the meaning of a sentence. Compare:

*Jane phoned me yesterday.* (Not somebody else.)

*Jane **phoned** me yesterday.* (She didn't come to see me.)

*Jane phoned **me** yesterday.* (She didn't phone you.)

*Jane phoned me **yesterday**.* (Not today.)

We often stress auxiliary verbs. This can make the whole sentence sound more emphatic, or can emphasise a contrast (see above). Most auxiliary verbs change their pronunciation when they are stressed (see 616).

*You **have** grown!*

*I **am** telling the truth – you **must** believe me!*

In emphatic sentences without auxiliary verbs we add *do* to carry stress.

*Do sit down.*            *She **does** like you.*

*If he **does** decide to come, let me know, will you?*

With stressed auxiliary verbs, word order can change (see 24.9). Compare:

*You have certainly grown.*     *You **certainly have** grown!*

## 3  vocabulary: special words

Words such as *so, such, really* and *just* can show emphasis.

*Thank you **so** much. It was **such** a lovely party. I **really** enjoyed it.*

*I just LOVE the way she talks.* (Note: *love* is stressed, not *just*.)

Swearwords (see 575) are often used for emphasis in an informal style.

*That's a **bloody** good idea.*

Question words can be emphasised by adding *ever* (see 624), *on earth* or *the hell* (very informal).

***Why ever** did he marry her?*

***What on earth** is she doing here?*        ***Where the hell** have you been?*

## 4  structures

If we can move words to an unusual position, this usually gives them more importance. Words are often 'fronted' for this reason (see 513).

***That film** – what did you think of it?*        ***Asleep**, then, were you?*

*I knew he was going to cause trouble, and **cause trouble** he did!*        ▶

'Cleft' structures with *it, what* etc can be used to focus on particular parts of a sentence and give them extra importance (see 130–131).
> *It was John who paid for the drinks.*
> *What I need is a good rest.*

*Do* can be used to emphasise an affirmative verb (see above).
> *She **does seem** to be trying.*     ***Do come** in.*

*Myself, yourself* etc can be used to emphasise nouns (see 493).
> *I got a letter from the Managing Director **himself.***

*Indeed* can be used to emphasise *very* with an adjective or adverb (see 273).
> *I was **very** surprised **indeed.***

*Very* can emphasise superlatives, *next, last, first* and *same* (see 140.4).
> *I'd like a bottle of your **very best** wine.*
> *The letter arrived on the **very next** day.*
> *We were born in the **very same** street in the **very same** year.*

Repetition can be used for emphasis (see 500.7).
> *She looks **much, much** older than she used to.*

# 185 **end** and **finish**: verbs

## 1 both used

These verbs have similar meanings, and are often both possible.
> *What time does the concert **end/finish**?*
> *Term **ends/finishes** on June 23.*

## 2 completing an activity

When we talk about completing something that we are doing, we usually prefer *finish*.
> *She's always starting something new, but she never **finishes** anything.*
> *You'll never **finish** that hamburger – it's too big for you.*
> *Are you still writing letters? ~ No, I've **finished**.*

## 3 changes

*End* is more common when there is an important change.
> *I decided it was time to **end** our affair.*
> *It's time to **end** the uncertainty – the Prime Minister must speak out.*
> *The Second World War **ended** in 1945.*

We also prefer *end* to talk about a special way of bringing something to a close or 'shaping' the end of something.
> *How do you **end** a letter to somebody you don't know?*
> *The ceremony **ended** with a speech from the President.*

*End* is often used to talk about physical shapes.
> *The road **ended** in a building site.* (NOT ~~The road finished~~ . . .)
> *Nouns that **end** in -s have plurals in -es.*

## 4 *-ing* forms

*Finish*, but not *end*, can be followed by an *-ing* form (see 296).
> *I **finished teaching** at 3.00.* (NOT ~~I ended teaching~~ . . .)

## 186 enjoy

*Enjoy* normally has an object.

> *Did you **enjoy the party**? ~ Yes, I **enjoyed it** very much.* (NOT ~~I enjoyed very much.~~)

To talk about having a good time, we can use *enjoy myself/yourself* etc.

> *I really **enjoyed myself** when I went to Rome.*
> *We're going to Paris for the weekend. ~ **Enjoy yourselves**!*

('*Enjoy!*' with no object is possible, especially in informal AmE.)

*Enjoy* can be followed by *-ing*.

> *I don't **enjoy looking** after small children.* (NOT ...~~enjoy to look~~...)

## 187 enough

### 1 adjective/adverb + *enough*

*Enough* usually follows adjectives and adverbs.

> *Is it **warm enough** for you?* (NOT ...~~enough warm~~...)
> *You're not driving **fast enough**.*

### 2 *enough* + noun

*Enough* can also be used before a noun as a determiner.

> *Have you got **enough milk**?*     *There aren't **enough glasses**.*

*Enough* is occasionally used after a noun, but this is rare in modern English except in a few expressions.

> *If only we had **time enough** ...*
> *I was **fool enough** to believe him.*

### 3 position with adjective + noun

When *enough* modifies an adjective and noun together, it comes before the adjective. Compare:

> *We haven't got **enough big** nails.*
>> (= We need more big nails – *enough* modifies *big nails*.)
> *We haven't got **big enough** nails.*
>> (= We need bigger nails – *enough* modifies *big*.)

### 4 *enough* or *enough of*?

Before determiners (e.g. *a, the, my, this, that*) and pronouns, we use *enough of*. Compare:

> – *I don't know **enough** French to read this.* (NOT ...~~enough of French~~...)
>   *I don't understand **enough of the** words in the letter.*
> – *We haven't got **enough** blue paint.* (NOT ...~~enough of blue paint.~~)
>   *We haven't got **enough of that** blue paint.*
> – *You didn't buy **enough** cards.* (NOT ...~~enough of cards~~)
>   *You didn't buy **enough of them**.*

Note the idiomatic structure *I've had enough of ...*. This can be followed by a noun without a determiner.

> *I've **had enough of** mathematics; I'm going to give it up.*
> *She's **had enough of** England; she's going back home.*     ▶

## 5 *enough* without a noun

*Enough* can be used alone without a noun to refer to an amount, if the meaning is clear.

> *Half a pound of carrots will be **enough**.*
> *That's **enough**, thank you.*
> *Enough is **enough**.*
> BUT NOT ~~*The meat is enough.*~~
> (The meat is not an amount.)

## 6 *enough* + infinitive; structure with *for*

We can use an infinitive structure after *enough*.

> *She's old enough **to do** what she wants.*
> *I haven't got enough money **to buy** a car.*

Infinitives can be introduced by *for* + **noun/pronoun**.

> *It's late enough **for the staff to stop** work.*
> *There was just enough light **for us to see** what we were doing.*

## 7 *It's small enough to put in your pocket,* etc

The subject of the sentence can be the object of the following infinitive. (For more about this structure, see 284.4.) Object pronouns are not normally used after the infinitive in this case.

> ***The radio**'s small enough **to put** in your pocket.*
> (NOT *... ~~to put it in your pocket.~~*)
> ***Those tomatoes** aren't ripe enough **to eat**.* (NOT *... ~~to eat them.~~*)

However, object pronouns are possible in structures with *for*.

> *The radio was small enough **for** me to put (**it**) in my pocket.*
> *Those tomatoes aren't ripe enough **for** the children to eat (**them**).*

For other examples of *for* + **object** + **infinitive**, see 291.
For similar structures with *too* and *too much/many*, see 595–596.

## 8 *the* = *enough*; leaving out *enough*

The article *the* can be used to mean 'enough'.

> *I hardly had **the** strength to take my clothes off.*
> *I didn't quite have **the** money to pay for a meal.*

*Time* and *room* are often used to mean 'enough time' and 'enough room'.

> *Have you got **time** to look at this letter?*
> *There isn't **room** for everybody to sit down.*

# 188 especial(ly) and special(ly)

## 1 *especially* and *specially*

*Especially* and *specially* can often both be used with the same meaning.

> *It was not (**e**)**specially** cold.*

## 2 *especially* meaning 'above all'

*Especially* is often used to mean 'above all'.

> *We play a lot of tennis, **especially** on Sundays.*

*The children are very noisy, **especially** when we have visitors.*
*I like all kinds of fruit, **especially** apples.*
*Especially* follows a subject.
*All my family like music. **My father, especially**, goes to as many concerts as he can.* (NOT ... ~~Especially my father goes~~ ...)

## 3 *especially* before prepositions and conjunctions

We prefer *especially* before prepositions and conjunctions.
*We go skiing quite a lot, **especially** in February.*
*I drink a lot of coffee, **especially** when I'm working.*

## 4 *specially* with past participles

*Specially* is used with a past participle to mean 'for a particular purpose'.
*These shoes were **specially made** for me.*
*The song was **specially written** for his birthday.*

## 5 *especial* and *special*

The adjective *especial* is rare. We normally use *special*.
*He took **special** trouble over his work.*

# 189 even

## 1 meaning

*Even* suggests the idea of a surprising extreme: 'more than we expect'; *not even* suggests 'less than we expect'.
*She's rude to everybody. She's **even** rude to the police.*
*He can't **even** write his own name.*

## 2 position

*Even* most often goes with the verb, in mid-position (see 24).
*She has broken all her toys. She **has even broken** her bike.* (NOT ~~Even she has broken~~ ...)
*He speaks lots of languages. He **even speaks** Esperanto.*
*They're open every day. They're **even** open on Christmas Day.*
*Even* goes at the beginning of a clause when it refers just to the subject; and it can go just before other words and expressions that we want to emphasise.
*Anybody can do this. **Even a child** can do it.*
*I work every day, **even on Sundays**.*
*I haven't written to anybody for months – **not even my parents**.*

## 3 *even* and *also*

*Also* (see 46) is not used to talk about surprising extremes.
*Everybody helped with the packing – **even** the dog.* (NOT ... ~~also the dog.~~)

## 4 *even if* and *even though*

*Even* is not used as a conjunction, but we can use *even* before *if* and *though*.
***Even if** I become a millionaire, I shall always be a socialist.* (NOT ... ~~Even I become~~ ...)
***Even though** I didn't know anybody at the party, I had a nice time.*
(NOT ~~Even although~~ ...)

▶

*I wouldn't marry you **even if** you were the last man in the world.*
We sometimes use *if* to mean *even if*.
*I'll do it **if** it kills me.* (= ... even if it kills me.)

## 5  even so; even now

*Even so* means 'however', 'in spite of that'.
*He seems nice. **Even so**, I don't really trust him.* (NOT *... ~~Even though, I don't really trust him.~~*)
*Even now* can mean 'in spite of everything that has happened'.
*He left her ten years ago, but **even now** she still loves him.*

# 190  eventual(ly)

*Eventual* and *eventually* mean 'final(ly)', 'in the end', 'after all that'. We use them to say that something happens after a long time or a lot of effort.
*The chess game lasted for three days. Androv was the **eventual** winner.*
*The car didn't want to start, but **eventually** I got it going.*
We use *at last* (see 204), not *eventually*, to give news.
*Steve has found a job **at last**!* (NOT *~~Steve has eventually found a job!~~*)
*Eventual* and *eventually* are 'false friends' for people who speak some languages. They do not mean the same as, for instance, French *éventuel* or *éventuellement*, and are not used to express the idea of possibility. For this meaning we use *possible, perhaps, if, may, might* etc.
*In our new house I'd like to have a spare bedroom for **possible** visitors.*
(NOT *... ~~eventual visitors.~~*)
*I'm not sure what I'll do next year. I **might** go to America if I can find a job.*
(NOT *... ~~Eventually I'll go to America~~...*)

# 191  ever

## 1  *ever* meaning 'at any time'

*Ever* is a 'non-affirmative word' (see 381). It is used especially in questions to mean 'at any time'. Compare:
*Do you **ever** go to Ireland on holiday?* (= at any time)
*We **always** go to Ireland on holiday.* (= every time)
*We **never** have holidays in England.* (= at no time)
*Ever* is possible in negative clauses, but *never* is more usual than *not ever*.
*I **don't ever** want to see you again.* (OR *I **never** want ...*)
We also use *ever* after *if*, and with words that express a negative idea (like *nobody, hardly* or *stop*).
*Come and see us **if** you are **ever** in Manchester.*
*Nobody **ever** visits them.*                 *I **hardly ever** see my sister.*
*I'm going to **stop** her **ever** doing that again.*

## 2  with comparatives, superlatives, *as* and *only*

*Ever* is used in affirmative clauses in comparisons and with *only*.
*You're looking **lovelier than** ever.*
*What is the **best** book you've **ever** read?*

*It's the **largest** picture **ever** painted.*
*He's as charming **as ever**.*
*She's the **only** woman **ever** to have climbed Everest in winter.*

### 3  *ever* + perfect

*Ever* is often used with perfect tenses (see 455, 423) to mean 'at any time up to now/then'.
*Have you **ever been** to Greece?*
*Had you **ever thought** of getting married before you met June?*

### 4  *ever* and *before*; *ever before*

*Ever* and *before* can both be used to mean 'at any time in the past', but there is a difference. *Before* (or *ever before*) refers to a present event, and asks whether it has happened at another time.
*Have you (ever) been to Scotland **before**?* (The hearer is probably in Scotland.)
*Ever* (without *before*) does not refer to a present event.
*Have you **ever** been to Africa?* (The hearer is not in Africa.)

### 5  *ever* meaning 'always'

*Ever* is not normally used to mean 'always'.
*I shall **always** remember you.* (NOT ~~I shall ever remember you.~~)
But *ever* is sometimes used to mean 'always' in compound expressions with adjectives and participles.
| | |
|---|---|
| *his **ever-open** mouth* | *an **ever-increasing** debt* |
| ***evergreen** trees* | *his **ever-loving** wife* |

*Ever* also means 'always' in *forever* (or *for ever*) and *ever since*, and in a few other expressions like *ever after* and *Yours ever* (used at the end of letters).
*I shall love you **forever**.*          *I've loved you **ever since** I met you.*

For *who ever, what ever* etc, see 624.
For *whoever, whatever* etc, see 625.
For *forever* with progressive forms, see 472.

## 192  ever so, ever such

These expressions are often used in informal British English to mean 'very'.
*She's **ever so** nice.*          *It's **ever such** a good film.*

For the difference between *so* and *such*, see 569.

## 193  every (one)

### 1  *every* + singular

*Every* is a determiner (see 154). We normally use it before a singular noun (but see paragraph 6). If the noun is a subject, its verb is also singular.

> *every* + singular noun (+ singular verb)

*I see her **every day**.* (NOT . . . ~~every days.~~)
***Every room** is being used.* (NOT ~~Every room are~~ . . .)

▶

## 2  *every one of*

We use *every one of* before a pronoun or a determiner (for example *the, my, these* – see 154). The pronoun or noun is plural, but a following verb is singular.

> *every one of us/you/them* (+ singular verb)
> *every one of* + determiner + plural noun (+ singular verb)

*His books are wonderful. I've read **every one of them**.*
*__Every one of the children was__ crying.*

## 3  *every one* without a noun

We can drop a noun and use *every one* alone, if the meaning is clear.
*His books are great. **Every one's** worth reading.*

## 4  negative structures

To negate *every*, we normally use *not every*.
*__Not every__ kind of bird can fly.*
(More natural than *Every kind of bird cannot fly.*)

## 5  pronouns and possessives

When a pronoun or possessive is used later in a clause to refer back to *every (one)*, the later word can usually be either singular (more formal) or plural (less formal).
*__Every__ person made **his/her** own travel arrangements.*
*__Every__ person made **their** own travel arrangements.*
*I told **every single** student what I thought of **him/her/them**.*
But if we are talking about something that concerns every member of a group at the same time, a plural word is necessary.
*When **every passenger's** ticket had been checked, the door opened and **they** all got on.* (NOT *. . . and he/she all got on.*)

## 6  *every* + plural noun

*Every* is used before a plural noun in expressions that refer to intervals.
*I see her **every few days**.*          *There's a meeting **every six weeks**.*
*She had to stop and rest **every two or three steps**.*

## 7  *everybody* etc

*Everybody, everyone, everything* and *everywhere* are used with singular verbs, like *every*.
*__Everybody has__ gone home.* (NOT *Everybody have . . .*)
*__Everything__ I like **is** either illegal, immoral or fattening.*
*I found that **everywhere was** booked up.*
When possessives and pronouns refer back to *everybody/one*, they can usually be either singular (more formal) or plural (less formal). Sometimes only a plural word makes sense. Compare:
*Has **everybody** got **his or her** ticket?* (more formal)
*Has **everybody** got **their** tickets?* (less formal)
*When **everybody** had finished eating, the waiters took away **their** plates.*
     (NOT *. . . his or her plate.*)
Note that *everyone* (= 'everybody') does not mean the same as *every one* (which can refer to things as well as people – see paragraph 2 above).

## 8  *everyday*

*Everyday* is an adjective meaning 'ordinary', 'usual', 'routine'. It is not the same as the adverbial expression *every day*. Compare:

> In **everyday** *life, you don't often find an elephant in a supermarket.*
> *You don't see elephants* **every day**.

## 9  common expressions

Note the following common expressions with *every*.
*every single*
> *She visits her mother* **every single** *day.*

*every other*
> *We meet* **every other** *Tuesday.* (= . . . every second Tuesday.)

*every so often; every now and then*
> *We go out for a drink together* **every so often** / **every now and then**.

For the difference between *every* and *each*, see 170.
For *every* and *all*, see 39.            For *every* and *any*, see 56.
For more information about *everybody/everyone*, see 548.

# 194  except and except for

## 1  *except for* before nouns

We generally use *except for* before noun phrases.
> *I've cleaned the house* **except for** *the bathroom.*
> *The garden was empty* **except for** *one small bird.*

## 2  *except (for)* after *all, any* etc

After generalising words like *all, any, every, no, everything, anybody, nowhere, nobody, whole*, we often leave out *for*.
> *I've cleaned* **all** *the rooms* **except (for)** *the bathroom.*
> *He ate* **everything** *on his plate* **except (for)** *the beans.*
> **Nobody** *came* **except (for)** *John and Mary.*

But this does not happen **before** *all*, etc.
> **Except for** *John and Mary,* **nobody** *came.* (NOT ~~Except John and Mary, nobody came.~~)

## 3  *except* before prepositions and conjunctions

We use *except*, not *except for*, before prepositions and conjunctions.
> *It's the same everywhere* **except in** *Scotland.*
> (NOT . . . ~~except for in Scotland.~~)
> *He's good-looking* **except when** *he smiles.*
> *This room is no use* **except as** *a storeroom.*
> *The holiday was nice* **except that** *there wasn't enough snow.*

## 4  *except (for)* + pronoun

After *except (for)* we use object pronouns, not subject pronouns.
> *Everybody understood* **except (for)** *me.* (NOT . . . ~~except I.~~)
> *We're all ready* **except (for)** *her.*

▶

## 5   except + verb: *he does nothing except eat*

A common structure is *do ... except* + infinitive without *to*.
> *He **does** nothing **except eat** all day.*
> *I'll **do** everything for you **except cook**.*
In other cases an *-ing* form is usually necessary.
> *She's not interested in anything **except skiing**.*
> *You needn't worry about anything **except having** a great time.*

## 6   except and *without*

*Except (for)* is only used to talk about exceptions to generalisations. In other cases, *without* or *but for* may be better. Compare:
> *Nobody helped me **except** you.*
> ***Without / But for** your help, I would have failed.*
>    (NOT *~~Except for your help, I would have failed.~~*)

For the use of *but* to mean 'except', see 116.
For the difference between *except, besides* and *apart from*, see 102.

# 195   exclamations: structures

Exclamations are often constructed with *how* and *what* or with *so* and *such*; negative question forms are also common.

## 1   exclamations with *how*

These are often felt to be a little formal or old-fashioned.

> how + adjective

*Strawberries! **How nice!***

> how + adjective/adverb + subject + verb

***How cold** it is!* (NOT *~~How it is cold!~~*)
***How beautifully** you sing!* (NOT *~~How you sing beautifully!~~*)

> how + subject + verb

***How** you've grown!*

For the structure of expressions like *How strange a remark*, see 14.

## 2   exclamations with *what*

> what a/an (+ adjective) + singular countable noun

***What a** rude man!* (NOT *~~What rude man!~~*)
***What a** nice dress!* (NOT *~~What nice dress!~~*)
***What a** surprise!*

> what (+ adjective) + uncountable/plural noun

***What** beautiful weather!* (NOT *~~What a beautiful weather!~~*)
***What** lovely flowers!*
***What** fools!*

> what + object + subject + verb (note word order)

***What** a beautiful smile **your sister has!*** (NOT *... ~~has your sister!~~*)

## 3  exclamations with *so* and *such*

> *so* + adjective

*You're **so kind**!*

> *such a/an* (+ adjective) + singular countable noun

*He's **such a nice boy**! (NOT . . . ~~a such nice boy!~~)*

> *such* (+ adjective) + uncountable/plural noun

*They talk **such rubbish**! (NOT . . . ~~such a rubbish!~~)*
*They're **such kind people**! (NOT . . . ~~so kind people!~~)*

For more information about *such* and *so*, see 569.

## 4  negative question forms

> ***Isn't** the weather nice!*          ***Hasn't** she grown!*

Americans and some British speakers may use ordinary (non-negative)
question forms in exclamations.

> *Boy, **am I** hungry!*
> *Wow, **did she** make a mistake!*
> ***Was I** furious!*

For more information about negative questions, see 368.

# 196  expect, hope, wait and look forward

## 1  *expect* and *hope*: difference of meaning

*Expecting* is mental rather than emotional. If I *expect* something to happen, I
have a good reason to think it will in fact happen. *Hoping* is more emotional. If
I *hope* for something to happen, I would like it to happen, but I do not know
whether it will. Compare:
– *I'm **expecting** John to phone at three o'clock.*
 *I **hope** he's got some good news.*
– *Lucy's **expecting** a baby.* (= She's pregnant.)
 *She's **hoping** it will be a girl.*
One can *expect* good or bad things, but one only *hopes* for things that one
wants.
> *I **expect** it will rain at the weekend. But I **hope** it won't.*

## 2  *expect* and *wait*: difference of meaning

One *waits* when somebody or something is late, when one is early for
something, or when one wants time to pass so that something will happen.
*Waiting* is often physical – the word suggests, for example, standing or sitting
somewhere until something happens.
Compare:
– *I'm **expecting** a phone call from John at three o'clock.* (NOT ~~I'm waiting for a~~
 ~~phone call from John at three o'clock.~~)
 *I hope he rings on time. I hate **waiting** for people to phone.* (NOT ~~I hate~~
 ~~expecting people to phone.~~)

▶

– *He **expects** to get a bike for his birthday.* (= He thinks he'll get one.)
*It's hard to **wait** for things when you're five years old.*
– *I **expected** her at ten, but she didn't turn up.*
*I **waited** for her till eleven, and then went home.*
*Can't wait* often expresses impatience.
*I **can't wait** for the holidays!*
When we say that we *expect* a person, this usually means that he/she is coming to our home, office etc. Compare:
*Come and see me this afternoon. I'll **expect** you at 4.00.*
*Let's meet at the cinema. I'll be there at 6.00.* (NOT ~~I'll expect you at 6.00.~~)

## 3  *look forward*: meaning

*Look forward* means 'think about (something in the future) with pleasure'. One *looks forward* to something that is certain to happen, and that one is glad about.
*He's **looking forward** to his birthday.*
*See you on Sunday.* ~ *I **look forward** to it.*

## 4  all four expressions compared

Compare:
*I **expect** to hear from her.* (= I'm pretty sure I'll get a letter from her.)
*I **hope** to hear from her.* (= I'm not sure whether she'll write, but I would like her to.)
*I'm **waiting** to hear from her.* (= I need her letter to come; perhaps it's late.)
*I **look forward** to hearing from her.* (= I feel pleasure at the thought that I will hear from her.)

## 5  structures

a  + object: *expect, hope for, wait for, look forward to*

Compare:
*We're **expecting** rain soon.*
*We're **hoping for** a lot of rain – the garden's very dry.*
*We've **been waiting for** rain for weeks.*
*I'm **looking forward to** the autumn.*

b  + infinitive (with *to*): *expect/hope/wait*

*We **expect to spend** the summer in France.*
*We **hope to see** Annemarie while we're there.*
*But we're still **waiting to hear** from her.*
(BUT NOT ~~I'm looking forward to see Annemarie.~~)
Before an infinitive, simple and progressive forms of *hope* and *expect* can often be used with little difference of meaning.
*We **hope** / We're **hoping** to get to Scotland next weekend.*
*We **expect** / We're **expecting** to hear from Lucy today.*

c   + object + infinitive: *expect, hope for, wait for*

>*I **expect him to arrive** about ten o'clock.*
>*We're **hoping for John to come up** with some new ideas.*
>*I'm still **waiting for Harry to pay** me back that money.*

*Expect* is often used with **object + infinitive** to talk about people's duties.

>*We **expect you to work** on the first Saturday of every month.*

Passive versions of the structure are also common.

>*Staff **are expected to start** work punctually at 8.30.*

d   + *-ing* form: *look forward to*

*Look forward* can be followed by *to . . . ing*, but not by an infinitive (see 298.2 ).

>*I **look forward to meeting** you.* (NOT *. . . to meet you.*)
>*I **look forward to hearing** from you.* (common formula at the end of a letter)

Simple and progressive forms can often be used with little difference of meaning.

>*I **look forward** / I'm **looking forward** to the day when the children leave home.*

e   + *that*-clause: *expect, hope*

>*I **expect (that)** she'll be here soon.*   *I **hope (that)** I'll recognise her.*
>(BUT NOT *I'm waiting that she arrives.*)

Before a *that*-clause, progressive forms of *expect* are not normally used.

>*I **expect (that)** she'll be here soon.* (NOT *I'm expecting (that). . .*)

*I expect (that) . . .* can be used to talk about the present or past, with the meaning of 'I suppose', 'I have good reason to think'.

>*I **expect** you're all tired after your journey.*
>*Sarah isn't here. I **expect** she was too tired to come.*

Before a *that*-clause, simple and progressive forms of *hope* can often be used with little difference of meaning.

>*We **hope** / We're **hoping** you can come and stay with us soon.*

*Hope* is often followed by a present tense with a future meaning (see 250).

>*I hope she **doesn't** miss the train.*

f   *expect something of somebody*

This structure refers to people's feelings about how other people ought to behave.

>*My parents **expected too much of me** when I was at school – they were terribly upset when I failed my exams.*

For *hope* and *expect* in negative clauses, see 369.
For *not* and *so* after *hope* and *expect*, see 539.
For *and* after *wait*, see 53.     For *wish*, see 630.

# 197 experiment and experience

An *experiment* is a test which somebody does to see what the result will be, or to prove something. *Experiment* is generally used with the verb *do*. There is also a verb *to experiment*.

>*We **did an experiment** in the chemistry lesson, to see if you could get chlorine gas from salt.* (NOT *We did an experience . . .*)

▶

*I'm **experimenting** with a new perfume.*
An *experience* is something that you live through; something that happens to you in life. *Experience* is generally used with the verb *have*. There is also a verb *to experience*.

> *I had a lot of interesting **experiences** during my year in Africa.* (NOT ~~I made a lot of interesting experiences~~ ...)
> *Have you ever **experienced** the feeling that you were going mad?* (NOT ~~Have you ever experimented the feeling~~ ...?)

The uncountable noun *experience* means 'the knowledge that you get from doing things'.

> *Sales person wanted – **experience** unnecessary.*

## 198 explain

After *explain*, we use *to* before an indirect object.

> *I explained my problem **to her**.* (NOT ~~I explained her my problem.~~)
> *Can you explain **to me** how to get to your house?* (NOT ~~Can you explain me~~ ...?)

## 199 fairly, quite, rather and pretty: adverbs of degree

### 1 fairly

*Fairly* generally modifies adjectives and adverbs. It does not suggest a very high degree: if you say that somebody is *fairly nice* or *fairly clever*, for example, he or she will not be very pleased.

> *How was the film? ~ **Fairly** good. Not the best one I've seen this year.*
> *I speak Russian **fairly** well – enough for everyday purposes.*

### 2 quite

*Quite* (especially in British English) suggests a higher degree than *fairly*.

> *How was the film? ~ **Quite** good. You ought to go.*
> *It's **quite** a difficult book – I had trouble with it.*
> *He's lived in St Petersburg, so he speaks Russian **quite** well.*

*Quite* can modify verbs and nouns.

> *I **quite enjoyed** myself at your party.*     *The room was **quite a mess**.*

For word order rules, the use of *quite* to mean 'completely', and other details, see 489.

### 3 rather

*Rather* is stronger than *quite*. It can suggest 'more than is usual', 'more than was expected', 'more than was wanted', and similar ideas.

> *How was the film? ~ **Rather** good – I was surprised.*
> *Maurice speaks Russian **rather** well. People often think he is Russian.*
> *I think I'll put the heating on. It's **rather** cold.*
> *I've had **rather** a long day.*

*Rather* can modify verbs (especially verbs that refer to thoughts and feelings) and nouns.

> I **rather think** *we're going to lose.*        *She **rather likes** gardening.*
> *It was **rather a disappointment**.*

For word order rules and other details of the use of *rather*, see 490.

### 4 pretty

*Pretty* (informal) is like *rather*, but only modifies adjectives and adverbs.

> *How's things? ~ **Pretty** good. You OK?*
> *You're driving **pretty** fast.*

*Pretty well* means 'almost'.

> *I've **pretty well** finished.*

## 200 far and a long way

### 1 far in questions and negatives

*Far* is most common in questions and negative clauses.

> *How **far** did you walk?*        *The youth hostel is not **far** from here.*

In affirmative clauses we usually prefer *a long way*.

> *We walked **a long way**.* (NOT *We walked far.*)
> *The station is **a long way** from here.*
>   (More natural than *The station is far from here.*)

### 2 far in affirmative clauses

However, *far* is normal in affirmative clauses with *too, enough, as* and *so*.

> *She's gone **far enough**. ~ A bit **too far**.*
> *It's ready **as far** as I know.*
> *Any problems? ~ OK **so far**.*

### 3 far with comparatives etc

*Far* is also used (in all kinds of clauses) to modify comparatives, superlatives and *too*.

> *She's **far older** than her husband.*
> *This bike is **by far the best**.*
> *You're **far too young** to get married.*

### 4 before a noun: a far country

*Far* can be used as an adjective before a noun, meaning 'distant'. This is rather formal and old-fashioned.

> *Long ago, in a **far** country, there lived a woman who had seven sons.*

*Much, many* and *long* (for time) are also more common in questions and negative sentences (see 357 and 330).

## 201 farther and further

### 1 distance

We use both *farther* and *further* to talk about distance. They mean the same.
   *Edinburgh is **farther/further** away than York.*

### 2 'additional'

*Further* (but not *farther*) can mean 'additional', 'extra', 'more advanced'.
   *For **further** information, see page 6.     College of **Further** Education*

## 202 feel

*Feel* has several different meanings. Progressive forms can be used with some meanings, but not with others. *Feel* can be a 'link verb' (see 328), followed by an adjective or noun complement. It can also be an ordinary verb, followed by a direct object.

### 1 link verb: *I feel fine*

*Feel* can be used to talk about one's physical or mental sensations. Adjective or (in British English) noun complements are used.
   *I **feel** fine.     Do you **feel** happy?*
   *Andrew was beginning to **feel** cold.*
   *When Louise realised what she had done, she **felt** a complete idiot.* (BrE)
In this sense *feel* is not normally used with reflexive pronouns (*myself* etc).
   *He always **felt** inferior when he was with her.*
      (More natural than *He always felt himself inferior . . .*)
To talk about feelings that are going on at a particular moment, simple or progressive forms can be used. There is little difference of meaning.
   *I **feel** fine. / I'm **feeling** fine.*
   *How **do** you **feel**? / How **are** you **feeling**?*

### 2 link verb: *That feels nice!*

*Feel* can also be used to say that something causes sensations. Progressive forms are not used.
   *That **feels** nice!     The glass **felt** cold against my lips.*

### 3 link verb: *feel like; feel as if/though*

*Feel* can be followed by *like* or *as if/though*.
   *My legs **feel like** cotton wool.*
   *Alice **felt as if/though** she was in a very nice dream.*
      (*Alice felt like she was . . .* is also possible – see 74.)

### 4 *feel like* meaning 'want'

*Feel like* can also mean 'want', 'would like'.
   *I **feel like** a drink. Have you got any beer?*
In this sense, *feel like* is often followed by an *-ing* form.
   *I **felt like** laughing, but I didn't dare.*

Compare:
>  I *felt like* swimming. (= I wanted to swim.)
>  I *felt like / as if* I was swimming. (= It seemed as if I was swimming.)

## 5 ordinary verb: reactions and opinions

*Feel* is often used to talk about reactions and opinions. Progressive forms are not usually used in this case.
>  I *feel sure* you're right. (NOT ~~I'm feeling sure~~ . . .)
>  He says he *feels doubtful* about the new plan.

*That*-clauses are common.
>  I *feel (that)* she's making a mistake.

A structure with **object + *to be* + complement** is possible in a formal style, but it is not very often used.
>  I *felt her to be unfriendly.* (More normal: *I felt that she was unfriendly.*)

There is also a structure *feel it* (+ *to be*) + **adjective/noun**.
>  We *felt it necessary* to call the police.
>  I *felt it (to be) my duty* to call the police.

## 6 ordinary verb: 'receive physical sensations'

*Feel* can be used with a direct object to talk about the physical sensations that come to us through the sense of touch.
>  I suddenly *felt an insect* crawling up my leg.

Progressive forms are not used, but we often use *can feel* to talk about a sensation that is going on at a particular moment.
>  I *can feel* something biting me!

## 7 ordinary verb: 'touch'

*Feel* can also be used with a direct object to mean 'touch something to learn about it or experience it'. Progressive forms are possible.
>  *Feel the photocopier.* It's very hot.
>  What are you doing? ~ *I'm feeling the shirts* to see if they're dry.

# 203 female and feminine; male and masculine

*Female* and *male* refer to the sex of people, animals and plants.
>  A *female* fox is called a vixen.          A *male* duck is called a drake.

*Feminine* and *masculine* are used for qualities and behaviour that are felt to be typical of men or women.
>  She has a very *masculine* laugh.
>  It was a very *feminine* bathroom.

*Feminine* and *masculine* are used for grammatical forms in some languages.
>  The word for 'moon' is *feminine* in French and *masculine* in German.

# 204   finally, at last, in the end and at the end

## 1   finally

*Finally* can suggest that one has been waiting a long time for something. In this sense, it often goes in mid-position (with the verb – see 24).

> *After trying three times, she **finally** managed to pass her exam.*
> *Steve has **finally** found a job.*

*Finally* can also introduce the last element in a series, like *lastly* (see 157.10).

> *We must increase productivity. We must reduce unemployment. And **finally**, we must compete in world markets.*

## 2   at last

*At last* also suggests – very strongly – the idea of impatience or inconvenience resulting from a long wait or delay.

> *James has paid me that money **at last**.*
> *When **at last** they found him he was almost dead.*

*At last* can be used as an exclamation. (*Finally* cannot be used in this way.)

> ***At last**! Where the hell have you been?*

Note that *lastly* (introducing the last item in a series) is not the same as *at last*.

> *Firstly, we need to increase profits. Secondly, ... Thirdly, ... And **lastly**, we need to cut down administrative expenses.* (NOT *...And at last we need to cut down...*)

## 3   in the end

*In the end* suggests that something happens after changes or uncertainty.

> *We made eight different holiday plans, but **in the end** we went to Brighton.*
> *I left in the middle of the film. Did they get married **in the end**?*
> *The tax man will get you **in the end**.*

Another use of *in the end* is to mean 'after we have considered everything'.

> ***In the end**, you can't get fit without exercise.*
> ***In the end**, Mother knows best.*

## 4   at the end

*At the end* simply refers to the position of something. There is no sense of waiting or delay.

> *A declarative sentence has a full stop **at the end**.*
> *I wish I was paid at the beginning of the week and not **at the end**.*

For *eventually*, see 190.

# 205   finished

*Finished* can be used as an adjective meaning 'ready'.

> *Is the report **finished** yet?*

With personal subjects, *to be finished* is often used in an informal style with the same meaning as *to have finished*.

> *How soon will you **be/have finished**, dear?*
> *I went to get the car from the garage, but they **weren't/hadn't finished**.*

# 206 fit and suit

These words do not mean exactly the same.
*Fit* refers to size and shape: if your clothes *fit* you, they are neither too big nor too small.

> *These shoes don't fit me – have you got a larger size?*

*Suit* refers to style, colour etc.

> *Red and black are colours that suit me very well.* (NOT . . . ~~colours that fit me very well.~~)
> *Do you think this style suits me?*

*Suit* can also be used to say whether arrangements are convenient.

> *Tuesday would suit me very well for a meeting.*

# 207 for: purpose and cause

## 1 people's purposes: *I went for an interview*

*For* can be used to talk about somebody's purpose in doing something, but only when it is followed by a noun.

> *We stopped at the pub for a drink.*
> *I went to the college for an interview with Professor Taylor.*

*For* is not used before a verb in this sense. The infinitive alone is used to express a person's purpose (see 289).

> *We stopped at the pub to have a drink.* (NOT . . . ~~for having a drink~~ OR ~~for to have a drink~~)
> *I went to the college to see Professor Taylor.* (NOT . . . ~~for seeing Professor Taylor.~~)

## 2 the purposes of things: *-ing* forms and infinitives

*For* can be used before the *-ing* form of a verb to express the 'purpose' of a thing – what it is used for – especially when the thing is the subject.

> *Is that cake for eating or just for looking at?*
> *An altimeter is used for measuring height above sea level.*

When the clause has a person as subject, an infinitive is often used to express the purpose of a thing.

> *We use altimeters to measure height above sea level.*

## 3 causes of reactions

*For . . .ing* can also be used after a description of a positive or negative reaction, to explain the behaviour that caused it.

> *We are grateful to you for helping us out.*
> *I'm angry with you for waking me up.*
> *They punished the child for lying.*
> *He was sent to prison for stealing.*

# 208 for, since, in and from: time

## 1 *for*

We use *for* for duration – to say how long something lasts.

> *for* + period of time

> *I studied the guitar **for three years** at school.*
> *That house has been empty **for six months**.*
> *We go away **for three weeks** every summer.*
> *My boss will be in Italy **for the next ten days**.*

To measure duration up to the present, we use a present perfect tense (see 460), not a present tense.

> *I've **known** her for a long time.* (NOT ~~I know her for a long time.~~)
> *We've **lived** here for 20 years.* (NOT ~~We live here for 20 years.~~)

A present tense with *for* refers to duration into the future. Compare:

> *How long **are** you here **for**?* (= Until when . . .?)
> *How long **have** you **been** here **for**?* (= Since when . . .?)

We can often leave out *for* in an informal style, especially with *How long . . .?* And *for* is not usually used before *all*.

> *How long have you been waiting **(for)**?*
> *We've been here **(for)** six weeks.*      *I've had a headache **all day**.*

## 2 *for* and *since* with perfect tenses: the difference

*For* and *since* can both be used with a present perfect to talk about duration up to the present. They are not the same. Compare:

> *for* + period

> *I've known her **for three days**.* (NOT *. . . ~~since three days.~~*)
> *It's been raining **for weeks**.*

> *since* + starting point

> *I've known her **since Tuesday**.*
> *It's been raining **since the beginning of the month**.*

With a past perfect, *for* and *since* refer to duration up to a particular past moment.

> *She'd been working there **for a long time**.* (NOT *. . . ~~since a long time.~~*)
> *She'd been working there **since 1988**.*

## 3 *in* after negatives and superlatives (AmE)

After negatives and superlatives, *in* can be used to talk about duration. This is especially common in American English.

> *I **haven't seen** him **for/in months**.*
> *It was the **worst** storm **for/in ten years**.*

## 4 *from* and *since*

*From* and *since* give the starting points of actions, events or states: they say when things begin or began.

> *from/since* + starting point

> *I'll be here **from three o'clock** onwards.*

*I work **from nine** to five.*
***From now** on, I'm going to go running every day.*
***From his earliest childhood** he loved music.*
*I've been waiting **since six o'clock**.*
*I've known her **since January**.*

We use *since* (with a perfect tense) especially when we measure duration from a starting point up to the present, or up to a past time that we are talking about.

*I've been working **since** six o'clock, and I'm getting tired.* (NOT ~~I've been working from six o'clock...~~)
*I **had been working since** six o'clock, and I was getting tired.*

*From* is used in other cases.

*The shop was open **from eight** in the morning, but the boss didn't arrive till ten.* (NOT ~~The shop was open since eight...~~)
*I'll be at home **from Tuesday morning (on)**.* (NOT ... ~~since Tuesday morning.~~)

*From* is sometimes possible with a present perfect, especially in expressions that mean 'right from the start'.

*She's been like that **from her childhood**.* (OR ... ***since** her childhood.*)
***From/Since** the moment they were married, they've quarrelled.*
***From/Since** the dawn of civilisation, people have made war.*

For *from ... to* and *from ... until*, see 602.
For more about tenses with *since*, see 522.
For *since* meaning 'as' or 'because', see 72.

## 209 forget and leave

We can use *forget* to talk about accidentally leaving things behind.
*Oh damn! I've **forgotten** my umbrella.*

However, we normally use *leave* if we mention the place.
*Oh damn! I've **left** my umbrella at home.* (NOT ~~I've forgotten my umbrella at home.~~)

## 210 fun and funny

*Fun* is normally an uncountable noun. It can be used after *be* to say that things or people are enjoyable or entertaining.
*The party was **fun**, wasn't it?* (NOT ~~The party was funny.~~)
*Anne and Eric are a lot of **fun**.*

In informal English, *fun* can also be used as an adjective before a noun.
*That was a real **fun party**.*

*Funny* is an adjective, and is used to say that something makes you laugh.
*Why are you wearing that **funny** hat?*

Note that *funny* has another meaning: 'strange', 'peculiar'.
*A **funny** thing happened.* ~ *Do you mean **funny** ha-ha or **funny** peculiar?*

# 211 future (1): introduction

There are several ways to use verbs to talk about the future in English. This is a complicated area of grammar: the differences between the meanings and uses of the different structures are not easy to analyse and describe clearly. In many, but not all situations, two or more structures are possible with similar meanings.

## 1 *will/shall*

When we are simply giving information about the future, or talking about possible future events which are not already decided or obviously on the way, we usually use *will* (or *I/we shall*) + **infinitive**. This is the most common way of talking about the future. For details, see 212.

> Nobody **will** ever **know** what happened to her.
>
> I think Liverpool **will win**.        I **shall** probably **be** home late tonight.

*Will* and *shall* are also used to express our intentions and attitudes towards other people: they are common in offers, requests, threats, promises and announcements of decisions. For details, see 217.

> **Shall** I **carry** your bag?        I**'ll hit** you if you do that again.
>
> I**'ll phone** you tonight.
>
> You can have it for half price. ~ OK. I'll buy it.

## 2 present forms: *I'm leaving; I'm going to leave*

When we talk about future events which have some present reality – which have already been planned or decided, or which we can see are on the way – we often use present forms. The present progressive is common. For details, see 214.

> I**'m seeing** John tomorrow.        What **are** you **doing** this evening?

The present progressive of *go* (*be going to . . .*) is often used as an auxiliary verb to talk about the future. For details, see 213.

> Sandra **is going to have** another baby.
>
> When **are** you **going to get** a job?

These present forms are especially common in speech (because conversation is often about future events which are already planned, or which we can see are on the way).

## 3 simple present: *the train leaves . . .*

The simple present can also be used to talk about the future, but only in certain situations. For details, see 215.

> The train **leaves** at half past six tomorrow morning.

## 4 other ways of talking about the future

We can use the future perfect to say that something will be completed, finished or achieved by a certain time. For details, see 219.

> By next Christmas we**'ll have been** here for eight years.

The future progressive can be used to say that something will be in progress at a particular time. For details, and other uses of this tense, see 220.

> This time tomorrow I**'ll be lying** on the beach.

*Be about* + **infinitive** (see 5) suggests that a future event is very close.
*The plane's **about to take off**. Is your seat belt done up?*
*Be* + **infinitive** is used to talk about plans, arrangements and schedules, and to give instructions. For details, see 91.
*The President **is to visit** Beijing in January.*
*You're **not to tell** anybody about this.*

## 5 'future in the past'

To say that something was still in the future at a certain past time, we can use a past form of one of the future structures. For details, see 221.
*Something **was going to** happen that **was to** change the world.*
*I knew she **would** arrive before long.*

## 6 subordinate clauses

In many subordinate clauses we refer to the future with present tenses instead of *shall/will* + **infinitive**. For details, see 580.
*Phone me when you **have** time.* (NOT ... *when you'll have time.*)
*I'll think of you when I'**m lying** on the beach next week.*
    (NOT ... *when I'll be lying on the beach ...*)
*I'll follow him wherever he **goes**.* (NOT ... *wherever he'll go.*)
*You can have anything I **find**.* (NOT ... *anything I'll find.*)

# 212 future (2): will/shall (information and prediction)

## 1 forms

> *will* + infinitive without *to*

*It **will be** cold tomorrow.*
*Where **will** you **spend** the night?*
Some British people use *I shall* and *we shall* instead of *I/we will*, with no difference of meaning in most situations. (For cases where there is a difference, see 217.) *Shall* is unusual in American English in most situations (but see 217).
Contractions: *I'll, you'll* etc; *shan't* /ʃɑːnt/ (BrE only), *won't* /wəʊnt/

## 2 use: giving information about the future; predicting

*Will* (or *shall*) + **infinitive** is used to give (or ask for) information about the future.
*It'**ll be** spring soon.     **Will** all the family **be** at the wedding?*
*We **shall need** the money on the 15th.*
*Karen **will start** work some time next week.*
*In another thirteen minutes the alarm **will go** off. This **will close** an electrical contact, causing the explosive to detonate.*
We often use *will/shall* in predictions of future events – to talk about what we think, guess or calculate will happen.
*Tomorrow **will be** warm, with some cloud in the afternoon.*
*Who do you think **will win** on Saturday?*
*I **shall be** rich one day.     You'**ll** never **finish** that book.*

▶

### 3 conditional use

*Will/shall* is often used to express conditional ideas, when we say what *will happen if* something else happens.

> He'll **have** an accident **if** he goes on driving like that.
> **If** the weather's fine, we'll **have** the party in the garden.
> Look out – you'll **fall!** (If you're not more careful.)
> Come out for a drink. ~ No, I'll **miss** the film on TV **if** I do.
> Don't leave me. I'll **cry!**

### 4 future events already decided: *will* not used

When future events are already decided, or when we can 'see them coming', we often prefer a present form (usually present progressive or *going to* . . .).

> I'm **seeing** the headmaster on Monday.    My sister's **going to have** a baby.

For details, see 213, 214 and 216.

### 5 not used in subordinate clauses: *when I arrive*

In subordinate clauses, we usually use present tenses instead of *will/shall* (see 580.2).

> I'll phone you when I **arrive.** (NOT . . . ~~when I will arrive.~~)

For exceptions, see 580.4,8, 260.

### 6 other uses of *will* and *shall*

*Will* and *shall* are not only used to give and ask for information about the future. They can also be used to express 'interpersonal' meanings such as requests, offers, orders, threats and promises. For details, see 217.

> **Shall** I **open** a window?        I'll **break** his neck!
> **Will** you **get** here at nine tomorrow, please?

For information about all uses of *will*, see 629.

## 213 future (3): going to ...

### 1 a present tense

This structure is really a present tense (the present progressive of *go*). We use it to talk about future actions and events that have some *present reality*. If we say that something in the future *is going to happen*, it is usually already planned or decided, or it is starting to happen, or we can see it coming now. The structure is very common in an informal style, especially in speech (because conversation is often about future actions and events of this kind).

### 2 plans: *We're going to get a new car*

We use *be going* + **infinitive** to talk about plans, especially in an informal style. This structure often emphasises the idea of intention, or a decision that has already been made.

*We're going to get a new car soon.*
*John says he's going to phone this evening.*
*When are you going to get your hair cut?*
*I'm going to keep asking her out until she says 'Yes'.*
*I'm going to stop him reading my letters if it's the last thing I do.*

## 3 things that are on the way: *She's going to have a baby*

Another use of the *going-to* structure is to predict the future on the basis of present evidence – to say that a future action or event is on the way, or starting to happen.

*Sandra's going to have another baby in June.*
*Look at the sky. It's going to rain.     Look out! We're going to crash!*

## 4 commands and refusals

*Going to* . . . can be used to insist that people do things or do not do things.
*You're going to finish that soup if you sit there all afternoon!*
*She's going to take that medicine whether she likes it or not!*
*You're not going to play football in my garden.*
It is also used in emphatic refusals.
*I'm not going to sit up all night listening to your problems!*

## 5 *gonna*

In informal speech, *going to* is often pronounced /gənə/. This is sometimes shown in writing as *gonna*, especially in American English.
*Nobody's gonna talk to me like that.*

For *was going to, has been going to* etc, see 221.
For *going to* . . . compared with the present progressive, see 214.2.
For a comparison with *will*, see 216.

# 214 future (4): present progressive

## 1 present reality: *I'm washing my hair this evening*

We use the present progressive for future actions and events that have some present reality. It is most common in discussions of personal arrangements and fixed plans, when the time and place have been decided.

*What are you doing this evening? ~ I'm washing my hair.*
*I'm seeing Larry on Saturday.*
*We're travelling round Mexico next summer.*
*Did you know I'm getting a new job?*
*What are we having for dinner?*
*My car's going in for a service next week.*

We often use the present progressive with verbs of movement, to talk about actions which are just starting.

*Are you coming to the pub?*
*I'm just popping out to the post office. Back in a minute.*
*Get your coat on! I'm taking you down to the doctor!*

Note that the simple present is not often used to talk about the future (see 215).

*What are you doing this evening?* (NOT ~~What do you do this evening?~~)  ▶

## 2 present progressive and *going to* ... : differences

In many cases, both structures can be used to express the same idea.
*I'm washing / going to wash my hair this evening.*
But there are some differences. For example, we prefer *going to* ... when we are talking not about fixed arrangements, but about intentions and decisions. Compare:
– *I'm seeing Phil tonight.* (emphasis on arrangement)
  *I'm really going to tell him what I think of him.* (emphasis on intention: NOT ~~I'm really telling him~~ ...)
– *Who's cooking lunch?* (asking what has been arranged)
  *Who's going to cook lunch?* (asking for a decision)
Because the present progressive is used especially for personal arrangements, it is not generally used to make predictions about events that are outside people's control.
*It's going to snow before long.* (NOT ~~It's snowing before long.~~)
*I can see that things are going to get better soon.* (NOT ... ~~things are getting better soon.~~)
And the present progressive is used for actions and events, but not usually for permanent states. Compare:
*Our house is getting / is going to get new windows this winter.*
*Their new house is going to look over the river.* (NOT ~~Their new house is looking over the river.~~)

## 3 commands and refusals

The present progressive can be used to insist that people do things or do not do things.
*You're finishing that soup if you sit there all afternoon!*
*She's taking that medicine whether she likes it or not!*
*You're not wearing that skirt to school.*
The present progressive is common in emphatic refusals.
*I'm sorry, you're not taking my car.*
*I'm not washing your socks – forget it!*

For a comparison with *will*, see 216.

# 215 future (5): simple present

## 1 timetables etc: *The summer term starts* ...

We can sometimes use the simple present to talk about the future. This is common when we are talking about events which are part of a timetable, a regular schedule or something similar.
*The summer term starts on April 10th.*
*What time does the bus arrive in Seattle?*
*My plane leaves at three o'clock.*
*Are you on duty next weekend?*
*The sun rises at 6.13 tomorrow.*
*Will* is also usually possible in these cases.

## 2 subordinate clauses: *when she gets a job*

The simple present is often used with a future meaning in subordinate clauses
– for example after *what, where, when, until, if, than*. For details, see 580.
*I'll tell you **what** I **find out**.* (NOT *. . . ~~what I'll find out~~.*)
*She'll pay us back **when** she **gets** a job.* (NOT *. . . ~~when she'll get a job~~.*)
*Alex will see us tomorrow **if** he **has** time.* (NOT *. . . ~~if he will have time~~.*)

## 3 instructions: *Where do I pay?*

Occasionally the simple present is used with a future meaning when asking for
and giving instructions.
*Where **do** I **pay?*** *Well, what **do** we **do** now?*
*So when you get to London you **go** straight to Victoria Station, you **meet** up
with the others, Ramona **gives** you your ticket, and you **catch** the 17.15
train for Dover. OK?*

## 4 other cases

In other cases, we do not usually use the simple present to talk about the
future.
*Lucy's **coming** for a drink this evening.* (NOT *~~Lucy comes~~ . . .*)
*I promise I'll **phone** you this evening.* (NOT *~~I promise I phone you this
evening~~.*)
*There's the doorbell.* ~ *I'll **go**.* (NOT *. . . ~~I go~~.*)

# 216 future (6): present forms or **will**?

*Will* is the 'basic' structure for talking about the future. We use *will* if there is
not a good reason for using present forms.

## 1 present reality

We prefer present forms (present progressive or *going to* . . .) when we are
talking about future events that have some present reality (see 213–214). In
other cases we use *will*. Compare:
– *I'm **seeing** Janet on Tuesday.* (The arrangement exists now.)
  *I wonder if she'll **recognise** me.* (not talking about the present)
– *We're **going to get** a new car.* (The decision already exists.)
  *I hope it **will be** better than the last one.* (not talking about the present)

## 2 predictions: thinking and guessing about the future

In predictions, we use *going to* when we have outside evidence for what we say
– for example black clouds in the sky, a person who is obviously about to fall.
*See those clouds? It's **going to rain**.* (NOT *~~See those clouds? It will rain~~.*)
*Look – that kid's **going to fall** off his bike.* (NOT *~~Look! That kid'll fall off his
bike~~.*)
We prefer *will* for predictions when there is not such obvious outside evidence
– when we are talking more about what is inside our heads: what we know, or
believe, or have calculated. (When we use *will*, we are not showing the listener
something; we are asking him or her to believe something.) Compare: ▶

- *Look out – we're going to crash!* (There is outside evidence.)
  *Don't lend him your car. He's a terrible driver – he'll crash it.* (the speaker's knowledge)
- *I've just heard from the builder. That roof repair's going to cost £7,000.* (outside evidence – the builder's letter)
  *I reckon it'll cost about £3,000 to put in new lights.* (the speaker's opinion)
- *Alice is going to have a baby.* (outside evidence – she is pregnant now)
  *The baby will certainly have blue eyes, because both parents have.* (speaker's knowledge about genetics)

# 217 future (7): will and shall (interpersonal uses)

## 1 differences between *will* and *shall*

*Will* and *shall* are not only used for giving information about the future. They are also common in offers, promises, orders and similar kinds of 'interpersonal' language use. In these cases, *will* (or *'ll*) generally expresses willingness or wishes (this is connected with an older use of *will* to mean 'wish' or 'want'). *Shall* expresses obligation (like a more direct form of *should*).

## 2 announcing decisions: *will*

We often use *will* when we tell people about a decision as we make it, for instance if we are agreeing to do something.
    *OK. We'll buy the tickets. You can buy supper after the show.*
    *The phone's ringing. ~ I'll answer it.* (NOT ~~I'm going to answer it.~~)
    *Remember to phone Joe, won't you? ~ Yes, I will.*
*Shall* is not used in this way.
    *You can have it for £50. ~ OK. I'll buy it.* (NOT . . . ~~I shall buy it.~~)
Note that the simple present is not normally used to announce decisions.
    *I think I'll go to bed.* (NOT ~~I think I go to bed.~~)
    *There's the doorbell. ~ I'll go.* (NOT . . . ~~I go.~~)
To announce decisions that have already been made, we generally prefer *going to . . .* or the present progressive (see 213–214).
    *Well, we've agreed on a price, and I'm going to buy it.*
    *I've made my decision and I'm sticking to it.*
Stressed *will* can express determination.
    *I will stop smoking! I really will!*

## 3 promises and threats: *will*

We often use *will/'ll* in promises and threats. Note that the simple present is not possible in these cases.
    *I promise I won't smoke again.* (NOT ~~I promise I don't smoke~~ . . .)
    *I'll phone you tonight.* (NOT ~~I phone~~ . . .)
    *I'll hit you if you do that again.     You'll suffer for this!*
*Shall* is also possible in British English after *I* and *we*, but it is less common than *will*.
    *I shall give you a teddy bear for your birthday.*
In older English, *shall* was often used with second and third person subjects in promises and threats. This is now very unusual.
    *You shall have all you wish for.     He shall regret this.*

## 4  refusals: *won't*

*Will not* or *won't* is used to refuse, or to talk about refusals.
> *I don't care what you say, I **won't do** it.*
> *The car **won't start**.*

## 5  asking for instructions and decisions: *shall*

Questions with *shall I/we* are used (in both British and American English) to ask for instructions or decisions, to offer services, and to make suggestions. *Will* is not used in this way.
> ***Shall I open** a window?* (NOT ~~Will I open a window?~~)
> ***Shall I carry** your bag?*
> *What time **shall we come** and see you?*
> *What on earth **shall we do**?*
> ***Shall we go** out for a meal?*
> *Let's go and see Lucy, **shall we**?*

## 6  giving instructions and orders: *will*

We can use *Will you ... ?* to tell or ask people to do things. (In polite requests, *Would you ... ?* is preferred – see 633.5.)
> ***Will you** get me a newspaper when you're out?*
> ***Will you** be quiet, please!   Make me a cup of coffee, **will you**?*

For reporting of interpersonal *shall* in indirect speech, see 278.4.

# 218  future (8): will/shall, going to and present progressive (advanced points)

## 1  *will/shall* and present forms: both possible

The differences between the structures used to talk about the future are not always very clear-cut. *Will/shall* and present forms (especially *going to ...* ) are often both possible in the same situation, if 'present' ideas like intention or fixed arrangement are a part of the meaning, but not very important. The choice can depend on which aspect we wish to emphasise.
- *What **will** you **do** next year?* (open question about the future; perhaps no clear plans have been made)
  *What **are** you **doing** next year?* (emphasis on fixed arrangements)
  *What are you **going to do** next year?* (emphasis on intentions)
- *All the family **will be** there.*
  *All the family **are going to be** there.*
- *If your mother comes, you'**ll have** to help with the cooking.*
  *If your mother comes, you'**re going to have** to help with the cooking.*   ▶

– *You **won't believe** this.*
*You're **not going to believe** this.*
– *Next year **will be** different.*
*Next year **is going to be** different.*
– *John **will explain** everything to you.*
*John's **going to explain** everything to you.*

Both *going to* . . . (see 213) and stressed *will* (see 217.2) can express a strong intention or determination.

*I'm really **going to stop** smoking!    I really **will stop** smoking!*

In cases like these, the different forms are all correct, and it is unimportant which one is chosen.

## 2  official arrangements

*Will* is often used, rather than present forms, in giving information about impersonal, fixed arrangements – for example official itineraries. Compare:

*We're **meeting** Sandra at 6.00.*
*The Princess **will arrive** at the airport at 14.00. She **will meet** the President at 14.30, and **will then** attend a performance of traditional dances.*

## 3  predictions as orders

Predictions can be used as a way of giving orders - instead of telling somebody to do something, the speaker just says firmly that it will happen. This is common in military-style orders.

*The regiment **will attack** at dawn.*
*You **will start** work at six o'clock sharp.*

## 4  different meanings of *will you* ...?

With a verb referring to a state, *will you* ...? asks for information.

*How soon **will you know** your holiday dates?*
*Will you be here next week?*

With a verb referring to an action, *will you* ...? usually introduces an order or request (see 217.6).

*Will you turn off that music!*
*Will you do the shopping this afternoon, please?*

To ask for information about planned actions, we use a present form (see 213–214) or the future progressive (see 220).

*When **are you going to see** Andy?*
*Are you **doing** the shopping this afternoon?*
*Will you **be doing** the shopping ...?*

## 5  expressing certainty about the present or past

We can use *will* to talk about the present – to say what we think is probably or certainly the case.

*There's somebody at the door. ~ That'll be the postman.*
*Don't phone them now – they'll be having dinner.*

*Will have* . . . can express similar ideas about the past.

*As you **will have noticed**, there is a new secretary in the front office.*
*It's no use expecting Barry to turn up. He'll **have forgotten**.*

For more about this and other uses of *will*, see 629.

## 6   obligation: *shall*

In contracts and other legal documents, *shall* is often used with third-person subjects to refer to obligations and duties.

> The hirer **shall be** responsible for maintenance of the vehicle.

In normal usage, we prefer *will*, *must* or *should* to express ideas of this kind.

# 219   future (9): future perfect (they will have finished)

> *will have* + past participle

We can use the future perfect to say that something will be finished or complete by a certain time in the future.

> The builders say they **will have finished** the roof by Tuesday.
> **I'll have spent** all my holiday money by the end of the week.

*Shall* can be used instead of *will* after *I* and *we* (see 212.1).

> I **shall have spent** . . .

A progressive form can be used to talk about a continuous activity.

> **I'll have been teaching** for twenty years this summer.

For *will have* . . . used to express certainty about the past (e.g. *It's no use phoning – he'll have left by now*), see 218.5, 629.

# 220   future (10): future progressive

> *shall/will* + *be* + . . .*ing*

## 1   events in progress in the future

We can use the future progressive to say that something will be in progress (going on) at a particular moment in the future.

> This time tomorrow **I'll be lying** on the beach.
> Good luck with the exam. **We'll be thinking** of you.

## 2   events that are fixed or expected to happen

The future progressive is also used (without a progressive meaning) to refer to future events which are fixed or decided, or which are expected to happen in the normal course of events.

> Professor Baxter **will be giving** another lecture on Roman glass-making at the same time next week.
> **I'll be seeing** you one of these days, I expect.

## 3   no idea of making decisions

The future progressive is useful if we want to show that we are not talking about making decisions, but about things that will happen 'anyway'.

> Shall I pick up the laundry for you? ~ Oh, no, don't make a special journey.
> ~ It's OK. **I'll be going** to the shops anyway.                    ▶

The tense can be used to make polite enquiries about people's plans. (By using the future progressive to ask 'What have you already decided?', the speaker shows that he/she does not want to influence the listener's intentions.) Compare:

>*Will you **be staying** in this evening?* (very polite enquiry, suggesting 'I simply want to know your plans')
>*Are you **going to stay** in this evening?* (pressing for a decision)

This usage is possible with verbs that do not normally have progressive forms (see 471).

>*Will you be **wanting** lunch tomorrow?*

### 4 progressive form with *going to*

A progressive form of the *going to* structure is also possible.

>*I'm **going to be working** all day tomorrow, so I won't have time to shop.*

For *will be . . .ing* used to express certainty about the present (e.g. *Don't phone now – they'll be having lunch*), see 218.5, 629.

## 221 future (11): future in the past

Sometimes when we are talking about the past, we want to talk about something which was in the future at that time – which had not yet happened. To express this idea, we use the structures that are normally used to talk about the future (see 211–220), but we make the verb forms past. For example, instead of *is going to* we use *was going to*; instead of the present progressive we use the past progressive; instead of *will* we use *would*; instead of *is to* we use *was to*.

>*Last time I saw you, you **were going to start** a new job.*
>*I had no time to shop because I **was leaving** for Germany in two hours.*
>*In 1988 I arrived in the town where I **would spend** ten years of my life.*
>*I went to have a look at the room where I **was to talk** that afternoon.*

Perfect forms of *be going to* are also possible.

>*I've **been going to write** to you for ages, but I've only just found time.*

For **was to have** + **past participle** (e.g. *She was to have taken over my job, but she fell ill*), see 91.1.

## 222 gender (references to males and females)

English does not have many problems of grammatical gender. Usually, people are *he* or *she* and things are *it*. Note the following points.

### 1 animals, cars, ships and countries

People sometimes call animals *he* or *she*, especially when they are thought of as having personality, intelligence or feelings. This is common with pets and domestic animals like cats, dogs and horses.

>*Once upon a time there was a rabbit called Joe. **He** lived . . .*
>*Go and find the cat and put **her** out.*

In these cases, *who* is often used instead of *which*.

>*She had an old dog **who** always slept in her bed.*

Some people use *she* for cars, motorbikes etc; sailors often use *she* for boats and ships (but most other people use *it*).

> *How's your new car?* ~ *Terrific.* **She's** *running beautifully.*
> *The ship's struck a rock.* **She's** *sinking!*

We can use *she* for countries, but *it* is more common in modern English.

> *France has decided to increase* **its** *trade with Romania.*
> (OR ... **her** *trade* ...)

## 2   *he or she*

Traditionally, English has used *he/him/his* when the sex of a person is not known, or in references that can apply to either men or women, especially in a formal style.

> *If a student is ill,* **he** *must send* **his** *medical certificate to the College office.*
> *If I ever find the person who did that, I'll kill* **him**.

Many people now regard such usage as sexist and try to avoid it. *He or she, him or her* and *his or her* are common.

> *If a student is ill,* **he or she** *must send a medical certificate* ...

## 3   unisex *they*

In an informal style, we often use *they* to mean 'he or she', especially after indefinite words like *somebody, anybody, nobody, person*. This usage is sometimes considered 'incorrect', but it has been common in educated speech for centuries. For details, see 528.

> *If anybody wants my ticket,* **they** *can have it.*
> *There's somebody at the door.* ~ *Tell* **them** *I'm out.*
> *When a person gets married,* **they** *have to start thinking about* **their**
>   *responsibilities.*

## 4   *actor* and *actress* etc

A few jobs and positions have different words for men and women. Examples:

| Man | Woman | Man | Woman |
|---|---|---|---|
| *actor* | *actress* | *monk* | *nun* |
| *(bride)groom* | *bride* | *policeman* | *policewoman* |
| *duke* | *duchess* | *prince* | *princess* |
| *hero* | *heroine* | *steward* | *stewardess* |
| *host* | *hostess* | *waiter* | *waitress* |
| *manager* | *manageress* | *widower* | *widow* |

A *mayor* can be a man or a woman; in Britain a *mayoress* is the wife of a male mayor.

Some words ending in *-ess* (e.g. *authoress, poetess*) have gone out of use (*author* and *poet* are now used for both men and women). The same thing is happening to *actress* and *manageress*. *Steward* and *stewardess* are being replaced by other terms such as *flight attendant*, and *police officer* is often used instead of *policeman/woman*.

## 5   words ending in *-man*

Some words ending in *-man* do not have a common feminine equivalent (e.g. *chairman, fireman, spokesman*). As many women dislike being called, for example, 'chairman' or 'spokesman', these words are now often avoided in ►

references to women or in general references to people of either sex. In many cases, *-person* is now used instead of *-man*.

> *Alice has just been elected* **chairperson** *(or* **chair***) of our committee.*
> *A* **spokesperson** *said that the Minister does not intend to resign.*

In some cases, new words ending in *-woman* (e.g. *spokeswoman*) are coming into use. But there is also a move to choose words, even for men, which are not gender-marked (e.g. *supervisor* instead of *foreman*, *ambulance staff* instead of *ambulance men*, *firefighter* instead of *fireman*).

### 6   man

*Man* and *mankind* have traditionally been used for the human race.

> *Why does* **man** *have more diseases than animals?*
> *That's one small step for a man, one giant leap for* **mankind***.*
>   (Neil Armstrong, on stepping onto the moon)

Some people find this usage sexist, and prefer terms such as *people*, *humanity* or *the human race*. Note also the common use of *synthetic* instead of *man-made*.

### 7   titles

*Ms* (pronounced /mɪz/ or /məz/) is often used instead of *Mrs* or *Miss*. Like *Mr*, it does not show whether the person referred to is married or not.

For more information about names and titles, see 363.

## 223   get (1): basic structures

*Get* is one of the commonest words in English, and is used in many different ways. It is sometimes avoided in a very formal style, but it is correct and natural in most kinds of speech and writing. The meaning of *get* depends on what kind of word comes after it. With a direct object, the basic meaning is 'obtain', 'come to have'; with other kinds of word, the basic meaning is 'become', 'come to be'.

### 1   *get + noun/pronoun: I got a letter*

With a direct object (noun or pronoun), *get* usually means 'receive', 'fetch', 'obtain', 'catch' or something similar. The exact meaning depends on the object.

> *I* **got a letter** *from Lucy this morning.*
> *Can you come and* **get me** *from the station when I arrive?*
> *If I listen to loud music I* **get a headache***.*
> *If you* **get a number 6 bus***, it stops right outside our house.*

*Get* can be used with two objects (see 610).

> *Let me* **get you a drink***.*

Other meanings are sometimes possible.

> *I didn't* **get** *the joke.* (= understand)
> *I'll* **get** *you for this, you bastard.* (= punish, make suffer)

*Get* + noun is not normally used to mean 'become'. To express this meaning, we can use *get to be* + noun (see paragraph 6 below).

> *Wayne's* **getting to be** *a lovely kid.* (NOT ~~Wayne's getting a lovely kid.~~)

## 2 get + adjective: *getting old*

Before an adjective, *get* usually means 'become'.

*As you **get old**, your memory **gets worse**.*
*My feet are **getting cold**.*

With **object + adjective**, the meaning is 'make somebody/something become'.

*It's time to **get the kids ready** for school.*
*I can't **get my hands warm**.*
*We must **get the house clean** before Mother arrives.*

For **go + adjective** (*go green, go blind* etc), and the differences between *get, go, become, turn* etc, see 128.

## 3 get + adverb particle or preposition: *get out*

Before an adverb particle (like *up, away, out*) or a preposition, *get* nearly always refers to a movement of some kind. (For the difference between *get* and *go*, see 225.)

*I often **get up** at five o'clock.*
*I went to see him, but he told me to **get out**.*
*Would you mind **getting off** my foot?*

In some idioms the meaning is different – e.g. *get to a place* (= arrive at . . .); *get over something* (= recover from); *get on with somebody* (= have a good relationship with).

With an object, the structure usually means 'make somebody/something move'.

*You can't **get him out of** bed in the morning.*
*Would you mind **getting your papers off** my desk?*
*Have you ever tried to **get toothpaste back** into the tube?*
*The car's OK – it **gets me from** A to B.*

## 4 get + past participle: *get washed, dressed, married* etc

*Get* can be used with a past participle. This structure often has a reflexive meaning, to talk about things that we 'do to ourselves'. Common expressions are *get washed, get dressed, get lost, get drowned, get engaged/married/divorced*.

*You've got five minutes to **get dressed**.*
*She's **getting married** in June.*

## 5 passive auxiliary: *He got caught*

*Get* + past participle is also used to make passive structures, in the same way as *be* + past participle.

*My watch **got broken** while I was playing with the children.*
*He **got caught** by the police driving at 120 mph.*
*I **get paid** on Fridays.*     *I never **get invited** to parties.*

This structure is mostly used in an informal style, and it is not often used to talk about longer, more deliberate, planned actions.

*Our house **was built** in 1827.* (NOT ~~Our house got built in 1827.~~)
*Parliament **was opened** on Thursday.* (NOT ~~Parliament got opened . . .~~)     ▶

## 6  *get ...ing; get + infinitive*

*Get ...ing* is sometimes used informally to mean 'start ...ing', especially in the expressions *get moving, get going*.

> *We'd better **get moving** – it's late.*

With an infinitive, *get* can mean 'manage', 'have an opportunity' or 'be allowed'.

> *We didn't **get to see her** – she was too busy.*
> *When do I **get to meet** your new boyfriend?*

*Get + infinitive* can also suggest gradual development.

> *He's nice when you **get to know** him.*
> *You'll **get to speak** English more easily as time goes by.*
> *Wayne's **getting to be** a lovely kid.*

## 7  *got* and *gotten*

In British English the past participle of *get* is *got*. In American English the past participle is *gotten* (e.g. *You've **gotten** us in a lot of trouble.*) except in the structure *have got* (see 237).

# 224  get (2): + object + verb form

## 1  causative: *Don't get him talking*

*Get + object + ...ing* means 'make somebody/something start ...ing'.

> *Don't **get him talking** about his illnesses.*
> *Once we **got the heater going** the car started to warm up.*

## 2  causative: *Get Penny to help us*

*Get + object + infinitive* means 'make somebody/something do something' or 'persuade somebody/something to do something': there is often an idea of difficulty.

> *I can't **get that child to go** to bed.*
> ***Get Penny to help** us if you can.*      *See if you can **get the car to start**.*

For *have + object + infinitive* (meaning 'order/instruct somebody to do something'), see 238.1.

## 3  causative: *get something done*

*Get + object + past participle* can mean 'cause something to be done by somebody else'. The past participle has a passive meaning.

> *I must **get my watch repaired**.* (= I want my watch to be repaired.)
> *I'm going to **get my hair cut** this afternoon.*

*Have* is used in a similar structure: see 238.2.

## 4  experience: *We got our roof blown off*

*Get + object + past participle* can sometimes be used in the sense of 'experience'.

> *We **got our roof blown off** in the storm last week.*

This idea is more often expressed with have (e.g. *We had our roof blown off.*) – see 238.3.

**5** *Get the children dressed*

We can also use *get* + **object** + **past participle** to talk about completing work on something.

> *It will take me another hour to* ***get the washing done***.
> *After you've* ***got the children dressed***, *can you make the beds?*

# 225 **get** and **go**: movement

*Go* is used to talk about a whole movement.
*Get* is used when we are thinking mainly about the end of a movement – the arrival. Compare:

> – *I* ***go*** *to work by car and Lucy* ***goes*** *by train.*
>   *I usually* ***get*** *there first.*
> – *I* ***went*** *to a meeting in Bristol yesterday.*
>   *I* ***got*** *to the meeting at about eight o'clock.*

We often use *get* to suggest that there is some difficulty in arriving.

> *It wasn't easy to* ***get*** *through the crowd.*
> *I don't know how we're going to* ***get*** *over the river.*
> *Can you tell me how to* ***get*** *to the police station?*

For *get* and *go* meaning 'become', see 128.

# 226 **give** with action-nouns

**1** *give a cough*, etc

We can replace certain verbs by a structure with *give* and a noun. This often happens in BrE, for example, with verbs referring to sounds made by people (e.g. *cough, cry, scream, chuckle, laugh, shout*).

> *He* ***gave a cough*** *to attract my attention.*
> *Suddenly she* ***gave a loud scream*** *and fell to the ground.*

**2** *give somebody a smile*, etc

The structure is also used with an indirect object (in both BrE and AmE) to replace transitive verbs, especially in an informal style. Common expressions:

*give somebody a smile, a look, a kiss, a hug, a ring* (BrE = a phone call)
*give something a push, a kick*
*give it a try, a go* (BrE = a try), *a shot* (AmE = a try)
*give it a miss* (BrE)
*not give it a thought*

> *She* ***gave me a strange look***.
> *I'll* ***give you a ring*** *if I hear anything.*
> *If the car won't start, we'll* ***give it a push***.
> *Perhaps salt will make it taste better.* ~ *OK, let's* ***give it a try***.
> *Are you coming to the film?* ~ *No, I'm tired. I'll* ***give it a miss***. (BrE)
> *He seemed to be in a bad temper, but I didn't* ***give it a thought***.

For taboo expressions like *I don't give a damn/shit* etc, see 575.
For other structures in which nouns replace verbs, see 598.
For more about structures with *give*, see 610.

# 227 go/come for a ...

We can use the structure *go/come for a ...* in some fixed expressions referring to actions, mostly leisure activities. Using this structure makes the action sound casual and probably rather short. (Compare *go ...ing* – see 228.) Common examples:

*go/come for a walk, a run, a swim, a ride, a drive, a drink, a meal*
*go for a bath, a shower, a pee/piss* (taboo – see 575).

> *We need some fresh air. Let's **go for a walk**.*
> *Would you like to **come for a drink** this evening?*
> *I'm **going for a shower**. Can you answer my phone if it rings?*

This structure is only used with certain action-nouns – we would probably not say, for example, *Come for a ski with us* or *I'm going for a read*.

For other structures in which nouns are used to refer to actions, see 598.

# 228 go/come ...ing

## 1 *go ...ing*

We use *go* with an *-ing* form to talk about activities in which people move about, and which do not have a fixed beginning or end. The structure is common in expressions referring to sport and leisure activities – for example *go climbing, go dancing, go fishing, go hunting, go riding, go sailing, go shooting, go skating, go skiing, go swimming, go walking.*

> *Let's **go climbing** next weekend.*
> *Did you **go dancing** last Saturday?*

*Go ...ing* is also used to talk about looking for or collecting things.

> *I think I'll **go shopping** tomorrow.*
> *In June all the students **go looking** for jobs.*
> *Anne's **going fruit-picking** this weekend.*

We do not use *go ...ing* to talk about activities that have a more definite beginning and end (NOT *go boxing, go watching a football match*).

## 2 *come ...ing*

*Come ...ing* is also possible in certain situations (for the difference between *come* and *go*, see 134).

> ***Come swimming*** *with us tomorrow.*

## 3 prepositions

Note that prepositions of place, not direction, are used after *go/come ...ing*.

> *I went swimming **in** the river.* (NOT *I went swimming to the river.*)
> *She went shopping **at** Harrods.* (NOT *... to Harrods.*)

# 229 gone with be

Gone can be used like an adjective after be, to say that somebody is away, or that something has disappeared or that there is no more.

> She's **been gone** for three hours – what do you think she's doing?
> You can go out shopping, but don't **be gone** too long.
> When I came back my car **was gone**.      Is the butter all **gone**?

For been used as a past participle of go or come, see 95.

# 230 had better

## 1 meaning

We use had better to give strong advice, or to tell people what to do (including ourselves).

> You'd **better** turn that music down before your Dad gets angry.
> It's seven o'clock. I'd **better** put the meat in the oven.

Had better refers to the immediate future. It is more urgent than should or ought. Compare:

> I really **ought** to go and see Fred one of these days. ~ Well, you'd **better** do it soon – he's leaving for South Africa at the end of the month.

Had better is not used in polite requests. Compare:

> **Could you** help me, if you've got time? (request)
> **You'd better** help me. If you don't, there'll be trouble. (order/threat)

Note that had better does not usually suggest that the action recommended would be better than another one that is being considered – there is no idea of comparison. The structure means 'It would be good to . . .', not 'It would be better to . . .'.

## 2 forms

Had better refers to the immediate future, but the form is always past (have better is impossible). After had better we use the infinitive without to.

> It's late – you **had** better **hurry** up.
>     (NOT . . . ~~you have better~~ . . .)
>     (NOT . . . ~~you had better hurrying / to hurry~~ . . .)

We normally make the negative with **had better not + infinitive**.

> You'd **better not wake** me up when you come in.
>     (You hadn't better wake me . . . is possible but very unusual.)

A negative interrogative form Hadn't . . . better . . .? is possible.

> **Hadn't** we **better** tell him the truth?

Normal unemphatic short answer forms are as follows:

> Shall I put my clothes away? ~ **You'd better!**
> He says he won't tell anybody. ~ **He'd better not.**

Had is sometimes dropped in very informal speech.

> **You better** go now.      I **better** try again later.

## 231 half

### 1 *half (of)*

We can use *half* or *half of* before a noun with a determiner (article, possessive or demonstrative). We do not normally put *a* or *the* before *half* in this case.

> *She spends **half (of) her time** travelling.* (NOT *She spends a/the half...*)
> *I gave him **half (of) a cheese pie** to keep him quiet.*

When *half (of)* is followed by a plural noun, the verb is plural.

> *Half (of) my friends live abroad.* (NOT *Half of my friends lives...*)

*Of* is not used in expressions of measurement and quantity.

> *I live **half a mile** from here.* (NOT *...half of a mile...*)
> *I just need **half a loaf** of bread.* (NOT *...half of a loaf...*)

We use *half of* before pronouns.

> *Did you like the books?* ~ *I've only read **half of them**.*

### 2 no following noun

*Half* can be used without a following noun, if the meaning is clear.

> *I've bought some chocolate. You can have **half**.* (NOT *...the half.*)

### 3 *the half*

We use *the* before *half* if we are saying which half we mean. Before a noun, *of* is used in this case.

> *Would you like **the big half** or **the small half**?*
> *I didn't like **the second half of** the film.*

### 4 *half a* and *a half*

*Half* usually comes before the article *a/an*, but it is possible to put it after in expressions of measurement.

> *Could I have **half a pound** of grapes?* (OR *...a half pound...*)

### 5 *one and a half*

The expression *one and a half* is plural. Compare:

> *I've been waiting for **one and a half hours**.* (NOT *...one and a half hour.*)
> *I've been waiting for **an hour and a half**.*

For more information about numbers and counting expressions, see 389.
For *half* in clock times (e.g. *half past two*), see 579.

## 232 happen to ...

*Happen* can be used with a following infinitive to suggest that something happens unexpectedly or by chance.

> *If you **happen to see** Joan, ask her to phone me.*
> *One day I **happened to get** talking to a woman on a train, and she turned out to be a cousin of my mother's.*

In sentences with *if* or *in case*, the idea of *by chance* can be emphasised by using *should* before *happen*.

> *Let me know if you **should happen** to need any help.*
> *I'll take my swimming things, in case I **should happen** to find a pool open.*

# 233  **hardly, scarcely** and **no sooner**

These three expressions can be used (often with a past perfect tense – see 423) to suggest that one thing happened very soon after another. Note the sentence structure:

> ... *hardly* ... *when/before* ...
> ... *scarcely* ... *when/before* ...
> ... *no sooner* ... *than* ...

*I had **hardly/scarcely** closed my eyes **when** the phone rang.*
*She was **hardly/scarcely** inside the house **before** the kids started screaming.*
*I had **no sooner** closed the door **than** somebody knocked.*
*We **no sooner** sat down in the train **than** I felt sick.*

In a formal or literary style, inverted word order is possible (see 302).

> ***Hardly had I** closed my eyes when I began to imagine fantastic shapes.*
> ***No sooner had she** agreed to marry him than she started to have doubts.*

# 234  **have** (1): introduction

*Have* is used in several different ways:

a  as an auxiliary verb, to make perfect verb forms
   ***Have** you **heard** about Peter and Corinne?*
   *I remembered his face, but I **had forgotten** his name.*

b  to talk about possession, relationships and other states
   *They **have** three cars.*
   ***Have** you **got** any brothers or sisters?*
   ***Do** you often **have** headaches?*

c  to talk about actions and experiences
   *I'm going to **have** a bath.*
   *We're **having** a party next weekend.*

d  with an infinitive, to talk about obligation (like *must*)
   *I **had to work** last Saturday.*

e  with object + verb form, to talk about causing or experiencing actions
   and events
   *He soon **had everybody laughing**.*
   *I must **have my shoes repaired**.*
   *We **had our car stolen** last week.*

For details of the different structures and meanings, see the following sections.

For contractions (*I've, haven't* etc), see 143.
For weak forms, see 616.
For **had better** + **infinitive**, see 230.

## 235 have (2): auxiliary verb

*have* + past participle

### 1 perfect verb forms

We use *have* as an auxiliary verb with past participles, to make 'perfect' verb forms.

> *You've heard about Peter and Corinne?* (present perfect: see 455–460)
> *I realised that I had met him before.* (past perfect: see 423–425)
> *We'll have been living here for two years next Sunday.*
>  (future perfect: see 219)
> *I'd like to have lived in the eighteenth century.*
>  (perfect infinitive: see 280)
> *Having been there before, he knew what to expect.*
>  (perfect participle: see 408.2a)

### 2 questions and negatives

Like all auxiliary verbs, *have* makes questions and negatives without *do*.

> *Have you heard the news?* (NOT ~~Do you have heard~~...?)
> *I haven't seen them.* (NOT ~~I don't have seen them.~~)

### 3 progressive forms

There are no progressive forms of the auxiliary verb *have*.

> *I haven't seen her anywhere.* (NOT ~~I'm not having seen her anywhere.~~)

For contractions, see 143.
For weak forms, see 616.

## 236 have (3): actions

### 1 meaning and typical expressions

We often use **have + object** to talk about actions and experiences, especially in an informal style.

> *Let's have a drink.*
> *I'm going to have a bath.*
> *I'll have a think* (BrE) *and let you know what I decide.*
> *Have a good time.*

In expressions like these, *have* can be the equivalent of 'eat', 'drink', 'enjoy', 'experience' or many other things - the exact meaning depends on the following noun. Common expressions:

> *have breakfast / lunch / supper / dinner / tea / coffee / a drink / a meal*
> *have a bath / a wash / a shave / a shower*
> *have a rest / a lie-down / a sleep / a dream*
> *have a good time / a bad day / a nice evening / a day off / a holiday*
> *have a good journey / flight / trip etc*
> *have a talk / a chat / a word with somebody / a conversation / a disagreement /*
>  *a row / a quarrel / a fight*

*have a swim / a walk / a ride / a dance / a game of tennis* etc
*have a try / a go*
*have a look*
*have a baby* (= give birth)
*have difficulty / trouble (in)* …*ing*
*have an accident / an operation / a nervous breakdown*

Note American English *take a bath/shower/rest/swim/walk.*
*Have* can also be used to mean 'receive' (e.g. *I've had a phone call from Sue*).

## 2 grammar

In this structure, we make questions and negatives with *do*. Progressive forms are possible. Contractions and weak forms of *have* are not used.
**Did** *you* **have** *a good holiday?* (NOT ~~Had you a good holiday?~~)
*What are you doing?* ~ *I'm **having** a bath.*
*I **have** lunch at 12.30 most days.* (NOT ~~I've lunch~~ …)

For other common structures in which nouns are used to talk about actions, see 598.

# 237 have (4): have (got) – possession, relationships and other states

## 1 meanings

We often use *have* to talk about states: possession, relationships, illnesses, the characteristics of people and things, and similar ideas.
*Her father **has** a flat in Westminster.*
*They hardly **have** enough money to live on.*
**Do** *you* **have** *any brothers or sisters?*
*The Prime Minister **had** a bad cold.*
*My grandmother **didn't have** a very nice personality.*
Sometimes *have* simply expresses the fact of being in a particular situation.
*She **has** a houseful of children this weekend.*
*I think we **have** mice.*

## 2 progressive forms not used

Progressive forms of *have* are not used for these meanings.
*She **has** three brothers.* (NOT ~~She is having three brothers.~~)
**Do** *you* **have** *a headache?* (NOT ~~Are you having a headache?~~)

## 3 questions and negatives with *do*

In American English and modern British English, questions and negatives are commonly formed with *do*.
**Does** *the house* **have** *a garden?*
*Her parents **did** not **have** very much money.*

▶

## 4 shorter question and negative forms: *Have you ...?; she has not*

Short question and negative forms (e.g. *Have you ...?, she has not*) were common in older English. In modern English they are rather formal and uncommon (except in a few fixed expressions like *I haven't the faintest idea*). They are not normally used in American English.
- *Have you an appointment?* (formal BrE only)
  *Do you have an appointment?* (AmE/BrE)
- *Angela has not the charm of her older sisters.* (formal BrE only)
  *Angela does not have the charm ...* (AmE/BrE)

## 5 have got

In conversation and informal writing, we often use the double form *have got*.
  *I've got a new boyfriend.* (More natural in speech than *I have a new boyfriend.*)
  *Has your sister got a car?*    *I haven't got your keys.*
Note that *have got* means exactly the same as *have* in this case – it is a present tense of *have*, not the present perfect of *get*.

## 6 have got (details)

*Do* is not used in questions and negatives with *got*.
  *Have you got a headache?* (NOT *Do you have got...*)
  *The flat hasn't got a proper bathroom.* (NOT *The flat doesn't have got...*)
*Got*-forms of *have* are not used in short answers or tags.
  *Have you got a light?* ~ *No, I haven't.* (NOT *No, I haven't got.*)
  *Anne's got a bike, hasn't she?*
*Got*-forms of *have* are less common in the past tense.
  *I had flu last week.* (NOT *I had got flu...*)
  *Did you have good teachers when you were at school?*
*Got* is not generally used with infinitives, participles or *-ing* forms of *have*: you cannot usually say *to have got a headache* or *having got a brother*. The infinitive of *have got* is occasionally used after modal verbs (e.g. *She must have got a new boyfriend*).
*Have got* is rather less common in American English, especially in questions and negatives.
In very informal American speech, people may drop *'ve* (but not *'s*) before *got*.
  *I('ve) got a problem.*
*Got*- and *do*-forms may be mixed in American English, especially when short answers, reply questions and tags follow *got*-forms.
  *I've got a new apartment.* ~ *You do?*

## 7 repetition: *got* not used

When we are talking about repeated or habitual states, *got*-forms of *have* are less often used. Compare:
- *I have / I've got toothache.*
  *I often have toothache.*
- *Do you have / Have you got time to go to London this weekend?*
  *Do you ever have time to go to London?*
- *Sorry, I don't have / haven't got any beer.*
  *We don't usually have beer in the house.*

## 8 repetition: a change in British English

Traditionally, *do*-forms of *have* were used in British English mostly to express habit or repetition. Compare (BrE):

> *Do you often **have** meetings?*
> ***Have** you (got) a meeting today?*

In modern British English (which is heavily influenced by American English), *do*-forms are common even when there is no idea of repetition.

> *Do you **have** time to go to the beach this weekend?* (AmE / modern BrE)

# 238  have (5): + object + verb form

*Have* can be followed by **object + infinitive (without *to*)**, **object + -*ing***, and **object + past participle**.

## 1 causative: *have somebody do/doing something*

*Have* + **object** + **infinitive** can mean 'cause somebody to do something'. This is mostly used in American English, to talk about giving instructions or orders.

> *I'm ready to see Mr Smith. **Have him come in**, please.*
> *The manager **had everybody fill out** a form.*

The structure with an -*ing* form can mean 'cause somebody to be doing something' (BrE and AmE).

> *He **had us laughing** all through the meal.*

For *get* + **object** + **infinitive** (meaning 'persuade somebody/something to do something'), see 224.2.

## 2 causative: *have something done*

*Have* + **object** + **past participle** can mean 'cause something to be done by somebody else'. The past participle has a passive meaning.

> *I must **have my watch repaired**. (= I want my watch to be repaired.)*
> *I'm going to **have my hair cut** this afternoon.*
> *If you don't get out of my house I'll **have you arrested**.*

*Get* is used in a similar structure: see 224.3.

## 3 experience: *have something happen/happening*

In the structure *have* + **object** + **infinitive/. . .*ing***, *have* can mean 'experience'.

> *I **had a very strange thing happen** to me when I was fourteen.*
> *We **had a gipsy come** to the door yesterday.*
> *It's lovely to **have children playing** in the garden again.*
> *I looked up and found we **had water dripping** through the ceiling.*

Note the difference between the infinitive in the first two examples (for things that happened), and the -*ing* form in the last two (for things that are/were happening). This is like the difference between simple and progressive tenses (see 461, 422).

▶

### 4 experience: *We had our roof blown off*

*Have* + **object** + **past participle** can also be used in the sense of 'experience'.
Again, the past participle has a passive meaning.

> We **had our roof blown off** in the storm.
> King Charles **had his head cut off**.
> She's just **had a short story published** in a magazine.

### 5 *I won't have ...*

*I won't have* + **object** + **verb form** can mean 'I won't allow ...'

> I won't **have you telling** me what to do.
> I won't **have my house turned** into a hotel.

## 239 have (6): have (got) to

### 1 meaning: obligation, certainty

We can use *have (got)* + **infinitive** to talk about obligation: things that it is
necessary for us to do. The meaning is quite similar to *must*; for the
differences, see 361.1.

> Sorry, **I've got to go** now.
> Do you often **have to travel** on business?

*Have (got)* + **infinitive** can also be used, like *must*, to express certainty. (This
used to be mainly an American English structure, but it is now becoming
common in British English.)

> I don't believe you. You **have (got) to be** joking.
> Only five o'clock! **It's got to be** later than that!

### 2 grammar: with or without *do; got*

In this structure, *have* can be used like an ordinary verb (with *do* in questions
and negatives), or like an auxiliary verb (without *do*). *Got* is usually added to
present-tense auxiliary-verb forms.

> When **do you have** to be back?    When **have you (got)** to be back?

*Have got to* is not normally used to talk about repeated obligation.

> I usually **have to be** at work at eight. (NOT ~~I've usually got to~~...)

Progressive forms are possible to talk about temporary continued obligation.

> **I'm having to work** very hard at the moment.

For more details of the use of *do*-forms and *got*-forms of *have*, see 237.

### 3 future: *have (got) to* or *will have to*

To talk about the future, we can use *have (got) to* if an obligation exists now;
we use *will have to* for a purely future obligation. Compare:

> **I've got to get up** early tomorrow – we're going to Devon.
> One day everybody **will have to ask** permission to buy a car.

*Will have to* can be used to tell people what to do. It 'distances' the
instructions, making them sound less direct than *must* (see 361).

> You can borrow my car, but you'll **have to bring** it back before ten.

For more about 'distancing', see 436.

## 4 pronunciation of *have to; gotta*

*Have to* is often pronounced /ˈhæftə/.
*He'll have to* /ˈhæftə/ *get a new passport soon.*
Note the spelling *gotta*, sometimes used in informal American English (for instance in cartoon strips) to show the conversational pronunciation of *got to*.
*I **gotta** call home.    A man's **gotta** do what a man's **gotta** do.*

# 240 headlines

## 1 special language

Headlines are the short titles above news reports (e.g. *RUSSIAN WOMAN LANDS ON MOON*). English news headlines can be very difficult to understand. One reason for this is that headlines are often written in a special style, which is very different from ordinary English. In this style there are some special rules of grammar, and words are often used in unusual ways.

## 2 grammar

a   Headlines are not always complete sentences. Many headlines consist of noun phrases with no verb.
   *MORE WAGE CUTS        HOLIDAY HOTEL DEATH*
   *EXETER MAN'S DOUBLE MARRIAGE BID*

b   Headlines often contain strings of three, four or more nouns; nouns earlier in the string modify those that follow.
   *FURNITURE FACTORY PAY CUT ROW*
   Headlines like these can be difficult to understand. It sometimes helps to read them backwards. *FURNITURE FACTORY PAY CUT ROW* refers to a *ROW* (disagreement) about a *CUT* (reduction) in *PAY* at a *FACTORY* that makes *FURNITURE*.

c   Headlines often leave out articles and the verb *be*.
   *SHAKESPEARE PLAY IMMORAL SAYS HEADMASTER*
   *SCHOOLBOY WALKS IN SPACE*

d   In headlines, simple tenses are often used instead of progressive or perfect forms. The simple present is used for both present and past events.
   *BLIND GIRL CLIMBS EVEREST* (= ... has climbed ...)
   *STUDENTS FIGHT FOR COURSE CHANGES* (= ... are fighting ...)
   The present progressive is used to talk about changes. *Be* is usually dropped.
   *BRITAIN GETTING WARMER, SAY SCIENTISTS*
   *TRADE FIGURES IMPROVING*

e   Many headline words are used as both nouns and verbs, and nouns are often used to modify other nouns (see paragraph 2b). So it is not always easy to work out the structure of a sentence. Compare:
   *US CUTS AID TO THIRD WORLD* (= The US reduces its help ... *CUTS* is a verb, *AID* is a noun.)                                                    ▶

*AID CUTS ROW* (= There has been a disagreement about the reduction in aid. *AID* and *CUTS* are both nouns.)
*CUTS AID REBELS* (= The reduction is helping the revolutionaries. *CUTS* is a noun, *AID* is a verb.)

f   Headlines often use infinitives to refer to the future.
*PM TO VISIT AUSTRALIA*
*HOSPITALS TO TAKE FEWER PATIENTS*
*For* is also used to refer to future movements or plans.
*TROOPS FOR GLASGOW?* (= Are soldiers going to be sent to Glasgow?)

g   Auxiliary verbs are usually dropped from passive structures.
*MURDER HUNT: MAN HELD* (= ... a man is being held by police. )
*SIX KILLED IN EXPLOSION* (= Six people have been killed ...)
Note that forms like *HELD*, *ATTACKED* are usually past participles with passive meanings, not past tenses (which are rare in headlines). Compare:
– *AID ROW: PRESIDENT ATTACKED* (= ... the President has been attacked.)
*AID ROW: PRESIDENT ATTACKS CRITICS*
    (= ... the President has attacked her critics.)
– *BOY FOUND SAFE* (= The missing boy has been found safe; he is safe.)
*BOY FINDS SAFE* (= A boy has found a safe.)

h   *As* and *in* are often used instead of longer connecting expressions.
*HOSPITAL BOSS AXED AS PATIENTS DIE* (= ... because patients die.)
*FOOTBALL MANAGER IN CAR CRASH*

i   A colon (:) is often used to separate the subject of a headline from what is said about it.
*STRIKES: PM TO ACT*   *MOTORWAY CRASH: DEATH TOLL RISES*
Quotation marks ('...') are used to show that words were said by somebody else, and that the report does not necessarily claim that they are true.
*CRASH DRIVER 'HAD BEEN DRINKING'*
A question mark (?) is often used when something is not certain.
*CRISIS OVER BY SEPTEMBER?*

For other styles with special grammar, see 1.

## 3   vocabulary

Short words save space, and so they are very common in headlines. Some of the short words in headlines are unusual in ordinary language (e.g. *curb*, meaning 'restrict' or 'restriction'), and some are used in special senses which they do not often have in ordinary language (e.g. *bid*, meaning 'attempt'). Other words are chosen not because they are short, but because they sound dramatic (e.g. *blaze*, which means 'big fire', and is used in headlines to refer to any fire). The following is a list of common headline vocabulary.

**act**  take action; do something
*FOOD CRISIS: GOVERNMENT TO ACT*
**aid**  military or financial help; to help
*MORE AID FOR POOR COUNTRIES*
*UNIONS AID HOSPITAL STRIKERS*
**alert**  alarm, warning
*FLOOD ALERT ON EAST COAST*

**allege** make an accusation
*WOMAN ALLEGES UNFAIR TREATMENT*
**appear** appear in court accused of a crime
*MP TO APPEAR ON DRUGS CHARGES*
**axe** abolish, close down; abolition, closure
*COUNTRY BUS SERVICES AXED*
*SMALL SCHOOLS FACE AXE*

**BA** British Airways
*BA MAKES RECORD LOSS*
**back** support
*AMERICA BACKS BRITISH PEACE MOVE*
**ban** forbid, refuse to allow something; prohibition
*US BANS STEEL IMPORTS*
*NEW BAN ON DEMONSTRATIONS*
**bar** refuse/refusal to allow entry
*HOTEL BARS FOOTBALL FANS*
*NEW BAR ON IMMIGRANTS*
**bid** attempt
*JAPANESE WOMEN IN NEW EVEREST BID*
**blast** explosion; criticise violently
*BLAST AT PALACE*
*PM BLASTS CRITICS*
**blaze** fire
*SIX DIE IN HOTEL BLAZE*
**block** stop, delay
*TORIES BLOCK TEACHERS' PAY DEAL*
**blow** bad news; discouragement; unfortunate happening
*SMITH ILL: BLOW TO WORLD CUP HOPES*
**bolster** give support/encouragement to
*EXPORT FIGURES BOLSTER CITY CONFIDENCE*
**bond** political/business association
*NEW TRADE BONDS WITH ICELAND*
**boom** big increase; prosperous period
*SPENDING BOOM OVER, SAYS MINISTER*
**boost** encourage(ment); to increase; an increase
*PLAN TO BOOST EXPORTS*
**brink** edge (of disaster)
*WORLD ON BRINK OF WAR*
**Brussels** the European Community parliament and administration
*BRUSSELS BANS BRITISH BLACKBERRY WINE*

**call (for)** demand/appeal (for)
*CALL FOR STRIKE TALKS*
*HOSPITAL ROW: MP CALLS FOR ENQUIRY*
**campaign** organised effort to achieve social or political result
*MP LAUNCHES CAMPAIGN FOR PRISON REFORM*
**cash** money
*MORE CASH NEEDED FOR SCHOOLS*
**charge** accusation (by police)
*THREE MEN HELD ON BOMB CHARGE*

▶

**chop**  abolition, closure
*300 BANK BRANCHES FACE CHOP*
**City**  London's financial institutions
*NEW TRADE FIGURES PLEASE CITY*
**claim**  (make) a statement that something is true (especially when there may be disagreement); **pay claim** demand for higher wages
*SCIENTIST CLAIMS CANCER BREAKTHROUGH*
*RACISM CLAIM IN NAVY*
*TEACHERS' PAY CLAIM REJECTED*
**clamp down on**  deal firmly with (usually something illegal)
*POLICE TO CLAMP DOWN ON SPEEDING*
**clash**  quarrel, fight (noun or verb)
*PM IN CLASH OVER ARMS SALES*
*STUDENTS CLASH WITH POLICE*
**clear**  find innocent
*DOCTOR CLEARED OF DRUGS CHARGE*
**Commons**  the House of Commons (in Parliament)
*MINISTERS IN COMMONS CLASH OVER HOUSING*
**con**  swindle
*TEENAGERS CON WIDOW OUT OF LIFE SAVINGS*
**crackdown**  firm application of the law
*GOVERNMENT PROMISES CRACKDOWN ON DRUGS DEALERS*
**crash**  financial failure
*BANK CRASH THREATENS TO BRING DOWN GOVERNMENT*
**curb**  restrict; restriction
*NEW PRICE CURBS*
**cut**  reduce; reduction
*BRITAIN CUTS OVERSEAS AID*
*NEW HEALTH SERVICE CUTS*
**cutback**  reduction (usually financial)
*TEACHERS SLAM SCHOOL CUTBACKS*

**dash**  (make) quick journey
*PM IN DASH TO BLAST HOSPITAL*
**deadlock**  disagreement that cannot be solved
*DEADLOCK IN PEACE TALKS*
**deal**  agreement, bargain
*TEACHERS REJECT NEW PAY DEAL*
**demo**  demonstration
*30 ARRESTED IN ANTI-TAX DEMO*
**dole**  unemployment pay
*DOLE QUEUES LENGTHEN*
**drama**  dramatic event; tense situation
*PRINCE IN AIRPORT DRAMA*
**drive**  united effort
*DRIVE TO SAVE WATER*
**drop**  give up, get rid of; fall (noun)
*GOVERNMENT TO DROP CHILD LABOUR PLAN*
*BIG DROP IN INDUSTRIAL INVESTMENT*
**due**  expected to arrive
*QUEEN DUE IN BERLIN TODAY*

**duo**  two people
  *HANDICAPPED DUO ROW ACROSS ATLANTIC*

**EU**  The European Union
  *EU TRADE MINISTERS TO MEET*
**edge**  move gradually
  *WORLD EDGES TOWARDS WAR*
**envoy**  ambassador
  *FRENCH ENVOY DISAPPEARS*

**face**  be threatened by
  *HOSPITALS FACE MORE CUTS*      *STRIKERS FACE SACK*
**feud**  long-lasting quarrel or dispute
  *FAMILY FEUD EXPLODES INTO VIOLENCE: SIX HELD*
**find**  something that is found
  *BEACH FIND MAY BE BONES OF UNKNOWN DINOSAUR*
**firm**  determined not to change
  *PM FIRM ON TAX LEVELS*
**flak**  heavy criticism
  *GOVERNMENT FACES FLAK OVER VAT*
**flare**  begin violently
  *RIOTS FLARE IN ULSTER*
**foil**  prevent somebody from succeeding
  *TWELVE-YEAR-OLD FOILS BANK RAIDERS*
**fraud**  swindle, deceit
  *JAIL FOR TICKET FRAUD MEN*
**freeze**  keep(ing) prices etc at their present level; block(ing) a bank account
  *MINISTER WANTS TWO-YEAR PAY FREEZE*
  *DRUG PROFITS FROZEN*
**fuel**  provide reason for growth (of anger, protest etc)
  *PAY FREEZE FUELS UNION ANGER*

**gag**  censor(ship), prevent(ion) from speaking
  *AFRICAN PRESIDENT ACTS TO GAG PRESS*
**gems**  jewels
  *£2m GEMS STOLEN*
**go**  resign; be lost, disappear
  *PM TO GO?*
  *4,000 JOBS TO GO IN NORTH*
**go for**  be sold for
  *PICASSO DRAWING GOES FOR £5m*
**go-ahead**  approval
  *SCOTTISH ROAD PLAN GETS GO-AHEAD*
**grab**  take violently
  *INVESTORS GRAB SHARES IN SCOTTISH COMPANIES*
**grip**  control; hold tightly
  *REBELS TIGHTEN GRIP ON SOUTH*
  *COLD WAVE GRIPS COUNTRY*
**gun down**  shoot
  *TERRORISTS GUN DOWN PRIEST*

▶

**hail**  welcome, praise
*PM HAILS PEACE PLAN*
**halt**  stop
*CAR PLANT TO HALT PRODUCTION*
**haul**  amount stolen in robbery, or seized by police or customs
*TRAIN ROBBERY: BIG GOLD HAUL*
*RECORD DRUGS HAUL AT AIRPORT*
**head**  lead; leader
*PM TO HEAD TRADE MISSION*
*COMMONWEALTH HEADS TO MEET IN OTTAWA*
**head for/to**  move towards
*ECONOMY HEADING FOR DISASTER, EXPERTS WARN*
**heed**  pay attention to
*GOVERNMENT MUST HEED DIVORCE FIGURES, SAYS BISHOP*
**hike**  (AmE) rise in costs, prices etc
*INTEREST HIKE WILL HIT BUSINESS*
**hit**  affect badly
*SNOWSTORMS HIT TRANSPORT*
**hit out at**  attack (with words)
*PM HITS OUT AT CRITICS*
**hitch**  problem that causes delay
*LAST-MINUTE HITCH DELAYS SATELLITE LAUNCH*
**hold**  arrest; keep under arrest
*MAN HELD AFTER STATION BLAST*
*POLICE HOLD TERROR SUSPECT*

**in (the) red**  in debt; making a financial loss
*BRITISH STEEL IN RED*
**IRA**  Irish Republican Army
*IRA LEADER MAKES STATEMENT*

**jail**  prison
*JAIL FOR PEACE MARCHERS*
**jobless**  unemployed (people)
*THREE MILLION JOBLESS BY APRIL?*

**key**  important, vital
*KEY WITNESS VANISHES*

**landslide**  victory by large majority in election
*LANDSLIDE FOR NATIONALISTS*
**lash**  criticise violently
*BISHOP LASHES TV SEX AND VIOLENCE*
**launch**  send (satellite etc) into space; begin (campaign etc); put (new
product) on market
*SPACE TELESCOPE LAUNCH DELAYED*
*ENVIRONMENT MINISTER LAUNCHES CAMPAIGN FOR CLEANER
  BEACHES*
*BRITISH FIRM LAUNCHES THROW-AWAY CHAIRS*
**lead**  clue (in police enquiry)
*NEW LEAD IN PHONEBOX MURDER CASE*

**leak**  unofficial publication of secret information
*PM FURIOUS OVER TAX PLAN LEAKS*
**leap**  big increase
*LEAP IN IMPORTS*
**life**  imprisonment 'for life'
*LIFE FOR AXE MURDERER*
**link**  connection, contact
*NEW TRADE LINKS WITH PERU*
**loom**  threaten to happen
*VAT ON FOOD: NEW ROW LOOMS*
**Lords**  the House of Lords (in Parliament)
*LORDS VOTE ON DOG REGISTRATION*
**lotto**  the national lottery
*DANCING GRANDMOTHER IN RECORD LOTTO WIN*

**mar**  spoil
*CROWD VIOLENCE MARS CUP FINAL*
**mercy**  intended to save lives
*DOCTOR IN MERCY DASH TO EVEREST*
**mission**  delegation (official group sent to conference etc)
*SHOTS FIRED AT UN MISSION*
**mob**  angry crowd; organised crime / Mafia (AmE)
*MOBS RAMPAGE THROUGH CITY STREETS*
*MOB LEADERS HELD*
**move**  step towards a particular result (often political)
*MOVE TO BOOST TRADE LINKS WITH JAPAN*
**MP**  Member of Parliament
*MP DENIES DRUGS CHARGE*
**MEP**  Member of the European Parliament
*MEPS WANT MORE PAY*

**nail**  force somebody to admit the truth
*MP NAILS MINISTER ON PIT CLOSURE PLANS*
**net**  win, capture
*TWO SISTERS NET £3m IN POOLS WIN*
**no 10**  the Prime Minister's residence (No 10 Downing Street)
*ANOTHER PETITION HANDED IN AT No 10*

**OAP**  old age pensioner; anybody over 65
*OAPS MARCH AGAINST WAR PLANS*
**odds**  chances, probability
*JONES RE-ELECTED AGAINST THE ODDS*
**on**  about, on the subject of, concerning
*NEW MOVE ON PENSIONS*
**opt (for)**  choose
*WALES OPTS FOR INDEPENDENCE*
**oust**  drive out, replace
*MODERATES OUSTED IN UNION ELECTIONS*
**out to**  intending to
*NATIONALISTS OUT TO CAPTURE MASS VOTE*

▶

**over** about, on the subject of, because of
*ROW OVER AID CUTS*

**pact** agreement
*DEFENCE PACT RUNS INTO TROUBLE*
**pay** wages
*TRANSPORT PAY TALKS BREAK DOWN*
**PC** police constable
*PC SHOT IN BANK RAID*
**peak** high point
*BANK LENDING HITS NEW PEAK*
**peer** lord; Member of the House of Lords
*PEERS REJECT GOVERNMENT WAGE-FREEZE BAN*
**peg** hold (prices etc) at present level
*BANKS PEG INTEREST RATES*
**pensioner** old age pensioner; anybody over 65
*PENSIONER SKIS DOWN MONT BLANC*
**peril** danger
*FLOOD PERIL IN THAMES VALLEY*
**pit** coal mine
*PIT TURNED INTO MUSEUM*
**plant** factory
*STEEL PLANT BLAZE*
**plea** call for help
*BIG RESPONSE TO PLEA FOR FLOOD AID*
**pledge** promise
*GOVERNMENT GIVES PLEDGE ON JOBLESS*
**PM** Prime Minister
*EGG THROWN AT PM*
**poised to** ready to, about to
*TORIES POISED TO MAKE ELECTION GAINS*
**poll** election; public opinion survey
*TORIES AHEAD IN POLLS*
**pools** football pools: a form of gambling in which people guess the results of football matches
*SISTERS SHARE BIG POOLS WIN*
**premier** head of government
*GREEK PREMIER TO VISIT UK*
**press** the newspapers
*BID TO GAG PRESS OVER DEFENCE SPENDING*
**press (for)** urge, encourage, ask for urgently
*MINISTER PRESSED TO ACT ON HOUSING*
*OPPOSITION PRESS FOR ENQUIRY ON AIR CRASHES*
**probe** investigation; investigate
*CALL FOR STUDENT DRUGS PROBE*
*POLICE PROBE RACING SCANDAL*
**pull out** withdraw; **pull-out** withdrawal
*US PULLS OUT OF ARMS TALKS*
*CHURCH CALLS FOR BRITISH PULL-OUT FROM ULSTER*
**push (for)** ask for, encourage
*SCHOOLS PUSH FOR MORE CASH*

**quake** earthquake
*HOUSES DAMAGED IN WELSH QUAKE*
**quit** resign, leave
*CHURCH LEADER QUITS*
*MINISTER TO QUIT GOVERNMENT*
**quiz** question (verb)
*POLICE QUIZ MILLIONAIRE SUPERMARKET BOSS*

**raid** enter and search; attack (noun and verb), rob, robbery
*POLICE RAID DUCHESS'S FLAT*
*BIG GEMS RAID*
**rampage** riot
*FOOTBALL FANS RAMPAGE THROUGH SEASIDE TOWNS*
**rap** criticise
*DOCTORS RAP NEW MINISTRY PLANS*
**rates** (bank) interest rates
*RATES RISE EXPECTED*
**record** bigger than ever before
*RECORD LOSS BY INSURANCE FIRM*
**riddle** mystery
*MISSING ENVOY RIDDLE: WOMAN HELD*
**rift** division, disagreement
*LABOUR RIFT OVER DEFENCE POLICY*
**rock** shock, shake
*BANK SEX SCANDAL ROCKS CITY*
*IRELAND ROCKED BY QUAKE*
**row** noisy disagreement, quarrel
*NEW ROW OVER PENSION CUTS*
**rule out** reject the possibility of
*PM RULES OUT AUTUMN ELECTION*

**sack** dismiss(al) from job
*STRIKING POSTMEN FACE SACK*
**saga** long-running news story
*NEW REVELATIONS IN BANK SEX SAGA*
**scare** public alarm, alarming rumour
*TYPHOID SCARE IN SOUTHWEST*
**scoop** win (prize etc)
*PENSIONER SCOOPS LOTTO FORTUNE*
**scrap** throw out (as useless)
*GOVERNMENT SCRAPS NEW ROAD PLANS*
**seek** look for
*POLICE SEEK WITNESS TO KILLING*
**seize** take (especially in police and customs searches)
*POLICE SEIZE ARMS AFTER CAR CHASE*
*£3m DRUGS SEIZED AT AIRPORT*
**set to** ready to; about to
*INTEREST RATES SET TO RISE*
**shed** get rid of
*CAR FIRM TO SHED 5,000 JOBS*

▶

**slam**  criticise violently
  *BISHOP SLAMS DEFENCE POLICY*
**slash**  cut, reduce drastically
  *GOVERNMENT TO SLASH HEALTH EXPENDITURE*
**slate**  criticise
  *PM SLATES BISHOP*
**slay**  (AmE) murder
  *FREEWAY KILLER SLAYS SIX*
**slump**  fall (economic)
  *EXPORTS SLUMP      CITY FEARS NEW SLUMP*
**snatch**  rob, robbery
  *BIG WAGES SNATCH IN WEST END*
**soar**  rise dramatically
  *IMPORTS SOAR FOR THIRD MONTH*
**spark**  cause (trouble) to start
  *REFEREE'S DECISION SPARKS RIOT*
**split**  disagree(ment)
  *CABINET SPLIT ON PRICES POLICY*
**spree**  wild spending expedition
  *BUS DRIVER SPENDS £30,000 IN THREE-DAY CREDIT CARD SPREE*
**stake**  financial interest
  *JAPANESE BUY STAKE IN BRITISH AIRWAYS*
**storm**  angry public disagreement
  *STORM OVER NEW STRIKE LAW*
**storm out of**  leave angrily
  *TEACHERS' LEADERS STORM OUT OF MEETING*
**stun**  surprise, shock
  *JOBLESS FIGURES STUN CITY*
**surge**  sudden increase; rise suddenly
  *SURGE IN JOBLESS FIGURES*
**swap**  exchange
  *HEART SWAP BOY BETTER*
**sway**  persuade
  *HOSPITAL PROTEST SWAYS MINISTERS*
**switch**  to change; a change
  *DEFENCE POLICY SWITCH*
**swoop**  to raid; a police raid
  *POLICE IN DAWN SWOOP ON DRUGS GANG*

**threat**  danger
  *TEACHERS' STRIKE THREAT*
**toll**  number killed
  *QUAKE TOLL MAY BE 5,000*
**top**  (adj) senior, most important
  *TOP BANKER KIDNAPPED*
**top**  (verb) exceed
  *IMPORTS TOP LAST YEAR'S FIGURES*
**Tory**  Conservative
  *VICTORY FOR TORY MODERATES*
**trio**  three people
  *JAILBREAK TRIO RECAPTURED*

**troops** soldiers
*MORE TROOPS FOR BORDER AREA*

**UK** The United Kingdom (of Great Britain and Northern Ireland)
*BRUSSELS CRITICISES UK JAIL CONDITIONS*
**Ulster** Northern Ireland
*PM IN SECRET TRIP TO ULSTER*
**UN** The United Nations
*UN IN RED: CANNOT BALANCE BUDGET*
**urge** encourage
*GOVERNMENT URGED TO ACT ON POLLUTION*
**US** The United States of America
*US URGED TO PULL OUT OF MIDDLE EAST*

**VAT** value added tax
*NEXT, VAT ON BABYFOOD?*
**vow** promise
*EXILED PRESIDENT VOWS TO RETURN*

**walk out** leave in protest
*CAR WORKERS WALK OUT OVER WAGE FREEZE*
**web** world-wide web, internet
*WEB SHOPPING UP BY 50% IN TWO YEARS*
**wed** marry
*BISHOP TO WED ACTRESS*

# 241 hear and listen (to)

## 1 *hear*: meaning

*Hear* is the ordinary word to say that something 'comes to our ears'.
> *Suddenly I **heard** a strange noise.* (NOT *Suddenly I listened to a strange noise.*)
> *Can you **hear** me?*

## 2 *listen (to)*: meaning

*Listen (to)* is used to talk about paying attention to sounds that are going on, in progress. It emphasises the idea of concentrating, trying to hear as well as possible. You can hear something without wanting to, but you can only listen to something deliberately. Compare:
> *I **heard** them talking upstairs, but I didn't really **listen** to their conversation.*
> ***Listen** carefully, please.* ~ *Could you speak louder? I can't **hear** you very well.*
> *I didn't **hear** the phone because I was **listening** to the radio.*

## 3 complete experiences: *hear*

*Listen (to)* is mostly used to talk about concentrating on experiences that are going on, in progress. To talk about the result of listening: experiencing or

▶

understanding the whole of a performance, speech, piece of music, broadcast or other communication, we generally use *hear*. Compare:

- *When she arrived, I was **listening to** a record of Brendel playing Beethoven.* (NOT *...~~I was hearing~~...*)

  *I once **heard** Brendel play all the Beethoven concertos.* (NOT *I ~~once listened to Brendel play~~...*)

- *I wish I had more time to **listen to** the radio.* (NOT *...~~to hear the radio.~~*)

  *Did you **hear** / **listen to** the news yesterday?*

### 4  *hear* not used in progressive forms

*Hear* is not usually used in progressive forms. To say that one hears something at the moment of speaking, *can hear* is often used, especially in British English (see 125).

*I **can hear** somebody coming.* (NOT *~~I am hearing~~...*)

### 5  *listen* and *listen to*

When there is no object, *listen* is used without *to*. Compare:

**Listen!** (NOT *~~Listen to!~~*)    **Listen to** me! (NOT *~~Listen me!~~*)

There are similar differences between *see, look (at)* and *watch*. See 506.
For *hear* + object + infinitive/-*ing*, see 242.

# 242  hear, see etc + object + verb form

### 1  object + infinitive or -*ing* form

*Hear, see, watch, notice* and similar verbs of perception can be followed by object + infinitive (without *to*) or object + -*ing* form.

*I **heard him go** down the stairs.*    *I **heard him going** down the stairs.* (NOT *~~I heard him went down the stairs.~~*)

There is often a difference of meaning. After these verbs, an infinitive suggests that we hear or see the whole of an action or event; an -*ing* form suggests that we hear or see something in progress, going on. Compare:

- *I **saw her cross** the road.* (= I saw her cross it from one side to the other.)

  *I **saw her crossing** the road.* (= I saw her in the middle, on her way across.)

- *I once **heard him give** a talk on Japanese politics.*

  *As I walked past his room I **heard him talking** on the phone.*

- **Watch me jump** over the stream.

  *I like to **watch people walking** in the street.*

- *I **heard the bomb explode**.* (NOT *~~I heard the bomb exploding.~~*)

  *I **saw the book lying** on the table.* (NOT *~~I saw the book lie~~...*)

A progressive form can suggest repetition.

*I **saw her throwing** stones at the other children.*

After *can see/hear* (which refer to actions and events that are in progress – see 125), only the -*ing* structure is used.

*I **could see** John **getting** on the bus.* (NOT *~~I could see John get~~...*)

These structures can be used after passive forms of *hear* and *see*. In this case, the infinitive has *to*.

He **was** never **heard to say** 'thank you' in his life. (NOT ~~He was never heard say~~...)

Justice must not only be done; it must **be seen to be done**.

She **was seen walking** away from the accident.

Passive forms of *watch* and *notice* are not used in this way.

## 2 possessives not used

After these verbs, possessives cannot be used with *-ing* forms.

I saw **Mary** crossing the road. (NOT ~~I saw Mary's crossing the road.~~)

## 3 object + past participle

In this structure, the past participle has a passive meaning.

I **heard my name repeated** several times. (= My name was repeated.)

Have you ever **seen a television thrown** through a window?

The idea of 'action or event in progress' can be given by a progressive form (**being** + **past participle**).

As I watched the tree **being cut** down ...

I woke up to hear the bedroom door **being opened** slowly.

These structures are not possible after passive forms of *hear* and *see*.

## 4 *look at*

*Look at* can be followed by **object + -ing form**, and in American English also by **object + infinitive**.

Look at him **eating!**   Look at him **eat!** (AmE)

For more about verbs that can be followed by both infinitives and *-ing* forms, see 299.
For the difference between *hear* and *listen*, see 241.
For *see, look* and *watch*, see 506.

# 243 hear, see etc with **that**-clause

The present-tense forms *I hear (that)* ... and *I see (that)* ... are often used to introduce pieces of news which one has heard, read or seen on television.

**I hear (that)** Alice is expecting a baby.

**I see (that)** the firemen are going on strike.

Some other verbs can be used like this. Common examples are *understand* and *gather*. These are often used to check information.

**I understand** you're moving to a new job. ~ Yes, that's right.

**I gather** you didn't like the party. ~ What makes you say that?

# 244 help

After *help*, we can use **object + infinitive** (with or without *to*).

Can you **help me (to) find** my ring? (NOT ~~Can you help me finding my ring?~~)

Thank you so much for **helping us (to) repair** the car.

Our main task is to **help the company (to) become** profitable.

*Help* can also be followed directly by an infinitive without an object.

Would you like to **help wash up**?

For the expression *can't help ...ing*, see 126.

## 245 here and there

We use *here* for the place where the speaker/writer is, and *there* for other places.

(on the telephone) *Hello, is Tom **there**? ~ No, I'm sorry, he's not **here**.*
(NOT *...~~he's not there.~~*)
*Don't stay **there** in the corner by yourself. Come over **here** and talk to us.*
Note that *here* and *there* cannot normally be used as nouns.
*This place is terrible.      It is terrible here.* (BUT NOT *~~Here is terrible.~~*)
*Did you like that place?* (BUT NOT *~~Did you like there?~~*)

There are similar differences between *this* and *that* (see 589), *come* and *go* (see 134) and *bring* and *take* (see 112).
For *here's* and *there's* followed by plural nouns, see 532.4.
For inverted word order after *here* and *there*, see 303.1.
For *Here you are*, see 545.18.

## 246 high and tall

### 1 What kind of things are *tall*?

We use *tall* mostly for people, trees, buildings with many floors, and a few other things which are higher than they are wide (e.g. factory chimneys or electricity pylons).
*How **tall** are you?* (NOT *~~How high are you?~~*)
*There are some beautiful **tall** trees at the end of our garden.*
In other cases we usually prefer *high*.
*Mount Elbrus is the **highest** mountain in Europe.*
*The garden's got very **high** walls.*

### 2 measurements

In measurements, we use *tall* for people, but we prefer *high* for things. Compare:
*I'm 1m 93 **tall**.      That tree is about 30m **high**.*

### 3 distance above the ground

We use *high* to talk about distance above the ground. A child standing on a chair may be *higher* than her mother, although she is probably not *taller*.
*That shelf is too **high** for me to reach.*
*The clouds are very **high** today.*

### 4 parts of the body

Parts of the body can be *long*, but not *tall*.
*Alex has got beautiful **long** legs.* (NOT *... ~~tall legs.~~*)

## 247 hire, rent and let

### 1 *hire* and *rent*

*Hire* and *rent* can mean: 'pay for the use of something'. In British English, *rent* is used for arrangements involving a long period of time (one rents a house, a flat, a TV). For shorter periods (e.g. paying for a car, a boat, evening dress) *rent* and *hire* can both be used.

> *How much does it cost to **rent** a two-room flat?*
> *I need to **hire/rent** a car for the weekend.*

*Hire (out)* and *rent (out)* can also mean 'sell the use of something'.

> *There's a shop in High Street that **hires/rents (out)** evening dress.*

In American English, *rent* is the normal word for both longer and shorter arrangements; *hire*, in American English, normally means 'employ'.

## 2 let

*Let* is used in British English, like *rent (out)*, to talk about selling the use of rooms, houses etc.

> *We **let** the upstairs room to a student.*

# 248 holiday and holidays

In British English, the plural *holidays* is often used for the 'long holiday' of the year. In other cases we normally use the singular *holiday*. Compare:

> *Where are you going for your summer **holiday(s)**?*
> *We get five days' Christmas **holiday** this year.*
> *Next Monday is a public **holiday**.*

The singular is used in the British expression *on holiday* (note the preposition).

> *I met Marianne **on holiday** in Norway.* (NOT ... ~~on/in holidays~~ ...)

Americans more often use the word *vacation*. (In British English, *vacation* is mainly used for the periods when universities are not teaching.) *Holiday* is most often used in American English for a day of publicly observed celebration (such as Thanksgiving) when people do not have to work.

# 249 home

## 1 articles and prepositions

No article is used in the expression *at home* (meaning 'in one's own place').

> *Is anybody **at home**?* (NOT ... ~~at the home?~~)

*At* is often dropped, especially in American English.

> *Is anybody **home**?*

*Home* (without *to*) can be used as an adverb referring to direction.

> *I think I'll go **home**.* (NOT ... ~~to home.~~)

There is no special preposition in English to express the idea of being at somebody's home (like French *chez*, German *bei*, Danish/Swedish/Norwegian *hos* etc). One way of saying this is to use *at* with a possessive.

> *We had a great evening **at Philip's**.*
> *Ring up and see if Jacqueline is **at the Smiths'**, could you?*

Possessive pronouns cannot be used in this way, though.

> *Come round to my place for a drink.* (NOT ... ~~to mine~~ ...)          ▶

## 2 *house* and *home*

*House* is an emotionally neutral word: it just refers to a particular type of building. *Home* is used more personally: it is the place that somebody lives in, and can express the idea of emotional attachment to a place. Compare:

*There are some horrible new **houses** in our village.*
*I lived there for six years, but I never really felt it was my **home**.*

## 250 hope

### 1 tenses after *hope*

After *I hope*, we often use a present tense with a future meaning.

*I hope she **likes** (= will like) the flowers.*
*I hope the bus **comes** soon.*

For a similar use of present tenses after *bet*, see 103.

### 2 negative sentences

In negative sentences, we usually put *not* with the verb that comes after *hope*.

*I hope she **doesn't wake up**.* (NOT ~~I don't hope she wakes up.~~)

For negative structures with *think, believe* etc, see 369.

### 3 special uses of past tenses

We can use *I was hoping* ... to introduce a polite request.

*I **was hoping** you could lend me some money.*
*I had hoped* ... refers to hopes for things that did not happen.
*I **had hoped** that Jennifer would study medicine, but she didn't want to.*

For more about the use of past tenses in polite requests, see 436.
For *I hope so/not*, see 539.
For the differences between *hope, expect, wait* and *look forward*, see 196.

## 251 hopefully

One meaning of *hopefully* is 'full of hope', 'hoping'.

*She sat there waiting **hopefully** for the phone to ring.*
Another, more recent meaning is 'it is to be hoped that' or 'I hope'.
***Hopefully**, inflation will soon be under control.*
***Hopefully** I'm not disturbing you?*

## 252 how

### 1 use and word order

*How* is used to introduce questions or the answers to questions.

***How** did you do it?*
*Tell me **how** you did it.*
*I know **how** he did it.*

We also use *how* in exclamations (see 195). The word order is not the same as in questions. Compare:
– *How cold **is it**?*
  *How cold **it is**!*
– *How **do you like** my hair?*
  *How **I love** weekends!* (NOT *How do I love weekends!*)
– *How **have you** been?*
  *How **you've** grown!* (NOT *How have you grown!*)
When *how* is used in an exclamation with an adjective or adverb, this comes immediately after *how*.
  *How **beautiful** the trees are!* (NOT *How the trees are beautiful!*)
  *How **well** she plays!* (NOT *How she plays well!*)

For the difference between *how* and *what like*, see 253.

## 2 with adjectives/adverbs: *how*, not *how much*

We use *how*, not *how much*, before adjectives and adverbs.
  *How **tall** are you?* (NOT *How much tall are you?*)
  *Show me how **fast** you can run.* (NOT *. . . how much fast . . .*)

## 3 comparisons: *how* not used

In comparisons we use *as* or *like* (see 326) or *the way* (see below), not *how*.
  *Hold it in both hands, **as / like / the way** Mummy does.*
      (NOT *. . . how Mummy does.*)

## 4 *how, what* and *why*

These three question words can sometimes be confused. Note particularly the following common structures.
  ***How** do you know?* (NOT *Why do you know?*)
  ***What** do you call this?* (NOT *How do you call this?*)
  ***What's** that . . . called?* (NOT *How is that . . . called?*)
  ***What** do you think?* (NOT *How do you think?*)
  ***What? What** did you say?* (NOT *How? How did you say?*)
  ***Why** should I think that?*
Both *What about . . .?* and *How about . . .?* are used to make suggestions, and to bring up points that have been forgotten.
  ***What/How about** eating out this evening?*
  ***What/How about** the kids? Who's going to look after them?*
In exclamations (see 195), *what* is used before noun phrases; *how* is used before adjectives (without nouns), adverbs and verb phrases.
  ***What** a marvellous house!*
  ***How** marvellous!    **How** you've changed!*

## 5 *how much, how many, how old, how far* etc

Many interrogative expressions of two or more words begin with *how*. These are used to ask for measurements, quantities etc. Examples:
  *How **much** do you weigh?*
  *How **many** people were there?*
  *How **old** are your parents?*
  *How **far** is your house?    How **often** do you come to New York?*    ▶

Note that English does not have a special expression to ask for ordinal numbers (*first, second* etc).

> *It's our wedding anniversary. ~ Congratulations. Which one?* (NOT *... the how-manyeth?*)

## 6 *how*-clauses in sentences

*How*-clauses are common as the objects of verbs like *ask, tell, wonder* or *know*, which can introduce indirect questions.

> *Don't ask me **how the journey was**.*
> *Tell us **how you did it**.*
> *I wonder **how animals talk to each other**.*
> *Does anybody know **how big the universe is**?*

*How*-clauses can also be used as subjects, complements or adverbials, especially in a more informal style.

> ***How you divide up the money*** *is your business.* (subject)
> *This is **how much I've done** since this morning.* (complement after *be*)
> *I spend my money **how I like**.* (adverbial)

## 7 *the way*

*The way* (see 615) can often be used instead of non-interrogative *how*. Note that *the way* and *how* are not used together.

> *Look at **the way** those cats wash each other.* OR *Look at **how** those cats ...*
> (NOT *... the way how those cats wash ...*)
> ***The way** you organise the work is for you to decide.* OR ***How** you organise ...*
> (NOT *The way how you organise ...*)

For *how to ...*, see 286.        For *how ever*, see 624.
For *learn how to ...*, see 317.   For *however*, see 49, 157.3, 625.

# 253 how and what ... like?

## 1 changes: *How's Ron?*

We generally use *how* to ask about things that change – for example people's moods and health. We prefer *what ... like* to ask about things that do not change – for example people's character and appearance. Compare:

– ***How's Ron?*** *~ He's very well.*
  ***What's Ron like?*** *~ He's quiet and a bit shy.*
– ***How** does she look today?* *~ Tired.*
  ***What** does she look **like**?* *~ Short and dark, pretty, cheerful-looking.*

## 2 reactions: *How was the film?*

We often use *how* to ask about people's reactions to their experiences. *What ... like* is also possible.

> ***How** was the film?* *~ Very good.* (OR ***What** was the film **like** ...?*)
> ***How's** your steak?*     ***How's** the new job?*

# 254  -ic and -ical

Many adjectives end in *-ic* or *-ical*. There is no general rule to tell you which form is correct in a particular case.

## 1  some adjectives normally ending in *-ic*

| | | | |
|---|---|---|---|
| academic | dramatic | linguistic | semantic |
| algebraic | egoistic | majestic | syntactic |
| arithmetic | emphatic | neurotic | systematic |
| artistic | energetic | pathetic | tragic |
| athletic | fantastic | pedagogic | |
| catholic | geometric | phonetic | |
| domestic | strategic | public | |

*arithmetical, geometrical* and *pedagogical* also occur.
Some of these words ended in *-ical* in older English (e.g. *fantastical, majestical, tragical*).
New adjectives which come into the language generally end in *-ic*, except for those ending in *-logical*.

## 2  some adjectives ending in *-ical*

*biological* (and many other adjectives ending in *-logical*)

| | | | |
|---|---|---|---|
| chemical | fanatical | medical | surgical |
| critical | logical | musical | tactical |
| cynical | mathematical | physical | topical |
| grammatical | mechanical | radical | |

## 3  differences of meaning

In some cases, both forms exist but with a difference of meaning.

a  *classic* and *classical*

*Classic* usually refers to a famous traditional style.
> He's a **classic** 1960s hippy who has never changed.
> She buys **classic** cars and restores them.

*Classical* refers to the culture of ancient Greece and Rome, or to European works of art of the so-called 'classical' period in the 18th century.
> She's studying **classical** languages and literature at Cambridge.

*Classical music* means 'serious' music, not pop or jazz.
> It's hard to learn **classical** guitar.

b  *comic* and *comical*

*Comic* is the normal adjective for artistic comedy.
> **comic** verse    **comic** opera
> Shakespeare's **comic** technique

*Comical* is a rather old-fashioned word meaning 'funny'.
> a **comical** expression

▶

c   *economic* and *economical*

*Economic* refers to the science of economics, or to the economy of a country.
   ***economic*** *theory*     ***economic*** *problems*
*Economical* means 'not wasting money'.
   *an **economical** little car*     *an **economical** housekeeper*

d   *electric* and *electrical*

*Electric* is used with the names of particular machines that work by electricity.
   *an **electric** motor*     ***electric*** *blankets*
Note also: *an **electric** shock*; *an **electric** atmosphere* (full of excitement).
*Electrical* is used before more general words.
   ***electrical*** *appliances*     ***electrical*** *equipment*
   ***electrical*** *component*     ***electrical*** *engineering*

e   *historic* and *historical*

*Historic* is used especially for historically important places, remains, customs etc, and for moments which 'make history'.
   *We spent our holiday visiting **historic** houses and castles in France.*
   *Our two countries are about to make a **historic** agreement.*
*Historical* means 'connected with the study of history' or 'really existing in history'.
   ***historical*** *research*     *a **historical** novel*
   ***historical*** *documents*     *Was King Arthur a **historical** figure?*

f   *magic* and *magical*

*Magic* is the more common word, and is used in a number of fixed expressions.
   *a **magic** wand* (= a magician's stick)
   *the **magic** word*     *a **magic** carpet*
*Magical* is sometimes used instead of *magic*, especially in metaphorical senses like 'mysterious', 'wonderful' or 'exciting'.
   *It was a **magical** experience.*

g   *politic* and *political*

*Politic* is a rather unusual word for 'wise', 'prudent'.
   *I don't think it would be **politic** to ask for a loan just now.*
*Political* means 'connected with politics'.
   ***political*** *history*     *a **political** career*

## 4   adverbs

Note that whether the adjective ends in *-ic* or *-ical*, the adverb ends in *-ically* (pronounced /ɪkli/). The one common exception is *publicly* (NOT ~~publically~~).

## 5   nouns ending in *-ics*

Many nouns ending in *-ics* are singular (e.g. *physics*, *athletics*). Some can be either singular or plural (e.g. *mathematics*, *politics*). For details, see 524.3.

# 255 idioms, collocations and fixed expressions

## 1 What are idioms?

An expression like *turn up* (meaning 'arrive'), *break even* (meaning 'make neither a profit nor a loss') or *a can of worms* (meaning 'a complicated problem') can be difficult to understand, because its meaning is different from the meanings of the separate words in the expression. (If you know *break* and *even*, this does not help you at all to understand *break even*.) Expressions like these are called 'idioms'. Idioms are usually special to one language and cannot be translated word for word (though related languages may share some idioms).

## 2 verbs with particles or prepositions

Common short verbs like *bring, come, do, get, give, go, have, keep, make, put,* and *take* are very often used with prepositions or adverb particles (e.g. *on, off, up, away*) to make two-word verbs. These are called 'prepositional verbs' or 'phrasal verbs', and many of them are idiomatic.

> *Can you **look after** the cats while I'm away?*
> *She just doesn't know how to **bring up** children.*
> *I **gave up** chemistry because I didn't like it.*

Many of these two-word verbs are especially common in informal speech and writing. Compare:

> – *What time are you planning to **turn up**?* (informal)
> ***Please let us know when you plan to arrive.*** (more formal)
> – *Just **keep on** till you **get to** the crossroads.* (informal)
> ***Continue as far as** the crossroads.* (formal)

For details of phrasal and prepositional verbs, see 599–600.

## 3 collocations (conventional word combinations)

We can say *I fully understand*, but not *I fully like; I rather like*, but not *I rather understand; I firmly believe*, but not *I firmly think*. Somebody can be a *heavy smoker* or a *devoted friend*, but not *a devoted smoker* or *a heavy friend*. Expressions like these are also idiomatic, in a sense. They are easy to understand, but not so easy for a learner to produce correctly. One can think of many adjectives that might be used with *smoker* to say that somebody smokes a lot – for example *big, strong, hard, fierce, mad, devoted*. It just happens that English speakers have chosen to use *heavy*, and one has to know this in order to express the idea naturally and correctly. These conventional combinations of words are called 'collocations', and all languages have large numbers of them. Some more examples:

> *a crashing bore* (BUT NOT *a crashing nuisance*)
> *a burning desire* (BUT NOT *a blazing desire*)
> *a blazing row* (BUT NOT *a burning row*)
> *highly reliable* (BUT NOT *highly old*)
> *a golden opportunity* (BUT NOT *a golden chance*)
> *change one's mind* (BUT NOT *change one's thoughts*)
> *Thanks a lot.* (BUT NOT *Thank you a lot.*)

▶

## 4 situational language: fixed expressions

The expressions that are used in typical everyday situations are often idiomatic in the same sense. With the help of a dictionary and a grammar, one could invent various possible ways of expressing a particular common idea, but generally there are only one or two ways that happen to be used by English speakers, and one has to know what they are in order to speak or write naturally. Some examples:

*Could you check the oil?* (More natural than *Could you inspect the oil?* or *Could you see how much oil there is in the engine?*)

*Is it a direct flight or do I have to change?* (More natural than *Does the plane go straight there or do I have to get another one?*)

*Sorry I kept you waiting.* (More natural than *Sorry I made you wait.*)

*Could I reserve a table for three for eight o'clock?* (More natural than *Could you keep me a table for three persons for eight o'clock?*)

Other fixed expressions are used as parts of sentences – useful introductions, conclusions or frames for the things that people want to say.

*Let me know when/where/what/how …*

| | |
|---|---|
| *The best thing would be to …* | *(do something) as a favour.* |
| *The point is …* | *… is more trouble than it's worth.* |
| *I wouldn't be surprised if …* | *I'll … on condition that you.* |

## 5 using idioms, collocations and fixed expressions.

Idioms, collocations and fixed expressions are common in all kinds of English, formal and informal, spoken and written. Informal spoken language is often very idiomatic.

Students should not worry because they do not know all the expressions of this kind that are commonly used by English speakers. If they use non-idiomatic ways of expressing ideas, they will normally be understood, and English speakers do not expect foreigners to speak perfect natural English. It is therefore not necessary for students to make great efforts to memorise idioms, collocations etc: they will learn the most common ones naturally along with the rest of their English. In particular, note that books of idioms often contain expressions which are slangy, rare or out of date, and which students should avoid unless they understand exactly how and when the expressions are used. This is especially true of colourful idioms like, for example, *raining cats and dogs, as cross as two sticks* (= angry) or *kick the bucket* (= die). If students try consciously to fill their speech and writing with such expressions the effect will probably be very strange.

It is, however, helpful for learners to have a good up-to-date dictionary of collocations (for example the *Oxford Dictionary of Collocations*) in order to become aware of the most common word combinations.

For more about formal and informal language, see 311.
For slang, see 533.

# 256 if (1): introduction

## 1 uncertain events and situations

In clauses after *if*, we usually talk about uncertain events and situations: things which may or may not happen, which may or may not be true, etc.

> *Ask John **if he's staying tonight**.* (He may or may not be staying.)
> ***If I see Annie**, I'll give her your love.* (I may or may not see Annie.)

## 2 conditions

An *if*-clause often refers to a condition – something which must happen so that something else can happen.

> *If you get here before eight, we can catch the early train.*
> *Oil floats if you pour it on water.*

Clauses of this kind are often called 'conditional' clauses. Verb phrases with *would/should* are also sometimes called 'conditional'.

## 3 'first', 'second' and 'third' conditionals; other structures

Some students' grammars concentrate on three common sentence structures with *if*, which are often called the 'first', 'second' and 'third' conditionals.

**'first conditional'**

| *if* + present | *will* + infinitive |
|---|---|
| If we play tennis | I'll win. |

**'second conditional'**

| *if* + past | *would* + infinitive |
|---|---|
| If we played tennis | I would win. |

**'third conditional'**

| *if* + past perfect | *would have* + past participle |
|---|---|
| If we had played tennis | I would have won. |

These are useful structures to practise. However, students sometimes think that these are the only possibilities, and become confused when they meet sentences like *If she didn't phone this morning, then she's probably away* ('What's this? A fourth conditional?'). It is important to realise that *if* is not only used in special structures with *will* and *would*; it can also be used, like other conjunctions, in ordinary structures with normal verb forms. For details, see the following sections.

## 4 position of *if*-clause

An *if*-clause can come at the beginning or end of a sentence. When an *if*-clause comes first, it is often separated by a comma.  ▶

Compare:
> *If you eat too much, you get fat.*
> *You get fat if you eat too much.*

For other meanings of *if*, see 261.10–13.
For *if* and *whether* in indirect speech, see 276, 621.
For *if not* and *unless*, see 601.
For more information about *would/should*, see 633.
For the difference between *if* and *in case*, see 271.
For *even if*, see 189.4.

# 257  if (2): ordinary structures

> *If you didn't study physics at school, you won't understand this book.*
> *I'll give her your love if I see her.*

## 1  the same tenses as with other conjunctions

When we are not talking about 'unreal' situations (see 258), we use the same tenses with *if* as with other conjunctions. Present tenses are used to refer to the present, past tenses to the past, and so on. Compare:

– *Oil floats if you pour it on water.*
  *Iron goes red when it gets very hot.*
– *If John didn't come to work yesterday, he was probably ill.*
  *As John didn't come to work yesterday, he was probably ill.*
– *If you didn't study physics at school, you won't understand this book.*
  *Because you didn't study physics at school, you won't understand this book.*

## 2  present tense with future meaning

In an *if*-clause, we normally use a present tense to talk about the future. This happens after most conjunctions (see 580). Compare:

– *I'll give her your love if I see her.* (NOT . . . *if I will see her.*)
  *I'll give her your love when I see her.* (NOT . . . *when I will see her.*)
– *If we have fine weather tomorrow, I'm going to paint the windows.*
  *As soon as we have fine weather, I'm going to paint the windows.*

For *if + will* (e.g. *if it will make you feel better*), see 260.
For *if + will* in reported speech (e.g. *I don't know if I'll be ready*), see 276.

# 258  if (3): special structures with past tenses and would

> *If I knew her name, I would tell you.*
> *What would you do if you lost your job?*

## 1  unreal situations

We use special structures with *if* when we are talking about unreal situations – things that will probably not happen, situations that are untrue or imaginary, and similar ideas. In these cases, we use past tenses and *would* to 'distance' our language from reality.

## 2   if + past; *would* + infinitive without *to*

To talk about unreal or improbable situations now or in the future, we use a past tense in the *if*-clause (even though the meaning is present or future), and *would* + **infinitive** (without *to*) in the other part of the sentence.

> *If I **knew** her name, I **would tell** you.* (NOT ~~If I know~~...)
>> (NOT ~~If I would know~~...) (NOT ...~~I will tell you.~~)
> *She **would be** perfectly happy if she **had** a car.*
> *What **would** you **do** if you **lost** your job?*

This structure can make suggestions sound less definite, and so more polite.

> *It **would be** nice if you **helped** me a bit with the housework.*
> ***Would** it **be** all right if I **came** round about seven tomorrow?*

## 3   *would, should* and *'d*

After *I* and *we*, *should* can be used with the same meaning as *would*. (*Would* is more common in modern English; *should* is rare in AmE.)

> *If I **knew** her name, I **should** tell you.*
> *If I **married** you, we **should** both be unhappy.*

We use *'d* as a contraction (see 143).

> *We**'d** get up earlier if there was a good reason to.*

For *I should*... meaning 'I advise you to...', see 264.2.
For *would* in the *if*-clause, see 262.
For *should* in the *if*-clause, see 261.1.

## 4   *if I were* etc

We often use *were* instead of *was* after *if*. This is common in both formal and informal styles. In a formal style *were* is more common than *was*, and many people consider it more correct, especially in American English. The grammatical name for this use of *were* is 'subjunctive' (see 567).

> *If I **were** rich, I would spend all my time travelling.*
> *If my nose **were** a little shorter I'd be quite pretty.*

For the expression *If I were you*..., see 264.

## 5   ordinary tense-use or special tense-use? *If I come* or *if I came*?

The difference between, for example, *if I come* and *if I came* is not necessarily a difference of time. They can both refer to the future; but the past tense suggests that a future situation is impossible, imaginary or less probable. Compare:

– *If I **become** President, I'll*... (said by a candidate in an election)
   *If I **became** President, I'd*... (said by a schoolboy)
– *If I **win** this race, I'll*... (said by the fastest runner)
   *If I **won** this race, I'd*... (said by the slowest runner)
– *Will it be all right if I **bring** a friend?* (direct request)
   *Would it be all right if I **brought** a friend?* (less direct, more polite)

## 6   *could* and *might*

We can use *could* to mean 'would be able to' and *might* to mean 'would perhaps' or 'would possibly'. ▶

*If I had another £500, I **could** buy a car.*
*If you asked me nicely, I **might** get you a drink.*

For other cases where a past tense has a present or future meaning, see 426.
For *if only*, see 265.

# 259  if (4): unreal past situations

> *If you had worked harder, you would have passed your exam.*

## 1  *if* + past perfect; *would have* + past participle

To talk about past situations that did not happen, we use a past perfect tense
in the *if*-clause, and ***would have* + past participle** in the other part of the
sentence.

*If you **had asked** me, I **would have told** you.*
(NOT ~~If you would have asked me~~...)
(NOT ~~If you asked me~~...)      (NOT ...~~I had told you.~~)
*If you **had worked** harder, you **would have passed** your exam.*
*I'd **have been** in bad trouble if Jane **hadn't helped** me.*

## 2  *could have . . .* and *might have . . .*

We can use *could have* + **past participle** to mean 'would have been able to . . .',
and *might have* + **past participle** to mean 'would perhaps have . . . ' or 'would
possibly have . . .'.

*If he'd run a bit faster, he **could have won**.*
*If I hadn't been so tired, I **might have realised** what was happening.*

## 3  present use: situations that are no longer possible

We sometimes use structures with *would have* . . . to talk about present and
future situations which are no longer possible because of the way things have
turned out.

*It **would have been** nice to go to Australia this winter, but there's no way we
can do it.* (OR *It would be nice* . . .)
*If my mother hadn't knocked my father off his bicycle thirty years ago, I
**wouldn't have been** here now.* (OR . . . *I wouldn't be here now.*)

# 260  if (5): if . . . will

> *I'll give you £100 if it will help you to go on holiday.*
> *If Ann won't be here, we'd better cancel the meeting.*
> *I don't know if I'll be ready in time.*
> *If you will come this way* . . .
> *If you will eat so much* . . .

We normally use a present tense with *if* (and most other conjunctions) to refer
to the future (see 580).

*I'll phone you if I **have** time.* (NOT ...~~if I will have time.~~)
But in certain situations we use *if* . . . *will*.

## 1   results

We use *will* with *if* to talk about what will happen because of possible future actions – to mean 'if this will be the later result'. Compare:
– *I'll give you £100 if I* **win** *the lottery.* (Winning the lottery is a condition – it must happen first.)
  *I'll give you £100 if it'll* **help** *you to go on holiday.* (The holiday is a result – it follows the gift of money.)
– *We'll go home now if you* **get** *the car.* (condition)
  *We'll go home now if it* **will make** *you feel better.* (result)

## 2   'If it is true now that ...'

We use *will* with *if* when we are saying 'if it is true now that ...' or 'if we know now that ...'.
  *If Ann* **won't be** *here on Thursday, we'd better cancel the meeting.*
  *If prices* **will** *really* **come** *down in a few months, I'm not going to buy one now.*

## 3   indirect questions: *I don't know if ...*

We can use *will* after *if* in indirect questions (see 276).
  *I don't know if I'll be ready in time.* (NOT ... ~~if I'm ready in time.~~)

## 4   polite requests

We can use *if* + *will* in polite requests. In this case, *will* is not a future auxiliary; it means 'are willing to' (see 629.4).
  *If you* **will come** *this way, I'll show you your room.*
  *If your mother* **will fill in** *this form, I'll prepare her ticket.*
*Would* can be used to make a request even more polite.
  *If you* **would come** *this way ...*

## 5   insistence

Stressed *will* can be used after *if* to suggest insistence.
  *If you* WILL *eat so much, it's not surprising you feel ill.*

# 261   if (6): other points

## 1   *if ... should; if ... happen to*

We can suggest that something is unlikely, or not particularly probable, by using *should* (not *would*) in the *if*-clause.
  *If you* **should** *run into Peter, tell him he owes me a letter.*
*If ... happen to* has a similar meaning.
  *If you* **happen** *to pass a supermarket, perhaps you could get some eggs.*
*Should* and *happen to* can be used together.
  *If you* **should happen to** *finish early, give me a ring.*
*Would* is not common in the main clause in these structures.
  *If he should be late, we'll* *have to start without him.*
    (NOT ... ~~we'd have to start without him.~~)                    ▶

## 2   *if ... was/were to*

This is another way of talking about unreal or imaginary future events.

> *If the boss **was/were to come in** now, we'd be in real trouble.*
>     (= If the boss came ...)
> *What would we do if I **was/were to lose** my job?*

It can be used to make a suggestion sound less direct, and so more polite.

> *If **you were to move** your chair a bit, we could all sit down.*

This structure is not normally used with verbs like *be* or *know*, which refer to continuing situations.

> *If I **knew** her name ...* (NOT ~~If I were to know her name~~ ...)

For the difference between *was* and *were* after *if*, see 258.4.

## 3   *if it was/were not for*

This structure is used to say that one event or situation changes everything.

> *If it **wasn't/weren't for** his wife's money he'd never be a director.*
>     (= Without his wife's money ...)
> *If it **wasn't/weren't for** the children, we could go skiing next week.*

To talk about the past we use *If it had not been for*.

> *If it **hadn't been for** your help, I don't know what I'd have done.*

*But for* can be used to mean 'if it were not for' or 'if it had not been for'.

> *But for your help, I don't know what I'd have done.*

## 4   leaving out *if*: conversational

*If* is sometimes left out at the beginning of a sentence in a conversational style, especially when the speaker is making conditions or threats.

> *You want to get in, you pay like everybody else.* (= If you want ...)
> *You touch me again, I'll kick your teeth in.*

## 5   leaving out *if*: formal inversion-structures

In formal and literary styles, *if* can be dropped and an auxiliary verb put before the subject. This happens mostly with *were*, *had* and *should*.

> ***Were she** my daughter, ...* (= If she were my daughter ...)
> ***Had I** realised what you intended, ...* (= If I had realised ...)
> ***Should you** change your mind, ...* (= If you should change ...)

Negatives are not contracted.

> ***Had we not** missed the plane, we would all have been killed in the crash.*
>     (NOT ~~Hadn't we missed~~ ...)

For other uses of inverted word order, see 302–303.

## 6   leaving out words after *if*

We sometimes leave out **subject + *be*** after *if*. Note the common fixed expressions *if necessary, if any, if anything, if ever, if in doubt*.

> *I'll work late tonight **if necessary**.* (= ... if it is necessary)
> *There is little **if any** good evidence for flying saucers.*
> *I'm not angry. **If anything**, I feel a little surprised.*
> *He seldom **if ever** travels abroad.*
> ***If in doubt**, ask for help.* (= If you are in doubt ...)

*If about to go on a long journey, try to have a good night's sleep.*

For more details of ellipsis (structures with words left out), see 177–182.

## 7   *if so* and *if not*

After *if*, we can use *so* and *not* instead of repeating a whole clause.
> *Are you free?* **If so**, *let's go out for a meal.* (= ... If you are free ...)
> *I might see you tomorrow.* **If not**, *then it'll be Saturday.* (= ... If I don't see you tomorrow ...)

## 8   extra negative

An extra *not* is sometimes put into *if*-clauses after expressions suggesting doubt or uncertainty.
> *I wonder* **if** *we* **shouldn't ask** *the doctor to look at Mary.*
> > (= I wonder if we should ask ...)
> *I wouldn't be surprised* **if** *she* **didn't** *get married soon.*
> > (= ... if she got married soon.)

## 9   *if ... then*

We sometimes construct sentences with *if ... then* to emphasise that one thing depends on another.
> **If** *she can't come to us,* **then** *we'll have to go and see her.*

## 10   *if* meaning 'even if'

We can use *if* to mean 'even if' (see 189.4).
> *I'll finish this job* **if** *it takes all night.*
> *I wouldn't marry you* **if** *you were the last man in the world.*

## 11   admitting facts with *if*

An *if*-clause can be used to admit a fact when giving a reason for it.
> **If** *I'm a bit sleepy, it's because I was up all night.*

## 12   *if* meaning 'I'm saying this in case'

*If*-clauses are quite often used to explain the purpose of a remark – to suggest 'I'm saying this in case ...'
> *There's some steak in the fridge* **if** *you're hungry.*
> **If** *you want to go home, Anne's got your car keys.*

## 13   *if* meaning 'although'

In a formal style, *if* can be used with a similar meaning to *although*. This is common in the structure *if* + **adjective** (with no verb). *If* is not as definite as *although*; it can suggest that what is being talked about is a matter of opinion, or not very important.
> *His style,* **if** *simple, is pleasant to read.*
> *The profits,* **if** *a little lower than last year's, are still extremely healthy.*

The same kind of idea can be expressed with *may ... but* (see 342).
> *His style* **may** *be simple,* **but** *it is pleasant to read.*

## 262 if (7): other structures found in spoken English

### 1 *would* in both clauses

Conditional *would* is sometimes used in both clauses of an *if*-sentence. This is very informal, and is not usually written. It is common in spoken American English.

> It **would** be good if we**'d** get some rain.
> How **would** we feel if this **would** happen to our family?

For *if . . . would* in polite requests, see 260.4.

### 2 *'d have . . . 'd have*

In informal spoken English, *if*-clauses referring to the past are sometimes constructed with *'d have*. This is frequently considered incorrect, but happens quite often in educated people's speech. It is not normally written.

> If I**'d have** known, I'd have told you.
> It would have been funny if she**'d have** recognised him.

### 3 *had've* and *would've*

Instead of the contracted *'d* in these structures, full forms are sometimes used for emphasis or in negatives. Both *had* and *would* occur. The following are genuine examples taken from conversation.

> I didn't know. But if I **had've** known . . .
> We would never have met if he **hadn't have** crashed into my car.
> If I **would've** had a gun, somebody might have got hurt.
> If you **wouldn't have** phoned her we'd never have found out what was happening.

### 4 mixed tenses

Sometimes a simple past tense is used with *if* where a past perfect would be normal. This is more common in American English.

> If I **knew** you were coming I'd have baked a cake.
> If I **had** the money with me I would have bought you one.
> If I **didn't have** my walking boots on I think I would have really hurt my foot.

## 263 if (8): other words with the same meaning

Many words and expressions can be used with a similar meaning to *if*, and often with similar structures. Some of the commonest are *imagine (that)*, *suppose (that)*, *supposing (that)* (used to talk about what might happen), and *providing (that)*, *provided (that)*, *as/so long as*, *on condition (that)* (used to make conditions).

> **Imagine** we could all fly. Wouldn't that be fun!
> **Supposing** you'd missed the train. What would you have done?
> You can borrow my bike **providing/provided** you bring it back.
> I'll give you the day off **on condition that** you work on Saturday morning.
> You're welcome to stay with us **as/so long as** you share the expenses.

For suggestions with *suppose, supposing* and *what if*, see 571.

## 264 if I were you

### 1 advice

We often use the structure *If I were you ...* to give advice.
> *I shouldn't worry if I were you.*
> *If I were you, I'd get that car serviced.*
*If I was you* is also possible. Some people consider it incorrect (see 258.4).

### 2 *I should/would ...*

Sometimes we leave out *If I were you*, and just use *I should ...* or *I would ...* to give advice.
> *I shouldn't worry.     I would get that car serviced.*
In this case, *I should/would* is similar to *you should/would*.

## 265 if only

We can use *If only ...!* to say that we would like things to be different. It means the same as *I wish ...* (see 630), but is more emphatic. The clause with *if only* often stands alone, without a main clause. Tense use is as follows:

a past to talk about the present

> *If only I knew more people!     If only I was better-looking!*
We can use *were* instead of *was* (see 258.4).
> *If only your father were here!*

b *would* + infinitive (without *to*) to talk about the future

> *If only it would stop raining, we could go out.*
> *If only somebody would smile!*

c past perfect to talk about the past

> *If only she hadn't told the police, everything would have been all right.*

## 266 ill and sick

*Ill* and *sick* are both used to mean 'unwell'. (In American English *ill* is less usual except in a formal style.)
> *George didn't come in last week because he was ill/sick.*
*Ill* is not very common before a noun.
> *I'm looking after my sick mother.* (More normal than ... *my ill mother.*)
*Be sick* can meant 'vomit' (= bring food up from the stomach).
> *I was sick three times in the night.*

# 267 immediately, the moment etc: conjunctions

In British English, *immediately* and *directly* can be used as conjunctions, to mean 'as soon as'.

> *Tell me **immediately** you have any news.*
> *I knew something was wrong **immediately** I arrived.*
> ***Directly** I walked in the door, I smelt smoke.*

*The moment (that)*, *the instant (that)*, *the second (that)* and *the minute (that)* can be used in the same way (in both British and American English).

> *Telephone me **the moment (that)** you get the results.*
> *I loved you **the instant (that)** I saw you.*

# 268 imperatives

## 1 forms and use

In sentences like *Come here, Be quiet, Have a drink* or *Don't worry about it*, the verb forms *come, be, have* and *don't worry* are called 'imperatives'. Affirmative imperatives have the same form as the infinitive without *to*; negative imperatives are constructed with *do not* (*don't*).

Imperatives are used, for example, to tell or ask people to do things, to make suggestions, to give advice or instructions, to encourage and offer, and to express wishes for people's welfare.

> ***Look** in the mirror before you drive off.*
> *Please **do not lean** out of the window.*
> ***Tell** him you're not free this evening.*
> ***Try** again – you nearly did it.*
> ***Have** some more tea.*
> ***Enjoy** your holiday.*

An imperative followed by *and* or *or* can mean the same as an *if*-clause.

> ***Walk** down our street any day **and** you'll see kids playing.*
> (= If you walk ...)
> ***Shut up or** I'll lose my temper.* (= If you don't shut up ...)
> ***Don't do** that again **or** you'll be in trouble.*

## 2 emphatic imperative: *Do sit down*

We can make an emphatic imperative with *do*.

> ***Do sit** down.      **Do be** more careful.      **Do forgive** me.*

## 3 passive imperative: *get vaccinated*

To tell people to arrange for things to be done to them, we often use **get + past participle**.

> ***Get vaccinated** as soon as you can.*

For more about *get* as passive auxiliary, see 223.5.

## 4  *do(n't) be*

Although *do* is not normally used as an auxiliary with *be* (see 90), this happens in negative imperatives.

> **Don't be** *silly!*

*Do be* can begin emphatic imperatives.

> **Do be** *quiet!*

## 5  subject with imperative

The imperative does not usually have a subject, but we can use a noun or pronoun to make it clear who we are speaking to.

> **Mary come** *here* – **everybody else stay** *where you are.*
> **Somebody answer** *the phone.*     **Relax, everybody.**

*You* before an imperative can suggest emphatic persuasion or anger.

> **You** *just* **sit down** *and relax for a bit.*     **You take** *your hands off me!*

Note the word order in negative imperatives with pronoun subjects.

> **Don't you** *believe it.* (NOT ~~You don't believe it.~~)
> **Don't anybody** *say a word.* (NOT ~~Anybody don't say~~ . . .)

## 6  question tags

After imperatives, common question tags (see 487–488) are *will you? would you? can you?* and *could you?*

> *Give me a hand,* **will you?**
> *Wait here for a minute,* **would you?**
> *Get me something to drink,* **can you?**

*Can't you* and *won't you* are more emphatic.

> *Be quiet,* **can't you?**     *Sit down,* **won't you?**

After negative imperatives, *will you?* is used.

> *Don't tell anybody,* **will you?**

## 7  word order with *always* and *never*

*Always* and *never* come before imperatives.

> **Always remember** *what I told you.* (NOT ~~Remember always~~ . . .)
> **Never speak** *to me like that again.*

## 8  *let*

English does not have a first-person imperative (used to suggest that 'I' or 'we' should do something) or a third-person imperative (for other people, not the hearer). These ideas are often expressed by a structure with *let*.

> **Let** *me see. Do I need to go shopping today?*     **Let's** *go home.*
> **Let** *him wait.*

For more details of this structure, see 323.

# 269  **in** and **into, on** and **onto**: prepositions

## 1  position and direction

We generally use *in* and *on* to talk about the positions of things – where they **are**; and *into* and *onto* to talk about directions and destinations – where things are **going**. Compare:

▶

– *A moment later the ball was **in** the goal.*
*The ball rolled slowly **into** the goal.* (NOT *. . . ~~rolled slowly in the goal.~~*)
– *She was walking **in** the garden.*     – *The cat's **on** the roof again.*
*Then she walked **into** the house.*      *How does it get **onto** the roof?*
Note that *into* and *onto* are normally written as single words. *On to* is also
possible in British English.

## 2   *in* and *on* for movement

After some verbs (e.g. *throw, jump, push, put, fall*) we can use both *in* and *into*,
or *on* and *onto*, to talk about directional movement. We prefer *into/onto* when
we think of the movement itself, and *in/on* when we think more of the end of
the movement – the place where somebody or something will be. Compare:
– *The children keep jumping **into** the flowerbeds.*
*Go and jump **in** the river.*
– *In the experiment, we put glowing magnesium **into** jars of oxygen.*
*Could you put the ham **in** the fridge?*
– *He was trying to throw his hat **onto** the roof.*
*Throw another log **on** the fire.*
We use *in* and *on* after *sit down* and *arrive.*
*He sat down **in** the armchair, and I sat down **on** the floor.* (NOT *He sat down
~~into. . .~~ OR ~~I sat down onto. . .~~*)
*We arrive **in** Athens at midday.* (NOT USUALLY *We arrive into Athens . . .*)

For *arrive at . . .*, see 81.

## 3   *into* for change

We normally use *into* after verbs suggesting change.
*When she kissed the frog, it **changed into** a handsome prince.*
(NOT *. . . ~~changed in a handsome prince.~~*)
*Can you **translate** this **into** Chinese?* (NOT *. . . ~~translate this in Chinese?~~*)
*Cut* can be followed by *into* or *in.*
*Cut the onion **in(to)** small pieces.*
And note the expression *in half.*
*I broke it **in half.*** (NOT *. . . ~~into half.~~*)

## 4   *in* and *on* as adverbs

*In* and *on* are used as adverbs for both position and movement.
*I stayed **in** last night.*     *Come **in!*** (NOT *~~Come into!~~*)
*What have you got **on**?*     *Put your coat **on**.*

For the difference between *in* and *to*, see 270.

# 270   in and to

## 1   *go to school in . . .* etc

After expressions like *go to school, go to work*, we use *in*, not *to*, to say where
the school, work etc is located.
*He went to school **in** Bristol.* (NOT *He went to ~~school to Bristol.~~*)
*At* is also possible. (For the difference between *in* and *at*, see 81.)
*She went to university **at/in** Oxford.*

## 2 *arrive* etc

We use *in* (or *at*), not *to*, after *arrive* and *land*.
> *We **arrive in** Bangkok on Tuesday morning.* (NOT ~~We arrive to Bangkok~~...)
> *What time do we **land at** Barcelona?* (NOT ...~~land to Barcelona?~~)

# 271 **in case** and **if**

## 1 precautions

*In case* is mostly used to talk about precautions – things which we do in order to be ready for possible future situations.
> *I always take an umbrella **in case** it rains.* (= ... because it might rain.)

To talk about the future, we use a present tense after *in case* (see 580).
> *I've bought a chicken **in case** your mother **stays** to lunch.* (NOT ...~~in case~~
> ~~your mother will stay~~...)

## 2 *in case ... should*

We often use ***should* + infinitive** (with a similar meaning to *might*) after *in case*. This adds the meaning 'by chance'.
> *I've bought a chicken **in case** your mother **should stay** to lunch.*

This structure is especially common in sentences about the past.
> *I wrote down her address **in case** I **should forget** it.*

The meaning 'by chance' can also be expressed by *(should) happen to*.
> *We took our swimming things **in case** we **happened to** find a pool.*
> (OR ... *in case* we ***should happen to*** *find a pool.*)

## 3 *in case* and *if*

*In case* and *if* are normally used in quite different ways.
'Do A *in case* B happens' means 'Do A (first) because B might happen later'.
'Do A *if* B happens' means 'Do A if B has already happened'. Compare:
– *Let's buy a bottle of wine **in case** Roger comes.*
> (= Let's buy some wine now because Roger might come later.)
> *Let's buy a bottle of wine **if** Roger comes.* (= We'll wait and see. If Roger
> comes, then we'll buy the wine. If he doesn't we won't.)
– *I'm taking an umbrella **in case** it rains.*
> *I'll open the umbrella **if** it rains.* (NOT ~~I'll open the umbrella in case it rains.~~)
– *People insure their houses **in case** they catch fire.* (NOT ...~~if they catch fire.~~)
> *People telephone the fire brigade **if** their houses catch fire.* (NOT ...~~telephone~~
> ...~~in case their houses catch fire.~~)

## 4 *in case of*

The prepositional phrase *in case of* has a wider meaning than the conjunction *in case*, and can be used in similar situations to *if*.
> ***In case of*** *fire, break glass.* (= If there is a fire ...)

## 272 in spite of

*In spite of* is used as a preposition. ***In spite of* + noun** means more or less the same as ***although* + clause**.

> *We went out **in spite of** the rain.* (= . . . although it was raining.)
> *We understood him **in spite of** his accent.*
> (= . . . although he had a strong accent.)

*In spite of* is the opposite of *because of.* Compare:

> *She passed her exams **in spite of** her teacher.* (She had a bad teacher.)
> *She passed her exams **because of** her teacher.* (She had a good teacher.)

*In spite of* can be followed by an *-ing* form.

> ***In spite of having** a headache I enjoyed the film.*

*In spite of* cannot be followed directly by a *that*-clause. Instead, we can use *in spite of the fact that.*

> *He is good company, **in spite of the fact that** he talks all the time.*

This is rather heavy: *although* means the same, and is more common.

In more formal English, *despite* can be used in the same way as *in spite of.*

## 273 indeed

### 1 *very . . . indeed*

*Indeed* is often used to emphasise *very* with an adjective or adverb.

> *I was **very pleased indeed** to hear from you.*
> *He was driving **very fast indeed**.*          *Thank you **very much indeed**.*

*Indeed* is unusual in this sense without *very*, and is not normally used after *extremely* or *quite.*

> (NOT *He was driving fast indeed.*)
> (NOT *He was driving quite/extremely fast indeed.*)

### 2 *indeed* with verb

*Indeed* can also be used after *be* or an auxiliary verb in order to suggest confirmation or emphatic agreement. This is rather formal. It is common in short answers (see 517).

> *We are **indeed** interested in your offer, and would be glad to have prices.*
> *It's cold. ~ It is **indeed**.*
> *Henry made a fool of himself. ~ He did **indeed**.*

## 274 indirect speech (1): introduction

### 1 direct and indirect speech

When we report people's words, thoughts, beliefs etc, we can give the exact words (more or less) that were said, or that we imagine were thought. This kind of structure is called 'direct speech' (though it is used for reporting thoughts as well as speech).

> *So he said, '**I want to go home**,' and just walked out.*
> *She asked '**What do you want?**'*
> *And then I thought, '**Well, does he really mean it?**'*

We can also make somebody's words or thoughts part of our own sentence, using conjunctions (e.g. *that*), and changing pronouns, tenses and other words where necessary. This kind of structure is called 'indirect speech' or 'reported speech'.

> *So he said that **he wanted to go home**, and just walked out.*
> *She asked **what I wanted**.*
> *And then I wondered **whether he really meant it**.*

These two structures cannot normally be mixed.

> *She said to me **'I have got no money'**.* OR *She said to me **that she had got no money**.* BUT NOT *She said to me that I have got no money.*

For punctuation in direct speech, see 476, 478.
For reporting verbs and word order, see 156.

## 2 change of situation

Words that are spoken or thought in one place by one person may be reported in another place at a different time, and perhaps by another person. Because of this, there are often grammatical differences between direct and indirect speech. For example:

> BILL (on Saturday evening): *I don't like this party. I want to go home now.*
> PETER (on Sunday morning): *Bill said that **he didn't like the** party, and **he wanted** to go home.*

These differences are mostly natural and logical, and it is not necessary to learn complicated rules about indirect speech in English.

## 3 pronouns

A change of speaker may mean a change of pronoun.
In the above example, Bill says *I* to refer to himself. Peter, talking about what Bill said, naturally uses *he*.

> *Bill said that **he** didn't like* ... (NOT *Bill said that I didn't like* ...)

## 4 'here and now' words

A change of place and time may mean changing or dropping words like *here*, *this*, *now*, *today*. Peter, reporting what Bill said, does not use *this* and *now* because he is no longer at the party.

> *Bill said that he didn't like **the** party* ...
>    (NOT *Bill said that he didn't like this party* ...)
> *... he wanted to go home.* (NOT *... to go home now.*)

Some other 'here and now' words: *next*, *last*, *yesterday*, *tomorrow*. Compare:

- DIRECT: *I'll be back **next week** .*
  INDIRECT: *She said she'd be back **the next week**, but I never saw her again.*
- DIRECT: *Ann got her licence **last Tuesday**.*
  INDIRECT: *He said Ann had got her licence **the Tuesday before**.*
- DIRECT: *I had an accident **yesterday**.*
  INDIRECT: *He said he'd had an accident **the day before**.*
- DIRECT: *We'll be there **tomorrow**.*
  INDIRECT: *They promised to be there **the next day**.*    ▶

## 5 tenses

A change of time may mean a change of tense.

*Bill said that he **didn't** like the party* ... (NOT ~~Bill said that he doesn't like the party~~ ... – when Peter is talking, the party is finished.)

For details of tense changes in indirect speech, see 275.

## 6 dropping *that*

The conjunction *that* is often dropped, especially after common reporting verbs (e.g. *say, think*) in informal speech. For more details, see 584.

*She **said (that)** she'd had enough.     I **think (that)** you're probably right.*

# 275 indirect speech (2): tenses

## 1 past reporting verbs: *He said he didn't like the party.*

When we report what somebody said or thought, it is usually natural to use different tenses from the original speaker (because we are talking at a different time).

> BILL (on Saturday evening): *I **don't like** this party. I **want** to go home now.* (present tenses)

> PETER (on Sunday morning): *Bill said that he **didn't like** the party, and he **wanted** to go home.* (past tenses)

It would be strange for Peter to say on Sunday *'Bill said that he doesn't like the party'*, just as it would be strange for Peter to say, on Sunday, *'Bill doesn't like the party yesterday and goes home'*. The tenses used in indirect speech are usually just the tenses that are natural for the situation – see the examples below.

## 2 typical tense changes after past reporting verbs

*will → would*
>   DIRECT:    *The exam **will** be difficult.*
>   INDIRECT: *They said that the exam **would** be difficult.*

**simple present → simple past**
>   DIRECT:    *I **need** help.*
>   INDIRECT: *She thought she **needed** help.*

**present progressive → past progressive**
>   DIRECT:    *My English **is getting** better.*
>   INDIRECT: *I knew my English **was getting** better.*

**present perfect → past perfect**
>   DIRECT:    *This **has been** a wonderful holiday.*
>   INDIRECT: *She told me that it **had been** a wonderful holiday.*

**past → past perfect**
>   DIRECT:    *Ann **grew** up in Kenya.*
>   INDIRECT: *I found out that Ann **had grown** up in Kenya.*

*can → could*
>   DIRECT:    *I **can** fly!*
>   INDIRECT: *Poor chap – he thought he **could** fly.*

*may → might*
    DIRECT:    *We **may** come back early.*
    INDIRECT: *They said they **might** come back early.*
**Past perfect tenses do not change.**
    DIRECT:    *I arrived late because I **had lost** the address.*
    INDIRECT: *He said he had arrived late because he **had lost** the address.*

### 3  *would, could* etc: no change

Past modal verbs are usually unchanged in indirect speech.
    DIRECT:    *It **would** be nice if we **could** meet.*
    INDIRECT: *He said it **would** be nice if we **could** meet.*

For more details, see 278.3.

### 4  *I told them I was British*

After past reporting verbs, we usually change the original tenses even if the things the original speaker said are still true.
  – DIRECT:    *I'm British.*
    INDIRECT: *I told the police I **was** British.* (The speaker still is British.)
  – DIRECT:    *You **can** use my car today.*
    INDIRECT: *Your mother said I **could** use her car today. Have you got the keys?*
  – DIRECT:    *How old **are** you?*
    INDIRECT: *Didn't you hear me? I asked how old you **were**.*
  – DIRECT:    *That **is** my seat.*
    INDIRECT: *Sorry, I didn't realise this **was** your seat.*
However, it is often also possible to keep the original speaker's tenses in these cases.
    *Didn't you hear me? I asked how old you **are**.*

For details, see 278.2.

### 5  *He says, I'll tell her* etc.

After present, future and present perfect reporting verbs, tenses are usually the same as in the original (because there is no important change of time).
  – DIRECT:    *I **don't** want to play any more.*
    INDIRECT: *He says he **doesn't** want to play any more.*
  – DIRECT:    *We **need** some help..*
    INDIRECT: *I'll tell her you **need** some help.*
  – DIRECT:    *Taxes **will** be raised.*
    INDIRECT: *The government has announced that taxes **will** be raised.*

## 276  indirect speech (3): questions and answers

### 1  word order: *I asked where Alice was*

In reported questions the subject normally comes before the verb in standard English, and auxiliary *do* is not used.
  – DIRECT:    *Where's Alice?*
    INDIRECT: *I asked **where Alice was**.* (NOT *... ~~where was Alice.~~*)    ▶

- DIRECT: *When are you leaving?*
  INDIRECT: *He wanted to know **when I was leaving**.* (NOT ... ~~when was I leaving.~~)
- DIRECT: *What do I need?*
  INDIRECT: *She asked **what she needed**.* (NOT ... ~~what did she need.~~)
- DIRECT: *Where are the President and his wife staying?*
  INDIRECT: *I asked **where the President and his wife were staying**.* (NOT ~~Where were staying~~...)

The same structure is used for reporting the answers to questions.

> *I knew **how they felt**.* (NOT ... ~~how did they feel.~~)
> *Nobody told me **why I had to sign** the paper.* (NOT ... ~~why did I have to sign~~...)

## 2 no question marks

Question marks are not used in reported questions.

> *We asked **where the money was**.* (NOT ... ~~where the money was?~~)

## 3 *yes/no* questions: *He asked if ...*

Yes/no questions are reported with *if* or *whether* (for the difference, see 621).

> *The driver asked **if/whether** I wanted the town centre.*
> *I don't know **if/whether** I can help you.*

In reported questions, we do not use a present tense after *if* to talk about the future.

> *I'm not sure **if I'll see her tomorrow**.* (NOT ... ~~if I see her tomorrow.~~)

## 4 *say* and *tell*: answers, not questions

*Say* and *tell* are not used to report questions.

> (NOT ~~The driver said whether I wanted the town centre.~~)

But *say* and *tell* can introduce the answers to questions.

> *Please **say whether you want** the town centre.*
> *He never **says where he's going**.*     *I told her **what time it was**.*

For the difference between *say* and *tell*, see 504.

# 277 indirect speech (4): infinitives

## 1 *He promised to write*

Speech relating to actions (e.g. promises, agreements, orders, offers, requests, advice and suggestions) is often reported with infinitives.

> *He promised **to write**.*     *She agreed **to wait** for me.*
> *Ann has offered **to baby-sit** tonight.*

**Object + infinitive** is common with *ask, advise, tell* and *order* (but not with *promise* or *offer*).

> *I told **Andrew to be** careful.*
> *The landlady has asked **us to be** quiet after nine o'clock.*
> *I advise **you to think** again before you decide.*
> *The policeman told **me not to park** there.*

## 2  *He asked her how to ...*

The structure **question word + infinitive** is common (see 286). It often corresponds to a direct question with *should*.

> *He asked her **how to make** a white sauce.* ('How should I make a white sauce?')
>
> *Don't tell me **what to do**.*  *I've forgotten **where to put** the keys.*
>
> *I didn't know **whether to laugh or cry**.*

## 3  *suggest, say*: infinitives not used

We do not use infinitive structures after *suggest* (see 570) or (usually) after *say*. However, after these and many other verbs, instructions etc can be reported with *that*-clauses, usually with modal verbs (see 353–354).

> *I **suggested that he should try** the main car park.* (NOT ~~I suggested him to try~~ ...)
>
> *The policeman **said that I mustn't park** there.* (NOT ~~The policeman said me not to park there.~~)
>
> *I told Andrew **that he ought to be** careful.*

Subjunctives (see 567) and *-ing* forms are also possible after some verbs, e.g. *suggest*.

> *I **suggested that he try** the main car park.*
>
> *I **suggested trying** the main car park.*

For the structures that are possible after particular verbs, see a good dictionary.

# 278  indirect speech (5): advanced points

## 1  reporting past tenses

In indirect speech, a speaker's past tenses are often reported using past perfect tenses.

> – DIRECT:   *I've just **written** to John.*
> INDIRECT: *She told me she **had** just **written** to John.*
> – DIRECT:   *I **saw** Penny at the theatre a couple of days ago.*
> INDIRECT: *In his letter, he said he'**d seen** Penny at the theatre a couple of days before.*

However, past perfect tenses are not always used, especially if the time relationships are clear without a change from past to past perfect.

> *This man on TV said that dinosaurs **were** around for 250 million years.* (NOT ... ~~that dinosaurs had been around~~ ...)
>
> *I told you John **(had) phoned** this morning, didn't I?*
>
> *We were glad to hear you **(had) enjoyed** your trip to Denmark.*

## 2  reporting present and future tenses

If somebody talked about a situation that has still not changed – that is to say, if the original speaker's present and future are still present and future – a reporter can often choose whether to keep the original speaker's tenses or to change them, after a past reporting verb. Both structures are common.

> – DIRECT:   *The earth **goes** round the sun.*
> INDIRECT: *He proved that the earth **goes/went** round the sun.*   ▶

– DIRECT:     *How old **are** you?*
INDIRECT: *Are you deaf? I asked how old you **are/were**.*
– DIRECT:     *It **will** be windy tomorrow.*
INDIRECT: *The forecast said it **will/would** be windy tomorrow.*

We are more likely to change the original speaker's tenses if we do not agree with what he/she said, if we are not certain of its truth, or if we wish to make it clear that the information comes from the original speaker, not from ourselves.

> *The Greeks thought that the sun **went** round the earth.* (NOT ... ~~that the sun goes round the earth.~~)
> *She just said she **was** fourteen! I don't believe her for a moment.*
> *He announced that profits **were** higher than forecast.*

## 3 modal verbs in indirect speech

The modals *would, should, could, might, ought* and *must* are usually unchanged after past reporting verbs in indirect speech. This is also true of *needn't* (see 366) and *had better* (see 230).

– DIRECT:     *It **would** be nice if I **could** see you again.*
INDIRECT: *He said it **would** be nice if he **could** see me again.*
– DIRECT:     *It **might** be too late.*
INDIRECT: *I was afraid that it **might** be too late.*
– DIRECT:     *It **must** be pretty late. I really **must** go.*
INDIRECT: *She said it **must** be pretty late and she really **must** go.*
– DIRECT:     *You **needn't** pretend to be sorry.*
INDIRECT: *I said he **needn't** pretend ...*

First-person *shall* and *should* may be reported as *would* in indirect speech (because of the change of person).

DIRECT:     *We **shall/should** be delighted to come.*
INDIRECT: *They said they **would** be delighted to come.*

For *had to* as a past of *must*, see 358, 360.

## 4 reporting 'Shall I ...?'

There are different ways of reporting questions beginning *Shall I ...?*, depending on whether the speaker is asking for information or making an offer.

– DIRECT:     ***Shall I** be needed tomorrow?* (information)
INDIRECT: *He wants to know if he **will** be needed tomorrow.*
– DIRECT:     ***Shall I** carry your bag?* (offer)
INDIRECT: *He wants to know if he **should/can** carry your bag.*

## 5 conditionals

After past reporting verbs, sentences with *if* and *would* are usually unchanged.

DIRECT:     *It **would** be best if we **started** early.*
INDIRECT: *He said it **would** be best if they **started** early.*

However, *if*-sentences that refer to 'unreal' situations can change as follows.

DIRECT:     *If I **had** any money I'**d buy** you a drink.*
INDIRECT: *She said if she **had had** any money she **would have bought** me a drink.* (OR *She said if she **had** any money she **would buy** ...*)

## 6 negative questions

Negative questions often express emotions such as surprise or enthusiasm (see 368), and these are usually reported in special ways.

- DIRECT: *Don't the children like ice-cream?*
  INDIRECT: ***She was surprised*** *that the children didn't like ice-cream.*
  (NOT ~~She asked if the children didn't like ice-cream.~~)
- DIRECT: *Isn't she lovely!*
  INDIRECT: ***I remarked*** *how lovely she was.* (NOT ~~I asked if she wasn't lovely.~~)

## 7 word order with *what, who* and *which*

Questions beginning *who/what/which* + *be* can ask for a subject or a complement. Compare:

> *Who is the best player here?* (This asks for a subject: a possible answer is *John is the best player here.*)
> *What is the time?* (This asks for a complement: a possible answer is *The time is 4.30,* NOT ~~4.30 is the time.~~)

When we report the first kind of question (where *who/what/which* + *be* asks for a subject), two word orders are possible.

- DIRECT: *Who's the best player here?*
  INDIRECT: *She asked me **who was the best player.***
  *She asked me **who the best player was.***
- DIRECT: *What's the matter?*
  INDIRECT: *I asked **what was the matter.***
  *I asked **what the matter was.***
- DIRECT: *Which is my seat?*
  INDIRECT: *She wondered **which was her seat.***
  *She wondered **which her seat was.***

This does not happen when *who/what/which* asks for a complement.

> DIRECT: *What's the time?*
> INDIRECT: *She asked **what the time was.*** (NOT USUALLY *She asked what was the time.*)

## 8 *She's written I don't know how many books*

Complicated structures can be produced in informal speech when reporting expressions are put into sentences with question-word clauses or relatives.

> *She's written **I don't know how many books.***
> *He's gone **I don't know where.***
> *This is the man who **Ann said would tell us about the church.***

For more about relative structures of this kind, see 498.15.
For more about embedding (clauses inside clauses) in general, see 515.

## 9 indirect speech without reporting verbs

In newspaper, radio and TV reports, reports of parliamentary debates, records of conferences, minutes of meetings etc, the indirect speech construction is often used with very few reporting verbs. The use of tenses is enough to make it clear that a text is a report.

▶

*The Managing Director began his address to the shareholders by summarising the results for the year. Profits on the whole **had been** high, though one or two areas **had been** disappointing. It **was**, however, important to maintain a high level of investment, and he **was** sure that the shareholders **would appreciate** ...*

In literary narrative, similar structures are common. The reported speech may be made more vivid by using direct question structures and 'here and now' words.

*At breakfast, Peter refused to go to school. Why should he spend all his time sitting listening to idiots? What use was all that stuff anyway? If he stayed at home he could read books. He might even learn something useful. His father, as usual, was unsympathetic. Peter had to go to school, by damn, and he had better get moving now, or there'd be trouble.*

# 279 infinitives (1): introduction

## 1 forms

Infinitives are forms like *(to) write, (to) stand*. Unlike verb tenses (e.g. *writes, stood*), infinitives do not usually show the actual times of actions or events. They usually refer to actions and events in a more general way, rather like *-ing* forms. (See 293–300).

Infinitives are generally used with *to*; for infinitives without *to*, see 281.

Besides simple infinitives like *(to) write*, there are also progressive infinitives (e.g. *(to) be writing*), perfect infinitives (e.g. *(to) have written*) and passive infinitives (e.g. *(to) be written*). For details of the various forms, see 280.

## 2 use

Infinitives have many functions. An infinitive can be used, for example, after *do* or a modal auxiliary verb as part of a verb phrase.

*Do you **think** she's ready?*
*We **must get** some more light bulbs.*

An infinitive can also be used, alone or with other words:

- as the subject or complement of a clause (see 290)
  ***To watch** him eating really gets on my nerves.*
  *The main thing is **to relax**.          It's nice **to talk** to you.*
- as the object or complement of a verb, adjective or noun (see 282–285)
  *I don't **want to talk**. I'm **anxious to contact** your brother.*
  *You have **the right to remain** silent.*
- to express a person's purpose (see 289)
  *He came to London **to look** for work.*

For full details of the uses of infinitives, see the following sections.

# 280 infinitives (2): forms

Besides the ordinary infinitive (e.g. *(to) go, (to) work*), there are also progressive, perfect and passive forms.

## 1 progressive infinitive: *(to) be ...ing*

Like other progressive forms (see 470), progressive infinitives suggest that actions and events are / were / will be continuing around the time that we are talking about.

*It's nice **to be sitting** here with you.*
*I noticed that he seemed **to be smoking** a lot.*
*This time tomorrow I'll **be lying** on the beach.*
    (future progressive tense: see 220)
*Why's she so late? She can't still **be working**.*

## 2 perfect infinitive: *(to) have* + past participle

Perfect infinitives can have the same kind of meaning as perfect tenses (see 427) or past tenses (see 421–422).

*It's nice **to have finished** work.* (= It's nice that I have finished.)
*I'm sorry not **to have come** on Thursday.* (= ... that I didn't come ...)

We often use perfect infinitives to talk about 'unreal' past events: things that did not happen, or that may not have happened (see 288).

*I meant **to have telephoned**, but I forgot.*
*You should **have told** me you were coming.*
*I may **have left** my umbrella at the restaurant.*

## 3 passive infinitive: *(to) be* + past participle

Passive infinitives have the same kind of meaning as other passive forms (see 412).

*There's a lot of work **to be done**.*      *She ought **to be told** about it.*
*That window must **be repaired** before tonight.*

Sometimes active and passive infinitives can have similar meanings, especially after a noun or *be* (see 287).

*There's a lot of work **to do** / **to be done**.*

## 4 combinations

Perfect progressive and perfect passive infinitives are common.

*I'd like **to have been sitting** there when she walked in.*
*They were lucky – they could **have been killed**.*

Progressive passive infinitives are possible but unusual.

*What would you like to be doing right now? ~ I'd like **to be being massaged**.*

Progressive perfect passive infinitives (e.g. *It must **have been being built** at the time*) are very unusual.

## 5 negative forms

Negative infinitives are normally made by putting *not* before the infinitive.

*Try **not to be** late.* (NOT USUALLY ~~Try to not be late.~~ OR ~~Try to don't be late.~~)
*You were silly **not to have locked** your car.*
*He's very busy. I'm afraid he **can't be disturbed**.*

▶

## 6 *to*

The marker *to* is normally used before infinitives (e.g. *He wanted to go*). Note that this *to* is not a preposition; after the preposition *to* we use *-ing* forms (see 298.2). For infinitives without *to* (e.g. *She let him go*), see 281.

## 7 split infinitive

A 'split infinitive' is a structure in which *to* is separated from the rest of the infinitive by an adverb.

*I'd like to really understand philosophy.*
*He began to slowly get up off the floor.*

Split infinitive structures are quite common in English, especially in an informal style. Some people consider them incorrect or careless, and avoid them if possible by putting the adverb in another position.

*He began slowly to get up off the floor.*

For details of the use of infinitives, see the following sections.
For the use of *to* instead of a whole infinitive (e.g. *I'd like to*), see 182.

# 281 infinitives (3): without **to**

We usually put *to* before the infinitive (e.g. *I want to know, It's nice to see you*). But we use the infinitive without *to* in some cases.

## 1 after modal auxiliary verbs

After the modal auxiliary verbs *will, shall, would, should, can, could, may, might* and *must*, we use the infinitive without *to*.

*I must go now.* (NOT ~~I must to go now.~~)
*Can you help me?*          *Do you think she might be joking?*
*I would rather go alone.*       *She will probably be elected.*

We also use the infinitive without *to* after *had better* (see 230), and sometimes after *need* and *dare* (see 366, 151).

*You'd better see what she wants.*
*She needn't do the washing up.*       *I daren't go out at night.*

The *to*-infinitive is used after *ought* (see 403).

## 2 after *let, make, hear* etc

Certain verbs are followed by **object + infinitive without *to***. They include *let, make, see, hear, feel, watch* and *notice*.

*She lets her children stay up very late.* (NOT ~~She lets her children to stay...~~
OR ~~She lets her children staying...~~)
*I made them give me the money back.*
*I didn't see you come in.*
*We both heard him say that I was leaving.*
*Did you feel the earth move?*

*Help* can also be used in this way (see 244).

*Could you help me (to) unload the car?*

This structure is also possible with *have* (see 238) and *know* (see 313).

*Have Mrs Hansen come in, please.* (especially AmE)
*I've never known him (to) pay for a drink.*

In passive versions of these structures (with *make, see, hear, help* and *know*) the infinitive with *to* is used.

> *He **was made to pay** back the money.*
> *She **was heard to say** that she disagreed.*

For more information about structures with *let*, see 322. For *make*, see 335.
For more information about *see, hear, watch* etc + **object** + **verb**, see 242.
For verbs that are followed by **object** + ***to*-infinitive**, see 283.

## 3 after *why (not)*

We can introduce questions and suggestions with *why (not)* + **infinitive without** *to*. For more details, see 628.

> ***Why pay** more at other shops? We have the lowest prices.*
> ***Why stand up** if you can sit down? **Why sit down** if you can lie down?*
> *You're looking tired. **Why not take** a holiday?*

## 4 after *and, or, except, but, than, as* and *like*

When two infinitive structures are joined by *and, or, except, but, than, as* or *like*, the second is often without *to*.

> *I'd like to lie down **and go** to sleep.*
> *Do you want to have lunch now **or wait** till later?*
> *We had nothing to do **except look** at the cinema posters.*
> *I'm ready to do anything **but work** on a farm.*
> *It's easier to do it yourself **than explain** to somebody else how to do it.*
> *It's as easy to smile **as frown**.*
> *I have to feed the animals as well **as look** after the children.*
> *Why don't you do something useful **like clean** the flat?*

*Rather than* is usually followed by an infinitive without *to*.

> ***Rather than wait** any more, I decided to go home by taxi.*

## 5 after *do*

Expressions like *All I did was, What I do is* etc can be followed by an infinitive without *to*.

> ***All I did was (to) give** him a little push.*
> ***What a fire-door does is (to) delay** the spread of a fire.*

# 282 infinitives (4): after verbs

After many non-auxiliary verbs, we can use the infinitives of other verbs.

> *It's **beginning to rain**.*
> *I don't **want to see** you again.*
> *She **seems to be crying**.*
> *I **expect to have finished** by tomorrow evening.*
> *The car **needs to be cleaned**.*

▶

Common verbs that can be followed by infinitives (for more detailed entries on some of these, see Index):

| afford | begin | fail | intend | prefer | seem |
|--------|-------|------|--------|--------|------|
| agree | care | forget | learn | prepare | start |
| appear | choose | go on | like | pretend | swear |
| arrange | consent | happen | love | propose | trouble |
| ask | continue | hate | manage | promise | try |
| attempt | dare | help | mean | refuse | want |
| (can't) bear | decide | hesitate | neglect | regret | wish |
| beg | expect | hope | offer | remember | |

Some of these verbs can be followed by **object + infinitive** (e.g. *I want her to be happy*). For details, see 283. A few verbs are followed by **verb + *for* + object + infinitive** (e.g. *I arranged for her to have violin lessons*). For details of these, see 291.7.

After some verbs we can use not only an infinitive but also an *-ing* form (sometimes with a difference of meaning). For details, see 299.

After some verbs, it is not possible to use an infinitive. Many of these can be followed by *-ing* forms (see 296).

*I enjoy sailing.* (NOT *I enjoy to sail.*)

For perfect infinitives after verbs, see 288.
For ***have* + infinitive** (e.g. *I have to go now*), see 239.
For ***be* + infinitive** (e.g. *You are to start tomorrow*), see 91.
For information about the structures that are possible with a particular verb, see a good dictionary.

## 283 infinitives (5): I want you to listen

Many verbs are followed by **object + infinitive**.

*I want **you to listen**.*

With some verbs (e.g. *want, allow*), a *that*-clause is impossible.

*She didn't **want me to go**.* (NOT *She didn't want that I go.*)

*They don't **allow people to smoke**.* (NOT *They don't allow that people smoke.*)

*I didn't **ask you to pay** for the meal.* (NOT *I didn't ask that you pay for the meal.*)

Some common verbs that can be followed by **object + infinitive**:

| advise | forbid | love | request |
|--------|--------|------|---------|
| allow | force | mean | teach |
| ask | get (see also 223) | need | tell |
| (can't) bear | hate | oblige | tempt |
| beg | help (see also 244) | order | trouble |
| cause | instruct | permit | want |
| command | intend | persuade | warn |
| compel | invite | prefer | wish (see also 630) |
| encourage | leave | recommend | |
| expect | like | remind | |

*Let, make, see, hear, feel, watch, notice, have,* and sometimes *know* and *help* are followed by object + infinitive without *to* (see 281).

> *Why won't you **let me explain**?*
> *I **heard her open** the door and go out.*

Some verbs cannot be followed by **object + infinitive**; for example *suggest.*

> *I **suggested that** she should go home.* (NOT *~~I suggested her to go home.~~*)

Many of the verbs listed above can also be followed by other structures such as an *-ing* form or a *that*-clause. For complete information, see a good dictionary.

For passive structures with these verbs, see 418.
For verbs that are followed by *for* + **object** + **infinitive** (e.g. *I arranged for her to go early*), see 291.7
For **object** + *to be* + **complement** after verbs of thinking and feeling (e.g. *I considered him to be an excellent choice*), see 607.
For structures with *take* (e.g. *The ferry took two hours to unload*), see 576.

# 284 infinitives (6): after adjectives

## 1 reactions and feelings: *pleased to see you*

Infinitives are often used after adjectives describing reactions and feelings.

> *I'm **pleased to see** you.*
> *John was **surprised to get** Ann's letter.*
> *She's **anxious to go** home.*
> *We're **happy to be** here.*
> *I was **shocked to see** how ill he was.*
> *Most people are **afraid to hear** the truth about themselves.*

Not all adjectives of this kind are followed by infinitives. Some are followed by **preposition + *-ing* form** (see 297), or by *that*-clauses (see 19). Some adjectives (e.g. *afraid, sure*) can be followed by either an infinitive or an *-ing* form, often with a difference of meaning: for details, see 299.

For structures with *for* (e.g. *She's anxious for the children to go home*), see 291–293.

## 2 other adjectives: *certain to win*

Besides adjectives referring to reactions and feelings, many other adjectives can be followed by infinitives. Examples: *right, wrong, stupid, certain* (see 299.15), *welcome, careful, due, fit, able* (see 3), *likely* (see 327), *lucky.*

> *We were **right to start** early.*　　*Be **careful not to wake** the children.*
> *I was **stupid to believe** him.*　　*It's very **likely to rain.***
> *She's **certain to win.***　　*You were **lucky not to be killed.***
> *You're **welcome to stay** as long as you like.*

For structures with preparatory *it* (e.g. *It is important to get enough sleep*), see 446.

## 3 superlatives etc: *the oldest athlete to win …*

Superlatives can be followed by an infinitive structure. The meaning is similar to an identifying relative clause (see 495).

> *He's the **oldest athlete** ever **to win** an Olympic gold medal.*
> (= … who has ever won …)　　　　　　　　　　　　　　　▶

This structure is also common with *first, second, third* etc, *next, last* and *only*.
> Who was the **first person to climb** Everest without oxygen?
> The **next to arrive** was Mrs Patterson.
> She's the **only scientist to have won** three Nobel prizes.

This structure is only possible when the noun with the superlative has a subject relationship with the infinitive.
> Is this the first time that you have stayed here?
> (NOT ... ~~the first time for you to stay here.~~ Time is not the subject of *stay*.)

## 4  easy to please

Some adjectives can be used with infinitives in a special structure, in which the subject of the clause is really the object of the infinitive. Examples are *easy, hard, difficult, impossible, good, ready,* and adjectives after *enough* and *too*.
> He's **easy to please**.
> (= To please him is easy. OR It is easy to please him.)
> Japanese is **difficult** for Europeans **to learn**.
> (= It is difficult for Europeans to learn Japanese.)
> His theory is **impossible to understand**.
> (= It is impossible to understand his theory.)
> Are these berries **good to eat**?    The apples were **ripe enough to pick**.
> The letters are **ready to sign**.    The box was **too heavy to lift**.

The structure often ends with a preposition (see 452).
> She's nice to talk **to**.            He's very easy to get on **with**.
> It's not a bad place to live **in**.

There is no object pronoun after the infinitive or preposition in these cases.
> Cricket is not very interesting to **watch**. (NOT ~~Cricket is not very interesting to watch it.~~)
> She's nice to talk **to**. (NOT ~~She's nice to talk to her.~~)

When the adjective is before a noun, the infinitive is usually after the noun.
> It's a **good wine to keep**. (NOT ~~It's a good to keep wine.~~)

*Easy, difficult* and *impossible* cannot be used in this structure when the subject of the clause is the subject of the following verb.
> She has difficulty learning maths. (NOT ~~She is difficult to learn maths.~~)
> Iron rusts easily. (NOT ~~Iron is easy to rust.~~)
> This material can't possibly catch fire. (NOT ~~This material is impossible to catch fire.~~)

For more about *enough/too* + **adjective** + **infinitive**, see 187, 595.
For **so** + **adjective** + **infinitive** (e.g. *Would you be so kind as to help me?*), see 538.8.
For information about the structures that are possible with a particular adjective, see a good dictionary.

# 285  infinitives (7): after nouns and pronouns

## 1  nouns related to verbs: *no wish to change*

We can use infinitives after some nouns which are related to verbs that can be followed by infinitives (e.g. *wish, decide, need*).
> I have no **wish to change**. (= I do not wish to change.)
> I told her about my **decision to leave**. (= I told her that I had decided to leave.)

*Is there any **need to ask** Joyce?* (= Do we need to ask Joyce?)
Not all nouns can be followed by infinitives in this way.

*I hate the **thought of getting** old.* (NOT ... ~~the thought to get old.~~)
And note that not all related verbs and nouns are followed by the same
structures. Compare:

- *I hope **to arrive**.*              – *I do not intend **to return**.*
  *There's no hope **of arriving**.*      *I have no intention **of returning**.*
- *She prefers **to live** alone.*
  *I understand her preference **for living** alone.*

Unfortunately there is no easy way to decide which structures are possible
after a particular noun. It is best to check in a good dictionary.

## 2 nouns related to adjectives: *You were a fool to agree*

We can also use infinitives after some nouns which are related to adjectives, or
which have an adjectival sense.

*You were a **fool to agree**.* (= You were foolish to agree.)
*What a **nuisance to have** to go!* (= How annoying to have to go!)
*It's a **pleasure to see** you again.* (= It's pleasant to see you again.)

## 3 purpose: *a key to open the door*

An infinitive can be used after a noun, or an indefinite pronoun like *something*,
to explain the purpose of a particular thing: what it does, or what somebody
does with it. The noun or pronoun can be the subject of the infinitive.

*Have you got a **key to open** this door?* (The key will open the door.)
*It was a **war to end** all wars.*
*I'd like **something to stop** my toothache.*

The noun or pronoun can also be the object of the infinitive.

*I need some more **books to read**.* (I will read the books.)
*Is there any **milk to put** on the cornflakes?*
*Did you tell her which **bus to take**?*      *Is there **anything to drink**?*

If the noun or pronoun is the object of the infinitive, we do not add an object
pronoun after the infinitive.

*I gave her a paper **to read**.* (NOT ... ~~a paper to read it.~~)
*He needs a place **to live** in.* (NOT ... ~~a place to live in it.~~)

*Some/any/nowhere* can also be followed by infinitives.

*The kids want **somewhere to practise** their music.*

## 4 *enough, too much* etc

Quantifiers like *enough, too much/many/little/few, plenty* etc are often
followed by **noun + infinitive**.

*There was **enough light to see** what I was doing.*
*There's **too much snow** (for us) **to be able** to drive.*
*We've got **plenty of time to see** the British Museum.*

*Enough* is often dropped before *room* and *time*.

*There's hardly **(enough) room to breathe** in here.*
*Do you think we'll have **(enough) time to do** some shopping?*     ▶

## 5 infinitive with preposition: *a friend to play with*

A noun can be followed by **infinitive + preposition**.

> *Mary needs a friend to play with.*
> *He's looking for a flat to live in.*

In a very formal style, another structure is possible: **noun + preposition + whom/which + infinitive**.

> *Mary needs a friend with whom to play.*
> *He's looking for a place in which to live.*

This is not possible when there is no preposition. One cannot say, for example, ~~I need a book which to read.~~

## 6 *the life to come* etc

In expressions like *the life to come* (= life after death), *the world to come*, *his wife to be* (= his future wife), the infinitive has a future meaning, and is similar to a relative clause with *be* (= the life/world that is to come, etc.)

For infinitives used to talk about people's purposes, see 289.
For passive infinitives (e.g. *There's work to be done.*), see 287.
For *for* + **object** + **infinitive** (e.g. *Is there any need for us to stay?*), see 291.5.
For infinitives after *first, next, last* or **superlative** + **noun** (e.g. *the first woman to climb Everest*), see 284.3.
For more about structures with prepositions at the end, see 452.

# 286 infinitives (8): who to . . . , what to . . . etc

## 1 indirect questions: *Tell us what to do*

In indirect speech (see 277.2), we can use an infinitive after the question words *who, what, where* etc (but not usually *why*). This structure expresses ideas such as obligation and possibility.

> *I wonder **who to invite**.* (= . . . who I should invite.)
> *Tell us **what to do**.*
> *Can you show me **how to get** to the station?* (= . . . how I can get to the station?)
> *I don't know **where to put** the car.*      *Tell me **when to pay**.*
> *I can't decide **whether to answer** her letter.*
> (BUT NOT ~~I can't understand why to do it.~~)

## 2 direct questions: *What shall we do?*

We do not usually begin a direct question with *How to . . .?, What to . . .?* etc. After question words, we often use *shall* and *should*.

> ***How shall** I tell her?* (NOT ~~How to tell her?~~)
> ***What shall** we do?* (NOT ~~What to do?~~)
> ***Who should** I pay?* (NOT ~~Who to pay?~~)

## 3 titles

*How to . . ., What to . . .* etc are often found as titles for instructions, information leaflets, books etc. (Note: these are not questions.)

> *HOW TO IMPROVE YOUR PRONUNCIATION*
> *WHAT TO DO IF FIRE BREAKS OUT*

For questions beginning *Why (not)* + **infinitive**, see 628.

# 287 infinitives (9): active and passive infinitive with similar meaning

## 1 obligation

We can use **noun + infinitive** to talk about obligation – things that people have to do. Active and passive infinitives are often both possible.

> *There's a lot of **work to do** / **to be done**.*
> *There are six **letters to post** / **to be posted**.*
> *Give me the names of the **people to contact** / **to be contacted**.*
> *The **people to interview** / **to be interviewed** are in the next room.*

We prefer active infinitives if we are thinking more about the person who will do the action.

> *I've got work **to do**.* (NOT *I've got work to be done.*)
> *They've sent **Jane** a form **to fill in**.*

We use passive infinitives if we are thinking more about the action, or the person/thing that the action is done to.

> *The **carpets to be cleaned** are in the garage.* (NOT *The carpets to clean...*)
> *His desk is covered with **forms to be filled in**.*

After *be*, we normally use passive infinitives in these cases.

> *These sheets **are to be washed**.* (NOT *These sheets are to wash.*)
> *This form **is to be filled in** in ink.* (NOT *This form is to fill in...*)
> *The cleaning **is to be finished** by midday.* (NOT *...is to finish...*)

## 2 to be seen/found/congratulated etc

Note the expressions *anywhere/nowhere to be seen/found*.

> *He wasn't **anywhere to be seen**.* (NOT *... anywhere to see.*)
> *Susan was **nowhere to be found**.* (NOT *...nowhere to find.*)

We also use passive infinitives to express value judgements with verbs like *congratulate, encourage, avoid*.

> *You are **to be congratulated**.* (NOT *...to congratulate.*)
> *This behaviour is **to be encouraged**.*

But note the common expression *to blame*, meaning 'responsible' (for some unfortunate event).

> *Nobody was **to blame** for the accident.*

## 3 nothing to do and nothing to be done etc

Note the difference between *nothing to do* and *nothing to be done*.

> *I'm bored – there's **nothing to do**.* (= There are no entertainments.)
> *There's **nothing to be done** – we'll have to buy a new one.*
> (= There's no way of putting it right.)

For structures like *She's easy to amuse*, see 284.4.
For structures with *take* (e.g. *The ferry took two hours to unload*), see 576.
For more about *be* + infinitive, see 91.

# 288 infinitives (10): **I'm glad to have left**

## 1 perfect or past meaning

Perfect infinitives (*to have gone, to have left* etc) can have the same kind of meaning as perfect or past tenses.

*I'm glad **to have left** school.* (= I'm glad that I have left ...)
*She was sorry **to have missed** Bill.* (= ... that she had missed Bill.)
*We hope **to have finished** the job by next Saturday.* (= ... that we will have finished ...)
*You seem **to have annoyed** Anne yesterday.* (= It seems that you annoyed Anne yesterday.)

## 2 perfect infinitive for 'unreal' past

After some verbs (e.g. *mean, be, would like*), perfect infinitives can refer to 'unreal' past situations that are the opposite of what really happened.

*I **meant to have telephoned**, but I forgot.* (or *I meant to telephone ...*)
*He **was to have been** the new ambassador, but he fell ill.*
*I wish I'd been there – I **would like to have seen** Harry's face when Nan walked in.*

With *would like, would prefer* and one or two other verbs, a double perfect infinitive is sometimes used in informal speech; the extra perfect infinitive does not change the meaning.

*I **would have liked to have seen** Harry's face.*

## 3 modals: *He could have killed himself*

After the modal verbs *could, might, ought, should, would* and *needn't*, we often use perfect infinitives to refer to unreal situations.

*Did you see him fall? He **could have killed** himself.*
(He did not kill himself.)
*You **should have written** – I was getting worried.*
(The person did not write.)
*I **would have gone** to university if my parents had had more money.*
(The speaker did not go to university.)
*She **needn't have sent** me flowers.*
(She did send flowers.)

Modal verbs with perfect infinitives can also refer to situations that are not unreal, but uncertain.

*She **could/should/ought to/may/will/must have arrived** by now.*

For more details, see the entries for the different modal verbs.

# 289 infinitives (11): purpose

## 1 *I sat down to rest*

We often use an infinitive to talk about a person's purpose – why he or she does something.

*I sat down **to rest**.* (NOT ~~I sat down for resting / for to rest.~~)
*He went abroad **to forget**.*

*I'm going to Austria **to learn German.***
***To switch on,** press red button.*
A *for*-structure (see 291) can be used to talk about a purpose that involves action by somebody else.
*I left the door unlocked **for Harriet to get in.***

**2** in order to; so as to

We can also use *in order to . . .* (more formal) or *so as to . . . .*
*He got up early **in order to have time to pack** .*
*I watched him **in order to know more about him.***
*I moved to a new flat **so as to be near my work.***
*In order to / so as to* are normal before negative infinitives.
*I'm going to leave now, **so as not to be** late.* (NOT ~~I'm going to leave now, not to be late.~~)

# 290 infinitives (12): subject, complement or object

**1** subject: *To practise is important / It's important to practise*

In older English, an infinitive clause could easily be the subject of a sentence.
***To practise regularly** is important.*
***To wait for people** who were late made him angry.*
In modern English, this is unusual in an informal style. We more often use *it* as a preparatory subject and put the infinitive clause later (see 446).
*It's important **to practise regularly.***
*It made him angry **to wait for people** who were late.*
We can also use an *-ing* structure at the beginning of a sentence as the subject, instead of an infinitive clause (see 295).
***Selling insurance** is a pretty boring job.*
    (More natural than *To sell insurance . . .*)

**2** complement: *Your task is to get across the river*

An infinitive clause can be used after *be* as a subject complement.
*Your task is **to get across the river** without being seen.*
*My ambition was **to retire at thirty.***
Sentences like these can also be constructed with preparatory *it* (see 446).
*It is your task **to get across the river** without being seen.*
*It was my ambition **to retire at thirty.***

**3** object: *I like to read the paper at breakfast*

Many verbs can have an infinitive clause as their object (see 283). Compare:
– *I like **cornflakes** for breakfast.* (noun object)
  *I like **to read the paper** at breakfast.* (infinitive clause as object)
– *She wants **some exercise.***
  *She wants **to dance.***

For structures like *He made it difficult to refuse*, see 447.

# 291 infinitives (13): for ... to ...

## 1 infinitive with its own subject

The structure *for* + **noun/pronoun** + **infinitive** is very common in English. It is used when an infinitive needs its own subject. Compare:
– *Ann will be happy to help you.* (Ann will help.)
  *Ann will be happy for the children to help you.* (The children will help.)
– *My idea was to learn Russian.*
  *My idea was for her to learn Russian.*
– *To ask Joe would be a big mistake.*
  *For you to ask Joe would be a big mistake.* (NOT ~~You to ask Joe would be~~ ...)
Note that the subject of the infinitive is the object of the preposition *for*. Object forms of pronouns are used.
  *Ann will be happy for them to help you.* (NOT ... ~~for they to help you.~~)

## 2 use

The structure is often used when we are referring to possibility, necessity or frequency, when we are expressing wishes, suggestions or plans for the future, and when we are giving personal reactions to situations. Like other infinitive structures, it is used especially after adjectives, nouns and verbs; it can also act as the subject of a clause. It often has the same meaning as a *that*-clause. Compare:
  *It's important for the meeting to start on time.*
  *It's important that the meeting should start on time.*

## 3 after adjectives: *anxious for us to see ...*

The structure *for* + **object** + **infinitive** can be used after certain adjectives which express wishes and other personal feelings about the importance or value of future events (e.g. *anxious, eager, delighted, willing, reluctant*).

> adjective + *for* + object + infinitive

*She's anxious for us to see her work.*
*I'm eager for the party to be a success.*
*Robert says he'd be delighted for Mary to come and stay.*

## 4 *It's impossible for ... to ...*

*For*-structures with preparatory *it* (see 446) are common with many adjectives expressing possibility, necessity, importance, urgency, frequency and value judgements.

> (...) *it* (...) + adjective + *for* + object + infinitive

*It's impossible for the job to be finished in time.*
*Would it be easy for you to phone me tomorrow?*
*It's important for the meeting to start at eight.*
*It seems unnecessary for him to start work this week.*
*I consider it essential for the school to be properly heated.*
*Is it usual for foxes to come so close to the town?*
*I thought it strange for her to be out so late.*
*It's not good for the oil tank to be so close to the house.*

Other common adjectives that are used in this way include *vital, necessary, pointless, unimportant, common, normal, unusual, rare, right, wrong.* Note that *likely* and *probable* are not used like this.

> She's **likely to arrive** this evening. (NOT ~~It's likely for her to arrive this evening.~~)
>
> It's **probable that she'll be** in a bad temper. OR She'll probably be . . . (NOT ~~It's probable for her to be~~ . . .)

## 5 after nouns: *It's a good idea for us to ...*

The structure can also be used after nouns in expressions with meanings similar to the adjectives listed above. Examples are: *time, a good/bad idea, plan, aim, need, request, mistake, shame.*

> It's **time for everybody to go** to bed.
>
> It's a good **idea for us to travel** in separate cars.
>
> There's a **plan for Jack to spend** a year in Japan.
>
> Our **aim is for students to learn** as quickly as possible.
>
> It was a big **mistake for them not to keep** John as manager.
>
> It was a real **shame for them not to win** after all their work.

## 6 *something for me to do*

*Something, anything, nothing* and similar words are often followed by *for* + object + infinitive.

> Have you got **something for me to do**?
>
> There's **nothing for the cats to eat**.
>
> Is there **anybody for Louise to play** with in the village?
>
> I must find **somewhere for him to practise** the piano.

## 7 after verbs: *ask for ... to ...*

*For*-structures are not normally used as objects after verbs.

> I need you to help me. (NOT ~~I need for you to help me.~~)

However, verbs which are normally followed by *for* (e.g. *ask, hope, wait, look, pay, arrange*) can often be used with *for* + object + infinitive.

> Anne **asked for the designs to be** ready by Friday.
>
> I can't **wait for them to finish** talking.
>
> Can you **arrange for the gold to be** delivered on Monday? (NOT . . . ~~for the gold being delivered.~~)

A few other verbs can be used like this, e.g. *suit* and *take (time).*

> When will it **suit you for us to call**?
>
> It **took** twenty minutes **for the smoke to clear**.

In informal American English, *like, hate, mean, intend* and some other verbs with similar meanings can be used with a *for*-structure. This is not usually possible in British English.

> I would **like for you to stay** as long as you want.
>
> She **hates for people to feel** sad.
>
> Did you **mean for John to mail** those letters?

▶

**8  after *too* and *enough***

A *for*-structure is often used after *too* and *enough*.

> This is much **too heavy for you to lift**.
> There are **too many people here for me to talk** to all of them.
> Do you think it's warm **enough for the snow to melt**?
> I explained **enough for her to understand** what was happening.

**9  as subject**

The *for*-structure can be the subject of a clause.

> **For us to fail** now would be a disaster.
> **For her to lose** the election would make me very happy.

However, it is more common for a structure with preparatory *it* to be used (see paragraph 4 above).

> **It** would make me very happy **for her to lose** the election.

**10  *for there to be***

The infinitive of *there is* (*there to be*) can be used after *for*.

> I'm anxious **for there to be** plenty of time for discussion.
> It's important **for there to be** a fire escape at the back of the building.

**11  *that*-clauses**

Instead of *for* + **object** + **infinitive**, a *that*-clause with *should* or a subjunctive (see 567) is often possible, especially when we want to express wishes, recommendations, suggestions and plans for the future. A *that*-clause is usually more formal than a *for*-structure.

> It is important **that there should be** a fire escape.
> I'm anxious **that the party should be** a success.
> His idea is **that we should travel** in separate cars.
> It is essential **that the meeting start** at eight.

For sentences like *He made it difficult for us to refuse*, see 447.

# 292  infinitives (14): other uses

**1  *I came home to find ...***

Infinitive clauses can be used to say what somebody found out or learnt at the end of a journey or task.

> I arrived home **to find that the house had been burgled**.

The idea of surprise or disappointment can be emphasised by using *only*.

> At last we got to Amy's place, **only to discover that she was away**.
> He spent four years studying, **only to learn that there were no jobs**.

**2  *To hear her talk, you'd think ...***

The infinitives of *see* and *hear* can be used to explain the reason for a false impression. The infinitive structure is usually followed by *you'd think* or a similar expression.

> **To see them, you'd think** they were married. But they only met yesterday.
> **To see him walk** down the street, **you'd never know** he was blind.
> **To hear her talk, you'd think** she was made of money.

# 293 -ing forms (1): introduction

## 1 'participles and 'gerunds'

We can use *-ing* forms (e.g. *smoking, walking*) not only as verbs, but also like adjectives or nouns. Compare:

> You're **smoking** *too much these days.* (verb: part of present progressive)
> *There was a* **smoking** *cigarette end in the ashtray.* (adjective describing *cigarette end*)
> **Smoking** *is bad for you.* (noun: subject of sentence)

When *-ing* forms are used as verbs or adjectives, they are often called 'present participles'. (This is not a very suitable name, because these forms can refer to the past, present or future.) When they are used more like nouns, they are often called 'gerunds'.

In *Practical English Usage* the expression '-*ing* form' is used except when there is a good reason to use one of the other terms. Noun-like uses of *-ing* forms ('gerunds') are discussed in the following entries. For their use to make progressive verb forms, see 470 and the entries on the present progressive, past progressive etc. Other ways of using *-ing* forms are discussed in 408–411 ('participles'), together with similar uses of 'past participles' (e.g. *invited, broken*).

## 2 perfect, passive and negative -ing forms

Note the structure of perfect, passive and negative *-ing* forms.

> **Having slept** *for twelve hours, I felt marvellous.* (perfect)
> *She loves* **being looked at**. (passive)
> **Not knowing** *what to do, I went home.* (negative)
> *She's angry about* **not having been invited**. (negative perfect passive)

For spelling rules, see 560–562.

## 3 -ing form or infinitive?

*-ing* forms are often used in similar ways to infinitives. For instance, they can follow certain verbs, adjectives or nouns (see 296–297). Compare:

> – *He agreed* **to wait**.
> *He suggested* **waiting**. (NOT *He suggested to wait.*)
> – *She's ready to listen.*
> *She's good at* **listening**. (NOT *She's good to listen.*)
> – *the need to talk*
> *the idea of* **talking** (NOT *the idea to talk*)

Unfortunately there is no easy way to decide which verbs, adjectives and nouns are followed by *-ing* forms, and which are followed by infinitives. It is best to check in a good dictionary.

Expressions with *-ing* forms can also be used as subjects in sentences, or as complements after *be*. Infinitives are also possible in these cases, but they are much less common in informal English. Compare:

> **Smoking cigarettes** *can kill you.* (More natural than *To smoke cigarettes can kill you.*)
> *My favourite activity is* **reading thrillers**. (More natural than *My favourite activity is to read thrillers.*)

▶

### 4 'participles' and 'gerunds': an unclear difference

The distinction between 'participles' and 'gerunds' is not always clear-cut, and it can sometimes be difficult to decide which term to use. For this reason, some grammarians prefer to avoid the terms 'participle' and 'gerund'. For a detailed discussion of this point, see Section 17.54 of *A Comprehensive Grammar of the English Language*, by Quirk, Greenbaum, Leech and Svartvik (Longman 1985).

## 294 -ing forms (2): a waiting room; a waiting train

*-ing* forms can be used before nouns. This can happen both with noun-like *-ing* forms ('gerunds') and adjective-like *-ing* forms ('participles'). The two structures do not have quite the same kind of meaning. Compare:
– *a **waiting** room* (= a room for waiting. *Waiting* is a gerund, used rather like a noun. Compare ***a guest room**.*)
  *a **waiting** train* (= a train that is waiting. *Waiting* is a participle, used rather like an adjective. Compare ***an early train**.*)
– *a **sleeping** pill* (***sleeping** is a gerund*)
  *a **sleeping** child* (***sleeping** is a participle*)
– ***working** conditions* (gerund)
  ***working** men and women* (participle)

## 295 -ing forms (3): subject, complement or object

### 1 *Smoking is bad for you*

An *-ing* form ('gerund') can be used, just like a noun, as the subject or complement of a verb.
  ***Smoking** is bad for you.* (subject)
  *My favourite activity is **reading**.* (complement)
Infinitives (e.g. *To smoke is bad for you*) are possible in these cases, but are formal and uncommon.
*-ing* forms can also be used as objects after certain verbs (see 296).
  *I hate **packing**.* (object)

### 2 *-ing form with its own object*

The *-ing* form subject, complement or object is used like a noun, but it is still a verb and can have its own object.
  ***Smoking** cigarettes is bad for you.*
  *My favourite activity is **reading** thrillers.*
  *I hate **packing** suitcases.*

### 3 *the opening of Parliament; my smoking*

We can often use determiners (for example *the, my, this*) with *-ing* forms.
  ***the** opening of Parliament*
  *Does **my** smoking annoy you?      I hate all **this** useless arguing.*
Possessive *'s* forms are also possible.
  ***John's** going to sleep during the wedding was rather embarrassing.*
  *She was angry at **Lina's** trying to lie to her.*

Subject pronouns are not possible.

*His shouting gets on my nerves.* (BUT NOT *He shouting*...)

Note that possessives and pronouns are not used before *-ing* forms if it is already clear who is being talked about.

*Thank you for **waiting**.* (NOT *Thank you for your waiting.*)

When an *-ing* form is used with an article, it cannot usually have a direct object. Instead, we can use an *of*-structure.

*the smoking **of** cigarettes* (NOT *the smoking cigarettes*)

*No* is often used with an *-ing* form to say that something is not allowed, or is impossible. This often happens in notices and after *there is*.

*NO SMOKING     NO PARKING     NO WAITING*

*Sorry – there's **no smoking** in the waiting room.*

*She's made up her mind; there's **no arguing** with her.*

### 4   object forms: *Do you mind me smoking?*

In an informal style it is more common to use object forms (like *me, John*) instead of possessives (*my, John's*) with *-ing* forms, especially when these come after a verb or preposition.

*Do you mind **me smoking**?     She was angry at **Lina trying** to lie to her.*

After some verbs (e.g. *see, hear, watch, feel*) possessives are not normally used with *-ing* forms.

*I saw **him getting** out of the car.* (NOT *I saw his getting*...)

### 5   *It's nice being with you*

We can use *it* as a preparatory subject or object for an *-ing* form (see 446–447).

*It's nice **being** with you.*

*I thought **it** pointless **starting** before eight o'clock.*

This is common with *any/no good, any/no use* and *(not) worth* (see 632).

*It's **no good** talking to him – he never listens.*

*Is **it any use** expecting them to be on time?*

*It's **no use** his/him apologising – I shall never forgive him.*

*I didn't think **it worth** complaining about the meal.*

### 6   nouns and *-ing* forms

When there is a noun which has a similar meaning to an *-ing* form, the noun is usually preferred.

*We're all excited about his **arrival**.* (NOT *...about his arriving.*)

## 296   -ing forms (4): after verbs

### 1   verbs that can be followed by *-ing* forms

After some verbs we can use an *-ing* form ('gerund'), but not normally an infinitive.

*I **enjoy travelling**.* (NOT *I enjoy to travel.*)

*He's **finished mending** the car.* (NOT *He's finished to mend*...)

*She's **given up smoking**.* (NOT *...given up to smoke.*)

*The doctor **suggested taking** a long holiday.* (NOT *The doctor suggested (me) to take*...)

▶

Some common verbs that are normally followed by -ing forms:

| | | | |
|---|---|---|---|
| *admit* | *dislike* | *give up* | *practise* |
| *appreciate* | *endure* | *(can't) help* | *put off* |
| *avoid* | *enjoy* | *imagine* | *resent* |
| *burst out* | *escape* | *involve* | *resist* |
| *(crying/laughing)* | *excuse* | *keep (on)* | *risk* |
| *consider* | *face* | *leave off* | *(can't) stand* |
| *contemplate* | *fancy* | *mention* | *suggest* |
| *delay* | *feel like* | *mind* | *understand* |
| *deny* | *finish* | *miss* | |
| *detest* | *forgive* | *postpone* | |

Some verbs can be followed by both -ing forms and infinitives – see paragraph 4 below.

Unfortunately there is no easy way to decide which structures are possible after a particular verb. It is best to check in a good dictionary.

## 2 verb + object + -ing form

Some of the verbs listed above, and some others, can be followed by **object + -ing form**.

*I **dislike people telling** me what to think.*
*I can't **imagine him working** in an office.*
*Nobody can **stop him doing** what he wants to.*
*He **spends all his time gardening**.*
*Did you **see her talking** to the postman?*

*Stop* (in an informal style) and *prevent* are often followed by **object + from + -ing form.**

*Try to **stop/prevent them (from) finding** out.*

Note that after many verbs we can use **possessive + -ing form** rather than **object + -ing form**, especially in a formal style. (See 295.3 for details.)

## 3 -ing form with passive meaning

After *deserve*, *need* and *require*, the -ing form has a passive sense. This structure is more common in British than American English.

*I don't think his article **deserves reading**.* (= ... deserves to be read.)
*Your hair **needs cutting**.* (= ... needs to be cut.)

In informal British English, *want* can also be used like this.

*The car **wants servicing**.* (= ... needs to be serviced.)

## 4 -ing form or infinitive

After some verbs, either an -ing form or an infinitive can be used. These include:

| | | | | |
|---|---|---|---|---|
| *advise* | *forbid* | *hear* | *prefer* | *start* |
| *allow* | *forget* | *intend* | *propose* | *stop* |
| *can't bear* | *go* | *like* | *regret* | *try* |
| *begin* | *go on* | *love* | *remember* | *watch* |
| *continue* | *hate* | *permit* | *see* | |

In some cases there is a difference of meaning: see 299.

For infinitives after verbs, see 282.

# 297 -ing forms (5): after nouns and adjectives

## 1 the idea of getting old; tired of listening

Some nouns and adjectives can be followed by *-ing* forms ('gerunds'). A preposition is normally used to connect the noun/adjective to the *-ing* form. Nouns/adjectives that are followed by *-ing* forms cannot usually be followed by infinitives (see paragraph 3 for some exceptions).

> I hate the **idea of getting** old. (NOT *... the idea to get old.*)
> The **thought of failing** never entered his head. (NOT *The thought to fail ...*)
> I'm **tired of listening** to this. (NOT *I'm tired to listen ...*)
> She's very **good at solving** problems. (NOT *... good to solve ...*)

Unfortunately there is no easy way to decide which nouns and adjectives can be followed by *-ing* forms. It is best to check in a good dictionary.

## 2 purpose: a machine for cutting

*For + -ing* **form** can be used after a noun, or after an indefinite pronoun such as *something* or *anything*, to explain the purpose of an object or material – what it is for.

> A strimmer is a **machine for cutting** grass and weeds.
> Have you got any **stuff for cleaning** silver?
> I need **something for killing** flies.

This structure is mostly used to talk in general about types of object and material. When we talk about somebody's purpose in using a particular object, we are more likely to use an infinitive (see 207.2).

> I must find something **to kill** that fly.

## 3 -ing form or infinitive

After a few nouns and adjectives, we can use either an *-ing* form or an infinitive. Normally there is little or no difference of meaning (see 299.13–16 for some exceptions).

> We have a good **chance of making / to make** a profit.
> I'm **proud of having won / to have won**.

For *be used to ... ing*, see 605.
For infinitives after nouns and adjectives, see 284–285.

# 298 -ing forms (6): without breaking; before starting

## 1 after all prepositions

When we put a verb after a preposition, we normally use an *-ing* form ('gerund'), not an infinitive.

> You can't make an omelette **without breaking** eggs. (NOT *... without to break eggs.*)
> Always check the oil **before starting** the car. (NOT *... before to start the car.*)
> We got the job finished **by working** sixteen hours a day.
> He's talking **about moving** to the country.
> They painted the house **instead of going** on holiday. (NOT *... instead to go ...*)

▶

## 2  to as a preposition: I look forward to ...ing

*To* is actually two different words. It can be an infinitive marker, used to show that the next word is an infinitive (e.g. *to swim, to laugh*). It can also be a preposition, followed for example by a noun (e.g. *She's gone to the park, I look forward to Christmas*).

When *to* is a preposition, it can be followed by the *-ing* form of a verb, but not normally by the infinitive. Common expressions in which this happens are *look forward to, object to, be used to, prefer (doing one thing to doing another), get round to, in addition to*.

In the following examples, note how the preposition *to* can be followed by either a noun or an *-ing* form.

– *I look forward to your next letter.*
  *I look forward to hearing from you.* (NOT ... ~~to hear from you.~~)
– *Do you object to Sunday work?*
  *Do you object to working on Sundays?*
– *I'm not used to London traffic.*
  *I'm not used to driving in London.*
– *I prefer the seaside to the mountains.*
  *I prefer swimming to walking.*
– *I'll get round to the washing up sooner or later.*
  *I'll get round to doing the washing up sooner or later.*

A few verbs and adjectives are used with *to* before nouns, but are followed by the infinitives of verbs. Examples are *agree, consent, entitled, inclined, prone*.

  *She agreed to our plan. / She agreed to do what we wanted.*
  *He's inclined to anger. / He's inclined to lose his temper.*

*Accustomed* can be followed by *to + -ing* form or an infinitive (see 299.11).

## 3  object + infinitive after for: for her to arrive

Note that some verbs are followed by *for* + object + infinitive. An *-ing* form is not usually possible in these cases.

  *We're still waiting for her to arrive.* (NOT ... ~~waiting for her arriving.~~)
  *Can you arrange for us to get tickets?* (NOT ... ~~for our getting tickets?~~)

For the difference between *used to* + infinitive and *be used to* + *-ing* form, see 604–5.
For *-ing* forms after conjunctions (e.g. *When planning a holiday . . .*), see 411.6.
For time clauses with *on* + *-ing* form, see 411.6.

# 299  -ing forms (7):
# remember, go on etc + -ing or infinitive

Some verbs and adjectives can be followed by either *-ing* forms ('gerunds') or infinitives.

  *I started playing / to play the violin when I was 10.*
  *She was proud of having won / to have won.*

With some of these verbs and adjectives, there is a difference of meaning.

## 1 *remember* and *forget*

*Remember/forget* + *-ing* form looks back at the past – at things that one did. *Forget ...ing* is used mostly in the phrase *I'll never forget ...ing*, and expressions with similar meanings.

> *I still remember buying my first bicycle.*
> *I'll never forget meeting the Queen.*

*Remember/forget* + **infinitive** looks forward in time – at things that one still has or still had to do at the moment of remembering or forgetting.

> *You must remember to fetch Mr Lewis from the station tomorrow.*
> *I forgot to buy the soap.*

## 2 *go on*

*Go on* + *-ing* form means 'continue'.

> *She went on talking about her illness until we all went to sleep.*

*Go on* + **infinitive** refers to a change of activity.

> *She stopped talking about that and went on to describe her other problems.*

## 3 *regret*

*Regret* + *-ing* form looks back at the past – at something that one is sorry that one did.

> *I regret leaving school at 14 – it was a big mistake.*

*Regret* + **infinitive** is used mostly in announcements of bad news.

> *We regret to inform passengers that the 14.50 train is one hour late.*
> *We regret to say that we are unable to help you.*

## 4 *advise, allow, permit* and *forbid*

In active clauses after these verbs, we use an *-ing* form if there is no object. If there is an object we use an infinitive. Compare:

> – *I wouldn't advise taking the car – there's nowhere to park.*
> *I wouldn't advise you to take the car ...*
> – *We don't allow/permit smoking in the lecture room.*
> *We don't allow/permit people to smoke in the lecture room.*
> – *The headmistress has forbidden singing in the corridors.*
> *The headmistress has forbidden children to sing ...*

Note the corresponding passive structures.

> – *Smoking is not allowed/permitted in the lecture room.*
> *People are not allowed/permitted to smoke in the lecture room.*
> – *Singing is forbidden.*          – *Early booking is advised.*
> *Children are forbidden to sing.*   *Passengers are advised to book early.*

## 5 *see, watch* and *hear*

After these verbs, the difference between **object + *-ing* form** and **object + infinitive** is like the difference between progressive and simple tenses. With *-ing* forms the verbs suggest that one pays attention to events or actions that are already going on; infinitives usually refer to complete events/actions which are seen/heard from beginning to end. (Note that these verbs are followed by the infinitive without *to*.) Compare:          ▶

– *I looked out of the window and **saw Mary crossing** the road.*
  *I **saw Mary cross** the road and **disappear** into the post office.*
– *As I passed his house I **heard him practising** the piano.*
  *I once **heard Brendel play** all the Beethoven concertos.*

For more details, see 242.

## 6  *try*

To talk about making an experiment – doing something to see what will happen – we use *try + -ing*.

> *I **tried sending** her flowers, **writing** her letters, **giving** her presents, but she still wouldn't speak to me.*

To talk about making an effort to do something difficult, we can use either *try* + **infinitive** or *try + -ing*.

> *I **tried to change** the wheel, but my hands were too cold.*
>   (OR *I **tried changing** the wheel . . .*)

## 7  *mean*

*Mean* in the sense of 'involve', 'have as a result' (see 348) can be followed by an *-ing* form.

> *If you want to pass the exam it will **mean studying** hard.*

In the sense of 'intend', *mean* is followed by an infinitive.

> *I don't think she **means to get** married for the moment.*

## 8  *learn* and *teach*

These verbs (and others with similar meanings) are followed by *-ing* forms mostly when we are referring to lessons or subjects of study.

> *She goes to college twice a week to **learn typing**.*
> *Mr Garland **teaches skiing** in the winter.*

Infinitives are preferred when we talk about the result of the study – about successfully learning a skill.

> *She **learnt to read** German at school, but she **learnt to speak** it in Germany.*
> *I **taught** myself **to type**.*

## 9  *like, love, hate* and *prefer*

After these four verbs, both infinitives and *-ing* forms can often be used without a great difference of meaning.

> *I **hate working** / **to work** at weekends.*
> *I don't get up on Sundays. I **prefer staying** / **to stay** in bed.*

*Like* + **infinitive** is used to talk about choices and habits. Compare:

> *I **like climbing** / **to climb** mountains (= I enjoy climbing.)*
> *When I pour tea I **like to put** the milk in first. (= I choose to; it's my habit.)*

After *would like, would prefer, would hate* and *would love*, infinitives are most often used.

> *I'd **like to tell** you something.* (NOT *I'd like telling you something.*)

*Can I give you a lift?* ~ *No thanks, I'd **prefer to walk**.* (NOT *. . . I'd prefer walking.*)

Compare:

> *Do you **like dancing**? (= Do you enjoy dancing?)*

*Would you like **to dance**?* (= Do you want to dance now?)

For more about *like*, see 325.
For details of structures with *prefer*, see 444.

## 10  *begin* and *start*

*Begin* and *start* can be followed by infinitives or *-ing* forms. Usually there is no important difference.

> *She **began playing** / **to play** the guitar when she was six.*
> *He **started talking** / **to talk** about golf, but everybody went out of the room.*

After progressive forms of *begin* and *start*, infinitives are preferred.

> *I'm **beginning to learn** karate.* (NOT ~~I'm beginning learning karate.~~)

Infinitives are also preferred with *understand*, *realise* and *know*.

> *I slowly **began to understand** how she felt.* (NOT . . . ~~began understanding~~ . . .)
> *He **started to realise** that if you wanted to eat you had to work.*
> (NOT . . . ~~started realising~~ . . .)

## 11  *attempt, intend, continue, can't bear, be accustomed to, be committed to*

After these words and expressions we can generally use either an *-ing* form or an infinitive without much difference of meaning.

> *I **intend telling** / **to tell** her what I think.*
> *I'm not **accustomed to giving/give** personal information about myself to strangers.*

For details of structures with *to + -ing*, see 298.2.

## 12  *-ing* form or infinitive of purpose: *stop*

Some verbs that are followed by *-ing* forms can also be followed by an infinitive of purpose (see 289). A common example is *stop*.

> *I **stopped running**.* (NOT . . . ~~I stopped to run.~~)
> *I **stopped to rest**.* (= . . . in order to rest.)

## 13  *afraid*

To talk about fear of things that happen accidentally, we prefer *afraid of + -ing*.

> *I don't like to drive fast because I'm **afraid of crashing**.*
> *Why are you so quiet?* ~ *I'm **afraid of waking** the children.*

In other cases we can use *afraid of + -ing* or *afraid + infinitive* with no difference of meaning.

> *I'm not **afraid of telling** / **to tell** her the truth.*

## 14  *sorry*

*Sorry for/about + -ing* is used to refer to past things that one regrets. (*That*-clauses are also very common in an informal style.)

> *I'm **sorry for/about losing** my temper this morning.*
> (OR *I'm **sorry that I lost** my temper.*)

*Sorry + perfect infinitive* (more formal) can be used with the same meaning.

> *I'm **sorry to have woken** you up.* (OR *I'm **sorry that I woke** you up.*) ▶

*Sorry* + **infinitive** is used to apologise for current situations – things that one is doing or going to do, or that one has just done.

> *Sorry to disturb you – could I speak to you for a moment?*
> *I'm sorry to tell you that you failed the exam.*
> *Sorry to keep you waiting – we can start now.*

## 15 *certain* and *sure*

*Certain/sure of* + *-ing* are used to refer to the feelings of the person one is talking about.

> *Before the game she felt certain of winning, but after a few minutes she realised it wasn't going to be so easy.*
> *You seem very sure of passing the exam. I hope you're right.*

*Certain/sure* + **infinitive** refer to the speaker's or writer's own feelings.

> *The repairs are certain to cost more than you think.* (NOT ~~The repairs are certain of costing~~ . . .)
> *Kroftova's sure to win – the other girl hasn't got a chance.*

Note that *He is sure to succeed* means 'I am sure that he will succeed'.

## 16 *interested*

To talk about reactions to things one learns, *interested* + **infinitive** is commonly used.

> *I was interested to read in the paper that scientists have found out how to talk to whales.*
> *I'm interested to see that Alice and Jake are going out together.*
> *I shall be interested to see how long it lasts.*

To talk about a wish to find out something, both *interested* + *-ing* and *interested* + **infinitive** are common.

> *I'm interested in finding out / to find out what she did with all that money.*
> *Aren't you interested in knowing / to know whether I'm pregnant?*

To talk about a wish to do something, we use *interested* with an *-ing* form.

> *I'm interested in working in Switzerland. Do you know anybody who could help me?* (NOT ~~I'm interested to work in Switzerland~~ . . .)

# 300 -ing forms (8): participles; progressive verbs

## 1 *a crying baby*

We can use *-ing* forms as adjectives before nouns.

> *I was woken by a crying baby.*
> *There is growing anger at the government's policies.*

When *-ing* forms are used like this, they are called 'present participles'. Their use is explained in 408–410.

## 2 *not knowing what to do* . . .

Participles can be used in another way. They can combine with other words into 'participle clauses'.

> *Not knowing what to do, I telephoned the police.*
> *Who's the girl dancing with your brother?*

For details of participle clauses, see 411.

### 3 progressive verbs

Present participles are also used to make progressive verb forms.

*It's raining.* (present progressive)
*She arrived just when I was leaving.* (past progressive)

For details of progressive forms, see 470 and the separate entries on the present progressive, past progressive etc.

## 301 instead of

### 1 preposition: *instead of*

*Instead* is not used alone as a preposition; we use the two words *instead of.*

*I'll have tea **instead of** coffee, please.* (NOT *. . . instead coffee . . .*)
*Can you work with Sally **instead of** me today, please?*

*Instead of* is not usually followed by an infinitive.

*I stayed in bed all day **instead of going** to work.* (NOT *. . . instead of (to) go to work.*)

### 2 *instead of* and *without*

*Instead* suggests that one person, thing or action replaces another. *Without* suggests that one person, thing etc is not together with another. Compare:

– *Ruth was invited to the reception, but she was ill, so Lou went **instead of** her.* (Lou replaced Ruth.) (NOT *. . . Lou went without her.*)
   *Max and Jake were invited, but Max was ill, so Jake went **without** him.* (Normally they would have gone together.)

– *She often goes swimming **instead of** going to school.* (Swimming replaces school.) (NOT *She often goes swimming without going to school.*)
   *She often goes swimming **without** telling her mother.* (Swimming and telling her mother should go together.) (NOT *She often goes swimming instead of telling her mother.*)

### 3 adverb: *instead*

*Instead* (without *of*) is an adverb. It usually begins or ends a clause.

*She didn't go to Greece after all. **Instead**, she went to America.*
*Don't marry Phil. Marry me **instead**.*

## 302 inversion (1): auxiliary verb before subject

We put an auxiliary verb (and non-auxiliary *have* and *be*) directly before the subject of a clause in several different structures.

### 1 questions

*Have your father and mother arrived?* (NOT *Have arrived your father and mother?*)
*Where is the concert taking place?* (NOT *Where is taking place the concert?*)
   (NOT *Where the concert is taking place?*)

Spoken questions do not always have this word order (see 481).

*You're coming tomorrow?*

Indirect questions do not usually have this order (see 276).

*I wondered what time the film was starting.* (NOT *. . . what time was the film starting.*)

▶

However, in formal writing inversion is sometimes used with *be* in indirect questions after *how*, especially when the subject is long.

*I wondered how reliable **was the information** I had been given.*

For more information about questions, see 480–486.

## 2 exclamations

Exclamations (see 195) often have the form of negative questions (see 368).

*Isn't it cold?*                      *Hasn't she got lovely eyes?*

In spoken American English, exclamations often have the same form as ordinary (non-negative) questions.

*Have you got a surprise coming!*     *Was I mad!*

In a rather old-fashioned literary style, inversion is sometimes found in exclamations after *how* and *what*.

*How beautiful **are the flowers**!*     *What a peaceful place **is Skegness**!*

## 3 with *may*

*May* can come before the subject in wishes.

*May all your wishes come true!*        *May he rot in hell!*

## 4 after *so, neither, nor*

In 'short answers' and similar structures, these words are followed by **auxiliary verb + subject**.

*I'm hungry. ~ So am I.*
*I don't like opera. ~ Neither/Nor do I.*

For more details of these structures, see 541 and 374.

## 5 after *as, than* and *so*

Inversion sometimes happens after *as, than* and *so* in a literary style.

*She was very religious, **as were most of her friends**.*
*City dwellers have a higher death rate **than do country people**.*
*So ridiculous **did she look** that everybody burst out laughing.*

## 6 conditional clauses

In formal and literary conditional clauses, an auxiliary verb can be put before the subject instead of using *if* (see 261.5).

*Were she my daughter ...* (= If she were my daughter ...)
*Had I realised what you intended ...* (= If I had realised ...)

Negatives are not contracted in this case.

*Had we not spent all our money already, ...* (NOT ~~Hadn't we spent~~ ...)

## 7 after negative and restrictive expressions

If a negative adverb or adverbial expression is put at the beginning of a clause for emphasis, it is usually followed by **auxiliary verb + subject**. These structures are mostly rather formal.

*Under no circumstances can we cash cheques.*
*At no time was the President aware of what was happening.*
*Not until much later did she learn who her real father was.*

The same structure is possible after a complete clause beginning *not until . . .*
>*Not until he received her letter did he fully understand her feelings.*

Inversion is also used after restrictive words like *hardly* (in BrE), *seldom, rarely, little* and *never*, and after **only** + **time expression**. This is formal or literary.
>*Hardly had I arrived when trouble started.* (BrE)
>*Seldom have I seen such a remarkable creature.*
>*Little did he realise the danger he faced.*
>*Never . . . was so much owed by so many to so few.* (Churchill)
>*Only then did I understand what she meant.*
>*Only after her death was I able to appreciate her.*
>*Not only did we lose our money, but we were nearly killed.*
>*Not a single word did he say.*

Inversion is not used after *not far . . .* and *not long . . .*
>*Not far from here you can see foxes.* (NOT *Not far from here can you . . .*)
>*Not long after that she got married.*

# 303 inversion (2): whole verb before subject

## 1 after adverbial expressions of place

When an adverbial expression of place or direction comes at the beginning of a clause, intransitive verbs are often put before their subjects. This happens especially when a new indefinite subject is being introduced. The structure is most common in literary and descriptive writing.
>*Under a tree was lying one of the biggest men I had ever seen.*
>*On the grass sat an enormous frog.*
>*Directly in front of them stood a great castle.*
>*Along the road came a strange procession.*

This structure is often used in speech with *here, there* and other short adverbs and adverb particles.
>*Here comes Freddy!* (NOT *Here Freddy comes.*)
>*There goes your brother.*
>*I stopped the car, and up walked a policeman.*
>*The door opened and out came Angela's boyfriend.*

If the subject is a pronoun, it goes before the verb.
>*Here she comes.* (NOT *Here comes she.*)     *Off we go!*

## 2 reporting

In story-telling, the subject often comes after reporting verbs like *said, asked, suggested* etc when these follow direct speech.
>*'What do you mean?' asked Henry.* (OR *. . . Henry asked.*)
>*'I love you,' whispered Jan.*

If the subject is a pronoun, it usually comes before the verb.
>*'What do you mean?' he asked.*

# 304 irregular verbs

## 1 common irregular verbs

This is a list of the more common irregular verbs. Students should check that they know all of them. For a complete list, see a good dictionary.

| Infinitive | Simple past | Past participle |
|---|---|---|
| arise | arose | arisen |
| awake | awoke | awoken |
| be | was, were | been |
| bear | bore | born(e) |
| beat | beat | beaten |
| become | became | become |
| begin | began | begun |
| bend | bent | bent |
| bet | bet, betted | bet, betted |
| bind | bound | bound |
| bite | bit | bitten |
| bleed | bled | bled |
| blow | blew | blown |
| break | broke | broken |
| bring | brought | brought |
| broadcast | broadcast | broadcast |
| build | built | built |
| burn | burnt/burned | burnt/burned |
| burst | burst | burst |
| buy | bought | bought |
| catch | caught | caught |
| choose | chose | chosen |
| come | came | come |
| cost | cost | cost |
| cut | cut | cut |
| deal | dealt /delt/ | dealt /delt/ |
| dig | dug | dug |
| do | did | done |
| draw | drew | drawn |
| dream | dreamt /dremt/ | dreamt /dremt/ |
|  | dreamed /driːmd/ | dreamed /driːmd/ |
| drink | drank | drunk |
| drive | drove | driven |
| eat | ate /et/ | eaten /ˈiːtən/ |
| fall | fell | fallen |
| feed | fed | fed |
| feel | felt | felt |
| fight | fought | fought |
| find | found | found |
| fly | flew | flown |

| Infinitive | Simple past | Past participle |
|---|---|---|
| forbid | forbade | forbidden |
| forget | forgot | forgotten |
| forgive | forgave | forgiven |
| freeze | froze | frozen |
| get | got | got |
| give | gave | given |
| go | went | gone/been |
| grow | grew | grown |
| hang | hung | hung |
| have | had | had |
| hear | heard /hɜːd/ | heard/hɜːd/ |
| hide | hid | hidden |
| hit | hit | hit |
| hold | held | held |
| hurt | hurt | hurt |
| keep | kept | kept |
| kneel | knelt | knelt |
| know | knew | known |
| lay | laid | laid |
| lead | led | led |
| lean | leant/leaned | leant/leaned |
| learn | learnt/learned | learnt/learned |
| leave | left | left |
| lend | lent | lent |
| let | let | let |
| lie | lay | lain |
| light | lit/lighted | lit/lighted |
| lose | lost | lost |
| make | made | made |
| mean | meant /ment/ | meant /ment/ |
| meet | met | met |
| pay | paid | paid |
| put | put | put |
| quit | quit/quitted | quit/quitted |
| read /riːd/ | read /red/ | read /red/ |
| ride | rode | ridden |
| ring | rang | rung |
| rise | rose | risen |
| run | ran | run |
| say | said /sed/ | said /sed/ |
| see | saw | seen |
| sell | sold | sold |
| send | sent | sent |
| set | set | set |

▶

| Infinitive | Simple past | Past participle |
|---|---|---|
| shake | shook | shaken |
| shine | shone /ʃɒn/ | shone /ʃɒn/ |
| shoot | shot | shot |
| show | showed | shown |
| shrink | shrank/shrunk | shrunk |
| shut | shut | shut |
| sing | sang | sung |
| sink | sank | sunk |
| sit | sat | sat |
| sleep | slept | slept |
| slide | slid | slid |
| smell | smelt/smelled | smelt/smelled |
| speak | spoke | spoken |
| speed | sped | sped |
| spell | spelt/spelled | spelt/spelled |
| spend | spent | spent |
| spill | spilt/spilled | spilt/spilled |
| spin | span/spun | spun |
| spit | spat | spat |
| split | split | split |
| spoil | spoilt/spoiled | spoilt/spoiled |
| spread | spread | spread |
| stand | stood | stood |
| steal | stole | stolen |
| stick | stuck | stuck |
| sting | stung | stung |
| strike | struck | struck |
| swear | swore | sworn |
| sweep | swept | swept |
| swing | swung | swung |
| swim | swam | swum |
| take | took | taken |
| teach | taught | taught |
| tear | tore | torn |
| tell | told | told |
| think | thought | thought |
| throw | threw | thrown |
| understand | understood | understood |
| wake | woke | woken |
| wear | wore | worn |
| win | won | won |
| wind /waɪnd/ | wound /waʊnd/ | wound /waʊnd/ |
| write | wrote | written |

## 2 verbs that are easily confused

| Infinitive | Simple past | Past participle |
|---|---|---|
| fall | fell | fallen |
| feel | felt | felt |
| fill | filled | filled |
| find<br>(= get back<br>  something lost) | found | found |
| found<br>(= start up an<br>  organisation or<br>  institution) | founded | founded |
| flow<br>(of a liquid = move) | flowed | flowed |
| fly<br>(= move in the air) | flew | flown |
| lay<br>(= put down flat) | laid | laid |
| lie<br>(= be down) | lay | lain |
| lie<br>(= say things that are<br>  not true) | lied | lied |

For more details of these three verbs, see 316.

| | | |
|---|---|---|
| leave | left | left |
| live | lived | lived |
| raise<br>(= put up) | raised | raised |
| rise<br>(= go/get up) | rose | risen |
| strike<br>(= hit) | struck | struck |
| stroke<br>(= pass the hand<br>  gently over) | stroked | stroked |
| wind /waɪnd/<br>(= turn, tighten a<br>  spring etc) | wound /waʊnd/ | wound /waʊnd/ |
| wound /wuːnd/<br>(= injure in a battle) | wounded | wounded |

▶

**3 notes**

- *Says* is pronounced /sez/.
- The old past participle *drunken* is used as an adjective in some expressions (e.g. *a drunken argument, drunken driving*), but these are not very common.
- *Prove* (regular) has an irregular past participle *proven* which is sometimes used instead of *proved*, especially as an adjective (e.g. *a proven liar*).
- *Speed* can also have regular forms, especially in the expression *speeded up*.
- *Sung* and *sunk* are sometimes used instead of *sang* and *sank*.
- *Burn, dream, lean, learn, smell, spell, spill* and *spoil* are all regular in American English. In British English, irregular past tenses and participles with *-t* are also common.
- *Dive* is regular in British English, but can be irregular in American:
  *dive – dived/dove* (/doʊv/) *– dived*
- *Fit* and *quit* are usually irregular in American English.
- The American past participle of *get* is either *got* or *gotten* (see 223.7).
- *Spit* has both *spit* and *spat* as past tense and participle in American English.
- Note the standard AmE pronunciations of *ate* (/eɪt/) and *shone* (/ʃoʊn/).

# 305 its and it's

These two words are often confused by native speakers of English as well as by foreign learners.
*Its* is a possessive word (like *my, your*).
  *Every country has **its** traditions.* (NOT *. . . ~~it's traditions.~~*)
*It's* is the contracted form of *it is* or *it has*.
  ***It's** raining again.* (NOT *~~Its raining again.~~*)
  *Have you seen my camera? **It's** disappeared.* (NOT *. . . ~~Its disappeared.~~*)

There is a similar difference between *whose* and *who's* – see 627.
For more about contractions, see 143.

# 306 it's time

**1 followed by infinitive**

*It's time* (or *it is time*) can be followed by an infinitive.
  ***It's time to buy** a new car.*
To say who should do something, we use *for* + object + infinitive (see 291).
  *It's time **for her to go** to bed.*

**2 followed by past tense with present meaning**

*It's time* can also be followed by a subject with a past tense verb. The meaning is present.
  ***It's time she went** to bed.*    ***It's time you washed** those trousers.*
  *I'm getting tired. **It's time we went** home.*
The expression *It's high time . . .* is often used in this structure in British English, to say that something is urgent.
  ***It's high time you got** a job.*

For other structures in which a past tense has a present or future meaning, see 426.

# 307 just

## 1 meanings

*Just* has several meanings.

### a time

*Just* often emphasises the idea of 'at this moment' or 'close to the present'.

> *I'll be down in a minute – I'm **just** changing my shirt.* (= right now)
> *Alice has **just** phoned.* (= a short time ago)
> *Keith's still around. I saw him **just** last week.* (= as recently as)

In expressions like *just after*, *just before* and *just when*, *just* suggests closeness to the time in question.

> *I saw him **just after** lunch.* (= . . . very soon after lunch.)

### b 'only', 'scarcely'

*Just* can mean 'only', 'nothing more than', 'scarcely'.

> *Complete set of garden tools for **just** £15.99!*
> *I **just want** somebody to love me – that's all.*
> *We **just caught** the train.*

This meaning can be emphasised by *only*.

> *There was **only just** enough light to read by.*

*Can/Could I just . . .?* can make a request seem less demanding.

> *Could I **just** use your phone for a moment?*

### c 'exactly'

*Just* often means 'exactly'.

> *What's the time? ~ It's **just** four o'clock.*
> *Thanks. That's **just** what I wanted.*
> *She's **just** as bad-tempered as her father.*

### d emphasiser

*Just* can emphasise other words and expressions, with the sense of 'simply', 'there's no other word for it'.

> *You're **just** beautiful.*     *I **just** love your dress.*

## 2 tenses

When *just* means 'a moment ago', past and present perfect tenses are both possible in British English. A present perfect is preferred when we are giving news. Compare:

> *Where's Eric? ~ He's **just gone** out.*     *Alice **has just left**.*
> *I've **just had** a brilliant idea.*
> *John **just phoned**. His wife's had a baby.* (The news is the baby, not the phone call.)

In American English a past tense is also common.

> *Where's Eric? ~ He **just went** out.*     *Alice **(has) just left**.*
> *I **just had** a brilliant idea.*

▶

## 3  *just now*

*Just now* can mean either 'at this moment' or 'a few moments ago'. Compare:
>  *She's not in **just now**. Can I take a message?*
>  *I saw Phil **just now**. He wanted to talk to you.*

When *just now* means 'a few moments ago', two positions are possible:

a  in end-position, usually with a past tense.
>  *I telephoned Ann **just now**.*

b  in mid-position (see 24) with the verb, with a present perfect or past tense.
>  *I('ve) **just now** realised what I need to do.*

# 308  kinds of English (1):
# standard English and dialects

'A language is a dialect that has an army and a navy.' (Max Weinreich)

'Dialect: A language variety that has everything going for it, except the government, the schools, the middle class, the law and the armed forces.'
>  (Tom McArthur)

## 1  What is 'standard English'?

After King Alfred's victory over the Vikings in 878, the government of Southern England came to be established in London, which later became the capital of the whole of Britain. Because of this, the English spoken in London and the East Midlands was gradually adopted as the 'official' variety of English. And as time went by, this dialect (and its later developments, profoundly influenced by Norman French), became the 'standard' language – the form of English generally accepted for use in government, the law, business, education and literature. Standard English, like all standard languages, is therefore largely the result of historical accident. If the Vikings, who held the north of England, had defeated Harold's army, the capital of modern Britain might well be York, and this book would be written in (and about) a very different kind of English.

## 2  What is a dialect?

Many people think that dialects are corrupted forms of a language, spoken by ignorant people who make mistakes because they have not learnt correct grammar. This is not at all true (for more about correctness, see 309). A standard language is not linguistically 'better' than other dialects; it is simply the dialect that has been adopted for official purposes such as government and education. All English dialects have a long history, going back to the distinct forms of speech of the Germanic and Scandinavian invaders who came from various parts of northern Europe to occupy Britain during the Middle Ages. And each of these dialects has a grammar that is as rich and systematic as standard English, even though it may be very different. Some examples of English dialect forms:

>  *I bain't ready.* (= I'm not ready.)
>  *He don't like it.*      *I wants a rest.*

*Where's them papers what I give you?*
*Can ye no help me?* (= Can't you help me?)
*They're not believing it.*
*She's after telling me.* (= She's told me.)
*Are youse coming or not?* (= Are you – plural – coming or not?)
*I ain't done nothing.* (= I haven't done anything.)

## 3 pronunciation: dialect and accent; 'received pronunciation'

A dialect is not the same as a regional accent (though they often go together). Many British people speak standard English, but with the typical accent of their part of the country. Other British people, however, combine standard English with a non-regional standard pronunciation. This (the so-called 'received pronunciation' or 'RP') is the pronunciation that has traditionally been used by a majority of British upper- and upper-middle-class people, though it has changed a good deal over the years. For a long time RP was considered more 'correct' than other accents, and its social dominance was reinforced by education and the media. This attitude is now changing, and there is less social prejudice in Britain than before against regional accents.

## 4 showing accent in writing

Writers may spell words in special ways to show a non-standard or conversational pronunciation – for example, apostrophes may be used in place of letters that are not pronounced. These spellings are common in cartoon strips. Some examples (mostly BrE):

*'e's gone 'ome.* (= He's gone home.)
*'elp yerself.* (= Help yourself.)
*Yer gettin' old.* (= You're getting old.)
*If I get me 'ands on yer...* (= If I get my hands on you ...)
*Where d'she put 'em?* (= Where did she put them?)
*C'mon, we're late.* (= Come on ...)
*C'n I 'ave a glass o' water?* (= Can I have a glass of water?)
*fish 'n' chips.* (= fish and chips)
*Come wi' me.* (= Come with me.)
*I dunno.* (= I don't know.)
*I gotta go.* (= I've got to go.)
*It's gonna rain.* (= It's going to rain.)
*I don't wanna play.* (= I don't want to play.)

*Gotta, gonna* and *wanna* are most common in AmE.

## 5 other standard forms of English

Standard British English is not, of course, the only standard form of English. American English also has a standard variety; this is different from standard British English in a number of ways (see 51). Other English-speaking countries, too, have their own standard versions of the language. Some of these are very close to British or American English; others (e.g. the developing Indian standard) are more clearly distinct.

▶

## 6 What kind of English should learners study?

For most learners, the best model is one or other of the two main standard varieties: British or American English. Neither of these is 'better' than the other, and they are both used and understood worldwide. The differences are generally unimportant: for details, see 51.

## 7 international English

As English is used more and more as a language of international communication, it seems possible that a new form of international English may develop. This could be a 'super-standard', with characteristics of both British and American English. International English could turn out to be simpler in some ways than the modern standard varieties, without some of their less important grammatical complications. It will be interesting to see what happens.

# 309 kinds of English (2): correctness

When people say that somebody's language is 'not correct', they may mean several different things.

## 1 slips and mistakes

People sometimes make slips of the tongue when they are talking.
*He works in Wildlife Conversation – I mean Conservation.*
Somebody can use a word wrongly because he or she is unsure of its meaning, or confuses it with another word.
*You're being very authoritative.* (meaning 'authoritarian')
And many people have trouble with spelling and punctuation.
*The firm has doubled it's profits this year.* (should be *its profits*)
Foreign learners may also make mistakes with points of grammar that do not cause problems for native speakers.
*I could not understanding the lecture.* (instead of *I could not understand . . .*)

## 2 dialect forms

Many people think that dialects are corrupt versions of the standard language, and that dialect forms are mistakes, made by ignorant people who have not learnt correct grammar. In fact, this is not at all true (see 308.2): dialects have their own systematic – but different – grammars. Teachers in British schools often tell children whose dialects have multiple negation, for example, that they are making mistakes if they say things like *I ain't done nothing*, because 'two negatives make a positive' (so *I ain't done nothing* is supposed to mean 'I have done something'). This is not, of course, the case: in the child's dialect, the sentence means 'I haven't done anything'. And if 'two negatives make a positive', then the teacher ought to be quite happy if the child says 'I ain't done nothing to nobody', since logically three negatives must make a negative! Dialect forms are not, therefore, incorrect in themselves. They are, however, out of place in styles where only the standard language is normally used. It would be inappropriate – in fact, incorrect – to use *I wants*, *he don't* or a double negative in a school essay, a job application, a newspaper article or a speech at a business conference.

## 3 divided usage

Speakers of a standard language often differ about small points of usage.
Where two different forms are common, people who use one form may claim
that theirs is the only 'correct' usage, and that people who use the other form
are making mistakes. Some examples from modern English:

| so-called 'only correct form' | so-called 'mistake' |
|---|---|
| *John and I went to the cinema.* | *John and me went to the cinema.* |
| *They're different from us.* | *They're different to us.* |
| *fewer people* | *less people* |
| *Somebody's dropped his or her keys.* | *Somebody's dropped their keys.* |
| *I'm unemployed at present.* | *I'm unemployed presently.* |

In fact, all of the so-called 'mistakes' listed above have been normal in
standard English for centuries, and are not wrong at all (though some of them
are more informal than the so-called 'only correct forms', and would be out of
place in a formal style). For details, see 429 (*I* and *me*), 155 (*different*), 320
(*less*), 528 (*their*) and 467 (*presently*).

## 4 prescriptive and descriptive rules

If people say that *less people* or *different to* is wrong, they are following a
prescriptive rule. Prescriptive rules are made by people who believe that they
can improve a language, or protect it against change. A lot of prescriptive rules
were made by eighteenth- and nineteenth-century British grammarians, often
because they thought that English grammar should imitate Latin, which was
considered a superior language. A typical example is the rule that 'split
infinitives' like *to boldly go*, where an adverb is put between *to* and the verb,
are wrong (a Latin infinitive is a single word, so cannot be split). Many people
still believe this, and try to avoid split infinitives, although the rule is
unrealistic (see 280.7). A similar rule said that sentences should not end in
prepositions (as in *What are you waiting for?* or *I don't like being shouted at.*).
In fact, it is quite normal for English sentences to end in prepositions (see 452).
Most prescriptive rules give misleading information, and have little effect on
the development of a language.

Descriptive rules simply say what happens in one form of a language (for
example standard written British English, standard spoken American English,
Yorkshire English, Dublin English or Singapore English), and not what some
people feel ought to happen. The rules in this book are descriptive of standard
British English.

## 5 When do mistakes become correct?

When somebody misuses a word or expression, this may influence other
people to make the same mistake. Sometimes a mistake becomes so
widespread that it becomes part of the language (this is one way in which
languages develop), and we can no longer realistically call it a 'mistake'. The
expression *oblivious of*, for example, originally meant 'forgetful of', but came
to be used to mean 'unconscious of'. A hundred years ago this was still a
mistake; now it is the normal use. The same thing is happening today with the
expression *a concerted effort*. This means 'an effort by people working
together', but some people now use it mistakenly to mean 'a strong effort'. ▶

If enough people follow the trend, this will sooner or later become the normal meaning, and the usage will have become correct.

# 310 kinds of English (3): spoken and written English

## 1 length and complexity; organisation of sentences

In writing, sentences can be planned in advance and revised, so there is time to build up complex structures. Spoken structures are usually simpler. Subjects, in particular, tend to be very short in speech. A typical written sentence:

*The group of young people who were sitting at the next table were making so much noise that my friends and I found it difficult to continue our conversation.*

In speech, we might say something more like:

*There were a lot of young people at the next table. They were making so much noise we couldn't talk.*

Written language is mostly made up of complete sentences. In conversation, complete sentences are often unnecessary.

*When are you seeing her? ~ Half past eight. ~ At your place? ~ No, at Andy's.*

Spoken sentences are often more loosely organised than written sentences, and the information may be 'spaced out' more by putting some of it before or after the main sentence (see 514).

*Last Wednesday it was, I was just going to work, . . .*
*This guy who rang up, he's an architect. Well, he said . . .*
*They work very hard, most of them.*

'Fronting' – putting something other than the subject at the beginning (see 513) – is more common in speech than in writing.

*People like that I just can't stand.     Strange people they are!*

## 2 structures

Some structures – for example, relative clauses with *whom* – are most common in a formal style. Since speech is more often informal, and writing is more often formal, these structures are most common in written English. Other structures – for example, contractions like *he's, can't* – are typically informal, and are most common in speech. (For more about formal and informal language, see 311.)  Some structures are common in speech, but hardly ever found in writing – for example, declarative questions (see 481):

*You live with your parents?*

certain conditional structures (see 262):

*It would be good if we'd get some rain.*

certain relative structures (see 498.16):

*It's ridiculous to sing songs that you don't know what they mean.*

and some kinds of ellipsis (see 179):

*Couldn't understand a word.*

Progressive and past verb forms are often used in speech in order to sound less definite or direct (see 436).

*I was hoping you could lend me some money.*

And structures whose purpose is to keep a conversation going (e.g. reply questions – see 484) are naturally only used in speech.

*We had a lovely holiday. ~ Did you?*

## 3   vocabulary

Written language often uses longer, less common words and expressions that are typical of a formal style (see 311), with a greater variety of synonyms. In speech, people usually prefer shorter, more common words, and they are more likely to keep repeating the same words. Phrasal verbs are common in speech, and are often replaced by more formal single words in writing. Compare:

> *I told him to get on the plane.*
> *She instructed the man to board the aircraft.*

# 311   kinds of English (4): formality

## 1   formal and informal language

Most people speak and write in different ways on different occasions. In some languages, for example, there are very complicated rules about how to speak to older or more important people. English does not have a system of this kind. However, there are some words and structures which are mostly used in *formal* situations, when people are careful about how they express themselves: for example in official notices, business letters or reports, meetings or conferences, or polite conversations with strangers. And some words and structures are mostly used in *informal* situations: for example in conversations with friends, or letters to one's family. Writing is more often formal, and speech is more often informal, but informal writing and formal speech are used when the situation makes them preferable.

> *Customer toilets are at the rear of the building.* (Printed notice in an Oxfordshire petrol station)
> *The toilets are outside round the back.* (Handwritten notice in the same petrol station, put up perhaps because the manager felt this would be easier for some of his customers to understand.)

Most words and expressions are neither formal nor informal, but neutral – English speakers do not have to know two ways of saying everything.

## 2   grammar

Some grammatical structures have different formal and informal versions. For example, contracted auxiliary verbs and negatives (see 143) are common in informal speech and writing. Compare:

> FORMAL:     *It has gone. It is not possible.*
> INFORMAL: *It's gone. It isn't possible.*

Prepositions come at the end of certain structures in informal language (see 452). Compare:

> FORMAL:     *In which century did he live?*
> INFORMAL: *Which century did he live in?*

Some relative structures are different (see 495). Compare:

> FORMAL:     *The man whom she married ...*
> INFORMAL: *The man she married ...*

Some determiners are followed more often by singular verb forms in formal language, and by plural forms in informal language (see 532.5). Compare:

> FORMAL:     *Neither of us likes him.*
> INFORMAL: *Neither of us like him.*

▶

Subject and object forms of pronouns (e.g. *I* and *me*) are used differently in formal and informal language (see 429). Compare:
– FORMAL: *It was **she who** first saw what to do.*
  INFORMAL: *It was **her that** first saw what to do.*
– FORMAL: ***Whom** did they elect?*
  INFORMAL: ***Who** did they elect?*
Ellipsis (leaving out words – see 177–182) is more common in informal language. Compare:
– FORMAL: ***Have you seen** Mr Andrews?*
  INFORMAL: ***Seen** John?*
– FORMAL: *We think **that** it is possible.*
  INFORMAL: *We think it's possible.*

## 3 vocabulary

Some words and expressions are used mainly in formal situations; in neutral or informal situations other words or expressions are used. And some words and expressions are only used in informal situations. Some examples:

– FORMAL: *commence*
  NEUTRAL/INFORMAL: *begin, start*
– FORMAL: *alight* (from a bus or train)
  NEUTRAL/INFORMAL: *get off*
– FORMAL: *I beg your pardon?*
  NEUTRAL/INFORMAL: *Pardon? Sorry?* (AmE *Excuse me? Pardon me?*)
  INFORMAL: *What?*
– FORMAL: *repair*
  NEUTRAL/INFORMAL: *mend* (BrE)
  INFORMAL: *fix*
– FORMAL: *acceptable, satisfactory*
  NEUTRAL/INFORMAL: *all right*
  INFORMAL: *OK*
– FORMAL: *I am (very) grateful to you.*
  NEUTRAL/INFORMAL: *Thank you.*
  INFORMAL: *Thanks.*

For structures used in polite requests and questions, see 435–7.
For formal and informal ways of using people's names and titles, see 363.
For the language used in particular social situations, see 545.
For taboo language, see 575.      For slang, see 533.
For the use of out-of-date grammar and vocabulary in ceremonies and other situations, see 392.

# 312 kinds of English (5): variation and change

Languages change over time. Younger people adopt newer forms of expression, while older people often resist change; so even people who speak the same standard language do not speak it in exactly the same way. There are several reasons for change.

## 1 communicative need

Several centuries ago, standard English had two second-person pronouns: *thou* (singular) and *ye* (plural). Modern English uses *you* for both. But people still feel the need to distinguish singular and plural, and so expressions like *you guys* (used for both men and women) are beginning to function as second person plural pronouns.

## 2 influence from other dialects

British English is heavily influenced by American English. Some structures which were not used by British speakers half a century ago are now as common as their older British equivalents.

*I **feel like** I'm getting a cold.* (Older British form: *I feel **as if** I'm getting a cold.*)

***Do you have** today's newspaper?* (Older British form: ***Have you (got)** today's newspaper?*)

## 3 Languages simplify themselves

As languages develop, complicated structures often become simpler and more regular. This may be happening with English conditional sentences – structures with *would* or *would have* in both clauses are quite common in speech.

*If you'**d have** asked I'**d have** told you.*

## 4 Small, less important distinctions are confused or disappear

Some irregular verb forms like *sank/sunk, sang/sung* or *lay/laid* are quite often confused in speech. Examples from the British radio:

*He wrote eight operas, all of which **sunk** without trace.*

*. . . a song she **sung** in yesterday's concert.*

Infinitives and *-ing* forms after verbs also sometimes get mixed up. An example from a letter:

*I now have pleasure **to enclose** the correct proposal form.* (instead of . . . *pleasure in enclosing . . .* )

When confusions like these become widespread, they can lead to language change. This may well happen with the possessive *'s* form: more and more people are leaving out the apostrophe or putting it in the 'wrong' place, so that this spelling convention might one day lose its importance and even disappear.

## 5 New forms and uses spread through the language

Progressive verb forms came into English a few hundred years ago, and gradually became used more and more widely. There are still a few verbs that are not generally used in progressive forms (see 471), but even these are losing their resistance. Some typical modern examples:

*I'**m understanding** French a lot better now.*

*How many eggs **were** you **wanting?***

## 6 'Underground' forms become respectable

Some forms have always existed in the language, but have been 'driven underground' by prescriptive rules (see 309.4), so that they have been avoided by careful speakers. People are now more tolerant of such forms, so they are becoming more common. Some examples:

***Here's** your papers.* (instead of *Here are . . .* – see 532.4)

*Somebody's left **their** umbrella behind.* (instead of . . . *his or her umbrella* – see 528)

***John and me** went to the cinema.      between **you and I***      ▶

## 7 Mistakes become part of the language

Sometimes a mistake is made by so many people that it becomes the normal form, and can no longer be called incorrect (see 309.5). This has happened with the word *data*. It was originally a plural, from a Latin word meaning 'given things', but it is now widely used as a singular uncountable noun. And recently people have started using *between ... to* instead of *between ... and* (e.g. *There were between 50 to 60 people on the bus*). This, too, could end up as a normal and correct expression.

## 8 Phonetically weak forms disappear

The weak form of *have* in *I've got* is so quiet that it is often not heard at all; and people are beginning to say *I got* instead of *I've got*. In time, this could become a new regular form.

## 9 some more examples of changes in modern English

- *Who* is replacing *whom*.
  **Who** *do you trust?* (George Bush's 1992 election slogan)
- *Will* and *would* have now practically replaced first-person *shall* and *should*.
  *We* **will be** *in touch soon.*     *I* **would be** *grateful for some help.*
- Subjunctive *were* is becoming less common.
  *If I* **was** *ten years younger I'd do the job myself.*     *I wish it* **was** *Friday.*
- Some adverbs without *-ly* are becoming more common.
  *You pronounced it* **wrong.**
- Comparatives and superlatives with *more* and *most* are gaining ground in two-syllable adjectives.
  *'Commoner' used to be commoner, but 'more common' is now* **more common.**
- Plural noun modifiers are becoming more common. For example, *antiques shop* is now as common as *antique shop*, and *drugs problem* is replacing *drug problem.*
- The (very old) use of *less* with plurals is becoming more respectable.
  *There were* **less** *people than I expected.*
- Some AmE prepositional uses and phrasal verb forms are moving into BrE.
  *The following trains will not run due to engineering work* **on weekends.**
    (instead of *...* **at weekends.**)
  *We* **met with** *the unions yesterday.* (instead of *We met the unions ...*)
  *Can I* **speak with** *Cathy?* (instead of *... speak to ...*)
  *We haven't seen Granny* **in ages.** (instead of *... for ages.*)
  *You have to* **fill out** *this form.* (instead of *... fill in ...*)
- The AmE use of a past tense with *just* and *already* is becoming common in BrE.
  *Peter* **just went** *out.* (instead of *Peter has just gone out.*)
  *I* **already told** *Jane about the party.*

# 313 know

## 1 *know how* + infinitive

*Know* is not followed directly by infinitives. We use know *how to* (see 286).
  I **know how to make** Spanish omelettes. (NOT ~~I know to make~~...)

## 2 object + infinitive

In a formal style, *know* is sometimes followed by **object + infinitive**.
  They **knew him to be** a dangerous criminal.
The passive equivalent is quite common in a formal style.
  He **was known to be** a dangerous criminal.
In a less formal style, *that*-clauses are more usual.
  They **knew that** he was a dangerous criminal.
*Know* means 'experience' in the common structure *I've never known* + **object**
+ **infinitive**; an infinitive without *to* is possible in British English.
  I've never **known it (to) rain** like this.

## 3 tenses

*Know* cannot usually be used in progressive forms (see 471).
  I **know** exactly what you mean. (NOT ~~I am knowing~~...)
A present perfect tense is used to say how long one has known somebody or
something. (See 460 for more details.)
  We've **known** each other since 1994. (NOT ~~We know each other since 1994.~~)

## 4 *know* and *know about/of*

*Know* + **object** is used mainly to talk about knowledge that comes from direct
personal experience. In other cases, we normally use *know about/of, have
heard of* or another structure. Compare:
  You don't **know** my mother, do you? ~ No, I've never met her.
  We all **know about** Abraham Lincoln. (NOT ~~We all know Abraham Lincoln.~~)

## 5 *know* and *find out* etc

*Know* is not normally used to talk about finding something out: to know
something is **to have learnt** it, not **to learn** it. To talk about getting knowledge
we can use for example *find out, get to know, learn, hear, can tell*.
  She's married. ~ Where did you **find** that **out**?
    (NOT ... ~~Where did you know that?~~)
  I want to travel round the world and **get to know** people from different
    countries. (NOT ...~~and know people~~...)
  He's from Liverpool, as you can **tell** from his accent.
    (NOT ...~~as you can know from his accent.~~)

## 6 *I know* and *I know it*

Note the difference between these two short answers.
  *I know* refers to facts – it could be completed by a *that*-clause.
  You're late. ~ **I know**. (= I know that I'm late.)
*I know it* generally refers to things – *it* replaces a noun.
  I went to a nice restaurant called The Elizabeth last night. ~ **I know it**.
    (= I know the restaurant.)
For ways of using *you know*, see 157.

# 314 last, the last, the latest

## 1 *last week, month* etc; *the last week, month* etc

*Last week, month* etc (without *the*) is the week, month etc just before this one.
If I am speaking in July, *last month* was June; in 2006, *last year* was 2005.
*The last week, month* etc is the period of seven/thirty/etc days up to the
moment of speaking. On July 15th 2006, *the last month* is the period from June
16th to July 15th; *the last year* is the 12 months starting in July 2005.
Compare:

– *I was ill **last week**, but I'm OK this week.* (NOT ~~I was ill the last week~~ . . .)
  *I've had a cold for **the last week**. I feel terrible.*
– *We bought this house **last year**.*
  *We've lived here for **the last year**, and we're very happy with the place.*

The difference between *next* and *the next* is similar. See 375.

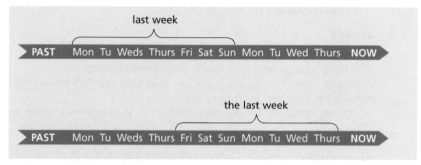

## 2 *the last three* . . . etc

Note the word order in expressions with numbers.

  *I've been busy for **the last three** months.* (NOT . . . ~~for the three last months.~~)

We generally say *the last few days/weeks* etc, not *the last days/weeks* etc.

  ***The last few days** have been busy.* (NOT ~~The last days~~ . . .)

## 3 the last in a series

*The last* can also mean 'the last in a series'.

  *In **the last** week of the holiday something funny happened.*
  *This is going to be **the last** Christmas I'll spend at home.*

## 4 *latest* and *last*

We can use *latest* to talk about something new, and *last* to mean 'the one
before'. Compare:

– *Her **latest** book's being published next week.* (NOT ~~Her last book~~ . . .)
  *She thinks it's much better than her **last** one.*
– *He's enjoying his **latest** job.* (NOT ~~He's enjoying his last job.~~)
  *But it doesn't pay as much as his **last** one.*

For tenses with *This is the last time* . . . etc, see 591.

## 315 later and in

With a time expression, we generally use *later* to mean 'after that time', and *in* to mean 'after now'. Compare:

*She got married on her 18th birthday; **six months later** she was divorced.*
*Penny's coming on July 1st, and Colin will arrive about **a week later**.*
*I'll see you **in a few days**.* (NOT ~~I'll see you a few days later~~.)

But without a time expression, *later* can be used to mean 'after now'.

*Bye! See you **later**!*

## 316 lay and lie

There are three similar verbs that can be confused: *lay* (regular except for spelling), *lie* (irregular) and *lie* (regular).

### 1 *lay*

*Lay* is a regular verb except for its spelling. Its forms are:

infinitive: *(to) lay*    past: *laid*
*-ing* form: *laying*    past participle: *laid*

*Lay* means 'put down carefully' or 'put down flat'. It has an object.

***Lay the tent** down on the grass and I'll see how to put it up.*
*I **laid the papers** on the table.* (NOT ~~I lay...~~)

Note the expressions ***lay a table*** (= put plates, knives etc on a table) and ***lay an egg*** (a bird's way of having a baby).

### 2 *lie* (irregular)

The forms of the irregular verb *lie* are:

infinitive: *(to) lie*    past: *lay*
*-ing* form: *lying*    past participle: *lain* (used mostly in a formal/literary style)

*Lie* (irregular) means 'be down', 'be/become horizontal'. It has no object.

*Don't **lie** in bed all day. Get up and do some work.* (NOT ~~Don't lay...~~)
*I **lay** down and closed my eyes.* (NOT ~~I laid down...~~)

### 3 *lie* (regular)

The regular verb *lie* (*lied*) means 'say things that are not true'.

*You **lied** to me when you said you loved me.*

### 4 dialect forms

In many British and American dialects, different forms of *lay* and irregular *lie* are used. *Lay* is often used in cases where standard English has *lie*.

*I'm going to **lay** down for a few minutes.* (Standard English ... *lie down* ...)

# 317  learn

## 1  forms

*Learn* is often irregular in British English (*learn/learnt*) and normally regular in American English (*learn/learned*). For other verbs like this, see 304.3.

For the adjective *learned* (/'lɜːnɪd/), see 18.

## 2  *learn (how) to ...*

To talk about consciously learning a method or technique for doing something, we can use *learn to ...* or *learn how to ...*
> *She enjoyed **learning (how) to look after young animals**.*
> *It's time you **learnt (how) to change the oil** in the car.*

When we talk about less conscious skills and other kinds of knowledge, we generally use *learn to ....*
> *Children usually **learn to walk** at around one year old.*
> *In the new job, I soon **learnt to keep my mouth shut**.*

# 318  least and fewest

## 1  *the least* as determiner: superlative of *little*

*The least* is used as a determiner before uncountable nouns; it is the superlative of *little* (= not much – see 329), and the opposite of *the most*.
> *I think I probably do **the least work** in this office.*

*The least* can be used without a noun if the meaning is clear.
> *Jan earns the most money in our family; Pete earns **the least**.*

We use *the least of* before plural abstract nouns to mean 'the smallest of'.
> *What will your mother think? ~ That's **the least of my worries**.*

## 2  'any ... at all'

With singular abstract nouns, *the least* can mean 'any ... at all'.
> *Do you think there's **the least chance** of Smith winning the election?*
> *What's the time? ~ I haven't got **the least idea**.*

## 3  *the fewest* as determiner: superlative of *few*

*The fewest* is used before plural nouns as the superlative of *few* (see 329).
> *The translation with **the fewest mistakes** isn't always the best.*

*Least* is often used instead of *fewest* before plural nouns (*... the **least** mistakes*), especially in an informal style. Some people feel this is incorrect.

## 4  *(the) least* with adjectives: the opposite of *(the) most* or *(the) ...est*

*(The) least* is used before adjectives in the same way as *(the) most* or *(the) ...est* (see 137), but with the opposite meaning.
> ***The least expensive** holidays are often the most interesting.*
> *I'm **least happy** when I have to work at weekends.*

For the use of *the* with superlatives, see 141.

## 5   *least* as adverb

*Least* can be used as an adverb (the opposite of *most*).
> *She always arrives when you **least** expect it.*
> *I don't much like housework, and I like cooking **least** of all.*

## 6   *at least*

*At least* means 'not less than (but perhaps more than)'.
> *How old do you think he is?* ~ *At least thirty.*
> *He's been in love **at least** eight times this year.*
We can also use *at least* as a discourse marker (see 157) to suggest that one thing is certain or all right, even if everything else is unsatisfactory.
> *We lost everything in the fire. But **at least** nobody was hurt.*

## 7   *not in the least*

We can use *not in the least* in a formal style to mean 'not at all', especially when talking about personal feelings and reactions.
> *I was not **in the least** upset by her bad temper.*

For *less* and *fewer*, see 320.

# 319   left

The past participle of *leave* – *left* – can be used in a special way, to mean 'remaining', 'not used', 'still there'.
> *What did you do with the money that was **left**?*
> *After the explosion, only two people were **left** alive.*
*Left* is common after *there is* and *have got*.
> *There's nothing **left** in the fridge.*
> *I **haven't got** any money **left**: can you get the tickets?*

# 320   less and fewer

## 1   the difference

*Less* is the comparative of *little* (used especially before uncountable nouns).
*Fewer* is the comparative of *few* (used before plural nouns). Compare:
> *I earn **less money** than a postman.*
> *I've got **fewer problems** than I used to have.*
*Less* is quite common before plural nouns, as well as uncountables, especially in an informal style. Some people consider this incorrect.
> *I've got **less problems** than I used to have.*                    ▶

## 2 *less/fewer* with and without *of*

*Less of* and *fewer of* are used before determiners (like *the*, *my* or *this*) and pronouns.

*I'd like to spend **less of my** time answering letters.*
*At the college reunions, there are **fewer of us** each year.*

Before nouns without determiners, *of* is not used.

*If you want to lose weight, eat **less** food.* (NOT ...~~less of food~~.)
***Fewer** people make their own bread these days.* (NOT ~~Fewer of people~~...)

## 3 *less* and *fewer* without nouns

Nouns can be dropped after *less* and *fewer* if the meaning is clear.

*Some people go to church, but **less/fewer** than 20 years ago.*

*Less* can be used as an adverb (the opposite of the adverb *more*).

*I worry **less** than I used to.*

## 4 *lesser*

*Lesser* is used in a few expressions (in a rather formal style) to mean 'smaller' or 'not so much'.

the ***lesser** of two evils*       *a **lesser**-known writer*

For *little* and *few*, see 329.
For *least* and *fewest*, see 318.
For the use of *much*, *far*, *a lot* etc with *fewer* and *less*, see 140.

# 321 lest

*Lest* has a similar meaning to *in case* (see 271) or *so that ... not* (see 543). It is rare in British English, and is found mostly in older literature and in ceremonial language. It is a little more common in formal American English.

*They kept watch all night **lest** robbers should come.*
*We must take care **lest** evil thoughts enter our hearts.*

*Lest* can be followed by a subjunctive verb (see 567).

*The government must act, **lest** the problem of child poverty **grow** worse.*

For more about older English, see 392.

# 322 let (1): structures

## 1 followed by infinitive without *to*

*Let* is followed by **object + infinitive without *to*.**

*We usually **let the children stay** up late on Saturdays.*
   (NOT ...~~let the children to stay / staying~~...)
*She didn't **let me see** what she was doing.* (NOT ...~~let me saw~~...)

Note the expressions *let ... know* (= tell, inform) and *let ... have* (= send, give).

*I'll **let you know** my holiday dates next week.*
*Could you **let me have** the bill for the car repair?*
*Let go of* means 'stop holding'.
*Don't **let go of** Mummy's hand.*

## 2  not used in passives

*Let* is unusual in passive forms; we prefer *allow*.
*After questioning he **was allowed** to go home.*

## 3  with object + preposition / adverb particle

*Let* can be followed by an object and a prepositional phrase or adverb particle expressing movement.
*You'd better **let the dog out** of the car.*
***Let him in**, could you?*      *Those kids **let my tyres down**.*

For more about infinitives without *to*, see 281.

# 323  let (2): introducing imperatives

*Let* can be used to introduce suggestions and orders, when these are not addressed to the hearer/reader (or not only to the hearer/reader). This structure can be considered a kind of imperative (see 268).

## 1  first-person plural imperative: *let's . . .*

We can use *let us* (formal) or *let's* (informal) to make suggestions or to give orders to a group that includes the speaker.
***Let us** pray.*      ***Let's** have a drink.*      *OK, **let's** all get moving.*
*Shall we?* is used as a question tag (see 487–488) in British English; *let's* can be used as a short answer.
***Let's** go for a walk, **shall we**? ~ Yes, **let's**.*
Negatives are *let us not / do not let us* (formal); *let's not / don't let's* (informal).
***Let us not** despair.* (formal)      ***Let's not** get angry.* (informal)
***Do not let us** forget those who came before us.* (formal)
***Don't let's** stay up too late tonight.* (informal)

## 2  first-person singular imperative: *let me . . .*

*Let me* is used to 'give instructions to oneself'; the expressions *Let me see* and *Let me think* are very common.
*What time shall we leave? ~ **Let me think**. Yes, Eight o'clock will be OK.*
*What's the best way to Manchester? **Let me see** – suppose I take the M6.*
***Let me** just get my coat and I'll be with you.*
In a very informal style, *let's* is often used to mean *let me* (see also 429.6).
***Let's** see. Suppose I take the M6 . . .*

## 3  third-person imperative: *let him . . .*

*Let* can also introduce a suggestion or order for someone or something else, not the speaker or hearer. This is common in formal and ceremonial language, but informal uses are also possible.      ▶

*Let the prayers begin.*
*Let our enemies understand that we will not hesitate to defend our territory.*
*Your boyfriend's going out with another girl.* ~ *Let him. I don't care.*
Note the structure with *let* + the infinitive of *there is*.
*Let there be no doubt in your minds about our intentions.*

# 324 life: countable or uncountable noun

When we talk about life in general, or about a kind of life, *life* is normally uncountable.
    *Life is complicated.*    *Ann enjoys life.*
    *I think I would enjoy city life.* (NOT ... ~~a city life.~~)
When we describe particular people's lives, *life* is normally countable.
    *My grandmother had a hard life.* (NOT ... ~~had hard life.~~)
    *My mother's parents lived interesting lives.*

For more about countable and uncountable nouns, see 148.

# 325 like: verb

## 1 not used in progressive forms

*Like* is not usually used in progressive forms (see 471).
    *What do you think of the soup?* ~ *I like it.* (NOT ... ~~I'm liking it.~~)

## 2 not used without an object

*Like* cannot normally be used without an object.
    *How do you feel about ballet?* ~ *I like it.* (NOT ... ~~I like.~~)
For exceptions, see paragraph 7 below.

## 3 *very much*: position

We can use *very much* with *like*, but not *very* alone.
    *I very much like ice cream.* (NOT ~~I very like ice cream.~~)
*Very much* does not come between *like* and its object (see 21).
    *I like you and your sister very much.* OR *I very much like you and your sister.*
    (NOT ~~I like very much you and your sister.~~)

## 4 *like ...ing*: enjoyment

To talk about enjoying activities in general, we can use *like ...ing* (especially in BrE) or *like* + infinitive.
    *I really like walking / to walk in the woods.*
    *Children always like listening / to listen to stories.*
To talk about enjoying something on one occasion, we use *like ...ing*.
    *I really liked working with him on his boat last week.*
*Like* + object + verb is possible.
    *I don't like people phoning / to phone me in the middle of the night.*

## 5  *like* + infinitive: choices and habits

We can use *like* + **infinitive** to talk about choices and habits.
> *I **like to do** the shopping early on Saturday mornings.*
> *When I'm pouring tea I **like to put** the milk in first.*

*Not like to* can mean 'think it better not to'.
> *Why didn't you tell me before?* ~ *I **didn't like to disturb** you at home.*

*Like* + **object** + **infinitive** is possible.
> *She **likes the children to go** to bed early during the week.*

## 6  *would like*

We use *would like* + **infinitive** as a polite way of saying 'want', especially in requests and offers.
> *I'd **like** two kilos of tomatoes, please.*
> ***Would** you **like** to dance?* ~ *Yes, OK.* (NOT ~~Would you like dancing?~~ ...)

*Do you like ...?* is not used in this way.
> (NOT ~~Do you like some more coffee?~~)

*Would like to* can be used instead of repeating a whole infinitive (see 182).
> *How about playing tennis?* ~ *I'd **like to**.*

Polite requests often begin *If you would like ...* ; the following clause is sometimes dropped.
> ***If you would like** to take a seat, I'll see if Mr Smithers is free.*
> ***If you would like** to come this way ...*

*Would* is sometimes dropped in this structure.
> ***If you like** to come this way ...*

For *would like* with a perfect infinitive (e.g. *I would like to have seen that.*), see 288.

## 7  *if you like* etc

When we offer people a choice, we often use *like* to mean 'want (to)' in subordinate clauses. Note that *to* is not used.
> *Can I go now?* ~ *If you **like**.* (NOT ~~If you like to.~~)
> *Do it **any** way you **like**.*    *Come **when** you **like**.*
> *You can sit **wherever** you **like**.*

# 326  like and as: similarity, function

We can use *like* or *as* to say that things are similar. We can also use *as* to talk about function – the jobs that people or things do.

## 1  *like* (similarity): *like me*

*Like* can be a preposition. We use *like*, not *as*, before a noun or pronoun to talk about similarity.

> *like* + noun/pronoun

> *My sister looks **like me**.* (NOT ...~~as me.~~)
> *He ran **like the wind**.* (NOT ...~~as the wind.~~)
> ***Like his parents**, he is a vegetarian.*

We can use *very*, *quite* and other adverbs of degree before *like*.
> *He's **very like** his father.*

▶

*She looks **a bit like** Queen Victoria.*
We can use *like* to give examples.
*She's good at scientific subjects, **like mathematics**.* (NOT *. . . as mathematics.*)
*In mountainous countries, **like Peru**, . . .*

## 2   *as* (similarity): *as I do*

*As* is a conjunction. We use it before a clause, and before an expression
beginning with a preposition.

> *as* + clause
> *as* + preposition phrase

*Nobody knows her **as I do**.*
*We often drink tea with the meal, **as they do** in China.*
*In 1939, **as in 1914**, everybody seemed to want war.*
*On Friday, **as on Tuesday**, the meeting will be at 8.30.*

## 3   *like I do* (informal)

In modern English, *like* is often used as a conjunction instead of *as*. This is
most common in an informal style.
*Nobody loves you **like I do**.*
*You look exactly **like your mother did** when she was 20.*

## 4   inverted word order: *as did all his family*

In a very formal style, *as* is sometimes followed by **auxiliary verb + subject**
(note the inverted word order – see 302).
*She was a Catholic, **as were** most of her friends.*
*He believed, **as did** all his family, that the king was their supreme lord.*

## 5   *as you know* etc

Some expressions beginning with *as* are used to introduce facts which are
'common ground' – known to both speaker/writer and listener/reader.
Examples are *as you know, as we agreed, as you suggested*.
***As you know**, next Tuesday's meeting has been cancelled.*
*I am sending you the bill for the repairs, **as we agreed**.*
There are some passive expressions of this kind – for example *as is well known;
as was agreed*. Note that there is no subject *it* after *as* in these expressions
(see 581).
***As is well known**, more people get colds in wet weather.* (NOT *As it is well
known . . .*)
*I am sending you the bill, **as was agreed**.* (NOT *. . . as it was agreed.*)

## 6   comparison with *as* and *like* after negatives

After a negative clause, a comparison with *as* or *like* usually refers only to the
positive part of what comes before.
*I don't smoke, **like Jane**.* (Jane smokes.)
*I am not **a Conservative**, **like Joe**.* (Joe is a Conservative.)
Before a negative clause, the comparison refers to the whole clause.
***Like Mary**, I don't smoke.* (Mary doesn't smoke.)
***Like Bill**, I am not a Conservative.* (Bill is not a Conservative.)

## 7 function or role: *He worked as a waiter*

Another use of *as* is to say what function or role a person or thing has – what jobs people do, what purposes things are used for, what category they belong to, etc. In this case, *as* is a preposition, used before a noun.

*He worked **as a waiter** for two years.* (NOT *. . . ~~like a waiter.~~*)
*Please don't use that knife **as a screwdriver**.*
*A crocodile starts life **as an egg**.*

Compare this use of *as* with *like*.

***As your brother**, I must warn you to be careful.* (I am your brother.)
***Like your brother**, I must warn you to be careful.* (I am not your brother, but he and I have similar attitudes.)

Note that *as* is usually pronounced /əz/ (see 616).
For comparisons with *as . . . as*, see 136.
For *like* used instead of *as if*, see 74.
For *What . . . like?*, see 253.
For *like* used to join two infinitive structures, see 281.4.

For *alike*, see 34.
For *the same as*, see 503.
For *such as*, see 568.6.

# 327 likely

## 1 meaning

*Likely* is an adjective with a similar meaning to *probable*.

*I don't think a Labour victory is **likely**.*    *The opposite is **unlikely**.*
*What's a **likely** date for the election?*    *Snow is very **unlikely**.*

Note also the informal adverb phrases *very/most likely*.

*I think she'll **very/most likely** be late.*

## 2 *it is (un)likely + that*-clause

We can use *it* as a preparatory subject or object for a *that*-clause (see 446.7).

***It's likely that** the meeting will go on late.*
*I thought **it unlikely that** she would come back.*

## 3 infinitive after *be (un)likely*

*Be + (un)likely* is often followed by an infinitive.

*I'm **likely to be** busy tomorrow.*
*Do you think it's **likely to rain**?*    *He's **unlikely to agree**.*

# 328 link verbs: be, seem, look etc

## 1 common link verbs

Some verbs are used to join an adjective or noun complement to a subject. These verbs can be called 'link verbs', 'copulas' or 'copular verbs'. Common examples: *be, seem, appear, look, sound, smell, taste, feel, become, get*.

*The weather **is** horrible.*    *I do **feel** a fool.*
*That car **looks** fast.*    *She **became** a racehorse trainer.*
*The stew **smells** good.*    *It's **getting** late.*

## 2 adjectives after link verbs

After link verbs we use adjectives, not adverbs. Compare:

▶

*He spoke intelligently.* (Intelligently is an adverb. It tells you about how the person spoke.)

*He seems intelligent.* (Intelligent is an adjective. It tells you about the person himself – rather like saying *He is intelligent. Seem* is a link verb.)

### 3 other uses

Some of these verbs are also used with other meanings as ordinary non-link verbs. They are then used with adverbs, not adjectives. Compare:

*The problem **appeared impossible**.* (NOT . . . ~~impossibly.~~)

*Isabel **suddenly appeared** in the doorway.* (NOT . . . ~~sudden~~ . . .)

Other verbs used in two ways like this are *look* (see 331), *taste* (see 577) and *feel* (see 202).

### 4 change

Some link verbs are used to talk about change, or the absence of change. The most common are: *become, get, grow, go, turn, stay, remain, keep.*

*It's **becoming** colder.*  
*How does she **stay** so young?*  
*It's **getting** colder.*  
*I hope you will always **remain** so happy.*  

*It's **growing** colder.*  
*Keep calm.*  
*The leaves **are going** brown.*  
*The leaves **are turning** brown.*

For the differences between these verbs, see 128.

### 5 other verbs followed by adjectives

Sometimes other verbs, too, can be followed by adjectives. This happens when we are really describing the subject of the sentence, and not the action of the verb. It is common in descriptions with *sit, stand, lie, fall.*

*The valley **lay quiet** and **peaceful** in the sun.*  
*She **sat motionless**, waiting for their decision.*  
*He **fell unconscious** on the floor.* (NOT . . . ~~unconsciously~~ . . .)

Adjectives can also be used in the structure **verb + object + adjective**, to describe the object of the verb.

*New SUPER GUB washes clothes SUPER WHITE.* (NOT . . . ~~WHITELY~~ . . .)  
*He pulled his belt **tight** and started off.* (NOT . . . ~~tightly~~ . . .)

For the difference between adjectives and adverbs, see 26.  
For cases like *drive slow, think positive*, see 27.2,4.  
For more about structures after verbs, see 606.  
See also the entries for particular link verbs.

## 329 (a) little and (a) few

### 1 uncountable and plural

We use the determiner *(a) little* with singular (usually uncountable) words, and we use *(a) few* with plurals. Compare:

*I have **little** interest in politics.*     *Few politicians are really honest.*  
*We've got **a little** bacon and **a few** eggs.*

### 2 of after (a) little and (a) few

We use *(a) little of* and *(a) few of* before a pronoun or determiner (for example *the, my, these* – see 154).

Compare:
- *Few people can say that they always tell the truth.*
  *Few of us can say that we always tell the truth.*
- *Could I try a little wine?*
  *Could I try a little of your wine?*
- *Only a few children like maths.*
  *Only a few of the children in this class like maths.*

## 3 use of *a*

There is a difference between *little* and *a little*, and between *few* and *a few*. Without *a*, *little* and *few* usually have rather negative meanings. They may suggest 'not as much/many as one would like', 'not as much/many as expected', and similar ideas.
> *The average MP has **little** real power.*
> ***Few** people can speak a foreign language perfectly.*

*A little* and *a few* are more positive: their meaning is generally closer to *some*. They may suggest ideas like 'better than nothing' or 'more than expected'.
> *Would you like **a little** soup?*
> *You don't need to go shopping. We've got **a few** potatoes and some steak.*

Compare:
- *Cactuses need **little** water.* (not much water)
  *Give the roses **a little** water every day.* (not a lot, but some)
- *His ideas are difficult, and **few** people understand them.*
  *His ideas are difficult, but **a few** people understand them.*

*Quite a few* (informal) means 'a considerable number'.
> *We've got **quite a few** friends in the village.*

## 4 formal and informal language

*Little* and *few* (with no article) are rather formal. In an informal style (e.g. ordinary conversation), we generally prefer *not much/many*, or *only a little/few*.
> *Come on! We haven't got **much** time!*
> ***Only a few** people speak a foreign language perfectly.*

However, *very little* and *very few* are possible in an informal style.
> *He's got **very little** patience and **very few** friends.*

## 5 *(a) little* and *(a) few* without nouns

We can drop a noun and use *(a) little/few* alone, if the meaning is clear.
> *Some more soup?* ~ *Just **a little**, please.*

## 6 not used after *be*

*(A) little* and *(a) few* are determiners (see 154). They are normally used before nouns, but not after *be*.
> *They had **little** hope.* (BUT NOT ~~*Their hope was little.*~~)

## 7 *(a) little* with adjectives and adverbs

*(A) little* can modify comparatives.
> *How are you?* ~ *A **little** better, thanks.*
> *The new model is **little faster** than the old one.*

▶

*Little* is not normally used to modify other adjectives or adverbs.
>  It's **not very interesting**. (NOT ~~It's little interesting~~.)

A *little* can be used, like *a bit* (see 107), before adjectives and adverbs with a critical or negative meaning.
>  You must forgive her – she's **a little confused**.
>  They arrived **a little late**.

Note also the expression *little known*.
>  He's studying the work of a **little known** German novelist.

For *less* and *fewer*, see 320.
For the adjective *little*, see 534.

# 330 long and (for) a long time

## 1 *long* in questions and negatives

*Long* (meaning '(for) a long time') is most common in questions and negative clauses, and with restrictive words like *hardly, seldom.*
>  Have you been waiting **long**?
>  It doesn't take **long** to get to her house.    She seldom stays **long**.

## 2 *(for) a long time* in affirmative clauses

In affirmative clauses we usually prefer *(for) a long time.*
>  I waited **(for) a long time**, but she didn't arrive. (NOT ~~I waited long~~...)
>  It takes **a long time** to get to her house. (NOT ~~It takes long~~...)

## 3 *long* in affirmative clauses

However, *long* is used in affirmative clauses with *too, enough, as* and *so*, and in a few other common expressions.
>  The meeting went on much **too long**.
>  I've been working here **long enough**. Time to get a new job.
>  You can stay **as long** as you want.
>  Sorry I took **so long**.    I'll be back **before long**.
>  She sits dreaming **all day long**. (also *all night/week/year long*)

*Long* is also used in affirmative clauses to modify adverbs and conjunctions.
>  We used to live in Paris, but that was **long before** you were born.
>  **Long after** the accident he used to dream that he was dying.
>  **Long ago**, in a distant country, there lived a beautiful princess.
>      (rather formal)

## 4 *for a long time* in negative clauses

When *for a long time* is used in a negative clause, it sometimes has a different meaning from *for long.* Compare:
– She didn't speak **for long**. (= She only spoke for a short time.)
  She didn't speak **for a long time**. (= She was silent for a long time.)
– He didn't work **for long**. (= He soon stopped working.)
  He didn't work **for a long time**. (= He was unemployed for a long time.)

The reason for the difference is to do with the 'scope of negation': in the first and third sentences, *not* goes with *for long*, but in the second and fourth *for a long time* is outside the influence of *not* (it could go at the beginning of the clause).

**5**  *How long are you here for?*

Questions like *How long are you here for?* refer to the future. Compare:
>  *How long are you here for?* ~ *Until the end of next week.*
>  *How long have you been here for?* ~ *Since last Monday.*

**6**  **comparative**

The comparative of *for a long time* is *(for) longer.*
>  *I hope you'll stay longer next time.* (NOT . . . *~~for a longer time.~~*)

For *no longer*, see 379.
*Much, many* and *far* are also more common in questions and negative clauses (see 357 and 200).

# 331  look

**1**  **link verb (= 'seem')**

Look can mean 'seem' or 'appear'. In this case it is a link verb (see 328) and can be followed by adjectives or nouns.
>  *You **look angry** – what's the matter?* (NOT *~~You look angrily~~*...)
>  *I **looked a real fool** when I fell in the river.*
>  *The garden **looks a mess**.*

To talk about a temporary appearance, we can use simple or progressive forms; there is not much difference of meaning.
>  *You **look** / You're **looking** very unhappy. What's the matter?*

Look can be followed by *like* or *as if* (see 74). Progressive forms are not usually used in this case.
>  *She **looks like** her mother.*
>  *It **looks as if** it's going to rain.* (NOT *~~It's looking as if~~*...)
>  *She **looks as if** she's dreaming.*
>  *She **looks like** she's dreaming.* (informal) (NOT *~~She looks like dreaming.~~*)

Look like ...*ing* ... (informal) is used with future reference in British English.
>  *It **looks like being** a wet night.* (= It looks as if it will be ...)

Look + infinitive is also sometimes used in informal British English.
>  *The team **look to repeat** their success.* (= It looks as if they will ...)

**2**  **ordinary verb = ('direct one's eyes')**

When *look* means 'direct one's eyes', it is used with adverbs, not adjectives. Before an object, a preposition is necessary (usually *at*).
>  *The boss **looked at** me angrily.* (NOT *~~The boss looked at me angry.~~*)

A preposition is not used when there is no object.
>  ***Look!** It's changing colour.* (NOT *~~Look at!~~*...)

**3**  **not followed by *if***

Before *if* or *whether*, we use *see* or *look to see*, not *look*.
>  *Could you **see if** Ann's in the kitchen?* (NOT *~~Could you look if Ann's in the kitchen?~~*)
>  *What are you doing?* ~ *I'm **looking to see whether** these batteries are OK.* (NOT *~~I'm looking whether~~*...)

▶

**4** *look after* and *look for; fetch*

These are not the same. *Look after* means 'take care of'; *look for* means 'try to find'. Compare:

*Could you **look after** the kids while I go shopping?*
*I spent ages **looking for** her before I found her.*

We use *fetch*, not *look for*, if we know where people or things are.

*I'm going to the station at three o'clock **to fetch** Daniel.* (NOT *. . . to look for Daniel.*)

For other uses of *look*, see a good dictionary.
For the difference between *look (at)*, *watch* and *see*, see 506.
For *Look!* and *Look here!* used in arguments, see 157.19.

## 332 lose and loose

*Lose* (pronounced /luːz/) is an irregular verb (*lose – lost – lost*).
*Loose* (pronounced /luːs/) is an adjective (the opposite of *tight*).

*I must be **losing** weight – my clothes all feel **loose**.* (NOT *I must be loosing weight . . .*)

## 333 [a] lot, lots, plenty, a great deal, a large amount, a large number, the majority

**1** **introduction; use of *of***

These expressions have similar meanings to the determiners *much*, *many* and *most*, but the grammar is not quite the same. In particular, *of* is used after these expressions even before nouns with no determiner. Compare:

– *There's not **a lot of** meat left.* (NOT *There's not a lot meat left.*)
*There's not **much** meat left.* (NOT *There's not much of meat left.*)
– *Plenty of shops open on Sunday mornings.* (NOT *Plenty shops . . .*)
*Many shops open on Sunday mornings.* (NOT *Many of shops . . .*)

For *much*, *many* and *most* with and without *of*, and other details of their use, see 356–357.

**2** *a lot of* and *lots of*

These are rather informal. In a more formal style, we prefer *a great deal of*, *a large number of*, *much* or *many*. (*Much* and *many* are used mostly in questions and negative clauses – see 357.) There is not much difference between *a lot of* and *lots of*: they are both used mainly before singular uncountable and plural nouns, and before pronouns. It is the subject, and not the form *lot/lots*, that makes a following verb singular or plural. So when *a lot of* is used before a plural subject, the verb is plural; when *lots of* is used before a singular subject, the verb is singular.

*A lot of time **is** needed to learn a language.*
*Lots of patience **is** needed, too.* (NOT *Lots of patience are needed, too.*)
*A lot of my friends **want** to emigrate.* (NOT *A lot of my friends wants . . .*)
*Lots of us **think** it's time for an election.*

## 3  *plenty of*

*Plenty of* is usually rather informal. It is used mostly before singular uncountables and plurals. It suggests 'enough and more'.

> *Don't rush. There's **plenty of time**.*     ***Plenty of shops** take cheques.*

## 4  *a great deal of, a large amount of* and *a large number of*

These are used in similar ways to *a lot of* and *lots of*, but are more formal. *A great deal of* and *a large amount of* are generally used with uncountable nouns.

> *Mr Lucas has spent **a great deal of time** in the Far East.*
> *I've thrown out **a large amount of old clothing**.*

*A large number of* is used before plurals, and a following verb is plural.

> *A **large number of problems** still **have** to be solved.* (More natural than *A large amount of problems . . .* or *A great deal of problems . . .*)

## 5  *the majority of*

*The majority of* (= 'most' or 'most of') is mostly used with plural nouns and verbs.

> ***The majority of criminals are** non-violent.*

## 6  measurement nouns

These expressions are not generally used before words for units of measure, like *pounds, years* or *miles*. Other words have to be used.

> *It cost **several** pounds.* (NOT ~~It cost a lot of pounds.~~)
> *They lived **many** miles from the town.* (NOT ~~They lived plenty of miles from the town.~~)

## 7  use without following nouns

These expressions can be used without nouns if the meaning is clear. In this case, *of* is not used.

> *How much did it cost? ~**A lot**.* (= A lot of money.)
> *We should be all right for cheese – I've bought **plenty**.*
> *He does not often speak, but when he does he says **a great deal**.*

## 8  use as adverbs

*A lot* and *a great deal* can be used as adverbs.

> *On holiday we walk and swim **a lot**.* (BUT NOT *. . . ~~we walk plenty~~* OR *. . . ~~swim lots.~~*)
> *The government seems to change its mind **a great deal**.*

## 334  loudly and aloud

*Loudly* is used (like *loud*) to talk about the strength of a noise. The opposite is *quietly*.

> *They were talking **so loudly** I couldn't hear myself think.*     ▶

*Aloud* is often used with the words *read* and *think*, to say that words are spoken, and not just 'said' silently in the head.

> *She has a very good pronunciation when she reads **aloud**.*
> *What did you say? ~ Oh, nothing. I was just thinking **aloud**.*

# 335 make: causative structures

## 1 object + infinitive

After *make* + object, we use the infinitive without *to* (see 281).

> *I made her **cry**.* (NOT ~~I made her to cry.~~ OR ~~I made her crying.~~)

Note that the infinitive must follow the object.

> *I can't make **the washing machine work**.* (NOT ~~I can't make work the washing machine.~~)

In passive structures the infinitive with *to* is used.

> *She **was made to repeat** the whole story.*

## 2 *make oneself understood*, etc

In a few cases *make* can be followed by *myself, yourself* etc and a past participle. The structure is common with *understood* and *heard*.

> *I don't speak good French, but I can make **myself understood**.* (NOT ... ~~make myself understand.~~)
> *She had to shout **to make herself heard**.*

## 3 with object + object complement: *make people welcome* etc

We can talk about an effect or change with *make* + object + adjective/noun (see 607).

> *She **made everybody welcome**.*
> *The rain **made the grass wet**.* (NOT ~~The rain made wet the grass.~~)

We do not use *make ... be* in this structure.

> *You have **made me a happy man**.* (NOT ~~You have made me be a happy man.~~)

For other structures and the difference between *make* and *do*, see 160.

# 336 make: prepositions

We usually say that something is *made of* a particular material.

> *Most things seem to be **made of** plastic these days.*
> *All our furniture is **made of** wood.*

When a material is changed into a completely different form to make something, we often use *make from*.

> *Paper is **made from** wood.* (NOT ~~Paper is made of wood.~~)

When we talk about the process of manufacture, we can also use *out of*.

> *He **made** all the window-frames **out of** oak; it took a long time.*

To mention one of several materials (e.g. in cooking), we can use *make with*.

> *The soup's good. ~ Yes, I **make** it **with** lots of garlic.*

## 337 marry and divorce

### 1 get married/divorced

In an informal style, *get married* and *get divorced* are more common than *marry* and *divorce* when there is no object.

*Lulu and Joe **got married** last week. (Lulu and Joe married ... is more formal.)*

*The Robinsons are **getting divorced**.*

In a more formal style, *marry* and *divorce* are preferred.

*Although she had many lovers, she never **married**.*

*After three very unhappy years they **divorced**.*

### 2 no preposition before object

Before a direct object, *marry* and *divorce* are used without prepositions.

*She **married a builder**. (*NOT* She married with a builder.)*

*Andrew's going to **divorce Carola**.*

### 3 get/be married to

We can also use *get/be married to* with an object.

*She **got married to** her childhood sweetheart.*

*I've **been married to** you for 25 years and I still don't understand you.*

## 338 may and might (1): introduction

### 1 grammar

*May* and *might* are modal auxiliary verbs (see 353–354).

a There is no *-s* in the third person singular.

*She **may** be here tomorrow. (*NOT* She mays...)*

*It **might** rain this afternoon.*

b Questions and negatives are made without *do*.

***May** I help you? (*NOT* Do I may...)*

*We **might not** be home before midnight.*

c After *may* and *might* we use the infinitive of other verbs, without *to*.

*You may **be** right. (*NOT* You may to be right.)*

*She might not **want** to come with us.*

d *May* and *might* do not have infinitives or participles (*to may, maying, mighted* do not exist). When necessary, we use other words.

*She wants **to be allowed** to open a bank account. (*NOT* ...to may open...)*

e *Might* does not normally have a past meaning. It is used in the same way as *may* to talk about the present and future. The difference is that *might* usually refers to situations which are less probable or less definite (see 339.2 and 340.1). *Might* also replaces *may* in past indirect speech (see 275). ▶

f However, certain past ideas can be expressed by *may* or *might* followed by a perfect infinitive (**have + past participle**).

> *She's late. I think she **may have missed** the train.*
> *Why did you do that? You **might have killed** yourself.*

g *Might* has a contracted negative *mightn't* (see 143). *Mayn't* is very unusual.

## 2 meanings

*May* and *might* are used mainly to talk about the chances of something happening, and to ask for and give permission (especially in a more formal style).

> *I **may** see you tomorrow.*
> *Do you think I **might** borrow your typewriter?*

*Can* and *could* are often used in similar ways to *may* and *might*. For the main differences, see 345. For *may* and *might* after *so that* and *in order that*, see 543.

# 339 may and might (2): chances etc

## 1 chances: *You may be right; We may go climbing*

We often use *may* and *might* to talk about the chance (possibility) that something will happen, or is happening.

> *We **may** go climbing in the Alps next summer.*
> *Peter **might** phone. If he does, ask him to ring later.*
> *I think Labour are going to win. ~ You **may** be right.*
> *Where's Emma? ~ I don't know. She **might** be out shopping, I suppose.*

*May well* and *might well* suggest stronger possibilities.

> *I think it's going to rain. ~ You **may well** be right – the sky's really black.*

## 2 *may* and *might*: the difference

*Might* is not often used as a past form of *may*: both *may* and *might* are used to talk about the present or future. *Might* is mostly used as a less definite or more hesitant form of *may*, suggesting a smaller chance – it is used when people think something is possible but not very likely. Compare:

> *I **may** go to London tomorrow.* (perhaps a 50% chance)
> *Joe **might** come with me.* (perhaps a 30% chance)

## 3 questions: *may* not used

*May* is not normally used to ask about the chance of something happening.

> *Are you **likely** to go camping this summer?* (NOT ~~May you go camping...?~~)
> *Has Emma gone shopping, **I wonder**?* (NOT ~~May Emma have gone shopping?~~)

But *may* is possible in indirect questions (for example after *Do you think*).

> *Do you think you **may** go camping this summer?*

*Might* can be used in direct questions, but this is rather formal.

> *Might you go camping?* (less natural than *Do you think you may/might ...?*)

## 4   two negatives: *may/might not* and *can't*

There are two ways to make *may/might* negative: with *may/might not* (= It is possible that ... not ...) and with *can't* (= It is not possible that ...) Compare:
–   *She* **may** *be at home.* (= Perhaps she is at home.)
   *She* **may not** *be at home.* (= Perhaps she is not at home.)
   *She* **can't** *be at home.* (= She is certainly not at home.)
–   *You* **might** *win.* (= Perhaps you will win.)
   *You* **might not** *win.* (= Perhaps you won't win.)
   *You* **can't** *win.* (= You certainly won't win.)

## 5   *might* meaning 'would perhaps'

*Might* (but not *may*) can have a conditional meaning (= would perhaps).
   *If you went to bed for an hour, you* **might** *feel better.*
      (= ... perhaps you would feel better.)
   *Don't play with knives. You* **might** *get hurt.* (= Perhaps you would get hurt.)

## 6   indirect speech: *might*

*Might* is used in past indirect speech when *may* was used in direct speech.
   *I* **may** *go to Scotland.* ~ *What?* ~ *I said I* **might** *go to Scotland.*

## 7   past: *might* + infinitive not used

*Might* + **infinitive** is not normally used to talk about past possibility (except in indirect speech).
   *I felt very hot and tired.* **Perhaps** *I* **was** *ill.* (NOT ... ~~I might be ill.~~)

## 8   *may/might have ...: She may have missed her train*

However, to say that it is possible that something happened or was true in the past, we can use *may/might have* + **past participle**.
   *Polly's very late.* ~ *She* **may have missed** *her train.* (= It is possible that she missed ...)
   *What was that noise?* ~ *It* **might have been** *a cat.*
*May/might have ...* can sometimes refer to the present or future.
   *I'll try phoning him, but he* **may have gone** *out by now.*
   *By the end of this year I* **might have saved** *some money.*

## 9   *might have ...: You might have killed yourself*

To say that something was possible but did not happen, we can use *might have ...*
   *You were stupid to try climbing up there. You* **might have killed** *yourself.*
   *If she hadn't been so bad-tempered, I* **might have married** *her.*
*May have ...* is now sometimes used with this meaning too; some people feel that this is not correct.
   *You were stupid to try climbing up there. You* **may have killed** *yourself.*
      (More normal: ... *You* **might have killed** *yourself.*)

For *might have ...* used to criticise people for not doing things, see 344.
For the use of *could have* + **past participle** in similar senses, see 124.7.      ▶

**10** **another use of *may/might*: typical occurrences**

In scientific and academic language, *may* is often used to talk about typical occurrences – things that can happen in certain situations.

*A female crocodile **may** lay 30-40 eggs.*
*The flowers **may** have five or six petals, pink or red in colour.*
*Children of divorced parents **may** have difficulty with relationships.*

With this meaning, *might* can be used to talk about the past.

*In those days, a man **might** be hanged for stealing a sheep.*

*Can* and *could* are used in a similar way, but are less formal. See 122.2,4.

# 340 may and might (3): permission

*May* and *might* are used for permission mostly in a formal style. They are much less common than *can* and *could*.

**1** **asking for permission: *May I put the TV on?***

*May* and *might* can both be used to ask for permission. *Might* is very polite and formal, and is mostly used in indirect question structures.

***May** I put the TV on?*
*I wonder if I **might** have a little more cheese.*
(More natural than *Might I have . . .?*)

**2** **giving and refusing permission: *You may / You may not***

*May* is used to give permission; *may not* to refuse permission or forbid.

*May I put the TV on? ~ Yes, of course you **may**.*
*May I borrow the car? ~ No, I'm afraid you **may not**.*
*Students **may not** use the staff car park.*

*Must not* is also used to forbid (see 360.3). It is a little stronger or more emphatic than *may not*.

*Students **must not** use the staff car park.*

**3** **talking about permission**

We do not usually use *may* and *might* to talk about permission which has already been given or refused, about freedom which people already have, or about rules and laws. Instead, we use *can, could* or *be allowed*.

*These days, children **can / are allowed to** do what they like.* (NOT *. . . children may do what they like.*)
*I **could / was allowed to** read what I liked when I was a child.* (NOT *I might read what I liked . . .*)
*Can you / Are you allowed to park on both sides of the road here?*
(More natural than *May you park . . .?*)

**4** **indirect speech**

However, *may* and *might* can be used to report the giving of permission. *May* is used after present reporting verbs, and *might* after past verbs.

*The Manager says that we **may** leave our coats in the downstairs toilet.*
*What are you doing here? ~ Peter said that I **might** look round.* (very formal)

# 341 **may** and **might** (4): **may** in wishes and hopes

*May* (but not *might*) is used in formal expressions of wishes and hopes.
> *I hope that the young couple **may** enjoy many years of happiness together.*
> *Let us pray that peace **may** soon return to our troubled land.*

*May* often comes at the beginning of the sentence.
> ***May** you both be very happy!*    ***May** God be with you.*
> ***May** the New Year bring you all your heart desires.*
> ***May** she rest in peace.* (prayer for a dead person)

# 342 **may** and **might** (5): may/might ... but

*May* (and sometimes *might*) can be used in a discussion rather like *although* or *even if*: to say that something is true, but that this makes no difference to the main argument. They are often followed by *but*.
> *He **may** be clever, but he hasn't got much common sense.* (= Even if he's clever, he ... OR Although he's clever, he ...)
> *It **may** be a comfortable car, but it uses a lot of petrol.*
> *She **might** have had a lovely voice when she was younger, but ...*

Note that in this structure, *may* and *might* can be used to talk about things that are definitely true, not just possible.
> *You **may** be my boss, but that doesn't mean you're better than me.*

# 343 **may** and **might** (6): may/might as well

This structure is used informally to suggest that one should do something because there is nothing better, nothing more interesting or nothing more useful to do. There is little difference between *may* and *might* in this case.
> *There's nobody interesting to talk to. We **may as well** go home.*
> *Shall we go and see Fred? ~OK, **might as well**.*

Note the difference between *may/might as well* and *had better* (see 230). Compare:
> *We **may as well** have something to eat.*
> (= There is nothing more interesting to do.)
> *We**'d better** have something to eat.*
> (= We ought to eat; there is a good reason to eat now.)

*Might as well* is also used to compare one unpleasant situation with another.
> *This holiday isn't much fun. We **might** just **as well** be back home.* (= Things wouldn't be any different if we were at home.)
> *You never listen – I **might as well** talk to a brick wall.*

# 344 **may** and **might** (7):
## requests, suggestions and criticisms

*Might* is often used in affirmative clauses to make requests and suggestions.
> *You **might** see if John's free this evening.*
> *You **might** try asking your uncle for a job.*

▶

The structure can be used to criticise. *Might have* + **past participle** is used to talk about the past.

> *You **might** ask before you borrow my car.*
> *She **might have told** me she was going to stay out all night.*

For the use of *could* in similar senses, see 124.7.

# 345 may and might (8): may/might and can/could

*May/might* are often used in similar ways to *can/could*. The main differences are as follows. For more details of these uses, see 121–124 and 338–340.

## 1 permission: *can/could* more common

*Can* and *could* are more common than *may* and *might*, which are used mostly in a formal style. Compare:

> ***Can** I look at your paper?*
> *Excuse me, **may** I look at your newspaper for a moment?*

There is an old belief that *may/might* are more 'correct' than *can/could* in this case, but this does not reflect normal usage.

## 2 'general' possibility: *can/could*, not *may/might*

We normally use *can* and *could* to say that things are possible in general: people are able to do them, the situation makes them possible, or there is nothing to stop them (see 122). *May* and *might* are not used in this way.

> *She's lived in France; that's why she **can** speak French.* (NOT . . . ~~that's why she may speak French.~~)
> *These roses **can** grow anywhere.* (NOT ~~These roses may grow anywhere.~~)
> ***Can** gases freeze?* (NOT ~~May gases freeze?~~)
> *In those days, everybody **could** find a job.* (NOT . . . ~~everybody might find a job.~~)

## 3 chances: *may/might/could*, not *can*

To talk about the chance (possibility) that something will happen, or is happening, we use *may*, *might* or *could*, but not *can*.

> *Where's Sarah?* ~ *She **may** be with Joe.* (NOT ~~She can be~~ . . .)
> *We **may** go to the Alps next summer.* (NOT ~~We can go~~ . . . ~~next summer.~~)

*Might* and *could* suggest a less strong possibility.

> *It **might/could** rain this evening, but I think it probably won't.*

*May* is not used in direct questions with this meaning.

> *Do you think you'll go to the Alps?* (NOT ~~May you go~~ . . .?)

## 4 negative sentences: *may/might not* and *can/could not*

*May/might not* means 'perhaps . . . not . . .'
*Can/could not* can mean 'it is certain that . . . not . . .' (see 359.2).
Compare:

> – *It **may/might not** rain tomorrow.* (= Perhaps it will not rain.)
>    *It **can't/couldn't** possibly rain tomorrow.* (= It will certainly not rain.)
> – *It **may not** be true.* (= Perhaps it is not true.)
>    *It **can't** be true.* (= It is certainly not true.)

– He **may/might not** have understood. (= Perhaps he did not understand.)
He **can't/couldn't** have understood. (= He certainly did not understand.)

# 346 maybe and perhaps

These two words mean the same. They are both common. In British English,
*perhaps* is used more often than *maybe* in a formal style.
**Maybe/Perhaps** *it'll stop raining soon.*
*Julius Caesar is* **perhaps** *the greatest of Shakespeare's early plays.*
*Perhaps* is often pronounced 'praps' by British people.

# 347 meals

There are regional and social differences in the names for meals.

## 1 British usage

a  midday: *dinner* or *lunch*

The midday meal is often called *dinner*, especially if it is the main meal of the
day. People who are 'higher' in the social scale usually call it *lunch*.

b  afternoon: *tea*

Some people have a light meal of tea and biscuits or cakes, called *tea*, at four or
five o'clock in the afternoon.

c  early evening: *(high) tea* or *supper*

Many people have a cooked meal around five or six o'clock. This is often called
*tea* or *high tea*; some people call it *supper*.

d  later evening: *supper* or *dinner*

A meal later in the evening is often called *supper* (and some people use the
same word for a bedtime snack). Some people use *dinner* for the evening meal
if it is the main meal of the day. A more formal evening meal with guests, or in
a restaurant, is usually called *dinner*.

## 2 American usage

Americans generally use *lunch* for the midday meal and *dinner* or *supper* for
the evening meal. However in rural areas it is still common for the main meal
of the day to be eaten at midday and called 'dinner', with the evening meal
being called 'supper'. Celebration meals at Christmas and Thanksgiving are
called *Christmas/Thanksgiving dinner*, even if they are eaten at midday.

# 348 mean

## 1 questions

Note the structure of questions with *mean*.
*Excuse me. What* **does** *'hermetic'* **mean**? (NOT ~~What means 'hermetic'?~~)  ▶

Note also the preposition in *What do you mean **by** 'hermetic'?* (= In what sense are you using the word?)

## 2 *mean* and *think*, *meaning* and *opinion*

*Mean* and *meaning* are 'false friends' for speakers of some European languages. They are not usually used for 'think' or 'opinion'.

> I **think** that Labour will win the next election. (NOT ~~I mean that Labour will win~~...)
>
> What's your **opinion**? (NOT ~~What's your meaning?~~)

## 3 structures

*Mean* (= intend, plan) can be followed by (**object**) + **infinitive**.

> Sorry – I didn't **mean to interrupt** you.
>
> Did you **mean John to post** those letters?

*Mean* (= involve, have as a result) can be followed by a noun or ...*ing*.

> The Fantasians have invaded Utopia. This **means war!**
>
> If you decide to try the exam, it will **mean studying** hard.

## 4 *I mean*

*I mean* is used informally as a 'discourse marker' (see 157) to introduce explanations or additional details.

> He's funny – **I mean**, he's really strange.
>
> It was a terrible evening. **I mean**, they all sat round and talked politics.
>
> Would you like to come out tonight? **I mean**, only if you want to, of course.

When *I mean* introduces a comment it can be close to *I think* or *I feel*, but it is not followed by *that*.

> A hundred pounds for a thirty hour week. **I mean**, it's not right, is it?
>
> (BUT NOT ~~I mean that it's not right~~...)

In informal speech, *I mean* often acts as a connector or 'filler', with little real meaning.

> Let's go and see Phil on Saturday. **I mean**, we could make an early start ...

*I mean* is also used to introduce corrections.

> She lives in Southport – **I mean** Southampton.

## 5 *What do you mean* ...?

*What do you mean* ...? can express anger or protest.

> **What do you mean**, I can't sing?
>
> **What do you mean** by waking me up at this time of night?

## 6 no progressive form

*Mean* is not normally used in progressive forms when it refers to meanings.

> What **does** that strange smile **mean**? (NOT ~~What is that strange smile meaning?~~)

But perfect progressive forms can be used to refer to intentions.

> I've **been meaning** to phone you for weeks.

# 349 means

## 1 singular and plural ending in *-s*

Both the singular and the plural of *means* end in *-s*.
> *In the 19th century a new **means** of communication was developed – the railway.* (NOT . . . ~~a new mean of communication~~ . . .)
> *There are several **means** of transport on the island.*

For other words with singular forms ending in *-s*, see 524.3.

## 2 *by all/any/no means*

*By all means* is not the same as *by all possible means*. It is used to give permission or to encourage somebody to do something, and means 'of course' or 'it is all right to . . .' Compare:
> *Can I borrow your sweater?* ~ ***By all means.***
> ***By all means** get a new coat, but don't spend more than £80.*
> *We must help her **by all possible means**.* (NOT ~~We must help her by all means.~~)

*By no means* (or *not by any means*) is not the opposite of *by all means*. It is similar to *definitely not*, or *not by a long way*.
> *Is that all you've got to say?* ~ ***By no means.***
> *Galileo was **by no means** the first person to use a telescope.*

# 350 measurements: 'marked' and 'unmarked' forms

Many adjectives that are used in measurements come in pairs (e.g. *tall/short, old/young, heavy/light, fast/slow*). The word that is used for the 'top' end of the measurement scale can usually be used in another sense, to talk about the quality in general. For instance, one can ask how *long* something is even if it is relatively short. Grammarians call these uses 'unmarked'. Compare:
– *She's very **tall** and he's very short.* (marked)
  *Exactly how **tall** are they both?* (unmarked) (NOT ~~Exactly how short are they both?~~)
– *Will you still love me when I'm **old**?* (marked)
  *He's only twenty-three years **old**.* (unmarked) (NOT . . . ~~twenty-three years young.~~)
– *Lead is one of the **heaviest** metals.* (marked)
  *Scales are used to measure how **heavy** things are.* (unmarked) (NOT . . . ~~how light things are.~~)
Some nouns are used in similar 'unmarked' ways. Compare:
– ***Age** brings wisdom but I'd rather have youth and stupidity.* (marked)
  *What is her exact **age**?* (unmarked) (NOT ~~What is her exact youth?~~)
– *The worst thing about the film was its **length**.* (marked)
  *What's the **length** of a football field?* (unmarked) (NOT ~~What's the shortness . . .?~~)

▶

# 351 mind: do you mind etc

## 1 meaning and use

*Mind* can mean 'dislike', 'be annoyed by', 'object to'. We use *mind* mostly in questions and negative clauses.

> **Do you mind** *the smell of tobacco?* ∼ *Not at all.*
> **Do you mind** *if we leave a bit earlier today?*
> *I* **don't mind** *if you use my car.*

After *mind*, we can use an *-ing* form, or **object + -ing form**.

> *Do you* **mind waiting** *a few minutes?* (NOT *. . . to wait . . .*)
> *I don't* **mind you coming** *in late if you don't wake me up.*

## 2 *Would you mind . . .?*

We can use *Would you mind . . .?* to ask people to do things, or to ask for permission.

> **Would you mind** *opening the window?* (= Please open . . .)
> **Would you mind** *if I opened the window?*

## 3 *Do/Would you mind my . . .ing?*

In a formal style, we sometimes use *my, your* etc with an *-ing* form after *mind* (see 295.3,4).

> *Do you mind* **my** *smoking?* (More common: . . . *me smoking?* or . . . *if I smoke?*)

## 4 answers

After *Would/Do you mind . . .?*, we use *No* or *Not at all* (more formal) to give permission (but we often add more words to make the meaning quite clear).

> *Do you mind if I look at your paper?* ∼ *No,* **please do** / **that's OK** / **sure**.

## 5 tenses

In subordinate clauses after *mind*, a present tense is usually used if we want to express a future meaning (see 580).

> *I don't mind what you* **do** *after you leave school.* (NOT *I don't mind what you will do . . .*)

# 352 miss

## 1 'fail to contact', 'be late for'

*Miss* often expresses the idea of failing to contact somebody/something, or being late for somebody/something.

> *How could he* **miss** *an easy goal like that?*
> *The station's about five minutes' walk, straight ahead. You can't* **miss** *it.*
> *If you don't hurry we'll* **miss** *the train.* (NOT *. . . lose the train.*)
> *You've just* **missed** *her – she went home five minutes ago.*

An *-ing* form can be used after *miss*.

> *I got in too late and* **missed seeing** *the news on TV.*

## 2 'be sorry to be without'

We can use *miss* to say that we are sorry because we are no longer with somebody, or no longer have something.

*Will you **miss** me when I'm away?*
*He's not happy in the country – he **misses** city life.*

Note that *regret* is not used in the same way. Compare:

*I **miss** working with you.* (= I'm sorry I'm no longer with you.)
*I **regret** working with you.* (= I'm sorry I was with you.)

## 3 'notice the absence of'

Another meaning of *miss* is 'notice that somebody/something is not there'.

*The child ran away in the morning, but nobody **missed** her for hours.*

## 4 *miss* not used

*Miss* is not used simply to say that somebody has not got something.

*In some of the villages they **haven't got** electricity.*
(NOT ...~~they miss electricity.~~)

In a formal style, the verb or noun *lack* can be used to express this idea.

*... they **lack** electricity.*
*I am sorry that **lack** of time prevents me from giving more details.*

## 5 *missing*

*Missing* is often used as an adjective, meaning 'lost'.

*When did you realise that the money was **missing**?*
*The **missing** children were found at their aunt's house.*

We can use *missing* after a noun. This often happens in clauses beginning with *there is*.

*There's **a page missing** from this book.*

In an informal style, a structure with *have ... missing* is also possible.

*We've got some plates **missing** – do you think Alan's borrowed them?*
*He **had** several teeth **missing**.*

# 353 modal auxiliary verbs: introduction

## 1 What are modal auxiliary verbs?

The verbs *can, could, may, might, will, would, shall* (mainly British English), *should, must* and *ought* are called 'modal auxiliary verbs'. They are used before the infinitives of other verbs, and add certain kinds of meaning connected with certainty, or with obligation and freedom to act (see next section).

## 2 grammar

a  Modal verbs have no *-s* in the third person singular.
*She **may** know his address.* (NOT ~~She mays~~ ...)

b  Questions, negatives, tags and short answers are made without *do*.
***Can** you swim?* (NOT ~~Do you can swim?~~) *~ Yes, **I can**.*
*He **shouldn't** be doing that, should he?* (NOT ~~He doesn't should~~ ...)

▶

c After modal auxiliary verbs, we use the infinitive without *to* of other verbs. *Ought* is an exception – see 403.

> *I must **water** the flowers.* (NOT *I must to water* . . .)

Progressive, perfect and passive infinitives are also possible (see 280).

> *I may not **be working** tomorrow.*
> *She was so angry she could **have killed** him.*
> *The kitchen ought **to be painted** one of these days.*

d Modal verbs do not have infinitives or participles (*to may, maying, mayed* do not exist), and they do not normally have past forms (though *would, could, should* and *might* can sometimes be used as past tenses of *will, can, shall* and *may*). Other expressions are used when necessary.

> *I'd like **to be able to** skate.* (NOT . . . *to can skate.*)
> *People really **had to** work hard in those days.* (NOT *People really musted work* . . .)

e However, certain past ideas can be expressed by a modal verb followed by a perfect infinitive (***have** + **past participle***).

> *You should **have told** me you were coming.*
> *I think I may **have annoyed** Aunt Mary.*

For details of these uses, see the entries on particular modal verbs.

f Modal verbs have contracted negative forms (*can't, won't* etc) which are used in an informal style. (*Shan't* and *mayn't* are only used in British English; *mayn't* is very rare.) *Will* and *would* also have contracted affirmative forms (*'ll, 'd*). For details, see 143. Some modals have both 'strong' and 'weak' pronunciations. For details, see 616.

g *There* is quite often used as a preparatory subject with modal verbs, especially when these are followed by *be* (see 586).

> ***There** may be rain later today.*

## 3 meanings

We do not normally use modal verbs to say that situations definitely exist or that particular events have definitely happened. We use them, for example, to talk about things which we expect, which are or are not possible, which we think are necessary, which we want to happen, which we are not sure about, which tend to happen, or which have not happened.

> *He **may arrive** any time.*
> *She **could be** in London or Paris or Tokyo – nobody knows.*
> *I **can't swim**.*
> *I think you **ought to see** a lawyer.*
> *We really **must tidy** up the garden.*
> *What **would you do** if you had a free year?*
> *Edinburgh **can be** very cold in winter.*
> *I think they **should have consulted** a doctor earlier.*
> *You **might have told** me Frances was ill.*

For further general information about the meanings of modal auxiliary verbs, see next section. For more detailed information, see the sections for each verb.

## 4 *need* and *used to*

*Need* (see 366) and *used to* (see 604) are sometimes used in similar ways to modal verbs.

> You **needn't** *wait for me.*
> *She* **used not** *to be so bad-tempered.*

# 354 modal auxiliary verbs: meanings

## 1 two kinds of meaning

Most of the meanings of modal verbs can be divided into two groups. One is to do with degrees of certainty: modal verbs can be used to say for instance that a situation is certain, probable, possible or impossible. The other is to do with obligation, freedom to act and similar ideas: modal verbs can be used to say that somebody is obliged to do something, that he/she is able to do something, that there is nothing to stop something happening, that it would be better if something happened (or did not), or that something is permitted or forbidden.

## 2 degrees of certainty

Modal verbs can express various degrees of certainty about facts, situations or events.

a   complete certainty (positive or negative): *shall, will, must, can't*
> *I* **shall** *be away tomorrow.*      *There's the phone. That***'ll** *be Tony.*
> *I* **shan't** *be late on Tuesday.*    *Things* **will** *be all right.*
> *It* **won't** *rain this evening.*      *You* **must** *be tired.*
> *That* **can't** *be John – he's in Dublin.*

b   probability (deduction; saying that something is logical or normal): *should, ought to*
> *She* **should** */* **ought to** *be here soon.*
> *It* **shouldn't** */* **oughtn't to** *be difficult to get there.*

c   possibility (talking about the chances that something is true or will happen): *may*
> *The water* **may** *not be warm enough to swim.*
> *We* **may** *be buying a new house.*

d   weak possibility: *might, could*
> *I* **might** *see you again – who knows?*
> *Things* **might** *not be as bad as they seem.*
> *We* **could** *all be millionaires one day.*

## 3 obligation and freedom to act

Modal verbs can express various aspects of obligation and freedom. (These uses of modal verbs are very important in the polite expression of requests, suggestions, invitations and instructions.)

a   strong obligation: *must, will, need*
> *Students* **must** *register in the first week of term.*
> *All sales staff* **will** *arrive for work by 8.40 a.m.*
> **Need** *I get a visa for Hungary?*

▶

b   prohibition: *must not, may not, cannot*
> Students **must not** use the staff car park.
> Books **may not** be taken out of the library.
> You **can't** come in here.

c   weak obligation; recommendation: *should, ought to, might, shall* (in questions)
> You **should** try to work harder.    You **might** see what John thinks.
> She really **ought to** wash her hair.    What **shall** we do?

d   willingness, volunteering, resolving, insisting and offering: *will, shall* (in questions)
> If you **will** come this way . . .
> I'll pay for the drinks.    She **will** keep interrupting
> people.
> I'll definitely work harder next term.    **Shall** I give you a hand?

e   permission: *can, could, may, might*
> You **can** use the car if you like.
> **Could** I talk to you for a minute?
> **May** we use the phone?
> Do you think I **might** take a break now?

f   absence of obligation: *needn't*
> You **needn't** work this Saturday.

g   ability: *can, could*
> She **can** speak six languages.
> Anybody who wants to **can** join the club.
> These roses **can** grow anywhere.
> When I was a baby I **could** put my foot in my mouth.
> You **could** get to my old school by bus, but not by train.

## 4   speaker's and hearer's point of view

Obligation, permission etc are usually seen from the speaker's point of view in statements and the hearer's in questions. Compare:

– **You must go and see Ann.** (**I** think it is necessary.)
  **Must you go and see Ann?** (Do **you** think it is necessary?)
– **You can borrow my car.** (**I** give permission.)
  **Can I borrow your car?** (Will **you** give permission?)

## 5   forms in indirect speech, after *if* etc

Instead of *can, will, shall* and *may*, we use *could, would, should* and *might* to express the same meanings in past indirect speech, (see 275), in some sentences after *if* (see 258), and in 'future in the past' sentences (see 221).

> I knew it **couldn't** be John.
> I told you you **wouldn't** be ready in time.
> If you stopped criticising, I **might** get some work done.
> I should be grateful if you **would** let me know your decision as soon as possible.
> They knelt in front of the child who **would** one day rule all England.

## 6  other meanings

Besides the meanings discussed in paragraphs 2 and 3, *will* and *would* are
used to talk about habitual behaviour or activity (see 629, 633).

*Most evenings he'll just sit in front of the TV and go to sleep.*
*When we were kids, my mum **would** take us out on bikes all round the
 countryside.*

*Used to* + **infinitive** (see 604) is similar to a modal verb structure in some ways.
It is used to talk about habitual behaviour or activity and (unlike *would*)
habitual states.

*I **used to** play a lot of tennis when I was younger.*
*The grass **used to** look greener when I was a child.*
  (NOT *The grass would look greener when I was a child.*)

## 7  subject-independence

An interesting, rather complicated point about modal verbs is that their
meaning usually 'spreads over' a whole clause. This means that one can
change a modal structure from active to passive, for example, without
affecting the meaning very much. Compare:
– *A child **could understand** his theory.*
 *His theory **could be understood** by a child.*
– *You **mustn't put** adverbs between the verb and the object.*
 *Adverbs **mustn't be put** between the verb and the object.*
– *Dogs **may** chase cats.*
 *Cats **may get chased** by dogs.*
With most other verbs that are followed by infinitives, their meaning is
attached to the subject, so that a change from active to passive changes the
sense of the sentence completely. Compare:
– *Dogs **like to chase** cats.*
 *Cats **like to be chased** by dogs.* (different and – of course – untrue)
– *Pete **wants to phone** Ann.*
 *Ann **wants to be phoned** by Pete.* (not the same meaning)

For more details of the use of the various modal verbs, see the entries for each verb.

# 355  more

## 1  *more* + noun

We can use *more* before a noun phrase as a determiner (see 154). We do not
generally use *of* when there is no other determiner (e.g. article or possessive).

*We need **more time**.* (NOT *... more of time.*)
*More university students are having to borrow money these days.*

However, *more of* is used directly before personal and geographical names.

*It would be nice to see **more of Ray and Barbara**.*
*Five hundred years ago, much **more of Britain** was covered with trees.* ▶

## 2 *more of* + determiner/pronoun

Before determiners (e.g. *a, the, my, this*) and pronouns, we use *more of*.
> Three **more of the** *missing climbers have been found.*
> *Could I have some* **more of that** *smoked fish?*
> *I don't think any* **more of them** *want to come.*

## 3 *more* without a noun

We can drop a noun after *more* if the meaning is clear.
> *I'd like some* **more,** *please.*

## 4 *one more* etc

Note the structure *one more, two more* etc + noun phrase.
> *There's just* **one more river** *to cross.*

## 5 *more* as an adverb

*More* can also be used as an adverb.
> *I couldn't agree* **more.**

*More and more* is used to talk about continual increase.
> *I hate this job* **more and more** *as the years go by.*

## 6 comparative structures

*More* is used to make the comparative forms of longer adjectives and most
adverbs (see 137–138).
> *As you get older you get* **more tolerant.**     *Please drive* **more slowly.**

For *no more, not any more/longer*, see 379.
For *far more, much more, many more* etc, see 140.

# 356 most

## 1 *most* (= 'the majority of') without *of*

*Most* can mean 'the majority of'. We do not use *the* before *most* with this
meaning.
> **Most** *children like ice cream.* (NOT ~~The most children~~...)

We do not generally use *of* after *most* when there is no other determiner
(e.g. article or possessive).
> **Most** *cheese is made from cow's milk.* (NOT ~~Most of cheese~~...)
> **Most** *Swiss people understand French.* (NOT ~~Most of Swiss people~~...)

However, *most of* is used directly before personal and geographical names.
> *I've read* **most of Shakespeare.**
> *The Romans conquered* **most of England.**

## 2 *most of* + determiner/pronoun

Before determiners (e.g. *a, the, my, this*) and pronouns, we use *most of*.
> **Most of the** *people here know each other.*
> **Most of my** *friends live abroad.* (NOT ~~Most my friends~~...)
> **Most of us** *thought he was wrong.*
> *He's eaten two pizzas and* **most of a** *cold chicken.*

## 3 *most* without a noun

We can drop a noun after *most* if the meaning is clear.
*Some people had difficulty with the lecture, but **most** understood.*

## 4 *the most* (= 'more than any other/others') with nouns

In comparisons (when *most* means 'more than any other/others') it is
normally used with *the* before nouns.
*Susan found **the most blackberries**.*
*The* is sometimes dropped in an informal style.
*Who earns **(the) most money** in your family?*

## 5 *(the) most* as an adverb

*(The) most* can also be used as an adverb. *The* is often dropped in an informal
style.
*They all talk a lot, but your little girl talks **(the) most**.*
*The truth hurts **most**.*

## 6 superlative adjectives and adverbs

*(The) most* is used to make the superlative forms of longer adjectives and most
adverbs (see 137–138).
*I wasn't as clever as the others, but I was **the most beautiful**.*
*I work **most efficiently** in the early morning.*

## 7 *most* meaning 'very'

*Most* can be used before adjectives to mean 'very' in evaluating expressions,
especially in a formal style.
*That is **most kind** of you.*     *Thank you for a **most interesting** afternoon.*
*The experience was **most distressing**.*

## 8 *mostly*

*Mostly* means 'in most (but not all) cases'. Compare:
*Your little girl talks **the most**.* (NOT *... talks mostly.*)
*She **mostly** talks about her friends.*

# 357 **much** and **many**

## 1 the difference

*Much* is used with singular (uncountable) nouns; *many* is used with plurals.
*I haven't got **much time**.*     *I don't know **many** of your **friends**.*

## 2 *much/many* + noun: without *of*

We do not generally use *of* after *much/many* when there is no other determiner
(e.g. article or possessive).
*She didn't eat **much** breakfast.* (NOT *... much of breakfast.*)
*There aren't **many** large glasses left.* (NOT *... many of large glasses left.*)
However, *much of* is used directly before personal and geographical names.
*I've seen too **much of** Howard recently.*     *Not **much of** Denmark is hilly.*

▶

### 3  *much/many of* + determiner + noun

Before determiners (e.g. *a, the, my, this*) and pronouns, we use *much of* and *many of*.

>*You can't see **much of a** country in a week.*
>*How **much of the** house do you want to paint this year?*
>*I won't pass the exam: I've missed too **many of my** lessons.*
>*How **many of you** are there?*

### 4  *much/many* without a noun

We can drop a noun after *much* or *many*, if the meaning is clear.

>*You haven't eaten **much**.*
>*Did you find any mushrooms? ~ Not **many**.*

Note that *much* and *many* are only used like this when a noun has been dropped.

>*There wasn't **much (food)**.* BUT NOT ~~*The food wasn't much.*~~ (Because you couldn't say ~~*The food wasn't much food.*~~)

*Many* is not usually used alone to mean 'many people'.

>*Many people **think** it's time for a change.*
>(More natural than *Many think . . .*)

### 5  not used in affirmative clauses

In an informal style, we use *much* and *many* mostly in questions and negative clauses. In most affirmative clauses they are unusual (especially *much*); other words and expressions are used instead.

>*How **much** money have you got? ~ I've got **plenty**.* (NOT ~~*I've got much.*~~)
>*He's got **lots of** men friends, but he doesn't know **many** women.*
>(More natural than *He's got many men friends . . .*)
>*Did you buy any clothes? ~ Yes, **lots**.* (NOT ~~*Yes, many.*~~)

In a formal style, *much* and *many* are more common in affirmative clauses.

>***Much** has been written about unemployment. In the opinion of **many** economists, . . .*

*Far* and *long* (= a long time) are also used mostly in questions and negative clauses. See 200 and 330.

### 6  after *so, as,* and *too*

*So much/many, as much/many* and *too much/many* are quite natural in affirmative clauses.

>*There was **so much** traffic that it took me an hour to get home.*
>*I play **as much** tennis as I can.    You make **too many** mistakes.*

### 7  *much* as adverb

We can use *much* as an adverb in questions and negative clauses.

>*Do you work **much** at weekends?    I don't travel **much** these days.*

We can also use *much* before comparative adjectives and adverbs, in affirmative clauses as well as questions and negatives.

>*She's **much older** than her brother.    I don't drive **much faster** than you.*

*Much* can be used before some verbs expressing enjoyment, preference and similar ideas, in affirmative clauses as well as questions and negatives, especially in a formal style.

*I **much appreciate** your help.*
*We **much prefer** the country to the town.*
*I didn't **much enjoy** the concert.*
*Very much* can be used in affirmative clauses as an adverb, but not usually before a noun. Compare:
*I **very much** like your new hairstyle.* (adverb)
*Thank you **very much**.* (adverb)
*There's a **whole lot of water** coming under the door.* (before noun)
(NOT *~~There's very much water coming~~*. . .)

For *much* and *very* with past participles (e.g. *much/very amused*), see 410.4.

# 358 must (1): introduction

## 1 grammar

*Must* is a modal auxiliary verb (see 353–354).

a There is no -*s* in the third person singular.
*He **must** start coming on time.* (NOT *~~He musts~~*. . .)

b Questions and negatives are made without *do*.
***Must you** go?* (NOT *~~Do you must go?~~*)
*You **mustn't** worry.* (NOT *~~You don't must worry.~~*)

c After *must*, we use the infinitive without *to* of other verbs.
*I must **write** to my mother.* (NOT *~~I must to write~~*. . .)

d *Must* has no infinitive or participles (*~~to must~~, ~~musting~~, ~~musted~~* do not exist), and it has no past tense. When necessary, we express similar meanings with other words, for example forms of *have to* (see 239).
*It's annoying **to have to** get up early on Sundays.* (NOT . . .*~~to must get up~~*. . .)
*He'll **have to** start coming on time.* (NOT *~~He'll must~~*. . .)
*She's always **had to** work hard.* (NOT *~~She's always musted~~*. . .)
*We **had to** cut short our holiday because my mother was ill.* (NOT *~~We musted~~*. . .)

e Some ideas about the past can be expressed by ***must have*** + **past participle** (see 359.4).
*I can't find my keys. I **must have left** them at home.*
*Must* can also be used with a past sense in indirect speech.
*Everybody told me I **must** stop worrying.*

f There is a contracted negative *mustn't* (/'mʌsnt/). *Must* has two pronunciations: a 'strong' pronunciation /mʌst/ and a 'weak' pronunciation /m(ə)st/. The weak pronunciation is used in most cases (see 616).

## 2 meanings

*Must* is used mostly to express the deduction or conclusion that something is certain (see 359), and (less often in American English) to talk about necessity and obligation (see 360).

▶

*You **must** be Anna's sister – you look just like her.*
*You really **must** get your hair cut.*

For differences between *must* and *have (got) to*, see 361.
For the difference between *must* and *should*, see 520.

# 359 must (2): deduction (concluding that something is certain)

## 1 statements: *Mary must have a problem*

*Must* can be used to express the deduction or conclusion that something is certain or highly probable: it is normal or logical, there are excellent reasons for believing it, or it is the only possible explanation for what is happening.

*If A is bigger than B, and B is bigger than C, then A **must** be bigger than C.*
*I'm in love. ~ You **must** be very happy.*
*Mary **must** have a problem – she keeps crying.*
*There's the doorbell. It **must** be Roger.*

## 2 negatives: *It can't be the postman*

*Must* is not often used to express certainty in negative clauses. We normally use *cannot/can't* to say that something is certainly not the case, because it is logically or practically impossible, or extremely improbable.

*If A is bigger than B, and B is bigger than C, then C **can't** be bigger than A.*
*It **can't** be the postman at the door. It's only seven o'clock.* (NOT *It mustn't be the postman* ...)
*She's not answering the phone. She **can't** be at home.*

However, *mustn't* is used in question tags (see 487–488) after *must*.

*It **must** be nice to be a cat, **mustn't** it?* (NOT *... can't it?*)

And *must not* is occasionally used, especially in American English, to say that there is evidence that something is not the case (see 361.4).

## 3 *need not / does not have to*

*Need not / needn't* is used (especially in British English) to say that something is not necessarily so; *does not have to* can also be used. *Must not* is not used in this sense.

*Look at those tracks. That must be a dog. ~ It **needn't** be – it could be a fox.*
*(*OR *... It doesn't have to be ...) (*NOT *... It mustn't be ...)*

## 4 *That must have been nice*

We can use ***must have*** + **past participle** to express certainty about the past.

*We went to Rome last month. ~ That **must have been** nice.*
*A woman phoned while you were out. ~ It **must have been** Kate.*

*Can* is used in questions and negatives.

*Where **can** John **have put** the matches? He **can't have thrown** them away.*

## 5 indirect speech

*Must* can be used after a past reporting verb as if it were a past tense.

*I felt there **must** be something wrong.*

## 6  *must* and *should*

*Should* can be used as a weaker form of *must* (see 520). Compare:
> Ann **must** be at home by now. (= I think she's certainly at home.)
> Ann **should** be at home by now. (= I think she's very probably at home.)

# 360  must (3): necessity and obligation

The following explanations apply particularly to British English. Americans often use *have (got) to* where British people use *must* (see 361). However, this use of *have (got) to* is becoming more common in British English under American influence.

## 1  statements: *I really must stop smoking*

In affirmative statements, we can use *must* to say what is necessary, and to give strong advice and orders to ourselves or other people.
> Plants **must** get enough light and water if they are to grow properly.
> British industry **must** improve its productivity.
> I really **must** stop smoking.
> You **must** be here before eight o'clock tomorrow.

*Must* is common in emphatic invitations.
> You really **must** come and see us soon.

## 2  questions: *Must I ...?*

In questions, we use *must* to ask about what the hearer thinks is necessary.
> **Must** I clean all the rooms?
> Why **must** you always leave the door open?

## 3  negatives: *You mustn't/can't ...*

We use *must not / mustn't* to say that it is wrong to do things, or to tell people not to do things. *Can't* is also possible.
> The government **mustn't/can't** expect people to work for no money.
> You **mustn't/can't** open this parcel until Christmas Day.

## 4  *mustn't* and *needn't / don't have to*

*Mustn't* is not used to say that things are unnecessary. This idea is expressed by *needn't, don't need to* (see 366) or *don't have to*.
> You **needn't** work tomorrow if you don't want to. OR You **don't have to** work ... (NOT ~~You mustn't ... if you don't want to.~~)
> You **don't need to** get a visa to go to Scotland. OR You **don't have to** get a visa ... (NOT ~~You mustn't get a visa to go to Scotland.~~)

## 5  past necessity and obligation

*Must* is not normally used to talk about past obligation (except in indirect speech – see below). This is because *must* is used mainly to influence people's behaviour – for example through orders or advice – and one cannot do this in the past. *Had to* is used to talk about obligation that existed in the past.
> I **had to** cycle three miles to school when I was a child.
> My parents **had to** work very hard to build up their business.

## 6 indirect speech

*Must* can be used after a past reporting verb as if it were a past tense.
> *The doctor said that I **must** stop smoking.*

Obligation can also be reported with *had to* and *would have to.*
> *The doctor said that I **had to** / **would have to** stop smoking.*

## 7 *must* and *should*

*Should* can be used as a weaker form of *must* (see 520). Compare:
> *That carpet **must** be cleaned.* (= It is absolutely necessary.)
> *That carpet **should** be cleaned.* (= It would be a good idea.)

# 361 must (4): advanced points

## 1 *must* and *have to*

In statements about obligation with *must* the obligation most often comes
from the speaker (and in questions, from the hearer). To talk about an
obligation that comes from 'outside' (for instance a regulation, or an order
from somebody else), we usually prefer *have to*. Compare:

- *I **must** do some more work; I want to pass my exam.*
  *In my job I **have to** work from nine to five.* (More natural than ... *I must
  work from nine to five.*)
- *We **must** go to New York soon and see your mother.*
  *My wife's an interpreter: she often **has to** go to New York.* (More natural than
  ... *she must often go to New York.*)
- *I **must** stop smoking.* (I want to.)
  *I've **got to** stop smoking.* (Doctor's orders.)
- *This is a terrible party. We really **must** go home.*
  *This is a lovely party, but we've **got to** go home because of the baby-sitter.*
- *I've got bad toothache. I **must** make an appointment with the dentist.*
  *I can't come to work tomorrow morning because I've **got to** see the dentist.*
- *You really **must** go to church next Sunday – you haven't been for ages.* (I am
  telling you to.)
  *Catholics **have to** go to church on Sundays.* (Their religion tells them to.)
- ***Must** you wear dirty old jeans all the time?* (Is it personally important
  for you?)
  *Do you **have to** wear a tie at work?* (Is there a regulation?)

*Have to* can also be used to talk about obligation coming from the speaker or
hearer, in the same way as *must*. This is normal in American English (which
uses *must* less often in this sense), and is becoming very common in British
English.
> *I really **have to** stop smoking.* (OR *I really must ...*)
> *Do I **have to** clean all the rooms?* (OR *Must I ...?*)

For *have to* and *have got to*, see 239.

## 2 future obligation: *will have to*, *have (got) to* and *must*

*Will have to* is used to talk about future obligation (*will must* is impossible –
see 358); but *have (got) to* is preferred when arrangements for the future have
already been made. Compare:

*When you leave school you'll* **have to** *find a job.*
*I've* **got to** *go for a job interview tomorrow.*
*Going to have to* is also possible.
*We're* **going to have to** *repair that window.*
*Must* can be used to give orders or instructions for the future.
*You can borrow my car, but you* **must** *bring it back before ten.*
*Will have to* can be used to 'distance' the instructions (see 436), making them
sound less like direct orders from the speaker.
*You can borrow my car, but you'll* **have to** *bring it back before ten.*
*Will need to* can be used in the same way (see 366.4).

### 3 talking about the past: *had to ...* and *must have ...*

*Had to* is used to talk about past obligation. *Must have* + **past participle** is used
to express certainty about the past (see 359.4). Compare:
*Edna isn't in her office. She* **had to** *go home.*
    (= It was necessary for her to go home.)
*Edna isn't in her office. She* **must have gone** *home.*
    (= It seems certain that she has gone home.)

### 4 a British-American difference: *can't* and *must not*

In American English, *must not* is often used when something is not logically
impossible, but when there is strong evidence for believing that it is not the
case. Compare:
– *He only left the office five minutes ago. He* **can't** *be home yet.* (It's logically
    impossible that he's home.)
    *She's not answering the doorbell. She* **must not** *be at home.* (It's not logically
    impossible that she's home, but it seems pretty certain that she isn't.)
– *The restaurant* **can't** *be open – the door's locked.*
    *That restaurant* **must not** *be any good – it's always empty.*
In British English, *can't* is normal for both meanings (though some people use
*must not* for the 'seems pretty certain' meaning). Compare:
*She walked past without saying 'Hello'. She* **must not** *have seen you.*
    (AmE; some British speakers.)
*She walked past without saying 'Hello'. She* **can't** *have seen you.*
    (most British speakers.)
Note that the contracted form *mustn't* is rare in AmE.

## 362 names: Florence, Homer etc

### 1 cities

The names of cities are often different in different languages – for example the
capital of Denmark, *København*, is called *Kopenhagen* in German, *Copenhague*
in French, and *Copenhagen* in Italian and English. Some examples of English
names for cities:
*The Hague, Brussels, Antwerp, Hanover, Cologne, Munich, Vienna, Lyons*
(now more usually *Lyon*), *Marseilles* (now more usually *Marseille*), *Milan,*
*Florence, Venice, Rome, Naples, Padua, Genoa, Leghorn* (now more usually
*Livorno*), *Turin, Geneva, Seville, Lisbon, Athens, Thessalonica, Prague,*
*Warsaw, Belgrade, Moscow, St Petersburg, Bucharest, Beirut, Damascus,* ▶

*Jerusalem, Peking* (now usually *Beijing*), *Bombay* (now usually *Mumbai*), *Calcutta* (now usually *Kolkata*).

## 2 classical names

The same is true of many classical Greek and Roman names. Some examples:
*Homer, Aeschylus, Livy, Horace, Ovid, Virgil, Aesop, Aristotle, Euclid, Sophocles, Mercury, Jupiter, Helen, Troy, Odysseus*

## 3 artists

The Italian artists Raffaello Sanzio and Tiziano are called *Raphael* and *Titian* in English.

## 4 countries

The names of countries, of course, also differ from one language to another (e.g. *Deutschland, Nemecko, Allemagne, Germany*). English versions are not listed here, as they are well known and can easily be found in any dictionary if needed.

# 363 names and titles: Peter; Mr Lewis

Names and titles are used both when talking about people and when talking to them. There are some differences.

## 1 talking about people

When we talk about people we can name them in four ways.

### a first name

We use first names mostly informally, for relatives, friends and children.
*Where's **Peter**? He said he'd be here at three.*
*How's **Maud** getting on at school?*

### b first name + surname

This is neutral – neither particularly formal nor particularly informal.
*Isn't that **Peter Connolly** the actor?*
*We're going on holiday with **Mary** and **Daniel Sinclair**.*

### c title (*Mr, Mrs* etc) + surname

This is more formal. We talk like this about people we do not know, or when we want to show respect or be polite.
*Can I speak to **Mr Lewis**, please?*
*We've got a new teacher called **Mrs Campbell**.*
*Ask **Miss Andrews** to come in, please.*
*There's a **Ms Sanders** on the phone.*
Note that it is less usual to talk about people by using title + first name + surname (e.g. *Mr John Parker*).

### d surname only

We often use just the surname to talk about men (and occasionally women) in public life – politicians, sports personalities, writers and so on.

*Do you think **Roberts** would make a good President?*
*The 5,000 metres was won by **Jones**.*
*I don't think **Eliot** is a very good dramatist.*
***Thatcher** was the first British woman Prime Minister.*

Surnames alone are sometimes used for employees (especially male employees), and by members of groups (especially all-male groups like soldiers, schoolboys, team members) when they refer to each other.

*Tell **Patterson** to come and see me at once.*
*Let's put **Billows** in goal and move **Carter** up.*

## 2 talking to people

When we talk to people we generally name them in one of two ways.

### a first name

This is informal, used for example to relatives, friends and children.
*Hello, **Pamela**. How are you?*

### b title + surname

This is more formal or respectful.
*Good morning, **Miss Williamson**.*

Note that we do not usually use both the first name and the surname of a person that we are talking to. It would be unusual to say *'Hello, Peter Matthews'*, for example.

Members of all-male groups sometimes address each other by their surnames alone (e.g. *'Hello, Smith'*), but this is unusual in modern English.

*Mr, Mrs* and *Ms* are not generally used alone.

*Excuse me. Can you tell me the time?* (NOT *Excuse me, Mr* or *Excuse me, Mrs.*)

*Doctor* can be used alone to talk to medical doctors whom one is consulting, but not usually in other cases.

***Doctor**, I've got this pain in my elbow.*

*Sir* and *madam* are used in Britain mostly by people in service occupations (e.g. shop assistants). Some employees call their male employers *sir*, and some schoolchildren call their teachers *sir* or *miss*. *Dear Sir* and *Dear Madam* are common ways of beginning letters to strangers (see 146) – note the capital letters. In other situations *sir* and *madam* are unusual in British English.

*Excuse me. Can you tell me the time?* (NOT *Excuse me, sir . . .* )

In American English, *sir* and *ma'am* are less formal than in British English, and are quite often used (especially in the South and West) when addressing people.

## 3 notes on titles

Note the pronunciations of the titles *Mr, Mrs* and *Ms* (used before names):
*Mr* /ˈmɪstə(r)/    *Mrs* /ˈmɪsɪz/    *Ms* /mɪz/ or /məz/

*Mr* (= *Mister*) is not normally written in full, and the other two cannot be. Like *Mr, Ms* does not show whether somebody is married or not. It is often used, especially in writing, to talk about or address women when one does not know (or has no reason to say) whether they are married. Many women also choose to use *Ms* before their own names in preference to *Mrs* or *Miss*. *Ms* is a relatively new title: it has been in common use in Britain since the 1970s, and a little longer in the United States.

▶

*Dr (= Doctor)* is used as a title for medical and other doctors (but see paragraph 2 for its use).
*Professor* does not mean 'teacher'; it is used only for heads of university departments and some other very senior university teachers.
Note that we do not normally combine two titles such as *Prof Dr* or *Mrs Dr*.

For ways of addressing people in letters, see 146.
For ways of introducing people, see 545.1.
For full stops with abbreviated titles and initials, see 2.

# 364 nationalities, countries and regions

## 1 introduction

In order to refer to a nation or region and its affairs it is usually necessary to know four words:
- the name of the country or region
    *Denmark, Japan, France, Catalonia*
- the adjective
    *Danish, Japanese, French, Catalan*
- the singular noun used for a person from the country
    *a Dane, a Japanese, a Frenchman/woman, a Catalan*
- the plural expression *the ...* used for the population as a whole
    *the Danes, the Japanese, the French, the Catalans*

Usually the singular noun is the same as the adjective (e.g. *Greek, Mexican*). The plural expression is usually the same as the adjective + -*s* (e.g. *the Greeks, the Mexicans*); words ending in -*ese*, and *Swiss*, have no -*s* (e.g. *the Japanese; the Swiss*). See paragraph 2 below for more examples.
However, there are a number of exceptions. Some of these are listed in paragraph 3.
All words of this kind (including adjectives) begin with capital letters.
    **American** literature (NOT ~~american literature~~)
The name of a national language is often the same as the national adjective.
    **Danish** *is difficult to pronounce.*    *Do you speak **Japanese**?*

## 2 Examples

| Country/region | Adjective | Person | Population |
|---|---|---|---|
| America (The United States) | American | an American | the Americans |
| Belgium | Belgian | a Belgian | the Belgians |
| Brazil | Brazilian | a Brazilian | the Brazilians |
| Europe | European | a European | the Europeans |
| Italy | Italian | an Italian | the Italians |
| Kenya | Kenyan | a Kenyan | the Kenyans |
| Morocco | Moroccan | a Moroccan | the Moroccans |
| Norway | Norwegian | a Norwegian | the Norwegians |
| Palestine | Palestinian | a Palestinian | the Palestinians |
| Russia | Russian | a Russian | the Russians |
| Tyrol | Tyrolean | a Tyrolean | the Tyroleans |

| Country/region | Adjective | Person | Population |
|---|---|---|---|
| Greece | Greek | a Greek | the Greeks |
| Iraq | Iraqi | an Iraqi | the Iraqis |
| Israel | Israeli | an Israeli | the Israelis |
| Thailand | Thai | a Thai | the Thais |
| China | Chinese | a Chinese (person) | the Chinese |
| Congo | Congolese | a Congolese (person) | the Congolese |
| Portugal | Portuguese | a Portuguese (person) | the Portuguese |
| Switzerland | Swiss | a Swiss | the Swiss |

## 3 exceptions

| Country/region | Adjective | Person | Population |
|---|---|---|---|
| Britain | British | a British person (Briton) | the British |
| England | English | an Englishwoman/man | the English |
| France | French | a Frenchman/woman | the French |
| Ireland | Irish | an Irishwoman/man | the Irish |
| Spain | Spanish | a Spaniard | the Spanish |
| The Netherlands/ Holland | Dutch | a Dutchwoman/man | the Dutch |
| Wales | Welsh | a Welshman/woman | the Welsh |
| Denmark | Danish | a Dane | the Danes |
| Finland | Finnish | a Finn | the Finns |
| Poland | Polish | a Pole | the Poles |
| Scotland | Scottish, Scotch | a Scot | the Scots |
| Sweden | Swedish | a Swede | the Swedes |
| Turkey | Turkish | a Turk | the Turks |

## Notes

a   *Scottish* is the usual word for the people and culture of Scotland; *Scotch* is used for whisky.

b   The word *Briton* is unusual except in newspaper headlines – for example *TWO BRITONS KILLED IN AIR CRASH*. *Brit* is sometimes used informally.

c   *English* is not the same as *British*, and is not used for Scottish, Welsh or Irish people (see 114).

d   Although *American* is the normal English word for United States citizens and affairs, people from other parts of the American continent may object to this use, and some people avoid it for this reason.   ▶

e *Arabic* is used for the language spoken in Arab countries; in other cases, the normal adjective is *Arab*. *Arabian* is used in a few fixed expressions and place names (e.g. *Saudi Arabian, the Arabian Sea*).

f Note the pronunciation of words like *Irishman/men, Dutchman/men*: the singular is the same as the plural (/ˈaɪrɪʃmən, ˈdʌtʃmən/).

# 365 near (to)

*Near* can be used as a preposition. *Near to* is also possible with the same meaning, but is less common.
> *We live **near (to)** the station.*
> *I put my bag down **near (to)** the door.*   *She was **near (to)** despair.*
> *Near (to)* can be followed by an *-ing* form.
> *I came very **near (to) hitting** him.*

For *-ing* forms after *to*, see 298.2.
For the difference between *nearest* and *next*, see 375.

# 366 need

## 1 ordinary verb: *Everybody needs to rest*

*Need* most often has ordinary verb forms: the third person singular has *-s*, and questions and negatives are made with *do*. *Need* is usually followed by an infinitive with *to*.
> *Everybody **needs to rest** sometimes.*
> *Do we **need to reserve** seats on the train?*

## 2 modal auxiliary forms: *he needn't; need I?*

*Need* can also have the same present-tense forms as modal auxiliary verbs: the third person singular has no *-s*, and questions and negatives are made without *do*. In this case, *need* is normally followed by an infinitive without *to*.
> *She **needn't reserve** a seat – there'll be plenty of room.*

These forms are used mainly in negative sentences (*needn't*); but they are also possible in questions, after *if*, and in other 'non-affirmative' structures (see 381).
> *You **needn't fill** in a form.*          *Need I **fill** in a form?*
> *I wonder if I **need fill** in a form.*
> *This is the only form you **need fill** in.*
>    (BUT NOT *~~You need fill in a form.~~*)

These forms are more common in BrE; in AmE *have to / don't have to* are preferred.

## 3 *needn't, need I?*: immediate necessity

These modal forms of *need* normally refer to immediate necessity. They are often used to ask for or give permission – usually permission not to do something. They are not used to talk about habitual, general necessity. Compare:

*It's OK – You **needn't** / **don't need to pay** for that phone call.*
*You **don't need to pay** for emergency calls in most countries.* (NOT ~~You needn't pay . . . in most countries.~~)

## 4 talking about the future

Present tense forms of *need* are used when making decisions about the future.
*  **Need** I **come** in tomorrow?*
*  Tell her she **doesn't need to work** tonight.*
*Will need to . . .* can be used to talk about future obligation, and give advice for the future. It can make orders and instructions sound less direct.
*  We'll **need to repair** the roof next year.*
*  You'll **need to start** work soon if you want to pass your exams.*
*  You'll **need to fill** in this form before you see the Inspector.*

For similar uses of *have to*, see 239.3.

## 5 *need . . .ing: The sofa needs cleaning*

After *need* an *-ing* form can be used with the same meaning as a passive infinitive, especially in BrE.
*  That sofa **needs cleaning** again.* (= . . . needs to be cleaned . . .)
A structure with **object + . . .ing** or **past participle** is also possible in some cases.
*  You **need your head examining**.* (BrE) (OR . . . *examined*.)

## 6 *need not have . . .*

If we say that somebody *need not have done something*, we mean that he or she did it, but that it was unnecessary – a waste of time.
*  You **needn't have woken** me up. I don't have to go to work today.*
*  I **needn't have cooked** so much food. Nobody was hungry.*
On the other hand, if we say that somebody *did not need to do something*, we are simply saying that it was not necessary (whether or not it was done). Compare:
*  I **needn't have watered** the flowers. Just after I finished it started raining.*
*  It started raining, so I **didn't need to water** the flowers.*
*Need never have . . .* is a more emphatic version of *need not have . . .* .
*  I **need never have** packed all that suncream – it rained every day.*

## 7 *need not* and *must not*

*Need not* or *do not need to* is used to say that there is no obligation; *must not* is used to say that there is an obligation not to do something. Compare:
*  You **needn't** tell Jennifer – she already knows.*
*  You **mustn't** tell Margaret – I don't want her to know.*
*Need not* is also sometimes used to say that something is not necessarily true.
*  She looks quite ill. I'm sure it's flu. ~ It **needn't** be – maybe she's just over-tired.*

For *there is no need to . . .*, see 587.2.

# 367 negative structures (1): basic rules

## 1 negative verb forms: auxiliary + *not*

We make negative verb forms by putting *not* after an auxiliary verb.
> *We **have not** forgotten you.*     *It **was not** raining.*     *She **can't** swim.*

*Do* is normally used if there is no other auxiliary verb.
> *I like the salad, but I **don't** like the soup.* (NOT *I like not the soup.*)

*Do* is followed by the infinitive without *to*.
> *I didn't **think**.* (NOT *I didn't to think, I didn't thinking* or *I didn't thought.*)

*Do* is not used with another auxiliary verb.
> *You **mustn't** worry.* (NOT *You don't must worry.*)

*Do* is not normally used with *be* (even when *be* is not auxiliary).
> *The supper **isn't** ready.* (NOT *The supper doesn't be ready.*)

For negative forms of *have, dare, need* and *used,* see the entries on these verbs.
For the dialect form *ain't,* see 143.4.
For negatives without *do* in older English (e.g. *I like him not*), see 392.
For negative subjunctives (e.g. *It's important that he not be disturbed*), see 567.2.

## 2 imperatives: *Don't worry*

Negative imperatives are made with *do not / don't* + infinitive (see 268).
> ***Do not expect** quick results.* (NOT *Expect not...*)
> ***Don't worry** – I'll look after you.* (NOT *Worry not...*)

*Do not / don't* is also used to make the negative imperative of *be.*
> ***Don't be** rude.*

## 3 infinitives and *-ing* forms: *It's important not to worry*

We put *not* before infinitives and *-ing* forms. *Do* is not used.
> *It's important **not to worry**.* (NOT *...to don't worry.*)
> *The best thing about a holiday is **not working**.*

## 4 other parts of a clause: *not his wife, not before six*

We can put *not* with other parts of a clause, not only a verb.
> *Ask Jake, **not his wife**.*     *Come early, but **not before six**.*
> *It's working, but **not properly**.*

We do not usually begin a sentence with ***not*** + **subject**. Instead, we use a
structure with *it*.
> *It was **not George** that came, but his brother.* (NOT *Not George came...*)

For the difference between *not* and *no* with nouns, see 382.

## 5 other negative words: *never, seldom* etc

Other words besides *not* can make a clause negative. Compare:
> *He's **not** at home.*     *He's **never** at home.*
> *He's **seldom / rarely / hardly ever** at home.*

We do not normally use the auxiliary *do* with these other words. Compare:
> *He **doesn't work**.*
> *He never **works**.* (NOT *He does never work.*)
> *He seldom / rarely / hardly ever **works**.*

However, *do* can be used for emphasis or contrast.
> *I never **did** like her.*

## 6 question tags: *You don't ..., do you?*

After negative clauses, question tags (see 487–488) are not negative.
> *You don't work on Sundays, **do you?***
> *You seldom work on Saturdays, **do you?*** (NOT *~~You seldom work on Saturdays, don't you?~~*)
> *She never smiled, **did she?***

The same thing happens after clauses with *little* and *few* (see 329).
> *There's **little** point in doing anything about it, **is there?*** (NOT *...~~isn't there?~~*)
> *He has **few** reasons for staying, **has he?***

## 7 'non-affirmative' words: *any* etc

We do not usually use *some, somebody* etc in negative clauses. Instead, we use the 'non-affirmative' words *any, anybody* etc. (see 381). Compare:
> *I've found some mushrooms.*     *I haven't found any mushrooms.*

# 368 negative structures (2): negative questions

## 1 structure

Contracted and uncontracted negative questions have different word order. (Uncontracted negative questions are usually formal.)

> auxiliary verb + *n't* + subject

> ***Doesn't she** understand?*
> *Why **haven't you** booked your holiday yet?*

> auxiliary verb + subject + *not*

> ***Does she not** understand?*
> *Why **have you not** booked your holiday yet?*

Non-auxiliary *have* and *be* go in the same position as auxiliary verbs.
> ***Hasn't she** any friends to help her?*     ***Aren't you** ready?*
> ***Have they not** at least a room to stay in?*     ***Is Mrs Allen not** at home?*

## 2 two meanings

Negative questions can have two different kinds of meaning. It is usually clear from the situation and context which kind of question is being asked.

### a 'It's true that ..., isn't it?'

A negative question can ask for confirmation of a positive belief. In this case the question expects the answer *Yes*, and means 'It's true that ... , isn't it?'
> ***Didn't you** go and see Helen yesterday? How is she?*
>     (= I believe you went and saw Helen yesterday ...)

Expressions of opinion can be made less definite by expressing them as negative questions (so that they ask for agreement).
> ***Wouldn't it** be better to switch the lights on?*

Negative questions of this kind are common in exclamations (see 195) and rhetorical questions (see 482).
> ***Isn't it** a lovely day!*
> *She's growing up to be a lovely person. ~ Yes, **isn't she!***
> ***Isn't the answer** obvious?* (= Of course the answer is obvious.)     ▶

b 'Is it true that ... not ...?'

A negative question can also ask for confirmation of a negative belief. In this case the question expects the answer *No*, and means 'Is it true that ... not ...?'

**Don't you** *feel well?* (= Am I right in thinking you don't feel well?)

*Oh, dear.* **Can't they** *come this evening?*

This kind of negative question can show that the speaker is surprised that something has not happened or is not happening.

**Hasn't the postman** *come yet?*

**Didn't the alarm** *go off? I wonder what's wrong with it.*

## 3 polite requests, invitations, offers, complaints and criticisms

Pressing invitations and offers often begin *Won't you ...? Wouldn't you ...?* or *Why don't you ...?*

**Won't you** *come in for a few minutes?*

**Wouldn't you** *like something to drink?*

**Why don't you** *come and spend the weekend with us?*

But in other cases we do not usually use negative questions to ask people to do things. This is done with ordinary questions, or with **negative statement + question tag**.

*Excuse me,* **can you** *help me for a moment?* (ordinary question, used as a request)

**You can't** *help me for a moment,* **can you?** (negative statement + question tag, common in informal requests)

BUT NOT ~~Can't you help me for a moment?~~

Negative questions may be understood as complaints or criticisms.

**Can't you** *lend me your pen for a minute?* (= something like 'Are you too selfish to lend me ...?')

**Don't you** *ever listen to what I say?*

## 4 *yes* and *no*

In a reply to a negative question, *Yes* suggests an affirmative verb, and *No* suggests a negative verb. Compare:

– *Haven't you written to Mary?* ~ *Yes.* (= I have written to her.)

*Haven't you told her about us?* ~ *No.* (= I haven't told her about us.)

– *Didn't the postman come this morning?* ~ *Yes, he did.*

*Didn't he bring anything for me?* ~ *No, he didn't.*

# 369 negative structures (3): think, hope, seem etc

## 1 *I don't think ...*

When we introduce negative ideas with *think, believe, suppose, imagine* and words with similar meanings, we usually make the first verb (*think* etc) negative, not the second.

*I* **don't think** *you've met my wife.*

(More natural than *I think you haven't met my wife.*)

*I* **don't believe** *she's at home.*

(More natural than *I believe she isn't at home.*)

However, surprise is often expressed with *I* **thought** + **negative**.

*Would you like a drink?* ~*I **thought** you'd **never** ask.*
*Hello! I **thought** you **weren't** coming.*

## 2   *I hope that . . . not . . .*

This does not happen with *hope.*
>*I **hope** it **doesn't** rain.* (NOT ~~I don't hope it rains.~~)

## 3   short answers: *I suppose not.*

In short answers, most of these verbs can be followed by *not* (see 539).
>*Are we going to see Alan again?* ~*I believe/suppose/hope **not.***

Another possible short answer construction is *I don't . . . so* (see 539).
>*Do you think it'll snow?* ~*I **don't** believe/suppose/think **so.***

*Hope* is not used in this structure.
>*I **hope not.*** (NOT ~~I don't hope so.~~)

*I don't think so* is more common than *I think not*, which is rather formal.

## 4   verbs followed by infinitives

Many verbs can be followed by infinitives (see 282). In an informal style we often prefer to make the first verb negative rather than the infinitive, although this may not change the meaning at all. This happens, for example, with *appear, seem, expect, happen, intend* and *want.*
>*Sibyl **doesn't seem** to like you.*
>    (Less formal than *Sibyl seems not to like you.*)
>*I **don't expect** to see you before Monday.*
>    (More natural than *I expect not to see you . . .*)
>*Angela and I were at the same university, but we **never happened** to meet.*
>    (Less formal than . . . *we happened never to meet.*)
>*I **don't want** to fail this exam.* (NOT ~~I want not to fail~~ . . .)
>*After I've finished this contract I **never intend** to teach again.*

# 370   negative structures (4): double negatives

## 1   English and other languages

In some languages, a negative word like *nobody, nothing* or *never* has to be used with a negative verb. In standard English, *nobody, nothing, never* etc are themselves enough to give a negative meaning, and *not* is unnecessary.
>*I opened the door, but I **could** see **nobody.*** (NOT ~~I couldn't see nobody.~~)
>*Tell them **nothing.*** (NOT ~~Don't tell them nothing.~~)
>*Your suggestion **will** help **neither** of us.* (NOT . . . ~~won't help neither~~ . . .)
>*Nothing matters now – everything's finished.* (NOT ~~Nothing doesn't matter~~ . . .)
>*I've **never** understood what she wants.* (NOT ~~I haven't never understood~~ . . .)

## 2   *nobody* and *not anybody,* etc

*Nobody, nothing, never* etc are rather emphatic. We often prefer to use *not anybody, not anything, not ever* etc. Note that *anybody, anything, ever* etc are not themselves negative words (see 381) – they have to be used with *not* to give a negative meaning.

▶

*I opened the door, but I **couldn't** see **anybody**.* (NOT *. . . ~~but I could see anybody.~~*)
   *Don't tell them **anything**.*
   *Your suggestion **won't** help **either** of us.*
At the beginning of a clause, only *nobody, nothing* etc are used.
   ***Nothing** matters.* (NOT *~~Not anything matters.~~*)
   ***Nowhere** is safe.*

## 3   double and multiple negatives and their meaning

Two or more negative words can be used in one clause, but then both words
normally have their full meaning. Compare:
   *Say **nothing**.* (= Be silent.)
   ***Don't** just say **nothing**. Tell us what the problem is.* (= Don't be silent . . .)
Multiple negatives are sometimes used instead of simple positive structures
for special stylistic effects. This is rather literary; in spoken English it can seem
unnatural or old-fashioned.
   ***Not** a day passes when I **don't** regret **not** having studied music in my youth.*
      (More natural: *Every day I regret not having studied music when I was
      younger.* OR *I wish I had studied music when I was younger.*)

## 4   dialects

In many British, American and other dialects, two or more negatives can be
used with a single negative meaning.
   *I **ain't** seen **nobody**.* (Standard English: *I haven't seen anybody.*)
   *I **ain't never** done **nothing** to **nobody**, and I **ain't never** got **nothing** from
      **nobody no** time.* (American song by Bert Williams)

For more information about *ain't*, see 143.4.

## 5   two negative ideas: *not . . . or / not . . . nor*

When *not* refers to two or more verbs, nouns, adjectives etc, we usually join
them with *or*.
   *He doesn't **smoke or drink**.* (NOT *~~He doesn't smoke nor drink.~~*)
   *She wasn't **angry or upset**.*
   *It's not **on the table or in the cupboard**.*
However, we can use *nor* after a pause, to separate and emphasise a second
verb, adjective etc.
   *Our main need is not food, **nor** money. It is education.* (More emphatic than
      *. . . food or money.*)
   *She didn't phone that day, **nor** the next day.* (More emphatic than *. . . or the
      next day.*)
Note that *neither* cannot be used in this way.

For the use of *neither . . . nor* to join two negative ideas (e.g. *He neither smokes nor drinks*),
   see 373.

## 6    *. . . I don't think* etc

In informal speech, expressions like *I don't think* or *I don't suppose* are often
added after negative statements. In this case, the extra negative makes no
difference to the meaning of the statement.

*She hasn't got much chance of passing the exam, **I don't think**.*
*We won't be back before midnight, **I don't suppose**.*

### 7 extra negative in expressions of doubt

In informal standard spoken English, a negative verb (without a negative meaning) is sometimes used after expressions of doubt or uncertainty.
> *I shouldn't be surprised if they **didn't** get married soon. (= . . . if they got married soon.)*
> *I wonder whether I **oughtn't** to go and see a doctor – I'm feeling a bit funny. (= . . . whether I ought to . . .)*

## 371 negative structures (5): ambiguous sentences

In a negative structure, *not* can refer to different parts of a sentence. Compare:
> *Arthur **didn't write** to Sue yesterday – he phoned her.*
> *Arthur **didn't write** to **Sue** yesterday – he wrote to Ann.*
> *Arthur **didn't write** to Sue **yesterday** – he wrote this morning.*

The exact meaning is shown in speech by stress and intonation, and even in writing it is usually clear from the context and situation. However, confusions sometimes arise. They can usually be avoided by reorganising the sentence. Compare:
> *The car crash didn't kill him. (Did he live, or did something else kill him?)*
> *It wasn't the car crash that killed him. (Only one possible meaning.)*

Negative sentences with *because*-clauses are often ambiguous.
> *I didn't sing **because Pam was there**.*

This sentence could mean 'My reason for not singing was that Pam was there' or 'My reason for singing was not that Pam was there'. The first meaning could be shown clearly by putting the *because*-clause at the beginning.
> *__Because Pam was there__, I didn't sing.*

## 372 neither (of): determiner

### 1 *neither* + singular noun

We use *neither* before a singular noun to mean 'not one and not the other (of two)'.
> *Can you come on Monday or Tuesday? ∼ I'm afraid **neither day** is possible.*

### 2 *neither of* + plural

We use *neither of* before a determiner (for example *the, my, these*), and before a pronoun. The noun or pronoun is plural.
> ***Neither of my** brothers can sing. (NOT ~~Neither my brothers can sing.~~)*
> ***Neither of us** saw it happen.*

After ***neither of*** + noun/pronoun, we use a singular verb in a formal style.
> *Neither of my sisters **is** married.*

In an informal style, a plural verb is possible.
> *Neither of my sisters **are** married.*

### 3 *neither* used alone

We can use *neither* without a noun or pronoun, if the meaning is clear. ▸

*Which one do you want?* ~ *Neither.*

## 4 pronunciation

In British English, *neither* can be pronounced both /'naɪðə(r)/ and /'niːðə(r)/. In American English, the usual pronunciation is /'niːðər/.

## 373 neither ... nor

This structure is used to join two negative ideas. (It is the opposite of *both . . . and.*) It is usually rather formal.

> *I **neither** smoke **nor** drink.* (less formal: *I don't smoke or drink.*)
> *The film was **neither** well made **nor** well acted.*

Sometimes more than two ideas are connected by *neither . . . nor.*

> *He neither **smiled, spoke,** nor **looked** at me.*

*Neither* cannot begin a complete clause in this structure.

> *He neither smiled . . . nor . . .* (BUT NOT ~~Neither he smiled~~ . . .)

When singular subjects are connected by *neither . . . nor,* the verb is normally singular, but it can be plural in a less formal style.

> *Neither James nor Virginia **was** at home.* (normal)
> *Neither James nor Virginia **were** at home.* (less formal)

See also *both . . . and* (111) and *either . . . or* (175).
For *not . . . or* and *not . . . nor,* see 370.5.

## 374 neither, nor and not ... either

### 1 *neither* and *nor*

We can use *neither* and *nor* as adverbs to mean 'also not'. *Neither* and *nor* come at the beginning of a clause, and are followed by inverted word order (see 302–303): **auxiliary verb + subject.**

> *I can't swim.* ~ ***Neither/nor can I.*** (NOT ~~I also can't.~~)
> *Ruth didn't turn up, and **neither/nor did Kate.*** (NOT *. . .* ~~and Kate didn't too.~~)

In American English, *nor* is not normally used after *and.*

### 2 *not either*

We can also use *not . . . either* with the same meaning and normal word order.

> *I can't swim.* ~ *I **can't either.***
> *Ruth didn't turn up, and Kate **didn't either.***

In very informal speech, *me neither* (and occasionally *me either,* especially in AmE) can be used instead of *I . . .n't either.*

> *I can't swim.* ~ *Me neither.*

### 3 one negative

Only one negative word (*not* or *neither*) is necessary to give a negative meaning.

> ***Neither** did Kate* OR *Kate **didn't** either.* (NOT ~~Neither didn't Kate~~ OR ~~Kate didn't neither~~)

For the pronunciation of *neither,* see 372.　　For *neither . . . nor,* see 373.
For other uses of *either,* see 174–175.　　For *not . . . or* and *not . . . nor,* see 370–375.
For *so am I, so do I* etc, see 541.
For the difference between *too/also* and *either* in negative sentences, see 47.

# 375 next and the next; nearest

## 1 next week, month etc; the next week, month etc

*Next week, month* etc (without *the*) is the week, month etc just after this one. If I am speaking in July, *next month* is August; in 2006, *next year* is 2007.

*The next week, month* etc is the period of seven/thirty/etc days starting at the moment of speaking. On July 15th 2006, *the next month* is the period from July 15th to August 15th; *the next year* is the period from July 2006 to July 2007. Compare:

– *Goodbye – see you **next week**.* (NOT *. . . see you the next week.*)
  *I'll be busy for **the next week**.* (= the seven days starting today)
– ***Next year** will be difficult.* (= the year starting next January)
  ***The next year** will be difficult.* (= the twelve months starting now)

The difference between *last* and *the last* is similar. See 314.

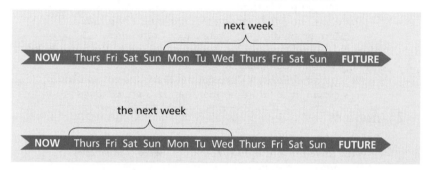

## 2 the next three . . . etc

Note the word order in expressions with numbers.
  *I'll be at college for **the next three years**.* (NOT *. . . the three next years.*)
We generally say *the next few days*, not *the next days*.
  ***The next few days** will be wet.*

## 3 next Sunday etc

When *next* is used with the names of days or months, it is not always clear exactly what is meant.
  *See you **next Sunday**.* ~ *Do you mean this coming Sunday or the one after?*
To avoid misunderstanding, one can say for example (1) *on Sunday, this Sunday, the/this Sunday coming, the/this coming Sunday* or *(on) Sunday this week,* and (2) *on Sunday week, a week on Sunday* or *(on) Sunday next week.*

## 4 place: next and nearest

*The nearest* is generally preferred for place - it means 'most near in space'.
  *Excuse me. Where's **the nearest** tube station?* (NOT *. . . the next tube station.*)
  *If you want to find Alan, just look in **the nearest** pub.*
*The next* can be used for place if we are talking about movement or direction. It means 'after this/that one'.
  *We get off at **the next** station.* (= the station that we will come to next.)
  *It's not on this shelf; it's on **the next** shelf up.*

▶

*Next* can also be used to talk about the nearest position in a row.
> *My girlfriend lives **next** door.*     *Who works in the **next** office?*
> *The people at the **next** table were having a terrible argument.*

*Next to* means 'beside'.
> *Come and sit **next to** me.*

# 376 no, none and not a/any

## 1 *no*: emphatic

*No* can be used instead of *not a* or *not any* when we want to emphasise a negative idea.
> *Would you believe it? There's **no** wardrobe in the bedroom!*
>> (More emphatic than ... *There isn't a wardrobe* ...)
> *Sorry I can't stop. I've got **no** time.*
>> (More emphatic than ... *I haven't got any time.*)
> *There were **no** letters for you this morning, I'm afraid.*
>> (More emphatic than *There weren't any letters* ...)

After *no*, countable nouns are usually plural unless the sense makes a singular noun necessary. Compare:
> *He's got **no children**.* (More natural than *He's got no child.*)
> *He's got **no wife**.* (More normal than *He's got no wives.*)

## 2 *none of*

Before a determiner (e.g. *the, my, this*) or a pronoun, we use *none of*.
> *She's done **none of the** work.* (NOT ... ~~no of the work~~.)
> *We understood **none of his** arguments.*
> *I've been to **none of those** places.*     *None of us speaks French.*

When we use *none of* with a plural noun or pronoun, the verb can be singular (a little more formal) or plural (a little more informal).
> *None of my friends **is** interested.* (more formal)
> *None of my friends **are** interested.* (more informal)

We can use *none* alone if the meaning is clear.
> *How many of the books have you read? ~ **None**.*

## 3 *not a/any*

We prefer *not a/any* in objects and complements when the sense is not emphatic. Compare:
> *He's **no** fool.* (= He's not a fool at all. – emphatic negative)
> *A whale is **not a** fish.* (NOT ~~A whale is no fish~~) – the sense is not emphatic.

## 4 subjects

*Not any* cannot normally be used with subjects. *No* and *none of* are used instead.
> *No brand of cigarette is completely harmless.* (NOT ~~Not any brand~~ ...)
> *No tourists ever came to our village.* (NOT ~~Not any tourists~~ ...)
> *None of my friends lives near me.* (NOT ~~Not any of my friends~~ ...)

## 5 *not* used to talk about two

We use *neither*, not *no* or *none*, to talk about two people or things (see 372).
> *Neither of my parents could be there.* (NOT ~~None of my parents~~ ...)

## 6   *nobody* etc

*Nobody, nothing, no one* and *nowhere* are used in similar ways to *no*.
> *I saw **nobody**.* (More emphatic than *I didn't see anybody*.)
> ***Nobody** spoke.* (NOT ~~*Not anybody spoke*~~.)

For *no* and *not*, see 382.          For more about *any*, see 55.
For *none* and *no one*, see 380.     For *no* as a modifying adverb (e.g. *no better*), see 57.

# 377   no doubt

*No doubt* means 'probably' or 'I suppose', not 'certainly'.
> ***No doubt** it'll rain soon.*
> *You're tired, **no doubt**. I'll make you a cup of tea.*

To say that something is certain, we can use *there is no doubt that* (formal),
*without any doubt* (formal), *certainly, definitely.*
> ***There is no doubt that** the world is getting warmer.* (NOT ~~*No doubt the world is getting warmer*~~.)
> *Cycling is **certainly** healthier than driving.* (NOT ~~*No doubt cycling is healthier than driving*~~.)

*Doubtless* is similar to *no doubt* (but more formal); *undoubtedly* is similar to
*there is no doubt that*.

For structures with the verb *doubt*, see 163.

# 378   no matter

## 1   conjunction

*No matter* can be used with *who, whose, what, which, where, when* and *how*.
These expressions are conjunctions, used to join clauses together. The
meaning is similar to 'it is not important who/what etc'.
> *I'll love you **no matter what** you do.*
> ***No matter where** you go, I'll follow you.*

We use a present tense with a future meaning after *no matter* (see 580).
> ***No matter where** you **go**, you'll find Coca-Cola.*
> *You'll be welcome no matter when you **come**.*

## 2   *no matter who* etc and *whoever* etc

The conjunctions *no matter who/what* etc are used rather like *whoever,
whatever* etc (see 625). Compare:
> – ***No matter what** you say, I won't believe you.*
> ***Whatever** you say, I won't believe you.*
> – *Phone me when you arrive, **no matter how** late it is.*
> *Phone me when you arrive, **however** late it is.*

However, clauses with *whoever/whatever/whichever* can be used as subjects or
objects. Clauses with *no matter who* etc cannot be used in this way.
> ***Whatever you do** is fine with me.* (BUT NOT ~~*No matter what you do is fine with me*~~.)
> *You can have **whichever you like**.* (BUT NOT ~~*You can have no matter which you like*~~.)

▶

### 3   *no matter* and *it doesn't matter*

Because *no matter . . .* is a conjunction, it must be used with two clauses.
>   *No matter when you come, you'll be welcome.* (BUT NOT ~~No matter when you come~~.)

To introduce just one clause, we can use *It doesn't matter.*
>   *It doesn't matter when you come.*

### 4   use without a verb

However, *no matter what* can be used at the end of a clause, without a following verb.
>   *I'll always love you, **no matter what**.* (= . . . no matter what happens.)

For sentences like *Something's the matter with my foot*, see 585.

## 379   no more, not any more, no longer, not any longer

We use *no more* with nouns to talk about quantity or degree – to say how much.
>   *There's **no more** bread.*

We do not use *no more* in standard modern English as an adverb to express the idea of actions and situations stopping. Instead, we use *no longer* (usually before the verb), *not . . . any longer* or *not . . . any more*.
>   *I **no longer** support the Conservative party.* (NOT ~~I no more support~~...)
>   *This **can't** go on **any longer**.*     *I'm **not** helping you **any more**.*

*Anymore* may be written as one word, especially in American English.
>   *Annie doesn't live here **anymore**.*

## 380   no one and none

### 1   *no one*

*No one* (also written *no-one* in British English) means the same as *nobody*. It cannot be followed by *of*.
>   *No one wished me a happy birthday.* (NOT ~~No one of my friends~~...)
>   *I stayed in all evening waiting, but **no one** came.*

### 2   *none*

To express the idea 'not a single one (of)', we can use *none (of)*, *not any (of)* or *not one (of)* (more emphatic). *No one* is not used in this way.
>   ***None of** my friends wished me a happy birthday.*
>   *I haven't read **any of** his books.*
>   ***Not one of** my shirts is clean.* (NOT ~~No one of my shirts~~...)
>   *Have you found any blackberries? ~ **Not one**.*

For more about *none*, see 376.

# 381 non-affirmative (or 'non-assertive') words

There are some words that are not often used in affirmative sentences – for example *any, anybody, ever, yet*. When we affirm or assert (that is, when we say that something is true) we normally use other words – for example *some, somebody, once, sometimes, already*. Compare:

- *Somebody telephoned.*
  *Did anybody telephone?*
- *I've bought you something.*
  *I haven't bought you anything.*
- *She's already here.*
  *Is she here yet?*

- *I sometimes go to the theatre.*
  *Do you ever go to the theatre?*
- *I met the Prime Minister once.*
  *Have you ever met the Prime Minister?*

Non-affirmative words are common not only in questions and negative sentences, but in other cases where we are not making affirmative statements – for example in *if*-clauses, after comparisons, and together with adverbs, verbs, prepositions, adjectives and determiners that have a negative kind of meaning.

*Let me know if you have any trouble.*
*I wonder if she found anything.*
*She writes better than anybody I know.*
*He seldom says anything.*
*I've hardly been anywhere since Christmas.*
*He denied that he had ever seen her.*
*Please forget that I ever told you anything about it.*
*I'd rather do it without anybody's help.*
*It's difficult to understand anything he says.*
*Few people have ever seen her laugh.*

For information about particular non-affirmative words, check in the Index to find the entries for the words in question.

# 382 not and no

To make a word, expression or clause negative, we use *not*.

*Not surprisingly, we missed the train.* (NOT ~~No surprisingly~~ ...)
*The students went on strike, but not the teachers.* (NOT ... ~~but no the teachers.~~)
*I can see you tomorrow, but not on Thursday.*
*I have not received his answer.*

We can use *no* with a noun or *-ing* form to mean 'not any', or 'not a/an'.

*No teachers went on strike.* (= There weren't any teachers on strike.)
*I've got no Thursdays free this term.* (= I haven't got any Thursdays ...)
*I telephoned, but there was no answer.* (= There wasn't an answer.)
*NO SMOKING*

Sometimes sentences constructed with **verb + *not*** and ***no* + noun** have similar meanings. The structure with *no* is usually more emphatic.

*There wasn't an answer. / There was no answer.*

# 383 not only

In the rather formal structure *not only . . . but also, not only* and *but also* can go
immediately before the words or expressions that they modify.

> We go there **not only in winter, but also in summer**.
> **Not only the bathroom** was flooded, **but also the rest** of the house.
> The place was **not only cold, but also damp**.

Mid-position with the verb (see 24) is also possible. In this case, *not only* is
generally used without *do*.

> She **not only sings** like an angel, but also dances divinely.
> She **not only plays** the piano, but also the violin.

*Not only* can be moved to the beginning of a clause for emphasis. It is then
followed by **auxiliary verb + subject**; *do* is used if there is no other auxiliary
(for more about this word order, see 302). *But* can be left out in this case.

> **Not only has she been** late three times; she has also done no work.
> **Not only do they need** clothing, but they are also short of water.

In informal English *not only . . . but also* is not very common; other structures
are generally preferred.

> We **don't only** go there in winter. We go in summer **too**.

# 384 noun + complement: what can follow a noun?

Many nouns, especially abstract nouns, can be followed by 'complements' –
other words and expressions that 'complete' their meaning. These
complements can be prepositional phrases, infinitive expressions or clauses
(with or without prepositions).

> Alan's **criticism of the plan** made him very unpopular.
> I hate the **thought of leaving** you.
> Does she understand the **need to keep** everything secret?
> I admire your **belief that** you are always right.
> There's still the **question of whether** we're going to pay her.

Many nouns can be followed by more than one kind of complement.

> He didn't give any **reason for the changes**.
> You've no **reason to get** angry.
> The main **reason why** I don't believe her is this.

Not all nouns can be followed by all kinds of complement.

> – the **idea of** marriage                – **freedom to** choose
>   the **idea that** I might get married      **freedom of** choice
>   (BUT NOT ~~the idea to get married~~)     (BUT NOT ~~freedom of choosing~~)

Note that a related noun and verb may have different kinds of complement.

> I have no **intention of resigning**.
> I do not **intend to resign**.

Unfortunately there is no easy way to decide which structures are possible
after a particular noun. It is best to check in a good dictionary.

For more information about *-ing* forms after nouns, see 297.
For infinitives after nouns, see 285.
For *should* in clauses after nouns, see 521.
For subjunctives in clauses after nouns, see 567.
For the prepositions that are used after some common nouns, see 449.
For prepositions before clauses, see 453.
For structures with preparatory *it* (e.g. *It's a pity that we can't see him*), see 446–447.

# 385 noun + noun (1): basic information

## 1 *milk chocolate; chocolate milk*

Many common ideas in English are expressed by **noun + noun** compounds. In
this structure, the first noun modifies or describes the second, a little like an
adjective. Compare:
- *milk chocolate* (a kind of chocolate)
  *chocolate milk* (a kind of milk)
- *a horse race* (a kind of race)
  *a race horse* (a kind of horse)
- *a book case* (a kind of case)
  *mineral water* (a kind of water)

**Noun + noun** expressions can often be changed into structures where the
second noun becomes a subject and the first an object.
> *an oil well* (= a well that produces oil)
> *a sheepdog* (= a dog that looks after sheep)
> *a Birmingham man* (= a man who comes from Birmingham)
> *the airport bus* (= the bus that goes to the airport)

## 2 the first noun is singular

Note that the first noun is usually singular in form, even if it has a plural
meaning. (For exceptions, see 531.)
> *a **shoe** shop* (= a shop that sells shoes)
> *a **horse** race* (= a race for horses)     ***trouser** pockets* (= pockets in trousers)
> *a **toothbrush*** (= a brush for teeth) *a **ticket** office* (= an office that sells tickets)

## 3 articles

Articles belonging to the first (modifying) noun are dropped in **noun + noun**
combinations.
> ***army** officers* (= officers in **the army**)
> *a **sun** hat* (= a hat that protects you against **the sun**)

## 4 more than two nouns

More than two nouns can be put together. A group of two nouns can modify a
third noun, these can modify a fourth, and so on.
> *oil production costs*     *road accident research centre*

This kind of structure is very common in newspaper headlines (see 240)
because it saves space.
> *FURNITURE FACTORY PAY CUT ROW*

## 5 other structures

Not all compound ideas can be expressed by a **noun + noun** structure.
Sometimes it is necessary to use a structure with *of* or another preposition;
sometimes a structure with possessive *'s* is used.
> *a feeling **of disappointment*** (NOT *a disappointment feeling*)
> *letters **from home*** (NOT *home letters*)     *cow's milk* (NOT *cow milk*)

For more details, see 386.                                                        ▶

## 6 pronunciation

Most **noun + noun** combinations have the main stress on the first noun.

a '*bicycle factory*     a '*fruit drink*     '*ski boots*     '*coffee beans*

However, there are quite a number of exceptions.

a *garden* '*chair*     a *fruit* '*pie*

The difference between noun modifiers and adjectival modifiers is sometimes shown by stress. Compare:

a '*French teacher* (noun modifier: *a person who teaches French*)

a *French* '*teacher* (adjective modifier: *a teacher who is French*)

To be sure of the stress on a particular combination, it is necessary to check in a good dictionary.

For the stressing of road and street names, see 502.

## 7 spelling

Some short, common **noun + noun** combinations are generally written together like single words.

*bathroom*     *lampshade*     *seaside*     (BUT NOT ~~railwaystation~~)

Others may be written with a hyphen (e.g. *letter-box*) or separately (e.g. *furniture shop*). In many cases usage varies, and some combinations can be found written in all three ways (e.g. *bookshop, book-shop* or *book shop*). Hyphens are becoming less common in modern English, and (except with very common short combinations like *bathroom*) it is usually acceptable to write the two words separately.

For more information about the spelling of different kinds of compounds, see 559.
For information about the spelling of particular **noun + noun** expressions, see a good dictionary.

# 386 noun + noun (2): advanced points

## 1 classifying expressions: *a sheepdog*

The **noun + noun** structure is mostly used to make 'classifying' expressions, which name a particular kind of thing.

*mountain plants* (a special group of plants)

*mineral water* (a sort of water)

a *sheepdog* (a particular kind of dog)

We use **noun + noun** especially to talk about things that belong to common well-known classes (so that the two nouns really describe a single idea). In other cases we prefer a preposition structure. Compare:

*the postman, the milkman, the insurance man* (all well-known kinds of people who may call regularly at a British home)

a *man from the health department* (not a regular kind of visitor)

More examples:

– He was reading a **history book**. (a common class of book)
He was reading a **book about the moon**. (NOT ~~a moon book~~)

– She was sitting at a **corner table** in the restaurant. (Restaurants often have corner tables.)

*Who's the **girl in the corner**?* (NOT ~~Who's the corner girl?~~)
– *What does that **road sign** say?*
*She was showing **signs of tiredness**.* (NOT *. . .* ~~tiredness signs.~~)

## 2 containers: *a matchbox; a box of matches*

**Noun + noun** is used for particular kinds of container.
*a matchbox     a paint tin     a coffee cup*
But we use the preposition structure (with *of*) to talk about a container together with its contents.
*a box of matches     a tin of paint     a cup of coffee*

## 3 units, selections and collections: *piece, group* etc

We also prefer the *of*-structure with words that refer to units, selections and collections, like *piece, slice, lump* (of sugar), *bunch* (of flowers), *blade* (of grass), *pack* (of cards), *herd, flock, group* and so on.
*a **piece of** paper* (NOT *a* ~~paper piece~~)
*a **bunch of** flowers* (NOT *a* ~~flower bunch~~)

## 4 'made of': *a silk dress; silken skin*

**Noun + noun** is normally used to say what things are made of.
*a silk dress     a stone bridge     an iron rod     a gold ring*
In older English, the *of*-structure was more common in this case (e.g. *a dress of silk, a bridge of stone*), and it is still used in some metaphorical expressions.
*He rules his family with a **rod of iron**.*
*The flowers were like a **carpet of gold**.*
A few pairs of nouns and adjectives (e.g. *gold, golden*) are used as modifiers with different meanings. Generally the noun simply names the material something is made of, while the adjective has a more metaphorical meaning. Compare:

*a **gold** watch          **golden** memories*
***silk** stockings        **silken** skin*
*a **lead** pipe           a **leaden** sky* (grey and depressing)
*a **stone** roof          a **stony** silence*

But *wooden* and *woollen* just mean 'made of wood/wool'.

## 5 measurement: *a five-litre can*

**Noun + noun** is used in measurements, with a number before the first noun. The number is usually joined to the first noun by a hyphen (-). Note that the first noun is normally singular in form in these cases.
*a **five-litre** can     a **ten-pound** note* (NOT *a* ~~five-litres can, a ten-pounds note~~)
*a **six-pound** chicken     a **three-mile** walk     a **five-day** course*
*a **two-person** tent     ten **two-hour** lessons*
The number *one* is often left out.
*a **(one-)pint** mug*
In fractions, the plural *-s* is not usually dropped.
*a **two-thirds** share* (NOT *a* ~~two-third share~~)
Exception: *three quarters* (*a **three-quarter** length coat*)          ▶

## 6 noun + 's + noun: *children's clothes; a bird's nest*

In some classifying expressions we use a structure with possessive *'s*.
This is common when we are talking about things that are used by a person or animal: the first noun refers to the user.

*children's clothes     a man's sweater*
*women's magazines     a bird's nest*

Generally, either both nouns are singular or both are plural.

*a child's toy     children's clothes*
but
*a women's magazine*

Not all 'used by' expressions have possessive *'s*.

*baby clothes     a birdcage*

British and American usage sometimes differ. Compare:

*a baby's bottle* (BrE)     *a baby bottle* (AmE)
*a baby's pram* (BrE)     *a baby carriage* (AmE)
*a doll's house* (BrE)     *a doll house* (AmE)

## 7 noun + 's + noun: *cow's milk; a hen's egg*

The *'s* structure is often used for products from living animals.

*cow's milk     lamb's wool*
*sheep's wool     a bird's egg     a hen's egg*
(B U T *camel hair, horsehair*)

When the animal is killed to provide something, we usually use **noun + noun**.

*calf skin     chamois leather     fox fur*
*chicken soup     a lamb chop     tortoise shell*

## 8 parts: *a man's leg; a table leg*

We use the *'s* structure to talk about parts of people's and animals' bodies.

*a man's leg     an elephant's trunk     a sheep's heart*

But to talk about parts of non-living things, we usually use the **noun + noun** structure.

*a table leg* (N O T *a table's leg*)
*a car door* (N O T U S U A L L Y *a car's door*)

## 9 pronunciation

Classifying expressions with possessive *'s* most often have the main stress on the first noun. Compare:

– *a 'doll's house* (a kind of house)
  *my brother's 'house* (not a kind of house)
– *'goat's milk* (a kind of milk)
  *the goat's 'tail* (not a kind of tail)

Here, too, there are exceptions.

*a child's 'bicycle* (a kind of bicycle)

For the use of structures with *'s* to talk about possession, relationships etc, see 440.

## 10 noun + noun, noun + 's + noun, or preposition structure?

This is a very complicated area of English grammar. The 'rules' given above show the general patterns, but unfortunately there is no easy way to be quite sure which structure is used to express a particular compound idea. The most common expressions will be learnt by experience; in cases of doubt, a good dictionary will often show which form is correct.

# 387 now (that)

*Now (that)* can be used as a conjunction. In an informal style, *that* is often dropped (see 584).

**Now (that)** *Andrew is married, he has become much more responsible.*
**Now** *the exams are over I can enjoy myself.*

# 388 nowadays

*Nowadays* is an adverb meaning 'these days', 'at the present time'.
*People seem to be very depressed* **nowadays.**
**Nowadays** *we think nothing of space travel.*
*Nowadays* cannot be used as an adjective.
*I don't like* **modern** *fashions.* (NOT ~~I don't like the nowadays fashions.~~)

# 389 numbers

## 1 fractions and decimals: *two fifths; nought point four*

We say simple fractions like this:

| | | | |
|---|---|---|---|
| $^1/_4$ | *a/one quarter* | $^{11}/_{16}$ | *eleven sixteenths* |
| $^1/_8$ | *an/one eighth* | $3^3/_4$ | *three and three quarters* |
| $^3/_7$ | *three sevenths* | $6^1/_8$ | *six and one eighth* |
| $^2/_5$ | *two fifths* | | |

More complex fractions can be expressed by using the word *over*.

$^{317}/_{509}$   *three hundred and seventeen* **over** *five hundred and nine*

We write and say decimals like this:

0.4     *nought* **point** *four* (NOT ~~nought comma four~~)
0.375   *nought point* **three seven five** (NOT ~~nought point three~~
        ~~hundred and seventy-five~~)
4.7     *four point seven*

For the difference between *a(n)* and *one* with numbers, see paragraph 11 below.

## 2 before nouns

With fractions below *1*, we use *of* before nouns.
*three quarters* **of** *an hour*
*seven tenths* **of** *a mile*
*a third* **of** *the students*
*Half* is not always followed by *of* (see 231).
**half** *an hour*       **half (of)** *the students*

▶

*Of* is also possible with decimals below *1*.
> *nought point six of a mile*
> *0.1625 cm      nought point one six two five of a centimetre*

However, decimals below *1* are often followed directly by plural nouns.
> *nought point six* **miles** (NOT ~~nought point six mile~~)
> *nought point one three two five* **centimetres**

Fractions and decimals over *1* are normally followed by plural nouns.
> *one and a half* **hours** (NOT ~~one and a half hour~~)
> *three and three eighths* **miles**
> *1.3* **millimetres** (NOT ~~1.3 millimetre~~)

Note also the structure *a . . . and a half*.
> *I've been waiting for* **an hour and a half**.

## 3 singular or plural verbs

Singular verbs are normally used after fractions, decimals, and other expressions referring to amounts and measurements (for more details, see 527).
> *Three quarters of a ton* **is** *too much.* (NOT ~~Three quarters of a ton are~~ . . .)
> *3.6 kilometres* **is** *about 2 miles.*

But plural verbs are used when we are talking about numbers of people or things, even after a singular fraction.
> *A third of the students* **are** *from abroad.* (NOT ~~A third of the students is~~ . . .)
> *Half of the glasses* **are** *broken.*

After expressions like *one in three, one out of five* + **plural noun**, both singular and plural verbs are possible.
> *One in three new cars* **break/breaks** *down in the first year.*

## 4 *nought, zero, nil* etc

The figure *0* is usually called *nought* in British English and *zero* in American English. When we say numbers one figure at a time, *0* is often called *oh* (like the letter *O*).
> *My account number is four one three* **oh** *six.*

In measurements of temperature, *0* is called *zero* in both British and American English. *Zero* is followed by a plural noun.
> **Zero degrees** *Celsius is thirty-two degrees Fahrenheit.*

Zero scores in team games are called *nil* (American *zero* or *nothing*). In tennis and similar games, the word *love* is used (originally from French *l'oeuf*, meaning 'the egg' – the figure *0* is egg-shaped).
> *And the score at half-time is: Scotland three, England* **nil**.
> *Forty-***love**; *Andrews to serve.*

## 5 telephone numbers

We say each figure separately, pausing after groups of three or four (not two). When the same figure comes twice, British people usually say *double*.
> *307 4922      three oh seven, four nine double two*
> *                     (AmE three zero seven, four nine two two)*

## 6 Roman numbers

Roman numbers (*I, II, III, IV* etc) are not common in modern English, but they are still used in a few cases – for example the names of kings and queens, page numbers in the introductions to some books, the numbers of paragraphs in some documents, the numbers of questions in some examinations, the figures on some old clock faces, and occasionally the names of centuries.

*It was built in the time of Henry V.*
*For details, see Introduction page ix.*
*Do question (vi) or question (vii), but not both.*
*a fine XVIII Century English walnut chest of drawers*

The Roman numbers normally used are as follows:

| | | | |
|---|---|---|---|
| 1 *I i* | 10 *X x* | 40 | *XL xl* |
| 2 *II ii* | 11 *XI xi* | 45 | *XLV xlv* |
| 3 *III iii* | 12 *XII xii* | 50 | *L l* |
| 4 *IV iv* | 13 *XIII xiii* | 60 | *LX lx* |
| 5 *V v* | 14 *XIV xiv* | 90 | *XC xc* |
| 6 *VI vi* | 19 *XIX xix* | 100 | *C c* |
| 7 *VII vii* | 20 *XX xx* | 500 | *D* |
| 8 *VIII viii* | 21 *XXI xxi* | 1000 | *M* |
| 9 *IX ix* | 30 *XXX xxx* | 1995 | *MCMXCV* |

## 7 cardinal and ordinal numbers: books, chapters etc; kings and queens

**After** a noun we usually use a cardinal number (*one, two* etc) instead of an ordinal number (*first, second* etc). This structure is common in titles. Compare:

*the fourth book – Book **Four*** *the third act – Act **Three***
*Mozart's thirty-ninth symphony – Symphony No. **39**, by Mozart*
*the third day of the course – Timetable for Day **Three***

However, the names of kings and queens are said with ordinal numbers.

*Henry VIII: Henry the **Eighth*** (NOT *Henry Eight*)
*Louis XIV: Louis the **Fourteenth***
*Elizabeth II: Elizabeth the **Second***

## 8 centuries

Note how the names of centuries relate to the years in them. The period from 1701 – 1800 is called the **18**th century (not the 17th); 1801 – 1900 is the **19**th century, etc.

## 9 floors

The *ground floor* of a British house is the *first floor* of an American house; the British *first floor* is the American *second floor*, etc.

## 10 *and*; punctuation

In British English we always put *and* between *hundred/thousand/million* and numbers below a hundred. In American English, *and* can be dropped.

| | |
|---|---|
| 310 | *three hundred **and** ten* (AmE also *three hundred ten*) |
| 5,642 | *five thousand, six hundred **and** forty-two* |
| 2,025 | *two thousand **and** twenty-five* |

▶

In measurements containing two different units, *and* is possible before the smaller, but is usually left out.

*two hours (**and**) ten minutes*
*two metres (**and**) thirty centimetres*

In writing we generally use commas (,) to divide large numbers into groups of three figures, by separating off the thousands and the millions. Full stops (.) are not used in this way.

*3,127* (NOT *3.127*)                          *5,466,243*

We do not always use commas in four-figure numbers, and they are not used in dates.

*4,126* OR *4126*                          *the year 1648*

Spaces are also possible.

*There are 1 000 millimetres in a metre.*

Note the hyphen between the tens and units in *twenty-one, twenty-two, thirty-six, forty-nine* etc.

## 11   *a* and *one*

We can say *an eighth* or *one eighth, a hundred* or *one hundred, a thousand* or *one thousand, a million* or *one million,* etc. *One* is more formal.

*I want to live for **a** hundred years.* (NOT *...for hundred years*)
*Pay Mr J Baron **one** thousand pounds.* (on a cheque)

*A* can only be used at the beginning of a number. Compare:

*a/**one** hundred*
*three thousand **one** hundred* (NOT *three thousand a hundred*)

*A thousand* can be used alone, and before *and,* but not usually before a number of hundreds. Compare:

*a/**one** thousand*                          *a/**one** thousand and forty-nine*
***one** thousand, six hundred and two*
    (More natural than *a thousand, six hundred and two.*)

We can use *a* or *one* with measurement words. The rules are similar.

*a/**one** kilometre* (BUT *one kilometre, six hundred metres*)
*an/**one** hour and seventeen minutes* (BUT *one hour, seventeen minutes*)
*a/**one** pound* (BUT *one pound twenty-five*)

## 12   numbers with determiners

Numbers can be used after determiners. Before determiners, a structure with *of* is necessary.

*You're **my one** hope.*
***One of my** friends gave me this.* (NOT *One my friend...*)

## 13   *eleven hundred* etc

In an informal style we often use *eleven hundred, twelve hundred* etc instead of *one thousand one hundred* etc. This is most common with round numbers between 1,100 and 1,900.

*We only got **fifteen hundred** pounds for the car.*

This form is used in historical dates (see 152).

*He was born in **thirteen hundred**.*
*It was built in **fifteen (hundred** and) twenty-nine.*

## 14 *billion*

A *billion* is a thousand million. (But in older British usage a *billion* was a million million.)

## 15 *five hundred* etc without -*s*

After a number, the words *dozen, hundred, thousand, million* and *billion* have no final -*s*, and *of* is not used. This also happens after *several* and *a few*. Compare:

- *five hundred* pounds          – *a few million* years
  *hundreds of* pounds               *millions of* years
- *several thousand* times
  It cost *thousands*.

Singular forms are used as modifiers before nouns in plural measuring expressions.

*a five-pound* note (NOT ~~*a five-pounds note*~~)
*a three-mile* walk          *a four-foot* deep hole
six *two-hour* lessons          *a six-foot* tall man
*a three-month*-old baby

In an informal style, we often use *foot* instead of *feet* in other structures, especially when we talk about people's heights.

*My father's just over six **foot** two.*

For the use of *be* in measurements, see 92.
For the use of possessive forms in expressions of time (e.g. *ten minutes' walk; four days' journey*), see 440–444.

## 16 British money (pre-euro)

There are 100 *pence* in a *pound*. Sums of money are named as follows:

*1p  one penny* (informal *one p* (/piː/) or *a penny*)
*5p  five pence* (informal *five p*)
*£3.75 three pounds seventy-five (pence)* OR *three pounds and seventy-five pence* (more formal)

Some people now use the plural *pence* as a singular in informal speech; *pound* is sometimes used informally as a plural.

*That's two pounds and one **pence**, please.*
*It cost me eight **pound** fifty.*

Singular forms are used in expressions like *a five-pound note* (see above). However, *pence* is often used instead of *penny* (*a five pence stamp*).

## 17 American money

There are 100 *cents* (¢) in a *dollar* ($). One-cent coins are called *pennies*; five-cent coins are *nickels*; ten-cent coins are *dimes*; a twenty-five cent coin is a *quarter*.

## 18 non-metric measures

In recent years, Britain has adopted some metric measurement units, but non-metric measures are still quite widely used. America uses mainly non-metric units. Approximate values are as follows:

▶

*1 inch (1 in) = 2.5 cm*
*12 inches = 1 foot (30 cm)*
*3 feet (3 ft) = 1 yard (90 cm)*
*5,280 feet / 1,760 yards = 1 mile (1.6 km)*
*5 miles = 8 km*
*1 ounce (1 oz) = 28 gm*
*16 ounces = 1 pound (455 gm)*
*2.2 pounds (2.2 lb) = 1 kg*
*14 pounds (14 lb) = 1 stone (6.4 kg)* (BrE only)
*1 British pint = 56.8 cl*
*1 US pint = 47.3 cl*
*8 pints (8 pt) = 1 gallon*
*1 British gallon = 4.55 litres*
*1 US gallon = 3.78 litres*
*1 acre = 4,840 square yards = 0.4 hectares*
*1 square mile = 640 acres = 259 ha*

British people measure their weight in *stones* and *pounds* or (more recently) in *kilograms*; Americans just use *pounds*. Height is measured in *feet*; distance can also be measured in *feet*, but longer distances are often measured in *yards*, especially in British English.

> *I weigh eight **stone** six.* (NOT ... ~~eight stones six~~)
> *We are now flying at an altitude of 28,000 **feet**.*
> *The car park's straight on, about 500 **yards** on the right.*

## 19 area and volume

We say, for example, that a room is *twelve feet **by** fifteen feet*, or that a garden is *thirty metres **by** forty-eight metres*.

A room *twelve feet by twelve feet* can be called ***twelve feet square***; the total area is *144 **square feet***.

A container *2 metres by 2 metres by 3 metres* has a volume of *12 **cubic metres***.

## 20 *a* and *per*

When we relate two different measures, we usually use *a/an*; *per* is often used in formal writing.

> *It costs two pounds **a** week.* (OR ... *£2 **per** week.*)
> *We're doing seventy miles **an** hour.* (OR ... *70 miles **per** hour / mph.*)

## 21 numbers not used as complements after *be*

Numbers are used as subjects or objects, but not usually as complements after *be*.

> *I've got three sisters.* (NOT ~~My sisters are three.~~)
> *There are twelve of us in my family.* (More natural than *We are twelve...*)

## 22 spoken calculations

Common ways of saying calculations in British English are:

$2 + 2 = 4$    *Two and two is/are four.* (informal)
           *Two plus two equals/is four.* (formal)

$7 - 4 = 3$    *Four from seven is/leaves three.* (informal)
           *Seven take away four is/leaves three.* (informal)
           *Seven minus four equals/is three.* (formal)

$3 \times 4 = 12$   *Three fours are twelve.* (informal)
              *Three times four is twelve.* (informal)
              *Three multiplied by four equals/is twelve.* (formal)

$9 \div 3 = 3$   *Three(s) into nine goes three (times).* (informal)
              *Nine divided by three equals/is three.* (formal)

## 23  example of a spoken calculation

Here, for interest, is a multiplication ($146 \times 281$) together with all its steps, in the words that a British English speaker might have used as he/she was working it out on paper before the days of pocket calculators.

$$
\begin{array}{r}
146 \\
\times\ 281 \\
\hline
29200 \\
11680 \\
146 \\
\hline
41026 \\
\end{array}
$$

*A hundred and forty-six times two hundred and eighty-one.*

beginning: *Put down two noughts. Two sixes are twelve; put down two and carry one; two fours are eight and one are nine; two ones are two.*

next line: *Put down one nought. Eight sixes are forty-eight; put down eight and carry four; eight fours are thirty-two and four is thirty-six; put down six and carry three; eight ones are eight and three is eleven.*

next line: *One times 146 is 146.*

addition: *Six and nought and nought is six; eight and four and nought is twelve; put down two and carry one; six and two are eight and one is nine and one is ten; put down nought and carry one; nine and one are ten and one is eleven; put down one and carry one; two and one are three and one are four.*

total: *forty-one thousand and twenty-six.*

Note how *is* and *are* can often be used interchangeably.

For ways of saying and writing dates, see 152.
For ways of telling the time, see 579.

# 390  of course

We use *of course (not)* to mean 'as everybody knows' or 'as is obvious'.
  *It looks as if the sun goes round the earth, but **of course** that's not true.*
  *We'll leave at eight o'clock. Granny won't be coming, **of course**.*
*Of course* can be used as a polite reply to a request.
  *Could you help me?* ~ ***Of course**.*
But *of course* is not always a very polite reply to a statement of fact.
  *It's cold.* ~ *It certainly is.* (NOT *Of course it is* – this would suggest that the first speaker had said something too obvious to be worth mentioning.)

For the use of *of course* to structure arguments, see 157.5.

# 391 often

*Often* is mostly used for habitual behaviour, to mean 'a lot of times on different occasions'. To say 'a lot of times on one occasion', we normally use another expression (e.g. *a lot of times, several times, keep* . . .*ing*). Compare:

> *I **often** fell in love when I was younger.*
>
> *I fell **several times** yesterday when I was skiing.* OR *I **kept falling** yesterday . . .*
>     (NOT ~~I often fell yesterday~~ . . .)

Note that *often* has two common pronunciations, with and without *t*: /'ɒfən/ and /'ɒftən/.

For the position of *often* and other adverbs of indefinite frequency, see 24.

# 392 older English verb forms

The English of a few hundred years ago was different in many ways from modern English – grammar, vocabulary, pronunciation and spelling have all changed greatly since Shakespeare's time. Some of the most striking differences are in the way verbs are used. Older English had distinct second-person singular verb forms ending in *-st*, with a corresponding second-person singular pronoun *thou* (object form *thee*, possessives *thy, thine* ). There were also third-person singular verb forms ending in *-th*, and *ye* could be used as a second-person plural pronoun.

> *Tell me what **thou knowest**.*     *How can I help **thee**?*
>
> *Where **thy** master **goeth**, there **goest thou** also.*
>
> *Oh come, all **ye** faithful.*

Older forms of *be* included second-person singular *art* and *wert*.

> *I fear thou **art** sick.*     ***Wert** thou at work today?*

Questions and negatives were originally made without *do*; later, forms with and without *do* (including affirmative forms with *do*) were both common.

> ***Came you** by sea or by land?*     ***Be not** afraid.*
>
> *They **know not** what they do.*     *Then he **did take** my hand and kiss it.*

Simple tenses were often used in cases where modern English has progressive forms.

> *We **go** not out today, for it **raineth**.*

Subjunctives (see 567) were more widely used than in modern English.

> *If she **be** here, then tell her I wait her pleasure.*

Inversion (see 302–303) was more common, and infinitives and past participles could come later in a clause than in modern English.

> *Now **are we** lost indeed.*
>
> *Hamlet, thou hast thy father much **offended**.* (Shakespeare)
>
> *And she me **caught** in her arms long and small*
>     *and therewithal so sweetly did me **kiss***
>     *and softly said 'Dear heart, how like you this?'* (Wyatt)

Some of these forms were still used in 19th-century and early 20th-century literature (particularly poetry) long after they had died out of normal usage. Modern writers of historical novels, films or plays often make their characters use some of these older forms in order to give a 'period' flavour to the language. And the forms also survive in certain contexts where tradition is especially valued – for example the language of religious services, public ceremonies and the law. Some dialects, too, preserve forms which have disappeared from the rest of the language – second-person singular pronouns (*tha, thee* etc) are still used by many people in Yorkshire.

## 393   once: adverb

When *once* means 'at some time', we use it for the past but not for the future. To refer to an indefinite future time, we can use *sometime* or *one day*. Compare:
– *I met her **once** in Venezuela.*
   ***Once** upon a time there was a beautiful princess.*
– *Come up and see me **sometime**.* (NOT *Come up and see me once.*)
   *We must go walking **one day**.* (NOT *We must go walking once.*)
When *once* has the more precise meaning of 'one time (not twice or three times)', it can be used to talk about any time, including the future.
   *I'm only going to say this **once**.*
Note that *at once* means 'immediately'.
   *Can I have the bill?* ∼*At once, sir.*

## 394   once: conjunction

*Once* can be used as a conjunction, meaning 'after', 'as soon as'. It often suggests that something is finished or completed, and is most often used with a perfect tense.
   ***Once** you've passed your test I'll let you drive my car.*
   ***Once** he had found somewhere to live he started looking for work.*
   ***Once** you know how to ride a bike you never forget it.*
Note that we do not use *that* after *once* (NOT *Once that you've passed your test . . .*).

For present perfect instead of future perfect after conjunctions, see 580.

## 395   one: substitute word

### 1   use

We often use *one* instead of repeating a singular countable noun.
   *Which is your boy?* ∼*The **one** in the blue coat.*
   *I'd like a cake. A big **one** with lots of cream.*
   *Can you lend me a pen?* ∼*Sorry, I haven't got **one**.*

### 2   a . . . one

We drop *a* if there is no adjective. Compare:
   *I'm looking for a flat. I'd like **a small one** with a garden.*
   *I'd like **one** with a garden.* (NOT *. . . a one with a garden.*)

▶

### 3 *ones*

*One* has a plural *ones*.
> *I'd like to try on those shoes. ~ Which **ones**? ~ The **ones** in the window.*
> *Green apples often taste better than red **ones**.*
> *What sort of sweets do you like? ~ **Ones** with chocolate inside.*

### 4 uncountable nouns

We do not use *one(s)* for uncountable nouns. Compare:
> *If you haven't got a fresh **chicken** I'll take a frozen **one**.*
> *If you haven't got fresh **cream** I'll take tinned (cream).* (NOT *... tinned one.*)

### 5 *which (one), this (one)* etc

We can leave out *one(s)* immediately after *which, this, that, another, either, neither* and superlatives.
> *Which (one) would you like? ~ This (one) looks the nicest.*
> *Let's have another (one).      Either (one) will suit me.*
> *I think my dog's the fastest (one).*

But we cannot leave out *one(s)* if there is an adjective.
> *This blue one looks the nicest.* (NOT *This blue looks ...*)

We nearly always leave out *ones* after *these* and *those*.
> *I don't think much of these.* (More natural than *... these ones.*)

### 6 not used after *my* etc, *some, several, a few, both* or a number

We do not use *one(s)* immediately after *my, your* etc, *some, several, (a) few, both* or a number.
> *Take your coat and pass me mine.* (NOT *... pass me my one.*)
> *Are there any grapes? ~ Yes, I bought some today.* (NOT *... I bought some ones today.*)
> *I'll take both.* (NOT *... both ones.*)
> *She bought six.* (NOT *... six ones.*)

But *one(s)* is used if there is an adjective.
> *I'll wear my old one.* (NOT *... my old.*)
> *I bought some sweet ones today.* (NOT *I bought some sweet today.*)
> *Has the cat had her kittens? ~ Yes, she's had four white ones.* (NOT *... four white.*)

### 7 *that of*

*One(s)* is not normally used after a noun with possessive *'s*. Instead, we can either just drop *one(s)*, or use a structure with *that/those of* (more formal).
> *A grandparent's job is easier than a parent's.* (NOT *... than a parent's one.*)
> *A grandparent's job is easier than that of a parent.* (NOT *... than the one of a parent.*)
> *Trollope's novels are more entertaining than those of Dickens.* (NOT *... than Dickens' ones / the ones of Dickens.*)

### 8 noun modifiers

*One(s)* is not generally used after noun modifiers.
> *Do you need coffee cups or tea cups?* (NOT *... or tea ones.*)

**9** *One(s)* **always refers back**

We use *one(s)* to avoid repeating a noun which has been mentioned before. It cannot normally be used in other cases.

> *Let's go and ask **the old man** for advice.* (NOT *... ~~ask the old one~~ ...*)

# 396 one, you and they:
## indefinite personal pronouns

**1** *one* **and** *you*: **meaning**

We can use *one* or *you* to talk about people in general, including the speaker and hearer.

> ***One/You*** *cannot learn a language in six weeks.*
> ***One/You*** *should never give people advice.*

**2** *one* **and** *you*: **formality and class**

*One* is more formal than *you* (and more common in writing than in speech). Compare:

> *If **you** want to make people angry, **you** just have to tell them the truth.*
> *If **one** wishes to make oneself thoroughly unpopular, **one** has merely to tell people the truth.*

*One* is often considered typical of more upper-class and intellectual usage, and is avoided by many people for this reason.

**3** *one* **and** *you*: **only used in generalisations**

*One* and *you* are only used in this way in very general statements, when we are talking about 'anyone, at any time'. Compare:

- ***One/You*** *can usually find people who speak English in Sweden.*
  *English is spoken in this shop.* OR *They speak English in this shop.* (NOT ~~*One speaks English*~~ *...* – the meaning is not 'people in general')
- ***One/You*** *should knock before going into somebody's room.*
  ***Somebody's*** *knocking at the door.* (NOT ~~*One is knocking*~~ *...*)
- *It can take **you/one** ages to get served in this pub.*
  *Thanks, **I'm** being served.* (NOT ~~*Thanks, one is serving me.*~~)

*One* generally has a singular meaning: 'any individual'; it is not used to refer to whole groups.

> ***We*** *speak a strange dialect where I come from.* (NOT ~~*One speaks a strange dialect where I come from.*~~)

**4** **people including the speaker/hearer**

*One* is not used for people who could not include the speaker; *you* is not used for people who could not include the hearer. Compare:

> ***One/You*** *must believe in something.*
> *In the sixteenth century **people** believed in witches.*
> (NOT *... ~~one/you believed in witches~~* – this could not include the speaker or hearer.)

▶

### 5   *one/you* as subject, object etc

*One* can be a subject or object; there is a possessive *one's* and a reflexive pronoun *oneself*.

>*He talks to **one** like a teacher.*          ***One's** family can be very difficult.*
>***One** should always give **oneself** plenty of time to pack.*

*You/your/yourself* can be used in similar ways.

### 6   *they*

*They* has a rather different, less general kind of meaning than *one* and *you*. It usually refers to a particular but rather vague group (for example the neighbours, the people around, the authorities).

>***They** don't like strangers round here.*
>***They**'re going to widen the road soon.*
>*I bet **they** put taxes up next year.*

Note also the common expression *they say* (= people say).

>***They say** her husband's been seeing that Mrs Hastings again.* (NOT ~~One says . . .~~)

# 397   one of ...

After *one of* we normally use a plural form.

>*one of our **cats*** (NOT ~~one of our cat~~)

Occasionally *one of* is used with a singular noun referring to a group.

>*Why don't you ask **one of the crew**?*

A following verb is normally singular.

>*One of our cats **has** disappeared.* (NOT ~~One of our cats have disappeared.~~)

After *one of*, a noun phrase must have a determiner (e.g. *the, my, those*).

>*one of **the**/my/those horses* (BUT NOT ~~one of horses~~)

*Of* cannot be dropped.

>*one **of** my friends* (NOT ~~one my friend~~ OR ~~one my friends~~)

For sentences like *She's one of the only women who have/has climbed Everest*, see 529.

# 398   only: focusing adverb

*Only* can be used as a 'focusing adverb' (see 24.6). It can refer to different parts of a sentence.

### 1   referring to the subject

*Only* normally comes before a subject that it refers to.

>***Only you** could do a thing like that.*
>***Only my mother** really understands me.*

### 2   referring to other parts of a sentence

When *only* refers to another part of a sentence, it often goes in 'mid-position' with the verb (see 24 for details).

>*She **only reads** biographies.*          *She **is only** on duty on Tuesdays.*
>*I **only like** swimming in the sea.*          *I've **only been** to India once.*
>*She **was only** talking like that because she was nervous.*

## 3 ambiguous sentences

Sometimes sentences with *only* are ambiguous (they can be understood in more than one way).

> *I only kissed your sister last night.* (The sense can be 'only kissed', 'only your sister' or 'only last night'.)

In speech, the meaning is usually clear because the speaker stresses the part of the sentence that *only* refers to. Even in writing, the context generally stops sentences like these from being really ambiguous. However, if necessary *only* can be put directly before the object, complement or adverbial expression that it refers to. This is rather formal. Compare:

> *They **only** play poker on Saturday nights.* (could be ambiguous)
> *They play **only poker** on Saturday nights.*
> *They play poker **only on Saturday nights**.*

The meaning can also be made more precise with a relative structure.

> *Poker is **the only game** (that) they play on Saturday nights.*
> *Saturday nights are **the only time** (that) they play poker.*

## 4 *only today* etc

*Only* with a time expression can mean 'as recently as', 'not before'.

> *I saw her **only today** – she looks much better.*
> *My shoes will **only** be ready **on Friday**.*
> ***Only then** did she realise what she had agreed to.*

For inverted word order after *only*, as in the last example above, see 302.

# 399 open

## 1 *open* and *opened*

We normally use *open*, not *opened*, as an adjective.

> *I can read you like an **open** book.* (NOT *... an opened book.*)
> *Are the banks **open** this afternoon?* (NOT *Are the banks opened ...?*)

*Opened* is used as the past tense and past participle of the verb *open*, to talk about the action of opening.

> *She **opened** her eyes and sat up.*    *The safe was **opened** with dynamite.*

## 2 when *open* is not used

Note that *open* is not the normal word to refer to the fastenings of clothes, or to switches or taps.

> *I can't **untie/undo** this shoelace.* (NOT *I can't open this shoelace.*)
> *How do you **unfasten** this belt?*
> *Could you **turn/switch** the radio **on**?* (NOT *... open the radio?*)
> *Who left the taps **turned on**?* (NOT *Who left the taps open?*)

For *closed* and *shut*, see 132.

## 400  opportunity and possibility

We often say that somebody *has the opportunity to do / of doing* something.
> *I **have the opportunity to go** to Denmark next year.* (= I **can** go ...)

*Possibility* is not often used in this structure. It is more normal to say that *there is a possibility of something happening.*
> *There's **a possibility of** my going to Denmark next year.* (= I **may** go ...)
> (NOT *I have the possibility to go to Denmark* ...)

## 401  opposite (adjective): position

We put the adjective *opposite* before a noun when we are talking about one of
a pair of things that naturally face or contrast with each other.
> *I think the picture would look better on the **opposite wall**.*
> *She went off in the **opposite direction**.*
> *I've got exactly the **opposite opinion** to yours.*
> *His brother was fighting on the **opposite side**.*

We put *opposite* after the noun when it means 'facing the speaker or listener'
or 'facing a person or place that has already been mentioned'.
> *I noticed that the **man opposite** was staring at me.* (NOT ... *the opposite man was staring at me.*)
> *You can see the cinema programmes on the **notice opposite**.*
> *The man she was looking for was in the **shop** directly **opposite**.*

For *opposite* and *in front of*, see 402.
For *opposite* and *contrary*, see 144.

## 402  opposite, facing and in front of

### 1  'across a road/room etc from': *opposite/facing*

We do not use *in front of* to mean 'across a road/river/room etc from'. This
idea is usually expressed with *opposite* or *facing*. (AmE also *across from*.)
> *There's a garage **opposite** my house.* (NOT ... *in front of my house.*)
> *She stood at the other side of the table **facing** me.* (NOT ... *in front of me.*)
> *The man sitting **across from** me was smoking a pipe.* (AmE)

### 2  *in front of* and *opposite*

Compare:
> *There's a bus stop **in front of** the school.*
> (The bus stop is on the same side of the road as the school.)
> *There's a bus stop **opposite** the school.*
> (The bus stop is on the other side of the road from the school.)

*In front of* is often the opposite of *behind*.
> *The woman **in front of** me in the post-office queue had a complicated problem. I always find myself **behind** people like that.*

### 3 *in front of* and *in the front of*

If you are **in front of** a place, vehicle etc you are outside it; if you are **in the front of** it you are inside. Compare:

> *We stood **in front of** her car so that she couldn't drive off.*
> *Her husband was sitting **in the front of** the car. He looked frightened.*

For the difference between *before* and *in front of*, see 98.

## 403 ought

### 1 forms

Ought is a modal auxiliary verb (see 353–354). The third person singular has no *-s*.

> *She **ought** to understand.* (NOT ~~She oughts~~ . . .)

Questions and negatives are made without *do*.

> ***Ought** we to go now?* (NOT ~~Do we ought~~ . . .?)
> *It **oughtn't** to rain today.*

After *ought*, we use the infinitive with *to* before other verbs. (This makes *ought* different from other modal auxiliary verbs.)

> *You ought **to see** a dentist.*

*To* is not used in question tags.

> *We ought to wake Helen, **oughtn't we**?* (NOT . . . ~~oughtn't we to?~~)

In American English, interrogative and contracted negative forms of *ought to* are rare; *should* is generally used instead.

> *He ought to be here soon, **shouldn't he**?*

In some English dialects, questions and negatives are made with *did* (e.g. *She didn't ought to do that*), but this structure is not used in standard English.

### 2 obligation: *I ought to phone Mother*

We can use *ought* to advise people (including ourselves) to do things; to tell people that they have a duty to do things; to ask about our duty. The meaning is very similar to that of *should*; it is not so strong as *must* (see 520). *Ought* is less frequent than *should*.

> *What time **ought** I to arrive?*
> *I really **ought** to phone Mother.*
> *People **ought** not to drive like that.*
> *He **ought** to get a medal for living with her.*
> *There **ought** to be traffic lights at this crossroads.*

### 3 deduction: *He ought to be here soon*

We can also use *ought* (like *should*) to say that we guess or conclude that something is probable (because it is logical or normal).

> *Henry **ought** to be here soon – he left home at six.*
> *We're spending the winter in Miami. ～ That **ought** to be nice.*
> *The weather **ought** to improve after the weekend.*  ▶

### 4   questions

The normal question forms of *ought* are rather formal. In an informal style they are often avoided, for example by using a structure with *think . . . ought* or by using *should*.

> **Do you think we ought** to go now? (Less formal than *Ought we to . . .?*)
> **Should** we go now?

### 5   *ought to have . . .*

*Ought* has no past form, but we can use **ought to have + past participle** to talk about things which were supposed to happen but did not.

> I **ought to have phoned** Ed this morning, but I forgot. (NOT ~~I ought to phone Ed this morning, but I forgot.~~)

The structure can also be used to make guesses or draw conclusions about things which are not certain to have happened.

> Bill **ought to have got** back home yesterday. Has anybody seen him?

It is also possible to talk about things that ought to have happened by now, or by a future time.

> Ten o'clock. She **ought to have arrived** at her office by now.
> We **ought to have finished** painting the house by the end of next week.

### 6   word order

Mid-position adverbs like *always, never, really* (see 24) can go before or after *ought* in a verb phrase. The position before *ought* is less formal.

> You **always ought** to carry some spare money. (less formal)
> You **ought always** to carry some spare money. (more formal)

In negative clauses, *not* comes before *to*.

> You ought **not to** go. / You **oughtn't to** go. (NOT ~~You ought to not go.~~)

## 404   out of

### 1   movement

The opposite of the preposition *into* is *out of*.

> She ran **out of** the room. (NOT ~~She ran out the room.~~ OR ~~She ran out from the room.~~)
> I took Harry's letter **out of** my pocket.

*Out of* is also used to mean 'through', when we mention the opening through which somebody/something goes out.

> I walked **out of the front door** without looking back.
> Why did you throw the paper **out of the window**?

In American English, *out* is normally used without *of* in this case.

> She turned and went **out the back door**. (AmE)

### 2   position

*Out of* can also be used to talk about position – the opposite of *in*.

> I'm afraid Mr Pallery is **out of** the office at the moment.

For *into* and *in*, see 269.

# 405 own

## 1 after possessives

We only use *own* after a possessive word. It cannot directly follow an article.
> *It's nice if a child can have **his or her own** room.* (NOT . . . ~~an own room.~~)
> *Car hire is expensive. It's cheaper to take **one's own** car.* (NOT . . . ~~the own car.~~)
> *I'm **my own** boss.*

## 2 a/some . . . of one's own

This structure makes it possible to include *a/an, some* or another determiner in the phrase.
> *I'd like to have **a car of my own**.*
> *It's time you found **some friends of your own**.*
> *He's got **no ideas of his own**.*

## 3 own with no following noun

We cannot use *mine, yours* etc with *own*, but we can drop a noun after *my own, your own* etc if the meaning is clear.
> *Would you like to use my pen?* ~ *No, thanks. I can only write with **my own**.* (NOT . . . ~~mine own.~~)

## 4 own and -self

The emphatic and reflexive pronouns *myself, yourself* etc (see 493) do not have possessive forms. *My own* etc is used instead.
> *I'll do it **myself**, and I'll do it in **my own** way.* (NOT . . . ~~in myself's way.~~)
> *She can wash **herself** and brush **her own** hair now.* (NOT . . . ~~brush herself's hair.~~)

## 5 on one's own

Note the two meanings of *on one's own*.
> *My mother lives **on her own**.* (without company)
> *Don't help him. Let him do it **on his own**.* (without help)

For *by oneself* used in similar ways, see 493.6.

# 406 paragraphs

Written English text is usually divided into blocks called 'paragraphs', to make it easier to read. Paragraphs can vary in length, from several hundred words (for example in literary or academic writing), to a few sentences (for example in journalism or letters). A paragraph division is usually shown by starting the text on a new line and 'indenting' (leaving a space at the beginning of the line). The paragraph divisions break the material up into easily 'digestible' sections, providing places where the reader can pause and think for a moment if necessary. And good writers can show the structure of their texts by making paragraph divisions in suitable places, for example when they move to a new stage in a story, a new point in a discussion or a new part of a description.

▶

*Bill decided that it was too late to start slimming, and put some more sugar in his coffee. The way things were, he needed all the help he could get. Everything was going wrong at work, everything had already gone wrong at home, and the weather in Edinburgh in November was lousy. The only remaining question was: should he commit suicide now or wait till after payday and get drunk first?*

*a new stage in the story* → *Three months ago everything had seemed so perfect. His boss had told him that he had an excellent future with the firm.*

*There are a lot of advantages to working at home. You don't have to travel to your job, you can choose your own working hours, you can take a day off if you want to, you don't waste time in endless unnecessary meetings, and – perhaps most important of all – you don't have a boss constantly checking up on you.*

*a new point in the discussion* → *On the other hand, it can be lonely working by yourself. Without colleagues around you . . .*

Another practice, common in typed letters and documents, is to leave a blank line without indenting.

*Dear Sirs*
*Three months ago I sent you an order for a set of glasses, together with a cheque in full payment. You wrote acknowledging my order, and said that the glasses would be dispatched within 15 days.*

*I have still not received the glasses, and repeated telephone calls to your office have had no result . . .*

# 407 part

*A* is usually dropped before *part of* if there is no adjective.
**Part of** *the roof was missing.* (BUT *A* **large part** *of the roof was missing.*)
**Part of** *the trouble is that I can't see very well.* (More natural than *A part of the trouble . . .*)
*Jan was in Australia* **part of** *last year.*

# 408 participles (-ing and -ed forms) (1): introduction

## 1 names

When -*ing* forms are used in certain ways, for example as parts of verb forms, or like adjectives (see below) they are called 'present participles'. Forms like *broken, gone, opened, started* are called 'past participles'. These are not very suitable names: both forms can be used to talk about the past, present or future.
*She was* **crying** *when I saw her.*
*Who's the man* **talking** *to Elizabeth?*
*This time tomorrow I'll be* **lying** *on the beach.*
*It was* **broken** *in the storm.*          *The kids are* **excited**.
*The new school is going to be* **opened** *next week.*

For the spelling of participles, see 560–562.
For -*ing* forms used like nouns ('gerunds'), in sentences like *Smoking is bad for you*, see 293–299.

## 2　use

a　verb forms

Participles are used with the auxiliary verbs *be* and *have* to make progressive, perfect and passive verb forms.

It **was raining** *when I got home.*
*I've forgotten your name.*　　　You'll **be told** *as soon as possible.*
Present and past participles can be put together to make progressive and perfect forms (e.g. *being employed, having arrived, having been invited*).

b　adjectives

Participles can be used like adjectives.

*I love the noise of **falling** rain.*　　　*John has become very **boring**.*
*She says she's got a **broken** heart.*　　*The house looked **abandoned**.*

c　adverbs

Sometimes participles are used like adverbs.
*She ran **screaming** out of the room.*

d　clauses

Participles can combine with other words into clause-like structures.
*Who's the fat man **sitting in the corner**?*
**Having lost all my money,** *I went home.*
*Most of the people **invited to the party** didn't turn up.*
**Rejected by all his friends,** *he decided to become a monk.*

For details of these uses, see the following sections.

# 409　participles (2): active and passive

## 1　active present participles, passive past participles

When *-ing* forms are used like adjectives or adverbs, they have similar meanings to active verbs.

***falling*** *leaves* (= leaves that fall)
*a meat-**eating** animal* (= an animal that eats meat)
*She walked out **smiling**.* (= She was smiling.)

Most past participles have passive meanings when they are used like adjectives or adverbs.

*a **broken** heart* (= a heart that has been broken)
*He lived alone, **forgotten** by everybody.* (= He had been forgotten by everybody.)

## 2　*interested* and *interesting* etc

*Interested, bored, excited* etc say how people feel.
*Interesting, boring* etc describe the people or things that cause the feelings.
Compare:

– *I was very **interested** in the lesson.* (NOT ~~I was very interesting in the lesson.~~)
*The lesson was really **interesting**.*　　　　　　　　　　　　　　▶

– *I didn't enjoy the party because I was **bored**.* (NOT *...~~because I was boring~~*.)
  *It was a terribly **boring** party.*
– *The children always get **excited** when Granny comes.* (NOT *~~The children~~*
  *~~always get exciting~~...*)
  *Granny takes the children to **exciting** places.*
– *His explanations make me very **confused**.* (NOT *...~~make me very confusing~~*.)
  *He's a very **confusing** writer.*

## 3 exceptions: *a fallen leaf, an escaped prisoner* etc

A few past participles can be used as adjectives with active meanings,
especially before nouns. Examples:

> *a **fallen** leaf* (= a leaf that has fallen)
> ***advanced** students* (= students who have advanced to a high level, NOT
>   students who have been advanced ...)

> | | |
> |---|---|
> | ***developed** countries* | *a **grown-up** daughter* |
> | ***increased** activity* | *an **escaped** prisoner* |
> | ***vanished** civilisations* | ***faded** colours* |
> | *a **retired** general* | ***swollen** ankles* |

> *Rescuers are still working in the ruins of the **collapsed** hotel.*

## 4 active past participles: advanced points

Some more past participles can be used with active meanings, but only with
adverbs. Examples:

> *a **well-read** person* (BUT NOT *a ~~read person~~*)
> *a **much-travelled** man*       *recently-**arrived** immigrants*
> *The train **just arrived** at platform six is the delayed 13.15 from Hereford.*

Some active past participles can be used after *be*. Examples:

> *She **is retired** now.*                *Those curtains **are** badly **faded**.*
> *My family **are** all **grown up** now.*       *This class **is** the most **advanced**.*

*Recovered, camped, stopped, finished* (see 205) and *gone* (see 229) are used in
this way after *be*, but not usually before nouns.

> *Why **are** all those cars **stopped** at the crossroads?* (BUT NOT *... a ~~stopped car~~*)
> *I hope you're fully **recovered** from your operation.*
> *We're **camped** in the field across the stream.*
> *I'll **be finished** in a few minutes.*       *Those days **are gone** now.*

# 410 participles (3): details

## 1 used as adjectives: *an interesting book*

Participles can often be used as adjectives before nouns, or after *be* and other
link verbs.

> | | |
> |---|---|
> | *an **interesting** book* | *a **lost** dog* |
> | *a **falling** leaf* | *The upstairs toilet window is **broken**.* |
> | ***screaming** children* | *His idea seems **exciting**.* |

Participles used as adjectives can have objects. Note the word order.

**English-speaking** *Canadians.* (NOT ~~speaking-English Canadians.~~)

*a* **fox-hunting** *man*     *Is that watch* **self-winding**?

Other compound structures with participles are also common before nouns.

**quick-growing** *trees*     **government-inspired** *rumours*

**home-made** *cake*     *the* **above-mentioned** *point*

*a* **recently-built** *house*

## 2 after nouns: *the people questioned*

We often use participles after nouns in order to define or identify the nouns, in the same way as we use identifying relative clauses (see 495).

*We couldn't agree on any of the* **problems discussed**.

(= . . . the problems that were discussed.) (NOT . . . ~~the discussed problems.~~)

*The* **people questioned** *gave very different opinions.*

(= The people who were questioned . . .) (NOT ~~The questioned people~~ . . .)

*I watched the match because I knew some of the* **people playing**. (NOT . . . ~~the playing people.~~)

*I got the only* **ticket left**. (NOT . . . ~~the only left ticket.~~)

*Those* is often used with a participle to mean 'the ones who are/were'.

*Most of* **those questioned** *refused to answer.*

**Those selected** *will begin training on Monday.*

## 3 differences of meaning

A few participles change their meaning according to their position. Compare:

– *a* **concerned** *expression* (= a worried expression)

*the people* **concerned** (= the people who are/were affected)

– *an* **involved** *explanation* (= a complicated explanation)

*the people* **involved** (= the same as *the people concerned*)

– *an* **adopted** *child* (= a child who is brought up by people who are not his/her biological parents)

*the solution* **adopted** (= the solution that is/was chosen)

## 4 *much* or *very* with past participles

When a past participle is part of a passive verb, we can put *much* or *very much* before it, but not *very*.

*He's* **(very) much admired** *by his students.* (NOT . . . ~~very admired~~ . . .)

*Britain's trade position has been* **(very) much weakened** *by inflation.*

(NOT . . . ~~very weakened~~ . . .)

When a past participle is used as an adjective, we usually prefer *very*. This is common with words referring to mental states, feelings and reactions.

*a* **very frightened** *animal* (NOT ~~a much frightened animal~~)

*a* **very shocked** *expression*

*The children were* **very bored**.

*She looked* **very surprised**.

Common exceptions:

*That's Alice, unless I'm* **(very) much mistaken**. (NOT . . . ~~unless I'm very mistaken.~~)

*He's* **well known** *in the art world.* (NOT . . . ~~very known~~ . . .)     ▶

With *amused*, *very* and *(very) much* are both possible.

> *I was **very amused** / **much amused** / **very much amused** by Miranda's performance.*

## 5 frightened by / frightened of

*By* is used after passive verbs to introduce the agent (the person or thing that does the action – see 413).

> *Most of the damage was caused **by your sister**.*

After past participles that are used like adjectives, we prefer other prepositions. Compare:

– *She was **frightened by** a mouse that ran into the room.*
> (*Frightened* is part of a passive verb referring to an action.)
> *She's always been terribly **frightened of** dying.*
> (*Frightened* is an adjective referring to a state of mind.)

– *The kids were so **excited by** the music that they kept screaming.*
> *Joe's **excited about** the possibility of going to the States.*

– *I was **annoyed by** the way she spoke to me.*
> *I'm **annoyed with** you.*

– *The burglar was **surprised by** the family coming home unexpectedly.*
> *I'm **surprised at/by** your attitude.*

– *He was badly **shocked by** his fall.*
> *We were **shocked at/by** the prices in London.*

Other examples:

> *His whereabouts are **known to** the police.*
> *The hills are **covered in** snow.*
> *The room was **filled with** thick smoke.*

## 6 special past participle forms

A few older forms of past participles are still used as adjectives before nouns in certain expressions.

| | |
|---|---|
| ***drunken** laughter/singing* etc | *a **sunken** wreck/ship* etc |
| *a **shrunken** head* | ***rotten** fruit/vegetables* etc |

# 411 participles (4): clauses

## 1 structures

Participles can combine with other words into participle clauses.

> *There's a woman **crying her eyes out** over there.*
> *Most of the people **invited to the reception** were old friends.*
> ***Not knowing what to do**, I telephoned the police.*
> ***Served with milk and sugar**, it makes a delicious breakfast.*

## 2 after nouns: *the people invited to the party*

Participle clauses can be used after nouns and pronouns.

> *We can offer you a **job cleaning cars**.*
> *There's **Neville, eating as usual**.*
> *In came **the first runner, closely followed by the second**.*
> *I found **him sitting at a table covered with papers**.*

Participle clauses are often very like relative clauses (see 494.5), except that they have participles instead of complete verbs.

*Who's **the girl dancing with your brother**?* (= . . . the girl who is dancing . . .)
*Anyone **touching that wire** will get a shock.* (= Anyone who touches . . .)
*Half of **the people invited to the party** didn't turn up.* (= . . . who were invited . . .)

Perfect participles are not often used in this way.

*Do you know anybody **who's lost a cat**?* (NOT ~~Do you know anybody having lost a cat?~~)

## 3 adverbial clauses: *Putting down my paper, I . . .*

Participle clauses can also be used in similar ways to full adverbial clauses, expressing condition, reason, time relations, result etc. (This can only happen, of course, when the idea of condition, reason etc is so clear that no conjunction is needed to signal it.) Adverbial participle clauses are usually rather formal.

*Used economically, one tin will last for six weeks.* (= If it is used . . .)
*Having failed my medical exams, I took up teaching.* (= As I had failed . . .)
*Putting down my newspaper, I walked over to the window.*
    (= After I had put down my newspaper, . . .)
*It rained for two weeks on end, completely ruining our holiday.*
    (= . . . so that it completely ruined our holiday.)

Note that *-ing* clauses can be made with verbs like *be*, *have*, *wish* and *know*, which are not normally used in progressive tenses (see 471). In these cases, the participle clause usually expresses reason or cause.

*Being unable to help in any other way, I gave her some money.*
*Not wishing to continue my studies, I decided to become a dress designer.*
*Knowing her pretty well, I realised something was wrong.*

## 4 subjects; misrelated participles

Normally the subject of an adverbial participle clause is the same as the subject of the main clause in a sentence.

*My wife had a talk with Sally, explaining the problem.* (*My wife* is the subject of *explaining*.)

It is often considered incorrect to make sentences with 'misrelated participles', where an adverb clause has a different subject from the main clause.

*Looking out of the window of our hotel room, there was a wonderful range of mountains.* (This could sound as if the mountains were looking out of the window.)

However, sentences like these are common and often seem quite natural, particularly when the main clause has preparatory *it* or *there* as a subject.

*Being French, it's surprising that she's such a terrible cook.*
*Having so little time, there was not much that I could do.*

'Misrelated participles' are normal in some fixed expressions referring to the speaker's attitude. Examples:

*Generally speaking, men can run faster than women.*
*Broadly speaking, dogs are more faithful than cats.*
*Judging from his expression, he's in a bad mood.*
*Considering everything, it wasn't a bad holiday.*
*Supposing there was a war, what would you do?*
*Taking everything into consideration, they ought to get another chance.* ▶

## 5 participle clauses with their own subjects

A participle clause can have its own subject. This happens most often in a
rather formal style.

*Nobody having any more to say, the meeting was closed.*
*All the money having been spent, we started looking for work.*
*A little girl walked past, her doll dragging behind her on the pavement.*
*Hands held high, the dancers circle to the right.*

The subject is often introduced by *with* when the clause expresses
accompanying circumstances.

*A car roared past with smoke pouring from the exhaust.*
*With Peter working in Birmingham, and Lucy travelling most of the week,
the house seems pretty empty.*

## 6 participle clauses after conjunctions and prepositions

*-ing* clauses can be used after many conjunctions and prepositions. They are
common with *after, before, since, when, while, on, without, instead of, in spite
of* and *as*. Note that *-ing* forms after prepositions can often be considered as
either participles or gerunds – the dividing line is not clear (see 293).

*After talking to you I always feel better.*
*After having annoyed everybody he went home.*
*Depress clutch before changing gear.*
*She's been quite different since coming back from America.*
*When telephoning from abroad, dial 1865, not 01865.*
*On being introduced, British people often shake hands.*
*They left without saying goodbye.*
*She struck me as being a very nervy kind of person.*

Clauses with past participles are possible (mostly in a formal style) after *if,
when, while, once* and *until*.

*If asked to look after luggage for someone else, inform police at once.*
*When opened, keep in refrigerator.*
*Once deprived of oxygen, the brain dies.*
*Leave in oven until cooked to a light brown colour.*

For clauses like *when ready*, see 73.4.

## 7 object complements

The structure **object + participle (clause)** is used after verbs of sensation
(e.g. *see, hear, feel, watch, notice, smell*) and some other verbs (e.g. *find, get,
have, make*).

*I saw a small girl standing in the goldfish pond.*
*Have you ever heard a nightingale singing?*
*I found her drinking my whisky.*
*We'll have to get the car repaired before Tuesday.*
*Do you think you can get the radio working?*
*We'll soon have you walking again.*
*I can make myself understood pretty well in English.*

For more about structures with *see* and *hear*, see 242. For *get*, see 224. For *have*, see 238. For *make*,
see 335.

# 412 passives (1): passive structures and verb forms

## 1 active and passive structures

Compare:
- *They **built** this house in 1486.* (active)
  *This house **was built** in 1486.* (passive)
- *Austrians **speak** German.* (active)
  *German **is spoken** in Austria.* (passive)
- *A friend of ours **is repairing** the roof.* (active)
  *The roof **is being repaired** by a friend of ours.* (passive)
- *This book **will change** your life.* (active)
  *Your life **will be changed** by this book.* (passive)

When A does something to B, there are often two ways to talk about it. If we want A (the doer) to be the subject, we use an active verb: *built, speak, is repairing*. If we want B (the 'receiver' of the action) to be the subject, we use: *was built, is spoken, is being repaired, will be changed*.

The object of an active verb corresponds to the subject of a passive verb.

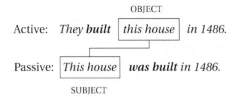

In most cases, the subject of an active verb is not expressed in the corresponding passive sentence. If it does have to be expressed, this usually happens in an expression with *by*; the noun is called the 'agent' (see 413).
   *This house was built in 1486 **by Sir John Latton**.*

## 2 passive verb forms

We normally make passive forms of a verb by using tenses of the auxiliary *be* followed by the past participle (= pp) of the verb. (For *get* as a passive auxiliary, see 223.5.) Here is a list of all the passive forms of an ordinary English verb.

| Name | Construction | Example |
|------|-------------|---------|
| (simple) future | *will be +pp* | *You'll **be told** soon enough.* |
| future perfect | *will have been +pp* | *Everything **will have been done** by Tuesday* |
| simple present | *am/are/is + pp* | *English **is spoken** here.* |
| present progressive | *am/are/is being + pp* | *Excuse the mess; the house **is being painted**.* |
| present perfect | *have/has been +pp* | *Has Mary **been told**?* |
| simple past | *was/were + pp* | *I **wasn't invited**, but I went.* |
| past progressive | *was/were being + pp* | *I felt as if I **was being watched**.* |
| past perfect | *had been + pp* | *I knew why I **had been chosen**.* |

▶

Future progressive passives (**will be being** + pp) and perfect progressive passives (**has been being** + pp) are unusual.
Examples of passive infinitives: *(to) be taken*; *(to) have been invited*.
Examples of passive *-ing* forms: *being watched*; *having been invited*.
Note that verbs made up of more than one word (see 599–600) can have passive forms if they are transitive.

>*The furniture **was broken up** for firewood.*
>*She likes **being looked at**.*     *I need **to be taken care of**.*
>*He hates **being made a fool of**.*

For more about structures with prepositions at the ends of clauses, see 452.

## 3   use of tenses

Passive tenses are normally used in the same way as active tenses. So for example the present progressive passive is used, like the present progressive active, to talk about things that are going on at the time of speaking (see 464).

>*The papers **are being prepared** now.*
>*The secretary **is preparing** the papers now.*

And the present perfect passive can be used, like the present perfect active, to talk about finished actions with present consequences (see 455).

>*Alex **has been arrested**!*     *The police **have arrested** Alex!*

## 4   verbs not used in the passive

Not all verbs can have passive forms. Passive structures are impossible with intransitive verbs (see 606.2) like *die* or *arrive*, which cannot have objects, because there is nothing to become the subject of a passive sentence. Some transitive verbs, too, are seldom used in the passive. Most of these are 'stative verbs' (verbs which refer to states, not actions). Examples are *fit, have, lack, resemble, suit*.

>*They **have** a nice house.* (BUT NOT ~~A nice house is had by them.~~)
>*My shoes **don't fit** me.* (BUT NOT ~~I'm not fitted by my shoes.~~)
>*Sylvia **resembles** a Greek goddess.* (BUT NOT ~~A Greek goddess is resembled by Sylvia.~~)
>*Your mother **lacks** tact.* (BUT NOT ~~Tact is lacked~~ . . .)
>*She **was having** a bath.* (BUT NOT ~~A bath was being had by her.~~)

## 5   confusing forms

Students often confuse active and passive verb forms in English. Typical mistakes:

>~~I was very interesting in the lesson.~~
>~~We were questioning by the immigration officer.~~
>~~She has put in prison for life.~~

Mistakes like these are not surprising, because:
1. *Be* is used to make both passive verb forms and active progressive tenses.
2. Past participles are used to make both passive verb forms and active perfect tenses. Compare:
   *He **was** calling.* (active – past progressive)
   *He **was** called.* (passive – simple past)
   *He **has** called.* (active – present perfect)

For active verb forms, see 10.

# 413 passives (2): agent

In a passive clause, we usually use *by* to introduce the agent – the person or thing that does the action, or that causes what happens. (Note, however, that agents are mentioned in only about 20 per cent of passive clauses.)
   *All the trouble was caused **by your mother**.*
   *These carpets are made **by children** who work twelve hours a day.*
Some past participles can be more like adjectives than verbs (see 410): for example *shocked, worried, frightened*. After these, we often use other prepositions instead of *by*.
   *I was **shocked at/by** your attitude.*
   *We were **worried about/by** her silence.*
   *Are you **frightened of** spiders?*
*With* is used when we talk about an instrument which is used by an agent to do an action (see 119).
   *He was shot (by the policeman) **with a rifle**.*

# 414 passives (3):
# When do we use passive structures?

## 1 interest in the action

We often choose passive structures when we want to talk about an action, but are not so interested in saying who or what does/did it. Passives without 'agents' (see 413) are common in academic and scientific writing for this reason.
   *Those pyramids **were built** around 400 AD.*
   *Too many books **have been written** about the Second World War.*
   *The results **have not** yet **been analysed**.*

▶

## 2 putting the news at the end

We often prefer to begin a sentence with something that is already known, or that we are already talking about, and to put the 'news' at the end. This is another common reason for choosing passive structures. Compare:

> John's **painting** my portrait. (active verb so that the 'news' – the portrait – can go at the end)
>
> Nice picture. ~ Yes, it **was painted** by my grandmother. (passive verb so that the 'news' – the painter – can go at the end)

## 3 keeping the same subject

In order to keep talking about the same person or thing, it may be necessary to switch from active to passive and back.

> He **waited** for two hours; then he **was seen** by a doctor; then he **was sent** back to the waiting room. He **sat** there for another two hours – by this time he **was getting** angry. Then he **was taken** upstairs and examined by a specialist, after which he **had to wait** for another hour before he **was allowed** to go home. (More natural than He waited for two hours; then a doctor saw him . . .)

## 4 putting heavier expressions at the end

Longer and heavier expressions often go at the end of a clause, and this can also be a reason for choosing a passive structure.

> I **was annoyed** by Mary **wanting to tell everybody what to do.**
>
> (More natural than **Mary wanting to tell everybody what to do** annoyed me – the phrase Mary . . . do would make a very long subject.)

## 5 meaning and grammar

Meaning and grammar do not always go together. Not all active verbs have 'active' meanings; for instance, if you say that somebody *receives* something or *suffers*, you are really saying that something is done to him/her. Some English active verbs might be translated by passive or reflexive verbs in certain other languages: e.g. *My shoes* **are wearing out**; *She* **is sitting**; *Suddenly the door* **opened**. And some English passives might be translated by active or reflexive verbs: e.g. *I* **was born** in 1956; *English* **is spoken** here.

Some verbs can be used in both active and passive forms with similar meanings: for example *to worry / to be worried*; *to drown / to be drowned* (see 165). Sometimes active and passive infinitives can be used with very similar meanings: for example *There's a lot of work to do / to be done* (for details, see 287).

For more about verbs like *open*, see 609.
For more about reflexive verbs, see 493.
For active and passive past participles, see 409.
For -*ing* forms with passive meanings after *need* and *want* (e.g. *My watch needs cleaning*), see 296.3.
For more about the way information is organised in sentences, see 512.

# 415 passives (4): verbs with two objects

Many verbs, such as *give, send, show, lend, pay, promise, refuse, tell, offer,* can be followed by two objects, an 'indirect object' and a 'direct object'. These usually refer to a person (indirect object) and a thing (direct object). Two structures are possible.

### A. verb + indirect object + direct object

*She gave her sister the car.*
*I had already shown the policewoman Sam's photo.*

### B. verb + direct object + preposition + indirect object

*She gave the car to her sister.*
*I had already shown Sam's photo to the policewoman.*

Both of these structures can be made passive.

### A. indirect object becomes subject of passive verb

**Her sister** *was given the car.*
**The policewoman** *had already been shown Sam's photo.*

### B. direct object becomes subject of passive verb

**The car** *was given to her sister.*
**Sam's photo** *had already been shown to the policewoman.*

The choice between the two passive structures may depend on what has been said before, or on what needs to be put last in the sentence (see 414.2,4).
Structure A (e.g. *Her sister was given the car.*) is the more common of the two. More examples:

*I've just **been sent** a whole lot of information.*
*You **were lent** ten thousand pounds last year.*
*The visitors **were shown** a collection of old manuscripts.*
*They **are being paid** a lot of money for doing very little.*
*He **was refused** a visa because he had been in prison.*
*We **will** never **be told** the real truth.*
*How much **have you been offered**?*

In structure B (e.g. *The car was given to her sister*), prepositions are sometimes dropped before indirect object pronouns.

*This watch was given **(to)** me by my father.*

*Explain* (see 198) and *suggest* (see 570) cannot be used in structure A.

**The problem was explained** *to the children.* (BUT NOT ~~The children were explained the problem.~~)

**A meeting place was suggested** *to us.* (BUT NOT ~~We were suggested a meeting place.~~)

For more details of verbs with two objects, see 610.
For more about prepositional verbs in the passive, see 416.

# 416 passives (5): verbs with prepositions

## 1 *look at, listen to, pay for* etc

The objects of prepositional verbs can become subjects in passive structures.

*We have looked **at the plan** carefully.* → ***The plan** has been carefully looked at.*

*Nobody listens **to her**.* → ***She** is never listened to.*

*Somebody has paid **for your meal**.* → ***Your meal** has been paid for.*

Note the word order. The preposition cannot be dropped.

*I don't like to be shouted **at**.* (NOT *~~I don't like to be shouted.~~*)

For more about prepositions at the ends of clauses, see 452.

## 2 *throw stones at, steal a bicycle from, give flowers to* etc

If there is already a direct object, the second object (after the preposition) cannot become a passive subject.

*They threw **stones at him**.* → ***Stones** were thrown at him.* (BUT NOT *~~He was thrown stones at.~~*)

*They stole **a bicycle from him**.* → ***A bicycle** was stolen from him.* (BUT NOT *~~He was stolen a bicycle from.~~*)

*They poured **water on us**.* → ***Water** was poured on us.* (BUT NOT *~~We were poured water on.~~*)

Note that possessive nouns or pronouns cannot become passive subjects, either.

*They called **Mr Archer's name**.* → ***Mr Archer's name** was called.* (BUT NOT *~~Mr Archer was name called.~~*)

*I broke **her mirror**.* → ***Her mirror** was broken.* (BUT NOT *~~She was mirror broken.~~*)

## 3 *give, send* etc

Verbs like *give, send, lend* can have two objects with no preposition (e.g. *They gave him a gold watch*). For the passive of this structure (e.g. *He was given a gold watch*), see 415.

For structures with *have* + object + past participle (e.g. *We had water poured on us*), see 238, 512.3.

# 417 passives (6): it was thought that ...

## 1 clause objects: *Nobody thought that she was a spy*

Some sentences have clauses as their objects. These cannot normally become the subjects of passive sentences.

*Nobody thought **that she was a spy**.* (BUT NOT *~~That she was a spy was thought by nobody.~~*)

*We felt **that he was the right man for the job**.* (BUT NOT *~~That he was ... was felt.~~*)

*The newspapers say **that his company is in trouble**.* (BUT NOT *~~That his company is in trouble is said ...~~*)

However, passive structures are often possible with preparatory *it* (see 446).
> *It **was thought** that she was a spy.*
> *It **was felt** that he was the right man for the job.*
> *It **is said** that his company is in trouble.*

## 2 infinitive objects: *They decided to ...*

A few verbs that are followed by infinitives (for example *decide, agree*) can also be used in passive structures beginning with *it*.
> *They **decided to meet** at twelve.* → *It **was decided** to meet at twelve.*
> *We **agreed to open** a new branch.* → *It **was agreed** to open a new branch.*

However, most verbs cannot be used in this way.
> *We **hope to make** a profit this year.* (BUT NOT ~~It is hoped to make~~ ...)

# 418 passives (7): He is believed to be ...

## 1 object + infinitive: *He asked me to send ...*

Many verbs can be followed by **object + infinitive** (see 283).
> *He **asked me to send** a stamped addressed envelope.*
> *We **chose Felicity to be** the Carnival Queen.*

In most cases, these structures can be made passive.
> *I **was asked to send** a stamped addressed envelope.*
> *Felicity **was chosen to be** the Carnival Queen.*
> *We **were told not to come** back.*
> *They **are allowed to visit** Harry once a week.*

## 2 verbs of thinking, feeling and saying

With verbs like *think, feel, believe, know* etc, the **object + infinitive** structure is rather formal and often unusual.
> *They **believe him to be** dangerous.* (more normal: *They believe that ...*)

However, the passive structure (e.g. *He is believed to be ...*) is common, and often occurs in news reports.
> *He **is believed to be** dangerous.*
> *Moriarty **is thought to be** in Switzerland.*
> *She **is known to have been** married before.*
> *It **is considered to be** the finest cathedral in Scotland.*

Note that with *say*, the infinitive structure is only possible in the passive.
> *His company **is said to be** in trouble.*
> (BUT NOT ~~They say his company to be in trouble.~~)

## 3 *hear, see, make* and *help*

These verbs can be followed, in active structures, by **object + infinitive** without *to* (see 281). In passive structures *to*-infinitives are used. Compare:
– *I saw him **come** out of the house.*
   *He was seen **to come** out of the house.*
– *They made him **tell** them everything.*
   *He was made **to tell** them everything.*
– *They helped him **(to) get** out of the country.*
   *He was helped **to get** out of the country.*

▶

## 4  preparatory *there*

With some verbs (e.g. *say, think, feel, report, presume, understand*), the passive
structure is possible with *there* as a 'preparatory subject'.

> *There are thought to be more than 3,000 different languages in the world.*
> (= It is thought that there are ...)
> *There was said to be disagreement between Ministers.*

## 5  perfect, progressive and passive infinitives

A passive verb can be followed by a perfect, progressive or passive infinitive.

> *He is believed to have crossed the frontier last night.*
> *I was told to be waiting outside the station at 6 o'clock.*
> *The hostages are expected to be released today.*

## 6  exceptions: *wanting* and *liking*

Verbs that refer to wanting, liking and similar ideas cannot usually be used in
passive structures with following infinitives.

> *Everybody **wanted Doris to be** the manager.* (BUT NOT ~~Doris was wanted to be the manager.~~)
> *We **like our staff to say** what they think.* (BUT NOT ~~Our staff are liked to say what they think.~~)

# 419  passives (8): he was considered a genius

After some verbs the direct object can be followed by an 'object complement' –
a noun or adjective which describes or classifies the object.

> *Queen Victoria considered him **a genius**.*
> *They elected Mrs Sanderson **President**.*
> *We all regarded Kathy as **an expert**.*
> *Most people saw him as **a sort of clown**.*
> *The other children called her **stupid**.*
> *You've made the house **beautiful**.*

In passive clauses these are subject complements; they come after the verb.

> *He was considered **a genius** by Queen Victoria.*
> *Mrs Sanderson was elected **President**.*
> *Kathy was regarded as **an expert**.*
> *He was seen as **a sort of clown**.*
> *She was called **stupid** by the other children.*
> *The house has been made **beautiful**.*

For more about object complements, see 607.

# 420 passives (9): **My suitcase is packed**

Some verbs refer to actions that produce a finished result. Examples are *cut*, *build*, *pack*, *close*. Other verbs do not: for example *push*, *live*, *speak*, *hit*, *carry*. The past participles of finished-result verbs, and some of their passive tenses, can have two meanings. They can refer to the action, or they can describe the result (rather like adjectives). Compare:

> *The theatre **was closed** by the police on the orders of the mayor.*
> (refers to the action of closing)
> *When I got there I found that the theatre **was closed**.*
> (refers to the state of being shut – the result of the action)

Because of this, for example, present passive forms can have similar meanings to present perfect passives.

> *The vegetables **are all cut up** – what shall I do now?* (= The vegetables have all been cut up . . .)
> *I got caught in the rain and my suit's **ruined**.* (= . . . has been ruined.)
> *I think your ankle **is broken**.* (= . . . has been broken.)
> *My suitcase **is packed**.* (= . . . has been packed.)

# 421 past (1): simple past (**I worked** etc)

This form is also called 'past simple'.

## 1 forms (regular verbs)

| Affirmative | Question | Negative |
|---|---|---|
| I worked | did I work? | I did not work |
| you worked | did you work? | you did not work |
| he/she/it worked | did he/she/it work? | he/she/it did not work |
| etc | etc | etc |

- Contracted negatives (see 143): *I didn't work, you didn't work* etc.
- Negative questions (see 368): *did I not work?* or *didn't I work?* etc.
- For the affirmative past forms of common irregular verbs, see 304.
- Questions and negatives of irregular verbs are made in the same way as those of regular verbs (with **did** + **infinitive**).

For details of question structures, see 480–486. For negatives, see 367–371.
For passive forms (e.g. *Work was done*), see 412.

## 2 pronunciation of *-ed*

The regular past ending *-ed* is pronounced as follows:
- /d/ after vowels and voiced consonants (except /d/):
  /ð/, /b/, /v/, /z/, /ʒ/, /dʒ/, /g/, /m/, /n/, /ŋ/, /l/
  *tried* /traɪd/   *lived* /lɪvd/   *used* /juːzd/   *failed* /feɪld/
- /t/ after unvoiced consonants (except /t/):
  /θ/, /p/, /f/, /s/, /ʃ/, /tʃ/, /k/
  *stopped* /stɒpt/   *passed* /pɑːst/   *laughed* /lɑːft/   *watched* /wɒtʃt/
  *worked* /wɜːkt/

▶

- /ɪd/ after /d/ and /t/
  *ended* /'endɪd/  *started* /'stɑːtɪd/

For adjectives like *aged, naked*, see 18.

## 3  spelling of regular affirmative past tense forms

| | |
|---|---|
| Most regular verbs:<br>add *-ed* | *work → worked*<br>*stay → stayed*<br>*show → showed*<br>*wonder → wondered*<br>*visit → visited*<br>*gallop → galloped* |
| Verbs ending in *-e*:<br>add *-d* | *hope → hoped*<br>*decide → decided* |
| Verbs ending in one stressed vowel<br>+ one consonant (except *w* or *y*):<br>double the consonant and add *-ed* | *shop → shopped*<br>*plan → planned*<br>*re'fer → referred*<br>*re'gret → regretted* |
| But (last syllable not stressed): | *'offer → offered*<br>*'visit → visited* |
| Verbs ending in consonant + *-y*:<br>change *y* to *i* and add *-ed* | *hurry → hurried*<br>*cry → cried*<br>*study → studied* |
| But (vowel + *-y*): | *play → played* |

Verbs ending in *-c* have *ck* in the past (e.g. *picnic → picnicked* ).
In British English, *-l* is doubled in the past after one short vowel even if the vowel is not stressed: *'travel → travelled*.

## 4  use

We use the simple past for many kinds of past events: short, quickly finished actions and happenings, longer situations, and repeated events.
> Peter **broke** a window last night.
> I **spent** all my childhood in Scotland.
> Regularly every summer, Janet **fell** in love.

The simple past is common in stories and descriptions of past events.
> One day the Princess **decided** that she **didn't like** staying at home all day, so she **told** her father that she **wanted** to get a job . . .

The simple past is often used with words referring to finished times.
> I **saw** John **yesterday morning**. He **told** me . . .

In general, the simple past tense is the 'normal' one for talking about the past; we use it if we do not have a special reason for using one of the other tenses.

For the simple past with a present or future meaning (e.g. *It's time you went*), see 426.
For special uses in subordinate clauses, see 580.

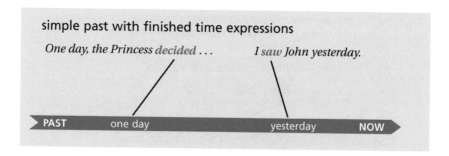

simple past with finished time expressions

*One day, the Princess decided . . .*   *I saw John yesterday.*

| PAST | one day | yesterday | NOW |

## 422   past (2): past progressive (**I was working** etc)

### 1   forms

> *was/were + -ing*
>
> *I was working.*
> *Were you listening to me?*      *She was not trying.*

For details of question structures, see 480–486. For negatives, see 367–371.
For passive forms (e.g. *Work was being done*), see 412.
For double letters in words like *sitting, stopping*, see 562.

### 2   use: *What were you doing at eight o'clock?*

We use the past progressive to say that something was in progress (going on) around a particular past time.

>   *What **were** you **doing** at eight o'clock yesterday evening? ~ I **was watching** TV.* (NOT *What did you do...? ~ I watched TV.*)
>   *When I got up this morning the sun **was shining**, the birds **were singing**, ...* (NOT *...the sun shone, the birds sang...*)

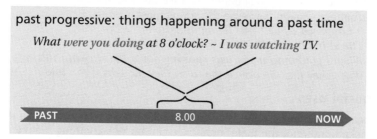

past progressive: things happening around a past time

*What were you doing at 8 o'clock? ~ I was watching TV.*

| PAST | 8.00 | NOW |

### 3   past progressive and simple past: 'background' events

We often use the past progressive together with a simple past tense. The past progressive refers to a longer 'background' action or situation; the simple past refers to a shorter action or event that happened in the middle of the longer action, or that interrupted it.

▶

*As I **was walking** down the road, I **saw** Bill.*
*The phone **rang** while I **was having** dinner.*
*Mozart **died** while he **was composing** the Requiem.*

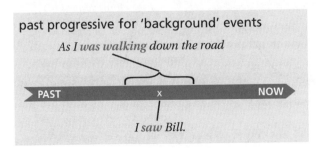

past progressive for 'background' events

*As I **was walking** down the road*

PAST     x     NOW

*I saw Bill.*

### 4 not used for repeated actions

The past progressive is not the normal tense for talking about repeated or habitual past actions. The simple past is usually used with this meaning.
*I **rang** the bell six times.* (NOT ~~I was ringing the bell six times.~~)
*When I was a child we **made** our own amusements.* (NOT ...~~we were making our own amusements.~~)
However, the past progressive is possible if the repeated actions form a 'background' for the main action.
*At the time when it happened, I **was travelling** to New York a lot.*

### 5 non-progressive verbs: *She said she believed*

Some verbs are not used in progressive forms (see 471).
*She said she **believed** Joe was dying.* (NOT ~~She said she was believing~~...)

### 6 used for shorter, temporary actions and situations

The past progressive, like other progressive forms (see 470), is used for temporary actions and situations. When we talk about longer, more permanent situations we use the simple past. Compare:
– *It happened while I **was living** in Eastbourne last year.*
  *I **lived** in London for ten years while I was a child.*
– *When I got home, water **was running** down the kitchen walls.*
  *When they first discovered the river, they thought it **ran** into the Atlantic.*

### 7 special uses

Because we often use the past progressive to talk about something that is a 'background', not the main 'news', we can make something seem less important by using this tense. Compare:
*I **had lunch** with the President yesterday.* (important piece of news)
*I **was having lunch** with the President yesterday, and she said...* (as if there was nothing special for the speaker about lunching with the President)
The past progressive is quite often used with verbs of saying: this gives more relative importance to the following verb – to what is said.
*John **was saying** that he still can't find a job.*

With *always, continually* and similar words, the past progressive can be used for things that happened repeatedly and unexpectedly or in an unplanned way (see 472).

> *Aunt Lucy **was always turning up** without warning and bringing us presents.*
> *I didn't like him – he **was continually borrowing** money.*

For the 'distancing' use of past progressives (e.g. *I was wondering whether you'd like to come out with me this evening*), see 436.

# 423 past perfect (1): basic information

This entry deals with the simple past perfect. For the past perfect progressive, see 425.

## 1 forms

> had + past participle
>
> *I had forgotten.*
> *Where had she been?*          *It hadn't rained for weeks.*

For passives (e.g. *The work had been done*), see 412.

## 2 meaning and use: earlier past

The basic meaning of the past perfect is 'earlier past'. A common use is to 'go back' for a moment when we are already talking about the past, to make it clear that something had already happened at the time we are talking about.

> *During our conversation, I realised that we **had met** before.* (NOT *I realised that we met before* OR *. . . have met before.*)
> *When I arrived at the party, Lucy **had** already **gone** home.* (NOT *. . . Lucy already went home.* OR *. . . has already gone home.*)

The past perfect is common after past verbs of saying and thinking, to talk about things that had happened before the saying or thinking took place.

> *I **told** her that I **had finished**.* (NOT *. . . that I (have) finished.*)
> *I **wondered** who **had left** the door open.*
> *I **thought** I **had sent** the cheque a week before.*

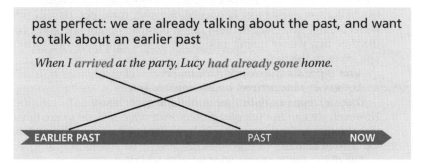

past perfect: we are already talking about the past, and want to talk about an earlier past

*When I arrived at the party, Lucy had already gone home.*

EARLIER PAST           PAST       NOW

▶

### 3 past perfect not used

The past perfect is normally only used as described above. The past perfect is not used simply to say that something happened some time ago, or to give a past reason for a present situation.

> *Alex Cary, who **worked** for my father in the 1980s, is now living in Greece.* (NOT ~~Alex Cary, who had worked for my father~~...)
>
> *I **left** some photos to be developed. Are they ready yet?* (NOT ~~I had left some photos~~...)

### 4 unreal events: *if* etc

After *if* (see 259), *wish* (see 630) and *would rather* (see 491), the past perfect can be used to talk about past events that did not happen.

> *If I **had gone** to university I would have studied medicine.*
> *I **wish** you **had told** me the truth.*
> *I'd **rather** she **had asked** me before borrowing the car.*

### 5 how long? past perfect, not simple past.

We use a past perfect, not a simple past, to say how long something had continued up to a past moment. A simple past perfect is used with 'non-progressive verbs' like *be, have* and *know*.

> *She told me that her father **had been** ill since Christmas.* (NOT ...~~that her father was ill since Christmas.~~)
>
> *I was sorry to sell my car. I **had had** it since College.* (NOT ...~~I had it since College.~~)
>
> *When they got married, they **had known** each other for 15 years.* (NOT ... ~~they knew each other for 15 years.~~)

With most other verbs, we use the past perfect progressive for this meaning (see 425).

For the difference between *since* and *for*, see 208.

## 424 past perfect (2): advanced points

### 1 past perfect or simple past with *after, as soon as*, etc

We can use time conjunctions (e.g. *after, as soon as, when, once*) to talk about two actions or events that happened one after the other. Usually the past perfect is not necessary in these cases, because we are not 'going back' from the time that we are mainly talking about, but simply moving forward from one event to the next.

> *After it **got** dark, we came back inside.*
> *As soon as Jane **arrived**, we sat down to eat.*
> *Once it **stopped** raining, we started the game again.*

However, we can use the past perfect with *after, as soon as* etc to emphasise that the first action is separate, independent of the second, completed before the second started.

> *She didn't feel the same **after** her dog **had died**.*
> *As soon as he **had finished** his exams, he went to Paris for a month.*

This use of the past perfect is especially common with *when*. (*When* has several meanings, so we often have to show the exact time relations by the verb form.) Compare:

– *When I **had opened** the windows, I sat down and had a cup of tea.*
   (NOT *When I opened the windows, I sat down* . . .: the first action was quite separate from the second.)
   *When I **opened** the window, the cat jumped out.* (More natural than *When I had opened the window,* . . .: one action caused the other.)

– *When I **had written** my letters, I did some gardening.* (NOT *When I wrote my letters, I did some gardening*.)
   *When I **wrote** to her, she came at once.*

## 2 unrealised hopes and wishes; things that did not happen

The past perfect can be used to express an unrealised hope, wish etc. *Had* is usually stressed in this case.

> *I HAD **hoped** we would leave tomorrow, but it won't be possible.*
> *He HAD **intended** to make a cake, but he ran out of time.*

## 3 past perfect with *It was the first/second . . . that . . .*

We use a past perfect after *it was the first/second . . . that . . .* and similar structures (see 591).

> *It was **the first time** that I **had heard** her sing.* (NOT *. . . that I heard* . . .)
> *It was **the fifth time** she **had asked** the same question.* (NOT *. . . she asked* . . .)
> *It was only **the second opera** I **had seen** in my life.* (NOT *. . . I saw* . . .)

For the past perfect with *before* (e.g. *He went out before I had finished my sentence*), see 97.3.

# 425 past perfect (3): progressive

## 1 forms: *had been + -ing*

> *I had been working.*          *Where had she been staying?*
> *They hadn't been listening.*

For double letters in words like *sitting, stopping,* see 562.

## 2 use We use the past perfect progressive to talk about actions or situations which had continued up to the past moment that we are thinking about, or shortly before it.

> *At that time we **had been living** in the caravan for about six months.*
> *When I found Mary, I could see that she **had been crying**.*
> *I went to the doctor because I **had been sleeping** badly.*          ▶

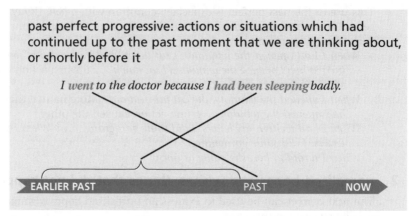

past perfect progressive: actions or situations which had continued up to the past moment that we are thinking about, or shortly before it

*I went to the doctor because I had been sleeping badly.*

EARLIER PAST          PAST          NOW

### 3 *how long?* past perfect progressive, not past progressive

We use a past perfect progressive, not a past progressive, to say how long something had been happening up to a past moment.

>*We'd been walking since sunrise, and we were hungry.* (NOT ~~We were walking since sunrise~~...)
>*When she arrived, she had been travelling for twenty hours.* (NOT ...~~she was travelling~~...)

For the difference between *since* and *for*, see 208.

### 4 progressive and simple: differences

Progressive forms are mostly used to talk about more temporary actions and situations. When we talk about longer-lasting or permanent situations we prefer simple forms. Compare:

>*My legs were stiff because I had been standing still for a long time.*
>*The tree that blew down had stood there for 300 years.*

Progressive forms generally emphasise the continuation of an activity; we use simple tenses to emphasise the idea of completion. Compare:

>*I had been reading science fiction, and my mind was full of strange images.*
>*I had read all my magazines, and was beginning to get bored.*

Some verbs are not normally used in progressive forms (see 471), even if the meaning is one for which a progressive form would be more suitable.

>*I hadn't known her for very long when we got married.* (NOT ~~I hadn't been knowing her~~...)

## 426 past verb form with present or future meaning

A past tense does not always have a past meaning. In some kinds of sentence we can use verbs like *I had, you went* or *I was wondering* to talk about the present or future.

## 1 after conjunctions, instead of *would*

In most subordinate clauses (e.g. after *if, supposing, wherever, what*), we use past tenses (and not *would ...*) to express 'unreal' or conditional ideas (see 580.6).

*If I **had** the money now I'd buy a car.*

*If you **caught** the ten o'clock train tomorrow you would be in Edinburgh by supper-time, unless the train **was** delayed, of course.*

*You look as if you **were** just about to scream.*

*Supposing we **didn't go** on holiday next year?*

*Would you follow me wherever I **went**?*

*In a perfect world, you would be able to say exactly what you **thought**.*

*Ten o'clock – it's time (that) you **went** home.*

*Don't come and see me today – I'd rather (that) you **came** tomorrow.*

*I wish (that) I **had** a better memory.*

## 2 distancing in questions, requests etc

We can make questions, requests and offers less direct (and so more polite) by using past tenses. (For more about 'distancing' of this kind, see 436.) Common formulae are *I wondered, I thought, I hoped, did you want*.

*I **wondered** if you were free this evening.*

*I **thought** you might like some flowers.*

***Did you want** cream with your coffee, sir?*

Past progressive forms (*I was thinking/wondering/hoping* etc) make sentences even less direct.

*I **was thinking** about that idea of yours.*

*I **was hoping** we could have dinner together.*

## 3 'past' modals

The 'past' modal forms *could, might, would* and *should* usually have present or future reference; they are used as less direct, 'distanced' forms of *can, may, will* and *shall*.

***Could** you help me for a moment?*    ***Would** you come this way, please?*

*I think it **might** rain soon.*    *Alice **should** be here soon.*

## 4 past focus on continuing situations

If we are talking about the past, we usually use past tenses even for things which are still true and situations which still exist.

*Are you deaf? I asked how old you **were**.*

*I'm sorry we left Liverpool. It **was** such a nice place.*

*Do you remember that nice couple we met on holiday? They **were** German, **weren't** they?*

*I got this job because I **was** a good driver.*

*Bill applied to join the police last week, but he **wasn't** tall enough.*

For more indirect speech examples, see 275, 278.

# 427  perfect verb forms

## 1  construction

Perfect verb forms are made with *have* + **past participle**.

> She **has lost** her memory. (present perfect)
> They **have been living** in France for the last year. (present perfect progressive)
> I told him that I **had** never **heard** of the place. (past perfect)
> When I went back to the village the house **had been pulled** down. (past perfect passive)
> We **will have finished** by tomorrow afternoon. (future perfect tense)
> I'm sorry **to have disturbed** you. (perfect infinitive)
> **Having seen** the film, I don't want to read the book. (perfect -*ing* form)

## 2  terminology and use

A perfect verb form generally shows the time of an event as being earlier than some other time (past, present or future). But a perfect form does not only show the time of an event. It also shows how the speaker sees the event – perhaps as being connected to a later event, or as being completed by a certain time. Because of this, grammars often talk about 'perfect aspect' rather than 'perfect tenses'.

For details of the use of the various perfect verb forms, see the individual entries in the book.

# 428  personal pronouns (1): basic information

## 1  terminology and use

The words *I, me, you, he, him, she, her, it, we, us, they* and *them* are usually called 'personal pronouns'. (This is a misleading name: *it, they* and *them* refer to things as well as people.)

Personal pronouns are used when more exact noun phrases are not necessary.

> *I'm tired.* (*I* replaces the name of any speaker.)
> *John's ill.* ***He'll** be away for a few days.* (NOT ... ~~John'll be away~~...)
> *Tell Mary I miss **her**.* (NOT ~~Tell Mary I miss Mary.~~)

## 2  subject and object forms: *I* and *me*, *he* and *him* etc

Personal pronouns (except *you*) have one form when they are used as subjects, and a different form for other uses – for example, when they are the objects of verbs or prepositions.

**Subject**: I    he    she    we    they
**Object**: me   him   her   us    them

Compare:

> – *I like dogs.*
>   *Dogs don't like **me**.*

> – *We sent **her** some flowers.*
>   *She sent **us** some flowers.*

## 3   other uses of object forms: *It was her*

*Me, him, her, us* and *them* are used not only as objects, but also as complements after *be*, and in short answers, especially in an informal style.

*Who said that?* ~ *(It was)* **her.**
*Who's there?* ~ **Me.**

In a more formal style, we use **subject form + verb** where possible.

*Who said that?* ~ **She did.** (BUT NOT ~~She.~~)

It is possible to use a subject form alone after *be* (e.g. *It is I; It was he*), but this is extremely formal, and is usually considered over-correct.

Object forms are also common in double subjects in informal speech.

***John and me** are going skiing this weekend.*

This is considered incorrect in more formal usage (see 429.1).

For sentences like *It's me that needs help*, see 429.3.

## 4   Personal pronouns cannot be left out

We cannot normally leave out personal pronouns, even if the meaning is clear without them (for some exceptions, see 429.11).

*It's raining.* (NOT ~~Is raining.~~)
*She loved the picture because **it** reminded her of home.* (NOT ... ~~because reminded her of home.~~)
*They arrested Alex and put **him** in prison.* (NOT ... ~~and put in prison.~~)
*Have some chocolate.* ~ *No, I don't like **it**.* (NOT ... ~~I don't like.~~)

## 5   One subject is enough

One subject is enough. We do not usually use a personal pronoun to repeat a subject that comes in the same clause.

***My car** is parked outside.* (NOT ~~My car it is parked outside.~~)
***The boss** really gets on my nerves.* (NOT ~~The boss he really gets on my nerves.~~)
***The situation** is terrible.* (NOT ~~It is terrible the situation.~~)

There are exceptions in very informal speech (see 514).

*He's not a bad bloke, **Jeff**.*
*It's a horrible place, **London**.*

For *it* as a preparatory subject or object, see 446–447.

## 6   personal and relative pronouns: *she* or *who*, not both

We do not use personal pronouns to repeat the meaning of relative pronouns (see 494.7).

*That's the girl **who** lives in the flat upstairs.* (NOT ... ~~who she lives~~ ...)
*Here's the money **(that)** you lent me.* (NOT ... ~~(that) you lent me it.~~)

## 7   *it* referring to *nothing*, the situation, etc.

*It* not only refers to the names of particular things. We can also use *it* to refer to indefinite pronouns like *nothing, anything, everything*.

***Nothing** happened, did **it**?*
***Everything's** all right, isn't **it**?*

▶

*It* can also refer to a whole fact, event or situation.

> *Our passports were stolen. **It** completely ruined our holiday.*
> *I did all I could, but **it** wasn't enough.*
> ***It's** terrible – everybody's got colds, and the central heating isn't working.*
> *Wasn't **it** lovely there!*

## 8 *it* as 'empty' subject: *it's ten o'clock*

We use *it* as a meaningless subject with expressions that refer to time, weather, temperature or distances.

> *It's ten o'clock.* (NOT ~~Is ten o'clock.~~)   *It's Monday again.*
> *It rained for three days.*   *It's thirty degrees.*
> *It's ten miles to the nearest petrol station.*

## 9 *it* used to identify

We use *it* for a person when we are identifying him or her.

> *Who's that over there?* ~ *It's John Cook.* (NOT ~~He's John Cook.~~)
> *Is that our waiter?* ~ *No, **it** isn't.* (NOT ~~No, he isn't.~~)
> On the phone: *Hello. **It's** Alan Williams.* (NOT *. . .* ~~I'm Alan Williams.~~)
> *It's your sister who plays the piano, isn't it?*

## 10 *we women, you men*

*We* and plural *you* (but not other personal pronouns) can be put directly before nouns.

> ***We women** know things that **you men** will never understand.*
> (BUT NOT ~~I woman know~~ *. . .* OR ~~They men will never~~ *. . .*)

For *you* used for people in general, see 396.
For the personal pronoun *one*, see 396.
For the use of *he* and *she* to refer to animals, ships etc, see 222.
For *they, them, their* with singular reference, see 528.
For the interrogative personal pronoun *who(m)*, see 623.

# 429 personal pronouns (2): advanced points

## 1 *John and me went; us women understand; between you and I*

We often use object forms in double subjects in informal speech.

> ***John and me** are going skiing this weekend.*
> ***Me and the kids** spent Sunday at the swimming pool.*

*Us* is sometimes used as a subject together with a noun.

> ***Us women** understand these things better than you men.*

And *I* is often used informally in double objects.

> *Between **you and I**, I think his marriage is in trouble.*
> *That's a matter for **Peter and I**.*
> *I often think of the old days and how you helped **Bertie and I**.* (letter from
>    Queen Elizabeth, wife of the future King George VI, to King Edward VIII).

These structures are often condemned as 'incorrect', but they have been common in educated speech for centuries. (There are examples of *me* in double subjects in Jane Austen's novels, written around 1800.) They are, however, restricted to a very informal style. They are not correct in formal speech or writing.

## 2  *as, than, but* and *except* + *me* or *I*

After *as* and *than*, object forms are generally used in an informal style.
> *My sister's nearly as tall **as me**.*
> *I can run faster **than her**.*

In a more formal style, subject forms are used, usually followed by verbs.
> *My sister's nearly as tall **as I am**.*
> *I can run faster **than she can**.*

*But* (meaning 'except') and *except* are followed by object forms (see 116, 194).
> *Nobody **but me** knew the answer.* (NOT ~~Nobody but I . . .~~)
> *Everybody **except him** can come.*

## 3  *It is/was me that . . . / I who . . .*

When a relative clause comes after an expression like *It is/was me/I*, there are two possibilities:

> object form + *that* (very informal)

> *It's **me that** needs your help.*
> *It was **him that** told the police.*

> subject form + *who* (very formal)

> *It is **I who** need your help.*
> *It was **he who** told the police.*

We can avoid being too formal or too informal by using a different structure.
> *He was the person / the one who told the police.*

## 4  mixed subject and object: *It's for him to decide*

Sometimes a pronoun is the object of a verb or preposition, but the subject of a following infinitive or clause. Normally an object form is used in this case.
> *It's for **him** to decide.* (NOT ~~It's for he to decide.~~)
> *I think it's a good idea for **you and me** to meet soon.*
> (Considered more correct than . . . *for you and I to meet soon.*)
> *Everything comes to **him** who waits.*
> (Considered more correct than . . . *to he who waits.*)

## 5  inclusive and exclusive *we*

Note that *we* and *us* can include or exclude the listener or reader. Compare:
> *Shall **we** go and have a drink?* (*We* includes the listener.)
> *We're going for a drink. Would you like to come with **us**?*
> (*We* and *us* exclude the listener.)

## 6  *us* meaning 'me'

In very informal British speech, *us* is quite often used instead of *me* (especially as an indirect object).
> *Give **us** a kiss, love.*

## 7  *Poor you!*

*You* can be modified by adjectives in a few informal expressions such as *Poor/Clever/Lucky (old) you!* (This occasionally happens also with *me*.)   ▶

## 8  *you*: different singular and plural forms

Although standard modern English uses *you* for both singular and plural, separate forms exist in certain varieties of English. Some speakers in Yorkshire use *thu* or *tha* as a singular subject form and *thee* as a singular object form. Some Irish and Scottish dialects have a separate plural form *ye*, *youse* or *yiz*. Many Americans (and increasingly, British people) use *you folks* or *you guys* (to both men and women) as an informal second-person plural.

*Hi, **you guys**. Listen to this.*

In southern US speech there is a second-person plural form *you all* (pronounced *y'all*), used instead of *you* when people wish to sound friendly or intimate; there is also a possessive *you all's* (pronounced *y'all's*).

*Hi, everybody. How're **you all** doing? What are **you all's** plans for Thanksgiving?*

For the older English forms *thee* and *thou*, see 392.

## 9  *he/she who . . .*

The structure *he/she who . . .* (meaning 'the person who . . .') is found in older literature.

***He who** hesitates is sometimes lost.*

But this is very unusual in modern English.

***The person who** leaves last should lock the door.* OR ***Whoever** leaves last . . .* (NOT ~~He/She who leaves last~~ . . .)

## 10  politeness

It is considered polite to use names or noun phrases, rather than *he*, *she* or *they*, to refer to people who are present.

***Dad** said I could go out. ~ No, I didn't.* (More polite than *He said I could go out.*)

***This lady** needs an ambulance.*

However, pronouns need to be used to avoid repetition (see 500).

*Dad said **he** didn't mind . . .* (NOT ~~Dad said Dad didn't mind~~ . . .)

It is considered polite to mention oneself last in double subjects or objects.

*Why don't **you and I** go away for the weekend?* (NOT ~~Why don't I and you~~ . . .?)

*The invitation was for **Tracy and me**.* (More polite than *. . . for me and Tracy*.)

## 11  leaving out personal pronouns

Personal pronouns cannot usually be left out (see 428.4).

*She loved the picture because **it** reminded her of home.* (NOT *. . . ~~because reminded her of home.~~*)

However, in informal speech, subject pronouns and/or auxiliary verbs are sometimes left out at the beginning of a sentence. For details of this, see 179.

***Can't** help you, I'm afraid.* (= I can't . . .)

***Seen** Paul?* (= Have you seen Paul?)

We seldom put *it* after *know*. See 313 for details.

*It's getting late. ~ I **know**.* (NOT *I ~~know it~~.*)

After certain verbs (e.g. *believe, think, suppose*), we use *so* rather than *it*. (For details, see 539.)

*Is that the manager?* ~ *I believe so.* (NOT . . . ~~I believe (it).~~)

And personal pronouns can be dropped after prepositions in descriptive structures with *have* and *with*.

*All the trees have got blossom on (them).*

*He was carrying a box with cups in (it).*

Object pronouns are not normally used in infinitive clauses if the object of the infinitive has just been mentioned (see 284.4).

*She's easy to please.* (NOT ~~She's easy to please her.~~)

*The pie looked too nice to eat.* (NOT . . . ~~too nice to eat it.~~)

*The bridge wasn't strong enough to drive over.* (NOT . . . ~~to drive over it.~~)

*This dish takes two hours to prepare.*

# 430 piece- and group-words

## 1 uncountable nouns: pieces

To talk about a limited quantity of something we can use a word for a piece or unit, together with *of*, before an uncountable noun. The most general words of this kind are *piece* and *bit*. *Bit* (informal) suggests a small quantity.

*a piece/bit of cake/bread*

*some pieces/bits of paper/wood*

*a piece/bit of news/information*

Other words are less general, and are used before particular nouns. Some common examples:

*a bar of chocolate/soap*

*a blade of grass*

*a block of ice*

*a drop of water/oil/vinegar*

*a grain of sand/salt/rice/corn/truth*

*an item of information/news/clothing/
furniture*

*a length of material*

*a loaf of bread*

*a lump of sugar/coal*

*a slice of bread/cake/meat*

*a speck of dust*

*a sheet of paper/metal/plastic*

*a stick of dynamite/chalk/celery*

*a strip of cloth/tape/land*

*a suit of clothes/armour*

## 2 not a ... of ...

Some words for small pieces can be used in a negative structure meaning 'no . . . at all'.

*There's not a grain of truth in what he says.*

*There hasn't been a breath of air all day.*

*We haven't got a scrap (of food) to eat.*

*He came downstairs without a stitch of clothing on.*

## 3 pairs

*Pair* is used for many things that normally go in twos, and with plural nouns that refer to some two-part objects (see 524.7).

*a pair of shoes/socks/earrings*

*a pair of glasses/binoculars*

*a pair of trousers/jeans/pyjamas*

*a pair of scissors/pliers*

▶

## 4  plural nouns: collections

Special words are used before certain plural nouns to talk about groups or collections.

*a **bunch** of flowers*    *a **crowd** of people*    *a **flock** of sheep/birds*
*a **herd** of cattle/goats*    *a **pack** of cards* (AmE *a **deck** of cards*)

*Set* is used before many uncountable and plural nouns referring to groups which contain a fixed number of things.

*a **set** of cutlery/napkins/dishes/tyres/sparking plugs/spanners*

For *a bit* as a modifier before adjectives and adverbs, see 107.
For *an amount, a lot, a large number* etc, see 333.
For *sort, type, kind* etc, see 551.

## 431  place: a place to live, etc

In an informal style, *place* can often be followed directly by an infinitive or relative clause, with no preposition or relative word.

*I'm looking for a **place to live**.* (More formal: ... *a place to live in*
or ... *a place in which to live*.)
*There's no **place to sit down**.*
*You remember the **place we had lunch**?* (= ... *the place (that) we had lunch
at?* OR ... *the place where we had lunch?*)

We do not use *a place where* before an infinitive.

*I'm looking for **a place (where) I can** wash my clothes.* (NOT ... *a place where
to wash my clothes.*)

'Go places' (informal) means 'become very successful in life'.

*That boy's going to **go places**, believe me.*

For similar structures with *way, time* and *reason*, see 498.6.

## 432  play and game

### 1  nouns

A *play* is a piece of dramatic literature for the theatre, radio or television.
*'Julius Caesar' is one of Shakespeare's early **plays**.*
A *game* is an activity like, for example, chess, football or bridge.
*Chess is a very slow **game**.* (NOT ... *a very slow play.*)
The uncountable noun *play* can be used to mean 'playing' in general.
*Children learn a great deal through **play**.*

### 2  verbs

People *act* in plays or films, and *play* games or musical instruments.
*My daughter is **acting** in her school play this year.*
*Have you ever **played** rugby football?*
*Play* can be used with the same meaning as *act* before the name of a character in a play or film.
*I'll never forget seeing Olivier **play** Othello.*

# 433 please and thank you

## 1 requests

We use *please* to make requests more polite.
*Could I have some more rice, **please?***
*Would you like some help? ~ Yes, **please**.*
Note that *please* does not change an order into a request. Compare:
*Stand over there.* (order)
***Please** stand over there.* (more polite order)
*Could you stand over there, **please?*** (polite request)
*Please do* is a rather formal answer to a request for permission.
*Do you mind if I open the window? ~ **Please do**.*

## 2 when *please* is not used

We do not use *please* to ask people what they have said.
*I've got a bit of a headache. ~ **I beg your pardon?***
(NOT ... *Please?*)
We do not use *please* when we give things to people.
*Have you got a pen I could use? ~ Yes, **here you are**.*
(NOT ... *Please.*)
*Please* is not used as an answer to *Thank you* (see below).
*Thanks a lot. ~ **That's OK**. (NOT ... *Please.*)*

## 3 *thank you* and *thanks*

*Thanks* is more informal than *thank you*. Common expressions:
*Thank you.* (NOT *Thanks you.*)
*Thank you very much.*
*Thanks very much.*
*Thanks a lot.* (BUT NOT *Thank you a lot.*)
*Thank God it's Friday.* (NOT *Thanks God ...*)
*Indeed* (see 273) can be used to strengthen *very much*.
*Thank you very much **indeed**.* (BUT NOT USUALLY *Thank you indeed.*)
*Thank you for / Thanks for* can be followed by an *-ing* form. Possessives are unnecessary and are not used.
*Thank you for **coming**. ~ Not at all. Thank you for **having** me.* (NOT *Thank you for your coming.*)
Some people say *Cheers* to mean *Thanks*.

## 4 accepting and refusing

We often use *Thank you / Thanks* like *Yes, please*, to accept offers.
*Would you like some potatoes? ~ **Thank you**. ~ How many?*
To make it clear that one wishes to refuse something, it is normal to say
*No, thank you / No, thanks.*
*Another cake? ~ **No, thanks**. I've eaten too many already.*
*Yes, thanks* is most often used to confirm that things are all right.
*Have you got enough potatoes? ~ **Yes, thanks**.*

▶

## 5   replies to thanks

In English, there is not an automatic answer to *Thank you*; British people, especially, do not usually answer when they are thanked for small things. If a reply is necessary, we can say *Not at all* (rather formal), *You're welcome, That's (quite) all right* or *That's OK* (informal). Some people say *No problem* (informal). Compare:

> *Could you pass the salt?* ~ *Here you are.* ~ *Thanks.* ~ (no answer)
> *Here's your coat.* ~ *Thanks.* ~ (no answer)
> *Thanks so much for looking after the children.* ~ **That's all right. Any time.**
>   (answer necessary)

For more about the language of common social situations, see 545.

## 434   point of view

*Point of view* can mean the same as *opinion*.
> *Thank you for giving us your **point of view** / **opinion**.*

But *from somebody's point of view* is not quite the same *as in somebody's view/ opinion*. It usually means 'as seen from somebody's position in life' (for example as a student, a woman, a Greek or a Catholic), and is used to say how somebody is affected by what happens. Compare:

– *In my opinion, war is always wrong.* (= I think war ...)
>   (NOT *From my point of view, war is always wrong.*)
> *He wrote about the war from the point of view of the ordinary soldier.*
– *In my view, it's a pretty good school.*
> *You have to judge a school from the child's point of view.*
– *In Professor Lucas's opinion, everybody should work a 20-hour week.*
> *From the employers' point of view, this would cause a lot of problems.*

## 435   politeness (1): using questions

### 1   requests: *Could you ...?*

We usually ask people to do things for us by making *yes/no* questions. (This suggests that the hearer can choose whether to agree or not.)

> *Could you tell me the time, please?* (much more polite than *Please tell me the time.*)

Some other typical structures used in requests:

> *Could you possibly tell me the way to the station?* (very polite)
> *Would you mind switching on the TV?*
> *Would you like to help me for a few minutes?*
> *You couldn't lend me some money, could you?* (informal)

Indirect *yes/no* questions are also used in polite requests.

> *I wonder if you could (possibly) help me for a few minutes.*

### 2   other structures: telling people to do things

If we use other structures (for example imperatives, *should, had better*), we are not asking people to do things, but telling or advising them to do things. These structures can therefore seem rude if we use them in requests, especially in conversation with strangers or people we do not know well. *Please* makes an order or instruction a little more polite, but does not turn it into a request. The following structures can be used perfectly correctly to give orders, instructions or advice, but they are not polite ways of requesting people to do things.

*Please answer by return of post.*    *You ought to tell me your plans.*
*Please help me for a few minutes.*    *You should shut the door.*
*Help me, would you?*    *You had better help me.*
*Carry this for me, please.*

## 3  shops, restaurants etc

Requests in shops, restaurants etc are usually more direct, and are not always expressed as questions. Typical structures:

**Can I have** *one of those, please?*    *I'd like to see the wine list, please.*
**Could I have** *a look at the red ones?*    *I would prefer a small one.*

*Give me ..., please* and *I want ..., please* are not normally considered polite. But in places where only a few kinds of thing are sold and not much needs to be said, it is enough just to say what is wanted and add *please*.

*'The Times', please.*    *Two cheeseburgers, please.*
*Black coffee, please.*    *Return to Lancaster, please.*

## 4  negative questions

Negative questions (see 368) are not used in polite requests.

*Could you give me a light?* (NOT ~~Couldn't you give me a light?~~ – this sounds like a complaint.)

But negative statements with question tags are used in informal requests.

*You couldn't give me a light, **could you?***
*I don't suppose you could give me a light, **could you?*** (very polite)

## 5  expressions of opinion

Expressions of opinion can also be made less direct by turning them into questions. Compare:

*It would be better to paint it green.* (direct expression of opinion)
*Wouldn't it be better to paint it green?* (less direct: negative question asking for agreement)
*Would it be better to paint it green?* (open question – very indirect)

For other rules of 'social language', see 545.

# 436  politeness (2): distancing verb forms

## 1  past tenses: *How much did you want to spend?*

We can make requests (and also questions, suggestions and statements) less direct (and so more polite) by using verb forms that suggest 'distance' from the immediate present reality. Past tenses are often used to do this.

*How much **did** you **want** to spend, sir?* (meaning 'How much do you want to spend?')
*How many days **did** you **intend** to stay?* (meaning '... do you intend ...')
*I **wondered** if you **were** free this evening.*

▶

## 2 progressives: *I'm hoping ...*

Progressive forms can be used in the same way. They sound more casual and less definite than simple forms, because they suggest something temporary and incomplete.

*I'm **hoping** you can lend me £10.* (less definite than *I hope ...*)

*What time **are** you **planning** to arrive?* (more casual-sounding than *Please let us know what time you plan to arrive.*)

*I'm **looking forward** to seeing you again.* (more casual than *I look forward ...*)

*I'm afraid we must **be going**.*

Past progressives give two levels of distancing.

*Good morning. I **was wondering**: have you got two single rooms?*

***Were** you **looking** for anything special?* (in a shop)

*I **was thinking** – what about borrowing Jake's car?*

## 3 future: *You'll need to ...*

Another way to distance something is to displace it into the future. *Will need/ have to* can be used to soften instructions and orders.

*I'm afraid you**'ll need** to fill in this form.*

*I**'ll have to** ask you to wait a minute.*

And *will* is sometimes used to say how much money is owed.

*That **will be** £1.65, please.*

Future progressive verbs are often used to enquire politely about people's plans (see 220).

***Will** you **be going** away at the weekend?*

## 4 modal verbs: *would, could* and *might*

The modal verbs *would, could* and *might* also make questions, requests and suggestions less direct.

*I thought it **would** be nice to have a picnic.*

*Hi! I thought I**'d** come over and introduce myself. My name's Andy.*

***Could** you give me a hand?*

***Could** I ask you to translate this for me?*

*We **could** ask Peter to help us.*

*I was wondering if you **might** be interested in a game of tennis.*

*I came in and ordered some shoes from you. ~ Oh yes, sir. When **would** that have been, exactly?*

*Would* is very often used to form requests and offers with verbs like *like* and *prefer*.

*What **would** you **like** to drink?*

Note the common use of *would* before verbs of saying and thinking, to make a statement sound less definite.

*I **would say** we'd do better to catch the earlier train.*

*This is what I **would call** annoying.*

*I **would think** we might stop for lunch soon.*

*I'm surprised you didn't like the film. I **would have thought** it was just your kind of thing.*

*We **would ask** passengers to have their tickets ready for inspection.*

### 5   conditional and negative expressions

Another way of distancing suggestions from reality is to make them conditional or negative.

>*It would be better **if** we turned it the other way up.*
>*What **if** we stayed at home for a change?*
>***Suppose** I gave Alice a call?*
>***If** you would come this way ...*
>*I wonder **if** you could lend me £5?*
>*I **don't suppose** you want to buy a car, do you?*
>*You **wouldn't like** to come out with us, by any chance?*
>*You **couldn't take** the children to school, could you?* (BUT NOT ~~Couldn't you take the children to school?~~ This sounds like a complaint – see 435.4.)

# 437   politeness (3): softening expressions

### 1   *quite, maybe, I think* etc

We can express our opinions and intentions less directly (and therefore more politely) by using softening expressions like *quite, rather, kind of, a bit, maybe* etc.

>*He's **quite** difficult to understand, isn't he?*
>*I find her **rather** bossy, don't you?*  ·  *The food's **a bit** expensive.*
>*This music's **kind of** boring.*  ·  ***Maybe** I'll go for a walk now.*

For more examples, see 157.16.

### 2   *I think I'll ...*

We can say that we are thinking of doing things, instead of expressing our intentions directly.

>*I **think** I'll go to bed in a few minutes.*
>*I'm **thinking** of going to London tomorrow.*
>*I'd quite like to start **thinking** about going home.*

### 3   *We would like to ...*

In a formal style, requests, invitations, suggestions etc are often introduced by *would like* instead of being expressed directly.

>*We **would like** to invite you to give a talk to our members on June 14th.*
>*I'd **like** to suggest that we take a vote.*
>*I **would like** to congratulate you on your examination results.*

# 438   politics and policy

*Politics* (usually singular but always with *-s* – see 524.3) is used to talk about government and related ideas.

>*I don't know much about **politics**, but I don't think this is a democracy.*
>*You talk beautifully – you should be in **politics**.*  ▶

*Policy* is used for people's rules of behaviour (not necessarily connected with politics).

> *After the war, British foreign* **policy** *was rather confused.* (NOT . . .~~British foreign politics~~ . . .)
> *It's not my* **policy** *to believe everything I hear.*
> *It's the firm's* **policy** *to employ a certain number of handicapped people.*

## 439 possessives (1): noun + 's (forms)

### 1 spelling

> singular noun + *'s*    *my* **father's** *car*
> plural noun + *'*     *my* **parents'** *house*
> irregular plural + *'s*  *the* **children's** *room,* **men's** *clothes,* **women's** *rights,*
>               *an old* **people's** *home*

We sometimes just add an apostrophe (') to a singular noun ending in -*s*, especially in literary and classical references.

> *Socrates' ideas.*     *Dickens' novels*

But *'s* is more common.

> *Mr Lewis's dog*

We can add *'s* or *'* to a whole phrase.

> *the man next door's wife*
> *Henry the Eighth's six wives*
> *the Smiths' new house*

Note the difference between, for example:

> *Joe and Ann's children* (one lot of children: Joe and Ann are their parents)
> *Joe's and Ann's children* (two separate lots of children: Joe's and Ann's)

### 2 pronunciation

The ending *'s* is pronounced just like a plural ending (see 525).

> *doctor's* /'dɒktəz/      *Madge's* /'mædʒɪz/
> *dog's* /dɒgz/        *Alice's* /'ælɪsɪz/
> *president's* /'prezɪdənts/   *James's* /'dʒeɪmzɪz/    *Jack's* /dʒæks/

The apostrophe in a word like *parents'* does not change the pronunciation at all. But with singular classical (ancient Greek and Roman) names ending in *s'*, we often pronounce a possessive *'s* even when it is not written.

> *Socrates'* /'sɒkrəti:zɪz / *ideas.*

### 3 possessive 's and other determiners

A noun cannot normally have an article or other determiner with it as well as a possessive word (see 154). Definite articles are usually dropped when possessives are used.

> *the car that is John's* = *John's car* (NOT ~~the John's car~~ OR ~~John's the car~~)

But a possessive word may of course have its own article.

> *the car that is* **the boss's** = *the boss's car*

When we want to use a noun with *a/an* or *this/that* etc as well as a possessive, we usually use the '*of mine*' construction (see 443).

> *She's* **a cousin of John's**. (NOT . . .~~a John's cousin.~~)
> *I saw that stupid* **boyfriend of Angie's** *yesterday.* (NOT . . .~~that Angie's stupid boyfriend~~ . . .)

### 4  possessive without a noun

We can use a possessive without a following noun, if the meaning is clear.
>*Whose is that? ~ **Peter's**.*

We often talk about shops, firms, churches and people's houses in this way.
The apostrophe is often dropped in the names of shops and firms.
>*I bought it at **Smiths**.     She got married at **St Joseph's**.*
>*We had a nice time at **John and Susan's** last night.*

In modern English, expressions like *the doctor, the dentist, the hairdresser, the butcher* are often used without *'s*.
>*Alice is at **the hairdresser('s)**.*

# 440  possessives (2): noun + 's (use)

### 1  meanings of the *'s* structure

We use the *'s* structure most often to talk about possessions, relationships and physical characteristics, especially when the first noun refers to a person or animal, or to a country, organisation or other group of living creatures.
>*That's my **father's** house.* (NOT *. . . the house of my father*)
>***Mary's** brother is a lawyer.* (NOT *The brother of Mary . . .*)
>*I don't like **Alice's** friends much.        **Pete's** eyes are like yours.*
>*There's something wrong with the **cat's** ear.*
>***Scotland's** climate is getting warmer.*
>*What do you think of the **company's** management?*

We also use the structure to talk about things that people etc produce.
>*I didn't believe the **girl's** story.        Have you read **John's** letter?*
>*What are **Norway's** main exports?*
>*The **government's** decision was extremely unwise.*

With some words for people's actions, we can use either *'s* or a structure with *of*.
>*the **Queen's** arrival* OR *the arrival **of the Queen***
>*the **committee's** second meeting* OR *the second meeting **of the committee***

An *of*-structure is preferred when the 'possessing' expression is very long. Compare:
>*My **sister's** husband.*
>*The husband **of the woman who sent you that strange letter**.*

### 2  *'s* not used: *the name of the street*

With nouns which are not the names of people, animals, countries etc, *'s* is less common, and a structure with a preposition (usually *of*) is more normal.
>*the name **of the street** (NOT the street's name)*
>*the back **of the room** (NOT the room's back)*
>*the roof **of the house** (NOT the house's roof)*
>*the top **of the page** (NOT the page's top)*

▶

However, both structures are possible in some expressions.

*the **earth's** gravity* OR *the gravity **of the earth***
*the **plan's** importance* OR *the importance **of the plan***
*the **concerto's** final movement* OR *the final movement **of the concerto***
*the **train's** arrival* OR *the arrival **of the train***
*the **world's** oldest mountains* OR *the oldest mountains **in the world***
   (NOT... ~~of the world~~) – see 139.7

Unfortunately, it is not possible to give useful general rules in this area: the choice of structure often depends on the particular expression.

### 3 subject

Note that the *'s* structure often corresponds to a sentence in which the first noun is the subject of *have* or some other verb.

*Joe's brother* (Joe **has** a brother)
*the **dog's** tail* (the dog **has** a tail)
*America's gold reserves* (America **has** gold reserves)
*the **manager's** decision* (the manager **made** a decision)
*Harris's novel* (Harris **wrote** a novel)

In a few cases, the first noun may correspond to the object of a verb.

*the **prisoner's** release* (they **released the prisoner**)

### 4 measurement of time: *a day's journey*

The *'s* structure (or the plural with *s'*) is often used to say how long things last.

*a **day's** journey*    *twenty minutes' delay*

**Noun + noun** structures are also possible in expressions with numbers (see 386.5).

*a **three-hour** journey*    *a **twenty-minute** delay*

### 5 other expressions of time: *yesterday's news*

We can also use the *'s* structure to talk about particular moments and events.

*yesterday's news*    *last Sunday's match*    *tomorrow's weather*

### 6 *worth*

Note the use of the *'s* structure before *worth*.

*a **pound's** worth of walnuts*    *three dollars' worth of popcorn*

For the *'s* structure in compound nouns (e.g. *a doll's house, cow's milk*), see 386.

## 441 possessives (3): my, your etc

### 1 What kind of words are they?

*My, your, his, her, its, our* and *their* are determiners (see 154), and are used at the beginning of noun phrases.

*my younger brother*    *your phone number*    *their plans*

They are also pronouns, because they stand for possessive noun phrases: *my younger brother* means 'the speaker's younger brother'; *their plans* means, for example, 'those people's plans' or 'the children's plans'.

They are not adjectives (although they are sometimes called 'possessive adjectives' in older grammars and dictionaries).

## 2   one's and whose

One's (see 396.5) and *whose* (see 496; 626) are also possessive determiners/
pronouns.
>*It's easy to lose **one's** temper when one is criticised.*
>*An orphan is a child **whose** parents are dead.*
>***Whose** bicycle is that?*

## 3   not used with other determiners

*My, your* etc are not used with other determiners like *the, a/an* or *this*.
>*She's lost **her** keys.* (NOT . . . ~~the her keys.~~)

If we want to use *a/an* or *this, that* etc with a possessive, we use the '. . . *of
mine*' structure (see 443).
>*A **friend of mine** has just invited me to Italy.* (NOT ~~A my friend~~ . . .)
>*How's **that brother of yours**?* (NOT . . . ~~that your brother?~~)

## 4   distributive use: *She told them to open their books,* etc

After a plural possessive, we do not normally use a singular noun in the sense
of 'one each'. (For details, see 530.)
>*The teacher told the children to open **their books**.* (NOT . . . ~~their book.~~)

## 5   articles instead of possessives

We sometimes use articles instead of *my, your* etc. This happens in
prepositional phrases which refer to the subject or object, mostly when we are
talking about blows, pains and other things that often happen to parts of
people's bodies.
>*The ball hit him **on the head**.*
>*She's got a pain **in the stomach**.*

In other cases we do not normally use articles instead of possessives.
>*She's got a parrot **on her shoulder**.* (NOT ~~She's got a parrot on the shoulder.~~)
>*Katy broke **her arm** mountain climbing.* (NOT ~~Katy broke the arm~~ . . .)
>*He stood there, **his eyes** closed and **his hands** in **his pockets**, looking half
>     asleep.* (NOT . . . ~~the eyes closed and the hands in the pockets~~ . . .)

## 6   spelling: *its, whose*

The possessives *its* and *whose* have no apostrophes. *It's* and *who's* are not
possessives, but contractions (see 143): they mean 'it is' or 'it has'; 'who is' or
'who has'. Compare:
>*The dog's in a good mood. **It's** just had **its** breakfast.*
>***Whose** little girl is that?* ~ *You mean the one **who's** making all that noise?*

For structures like *Do you mind my smoking?*, see 295.3.
For *my own, your own* etc, see 405.
For the older English form *thy*, see 392.
For southern AmE *you all's*, see 429.8.

# 442   possessives (4): mine, yours etc

*Mine, yours, his, hers, ours* and *theirs* are similar to *my, your* etc, but they are
not determiners, and are used without following nouns.                       ▶

Compare:
>  *That's* **my coat.**      *That coat is* **mine.**
>  *Which is* **your car?**      *Which car is* **yours?**

*Whose* can be used with a following noun (see 441) or without.
>  **Whose car** *is that?*      **Whose** *is that car?*

We do not use articles with *mine* etc.
>  *Can I borrow your keys? I can't find* **mine.** (NOT ~~I can't find the mine.~~)

*One's* cannot be used without a following noun; instead, we use *one's own.*
>  *It's nice to have a room of* **one's own.** (NOT ... ~~of one's.~~)

*Its* is not normally used without a following noun.
>  *I've had my breakfast, and the dog's had* **its breakfast** *too.* (NOT ... ~~and the dog's had its.~~)

For the older English form *thine*, see 392.

## 443 possessives (5): a friend of mine etc

We cannot usually put a possessive between another determiner and a noun.
We can say *my friend, Ann's friend, a friend* or *that friend*, but not ~~a my friend~~
or ~~that Ann's friend~~. Instead, we use a structure with *of* + **possessive**.

> determiner + noun + *of* + possessive

>  *That policeman is* **a friend of mine.**      *He's* **a cousin of the Queen's.**
>  *How's* **that brother of yours?**      *She's* **a friend of my father's.**
>  *I met* **another boyfriend of Lucy's** *yesterday.*
>  *Have you heard* **this new idea of the boss's?**
>  *He watched* **each gesture of hers** *as if she was a stranger.*
>  *My work is* **no business of yours.**

The structure has a variant in which a noun does not have possessive *'s*: this is
sometimes used when talking about relationships.
>  *He's* **a cousin of the Queen.**      *She's* **a friend of my father.**

The word *own* is used in a similar structure (see 405).
>  *I wish I had* **a room of my own.**

## 444 prefer

When we say that we prefer one activity to another, two *-ing* forms can be
used. The second can be introduced by *to* or *rather than* (more formal).
>  *I prefer* **riding to walking.** (NOT ~~I prefer riding to walk.~~)
>  *She prefers* **making** *toys for her children* **rather than buying** *them.*

*Prefer* can also be followed by an infinitive (this is normal after *would prefer*).
We can use an infinitive (without *to*) or an *-ing* form after *rather than* in this
case.
>  *She* **prefers to make** *toys for her children* **rather than buy/buying** *them.*
>  *I* **would prefer to stay** *at home* **rather than drive/driving** *to your mother's.*

For more about *to* with *-ing* forms, see 298.2.

# 445 prefixes and suffixes

The following are some of the most common and useful English prefixes and suffixes.

## 1 prefixes

| prefix | mainly added to | usual meaning | examples |
|---|---|---|---|
| a- | adj. | not, without | *amoral, asexual* |
| Anglo- | adj. | English | *Anglo-American* |
| ante- | adj., verbs, nouns | before | *antenatal, antedate anteroom* |
| anti- | adj., nouns | against | *antisocial, anti-war* |
| arch- | nouns | supreme, most | *archbishop, arch-enemy* |
| auto- | adj., nouns | self | *automatic, autobiography* |
| bi- | adj., nouns | two | *bilingual, bicycle* |
| cent(i)- | nouns | hundredth | *centimetre, centilitre* |
| co- | verbs, nouns | together (with) | *co-operate, co-pilot* |
| counter- | adj., verbs, nouns | against | *counteract counter-revolution(ary)* |
| cyber- | nouns | computer, internet | *cybercrime, cyberculture* |
| de- | verbs | reversing action | *defrost, deregulate* |
| | verbs | take away | *deforest* |
| dis- | adj., verbs, nouns | not, opposite | *disloyal, disappear disorder* |
| | verbs | reversing action | *disconnect, disinfect* |
| e- | nouns | electronic, internet | *email, e-commerce, e-book* |
| eco- | adj., nouns | environment | *eco-friendly, eco-tourism* |
| en- | nouns | put in | *endanger, encircle* |
| | adj. | make | *enrich, enable* |
| Euro- | adj., nouns | European | *Eurocentric, Europop* |
| ex- | nouns | former | *ex-husband* |
| extra- | adj. | exceptionally | *extra-special* |
| | adj. | outside | *extra-terrestrial* |
| fore- | verbs, nouns | before | *foretell, foreknowledge* |
| geo- | adj., nouns | earth | *geothermal, geophysics* |
| hyper- | adj., nouns | extreme(ly) | *hypercritical, hypertension* |
| ill- | past participles | badly | *ill-advised, ill-expressed* |
| in- (im- before p) (il- before l) (ir- before r) | adj. | not, opposite | *incomplete, insensitive impossible illegible irregular* |
| inter- | adj., verbs | between, among | *international, intermarry* ▶ |

| prefix | mainly added to | usual meaning | examples |
|--------|-----------------|---------------|----------|
| kilo- | nouns | thousand | *kilometre, kilogram* |
| mal- | adj., verbs, nouns | bad(ly) | *maltreat, malformed malfunction* |
| mega- | nouns | million | *megabyte* |
| | adj. (informal) | extremely | *mega-rich* |
| micro- | adj., nouns | very small | *microlight (aircraft), micrometer* |
| mid- | nouns | in the middle of | *mid-December, mid-afternoon* |
| milli- | nouns | thousandth | *millisecond* |
| mini- | nouns | little | *miniskirt, minicab* |
| mis- | verbs, nouns | wrong(ly) | *misunderstand, misconduct* |
| mono- | adj., nouns | one | *monogamous, monorail* |
| multi- | adj., nouns | many | *multilingual, multi-purpose* |
| neo- | adj., nouns | new(ly) | *neo-classical, neo-Nazi* |
| non- | nouns, adj. | not | *non-smoker, non-returnable* |
| omni- | adj. | all | *omnipresent* |
| out- | verbs, nouns | do/be more than | *outrun, outnumber* (vb.) |
| over- | adj., verbs | too much | *over-confident, overeat* |
| pan- | adj. | right across | *pan-American* |
| photo- | adj., nouns | light | *photoelectric, photosynthesis* |
| poly- | adj., nouns | many | *polyglot, polygon* |
| post- | adj., nouns | after | *post-modern, postwar* |
| pre- | adj., nouns | before | *premarital, prewar* |
| pro- | adj., nouns | for, in favour of | *pro-communist, pro-government* (adj.) |
| pseudo- | adj. | false | *pseudo-academic* |
| psycho- | adj., nouns | mind, mental | *psycho-analysis* |
| re- | verbs, nouns | again, back | *rebuild, reconstruction* |
| semi- | adj., nouns | half | *semi-conscious, semicircle* |
| socio- | adj., nouns | society | *socio-economic* |
| sub- | adj., nouns | below | *sub-standard, subconscious, subway* |
| super- | adj. nouns | more than, special | *supernatural, supermarket* |
| tele- | nouns | distant | *telescope* |
| thermo- | adj., nouns | heat | *thermo-electric, thermometer* |
| trans- | adj., verbs | across | *transatlantic, transplant* |
| tri- | adj., nouns | three | *tripartite, triangle* |

| prefix | mainly added to | usual meaning | examples |
|--------|-----------------|---------------|----------|
| ultra- | adj., nouns | extreme, beyond | *ultra-modern, ultrasound* |
| un- | adj., participles verbs | not, opposite reverse action | *uncertain, unexpected untie, undress* |
| under- | verbs, participles | too little | *underestimate, under-developed* |
| uni- | adj., nouns | one | *unilateral, unicycle* |
| vice- | nouns | deputy | *vice-chairman* |

## 2 suffixes that form nouns

| suffix | mainly added to | usual meaning | examples |
|--------|-----------------|---------------|----------|
| -age | verbs | instance of | *breakage, shrinkage* |
| -al | verbs | instance of | *refusal, dismissal* |
| -ance, -ancy | adj., verbs | process/state of | *reluctance, performance, expectancy* |
| -ation | verbs | process/state of | *exploration, starvation* |
| | verbs | product of | *organisation, foundation* |
| -ee | verbs | object of verb | *payee, employee* |
| -ence, -ency | adj., verbs | process/state of | *independence, presidency* |
| -er | nouns | belonging to | *teenager, Londoner* |
| -er/or | verbs | person/thing that does | *writer, driver, starter, editor* |
| -ess | nouns | female | *lioness, waitress* |
| -ette | nouns | small | *kitchenette* |
| -ful | nouns | amount held in | *spoonful, cupful* |
| -hood | nouns | quality, group, time of | *brotherhood, childhood* |
| -ing | nouns | quantity of material | *carpeting, tubing* |
| | nouns | activity | *farming, surfing* |
| -ism | nouns | belief, practice | *communism, impressionism* |
| -ity | adj. | quality of | *elasticity, falsity* |
| -ment | verbs | process/result of | *government, arrangement* |
| -ness | adj. | quality of | *meanness, happiness* |
| -ocracy | nouns | government by | *democracy* |
| -ology | nouns | study of | *sociology* |
| -phile | nouns | lover of | *Anglophile* |
| -phobe | nouns | hater, fearer of | *Anglophobe* |
| -phobia | nouns | irrational fear of | *arachnophobia* (fear of spiders) |
| -ship | nouns | status, state, quality of | *friendship, dictatorship* |

▶

## 3   suffixes that form nouns or adjectives

| suffix | mainly added to | usual meaning | examples |
|--------|-----------------|---------------|----------|
| -ese | place nouns | inhabitant of, language of | *Chinese, Vietnamese* |
| -(i)an | nouns | supporter of, related to | *Darwinian, republican* |
|  | nouns | citizen of | *Parisian, Moroccan* |
| -ist | nouns | practitioner of | *pianist, racist* |

## 4   suffixes that form adjectives

| suffix | mainly added to | usual meaning | examples |
|--------|-----------------|---------------|----------|
| -able | verbs | can be (done) | *washable, drinkable* |
| -al | nouns | related to | *accidental* |
| -centric | nouns | centred on | *Eurocentric* |
| -ed | nouns | having | *wooded, pointed, blue-eyed* |
| -ful | nouns | full of, providing | *useful, helpful* |
| -ic | nouns | related to | *electric* |
| -ical | nouns | related to | *philosophical, logical* |
| -ish | adj., nouns | rather (like) | *greenish, childish* |
|  | place nouns | inhabitant of, language of | *Scottish, Turkish* |
| -ive | verbs | can do, does | *attractive, selective* |
| -less | nouns | without | *careless, homeless* |
| -like | nouns | like | *childlike* |
| -ly | nouns | with the quality of | *friendly, motherly* |
| -ous | nouns | having | *virtuous, ambitious* |
| -proof | nouns | protected/-ing against | *bullet-proof, waterproof* |
| -ward | adj. | towards | *backward, northward* |
| -y | nouns | like, characterised by | *creamy, wealthy* |

## 5   suffixes that form adverbs

| suffix | mainly added to | usual meaning | examples |
|--------|-----------------|---------------|----------|
| -ly | adj. | in an (adjective) way | *calmly, slowly* |
| -ward(s) | adj. | towards | *backwards, northward(s)* |

## 6   suffixes that form verbs

| suffix | mainly added to | usual meaning | examples |
|--------|-----------------|---------------|----------|
| -ate | nouns | causative | *orchestrate, chlorinate* |
| -en | adj. | make, become | *deafen, ripen, harden* |
| -ify | adj., nouns | causative: make | *simplify, electrify* |
| -ise/-ize | adj., nouns | various | *modernise, symbolise* |

## 7 Note: negative words with no positive equivalent

Some words with negative prefixes have no positive opposite equivalent: for example, somebody can be *distressed,* but not ~~tressed~~. Other examples:
*dishevelled, disappoint, discard, disclose, disconcert, disfigure, dismiss, dispose, incessant, indelible, uncanny, uncouth, ungainly, unkempt, unnerved, unspeakable, unwieldy, unwitting*

For hyphens after *co-, ex-* etc, see 559.2d.

# 446 preparatory it (1): subject

## 1 *It's nice to talk to you*

When the subject of a clause is an infinitive expression, this does not normally come at the beginning. We usually prefer to start with the 'preparatory subject' *it,* and to put the infinitive expression later (long or complicated items are often put towards the end of a sentence – see 512). Preparatory *it* is common before *be* + **adjective/noun.**

> *It's nice **to talk** to you.* (More natural than *To talk to you is nice.*)
> *It was good of you **to phone.***
> *It was stupid of you **to leave** the door unlocked.*
> *It's important **to book** in advance.*
> *It's my ambition **to run** a three-hour marathon.*
> *It was a pleasure **to listen** to her.*
> *It upsets me **to hear** people arguing all the time.*

*It* can also be a preparatory subject for *for* + **object** + **infinitive** (see 291).

> *It will suit me best **for you to arrive** at about ten o'clock.*
> *It's essential **for the papers to be** ready before Thursday.*

## 2 *It's probable that we'll be late*

We also use preparatory *it* when the subject of a clause is itself a clause.

> *It's probable **that we'll be a little late.***
> *It doesn't interest me **what you think.***
> *It's surprising **how many unhappy marriages there are.***
> *It's exciting **when a baby starts talking.***

## 3 *It was nice seeing you*

*It* can be a preparatory subject for an *-ing* form. This is usually informal.

> *It was nice **seeing** you.*      *It's crazy her **going** off like that.*
> *It's worth **going** to Wales if you have the time.*
> *It's no use **trying** to explain – I'm not interested.*
> *It surprised me your not **remembering** my name.*

For more information about structures with *worth,* see 632.
For *there* as a preparatory subject with *any/no use,* see 587.2.

## 4 *It takes ... + infinitive*

We can use this structure to say how much time is necessary (see 576).

> *It **took** me months to get to know her.*
> *How long does **it take** to get to London from here?*

▶

### 5   *if, as if* and *as though*

*It* is used to introduce some clauses with *if*, *as if* and *as though*.
> *It looks **as if** we're going to have trouble with Ann again.*
> ***It's** not **as if** this was the first time she's been difficult.*
> *It will be a pity **if** we have to ask her to leave.*
> *But **it** looks **as though** we may have to.*

### 6   *It was my aunt who took Peter to London*

*It* can be used in 'cleft sentences' (see 131) with *who-* and *that-*clauses to emphasise one part of a sentence.
> ***It was my aunt** who took Peter to London yesterday, not my mother.*
> (emphasising *my aunt*)
> ***It was Peter that** my aunt took to London yesterday, not Lucy.*
> (emphasising *Peter*)

### 7   *It's amazing the way they work together*

*It* is not normally used as a preparatory subject for noun phrases.
> *The new concert hall is wonderful.* (NOT ~~It's wonderful the new concert hall.~~)

But in an informal style, *it* can be a preparatory subject for **noun + relative clause**.
> ***It's** wonderful **the enthusiasm that the children show**.*

This is very common with *the way . . .*
> ***It's** amazing **the way (that) they work together**.*
> ***It's** strange **the way you know what I'm thinking**.*

For passive structures with *it* as a preparatory subject, see 417.

## 447   preparatory it (2): object

### 1   *I find it difficult to talk to you.*

We can sometimes use *it* as a preparatory object. This happens when the object of a verb is an infinitive expression or a clause, and when this has an adjective or noun complement. For example, instead of saying 'I find **to talk to you difficult**', we prefer 'I find **it** difficult **to talk to you**'.

> subject + verb + *it* + complement + infinitive/clause

> *We found **it** tiring **to listen** to him.*
> *My blister made **it** a problem **to walk**.*
> *I thought **it** strange **that she hadn't written**.*
> *George made **it** clear **what he wanted**.*

Note that this structure is not normally used when there is no adjective or noun complement after the verb.
> *I cannot bear to see people crying.* (NOT ~~I cannot bear it to see people crying.~~)
> *I remember that we were very happy.* (NOT ~~I remember it that . . .~~)

But note the structure *I like/love/hate it when . . .*
> *I love **it** when you sing.*

Note also the idiom *I take it that . . .* (= I assume that . . .).
> *I take **it that** you won't be working tomorrow.*

## 2 *I found it strange being ...*

This structure is also possible with *-ing* form objects.
*I found it strange **being** in her house.*

## 3 *I would appreciate it if ...*

*It* is used as a preparatory object for an *if*-clause after *would appreciate*.
*I **would appreciate it if** you would keep me informed.* (NOT ~~I would~~ ~~appreciate if you would~~...)

## 4 owe and *leave*

Note the structures *owe it to somebody to ...* and *leave it to somebody to ...*
*We **owe it to society to** make our country a better place.*
*I'll **leave it to you to** decide.*

# 448 prepositions (1): introduction

## 1 meanings and use

It is difficult to learn to use prepositions correctly in a foreign language. Most English prepositions have several different functions (for instance, one well-known dictionary lists eighteen main uses of *at*), and these may correspond to several different prepositions in another language. At the same time, different prepositions can have very similar uses (*in the morning, on Monday morning, at night*). Many nouns, verbs and adjectives are normally used with particular prepositions: we say *the reason for, arrive at, angry with somebody, on a bus.* Often the correct preposition cannot be guessed, and one has to learn the expression as a whole. In some expressions English has no preposition where one may be used in another language; in other expressions the opposite is true. For details of some difficult cases of prepositional usage, see 449–454.

## 2 word order

In English, prepositions can come at the ends of clauses in certain structures, especially in an informal style. For details, see 452.

| | |
|---|---|
| *What are you thinking **about**?* | *She's not very easy to talk **to**.* |
| *You're just the person I was looking **for**.* | *I hate being shouted **at**.* |

## 3 *-ing* forms

When we use verbs after prepositions, we use *-ing* forms, not infinitives. For details, see 298, 454.
*She saved money **by giving** up cigarettes.*
When *to* is a preposition, it is also followed by *-ing* forms. (see 298.2).
*I look forward **to seeing** you soon.*

## 4 prepositions before conjunctions

Prepositions are sometimes dropped before conjunctions and sometimes not. For details, see 453.
*I'm not certain **(of) what** I'm supposed to do.*
*The question **(of) whether** they should turn back was never discussed.* ▶

## 5 prepositions and adverb particles

Words like *on, off, up, down* can function both as prepositions and as adverb
particles. For the difference, see 20. For verbs with prepositions and particles,
see 599, 600.

> *She ran **up** the stairs.* (preposition)
> *She rang me **up**.* (adverb particle)

# 449 prepositions (2):
# after particular words and expressions

It is not always easy to know which preposition to use after a particular noun,
verb or adjective. Here are some of the most common combinations which
cause difficulty to students of English. Alternatives are sometimes possible,
and American and British usage sometimes differ. There is only room for very
brief notes here; for more complete information about usage with a particular
word, consult a good dictionary.

**accuse** somebody **of** something (NOT ~~for~~)
> *She **accused** me **of** poisoning her dog.*

**afraid of** (NOT ~~by~~)
> *Are you **afraid of** spiders?*

**agree with** a person, opinion or policy
> *He left the firm because he didn't **agree with** their sales policy.*
> *I entirely **agree with** you.*

**agree about** a subject of discussion
> *We **agree about** most things.*

**agree on** a matter for decision
> *Let's try to **agree on** a date.*

**agree to** a suggestion
> *I'll **agree to** your suggestion if you lower the price.*

**angry with** (sometimes **at**) a person **for** doing something
> *I'm **angry with** her **for** lying to me.*

**angry about** (sometimes **at**) something
> *What are you so **angry about**?*

**anxious about** (= worried about)
> *I'm getting **anxious about** money.*

**anxious for** (= eager to have)
> *We're all **anxious for** an end to this misunderstanding.*

**anxious + infinitive** (= eager, wanting)
> *She's **anxious to find** a better job.*

**apologise to** somebody **for** something
> *I think we should **apologise to** the Smiths.*
> *I must **apologise for** disturbing you.*

**arrive at** or **in** (NOT ~~to~~)
> *What time do we **arrive at** Cardiff?*
> *When did you **arrive in** England?*

**ask:** see 79.

**bad at** (NOT ~~in~~)
  *I'm not **bad at** tennis.*
**believe** a person or something that is said (= accept as truthful/true
    – no preposition)
  *Don't **believe** her.      I don't **believe** a word she says.*
**believe in** God, Father Christmas etc (= believe that . . . exists; trust)
  *I half **believe in** life after death.*
  *If you **believe in** me I can do anything.*
**belong in/on/etc** (= go, fit, have its place in/on/etc)
  *Those glasses **belong on** the top shelf.*
**belong to** (= be a member of)
  *I **belong to** a local athletics club.*
**blue with** cold, **red with** anger etc
  *My hands were **blue with cold** when I got home*
**borrow**: see 109.


**care**: see 127.
**clever at** (NOT ~~in~~)
  *I'm not very **clever at** cooking.*
**congratulate/congratulations on** something
  *I must **congratulate** you **on** your exam results.*
  ***Congratulations on** your new job!*
**congratulate/congratulations on/for** doing something
  *He **congratulated** the team **on/for** having won all their games.*
**crash into** (NOT USUALLY ~~against~~)
  *I wasn't concentrating, and I **crashed into** the car in front.*


**depend/dependent on** (NOT ~~from~~ OR ~~of~~)
  *We may play football – it **depends on** the weather.*
  *He doesn't want to be **dependent on** his parents.*
  But: **independent of**
**details of**
  *Write now for **details of** our special offer.*
**die of** or **from**
  *More people **died of** flu in 1919 than were killed in the First World War.*
  *A week after the accident he **died from** his injuries.*
**different**: see 155.
**difficulty with** something, **(in)** doing something (NOT ~~difficulties to . . .~~)
  *I'm having **difficulty with** my travel arrangements.*
  *You won't have much **difficulty (in) getting** to know people in Italy.*
**disappointed with** somebody
  *My father never showed if he was **disappointed with** me.*
**disappointed with/at/about** something
  *You must be pretty **disappointed with/at/about** your exam results.*
[a] **discussion about** something
  *We had a long **discussion about** politics.*
[to] **discuss** something (no preposition)
  *We'd better **discuss** your travel plans.*
**divide into** (NOT ~~in~~)
  *The book is **divided into** three parts.*

▶

**dream of** (= think of, imagine)
*I often **dreamed of** being famous when I was younger.*
**dream about/of** (while asleep)
*What does it mean if you **dream about/of** mountains?*
**dress(ed) in** (NOT ~~with~~)
*Who's the woman **dressed in** green?*
**drive into** (NOT ~~against~~)
*Granny **drove into** a tree again yesterday.*

**enter into** an agreement, a discussion etc
*We've just **entered into** an agreement with Carsons Ltd.*
**enter** a place (no preposition)
*When I **entered** the room everybody stopped talking.*
**example of** (NOT ~~for~~)
*Sherry is an **example of** a fortified wine.*
**explain** something **to** somebody (NOT ~~explain somebody something~~)
*Could you **explain** this rule **to** me?*

**fight, struggle** etc **with**
*I've spent the last two weeks **fighting with** the tax office.*
**frightened of** or **by**: see 410.5.

**get in(to)** and **out of** a car, taxi or small boat
*When I **got into** my car, I found the radio had been stolen.*
**get on(to)** and **off** a train, plane, bus, ship, (motor)bike or horse
*We'll be **getting off** the train in ten minutes.*
**good at** (NOT ~~in~~)
*Are you any **good at** tennis?*

[the] **idea of** . . .ing (NOT ~~the idea to . . .~~)
*I don't like **the idea of getting** married yet.*
**ill with**
*The boss has been **ill with** flu this week.*
**impressed with/by**
*I'm very **impressed with/by** your work.*
**increase in** activity, output etc (NOT ~~of~~)
*I'd like to see a big **increase in** productivity.*
**independent, independence of** or **from**
*She got a job so that she could be **independent of** her parents.*
*When did India get its **independence from** Britain?*
**insist on** (NOT ~~to~~)
*George's father **insisted on** paying.*
**interest/interested in** (NOT ~~for~~)
*When did your **interest in** social work begin?*
*Not many people are **interested in** grammar.*
**interested to do /in doing** something: see 299.16

**kind to** (NOT ~~with~~)
*People have always been very **kind to** me.*

**lack of**
  *Lack of time prevented me from writing.*
**[to] lack** (no preposition)
  *Your mother lacks tact.*
**[to] be lacking in**
  *She is lacking in tact.*
**laugh at**
  *I hate being laughed at.*
**laugh about**
  *We'll laugh about this one day.*
**leave** somewhere (talking about the action of leaving)
  *I left London early, before the traffic got too heavy.*
**leave from** somewhere (talking about the place)
  *Does the plane leave from Liverpool or Manchester?*
**listen to**
  *If you don't listen to people, they won't listen to you.*
**look at** (= point one's eyes at)
  *Stop looking at me like that.*
**look after** (= take care of)
  *Thanks for looking after me when I was ill.*
**look for** (= try to find)
  *Can you help me look for my keys?*

**make, made of/from**: see 336.
**marriage to; get/be married to** (NOT ~~with~~)
  *Her marriage to Philip didn't last very long.*
  *How long have you been married to Sheila?*
**marry** somebody (no preposition)
  *She married her childhood sweetheart.*

**near (to)**: see 365.
**nice to** (NOT ~~with~~)
  *You weren't very nice to me last night.*

**operate on** a patient
*They operated on her yesterday evening.*

**pay for** something that is bought (NOT ~~pay something~~)
  *Excuse me, sir. You haven't paid for your drink.*
**pleased with** somebody
  *The boss is very pleased with you.*
**pleased with/about/at** something
  *I wasn't very pleased with/about/at my exam results.*
**polite to** (NOT ~~with~~)
  *Try to be polite to Uncle Richard for once*
**prevent ... from ...ing** (NOT ~~to~~)
  *The noise from downstairs prevented me from sleeping.*
**proof of** (NOT ~~for~~)
  *I want proof of your love. Lend me some money.*

▶

**reason for** (NOT ~~of~~)
*Nobody knows the **reason for** the accident.*
**remind of** (and see 499)
*She **reminds** me **of** a girl I was at school with.*
**responsible/responsibility for** (NOT ~~of~~)
*Who's **responsible for** the shopping this week?*
**rude to** (NOT ~~with~~)
*Peggy was pretty **rude to** my family last weekend.*
**run into** (= meet)
*I **ran into** Philip at Victoria Station this morning.*

**search** (without preposition) (= look through; look everywhere in/on)
*They **searched** everybody's luggage.*
*They **searched** the man in front of me from head to foot.*
**search for** (= look for)
*The customs were **searching for** drugs at the airport.*
**shocked at/by**
*I was terribly **shocked at/by** the news of Peter's accident.*
**shout at** (aggressive)
*If you don't stop **shouting at** me I'll come and hit you.*
**shout to** (= call to)
*Mary **shouted to** us to come in and swim.*
**smile at**
*If you **smile at** me like that I'll give you anything you want.*
**sorry about** something that has happened
*I'm **sorry about** your exam results.*
**sorry for/about** something that one has done
*I'm **sorry for/about** breaking your window.*
**sorry for** a person
*I feel really **sorry for** her children.*
**speak to; speak with** (especially AmE)
*Could I **speak to/with** your father for a moment?*
**suffer from**
*My wife is **suffering from** hepatitis.*
**surprised at/by**
*Everybody was **surprised at/by** the weather.*

**take part in** (NOT ~~at~~ OR ~~of~~)
*I don't want to **take part in** any more conferences.*
**think of/about** (NOT ~~think to~~)
*I'm **thinking of** studying medicine.*
*I've also **thought about** studying dentistry.*
**the thought of** (NOT ~~the thought to~~)
*I hate **the thought of** going back to work.*
**throw ... at** (aggressive)
*Stop **throwing** stones **at** the cars.*
**throw ... to** (in a game etc)
*If you get the ball, **throw** it **to** me.*
**translate into** (NOT ~~in~~)
*Could you **translate** this **into** Greek for me?*

**trip over**
*He **tripped over** the cat and fell downstairs.*
**typical of** (NOT ~~for~~)
*The wine's **typical of** the region.*

**write**: see 610.
**wrong with**
*What's **wrong with** Rachel today?*

For *of* after determiners like *some, most,* see 154.

# 450 prepositions (3): before particular words and expressions

This is a list of a few expressions which often cause problems. For other **preposition + noun** combinations, see a good dictionary.

**at** the cinema; **at** the theatre; **at** a party; **at** university
*What's on **at the cinema** this week?*

a book (written) **by** Joyce; a concerto (composed) **by** Mozart; a film (directed) **by** Orson Welles (NOT ~~of~~ OR ~~from~~)
*I've never read anything **by** Dickens.*
**by** car/bike/bus/train/boat/plane/land/sea/air; **on** foot (but **in** the car, **on** a bus etc)
*Let's take our time and go **by boat**.*

**for** ... reason
*My sister decided to go to America **for** several **reasons**.*

**from** ... point of view (NOT ~~according to~~ OR ~~after~~)
*Try to see it **from** my **point of view**.*

**in** ... opinion (NOT ~~according to~~ OR ~~after~~)
*In my **opinion**, she should have resigned earlier.*
**in** the end (= finally, after a long time)
*In the end, I got a visa for Russia.*
**at** the end (= at the point where something stops)
*I think the film's a bit weak **at the end**.*
**in** pen, pencil, ink etc
*Please fill in the form **in ink**.*
**in** a picture, photo etc (NOT ~~on~~)
*She looks much younger **in** this **photo**.*
**in** the rain, snow etc
*I like walking **in the rain**.*
**in** a suit, raincoat, shirt, skirt, hat etc
*Who's the man **in** the funny hat over there?*
**in** a ... voice
*Stop talking to me **in** that stupid voice.*

▶

**on** page 20 etc (NOT ~~in/at~~)
   *There's a mistake **on page 120**.*
**on** the radio; **on** TV; **on** the phone
   *Is there anything good **on TV** tonight?*
   *It's Mrs Ellis **on the phone**: she says it's urgent.*
**on** time (= at the planned time, neither late nor early)
   *Peter wants the meeting to start exactly **on time**.*
**in** time (= with enough time to spare, before the last moment)
   *He would have died if they hadn't got him to the hospital **in time**.*

# 451 prepositions (4): expressions without prepositions

This is a list of some common expressions in which we do not use prepositions, or can leave them out.

## 1 *discuss, enter, marry, lack, resemble* and *approach*

These verbs are normally followed by direct objects without prepositions.
   *We must **discuss your plans**. (NOT . . . ~~discuss about your plans.~~)*
   *Conversation stopped as we **entered the church**. (NOT . . . ~~entered in(to) the church.~~)*
   *She **married a friend** of her sister's. (NOT . . . ~~married with~~ . . .)*
   *He's clever, but he **lacks experience**. (NOT . . . ~~lacks of~~ . . .)*
   *The child does not **resemble either** of its parents. (NOT . . . ~~resemble to~~ . . .)*
   *The train is now **approaching London** Paddington. (NOT . . . ~~approaching to~~ . . .)*

## 2 *next, last* etc

Prepositions are not used before a number of common expressions of time beginning *next, last, this, that* (sometimes), *one, every, each, some, any* (in an informal style), *all*.
   *See you **next Monday**. (NOT . . . ~~on next Monday.~~)*
   *The meeting's **this Thursday**.            We met **one Tuesday** in August.*
   *I'll never forget meeting you **that afternoon**.*
   *Come **any day** you like.            The party lasted **all night**.*
Note also *tomorrow morning, yesterday afternoon* etc.

## 3 days of the week

In an informal style, we sometimes leave out *on* before the names of the days of the week.
   *Why don't you come for a drink **(on) Monday** evening?*

## 4 a meaning 'each'

No preposition is used in expressions like *three times a day, sixty miles an hour, eighty pence a kilo*.
   *Private lessons cost £20 **an hour**.*

For *per* in expressions like these, see 389.20

## 5 *What time ...?* etc

We usually leave out *at* before *what time*.
> ***What time** does Granny's train arrive?*
>> (More natural than *At what time ...?* )

In an informal style, we can also leave out *on* before *what/which day(s)*.
> ***What day** is your hair appointment?*
> ***Which day** do you have your music lesson?*

## 6 *about*

In an informal style, *at* is often dropped before ***about*** + **time expression**.
> *I'll see you **(at) about 3 o'clock**.*

## 7 'how long'

In an informal style, *for* is often left out in expressions that say how long
something lasts.
> *I've been here **(for) three weeks** now.     How long are you staying **(for)**?*

## 8 measurement expressions etc after *be*

Expressions containing words like *height, weight, length, size, shape, age,
colour* are usually connected to the subject of the clause by the verb *be*,
without a preposition.
> *He **is just the right height** to be a policeman.*
> *She's **the same age** as me.*
> *His head's **a funny shape**.*
> *I'm **the same weight** as I was twenty years ago.*
> ***What shoe size** are you?*
> ***What colour** are her eyes?* (NOT *Of what colour...?*)

## 9 *(in) this way* etc

We often leave out *in* (especially in informal speech) in expressions like
*(in) this way, (in) the same way, (in) another way* etc.
> *They plant corn **(in) the same way** their ancestors used to 500 years ago.*

## 10 *home*

We do not use *to* before *home* (see 249).
> *I'm going **home**.*

In informal English (especially American), *at* can be left out before *home*.
> *Is anybody **home**?*

## 11 *place*

In an informal style, *to* can be dropped in some expressions with the word
*place*. This is normal in American English.
> *Let's go **(to) some place** where it's quiet.*
> *I always said you'd go **places**.* (= become successful)

## 12 infinitive structures

Prepositions can be dropped in the structure **noun + infinitive + preposition**
(see 285.5).
> *She has no **money to buy food (with)**.*
> *We have an **hour to do it (in)**.*

▶

This is particularly common with the noun *place*.

> *We need **a place to live (in)**.*    *She had **no place to go (to)**.*

For the use of prepositions after *near*, see 365.

# 452 prepositions (5): at the ends of clauses

## 1 introduction

A preposition often connects two things: (1) a noun, adjective or verb that comes before it, and (2) a 'prepositional object' – a noun phrase or pronoun that comes after the preposition.

> *This is a present **for** you.*    *He's looking **at** her.*
> *I'm really angry **with** Joe.*    *They live **in** a small village.*

In some structures we may put the prepositional object at or near the beginning of a clause. In this case, the preposition does not always go with it – it may stay together with 'its' noun, adjective or verb at the end of the clause. This happens especially in four cases:

> *wh*-questions:    *Who's the present **for**?*
> relative structures:    *Joe's the person that I'm angry **with**.*
> passives:    *She likes to be looked **at**.*
> infinitive structures: *The village is pleasant to live **in**.*

## 2 *wh*-questions

When a question word is the object of a preposition, the preposition most often comes at the end of the clause, especially in informal usage.

> ***Who's** the present **for**? (**For whom** is the present? is extremely formal.)*
> ***What** are you looking **at**?*
> ***Who** did you go **with**?*
> ***Where** did she buy it **from**?*
> ***Which** flight is the general travelling **on**?*
> ***What** kind of films are you interested **in**?*

This also happens in indirect *wh*-questions, and in other *what*-clauses.

> *Tell me **what** you're worried **about**.*
> ***What** a lot of trouble I'm **in**!*

Some questions consist simply of **question word + preposition**.

> ***What with**?*    ***Who for**?*

However, this structure is unusual when there is a noun with the question word.

> *With **what money**? (NOT ~~What money with?~~)*

## 3 relative clauses

When a relative pronoun (see 494) is the object of a preposition, the preposition also often goes at the end of the clause, especially in informal usage.

> *Joe's the person **that** I'm angry **with**. (Less formal than ... **with whom** I am angry.)*
> *This is the house **(that)** I told you **about**.*
>     *(Less formal than ... **about which** I told you.)*
> *You remember the boy **(who)** I was going out **with**?*

> *She's the only woman (**who**) I've ever really been in love **with**.*
> *That's **what** I'm afraid **of**.*

Because *whom* is unusual in an informal style, it is very rare in clauses that end with prepositions (see 498.3,7).

## 4   passives

In passive structures (see 412–420), prepositions go with their verbs.

> *She likes **to be looked at**.*
> *I don't know where he is – his bed **hasn't been slept in**.*
> *Carol **was operated on** last night.*

## 5   infinitive structures

Infinitive complements (see 284–285) can have prepositions with them.

> *The village is pleasant **to live in**.*
> *She needs other children **to play with**.*
> *Can you get me a chair **to stand on**?*
> *I've got lots of music **to listen to**.*
> *Their house isn't easy **to get to**.*

## 6   exceptions

Many common adverbial expressions consist of **preposition + noun phrase** (e.g. *with great patience, in a temper*). In these cases, the preposition is closely connected with the noun, and is kept as near as possible to it; it cannot usually be moved to the end of a clause.

> *I admired **the patience with** which she spoke.* (NOT *. . . the patience she spoke with.*)

*During* and *since* are not normally put at the ends of clauses.

> ***During** which period did it happen?* (NOT *Which period did it happen during?*)
> ***Since** when have you been working for her?* (NOT *When have you been working for her since?*)

## 7   formal structures

In a more formal style, a preposition is often put earlier in questions and relative structures, before the question word or relative pronoun.

> ***With whom** did she go?*
> *It was the house **about which** he had told them.*
> *She was the only woman **with whom** he had ever been in love.*

This can also happen in infinitive complements, in a very formal style. A relative pronoun is used.

> *She needs other children **with whom to play**.*
> *It is a boring place **in which to live**.*

Note that after prepositions *which* and *whom* can be used, but not normally *who* and *that*.

Even in a very formal style, prepositions are not often put at the beginning of questions which have *be* as the main verb.

> *Who **is it for**, madam?* (NOT *For whom is it?*)

And the structures *where . . . to*, *what . . . like* and *what . . . for* have a fixed order.

> ***Where** shall I send it **to**?* (BUT NOT *To where shall I send it?*)

▶

*What does she look **like**?* (BUT NOT ~~Like what does she look?~~)
*What did you buy that **for**?* (BUT NOT ~~For what did you buy that?~~)
Prepositions cannot be moved away from passive verbs even in a formal style.
*In my family, money was never **spoken about**.* (NOT *. . .~~about money was~~*
~~never spoken.~~)

For more information about formal and informal language, see 311.
For sentences like *It's got a hole in (it); I like cakes with cream on (them)*, see 177.13.

# 453 prepositions (6): before conjunctions

Prepositions can be followed by conjunctions in some cases but not in others.

## 1 indirect speech: prepositions dropped before *that*

Prepositions are not used directly before the conjunction *that*. In indirect
speech – after words that refer to saying, writing, thinking etc – prepositions
are usually dropped before *that*-clauses. Compare:
- *I knew **about** his problems.*
  *I knew **that** he had problems.*
    (NOT *~~I knew about that he had problems.~~*)
- *She had no **idea of** my state of mind.*
  *She had no **idea that** I was unhappy.*
    (NOT *~~She had no idea of that I was unhappy.~~*)
- *I wasn't **aware of** the time.*
  *I wasn't **aware that** it was so late.*
    (NOT *~~I wasn't aware of that it was so late.~~*)

## 2 emotional reactions: prepositions dropped

Prepositions are also dropped before *that* after many common words that refer
to emotional reactions. Compare:
- *We are **sorry about** the delay.*    – *I was **surprised at** her strength.*
  *We are **sorry that** the train is late.*   *I was **surprised that** she was so strong.*
  (NOT *. . .~~sorry about that the train~~*  (NOT *. . .~~surprised at that she was~~* . . .)
  ~~is late.~~)

## 3 the fact that

In other cases (not involving indirect speech or words referring to emotional
reactions) prepositions cannot so often be dropped before *that*-clauses.
Instead, the expression *the fact* (see 583.3) is generally put between the
preposition and *that*.
> *The judge paid a lot of attention **to the fact that** the child was unhappy
> at home.* (NOT *~~The judge paid a lot of attention (to) that the child~~* . . .)
> *He said the parents were responsible **for the fact that** the child had run
> away.* (NOT *. . .~~responsible (for) that the child had run away.~~*)

## 4 question words

After some very common words like *tell, ask, depend, sure, idea, look*,
prepositions can be dropped before *who, which, what* and other question
words. This is especially common in indirect questions. Compare:

– *Tell* me *about* your trip.
  *Tell* me *(about)* *where* you went.
– *I asked* her *about* her religious beliefs.
  *I asked* her *whether* she believed in God.
    (More natural than *I asked her about whether she believed in God.*)
– *We may be late – it depends on the traffic.*
  *We may be late – it depends (on) how much traffic there is.*
– *I'm not sure of his method.*
  *I'm not sure how he does it.*
    (More natural than *I'm not sure of how he does it.*)
– *Look at this.*
  *Look (at) what I've got.*
In other cases it is unusual or impossible to leave out the preposition.
  *I'm worried about where she is.* (NOT ~~I'm worried where she is.~~)
  *The police questioned me about what I'd seen.* (NOT ~~The police questioned me what I'd seen.~~)
  *There's the question of who's going to pay.*
    (More natural than . . . *the question who's going to pay.*)
  *People's chances of getting jobs vary according to whether they live in the North or the South.* (NOT . . . ~~according whether . . .~~)
*If* does not normally follow prepositions; we use *whether* (see 621) instead.
  *I'm worried about whether you're happy.* (NOT ~~I'm worried about if . . .~~)

For the structures (with and without preposition) that are possible after a particular verb, noun or adjective, see a good dictionary.

## 454 prepositions (7): -ing forms and infinitives

Prepositions are not normally used before infinitives in English. After **verb/noun/adjective + preposition**, we usually use the *-ing* form of a following verb.
  *He insisted on being paid at once.* (NOT ~~He insisted on to be paid . . .~~)
  *I don't like the idea of getting married.* (NOT . . . ~~the idea of to get married.~~)
  *I'm not very good at cooking.* (NOT . . . ~~good at to cook.~~)
In some cases we drop the preposition and use an infinitive. Compare:
– *He asked for a loan.*            – *We're travelling for pleasure.*
  *He asked to borrow some money.*    *We're travelling to enjoy ourselves.*
– *She was surprised at his mistake.*
  *She was surprised to see what he had done.*
Sometimes two structures are possible. There is often a difference of meaning or use. For more details, see 299.
  *I'm interested in learning more about my family.*
  *I was interested to learn that my grandfather was Jewish.*

For details of the structures that are possible after a particular verb, noun or adjective, see a good dictionary.

# 455 present perfect (1): basic information

This entry deals with the simple present perfect. For the present perfect progressive, see 458–459.

## 1 forms

> *have/has* + past participle

*I have broken my glasses.*
*Have you finished?*    *She hasn't phoned.*

In older English, some present perfect forms were made with *be*, not *have* (e.g. *Winter is come*). This does not normally happen in modern English (for exceptions, see 205 and 213).

For details of question structures, see 480–486. For negatives, see 367–371.
For passive forms (e.g. *The work has been done*), see 412.

## 2 other languages

In some other languages there are verb forms which are constructed like the English present perfect (compare English *I have worked*, French *j'ai travaillé*, German *ich habe gearbeitet*, Italian *ho lavorato*, Spanish *he trabajado*). Note that the English present perfect is used rather differently from most of these.

## 3 finished events connected with the present

We use the present perfect especially to say that a finished action or event is connected with the present in some way. If we say that something has happened, we are thinking about the past and the present at the same time.

*I can't go on holiday because I have broken my leg.* (NOT *I can't go on holiday because I broke my leg.*)

We could often change a present perfect sentence into a present sentence with a similar meaning.

*I've broken my leg.* → *My leg is broken now.*
*Have you read the Bible.* → *Do you know the Bible?*
*Some fool has let the cat in.* → *The cat is in.*
*Utopia has invaded Fantasia.* → *Utopia is at war with Fantasia.*
*Mary has had a baby.* → *Mary now has a baby.*
*Our dog has died.* → *Our dog is dead.*
*All the wars in history have taught us nothing.* → *We know nothing.*

The present perfect is often used to express the idea of completion or achievement.

*At last! I've finished!*
*Have you done all the housework?*

We do not use the present perfect if we are not thinking about the present (see 456.1). Compare:

*I've travelled in Africa a lot.* (= I know Africa.)
*Some people think that Shakespeare travelled a lot in Germany.* (NOT *Some people think that Shakespeare has travelled* ...)

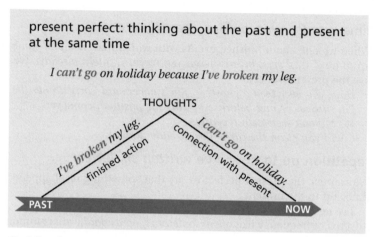

present perfect: thinking about the past and present at the same time

*I can't go on holiday because I've broken my leg.*

THOUGHTS

*I've broken my leg:* finished action

*I can't go on holiday:* connection with present

PAST — NOW

## 4 finished events: news

We normally use the present perfect to announce news of recent events.
> *Andy **has won** a big prize!*
> *Have you heard? Uncle George **has crashed** the car again.*
> *Here are the main points of the news. The pound **has fallen** against the dollar. The Prime Minister **has said** that the government's economic policies are working. The number of unemployed **has reached** five million. There **has been** a fire . . .*

After announcing news, we usually use the simple past to give more details. (see 456.5).
> *Uncle George **has crashed** the car again. He **ran** into a tree in High Street.*

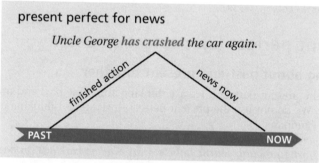

present perfect for news

*Uncle George has crashed the car again.*

finished action

news now

PAST — NOW

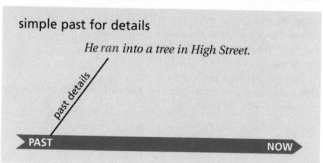

simple past for details

*He ran into a tree in High Street.*

past details

PAST — NOW

### 5 time words: *ever, before, recently* etc

When we talk about finished events with words that mean 'at some/any time up to now' (like *ever, before, never, yet, recently, lately, already*), we normally use the present perfect.

> *Have you **ever seen** a ghost?*     *She's **never said** 'sorry' in her life.*
> *I'm sure we've **met before**.*     *Has the postman **come** yet?*
> *We **haven't seen** Beth recently.*
> *Could you clean the car? ~ I've **already done** it.*

### 6 repetition up to now: *I've written six letters* ...

We can use the present perfect to say that something has happened several times up to the present.

> *I've **written** six letters since lunchtime.*

Adverbs of frequency like *often, sometimes, occasionally* are common with the present perfect.

> *How **often have** you **been** in love in your life?*
> *I've **sometimes thought** of moving to Australia.*

### 7 continuation up to now: *I've known her for years*

To talk about actions and situations that have continued up to the present, both the simple present perfect and the present perfect progressive are possible (depending on the kind of verb and the exact meaning – for details, see 459).

> *I've **known** her for years.* (NOT *I know her for years*. – see 460.1)
> *I've **been thinking** about you all day.*

For present perfect tenses in clauses referring to the future (e.g. *I'll take a rest when I've finished cleaning the kitchen*), see 580.

## 456 present perfect (2): perfect or past?

### 1 thinking about past and present together

We use the present perfect if we are thinking about the past and present together. We do not use the present perfect if we are not thinking about the present. Compare:

- *My sister **has learnt** French.* (She can speak French now.)
  *Shakespeare probably **learnt** Italian.* (NOT *Shakespeare has probably learnt Italian.*)
- *We've **studied** enough to pass the exam.* (The exam is still to come.)
  *We **studied** enough to pass the exam.* (The exam is over.)
- *Ann and Peter **have got** married!* (news)
  *My parents **got** married in Canada.*

We do not use the present perfect in story-telling.

> *Once upon a time a beautiful princess **fell** in love with a poor farmer.*
> (NOT *... has fallen in love ...*)

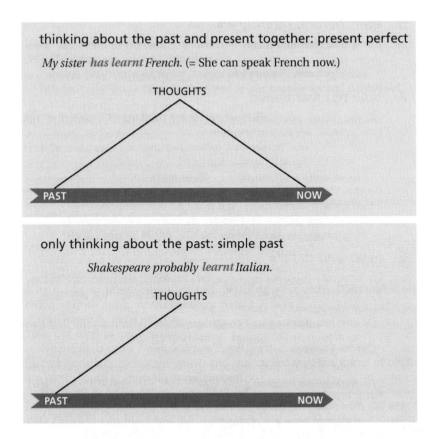

thinking about the past and present together: present perfect

*My sister **has learnt** French.* (= She can speak French now.)

THOUGHTS

PAST                                    NOW

only thinking about the past: simple past

*Shakespeare probably **learnt** Italian.*

THOUGHTS

PAST                                    NOW

## 2 finished-time words: present perfect not used

We do not often use the present perfect with words that refer to a completely finished period of time, like *yesterday, last week, then, when, three years ago, in 1970.* This is because the present perfect focuses on the present, and words like these focus on the past, so they contradict each other. Compare:
- *Have you seen Lucy anywhere?*
  *I saw Lucy yesterday.* (NOT ~~I have seen Lucy yesterday.~~)
- *Tom has hurt his leg; he can't walk.*
  *Tom hurt his leg last week.* (NOT ~~Tom has hurt his leg last week.~~)
- *What have you done with the car keys? I can't find them.*
  *What did you do then?* (NOT ~~What have you done then?~~)
- *My brother has had an accident. He's in hospital.*
  *When did the accident happen?* (NOT ~~When has the accident happened?~~)
- *All my friends have moved to London.*
  *Eric moved three years ago.* (NOT ~~Eric has moved three years ago.~~)

For tenses with *just* and *just now*, see 307.                    ▶

### 3   *ever, before, recently* etc

But with words that mean 'at some/any time up to now' (like *ever, before, never, yet, recently, already*), we normally use the present perfect (see 455.5).
> *Have you **ever been** to Chicago?     I've **seen** this film **before**.*

### 4   time not mentioned

We use the present perfect when we are thinking of a period of 'time up to now', even if we do not mention it.
> *Have you **seen** 'Romeo and Juliet'?* (= Have you ever seen it? or Have you seen the present production?)
> *You've **done** a lot for me.* (... up to now)

On the other hand, we do not use the present perfect when we are thinking of a particular finished time, even if we do not mention it.
> *Did you **see** 'Romeo and Juliet'?* (It was on TV last night.)
> *My grandfather **did** a lot for me.* (... when he was alive)

### 5   news and details

We normally use the present perfect to announce news (see 455.4).
But when we give more details, we usually change to a past tense.
> *Joe **has passed** his exam! He **got** 87%.*
> *There **has been** a plane crash near Bristol. Witnesses say that there **was** an explosion as the aircraft **was taking off**, ...*
> *The Prime Minister **has had** talks with President Kumani. During a three-hour meeting, they **discussed** the economic situation, and **agreed** on the need for closer trade links between the two countries.*

For more details, exceptions and notes on American usage, see 457.6.

## 457   present perfect (3): perfect or past (advanced points)

### 1   causes and origins: *Who gave you that?*

We normally use the present perfect when we are thinking about past events together with their present results (see 455.3).
> *I **can't come** to your party because I've **broken** my leg.*

However, we usually prefer a past tense when we identify the person, thing or circumstances responsible for a present situation (because we are thinking about the past cause, not the present result). Compare:
– *Look what John's **given** me!* (thinking about the gift)
  *Who **gave** you that?* (thinking about the past action of giving)
– *Some fool **has let** the cat in.*
  *Who **let** that cat in?*

Other examples:
> *Why are you crying? ~ Granny **hit** me.* (NOT ... ~Granny has hit me.)
> *I'm glad you **were** born.     How **did** you **get** that bruise?*
> *That's a nice picture. **Did** you **paint** it yourself?*
> *Some people think that 'Pericles' **was** not **written** by Shakespeare.*
> *The Chinese **invented** paper.* (NOT The Chinese have invented paper.)

## 2  expectation and reality: *You're older than I thought*

We use a past tense to refer to a belief that has just been shown to be true or false.

> *It's not as big as I **expected**. (NOT ... as I have expected.)*
> *You're older than I **thought**. (NOT ... than I have thought.)*
> *But you **promised** ... ! (NOT But you have promised... !)*
> *I **knew** you would help me! (NOT I have known...!)*

## 3  *today, this week* etc

With definite expressions of 'time up to now' (e.g. *today, this week*), perfect and past tenses are often both possible. We prefer the present perfect if we are thinking of the whole period up to now. We prefer the simple past if we are thinking of a finished part of that period. Compare:

– *I **haven't seen** John this week.* (the whole week up to now – present perfect more natural)

> *I **saw** John this week, and he said ...* (earlier in the week – simple past more natural)

– ***Has** Ann **phoned** today?* (meaning 'any time up to now')

> ***Did** Ann **phone** today?* (meaning 'earlier, when the call was expected')

## 4  *always, ever* and *never*

In an informal style, simple past tenses are sometimes possible with *always, ever* and *never* when they refer to 'time up to now'.

> *I **always knew** I could trust you.* (OR *I've always known ...*)
> *Did you **ever see** anything like that before?* (OR *Have you ever seen ...?*)

## 5  present perfect with past time expressions

Grammars usually say that the present perfect cannot be used together with expressions of finished time – we can say *I have seen him* or *I saw him yesterday*, but not *I have seen him yesterday*. In fact, such structures are unusual but not impossible (though learners should avoid them). They often occur in brief news items, where space is limited and there is pressure to announce the news and give the details in the same clause.

Here are some real examples taken from news broadcasts, newspaper articles, advertisements, letters and conversations.

> *Police **have arrested** more than 900 suspected drugs traffickers in raids throughout the country **on Friday and Saturday**.*
> *... a runner who's **beaten** Linford Christie **earlier this year**.*
> *A 24-year-old soldier **has been killed** in a road accident **last night**.*
> *The horse's trainer **has had** a winner here **yesterday**.*
> *... indicating that the geological activity **has taken place** a very long time ago.*
> *Perhaps what **has helped** us to win eight major awards **last year** alone ...*
> *I **have stocked** the infirmary cupboard **only yesterday**.*
> *I am pleased to confirm that Lloyds Bank ... **has opened** a Home Loan account for you **on 19th May**.*

▶

## 6   simple past for news

Recently, some British newspapers have started regularly using the simple past for smaller news announcements – probably to save space. This also happens on TV text news pages. Some authentic examples:

*An unnamed Ulster businessman **was shot** dead by terrorists . . .*
*A woman **was jailed** for six months after taking a baby boy from his mother.*
*Driving wind and rain **forced** 600 out of 2,500 teenagers to abandon the
    annual 'Ten Tor' trek across Dartmoor.*

## 7   American English

In American English the simple past is often used to give news.

*Did you **hear**? Switzerland **declared** / **has declared** war on Mongolia!*
    (BrE *Have you heard? Switzerland has declared war . . .*)
*Uh, honey, I **lost** / I've **lost** the keys* (BrE *. . . I've lost . . .*)
*Lucy just **called**.* (BrE *Lucy has just called.*)

In American English, it is also possible to use the simple past with indefinite past-time adverbs like *already, yet, ever* and *before.*

*Did you **eat already**?* OR **Have you eaten** . . .? (BrE *Have you eaten already?*)
*I **didn't call** Bobby yet* OR *I **haven't called** . . .* (BrE *I haven't called . . .*)

British English is changing under American influence, so some of these uses are becoming common in Britain as well.

For more about tenses with *just,* see 307.
For more about British-American differences, see 51.

## 8   bad rules (1): 'definite time'

Grammars sometimes say that the present perfect is not used with expressions referring to 'definite time'. This is confusing – the present perfect is not often used with **finished** time expressions, but it actually is very common with **definite** time expressions. Compare:

*I've **lived** here for **exactly** three years, seven months and two days.*
    (present perfect with very definite time-reference)
*Once upon a time a little girl **lived** with her mother in a lonely house in a
    dark forest.* (simple past with very indefinite time-reference)

## 9   bad rules (2): 'finished actions'

Note also that the choice between simple present perfect and simple past does not depend on whether we are talking about finished **actions**, as learners' grammars sometimes suggest (though it can depend on whether we are talking about finished **time periods**). Compare:

*That cat **has eaten** your supper.* (finished action – present perfect)
*I **ate** the last of the eggs this morning.* (finished action – simple past)

## 10   bad rules (3): 'recent actions'

The choice also does not depend directly on whether actions and events are recent. Recent events are more likely to be 'news', and we are more likely to be concerned about their present results, so many present perfect sentences are in fact about recent events. But it is possible to use the present perfect to talk about things that happened a long time ago. Compare:

*The French revolution **has influenced** every popular radical movement in Europe since 1800.* (200-year-old event – present perfect)
*Ann **phoned** five minutes ago.* (very recent event – simple past)

## 11 both possible

The difference between the present perfect and the simple past is not always very clear-cut. It often depends on our 'focus': are we thinking mostly about the present relevance of a past event, or about the past details? In some cases both present perfect and past are possible with little difference of meaning.

*We **(have) heard** that you have rooms to let.*
*Has Mark **phoned**?* OR *Did Mark **phone**?*
*I've **given** / I **gave** your old radio to Philip.*

# 458 present perfect (4): progressive (or 'continuous')

## 1 forms

> *have/has been + -ing*

*I have been thinking about you.*
*Have you been waiting long?*
*I haven't been studying very well recently.*

For double letters in words like *sitting, stopping,* see 562.

## 2 continuing actions and situations

We use the present perfect progressive to look back over actions and situations which started in the past and are still going on.

*I've **been working** very hard recently.*
*It's **been raining** all day. I'm tired of it.*
*House prices **have been going** up steadily all this year.*

We often use the present perfect progressive to talk about people's use of their time up to the present.

*Hi! What **have** you **been doing** with yourself? ~ I've **been trying** to write a novel.*
*That kid **has been watching** TV non-stop since breakfast.*

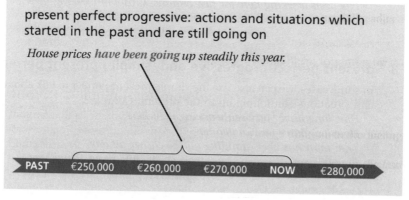

present perfect progressive: actions and situations which started in the past and are still going on

*House prices **have been going** up steadily this year.*

| PAST | €250,000 | €260,000 | €270,000 | NOW | €280,000 |

## 3 actions and situations that have just stopped

We also use the present perfect progressive for actions and situations which have just stopped, but which have present results.

*You look hot. ~ Yes, I've **been running.***
*Sorry I'm late. **Have** you **been waiting** long?*
*I must just go and wash. I've **been gardening.***

## 4 repeated actions

We can use the present perfect progressive for repeated as well as continuous activity.

*People **have been phoning** me all day.*
*I've **been waking** up in the night a lot. I think I'll see the doctor.*

## 5 time expressions: *recently, lately, this week, since ..., for ...,* etc

We often use the present perfect progressive with words that refer to a period of time continuing up to now, like *recently, lately, this week, since January, for the last three days.*

*The firm **has been losing** money **recently**.*
*John's **been walking** in Scotland **all this week**.*
*I've **been doing** a new job **since January**.*
*It's **been raining for the last three days**.*

For the difference between *since* and *for*, see 208.

## 6 not used with finished time expressions

We cannot use the present perfect progressive with expressions that refer to a finished period of time.

*You look tired. ~ Yes. I **was cycling** from midday until five o'clock.*
*(NOT ... I've been cycling from midday until five o'clock.)*

## 7 how long?

We use the present perfect progressive, not the present progressive, to talk about how long something has been happening.

*How long **have** you **been studying** English? (NOT How long are you studying ...?)*
*I've **been working** here for two months. (NOT I'm working here for two months.)*

For details, see 460.

## 8 present perfect progressive and (simple) present perfect

In some cases, we can also use the simple present perfect to talk about actions and situations continuing up to the present. Compare:
- *How long **have** you **been working** with her?*
 *How long **have** you **known** her?*
- *That man **has been standing** on the corner all day.*
 *For 900 years the castle **has stood** on the hill above the village.*

For the differences, see 459.

# 459 present perfect (5): simple or progressive?

## 1 non-progressive verbs

Some verbs are not used in progressive forms (see 471), even if the meaning is one for which a progressive form is more suitable. Common examples are *be*, *have* and *know*.

> *John's **been** ill all week.* (NOT ~~John's been being ill~~...)
> *She's **had** a cold since Monday.* (NOT ~~She's been having a cold~~...)
> *I've only **known** her for two days.* (NOT ~~I've only been knowing her~~...)

## 2 temporary or permanent

We use progressive forms mostly for shorter, temporary actions and situations. When we talk about longer-lasting or permanent situations we often prefer the simple present perfect. Compare:

> – *That man **has been standing** on the corner all day.*
> *For 900 years the castle **has stood** on the hill above the village.*
> – *I **haven't been working** very well recently.*
> *He **hasn't worked** for years.*
> – *I've **been living** in Sue's flat for the last month.*
> *My parents **have lived** in Bristol all their lives.*

Progressive and simple tenses are sometimes both possible, with a slight difference of emphasis.

> *It's **been raining** / It's **rained** steadily since last Saturday.*
> *Harry **has been working** / **has worked** in the same job for thirty years.*

We generally use the progressive to talk about continuous change or development, even if this is permanent.

> *Scientists believe that the universe **has been expanding** steadily since the beginning of time.*

## 3 *how much? how often?* simple present perfect

We use the simple present perfect to say how much we have done, or how often we have done something. Compare:

> – *I've **been planting** rose bushes all afternoon.*
> *Look at all the rose bushes I've **planted**!* (NOT ...~~I've been planting.~~)
> – *We've **been painting** the house.*
> *We've **painted** two rooms since lunchtime.* (NOT ~~We've been painting two rooms since lunchtime.~~)
> – *I've **been playing** a lot of tennis recently.*
> *I've **played** tennis three times this week.*

# 460 present perfect (6): present perfect or present?

## 1 *how long?* present perfect

We use a present perfect to say how long a situation or action has continued up to now. Compare:

> – *It's **raining** again.*
> *It's **been raining** since Christmas.* (NOT ~~It's raining since Christmas.~~)
> – *Are you **learning** English?*
> *How long **have** you **been learning**?* (NOT ~~How long are you learning?~~) ▶

– *I hear you're **working** at Smiths.* ~ *Yes, I've **been working** there for a month.*
  (NOT ~~*I'm working there for*~~ . . .)
– *I **know** her well.*
  *I've **known** her for years.* (NOT ~~*I know her for years.*~~)
– *My brother's a doctor.*
  *How long **has** he **been** a doctor?* (NOT ~~*How long is he a doctor?*~~)
Compare also:
  *How long **are** you here for?* (= until when; when are you leaving?)
  *How long **have** you **been** here for?* (= since when; when did you arrive?)

For the difference between simple and progressive forms, see 459.
For the difference between *since* and *for*, see 208.
For tenses with *since*, see 522.

## 2  This is the first time etc

We use a simple present perfect after *this is the first time that* . . . , *it's the second . . . that . . .* , and similar structures (see 591).
  *This is **the first time** that I've **heard** her sing.* (NOT ~~*This is the first time that I hear her sing.*~~)
  *It's **the fifth time** you've **asked** me the same question.*
  *This is only **the second** opera I've **ever** seen.*

For present perfect and simple present passives with similar meanings (e.g. *The shop has been / is closed*), see 420.

# 461  present tenses (1): introduction

## 1  the two present tenses

Most English verbs have two present tenses. Forms like *I wait, she thinks* are called 'simple present' or 'present simple'; forms like *I am waiting* or *she's thinking* are called 'present progressive' or 'present continuous'. The two present tenses are used in different ways.

## 2  general time: simple present

When we talk about permanent situations, or about things that happen regularly or all the time (not just around now), we usually use the simple present (see 462–463 for details).
  *My parents **live** near Dover.*          *Water **freezes** at 0° Celsius.*
  *I **go** to London about three times a week.*

## 3  around now: present progressive

When we talk about temporary continuing actions and events, which are just going on now or around now, we usually use a present progressive tense (see 464 for details).
  *What **are** you **doing**?* ~ *I'm **reading**.*
  *I'm **travelling** a lot these days.*

### 4 future time

Both present tenses can be used to talk about the future.
*I'll meet you when you **arrive**.*
*Come and see us next week if you**'re passing** through London.*

For the differences, see 463–464, 466.

# 462 present tenses (2): simple present (forms)

## 1 forms

| Affirmative | Question | Negative |
|---|---|---|
| I work | do I work? | I do not work |
| you work | do you work? | you do not work |
| he/she/it works | does he/she/it work? | he/she/it does not work |
| we work | do we work? | we do not work |
| they work | do they work? | they do not work |

– Contracted negatives (see 143): *I don't work, he doesn't work* etc
– Negative questions (see 368): *do I not work?* or *don't I work?* etc

For passives (e.g. *The work is done*), see 412.

## 2 spelling of third person singular forms

| | |
|---|---|
| Most verbs:<br>add *-s* to infinitive | *work → works*<br>*sit → sits*<br>*stay → stays* |
| Verbs ending in consonant + *y*:<br>change *y* to *i* and add *-es* | *cry → cries*<br>*hurry → hurries*<br>*reply → replies* |
| But (vowel + *y*): | *enjoy → enjoys* |
| Verbs ending in *-s, -z, -ch, -sh* or *-x*:<br>add *-es* to infinitive | *miss → misses*<br>*buzz → buzzes*<br>*watch → watches*<br>*push → pushes*<br>*fix → fixes* |
| Exceptions: | *have → **has***<br>*go → goes*<br>*do → does* |

## 3 pronunciation of third person singular forms

The pronunciation of the *-(e)s* ending depends on the sound that comes before it. The rules are the same as for the plural *-(e)s* ending – see 525.
Irregular pronunciations: *says* (/sez/, not /seɪz/); *does* (/dʌz/, not /duːz/).

# 463 present tenses (3): simple present (use)

## 1 general time: *It always rains in November*

We often use the simple present to talk about permanent situations, or about things that happen regularly, repeatedly or all the time.

What **do** frogs **eat**? (NOT ~~What are frogs eating?~~)
It always **rains** here in November.
I **play** tennis every Wednesday.
Alice **works** for an insurance company.

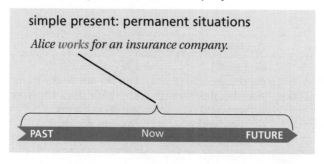

simple present: permanent situations

*Alice works for an insurance company.*

PAST — Now — FUTURE

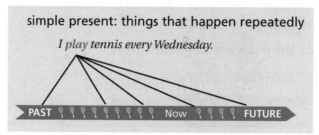

simple present: things that happen repeatedly

*I play tennis every Wednesday.*

PAST — Now — FUTURE

## 2 not used for things happening just around the present

We do not usually use the simple present to talk about temporary situations or actions that are only going on around the present. Compare:

- *Water **boils** at 100° Celsius.*
  *The kettle's **boiling** – shall I make tea?* (NOT ~~The kettle boils~~...)
- *It usually **snows** in January.*
  *Look – it's **snowing**!* (NOT ~~Look – It snows!~~)
- *I **play** tennis every Wednesday.*
  *Where's Bernard? ~ He's **playing** tennis.* (NOT ...~~He plays tennis.~~)

## 3 non-progressive verbs

However, the simple present is used for this 'around the present' meaning with verbs that do not have progressive forms (see 471).

I **like** this wine very much. (NOT ~~I'm liking~~ ...)
I **believe** you. (NOT ~~I'm believing you.~~)

## 4 talking about the future

We do not normally use the simple present to talk about the future.

*I promise I **won't** smoke any more.* (NOT ~~I promise I don't smoke any more.~~)

*We're **going** to the theatre this evening.* (NOT ~~We go to the theatre this evening.~~)

*There's the doorbell.* ~ *I'll **get** it.* (NOT ~~I get it.~~)

However, the simple present is used for 'timetabled' future events (see 215).

*His train **arrives** at 11.46.*     *I **start** my new job tomorrow.*

And the simple present is often used instead of *will* . . . in subordinate clauses that refer to the future. (For details, see 580).

*I'll kill anybody who **touches** my possessions.* (NOT . . . ~~who will touch~~ . . .)

*I'll phone you when I **get** home.* (NOT . . . ~~when I'll get home.~~)

The simple present is also used in suggestions with *Why don't you . . . ?*

*Why **don't** you **take** a day off tomorrow?*

## 5 series of events: demonstrations, commentaries, instructions, stories

When we talk about series of completed actions and events, we often use the simple present. This happens, for example, in demonstrations, commentaries, instructions and present-tense stories (see 465 for more details).

*First I **take** a bowl and **break** two eggs into it. Next . . .* (NOT ~~First I am taking a bowl~~ . . .)

*Lydiard **passes** to Taylor, Taylor **shoots** – and it's a goal!*

*How **do** I **get** to the station?* ~ *You **go** straight on to the traffic lights, then you **turn** left, . . . .*

*So I **go** into the office, and I **see** this man, and he **says** to me . . .*

## 6 *how long?* present tenses not used

We use a perfect tense, not a present tense, to say how long a present action or situation has been going on. (See 460 for details.)

*I've **known** her since 1960.* (NOT ~~I know her since 1960.~~)

# 464 present tenses (4): progressive (or 'continuous')

## 1 present progressive: forms

*am/are/is* + *-ing*

*I am waiting.*

*Are you listening?*     *She isn't working today.*

For double letters in words like *sitting*, *stopping*, see 562.
For passive forms (e.g. *The work **is being done***), see 412.

## 2 use: 'around now'

We use the present progressive to talk about temporary actions and situations that are going on now or 'around now': before, during and after the moment of speaking.

*Hurry up! We're all **waiting** for you!* (NOT ~~We all wait~~ . . .)

*What **are** you **doing**?* ~ *I'm **writing** letters.* (NOT . . . ~~I write letters.~~)

▶

*Why **are** you **crying**? Is something wrong?* (NOT ~~Why do you cry?~~...)
*He's **working** in Saudi Arabia at the moment.*

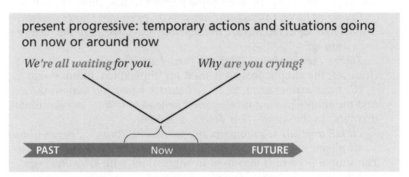

present progressive: temporary actions and situations going on now or around now

*We're all waiting for you.*    *Why are you crying?*

PAST        Now        FUTURE

## 3 repeated actions

The present progressive can refer to repeated actions and events, if these are just happening around the present (for more details, see 466).

*Why **is** he **hitting** the dog?*    *I'm **travelling** a lot these days.*

## 4 changes

We also use the present progressive to talk about developments and changes.

*That child's **getting** bigger every day.*    *House prices **are going** up again.*

## 5 talking about the future

We often use the present progressive to talk about the future (see 214).

*What **are** you **doing** tomorrow evening?*
*Come and see us next week if you're **passing** through London.*

## 6 things that happen all the time: not used

We do not normally use the present progressive to talk about permanent situations, or about things that happen regularly, repeatedly or all the time. Compare:

– *Look – the cat's **eating** your breakfast!*
*What **do** bears **eat**? ~ Everything.* (NOT ~~What are bears eating?~~...)
– *Why **is** that girl **standing** on the table?*
*Chetford Castle **stands** on a hill outside the town.* (NOT ...~~is standing~~...)
– *My sister's **living** at home for the moment.*
*Your parents **live** in North London, don't they?*

## 7 verbs not used in progressive forms

Some verbs are not used in progressive forms (see 471), even if the meaning is 'just around now'.

*I **like** this wine.* (NOT ~~I'm liking this wine.~~)
*Do you **believe** what he says?* (NOT ~~Are you believing...?~~)
*The tank **contains** about 7,000 litres at the moment.* (NOT ~~The tank is containing~~...)

## 8 how long? present tenses not used

We use a perfect tense, not a present tense, to say how long something has been going on. (See 460 for details.)

> *I've been learning English for three years.* (NOT ~~I'm learning English for three years.~~)

# 465 present tenses (5): stories, commentaries and instructions

## 1 stories

Present tenses are often used informally to tell stories. The simple present is used for the events – the things that happen one after another. The present progressive is used for 'background' – things that are already happening when the story starts, or that continue through the story. (This is like the difference between the simple past and past progressive: see 422.)

> *So I **open** the door, and I **look** out into the garden, and I **see** this man. He's **wearing** pyjamas and a policeman's helmet. 'Hello,' he **says** ...*
>
> *There's this Scotsman, you see, and he's **walking** through the jungle when he **meets** a gorilla. And the gorilla's **eating** a snake sandwich. So the Scotsman **goes** up to the gorilla ...*

The simple present is common in summaries of plays, stories, etc.

> *In Act I, Hamlet **sees** the ghost of his father. The ghost **tells** him ...*
>
> *Chapter 2: Henry **goes** to Scotland and **meets** the Loch Ness Monster.*

## 2 commentaries

In commentaries, the use of tenses is similar. The simple present is used for the quicker actions and events (which are finished before the sentences that describe them); the present progressive is used for longer actions and situations. There are more simple and fewer progressive tenses in a football commentary, for instance, than in a commentary on a boat race.

> *Smith **passes** to Devaney, Devaney to Barnes – and Harris **intercepts** ...*
>
> *Harris **passes** back to Simms, nice ball – and Simms **shoots**!*
>
> *Oxford **are pulling** slightly ahead of Cambridge now; they're **rowing** with a beautiful rhythm; Cambridge **are looking** a little disorganised ...*

## 3 instructions and demonstrations

We often use present tenses in a similar way to give instructions, demonstrations and directions.

> *OK, let's go over it again. You **wait** outside the bank until the manager **arrives**. Then you **radio** Louie, who's **waiting** round the corner, and he **drives** round to the front entrance. You and Louie **grab** the manager ...*
>
> *First I **put** a lump of butter into a frying pan and **light** the gas; then while the butter's **melting** I **break** three eggs into a bowl, like this ...*
>
> *How **do** I **get** to the station? ~ You **go** straight on to the traffic lights, then you **turn** left ...*

# 466 present tenses (6): advanced points

## 1 repeated actions: simple or progressive?

The present progressive can refer to repeated actions and events, if these are happening around the moment of speaking.

> Why *is* he *hitting* the dog?
> Jake's *seeing* a lot of Felicity these days.

But we do not use the present progressive for repeated actions and events which are not closely connected to the moment of speaking.

> I *go* to the mountains about twice a year. (NOT ~~I'm going to the mountains about twice a year.~~)
> Water *boils* at 100° Celsius. (NOT ~~Water is boiling at 100° Celsius.~~)

## 2 long-lasting changes

We use the present progressive for changes and developments, even if these are very long-lasting.

> The climate *is getting* warmer. (NOT ~~The climate gets warmer.~~)
> The universe *is expanding*, and has been since its beginning.

## 3 *You look lovely when you're smiling*

We use the simple present for regular or repeated actions and events; but we can use the present progressive for things that are going on around these actions and events.

> At seven, when the post *comes*, I'm usually *having* breakfast.
> She *doesn't like* to be disturbed if she's *working*.
> You *look* lovely when you're *smiling*.

## 4 *I promise* ... etc

Sometimes we do things by saying special words (e.g. promising, agreeing). We usually use the simple present in these cases.

> I *promise* never to smoke again. (NOT ~~I'm promising~~ ...)
> I *swear* that I will tell the truth ...
> I *agree*. (NOT ~~I am agreeing.~~)
> He *denies* the accusation. (NOT ~~He is denying~~ ...)

## 5 *I hear* etc

The simple present is used with a perfect or past meaning in introductory expressions like *I hear, I see, I gather, I understand* (see 243).

> I *hear* you're getting married. (= I have heard ...)
> I *see* there's been trouble down at the factory.
> I *gather* Peter's looking for a job.

Quotations are often introduced with *says*.

> No doubt you all remember what Hamlet *says* about suicide.
> It *says* in the paper that petrol's going up again.

## 6 *Here comes* ... etc

Note the structures *here comes* ... and *there goes* .... 

> *Here comes* your husband. (NOT ~~Here is coming~~ ...)
> *There goes* our bus – we'll have to wait for the next one.

### 7   *I feel / I'm feeling*

Verbs that refer to physical feelings (e.g. *feel, hurt, ache*) can often be used in simple or progressive tenses without much difference of meaning.

*How **do** you **feel**?* OR *How **are** you **feeling**?*
*My head **aches**.* OR *My head **is aching**.*

### 8   formal correspondence

Some fixed phrases that are used in letter-writing can be expressed either in the simple present (more formal) or in the present progressive (less formal).

*We **write** to advise you ...* (Less formal: *We **are writing** to let you know ...*)
*I **enclose** my cheque for £200.* (Less formal: *I **am enclosing** ...*)
*I **look forward** to hearing from you.* (Less formal: *I'm **looking forward** to hearing ...*)

For progressive forms with *always* and similar words (e.g. *She's always losing her keys*), see 472.
For progressive forms in general, see 470.
For the 'distancing' use of progressive forms, see 436.
For simple and progressive forms in older English, see 392.

## 467   presently

When *presently* means 'now, at present', it usually comes in mid-position with the verb (see 24).

*Professor Holloway is **presently** working on plant diseases.*
*The Manager is **presently** on holiday, but he will contact you on his return.*

An older meaning of *presently* (becoming less common) is 'not now, later', 'in a minute'.

With this meaning, *presently* usually comes in end-position, or separately as a short answer.

*He's having a rest now. He'll be down **presently**.*
*Mummy, can I have an ice-cream? ~ **Presently**, dear.*

## 468   price and prize

The *price* is what you pay if you buy something. A *prize* is what you are given if you have done something exceptional, or if you win a competition.

*What's the **price** of the green dress?* (NOT *... the prize of the green dress?*)
*She received the Nobel **prize** for physics.* (NOT *... the Nobel price ...*)

## 469   principal and principle

These two words have the same pronunciation. The adjective *principal* means 'main', 'most important'.

*What's your **principal** reason for wanting to be a doctor?* (NOT *... your principle reason ...*)

The noun *principal* means 'headmaster' or 'headmistress' (especially, in Britain, of a school for adults).

*If you want to leave early you'll have to ask the **Principal**.*

▶

A *principle* is a scientific law or a moral rule.
>Newton discovered the **principle** of universal gravitation. (NOT ... ~~the principal of universal gravitation.~~)
>She's a girl with very strong **principles**.

# 470 progressive (1): general

## 1 forms

Progressive verb forms (also called 'continuous' forms) are made with **be + -ing**.
>I **am waiting** for the shops to open. (present progressive)
>Your suit **is being cleaned**. (present progressive passive)
>She phoned while I **was cooking**. (past progressive)
>I didn't know how long she **had been sitting** there. (past perfect progressive)
>**Will** you **be going** out this evening? (future progressive)
>I'd like **to be lying** on the beach now. (progressive infinitive)

## 2 terminology and use

A progressive form does not simply show the time of an event. It also shows how the speaker sees the event – generally as ongoing and temporary, not completed or permanent. (Because of this, grammars often talk about 'progressive aspect' rather than 'progressive tenses'.) Compare:
>– I've **read** your letter. (completed action)
>I've **been reading** a lot of thrillers recently. (not necessarily completed)
>– The Rhine **runs** into the North Sea. (permanent)
>We'll have to phone the plumber – water**'s running** down the kitchen wall. (temporary)

When a progressive is used to refer to a short momentary action, it often suggests repetition.
>Why **are** you **jumping** up and down?
>The door **was banging** in the wind.

## 3 distancing

Progressive forms can make requests, questions and statements less direct. (They sound less definite than simple forms, because they suggest something temporary and incomplete.)
>**I'm hoping** you can lend me £10. (less definite than I hope ...)
>What time **are** you **planning** to arrive?
>**I'm looking** forward to seeing you again.
>I'm afraid we must **be going**.
>I **was wondering** if you had two single rooms.
>Will you **be going** away at the weekend?

For more about this kind of 'distancing', see 436.
For more details of the use of progressives, see the individual entries on the present progressive, past progressive etc.

# 471 progressive (2): non-progressive verbs

## 1 verbs not used in progressive ('continuous') forms

Some verbs are never or hardly ever used in progressive forms.

> I **like** this music. (NOT ~~I'm liking this music.~~)
> I rang her up because I **needed** to talk. (NOT ... ~~because I was needing to talk.~~)

Some other verbs are not used in progressive forms when they have certain meanings. Compare:

> I'm **seeing** the doctor at ten o'clock.
> I **see** what you mean. (NOT ~~I'm seeing what you mean.~~)

Many of these non-progressive verbs refer to states rather than actions. Some refer to mental states (e.g. *know, think, believe*); some others refer to the use of the senses (e.g. *smell, taste*).

Modal verbs (e.g. *can, must*) have no progressive forms. See 353.

## 2 common non-progressive verbs

Here is a list of some common verbs which are not often used in progressive forms (or which are not used in progressive forms with certain meanings).

**mental and emotional states**

| | | |
|---|---|---|
| *believe* | *(dis)like* | *see* (= understand) |
| *doubt* | *love* | *suppose* |
| *feel* (= have an opinion) | *prefer* | *think* (= have an opinion) |
| *hate* | *realise* | *understand* |
| *imagine* | *recognise* | *want* |
| *know* | *remember* | *wish* |

**use of the senses**

| | | |
|---|---|---|
| *feel* | *see* | *sound* |
| *hear* | *smell* | *taste* |

**communicating and causing reactions**

| | | |
|---|---|---|
| *agree* | *impress* | *promise* |
| *appear* | *look* (= seem) | *satisfy* |
| *astonish* | *mean* | *seem* |
| *deny* | *please* | *surprise* |
| *disagree* | | |

**other**

| | | |
|---|---|---|
| *be* | *deserve* | *measure* (= have length etc) |
| *belong* | *fit* | *need* |
| *concern* | *include* | *owe* |
| *consist* | *involve* | *own* |
| *contain* | *lack* | *possess* |
| *depend* | *matter* | *weigh* (= have weight) |

More details of the use of some of these verbs are given in other entries in the book. See the Index for references.

▶

## 3  progressive and non-progressive uses

Compare the progressive and non-progressive uses of some of the verbs listed above.

- *I'm feeling fine.* (OR *I feel fine.* – see 202.1)
  *I feel we shouldn't do it.* (NOT ~~I'm feeling we shouldn't do it.~~ – *feel* here = have an opinion.)
- *What are you thinking about?*
  *What do you think of the government?* (NOT ~~What are you thinking of the government?~~ – *think* here = have an opinion.)
- *I'm seeing Leslie tomorrow.*
  *I see what you mean.* (NOT ~~I'm seeing what you mean.~~ – *see* here = understand.)
- *Why are you smelling the meat? Is it bad?*
  *Does the meat smell bad?* (NOT ~~Is the meat smelling bad?~~ – see 535.)
- *I'm just tasting the cake to see if it's OK.*
  *The cake tastes wonderful.* (NOT ~~The cake's tasting wonderful.~~ – see 577.)
- *The scales broke when I was weighing myself this morning.*
  *I weighed 68 kilos three months ago – and look at me now!*
  (NOT ~~I was weighing 68 kilos~~ . . . – *weigh* here = have weight.)

Occasionally 'non-progressive' verbs are used in progressive forms in order to emphasise the idea of change or development.

> *These days, more and more people prefer / are preferring to take early retirement.*
> *The water tastes / is tasting better today.*
> *As I get older, I remember / I'm remembering less and less.*
> *I'm liking it here more and more as time goes by.*

*Need, want* and *mean* can have future or present perfect progressive uses.

> *Will you be needing the car this afternoon?*
> *I've just been invited to Sydney. It's wonderful – I've been wanting to go to Australia for years.*
> *I've been meaning to tell you about Andrew. He . . .*

## 4  can see etc

*Can* is often used with *see, hear, feel, taste, smell, understand* and *remember* to give a kind of progressive meaning, especially in British English. For details, see 125.

> *I can see Sue coming down the road.*
> *Can you smell something burning?*

## 5  -ing forms

Even verbs which are never used in progressive tenses have *-ing* forms which can be used in other kinds of structure.

> *Knowing her tastes, I bought her a large box of chocolates.*
> *I don't like to go to a country without knowing something of the language.*

## 472 **progressive** (3): with **always** etc

We can use *always*, *continually* and similar words with a progressive form to mean 'very often'.

*I'm **always losing** my keys.*
*Granny's nice. She's **always giving** people little presents.*
*I'm **continually running** into Paul these days.*
*That cat's **forever getting** shut in the bathroom.*

This structure is used to talk about things which happen very often (perhaps more often than expected), and which are unexpected or unplanned. Compare:

– *When Alice comes to see me, I **always meet** her at the station.*
(a regular, planned arrangement)
*I'm **always meeting** Mrs Bailiff in the supermarket.*
(accidental, unplanned meetings)
– *When I was a child, we **always had** picnics on Saturdays in the summer.*
(regular, planned)
*Her mother **was always arranging** little surprise picnics and outings.*
(unexpected, not regular)

## 473 **punctuation** (1):
## full stop, question mark and exclamation mark

### 1 **sentence division**

Full stops (AmE periods), question marks and exclamation marks (AmE exclamation points) are used to close sentences. After one of these, a new sentence has a capital letter.

*I looked out of the window. It was snowing again.*
*Why do we try to reach the stars? What is it all for?*
*They have no right to be in our country! They must leave at once!*

We do not normally put full stops, question or exclamation marks before or after grammatically incomplete sentences.

*She phoned me as soon as she arrived.* (NOT ~~She phoned me. As soon as she arrived.~~)
*In his job he has to deal with different kinds of people.* (NOT ~~In his job. He has to deal with different kinds of people.~~)
*Did you understand why I was upset?* (NOT ~~Did you understand? Why I was upset?~~)

However, sometimes we can emphasise a clause or phrase by separating it with a full stop and capital letter.

*People are sleeping out on the streets. In Britain. In the 21st century. Because there are not enough houses.*

### 2 **abbreviations**

Full stops can be used after abbreviations (see 2). This is more common in American English than in British English.

*Dr. Andrew C. Burke, M.A.* (OR *Dr Andrew C Burke, MA*)  ▶

### 3 indirect questions

We do not use question marks after indirect questions (see 276).

*I asked her what time it was.* (NOT ... ~~what time it was?~~)

# 474 punctuation (2): colon

## 1 explanations

A colon (:) usually introduces an explanation or further details.

*We decided not to go on holiday: we had too little money.*

*There was a problem with the car: it was losing oil.*

## 2 lists

A colon can introduce a list.

*The main points are as follows: (1) ... , (2) ... , (3) ....*

*We need three kinds of support: economic, moral and political.*

## 3 subdivisions

A colon can introduce a subdivision of a subject in a title or heading.

*punctuation: colon*

## 4 capitals

In British English, it is unusual for a capital letter to follow a colon (except at the beginning of a quotation). However, this can happen if a colon is followed by several complete sentences.

*My main objections are as follows:*

> *First of all, no proper budget has been drawn up.*
> *Secondly, there is no guarantee that ...*

In American English, colons are more often followed by capital letters.

## 5 letters

Americans usually put a colon after the opening salutation (*Dear ...*) in a business letter.

*Dear Mr. Callan:*

*I am writing to ...*

British usage prefers a comma or no punctuation mark at all in this case.

## 6 direct speech

Normally, direct speech is introduced by a comma in writing (see 476.9).

***Stewart opened his eyes and said,*** *'Who's your beautiful friend?'*

But a long passage of direct speech may be introduced by a colon.

*Introducing his report for the year,* ***the Chairman said:*** *'A number of factors have contributed to the firm's very gratifying results. First of all, ...'*

And a colon is used when direct speech is introduced by a name or short phrase (as in the text of a play, or when famous sayings are quoted).

POLONIUS: *What do you read, my lord?*

HAMLET:    *Words, words, words.*

***In the words of Murphy's Law:*** *'Anything that can go wrong will go wrong.'*

# 475  punctuation (3): semi-colon

## 1  instead of full stops

Semi-colons (;) are sometimes used instead of full stops, in cases where sentences are grammatically independent but the meaning is closely connected. Semi-colons are not nearly as common as full stops or commas.

> *Some people work best in the mornings; others do better in the evenings.*
> *It is a fine idea; let us hope that it is going to work.*

Commas are not usually possible in cases like these (see 476).

## 2  in lists

Semi-colons can also be used to separate items in a list, particularly when these are grammatically complex.

> *You may use the sports facilities on condition that your subscription is paid*
> *  regularly; that you arrange for all necessary cleaning to be carried out; that*
> *  you undertake to make good any damage; . . .*

For commas in lists, see 476.

# 476  punctuation (4): comma

Commas (,) generally reflect pauses in speech.

## 1  co-ordinate clauses

Clauses connected with *and,* *but* or *or* are usually separated by commas unless they are very short. Compare:
– *Jane decided to try the home-made steak pie, and Andrew ordered Dover sole*
> *  with boiled potatoes.*
> *Jane had pie and Andrew had fish.*
– *She had very little to live on, but she would never have dreamed of taking*
> *  what was not hers.*
> *She was poor but she was honest.*

## 2  subordinate clauses

When subordinate clauses begin sentences, they are often followed by commas. Compare:

> *If you are ever in London, come and see me.*
> *Come and see me if you are ever in London.*

Commas are not used before *that*-clauses.

> *It is quite natural that you should want to meet your father.* (NOT *It is quite*
> *natural, that . . .*)

## 3  grammatically separate sentences: commas not used

We do not usually put commas between grammatically separate sentences (in places where a full stop or a semi-colon would be possible – see 473 and 475).

> *The blue dress was warmer. On the other hand, the purple one was prettier.*
> OR *The blue dress was warmer; on the other hand . . .* (NOT *The blue dress*
> *was warmer, on the other hand . . .*)                                               ▶

## 4 unusual word order

If words or expressions are put in unusual places or interrupt the normal
progression of a sentence, we usually separate them off by commas.

*My father,* **however,** *did not agree.*
*Jane had,* **surprisingly,** *paid for everything.*
*We were,* **believe it or not,** *in love with each other.*
*Andrew Carpenter,* **the deputy sales manager,** *was sick.*

Two commas are necessary in these cases.

(NOT *Andrew Carpenter the deputy sales manager, was sick* . . .)

## 5 adjectives

After *be* and other 'link verbs' (see 328), commas are always used between
adjectives.

*The cowboy was* **tall, dark** *and handsome.*

Before a noun, we generally use commas between adjectives which give
similar kinds of information.

*This is an* **expensive, ill-planned, wasteful** *project.*

Commas are sometimes dropped between short adjectives.

*a* **tall(,) dark(,) handsome** *cowboy*

Commas cannot be dropped when adjectives or other modifiers refer to
different parts of something.

*a* **green, red** *and gold carpet* (NOT *a green red* . . .)
**concrete, glass** *and plastic buildings*

Commas are not normally used before a noun when adjectives give different
kinds of information.

*Have you met our* **handsome new financial** *director?* (NOT *. . . our*
*handsome, new, financial director?*)

## 6 identifying expressions: commas not used

When nouns are followed by identifying expressions which show exactly who
or what is being talked about, commas are not used. Compare:

– **The driver in the Ferrari** *was cornering superbly.* (The phrase *in the Ferrari*
identifies the driver.)
(NOT *The driver, in the Ferrari, was cornering superbly* OR *The driver in the*
*Ferrari, was cornering superbly.*)
*Stephens,* **in the Ferrari,** *was cornering superbly.* (The phrase *in the Ferrari*
does not identify the driver; he is already identified by his name,
*Stephens.*)

– **The woman who was talking on the phone** *gave Parker a big smile.*
*Mrs Grange,* **who was talking on the phone,** *gave Parker a big smile.*

For more about identifying and non-identifying relative clauses, see 495.

## 7 long subjects: commas not used

We do not usually put a comma after a subject, even if it is very long.

*The man from the Japanese Ministry of Education arrived* early.
(NOT *The man from the Japanese Minstry of Education, arrived early.*)
**What we need most of all** *is more time.* (NOT *What we need most of all, is* . . .)

### 8 lists

We can use commas to separate items in a series or list. A comma is not usually used with *and* between the last two items unless these are long. Compare:

> *I went to Spain, Italy, Switzerland, Austria and Germany.*
> *You had a holiday at Christmas, at New Year and at Easter.*
> *I spent yesterday playing cricket, listening to jazz records, and talking about the meaning of life.*

For semi-colons in lists, see 475.

### 9 direct speech

A comma is generally used between a reporting expression and a piece of direct speech.

> *He said, 'There's no way we can help her'.*

If a reporting expression follows a piece of direct speech, we usually put a comma instead of a full stop before the closing quotation mark.

> *'I don't like this one bit,' said Julia.*

### 10 indirect speech: no comma before *that* etc

We do not put commas before *that, what, where* etc in indirect speech structures.

> *Everybody realised that I was a foreigner.* (NOT *Everybody realised, that*...)
> *They quickly explained what to do.* (NOT *They quickly explained, what*...)
> *I didn't know where I should go.* (NOT *I didn't know, where*...)

### 11 numbers

Commas are used to divide large numbers into groups of three figures, by separating off the thousands and millions.

> *6,435* (NOT *6.435*)    *7,456,189*

We do not always use commas in four-figure numbers, and they are never used in dates.

> *3,164* OR *3164*    *the year 1946*

Spaces are sometimes used instead of commas.

> *There are 1 000 millimetres in one metre.*

We do not use commas in decimals (see 389.1).

> *3.5 = three point five* OR *three and a half* (NOT *3,5 three comma five*)

## 477 punctuation (5): dash

Dashes (–) are especially common in informal writing. They can be used in the same way as colons, semi-colons or brackets.

> *There are three things I can never remember – names, faces, and I've forgotten the other.*
> *We had a great time in Greece – the kids really loved it.*
> *My mother – who rarely gets angry – really lost her temper.*

▶

A dash can introduce an afterthought, or something unexpected and surprising.

>*We'll be arriving on Monday morning – at least, I think so.*
>*And then we met Bob – with Lisa, believe it or not!*

For the use of hyphens (as in *hard-working* or *co-operative*), see 559.

# 478 punctuation (6): quotation marks

Quotation marks can be single ('...') or double ("..."). They are also called 'inverted commas' in British English.

## 1 direct speech

We use quotation marks (single or double) when we quote direct speech. For quotations inside quotations, we use double quotation marks inside single (or single inside double).

>*'His last words,' said Albert, 'were "Close that bloody window".'*

## 2 special use of words

We often put quotation marks (usually single) round words which are used in special ways – for example when we talk about them, when we use them as titles, or when we give them special meanings.

>*People disagree about how to use the word 'disinterested'.*
>*His next book was 'Heart of Darkness'.*
>*A textbook can be a 'wall' between the teacher and the class.*

# 479 punctuation (7): apostrophe /əˈpɒstrəfiː/

We use apostrophes (') for three main reasons.

## 1 missing letters

Apostrophes replace letters in contracted forms (see 143).

>*can't* (= cannot)      *I'd* (= I would/had)
>*it's* (= it is/has)      *who's* (= who is/has)

## 2 possessives

We use apostrophes before or after possessive *-s* (see 439).

>*the **girl's** father      **Charles's** wife      my **parents'** house*

Possessive determiners and pronouns (e.g. *yours, its*) do not have apostrophes.

>*This money is **yours**.* (NOT ... ~~your's~~.)
>*The cat had not had **its** food yet.* (NOT ...~~it's food~~ ...)
>***Whose** house did she stay in?* (NOT ~~Who's~~ ...)

## 3 special plurals

Words which do not usually have plurals sometimes have an apostrophe when a plural form is written.

>*It is a nice idea, but there are a lot of **if's**.*

Apostrophes are used in the plurals of letters, and sometimes of numbers and abbreviations.

*He writes **b's** instead of **d's**.*
*It was in the early **1960's**.* (More usually: ... *1960s*.)
*I know two **MP's** personally.* (More usually: ... *MPs*.)

It is not correct to put apostrophes in normal plurals.

*JEANS – HALF PRICE* (NOT ~~JEAN'S~~ ...)

# 480 questions (1): basic rules

These rules apply to most written and spoken questions. For 'declarative questions' like *This is your car?* (in which the subject comes before the verb), see 481.

## 1 auxiliary verb before subject: *Have you ...?*

In a question, an auxiliary verb normally comes before the subject.

*When **is** Oliver leaving?* (NOT ~~When Oliver is leaving?~~)
*Have you** received my letter of June 17?* (NOT ~~You have received ...?~~)
*Why **are** you laughing?* (NOT ~~Why you are laughing?~~)
*What **are all those people** looking at?* (NOT ~~What all those people are looking at?~~)
*How much **does the room** cost?* (NOT ~~How much the room costs?~~)

## 2 do: *Do you like ...?*

If there is no other auxiliary verb, we use *do, does* or *did* to form a question.

*Do you like Mozart?* (NOT ~~Like you Mozart?~~)
*What **does** 'periphrastic' mean?* (NOT ~~What means 'periphrastic'?~~)
*Did you wash the car today?*

## 3 do not used with other auxiliaries

*Do* is not used together with other auxiliary verbs or with *be*.

*Can you** tell me the time?* (NOT ~~Do you can tell me the time?~~)
*Have you** seen John?* (NOT ~~Do you have seen John?~~)
*Are you** ready?*

## 4 infinitive after do: *What does he want?*

After *do*, we use the infinitive (without *to*).

*What does the boss **want?*** (NOT ~~What does the boss wants?~~)
*Did you **go** climbing last weekend?* (NOT ~~Did you went ...?~~ OR ~~Did you to go ...?~~)

## 5 only auxiliary verb before subject

Only the auxiliary verb goes before the subject, not the whole of the verb.

*Is your mother **coming** tomorrow?* (NOT ~~Is coming your mother tomorrow?~~)
*Is your daughter **having** a lesson today?* (NOT ~~Is having your daughter ...?~~)
*When **was** your reservation **made?*** (NOT ~~When was made your reservation?~~)

This happens even if the subject is very long.

*Where are **the President and his family** staying?* (NOT ~~Where are staying the President ...?~~)

▶

## 6 *Who phoned? / Who did you phone?*

When *who, which, what* or *whose* is the subject (or part of the subject), *do* is not normally used. Compare:
– *Who **phoned**?* (*Who* is the subject.)
  *Who **did** you **phone**?* (*Who* is the object.)
– *What **happened**?* (*What* is the subject.)
  *What **did** she **say**?* (*What* is the object.)
More examples:
  *Which **costs** more – the blue one or the grey one?* (NOT ~~Which does cost more...?~~)
  *Which type of battery **lasts** longest?* (NOT ~~Which type of battery does last longest?~~)
  *How many people **work** in your office?* (NOT ~~How many people do work...?~~)
But *do* can be used after a subject question word for emphasis, to insist on an answer.
  *Well, tell us – what **did happen** when your father found you?*
  *So who **did marry** the Princess in the end?*

## 7 indirect questions: *Tell me when you are leaving*

In an indirect question, we do not put an auxiliary before the subject, and we do not use a question mark. For details, see 276.
  *Tell me when **you are** leaving.* (NOT ~~Tell me when are you leaving?~~)

## 8 prepositions: *What are you talking about?*

Prepositions often come at the end of *wh*-questions, separated from their objects. (For details, see 452.)
  ***What** are you talking **about**?* (NOT ~~About what are you talking?~~)
  ***Who** did you buy the ticket **from**?*
  ***What** did you clean the floor **with**?*

For negative questions, see 368.
For ellipsis in questions (e.g. *Seen John? Coming tonight?*), see 179.

# 481 questions (2): declarative questions

In spoken questions, we do not always use 'interrogative' word order.
  ***You're** working late tonight?*
These 'declarative questions' are often used when the speaker thinks he/she knows or has understood something, but wants to make sure or express surprise. A rising intonation is common.
  ***This is** your car?* (= I suppose this is your car, isn't it?)
  ***That's** the boss? I thought he was the cleaner.*
  *We're going to Hull for our holidays. ~ **You're going** to Hull?*
This word order is not normally possible after a question word.
  ***Where are you** going?* (NOT ~~Where you are going?~~)

# 482 questions (3): rhetorical questions

## 1 questions that do not expect an answer

Questions do not always ask for information. In many languages, a question with an obvious answer can be used simply as a way of drawing attention to something. Questions of this kind are called 'rhetorical questions'.

*Do you know what time it is?* (= You're late.)
*Who's a lovely baby?* (= You're a lovely baby.)
*I can't find my coat. ~ What's this, then?* (= Here it is, stupid.)

Very often, a rhetorical question draws attention to a negative situation – the answer is obviously *No*, or there is no answer to the question.

*What's the use of asking her?* (= It's no use asking her.)
*How do you expect me to find milk on a Sunday night? Where am I going to find a shop open?* (= You can't reasonably expect ... There aren't any shops open.)
*Where's my money?* (= You haven't paid me.)
*I can run faster than you. ~ Who cares?* (= Nobody cares.)
*Are we going to let them do this to us?* (= We aren't ...)
*Have you lost your tongue?* (= Why don't you say anything?)
*What do you think you're doing?* (= You can't justify what you're doing.)
*Who do you think you are?* (= You aren't as important as your behaviour suggests.)
*Why don't you take a taxi?* (= There's no reason not to.)

## 2 *Why/How should ...?*

*Why should ...?* can be used aggressively to reject suggestions, requests and instructions.

*Ann's very unhappy. ~ Why should I care?*
*Could your wife help us in the office tomorrow? ~ Why should she? She doesn't work for you.*

*How should/would I know?* is an aggressive reply to a question.

*What time does the film start? ~ How should I know?*

## 3 negative *yes/no* questions

Negative *yes/no* questions (see 368) often suggest that the speaker wants the answer *Yes*, or some other positive response.

*Haven't I done enough for you?* (= I have done enough for you.)
*Didn't I tell you it would rain?* (= I told you ...)
*Don't touch that! ~ Why shouldn't I?* (= I have a perfect right to.)

# 483 questions (4): echo questions

## 1 *You're getting married?*

To question what has been said, a speaker may simply repeat ('echo') what he/she has heard. A rising intonation is common.

*I'm getting married. ~ You're getting married?*                    ▶

## 2 *Take a look at what?*

To question one part of a sentence, we can repeat the rest of the sentence, and put a stressed question word in place of the part we are asking about.

*Just take a look at that.* ~ **Take a look at what?**
*She's invited thirteen people to dinner.* ~ **She's invited how many?**
*We're going to Tierra del Fuego on holiday.* ~ **You're going where?**
*I've broken the fettle gauge.* ~ **You've broken the what?**

To question a verb, or the part of a sentence beginning with the verb, *do what* is used.

*She set fire to the garage.* ~ **She did what** *(to the garage)?*

## 3 repeating a question

A speaker may question a question, by repeating it with a rising intonation. Note that we use normal question structures with inverted word order, not indirect question structures, in this case.

*Where are you going?* ~ **Where am I going?** *Home.* (NOT . . . ~~Where I'm going?~~. . .)
*What does he want?* ~ **What does he want?** *Money, as usual.* (NOT . . . ~~What he wants?~~. . .)
*Are you tired?* ~ **Am I tired?** *Of course not.* (NOT . . . ~~Whether I'm tired?~~. . .)
*Do squirrels eat insects?* ~ **Do squirrels eat insects?** *I'm not sure.* (NOT . . . ~~Whether squirrels eat insects?~~. . .)

# 484 questions (5): reply questions (Was it? Did you?)

Short questions are often used in conversation to show that the listener is paying attention and interested. They are constructed with auxiliary verb + pronoun, like question tags (see 487).

*It was a terrible party.* ~ **Was it?** ~ *Yes* . . .

Note that these questions do not ask for information - they simply show that the listener is reacting to what has been said. More examples:

*We had a lovely holiday.* ~ **Did you?** ~ *Yes, we went* . . .
*I've got a headache.* ~ **Have you,** *dear? I'll get you an aspirin.*
*John likes that girl next door.* ~ *Oh,* **does he?**
*I don't understand.* ~ **Don't you?** *I'm sorry.*

Negative questions in reply to affirmative statements express emphatic agreement (like negative-question exclamations – see 195.4).

*It was a lovely concert.* ~ *Yes,* **wasn't it?** *I did enjoy it.*
*She's put on a lot of weight.* ~ *Yes,* **hasn't she?**

# 485 questions (6): question-word clauses

## 1 question-word clauses as objects

Clauses beginning with question words can refer both to questions and to the answers to questions. They often act as the objects of verbs – for example, when questions and their answers are reported (see 276).

> *I asked **who wanted to come**.*
> *She wondered **why he wasn't wearing a coat**.*
> *We need to decide **where Ann's going to sleep**.*
> *He told me **when he was arriving**, but I've forgotten.*
> *She explained **what the problem was**.*

## 2 other uses

Question-word clauses can act not only as objects, but also as subjects, complements or adverbials. This structure is often rather informal (especially with *how*-clauses – see 252).

> ***Who you invite** is your business.*     *A hot bath is **what I need**.*
> ***Where we stay** doesn't matter.*     *This is **how much I've done**.*
> *I'm surprised at **how fast she can run**.*
> *You can eat it **how you like**. (very informal)*

The 'preparatory *it*' structure is often used with subject clauses (see 446).

> *It's your business **who you invite**.*     *It doesn't matter **where we stay**.*

Question-word clauses can give more information about nouns. In this case they are called 'relative clauses' (see 494–498 for details).

> *There's that man **who threw stones at your dog**.*
> *The place **where Mary works** has just had a fire.*

# 486 questions (7): that-clauses

A *wh*-question usually refers to the main clause which starts with the question word. However, questions can also refer to subordinate *that*-clauses after verbs like *wish*, *think* or *say*.

> *Who do you wish **(that) you'd married**, then?*
> *How long do you think **(that) we should wait**?*
> *What did you say **(that) you wanted** for Christmas?*

*That* is usually dropped; it must be dropped when the question word refers to the subject of the subordinate clause.

> ***Who** do you think **is outside**?* (NOT ~~Who do you think that is outside?~~)
> ***What** do you suppose **will happen now**?* (NOT ~~What do you suppose that will happen now?~~)

# 487 question tags (1): basic information

## 1 What are question tags?

'Question tags' are the small questions that often come at the ends of sentences in speech, and sometimes in informal writing.

> *The film wasn't very good, **was it?*** ▶

Negatives are usually contracted. Full forms are possible in formal speech.

*That's the postman,* **isn't it?** *You take sugar in tea,* **don't you?**

*They promised to repay us within six months,* **did they not?** (formal)

Question tags can be used to check whether something is true, or to ask for agreement.

## 2 negative after affirmative, and vice versa

Question tags are used after affirmative and negative sentences, but not after questions.

*You're the new secretary,* **aren't you?**

*You're* **not** *the new secretary,* **are you?**

(BUT NOT *Are you the new secretary, aren't you?*)

To check information or ask for agreement, we most often put negative tags after affirmative sentences, and non-negative tags after negative sentences.

| + | − |
|---|---|

*It's cold,* **isn't it?**

| − | + |
|---|---|

*It's not warm,* **is it?**

For 'same-way' tags, see 488.7

## 3 auxiliaries

If the main sentence has an auxiliary verb (or non-auxiliary *be*), this is repeated in the question tag.

*Sally* **can** *speak French,* **can't she?**

*The meeting's at ten,* **isn't it?**

*You* **didn't** *speak to Luke,* **did you?**

*You* **wouldn't** *like a puppy,* **would you?**

If the main sentence has no auxiliary, the question tag has *do*.

*You like oysters,* **don't you?**

*Harry gave you a cheque,* **didn't he?**

## 4 negative words

Non-negative tags are used after sentences containing negative words like *never, no, nobody, hardly, scarcely* and *little*.

*You* **never** *say what you're thinking,* **do you?** (NOT *...don't you?*)

*It's* **no** *good,* **is it?** (NOT *...isn't it?*)

*It's* **hardly** *rained at all this summer,* **has it?**

*There's* **little** *we can do about it,* **is there?**

## 5  meaning and intonation

In speech, we can show the exact meaning of a question tag by the intonation. If the tag is a real question – if we really want to know something and are not sure of the answer – we use a rising intonation: the voice goes up.

*The meeting's at four o'clock, **isn't it?***

If the tag is not a real question – if we are sure of the answer – we use a falling intonation: the voice goes down.

*It's a beautiful day, **isn't it?***

In writing, the exact meaning of a question tag is normally clear from the context.

## 6  requests

We often ask for help or information by using the structure **negative statement + question tag**.
*You **couldn't** lend me a pound, **could you?***
*You **haven't** seen my watch anywhere, **have you?***

For details of other kinds of tags, see 514.

# 488  question tags (2): advanced points

## 1  *aren't I?*

The question tag for *I am* is *aren't I?*
*I'm late, **aren't I?***

## 2  imperatives

After imperatives, *won't you?* can be used to invite people politely to do things (especially in British English).
*Come in, **won't you?***
*Will/would/can/could you?* can all be used to tell or ask people to do things.
*Give me a hand, **will you?**    Open a window, **would you?***
*Can't* you expresses impatience.
*Shut up, **can't you?***
After a negative imperative, we use *will you?*
*Don't forget, **will you?***

## 3  *let's*

After *let's . . .* (in suggestions etc, see 323), we use *shall we?*
*Let's have a party, **shall we?***

## 4  *there*

*There* can be a subject in question tags.
*There's something wrong, **isn't there?***
*There weren't any problems, **were there?***
When *there's* introduces a plural subject (see 532.4), the tag is *aren't there?*
*There's some more **chairs** upstairs, **aren't there?***

▶

### 5  *it* and *they* with *nothing, nobody, somebody* etc

We use *it* in question tags to refer to *nothing* and *everything*.
> *Nothing can happen, can **it?***

We use *they* (see 528) to refer to *nobody, somebody* and *everybody* (and *no one* etc).
> *Nobody phoned, **did they?***
> *Somebody wanted a drink, **didn't they?** Who was it?*

### 6  non-auxiliary *have*

After non-auxiliary *have* (referring to states), question tags with *have* and *do* are often both possible. (*Do* is normal in American English.)
> *Your father **has** a bad back, **hasn't/doesn't he?***

For more about the use of *do* with *have*, see 236–239.

### 7  'same-way' question tags: *You're getting married, are you?*

Non-negative question tags are quite common after affirmative sentences. These are often used as responses to something that has been said, like 'reply questions' (see 484): the speaker repeats what he/she has just heard or learnt, and uses the tag to express interest, surprise, concern or some other reaction.
> *So **you're** getting married, **are you?** How nice!*
> *So **she thinks** she's going to become a doctor, **does she?** Well, well.*
> *You **think** you're funny, **do you?***

'Same-way' tags can also be used to ask questions. In this structure, we use the main sentence to make a guess, and then ask (in the tag) if it was correct.
> *Your **mother's** at home, **is she?**     This **is** the last bus, **is it?***
> *You **can** eat shellfish, **can you?***

*I'll ... shall I?* can be used to make offers.
> *I'll **hold** that for you, **shall I?***

Negative 'same-way' tags are occasionally heard; they usually sound aggressive.
> *I see. You **don't** like my cooking, **don't you?***

### 8  ellipsis: *Nice day, isn't it?*

In sentences with question tags, it is quite common to leave out pronoun subjects and auxiliary verbs. (This is called 'ellipsis'. For details, see 179.)
> *(It's a) **nice** day, **isn't it?**     (She was) **talking** to my husband, **was she?***

In very informal speech, a question tag can sometimes be used after a question with ellipsis.
> *Have a **good** time, **did you?**          Your **mother** at home, **is she?***
> *John **be** here tomorrow, **will he?***

For details of other kinds of tags, see 514.

### 9  *I (don't) think*

Note the use of question tags in sentences beginning with *I (don't) think* and similar expressions (see 179).
> *I think he's Norwegian, **isn't he?** (NOT ... ~~don't I?~~)*
> *I don't think it will rain, **will it?** (NOT ... ~~do I?~~)*
> *I suppose you're hungry, **aren't you?***

# 489 quite

## 1 two meanings

*Quite* has two meanings. Compare:
> *It's **quite** good, but it could be better.* (= It's OK, not bad.)
> *It's **quite** impossible.* (= It's completely impossible.)

*Good* is a 'gradable' adjective: things can be more or less good. With gradable words, *quite* usually means something like 'fairly' or 'rather' (see 199) in affirmative sentences. *Impossible* is non-gradable: things are either impossible or not; but they cannot be more or less impossible. With non-gradable words, *quite* means 'completely'. Compare:

– *I'm **quite** tired, but I can walk a bit further.*
  *I'm **quite** exhausted – I couldn't walk another step.*
– *It's **quite** surprising.* (similar to *fairly surprising*)
  *It's **quite** amazing.* (= absolutely amazing)
– *He speaks French **quite** well, but he's got a strong English accent.*
  *He speaks French **quite** perfectly.*
– *I **quite** like her, but she's not one of my closest friends.*
  *Have you **quite** finished?* (= Have you completely finished?)

In American English *quite* with gradable adjectives often means something like 'very', not 'fairly/rather'.

## 2 word order with nouns

*Quite* can be used with ***a/an* + noun**. It normally comes before *a/an* if there is a gradable adjective or no adjective.
> *It's **quite a nice** day.*
> *We watched **quite an interesting** film last night.*
> *She's **quite a** woman!*     *The party was **quite a** success.*

With non-gradable adjectives, *quite* normally comes after *a/an* in BrE.
> *It was **a quite perfect** day.* (AmE *It was quite a perfect day.*)

*Quite* is sometimes used before *the* to mean 'exactly', 'completely'.
> *He's going **quite the** wrong way.*     ***quite the** opposite*

## 3 comparisons

*Quite* is not used directly before comparatives.
> *She's **rather / much / a bit older** than me.* (BUT NOT *She's ~~quite older~~ . . .*)

But we use *quite better* to mean 'completely recovered' (from an illness).
*Quite similar* means 'fairly/rather similar'; *quite different* means 'completely different'.

## 4 *quite a bit/few/lot* etc

*Quite a bit* and *quite a few* (informal) mean almost the same as *quite a lot*.
> *We're having **quite a bit** of trouble with the kids just now.*
> *We thought nobody would be there, but actually **quite a few** people came.*

## 5 *not quite*

*Not quite* means 'not completely' or 'not exactly'. It can be used before adjectives, adverbs, verbs and nouns, including nouns with *the*.
> *I'm **not quite** ready – won't be a minute.*
> *She didn't run **quite fast** enough for a record.*
> *I don't **quite** agree.*     *That's **not quite** the colour I wanted.*

# 490 rather: adverb of degree (**rather good,** etc)

## 1 meaning

*Rather* can be used as an adverb of degree. The meaning is similar to 'quite' or 'fairly', but more emphatic (see 199). This use of *rather* is less common in American English.

>*The film was **rather** good.*    *Some people **rather** like being miserable.*
>*It's **rather** later than I thought.*    *I **rather** think we're going to lose.*

Rather often suggests 'more than usual', 'more than was expected', 'more than is wanted' and similar ideas.

>*How was the film? ~ **Rather** good – I was surprised.*
>*She sings **rather** well – people often think she's a professional.*
>*It's **rather** warm in here. Let's open a window.*

## 2 word order with articles

*Rather* generally comes before articles, but can also come after *a/an* if there is an adjective.

>*That's **rather the** impression I wanted to give.*
>*He's **rather a** fool.*
>*Jane's had **rather a good** idea.* (OR *Jane's had **a rather good** idea.*)

## 3 plural nouns

*Rather* is not normally used before a plural noun with no adjective.
(NOT ~~They're rather fools.~~)

# 491 rather: preference

## 1 *rather than*

This expression is normally used in 'parallel' structures: for example with two adjectives, adverbs, nouns, infinitives or -*ing* forms.

>*I'd call her hair **chestnut rather than brown**.*
>*I'd prefer to go **in August rather than in July**.*
>*We ought to invest in **machinery rather than buildings**.*
>*I prefer **starting** early **rather than leaving** things to the last minute.*

When the main clause has a *to*-infinitive, *rather than* is usually followed by an infinitive without *to* or an -*ing* form.

>*I decided **to write rather than phone/phoning**.*
>***Rather than use/using** the last of my cash, I decided **to write** a cheque.*

## 2 *would rather*

This expression means 'would prefer to', and is followed by the infinitive without *to*. We often use the contraction *'d rather*.

>***Would** you **rather stay** here or go home?*
>*How about a drink? ~ **I'd rather have** something to eat.*

The negative is *would rather not*.

>*I'd **rather not** go out tonight.* (NOT ~~I wouldn't rather...~~)

Note that *would rather like* does not mean 'would prefer'; in this expression, *rather* means 'quite', and does not suggest preference. Compare:

*I'd rather like a cup of coffee.* (= I'd quite like ...)

~ *Oh, would you? I'd rather have a glass of beer.* (= I'd prefer ...)

## 3 *would rather*: past tense with present or future meaning

We can use *would rather* to say that a person would prefer somebody to do something. We use a special structure with a past tense.

> *would rather* + subject + past tense

*I'd rather you went home now.*
*Tomorrow's difficult. I'd rather you came next weekend.*
*My wife would rather we didn't see each other any more.*
*Shall I open a window?* ~ *I'd rather you didn't.*

A present tense or present subjunctive is possible (e.g. *I'd rather he goes / he go home now*), but unusual. To talk about past actions, a past perfect tense is possible.

*I'd rather you hadn't done that.*

However, this kind of idea is usually expressed with *I wish* (see 630).

*I wish you hadn't done that.*

In older English, *had rather* was used in the same way as *would rather*. This structure is still found in grammars, but it is not normally used.

For other structures where a past tense has a present or future meaning, see 426.

## 4 *or rather*

People often use *or rather* to correct themselves.

*He's a psychologist – or rather, a psychoanalyst.* (NOT *... or better, a psychoanalyst.*)

## 5 *would rather* and *had better*

Note that *would rather* (= would prefer) is not the same as *had better* (= should) – see 230. Compare:

*I suppose I'd better clean the windows, but I'd rather watch TV.*

# 492 reason

The preposition *for* is used both before and after *reason*.

*What's the real reason for your depression?* (NOT *... reason of your depression?*)

*I need to talk to you for two reasons.*

Reason can be followed by a clause beginning *why* ... or *that* ....

*The reason why I came here was to be with my family.*

*Do you know the reason that they're closing the factory?*

In an informal style, *why/that* is often left out.

*The reason she doesn't like me is that I make her nervous.*

Some people consider it incorrect to use a *because*-clause as a complement after *reason* (as in *Sorry I'm late – the reason is because I overslept.*)

# 493 reflexive pronouns

## 1 What are reflexive pronouns?

Reflexive pronouns are *myself, yourself, himself, herself, itself, oneself, ourselves, yourselves, themselves.*

## 2 use: *I cut myself shaving*

A common use of reflexive pronouns is to talk about actions where the subject and object are the same person.
> *I cut **myself** shaving this morning.* (NOT ~~I cut me~~ . . .)
> *We got out of the water and dried **ourselves**.* (NOT . . . ~~dried us.~~)
> *I'm going to the shops to get **myself** some tennis shoes.*
> *Talking to **oneself** is the first sign of madness.*

Reflexive pronouns can also refer to possessives and objects.
> *His letters are all about **himself**.*
> *I'm going to tell **her** a few facts about **herself**.*
> *I love **you** for **yourself**, not for your money.*

## 3 after prepositions: *She took her dog with her*

After prepositions of place, we often use a personal pronoun (*me, you* etc) if the meaning is clear without using a reflexive. Compare:
> *She took her dog **with her**.* (NOT . . . ~~with herself.~~ She could hardly take her dog with somebody else.)
> *She's very pleased **with herself**.* (She could be pleased with somebody else.)

Other examples:
> *Close the door **after you**.*     *He was pulling a small cart **behind him**.*

## 4 emphatic use: *Do it yourself*

We can use reflexives as emphasisers, to mean 'that person/thing and nobody/ nothing else'.
> *It's quicker if you do it **yourself**.*     *The manageress spoke to me **herself**.*
> *The house **itself** is nice, but the garden's very small.*
> *I'll go and see the President **himself** if I have to.*

## 5 reflexives used instead of personal pronouns

Reflexives are sometimes used instead of personal pronouns after *as, like, but (for)* and *except (for)*.
> *These shoes are designed for heavy runners **like yourself**.* (OR . . . **like you**.)
> *Everybody was early **except myself**.* (OR . . . **except me**.)

Reflexives can also be used instead of personal pronouns in co-ordinated noun phrases.
> *There will be four of us at dinner: Robert, Alison, Jenny **and myself**.*
> (OR . . . *and I/me*.)

People often feel that these uses are fussy – too exact and unnecessary.

## 6 *by oneself*

*By myself/yourself* etc means 'alone, without company' or 'without help'.
> *I often like to spend time **by myself**.*
> *Do you need help?* ~ *No, thanks. I can do it **by myself**.*

## 7  *-selves* and *each other / one another*

Note the difference between *-selves* and *each other / one another* (see 171).
> *They talk to **themselves** a lot.* (Each of them talks to him/herself.)
> *They talk to **each other** a lot.* (Each of them talks to the other.)

## 8  *own*

There are no possessive reflexives. Instead, we use *my own, your own* etc.
> *I always type **my own** letters.* (NOT ... ~~myself's letters.~~)
> *The children have both got **their own** rooms.*

## 9  reflexives not used

Certain verbs (e.g. *wash, dress, shave*) have reflexive pronouns in some
languages but not in English.
> *Do you **shave** on Sundays?* (NOT ~~Do you shave yourself on Sundays?~~)
However, reflexives can be used if it is necessary to make it clear who does
the action.
> *She's old enough to **dress herself** now.*
> *The barber shaves all the people in the town who don't **shave themselves**.*
>     *So does he **shave himself** or not?*
Some other verbs which do not normally have reflexive pronouns:
> *Suddenly the door **opened**.* (NOT ~~Suddenly the door opened itself.~~)
> *His book's **selling** well.* (NOT ~~His book's selling itself well.~~)
> *Try to **concentrate**.* (NOT ~~Try to concentrate yourself.~~)
> *I **feel** strange.* (NOT ~~I feel myself strange.~~)
> *Hurry!* (NOT ~~Hurry yourself!~~)

For more about structures like *The door opened* and *His book's selling well*, see 609.

# 494  relatives (1): basic information

## 1  relative clauses: *the people who live next door*

Clauses beginning with question words (e.g. *who, which, where*) are often used
to modify nouns and some pronouns – to identify people and things, or to give
more information about them. Clauses used like this are called
'relative clauses'.
> *Do you know the people **who live next door**?*
> *Those **who want tickets** can get them from the office.*
> *There's a programme tonight **which you might like**.*
> *He lives in a village **where there are no shops**.*

## 2  relative pronouns: *who, whom, which*

When *who, whom* and *which* introduce relative clauses, they are called
'relative pronouns'. *Who(m)* refers to people and *which* to things.
> *What's the name of the tall man **who** just came in?* (NOT ... ~~the tall man
> which~~ ...)
> *It's a book **which** will interest children of all ages.* (NOT ... ~~a book who~~ ...)

## 3  subject and object

*Who* and *which* can be the subjects of verbs in relative clauses.
> *I like people **who smile** a lot.*
> *This is the key **which opens** the garage,*

▶

*Who(m)* and *which* can also be the objects of verbs in relative clauses. *Whom* is unusual in an informal style (see 623).

> *Do you remember the people **who we met** in Italy?* (*Who* is the object of *met.*)
>
> *I forget most of the films **which I see**.* (*Which* is the object of *see.*)

## 4   that = who/which

We often use *that* instead of *who* or *which*, especially in an informal style.

> *I like people **that** smile a lot.*
>
> *This is the key **that** opens the garage.*
>
> *Do you remember the people **that** we met in Italy?*
>
> *I forget most of the films **that** I see.*

## 5   all that, only ... that etc

*That* is especially common after quantifiers like *all, every(thing), some(thing), any(thing), no(thing), none, little, few, much, only*, and after superlatives.

> *Is this **all that's** left?* (More natural than ... *all which is left?*)
>
> *Have you got **anything that** belongs to me?* (More natural than ... *anything which* ...)
>
> *The **only** thing **that** matters is to find our way home.*
>
> *I hope the **little that** I've done has been useful.*
>
> *It's the **best** film **that's** ever been made about madness.*

Note that *what* (see 497) cannot be used in these cases.

> *All that you say is certainly true.* (NOT *All what you say* ...)

## 6   leaving out object pronouns: *the people we met*

Object pronouns can often be left out.

> *Do you remember **the people we met** in Italy?*
>
> *I forget most of **the films I see**.*        *All **I want** is your happiness.*

This is not possible in all relative clauses: see 495.

## 7   one subject or object is enough

As subjects or objects, *who(m), which* and *that* replace words like *she, him* or *it*: one subject or object in a relative clause is enough. Compare:

– *He's got a new girlfriend. **She** works in a garage.*
  *He's got a new girlfriend **who** works in a garage.* (NOT ... ~~who she works in a garage.~~)

– *This is Mr Rogers. You met **him** last year.*
  *This is Mr Rogers, **whom** you met last year.* (NOT ... ~~whom you met him last year.~~)

– *Here's an article. **It** might interest you.*
  *Here's an article **which** might interest you.* (NOT ... ~~which it might interest you.~~)

– *I've found the car keys. You were looking for **them**.*
  *I've found the car keys **that** you were looking for.* (NOT ... ~~that you were looking for them.~~)

## 8 whose: *a girl whose hair ...*

*Whose* is a possessive relative pronoun, used as a determiner before nouns. It replaces *his/her/its*. For more details, see 496.

> *I saw a girl **whose hair** came down to her waist.* (NOT ... ~~whose her hair came down~~...)

## 9 *which* referring to a whole clause

*Which* can refer not only to a noun, but also to the whole of a previous clause. Note that *what* cannot be used in this way.

> *He got married again a year later, **which** surprised everybody.* (NOT ...,~~what surprised everybody.~~)
>
> *She cycled from London to Glasgow, **which** is pretty good for a woman of 75.* (NOT *She cycled*... , ~~what is pretty good~~...)

## 10 relative *when, where* and *why*

*When* and *where* can introduce relative clauses after nouns referring to time and place. They are used in the same way as **preposition + *which*.**

> *I'll never forget the day **when** I first met you.* (= ... the day on which ...)
> *Do you know a shop **where** I can find sandals?* (= ... a shop at which ...)

*Why* is used in a similar way after *reason*.

> *Do you know the reason **why** she doesn't like me?* (= ... the reason for which ...)

# 495 relatives (2): identifying and non-identifying clauses

## 1 two kinds of relative clause

Some relative clauses identify or classify nouns: they tell us which person or thing, or which kind of person or thing, is meant. (In grammars, these are called 'identifying', 'defining' or 'restrictive' relative clauses.)

> *What's the name of the tall man **who just came in**?*
> *People **who take physical exercise** live longer.*
> *Who owns the car **which is parked outside**?*
> *Have you got something **that will get ink out of a carpet**?*

Other relative clauses do not identify or classify; they simply tell us more about a person or thing that is already identified. (In grammars, these are called 'non-identifying', 'non-defining' or 'non-restrictive' relative clauses.)

> *This is Ms Rogers, **who's joining the firm next week**.*
> *In 1908 Ford developed his Model T car, **which sold for $500**.*

There are several grammatical differences between the two kinds of relative clause. There are also stylistic differences: non-identifying clauses are generally more formal, and are less frequent in informal speech.

## 2 pronunciation and punctuation

Identifying relative clauses usually follow immediately after the nouns that they modify, without a break: they are not separated by pauses or intonation movements in speech, or by commas in writing. (This is because the noun would be incomplete without the relative clause, and the sentence would ▶

make no sense or have a different meaning.) Non-identifying clauses are normally separated by pauses and/or intonation breaks and commas. Compare:
- *The woman who does my hair* has moved to another hairdresser's.
  Dorothy*, who does my hair,* has moved to another hairdresser's.
- She married *a man that she met on a bus.*
  She married *a very nice young architect from Belfast, whom she met on a bus.*

Note how the identifying clauses cannot easily be left out.
  The woman has moved to another hairdresser's. (Which woman?)
  She married a man. (!)

When a non-identifying clause does not come at the end of a sentence, two commas are necessary.
  Dorothy*, who does my hair,* has moved ... (NOT ~~Dorothy, who does my hair has moved~~ ...)

### 3 use of *that*

*That* is common as a relative pronoun in identifying clauses. In non-identifying clauses, *that* is unusual. Compare:
- Have you got a book *which/that* is really easy to read?
  I lent him 'The Old Man and the Sea', *which* is really easy to read.
  (NOT ... ~~'The Old Man and the Sea', that is really easy to read.~~)
- Where's the girl *who/that* sells the tickets?
  This is Naomi, *who* sells the tickets. (NOT ~~This is Naomi, that sells the tickets.~~)

### 4 leaving out object pronouns

In identifying relative clauses, we often leave out object pronouns, especially in an informal style. In non-identifying clauses this is not possible. Compare:
- I feel sorry for *the man she married.*
  She met *my brother, whom she later married.* (NOT ~~She met my brother, she later married.~~)
- Did you like *the wine we drank last night?*
  I poured him *a glass of wine, which he drank at once.* (NOT ~~I poured him a glass of wine, he drank at once.~~)

## 496  relatives (3): whose

### 1 relative possessive

*Whose* is a relative possessive word, used as a determiner before nouns in the same way as *his, her, its* or *their*. It can refer back to people or things. In a relative clause, *whose + noun* can be the subject, the object of a verb or the object of a preposition.
  I saw a girl *whose beauty* took my breath away. (subject)
  It was a meeting *whose purpose* I did not understand. (object)
  Michel Croz, *with whose help* Whymper climbed the Matterhorn, was one of the first professional guides. (object of preposition)
  I went to see my friends the Forrests, *whose children* I used to look after when they were small. (object of preposition)

*Whose* can be used in both identifying and non-identifying clauses.

## 2 things: *of which; that . . . of*

Instead of *whose*, we can use *of which* or *that . . . of* (less formal) to refer to
things, and these are sometimes preferred. The most common word order is
**noun + of which** or **that . . . of**, but *of which . . . + noun* is also possible.
Compare the following four ways of expressing the same idea.

> He's written a book **whose name I've forgotten.**
> He's written a book **the name of which I've forgotten.**
> He's written a book **that I've forgotten the name of.**
> He's written a book **of which I've forgotten the name.**

We do not normally use **noun + of whom** in a possessive sense to talk about
people.

> *a man whose name I've forgotten* (NOT ~~a man of whom I've forgotten the name~~)

## 3 only used as a determiner

Relative *whose* is only used as a possessive determiner, before a noun. In other
cases we use *of which/whom* or *that . . . of*.

> He's married to a singer **of whom** you may have heard. OR . . . **that** you may
> have heard **of.** (NOT . . . ~~a singer whose you may have heard.~~)

## 4 formality

Sentences with *whose* are generally felt to be rather heavy and formal; in an
informal style other structures are often preferred. *With* (see 631) is a common
way of expressing possessive ideas, and is usually more natural than *whose* in
descriptions.

> *I've got some friends **with a** house that looks over a river.*
> (Less formal than . . . *whose house looks over a river.*)
> *You know that girl **with a** brother who drives lorries?*
> (Less formal than . . . *whose brother drives lorries?*)
> *She's married to the man over there **with the** enormous ears.*
> (More natural than . . . *the man over there whose ears are enormous.*)

For *whose* in questions, see 626.

# 497 relatives (4): what

## 1 meaning and use: *the thing(s) which*

*What* does not refer to a noun that comes before it. It acts as **noun + relative
pronoun** together, and means 'the thing(s) which'. Clauses beginning with
*what* can act as subjects, objects, or complements after *be*.

> **What she said** made me angry. (subject of *made*)
> *I hope you're going to give me **what I need**.* (object of *give*)
> *This is exactly **what I wanted**.* (complement)

For singular and plural verbs after *what* (e.g. *What we need most is/are books*), see 529. ▶

## 2  *what* not used

*What* is only used to mean 'the thing(s) which'. It cannot be used as an ordinary relative pronoun after a noun or pronoun.

We haven't got **everything that** you ordered. (NOT ...~~everything what~~...)
The **only thing that** keeps me awake is coffee. (NOT ~~The only thing what~~...)

We use *which*, not *what*, to refer to a whole clause that comes before (see 494.9).

Sally married Joe, **which** made Paul very unhappy. (NOT ...~~what made~~...)

## 3  *what* as a determiner

*What* can also be used as a determiner with a noun.

**What money** he has comes from his family. (= The money that he has ...)
I'll give you **what help** I can. (= ... any help that I can.)

# 498  relatives (5): advanced points

## 1  double use of relative pronouns

Note that relative pronouns have a double use: they act as subjects or objects inside relative clauses, and at the same time they connect relative clauses to nouns or pronouns in other clauses – rather like conjunctions.

## 2  relative pronouns as general-purpose connectors

In non-identifying clauses, the pronouns *who* and *which* sometimes act as general-purpose connecting words, rather like *and* + **pronoun**.

She passed the letter to Moriarty, **who** passed it on to me. (= ... and he passed it on ...)
I dropped the saucepan, **which** knocked over the eggs, **which** went all over the floor. (= ... and it knocked ... and they went ...)
I do a lot of walking, **which** keeps me fit. (= ... and this keeps me fit.)

## 3  *who* and *whom*

*Who* can be used as an object in identifying clauses in an informal style. *Whom* is more formal.

The woman **who** I marry will have a good sense of humour.
(More formal: The woman **whom** I marry ...)

In non-identifying clauses, *who* is less common as an object, though it is sometimes used in an informal style.

In that year he met Rachel, **whom** he was later to marry.
(OR ... Rachel, **who** he was later to marry. – informal)

## 4  *that* for people

*That* is often used in identifying relative clauses instead of *who/whom/which* (see 494.4). *That* is most common as an object, or as a subject instead of *which*. *That* can be used as a subject instead of *who*, but this is quite informal. Compare:

the people **that** I invited (normal)      the books **that** I lent you (normal)
the bus **that** crashed (normal)
the people **that** live next door (informal; the people who ... is preferred in a less informal style)

## 5  *which* as determiner; *in which case*

*Which* can be used as a determiner in relative clauses, with a general noun which repeats the meaning of what came before. This structure is rather formal, and is mainly used after prepositions, especially in some fixed phrases like *in which case* and *at which point.*

> She may be late, **in which case** we ought to wait for her.
> He lost his temper, **at which point** I decided to go home.
> He was appointed Lord Chancellor, **in which post** he spent the rest of his life.
> He spoke in Greek, **which language** I could only follow with difficulty.

## 6  *when, where* etc replaced by *that* or dropped

After common nouns referring to time, *when* is often replaced by *that* or dropped in an informal style.

> Come and see us **any time (that)** you're in town.
> I'll never forget **the day (that)** we met.
> That was **the year (that)** I first went abroad.

The same thing happens with *where* after *somewhere, anywhere, everywhere, nowhere* and *place* (but not after other words).

> Have you got **somewhere (that)** I can lie down for an hour?
> We need **a place (that)** we can stay for a few days. (BUT NOT ~~We need a house we can stay for a few days.~~)

After *way*, *in which* can be replaced by *that* or dropped in an informal style.

> I didn't like **the way (that)** she spoke to me.
> Do you know **a way (that)** you can earn money without working?

The same thing happens with *why* after *reason.*

> **The reason (that)** you're so bad-tempered is that you're hungry.

For more about *place*, see 431. For *way*, see 615. For *reason*, see 492.

## 7  position of prepositions

Prepositions can come either before relative pronouns (more formal) or at the ends of relative clauses (more informal). Compare:

- *He was respected by the people **with whom** he worked.* (formal)
  *He was respected by the people **(that)** he worked **with**.* (informal)
- *This is the room **in which** I was born.* (formal)
  *This is the room **(that)** I was born **in**.* (informal)

*Who* and *that* are not used after prepositions.

> ... the people **with whom** he worked. (NOT ... ~~the people with who/that he worked.~~)

For more about prepositions at the ends of clauses, see 452.

## 8  *some of whom, none of which* etc

In non-identifying clauses, quantifying determiners (e.g. *some, any, none, all, both, several, enough, many* and *few*) can be used with *of whom, of which* and *of whose*. The determiner most often comes before *of which/whom/whose*, but can sometimes come after it in a very formal style.

> They picked up five boat-loads of refugees, **some of whom** had been at sea for
> several months. (OR ... **of whom some** ...)
> ▶

*We've tested three hundred types of boot, **none of which** is completely*
*waterproof.* (OR ... *of which none* ...)
*They've got eight children, **all of whom** are studying music.* (OR ... *of whom*
*all are studying* ...)
*She had a teddy-bear, **both of whose** eyes were missing.*
This structure is also possible with other expressions of quantity, with
superlatives, with *first, second* etc, and with *last.*

| | | |
|---|---|---|
| *a number **of whom*** | *three **of which*** | *half **of which*** |
| *the majority **of whom*** | *the youngest **of whom*** | |

## 9  whatever, whoever etc

*Whatever* can be used rather like *what*, as **noun + relative pronoun** together.
*Take **whatever** you want.* (= ... anything that you want.)
Other words that can be used like this are *whoever, whichever, where,*
*wherever, when, whenever* and *how.*
*This is for **whoever** wants it.* (= ... any person that wants it.)
*I often think about **where** I met you.* (= ... the place where ...)
*We've bought a cottage in the country for **when** we retire.* (= ... the time
when ...)
***Whenever** you want to come is fine with me.* (= Any day that ...)
*Look at **how** he treats me.* (= ... the way in which ...)

For details of the use of *whoever, whatever* and other words ending in *-ever*, see 625.
For more about *how*-clauses, see 252.

## 10  reduced relative clauses: *the girl dancing*

A participle is often used instead of a relative pronoun and full verb.
*Who's the girl **dancing** with your brother?*
(= ... that is dancing with your brother?)
*Anyone **touching** that wire will get a shock.*
(= ... who touches ...)
*Half of the people **invited** to the party didn't turn up.*
(= ... who were invited ...)
*I found him sitting at a table **covered** with papers.*
(= ... which was covered with papers.)
Reduced structures are also used with the adjectives *available* and *possible.*
*Please send me all the tickets **available**.* (= ... that are available.)
*Tuesday's the only date **possible**.*

## 11  separating a noun from its relative pronoun

Relative pronouns usually follow their nouns directly.
*The **idea which** she put forward was interesting.* (NOT ~~The idea was~~
~~interesting which she put forward.~~)
*I rang up Mrs **Spencer, who** did our accounts.* (NOT ~~I rang Mrs Spencer up,~~
~~who did our accounts.~~)
However, a descriptive phrase can sometimes separate a noun from its relative
pronoun.
*I rang up Mrs **Spencer, the Manager's secretary, who** did our accounts.*

## 12 agreement of person

Most relative clauses have third-person reference; *I who . . .* , *you who . . .* and *we who . . .* are unusual, though they sometimes occur in a very formal style.

*You who pass by, tell them of us and say*
*For their tomorrow we gave our today.*
    (Allied war memorial at Kohima)

A different kind of first- and second-person reference is common in the relative clauses of cleft sentences (see 131). However, the verb is usually third-person, especially in an informal style.

*It's me that's responsible for the organisation.*
    (More formal: *It is I who am responsible . . .* )
*You're the one that knows where to go.* (NOT *. . . the one that know . . .*)

## 13 relative + infinitive: *a garden in which to play*

When a noun or pronoun is the object of a following infinitive, a relative pronoun is not normally used.

*I can't think of anybody to invite.* (NOT *. . . anybody whom to invite.*)

However, relative pronouns are possible with preposition structures.

*We moved to the country so that the children would have a garden in which to play.*
*He was miserable unless he had neighbours with whom to quarrel.*

This structure is rather formal, and it is more common to use **infinitive + preposition** without a relative pronoun.

*. . . so that the children would have a garden to play in.* (NOT *. . . which to play in.*)
*. . . unless he had neighbours to quarrel with.* (NOT *. . . whom to quarrel with.*)

## 14 relative clauses after indefinite noun phrases

The distinction between identifying and non-identifying clauses (see 495) is most clear when they modify definite noun phrases like *the car*, *this house*, *my father*, *Mrs Lewis*. After indefinite noun phrases like *a car*, *some nurses* or *friends*, the distinction is less clear, and both kinds of clause are often possible with slight differences of emphasis.

*He's got a new car that goes like a bomb.*
    (OR *He's got a new car, which goes like a bomb.*)
*We became friendly with some nurses that John had met in Paris.*
    (OR *We became friendly with some nurses, whom John had met in Paris.*)

In general, identifying clauses are used when the information they give is felt to be centrally important to the overall message. When this is not so, non-identifying clauses are preferred.

## 15 *somebody I know you'll like*

It is often possible to combine relative clauses with indirect statements and similar structures, e.g. *I know/said/feel/hope/wish (that) . . .* , especially in an informal style. Expressions like *I know*, *I said* etc come after the position of the relative pronoun.

*We're going to meet somebody (who/that) I know (that) you'll like.*
*It's a house (which/that) we feel (that) we might want to buy.*
*That's the man (who/that) I wish (that) I'd married.*

▶

Note that the conjunction (the second *that*) is usually dropped in this structure; it must be dropped if the relative pronoun is a subject.

> *This is the woman (who/that) Ann said could show us the church.*
>
> (NOT ~~This is the woman (who/that) Ann said that could show us~~ . . .)

In this structure, people sometimes use *whom* as a subject pronoun. This is not generally considered correct.

> *This is a letter from my father,* ***whom we hope will be out of hospital soon.***
>
> (More correct: . . . *who we hope will be out* . . .)

Relative clauses can also be combined with *if*-clauses in sentences like the following.

> *I am enclosing an application form,* ***which I should be grateful if you would sign and return.***

## 16   *a car that I didn't know how fast it could go,* etc

We do not usually combine a relative clause with an indirect question structure. However, this sometimes happens in informal speech.

> *I've just been to see an old friend* ***that I'm not sure when I'm going to see again.***
>
> *There's a pile of washing-up* ***that I just don't know how I'm going to do.***

There is no grammatically correct way of doing this when the relative pronoun is the subject of the relative clause. However, sentences like the following (with added pronouns) are also sometimes heard in informal speech. Some real examples:

> *I was driving a car* ***that I didn't know how fast it could go.***
>
> *It's ridiculous to sing songs* ***that you don't know what they mean.***
>
> *There's a control at the back* ***that I don't understand how it works.***
>
> *There's still one kid* ***that I must find out whether she's coming to the party or not.***

## 17   omission of subject

In a very informal style, a subject relative pronoun is sometimes dropped after *there is.*

> ***There's** a man at the door* ***wants to talk to you.***

## 18   double object

Occasionally a relative pronoun acts as the object of two verbs. This happens especially when a relative clause is followed by *before . . .ing, after . . .ing* or *without . . .ing.*

> *We have water* ***that it's best not to** **drink before boiling.*** (OR . . . *boiling* ***it.****)
>
> *I'm sending you a letter* ***that I want you to** **destroy after reading.*** (OR . . . *after reading* ***it.****)
>
> *He was somebody* ***that** *you could* **like without admiring.*** (OR . . . *admiring* ***him.****)

## 19 older English: *who* and *that which*

In older English, *who* could be used in a similar way to *what*, as **noun + relative pronoun** together, meaning 'the person who', 'whoever' or 'anybody who'. In modern English, this is very unusual.

> *Who steals my purse steals trash.* (Shakespeare, Othello)
> (Modern English: *Whoever/Anybody who ...*)

*That which* used to be used in the same way as *what*. This, too, is very unusual in modern English.

> *We have that which we need.* (Modern English: *We have what we need.*)

# 499 remind

## 1 meaning: *remind* and *remember*

These two verbs are not the same. *Reminding* somebody means 'making somebody remember'. Compare:
- *Remind me to pay the milkman.* (NOT *Remember me to pay*...)
  *I'm afraid I won't remember to pay the milkman.*
- *This sort of weather reminds me of my home.* (NOT *This sort of weather remembers me*...)
  *This sort of weather makes me remember my home.*

But note the special use of *remember* in *Remember me to your parents* and similar sentences.

## 2 structures

After *remind*, we can use an infinitive structure (for actions) or a *that*-clause (for facts).

> *Please remind me to go to the post office.* (NOT *Please remind me of going*...)
> *I reminded him that we hadn't got any petrol left.*

## 3 *remind ... of ...*

We use *remind ... of* to say that something/somebody makes us remember the past, or things that have been forgotten.

> *The smell of hay always reminds me of our old house in the country.*
> (NOT ... *reminds me our old house*...)
> *Remind me of your phone number.*

We can also use *remind ... of* to talk about similarities.

> *She reminds me of her mother.* (= She is like her mother.)

# 500 repetition

## 1 avoidance of repetition

In English, unnecessary repetition is usually considered to be a bad thing. Careful writers generally try not to use the same words and structures in successive clauses and sentences without a good reason; when expressions are repeated, it is often for deliberate emphasis or other stylistic purposes. Casual repetition is more common in informal language, but even in conversation people often sound monotonous or clumsy if they do not vary their sentence structure and vocabulary. Some kinds of repetition are actually ungrammatical in both writing and speech.

▶

## 2   unnatural/ungrammatical repetition

When we refer again to a person or thing that has already been mentioned, we normally use a pronoun instead of repeating the original noun phrase. When the reference is very close to the original mention, repetition (unless there is a special reason for it) is usually not only unnatural, but ungrammatical.

> *What's Rachel doing here?* ~ *She wants to talk to you.* (NOT . . . ~~Rachel wants to talk to you.~~)
> *We got that cat because the children wanted* ***it***. (NOT ~~We got that cat because the children wanted that cat.~~)
> *Dad's just cut* **himself** *shaving.* (NOT ~~Dad's just cut Dad shaving.~~)

This kind of thing happens with other words besides nouns.

> *I don't smoke.* ~ *I* ***do***. (NOT . . . ~~I smoke.~~)
> *Do you know if the bank's open?* ~ *I think* **so**. (NOT ~~I think the bank's open.~~)
> *She's staying at the Royal Hotel, so we said we'd meet her* **there**. (NOT . . . ~~so we said we'd meet her at the Royal Hotel.~~)

However, repetition is necessary and normal when alternatives are discussed.

> *Would you rather have potatoes or rice?* ~ ***Rice**, please.*
> *Shall we dance or go for a walk?* ~ *Let's* **go for a walk**.

For more details, see 177–182 (ellipsis) and 539 (*so*).

## 3   duplicated subjects and objects

We do not very often repeat a subject or object with the same verb.

> *That wall needs painting.*
> > (More normal than *That wall, it needs painting.*)
> *I saw my uncle yesterday.*
> > (More normal than *My uncle, I saw him yesterday.*)

However, this kind of repetition can happen in informal speech, when people announce a topic and then make a sentence about it (see 513).

> *That friend of your mother's –* **he's** *on the phone.*
> *Those bicycle wheels – I think we ought to put* **them** *in the garden shed.*

And sometimes a pronoun subject is repeated by a noun phrase 'tag' after the sentence (see 514).

> *She's a clever girl,* **your Anne**.

## 4   related verbs and nouns

We usually avoid putting related verbs and nouns together.

> – *We made wonderful* **plans**. OR *We* **planned** *wonderful things.*
> > (BUT NOT ~~We planned wonderful plans.~~)
> – *She* **wrote** *an interesting paper.* OR *She did an interesting piece of* **writing**.
> > (BUT NOT ~~She wrote an interesting piece of writing.~~)

There are some fixed expressions which are exceptions (e.g. *to sing a song, to live a good life, to die a violent death*).

## 5 *Wonderful, isn't it?* etc

There is a common kind of exchange in which one speaker gives his/her opinion of something, and the other speaker agrees by saying the same thing in other words which are at least as emphatic. Repetition is carefully avoided.

> *Glorious day.* ~ ***Wonderful**, isn't it?* (NOT ... ~~Glorious, isn't it?~~)
> *Terrible weather.* ~ ***Dreadful**.*
> *United didn't play very well, then.* ~ *Bloody **rubbish**.*

## 6 clumsy style

In writing, repetition is often considered clumsy even when it is not ungrammatical. Most of the repetitions in the following text would be avoided by a careful writer, by varying the structure and by careful use of synonyms (e.g. *tried/attempted, summarise / describe briefly, forecast/predict*).

> *In this report, I have tried to forecast likely developments over the next three years. In the first section, I have tried to summarise the results of the last two years, and I have tried to summarise the present situation. In the second section, I have tried to forecast the likely consequences of the present situation, and the consequences of the present financial policy.*

## 7 deliberate repetition

Speakers and writers can of course repeat vocabulary and structures deliberately. This may be done for emphasis.

> *I'm **very, very** sorry.*     *I want **every room** cleaned – **every** single **room**.*

Repeating somebody else's words may show surprise or disbelief.

> *I'm getting married.* ~ ***You're getting married**? Who to?*

Structural repetition can show how ideas are similar or related (by using the same structure for the same kind of item).

> *First of all, I **want to** congratulate you all on the splendid results. Secondly, I **want to** give you some interesting news. And finally, I **want to** thank you all ...*

## 8 literary examples

Here are two contrasting examples of repetition used deliberately for literary purposes. In the first, by John Steinbeck, structures and key vocabulary (especially nouns and verbs) are repeated and rhythmically balanced in order to create an impressive (or mock-impressive) effect – to make the story and characters sound striking and important.

> *This is the story of Danny and of Danny's friends and of Danny's house. It is a story of how these three became one thing, so that in Tortilla Flat if you speak of Danny's house you do not mean a structure of wood flaked with old white-wash, overgrown with an ancient untrimmed rose of Castile. No, when you speak of Danny's house you are understood to mean a unit of which the parts are men, from which came sweetness and joy, philanthropy, and, in the end, a mystic sorrow. For Danny's house was not unlike the Round Table, and Danny's friends were not unlike the knights of it. And this is the story of how the group came into being, of how it flourished and grew to be an organisation beautiful and wise. This story deals with the adventuring of Danny's friends, with the good they did, with their thoughts and their endeavors. In the end, this story tells how the talisman was lost and how the group disintegrated.*
>
> (John Steinbeck, *Tortilla Flat*)

▶

In contrast, the following text, by Ernest Hemingway, uses a kind of style which 'good' writers would normally avoid, repeating pronouns and simple structures in an apparently monotonous way. Hemingway's purpose is to show the simplicity of his hero, an uneducated old fisherman, by using a style that is supposed to reflect the way he thinks and speaks.

> *He did not remember when he had first started to talk aloud when he was by himself. He had sung when he was by himself in the old days and he had sung at night sometimes when he was alone steering on his watch in the smacks or in the turtle boats. He had probably started to talk aloud, when alone, when the boy had left. But he did not remember.*
> (Ernest Hemingway, *The Old Man and the Sea*)

## 501 [the] rest

*The rest* means 'what is left'. It is singular in form, and *the* is always used.
> *We only use three rooms.* **The rest** *of the house is empty.*

To talk about what is left after something has been used up, eaten, destroyed etc, we often use other words.
> *There were* **remains** *of the meal all over the floor.* (NOT ~~There were rests~~...)
> *Supper tonight is* **leftovers** *from lunch.* (NOT ...~~rests~~...)
> *If you divide 100 by 12,* **the remainder** *is 4.*

When *the rest* refers to a plural noun, it has a plural verb.
> *There are four chocolates for Penny, four for Joe and* **the rest are** *mine.*
> (NOT ...~~the rest is mine.~~)

## 502 road and street

### 1 the difference

A *street* is a road with houses on either side. We use *street* for roads in towns or villages, but not for country roads.
> *Cars can park on both sides of the* **street** *here.*
> *Our village has only got one* **street**.

*Road* is used for both town and country.
> *Cars can park on both sides of our* **road**.
> *The* **road** *out of our village goes up a steep hill.* (NOT ~~The street out of our village~~...)

### 2 street names: stress

In street names we normally stress the word *Road*, but the word before *Street*.
> *Marylebone 'Road        'Oxford Street*

## 503 the same

### 1 the same (as)

We normally use *the* before *same*.
> *Give me* **the same** *again, please.* (NOT ~~Give me same again, please.~~)

In a comparison, we use *the same (...) as*.
>*You've got **the same** idea **as** me.* (NOT ... ~~my same idea.~~)
>*Her hair's **the same** colour **as** her mother's.* (NOT ... ~~the same colour like~~ ...)

Note the expression *the very same* (= exactly the same).
>*Our birthdays are on **the very same** day.*

## 2  other structures

Before a clause, *the same ... that* or *the same ... who* can be used.
>*That's **the same** man **that/who** asked me for money yesterday.*

*As* is also possible before a clause, especially with a noun that is the object of the following verb.
>*He's wearing **the same** shirt **that/as** he had on yesterday.*

*As/who/that* can be left out when they refer to the object of the following verb.
>*He's wearing **the same shirt he had** on yesterday.*

Note also the expression *do the same*.
>*Why do you always try to **do the same** as your brother?*
>*Joe and Carol went on a camping holiday, and we're going to **do the same**.*

# 504  say and tell

## 1  meaning and use

Both *say* and *tell* are used with direct and indirect speech. (*Say* is more common than *tell* with direct speech.)
>*'Turn right,' I **said**.* (OR *'Turn right,' I **told** him.*)
>*She **said** that it was my last chance.* (OR *She **told** me that it was my last chance.*)

*Tell* is only used to mean 'instruct' or 'inform'. So we do not use *tell* with greetings, exclamations or questions, for example.
>*He **said**, 'Good morning.'* (BUT NOT ~~He told them, 'Good morning.'~~)
>*Mary **said**, 'What a nice idea.'* (BUT NOT ~~Mary told us, 'What a nice idea.'~~)
>*'What's your problem?' I **said**.* (BUT NOT ~~'What's your problem?' I told her.~~)

## 2  *say*: objects

*Say* is most often used without a personal object.
>*She **said** that she would be late.* (NOT ~~She said me~~ ...)

If we want to put a personal object after *say*, we use *to*.
>*And I **say to all the people** of this great country* ...

## 3  *tell*: objects

After *tell*, we usually say who is told.
>*She **told me** that she would be late.* (NOT ~~She told that~~ ...)

*Tell* is used without a personal object in a few expressions. Common examples: *tell the truth, tell a lie, tell a story/joke*.
>*I don't think she's **telling the truth**.* (NOT ... ~~saying the truth.~~)

Note also the use of *tell* to mean 'distinguish', 'understand', as in *tell the difference, tell the time*.
>*He's seven years old and he still can't **tell the time**.*

*Tell* is not used before objects like *a word, a name, a sentence, a phrase*.
>*Alice **said a naughty word** this morning.* (NOT ~~Alice told~~ ...)

▶

We do not usually use *it* after *tell* to refer to a fact.

> *What time's the meeting?* ~ *I'll* **tell you** *tomorrow.* (NOT ~~I'll tell you it tomorrow.~~)

## 4 infinitives

*Tell* can be used before **object + infinitive**, in the sense of 'order' or 'instruct'. *Say* cannot be used like this.

> *I* **told the children to go** *away.* (NOT ~~I said the children to go away.~~)

## 5 indirect questions

Neither *tell* nor *say* can introduce indirect questions (see 276).

> *Bill* **asked** *whether I wanted to see a film.* (NOT ~~Bill said whether I wanted to see a film.~~ OR ~~Bill told me whether . . .~~)

But *say* and *tell* can introduce the answers to questions.

> *Has she* **said** *who's coming?*
> *He only* **told** *one person where the money was.*

For *so* after *say* and *tell*, see 540.

# 505 see

## 1 progressive forms not used

When *see* means 'perceive with one's eyes', progressive ('continuous') forms are not normally used.

> **Do you see** *the woman in blue over there?* (NOT ~~Are you seeing . . .?~~)

To talk about seeing something at the moment of speaking, *can see* is often used, especially in British English (see 125).

> *I* **can see** *an aeroplane.* (AmE also *I see an airplane.*)
> (NOT ~~I am seeing an aeroplane.~~)

But we can say that somebody *is seeing things* if we mean that he/she is imagining things that are not there.

> *Look! A camel!* ~ *You're* **seeing things**.

When *see* means 'understand' or 'have heard' (see 243), progressive forms are not normally used.

> *We've got a problem.* ~ *I* **see**.
> *I* **see** *they're talking about putting up taxes again.*

## 2 changes

Progressive forms can be used for changes in people's ability to see.

> *I'm* **seeing** *much better since I got those new glasses.*
> *I'm* **seeing** *a lot of things in this book that I missed when I read it before.*

## 3 'meet', 'arrange' etc

When *see* means 'meet', 'interview', 'talk to', 'go out with' or 'arrange', 'supervise', progressive forms are possible.

> *I'm* **seeing** *the dentist tomorrow.*
> *Are you still* **seeing** *that Henderson woman?*
> *John's down at the docks. He's* **seeing** *that our stuff gets loaded properly.*

**4  other meanings: 'consider' etc**

*See* can mean 'consider', 'think', 'find out', 'discuss' or 'decide'.

> *Can I have a holiday next Monday? ~ I'll see.*
> *What time shall we go to the gym? ~ Let me see. How about 5 o'clock?*
> *Can you look out of the window and see if it's still snowing?*

A preposition is necessary before an object in these cases.

> *We'll see about that tomorrow.* (NOT ~~We'll see that tomorrow.~~)
> *You'd better see about that with Jim.* (NOT ~~You'd better see that with Jim.~~)

*See if . . . can* often means 'try to'.

> *See if you can get him to stop talking.*

For *see* + object + infinitive /*-ing* form, see 242.
For the difference between *see*, *look* and *watch*, see 506.

# 506  see, look (at) and watch

**1  see**

*See* is the ordinary verb to say that something 'comes to our eyes', whether or not we are paying attention.

> *Suddenly I **saw** something strange.* (NOT ~~Suddenly I looked at something strange.~~)
> *Did you **see** the article about the strike in today's paper?*

**2  look (at)**

We use *look* to talk about concentrating, paying attention, trying to see what is there. You can *see* something without wanting to, but you can only *look at* something deliberately. Compare:

> *I **looked at** the photo, but I didn't **see** anybody I knew.*
> *Do you **see** that man? ~ Yes. ~ **Look** again. ~ Good heavens! It's Moriarty!*
> *He **looked at** her with his eyes full of love.*

When *look* has an object it is followed by *at*. When there is no object there is no preposition. Compare:

> ***Look at** me!* (NOT ~~Look me!~~)     ***Look!*** (NOT ~~Look at!~~)

Note that *at* is often dropped before a *wh*-clause.

> ***Look (at) what** you've done!*
> ***Look who's** here!*                    ***Look where** you're going.*

**3  watch**

*Watch* is like *look at*, but suggests that something is happening or going to happen. We *watch* things that change, move or develop.

> ***Watch** that man – I want to know everything he does.*
> *I usually **watch** a football match on Saturday afternoon.*

**4  complete experiences: see**

*Watch* is typically used to talk about experiences that are going on, in progress. We often prefer *see* to talk about the whole of a performance, play, cinema film, match etc. Compare:

> *He got into a fight yesterday afternoon while he was **watching** a football match.* (NOT ~~. . . while he was seeing a football match.~~)
> *Have you ever **seen** Chaplin's 'The Great Dictator'?* (NOT ~~Have you ever watched Chaplin's 'The Great Dictator'?~~)

▶

## 5 watch TV

*Watch* is normally used with *TV*; *watch* and *see* are both used to talk about TV programmes and films.

> *You spend too much time **watching TV**.*
> *We **watched/saw a great film** on TV last night.*

## 6 see if/whether

*See* can be followed by *if/whether*, in the sense of 'find out'. *Look* and *watch* are not normally used in this way.

> ***See if** that suit still fits you.* (NOT ~~Look if that suit~~ . . .)
> *I'm looking to **see whether** there's any food left.* (NOT ~~I'm looking whether there's~~. . .)
> *Ring up and **see whether** she's in.*

For infinitives and *-ing* forms after these verbs, see 242.
For other meanings of *see* (and progressive uses), see 243, 471.
For other meanings of *look*, see 157.19.     For *if* and *whether*, see 621.
There are similar differences between *hear* and *listen (to)*. See 241.

# 507 seem

## 1 link verb: used with adjectives

*Seem* is a link verb (see 328); it is followed by adjectives, not adverbs.

> *You **seem angry** about something.* (NOT ~~You seem angrily~~. . .)

## 2 seem and seem to be

*Seem* is often followed by *to be*. We prefer *seem to be* when we are talking about objective facts – things that seem definitely to be true. *Seem* is used without *to be* when we are talking about subjective impressions. (The difference is not always clear-cut, and both are often possible.) Compare:

> – *The bus **seems to be** full.*
>   *She **seems** excited.*
> – *The doctors have done the tests, and he definitely **seems to be** mentally ill.*
>   *It **seems** crazy, but I think I'm in love with the postman.* (NOT ~~It seems to be crazy~~. . .)
> – *According to the experts, the north side of the castle **seems to be** about 100 years older than the rest.*
>   *He **seems** older than he is.* (NOT ~~He seems to be older than he is~~ – this would suggest that he might actually be older than he is.)
> – *She doesn't **seem to be** ready yet.*
>   *She **seems** (to be) very sleepy today.*

## 3 with nouns

*Seem to be* is normal before noun phrases.

*I looked through the binoculars: it **seemed to be** some sort of large rat.*
(NOT *. . . it seemed some sort of large rat.*)
*I spoke to a man who **seemed to be** the boss.* (NOT *. . . who seemed the boss.*)

However, *to be* can be dropped before noun phrases which express more subjective feelings.

*She **seems** (to be) a nice girl.*
*The cup **seemed** almost doll's size in his hands.*
*It **seems** a pity, but I can't see you this weekend.* (NOT *It seems to be a pity . . .*)

## 4 other infinitives

*Seem* can be followed by the infinitives of other verbs besides *be*.

*Ann **seems to need** a lot of attention.*

Perfect infinitives (see 280) are possible.

*The tax people **seem to have made** a mistake.*

To express a negative idea, we most often use a negative form of *seem*; but in a more formal style *not* can go with the following infinitive. Compare:

*He **doesn't seem to be** at home.*
*He **seems not to be** at home.* (formal)

Note the structure *can't seem to . . .*

*I **can't seem to** get anything right.*
(More formal: *I seem not to be able to get anything right.*)

## 5 *seem like*

We can use *like*, but not *as*, after *seem*.

*North Wales **seems (like)** a good place for a holiday.* (NOT *. . . seems as a . . .*)

## 6 *it seems*

*It* can be a preparatory subject (see 446) for *that-* and *as if*-clauses after *seem*.

*It **seems that** Bill and Alice have had a row.*
*It **seemed as if** the night was never going to end.*

## 7 *there seems*

*There* (see 586) can be a preparatory subject for *seem to be*.

*There **seems to be** some mistake.*

For *like* and *as*, see 326.   *Appear* is used in similar ways (see 58).

# 508 sensible and sensitive

A *sensible* person has 'common sense', and does not make stupid decisions.

*I want to buy that dress.* ~ *Be **sensible**, dear. It's much too expensive.*

A *sensitive* person feels things easily or deeply, and may be easily hurt.

*Don't shout at her – she's very **sensitive**.* (NOT *. . . very sensible.*)
*Have you got a sun cream for **sensitive** skin?* (NOT *. . . for sensible skin?*)

*Sensible* is a 'false friend' – similar words in some languages mean 'sensitive'.

# 509 sentence structure (1): basic word order

## 1 subject – verb – object/complement

In an affirmative sentence, the subject normally comes before the verb; objects or complements come after the verb.

*Ann smiled.*     *My father likes dogs.*     *Eric is a doctor.*

In a few affirmative structures the verb can come before the subject (e.g. *So can I, In came Mrs Parker*). See 302–303. For sentences that begin with the object (e.g. *Those people I can't stand*), see 513.

## 2 preparatory *it* and *there*

When the subject or object is an infinitive phrase or clause, we often put it at the end of a sentence, and use *it* as a preparatory subject or object (see 446–447).

*It's difficult* **to understand what he wants.**
*She made it clear* **that she disagreed.**

*There* can be a preparatory subject for an indefinite expression (see 587).

***There** is **a big spider** in the bath.*

## 3 direct and indirect objects

Indirect objects can come before direct objects (without a preposition) or after direct objects (with a preposition).

*She sent **the nurse some flowers**.*     *She sent **some flowers to the nurse**.*

For details, see 610.

## 4 questions: auxiliary before subject

Questions normally have the order **auxiliary verb – subject – main verb**.

*Have you seen Andrew?*     *Where was she going?*     *Did Mary phone?*

Indirect questions (see 276) have the subject before the verb.

*Do you know where **she was** going?*

## 5 negatives: auxiliary + *not*

Negative structures have *not* after an auxiliary verb.

*The train **did not** stop.* (NOT ~~The train stopped not.~~)

For word order in negative questions (e.g. *Why didn't she come? / Why did she not come?*), see 368.

## 6 adjectives before nouns

When adjectives are together with nouns, they usually come before them.

*an **interesting** book*     ***difficult** questions*

For the order of adjectives, see 15.     For exceptions and special cases, see 13.

## 7 adverbs: possible positions

Different adverbs can go in different places in a sentence: at the beginning, with the verb, or at the end. For details, see 21–25.

***Suddenly** I had a terrible thought.*
*The children had **probably** gone home.*     *I was playing **badly**.*

An adverb cannot normally come between a verb and its object.

*I **like** mushrooms very much.* (NOT ~~I like very much mushrooms.~~)

## 8   subordinate clauses (*after ... , if ..., because ..., etc*)

Adverbial subordinate clauses (beginning for example, *after, before, when, while, if, because*) can usually come either before or after the rest of the sentence (see 510.3).

> *After I left school I spent a year in China.* (OR *I spent a year in China after I left school.*)

## 9   prepositions: *in what ... / what ... in*

In an informal style, a preposition can be separated from its object in certain structures. For details, see 452. Compare:

> *In what hotel did the President stay?* (formal)
> *What hotel did the President stay in?* (informal)

For ways of arranging the information in a sentence, see 512.
For special structures in spoken English, see 514.
For word order in exclamations (e.g. *How kind you are!* ), see 195.
For word order with phrasal verbs (e.g. *She put out the cat / She put the cat out*), see 599.4.
For structures like *The older I get ...* , see 139.5.
For structures like *cold as/though she was,* see 71.
For structures like *so/how strange an experience,* see 14.
For *quite a ...* and *rather a ...* , see 489, 490.
For word order with *enough,* see 187.

# 510   sentence structure (2): conjunctions

## 1   What are conjunctions?

Conjunctions are words that join clauses into sentences.

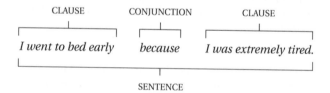

Conjunctions not only join clauses together; they also show how the meanings of the two clauses are related.

> *We brought the food **and** they supplied the drink.* (addition)
> *She was poor **but** she was honest.* (contrast)
> *We can go swimming, **or** we could stay here.* (alternative)
> *People disliked her **because** she was so rude.* (cause)
> *I'll phone you **when** I arrive.* (time)

## 2   two kinds

*And, but* and *or* are often called 'co-ordinating conjunctions'. They join pairs of clauses that are grammatically independent of each other.

▶

Other conjunctions, like *because, when, that* or *which*, are called 'subordinating conjunctions'. A subordinating conjunction together with its following clause acts like a part of the other clause.

ADVERB
*I'll phone you* | *tomorrow.*

ADVERB
*I'll phone you* | *when I arrive.*
(*When I arrive* is similar to *tomorrow* – it acts like an adverb in the
    clause *I'll phone you . . .* )

OBJECT
*He told me* | *a lie.*

OBJECT
*He told me* | *that he loved me.*
(*that he loved me* is similar to *a lie* – it is the object in the clause
    *He told me . . .* )

ADJECTIVE
*It's an* | *unanswerable* | *question.*

ADJECTIVE
*It's a question* | *which nobody can answer.*
(*which nobody can answer* is similar to *unanswerable* – it acts like an
    adjective in the clause *It's a question . . .* )

Some conjunctions are made up of two or more words.
    *I stayed an extra night* **so that** *I could see Ann.*
    *Let me know* **the moment that** *you arrive.*
In grammars, clauses that follow subordinating conjunctions are called 'subordinate clauses' or 'dependent clauses'.

## 3 position of subordinate clauses

Adverb clauses can usually go either first or last in a sentence (depending on what is to be emphasised – the most important information usually comes last).
- *While I was having a shower, I slipped on the floor.* (emphasises what
    happened)
    *I slipped on the floor while I was having a shower.* (emphasises when it
    happened)
- *If you need help, just let me know.*
    *Just let me know if you need help.*
- *Although the bicycle was expensive, she decided to buy it.*
    *She decided to buy the bicycle although it was expensive.*
- *Because she was too angry to speak, Ann said nothing.*
    *Ann said nothing, because she was too angry to speak.*

## 4 punctuation

Commas are often used to separate longer or more complicated clauses. Shorter pairs of clauses are often connected without commas. Compare:
    *I came home and the others went dancing.*
    *I decided to come home earlier than I had planned, and the others spent the
    evening at the local club.*

When a subordinate clause begins a sentence, it is more often separated by a comma, even if it is short. Compare:

*If you are passing, come in and see us.*
*Come in and see us if you are passing.*

For punctuation in relative clauses, see 495.

## 5  leaving words out

Words for repeated ideas can often be left out in the second of two co-ordinate clauses (see 178 for details), but not normally in a subordinate clause. Compare:

*She was depressed, **and didn't** know what to do.* (= and she didn't know what to do.)
*She was depressed, **because she didn't** know what to do.* (NOT ~~She was depressed, because didn't know~~ . . .)

However, after *if, when, while, until, once, unless* and *(al)though*, a pronoun subject and the verb *be* can often be dropped, especially in common fixed expressions like *if necessary.*

*I'll pay for you **if necessary**.* (= . . . if it is necessary.)
***If in doubt**, wait and see.* (= If you are in doubt . . .)
***When in Rome**, do as the Romans do.      Cook slowly **until ready**.*
***Once in bed**, I read for twenty minutes and then turned out the light.*

Many conjunctions that express time relations (*after, before, since, when, while, whenever, once* and *until*) can often be followed by *-ing* forms or past participles instead of subjects and full verbs (see 411.6).

*I always feel better **after talking** to you.*
*Some things are never forgotten, **once learnt**.*

## 6  conjunctions in separate sentences

Normally a conjunction connects two clauses into one sentence. However, sometimes a conjunction and its clause can stand alone. This happens, for example, in answers.

*When are you going to get up? ~ **When I'm ready**.*
*Why did you do that? ~ **Because I felt like it**.*
*I'm going out, Mum. ~ **As soon as you've brushed your hair**.*

Writers and speakers can also separate clauses for emphasis.

*This government has got to go. **Before it does any more damage**.*

Afterthoughts may also begin with conjunctions.

*OK, I did it. – **But I didn't mean to**.*

For tenses in subordinate clauses, see 580.
For structures in which *that* is dropped, see 584.
See also 494–498 (relative pronouns and clauses), 274–278 (indirect speech), and the individual entries on the various conjunctions.

# 511 sentence structure (3): problems with conjunctions

In most languages of European origin, clauses are joined together by conjunctions in similar ways. However, students who speak other languages may have some problems in using English conjunctions correctly.

## 1 one conjunction for two clauses

One conjunction is enough to join two clauses – we do not normally use two.
- *Although she was tired, she went to work.*
  *She was tired **but** she went to work.*
  (NOT *Although she was tired but she went to work.*)
- *Because I liked him, I tried to help him.*
  *I liked him, **so** I tried to help him.*
  (NOT *Because I liked him, so I tried to help him.*)
- *As you know, I work very hard.*
  *You know **that** I work very hard.*
  (NOT *As you know, that I work very hard.*)

However, we can use *and* or *or* together with a repeated conjunction.
  *We came back because we ran out of money, **and because** Ann got ill.*
  *She didn't write when I was ill, **or when** I got married.*

## 2 Relative pronouns are also conjunctions

Relative pronouns (*who, which* and *that* – see 494) join clauses like conjunctions.
  *There's the girl **who** works with my sister.*
A relative pronoun is like the subject or object of the verb that comes after it. So we do not need another subject or object.
  *I've got a friend **who** works in a pub.* (NOT *...who he works in a pub.*)
  *The man **(that)** she married was an old friend of mine.* (NOT *The man that she married him...*)
  *She always thanks me for the money **that** I give her.* (NOT *...the money that I give her it.*)

## 3 *that, where* and *when*

*That* is often used instead of *which* or *who(m)* (see 494–495).
  *There's the girl **that** works with my sister.*
But we do not usually use *that* instead of *when* or *where.*
  *August 31st is a national holiday, **when** everybody dances in the streets.*
    (NOT *...that everybody dances...*)
  *The house **where** I live is very small.* (NOT *The house that I live is very small.*)
But *that ... in* can mean the same as *where.*
  *The house **that** I live **in** is very small.*
*That* can be used instead of *where* and *when* in a few special cases (e.g. after *place, day*); for details, see 498.6.
  *I'll always remember **the day (that)** I met you.*

For conjunctions after prepositions, see 453.
For *now* as a conjunction, see 387. For *once*, see 394. For *the moment* and *immediately*, see 267.

# 512 sentence structure (4): information structure

## 1 different ways of organising information

When we talk about a situation, we can usually organise the information in various ways – for example, by choosing different elements of the situation as the subject of a clause or sentence.

*The storm blew Margaret's roof off.*
*Margaret's roof was blown off in the storm.*
*Margaret had her roof blown off in the storm.*

The way we choose to organise information in a clause or sentence can depend on what has been said before, on what the listener already knows, or on what we want to emphasise. This is a complicated area of English grammar. Some guidelines are given below.

## 2 normal order: important new information last

Most often, a clause or sentence moves from 'known' to 'new': from low to high information value. So we often choose as the subject a person or thing that is already being talked about or that has already been mentioned, or something that the speaker and hearer are both familiar with, or even some new information that is not the main point of the message. The important new information generally comes at the end of a clause or sentence.

*How's Joe these days? ~ Oh, fine. He's just got married to a very nice girl.*
  (More natural than . . . *A very nice girl's just got married to him.*)
*My father was bitten by a dog last week.*
  (More natural than *A dog bit my father last week.*)
*Our dog bit the postman this morning.*
  (More natural than *The postman was bitten by our dog this morning.*)
*I can't find my clothes. ~ Well, your trousers are under my coat.*
  (More natural than . . . *My coat's on your trousers.*)

To avoid beginning a clause with a completely new element, we can use the *there is* structure. For details, see 587.

*There's a cat on the roof.* (More natural than *A cat's on the roof.*)

For 'known' and 'new' information with *as, since* and *because*, see 72.

## 3 getting the right subject: actives, passives, etc

In many situations, there is an 'agent' (the person or thing who does something) and a 'patient' (the person or thing that something is done to). If we want to make the agent the subject, we can usually do this by choosing an active verb form (see 10).

*The storm blew Margaret's roof off.*
*Somebody's dropped ketchup all over the floor.*

If we want to make the patient the subject, we can usually do this by choosing a passive verb form (see 412).

*Margaret's roof was blown off in the storm.*
*Ketchup has been dropped all over the floor.*

If we want to make something else the subject, we can often do this by using a structure with *have* + **object** + **past participle** (see 238.3).

*Margaret had her roof blown off in the storm.*
*The floor has had ketchup dropped all over it.*

▶

Structures with *have* are often used to 'personalise' a situation by making a person the subject.

> *I've got the house full of children.* (Instead of *The house is full of children.*
>   OR *There are children all over the house.*)

We can often get the subject we want by choosing the right verb. Compare:

– *The biscuit factory employs 7,000 people.*
  *7,000 people work for the biscuit factory.*
– *He led the children through the silent streets.*
  *The children followed him through the silent streets.*

Some verbs can have both agent and patient subjects. For details, see 609.

> *She opened the door*      *The door opened.*

## 4 end-weight: *It worried me that she hadn't been in touch*

Longer and heavier structures usually come last in a clause or sentence. (These usually have the highest 'information-value' in any case.)

> *Children are sometimes discouraged by **the length of time it takes to learn a musical instrument**.* (More natural than *The length of time it takes to learn a musical instrument sometimes discourages children.*)

Because of this, we often use a structure with 'preparatory *it*' in order to move a clause or infinitive subject or object to the end of a sentence. For details, see 446–447.

> *It worried me **that she hadn't been in touch for so long**.*
>   (More natural than *That she hadn't been in touch for so long worried me.*)
> *It's important **to tell us everything you know**.*
>   (More natural than *To tell us everything you know is important.*)
> *He made it clear **that he was not in the least interested**.* (More natural than *He made that he was not in the least interested clear.*)

Adverbs do not normally separate the verb from the object in an English clause (see 21.1). However, a very long and heavy object may come after a shorter adverb. Compare:

> *She plays the violin **very well*** (NOT ~~*She plays very well the violin.*~~)
> *She plays **very well** almost any instrument that you can think of and several that you can't.*

End-weight can also affect the word order of indirect questions. Compare:

> *I'm not sure what the point **is**.*
> *I'm not sure what **is** the point of spending hours and hours discussing this.*

## 5 emphatic structures: *What I need is ...; Nice man, Joe*

There are various ways of giving extra emphasis to one part of a sentence. One way is to use a 'cleft sentence' with *it* or *what*: this emphasises one idea by putting everything else into a subordinate clause. For details, see 130–131.

> *It was **my mother** who finally called the police.*
> *What I need is **a hot bath and a drink**.*

If we move to the beginning of a sentence something that does not normally go there, this gives it extra emphasis. This kind of structure ('fronting') is common in speech, where intonation can make the information structure clear. For details, see 513.

> ***The other plans** we'll look at next week.*      ***Nice man**, Joe.*

For more information about emphasis, see 184.

# 513 sentence structure (5): fronting

## 1 *People like that I just can't stand*

Affirmative sentences most often begin with the grammatical subject.
> *I just can't stand people like that.*

If we begin a sentence with something else ('fronting'), this is often to make it the topic – the thing we are talking about – even though it is not the grammatical subject. This can also move the main new information to the end – its most natural position (see 512).
> ***This question*** *we have already discussed at some length.*
> ***All the other information which you need*** *I am putting in the post today.*
>   (from a business letter)
> ***Any video in our catalogue*** *we can supply, if available.* (Notice in music shop.)

Fronting is particularly common in speech.
> ***People like that*** *I just can't stand.*
> *(A)* ***fat lot of good*** *that does me.* (= 'That doesn't do me much good', but putting strong emphasis on *me*.)

Question-word clauses are often fronted.
> ***What I'm going to do next*** *I just don't know.*
> ***How she got the gun through customs*** *we never found out.*

## 2 *Very good lesson we had*

Fronting words in short sentences can also give them extra emphasis. This happens mostly in speech.
> ***Strange people*** *they are!*
> ***Very good lesson*** *we had yesterday.*     ***Last for ever*** *these shoes will.*

In a few exclamatory expressions, a noun is fronted before *that*, but this is uncommon in modern English.
> ***Fool*** *that I was!*

## 3 ellipsis: *Postman been?*

In a very informal style, articles, pronouns and auxiliary verbs are often left out, bringing a more important word to the front of the clause. This is called 'ellipsis': for details, see 179.
> ***Postman*** *been?*     ***Seen*** *John?*

Sometimes ellipsis is used to front a verb and/or complement, while the subject is put in a 'tag' (see 514) at the end.
> ***Likes*** *his beer, Stephen does.*
> ***Funny****, your brother.*     ***Nice day****, isn't it?*

## 4 adverbs etc: *Off we go!*

Many adverbs and adverbial expressions can go at the beginning of a clause (see 22). This often happens when we are using the adverbs to structure a piece of narrative or a description.
> *Once upon a time there were three little pigs. One day . . . Then . . . Soon after that . . . After dark, . . .*
> *Inside the front door there is . . . Opposite the living room is . . . On the right you can see . . . At the top of the stairs . . .*     ▶

Adverb particles are often fronted when giving instructions to small children.

>  ***Off*** *we go!*    ***Down*** *you come!*

Inversion (see 302–303) is necessary after some emphatic fronted adverbs and adverbial expressions.

>  *Under no circumstances **can we** accept cheques.* (NOT ~~*Under no circumstances we can*~~ . . .)
>  *Round the corner **came Mrs Porter**.*

## 5  fronting with *as* or *though*

Fronted adjectives and adverbs are possible in a structure with *as* or *though* (see 71).

>  ***Young as I was**, I realised what was happening.*
>  ***Tired though she was**, she went on working.*
>  ***Fast though she drove**, she could not catch them.*
>  ***Much as I respect his work**, I cannot agree with him.*

See also entries on basic word order (509), information structure (512), 'spacing out' information in speech (514), tags (514), emphasis (184) and cleft sentences (130–131).
For the use of passive and other structures to bring objects to the front, see 512.3, 414.1.

# 514  sentence structure (6):
# spoken structures and tags

## 1  *This guy who rang up, he's an architect*

In informal speech, we often 'space out' the different elements of a sentence, giving the hearer a little extra time to interpret each part before going on to the next.

>  *Last Wednesday **it was**, I was just going to work, . . .*
>  *It's terrible, **you know**, the unemployment down there.*

One way of spacing out information is to separate a subject or object, announce it at the front of a sentence, and then repeat it with a pronoun.

>  ***George Best** – now **he** was a good player.*
>  ***This guy** who rang up, **he's** an architect. Well, . . .*
>  ***That couple** we met in Berlin, we don't want to send **them** a card, do we?*
>  ***One of my brothers**, his wife's a singer, **he** says . . .*

This does not usually happen with pronoun subjects, but *me* and *myself* are occasionally detached and fronted.

>  ***Me**, I don't care.*
>  ***Myself**, I think you're making a big mistake.*

Another common way of separating part of a sentence is to introduce it with *You know* . . .

>  ***You know** Sylvia. Well, she . . .*

## 2  tags: *They work very hard, most of them*

We can space out information by putting some of it in a complete sentence and then adding more details at the end. The extra words at the end are called a 'tag'.

>  *They work very hard, **most of them**.*
>  *That's the doorbell, **I think**.    I don't mind, **to be honest**.*

It is possible to 'announce' the subject with a pronoun, and put the full subject in a tag.

> *He hasn't a chance,* **Fred.**    *He likes his beer,* **John.**
> *They're very polite,* **your children.**

In sentences like these, we often drop the pronoun at the beginning.

> *Hasn't a chance, Fred.*    *Likes his beer, John.*

We can also drop an unstressed form of *be*.

> *Very polite, your children.*
> *Living in the clouds, you lot.*    *Crazy, that driver.*

The tag can repeat the verb by using an auxiliary.

> *(He) hasn't a chance, Fred* **hasn't.**
> *(He) likes his beer, John* **does.**
> *(She) really got on my nerves, Sylvia* **did.**

### 3 emphasising tags: *You've gone mad, you have*

Sometimes a tag gives no new information, but simply repeats and emphasises the subject and verb.

> *You've gone mad,* **you have.**
> *I'm getting fed up,* **I am.**    *He likes his beer,* **he does.**

Pronouns are not usually used alone in tags, except for reflexives.

> *(I) don't think much of the party,* **myself.**

For more about dropping words ('ellipsis') at the beginning of a sentence, see 179.
For other uses of tags and similar structures, see 487–488 (question tags), 484 (reply questions) and 517 (short answers).

## 515 sentence structure (7): understanding complicated structures

### 1 clause inside clause: *Ann, when she finally ...*

Sometimes an adverb clause is put into the middle of another clause, separating a subject from its verb.

> subject + *if/when/after/because* ... + verb

> *Ann, when she finally managed to go to sleep, had a series of bad dreams.*

> *The government, if recent reports can be trusted, has decided not to raise interest rates.*

In these structures, a noun may not be the subject of a verb that comes just after it.

> *Mr Andrews, when he saw **the policeman, started** running as fast as he could.* (It was not the policeman who started running.)

Sentences like these can be hard for learners to understand, especially if they are long and complicated.

> *Mr Fisher, after he had completed his discussions with the bank manager, drew a large sum of money out of the bank and caught the next plane* ▸

to Paris. (A learner might think that it was the bank manager who took
the money and went to Paris.)

*One way of deciding what to do if you have difficulty in choosing the best
course of action is to toss a coin.* (Does the sentence say that the best
course of action is to toss a coin?)

## 2 *that picture of the children standing ...*

The same thing can happen when the subject of a sentence is followed by a
descriptive phrase or relative clause.

> subject + descriptive phrase/clause + verb

*That picture **of the children standing in front of the Palace talking to the
Prime Minister** is wonderful.* (The sentence does not say that the Prime
Minister is wonderful.)

*The tree **that Mary gave to my younger brother** is growing fast.*

*The reporter **who first made contact with the kidnappers** telephoned the
police immediately.* (Who telephoned?)

## 3 missing relative pronouns: *the film she was talking about*

When relative pronouns (*who/which/that*) are left out (see 494.6), this can
cause difficulty.

*It was a question a small child could have answered.* (= ... that a small child
could have answered.)

*The film she was talking about at Celia's party turned out to be very boring.*
(= ... the film which she was talking about ...)

*The manager of Brown's, the chemist's, has confirmed that bottles of
shampoo he took off the shelves after animal rights protesters claimed
to have put bleach into them did contain poisonous chemicals.* (= ...
bottles of shampoo which he took off ...)

*The really important point is that because he did not invite the one man he
certainly should have asked his father was angry.* (Does the sentence say
that he should have asked his father?)

## 4 missing *that*: *The man claimed he was ...*

We often leave out the conjunction *that* after verbs (see 584). This can make
complicated sentences more difficult to follow.

*The man who was arrested claimed he was somewhere else at the time of the
robbery.* (= ... claimed that he was ...)

*She insisted she thought he knew she was on the train.* (= She insisted that
she thought that he knew that ...)

In short news reports, *that* is sometimes left out after nouns.

*Officials did not accept his claim he was innocent.* (= ... that he was
innocent.)

*The Minister denied the suggestion he had concealed information from
Parliament.* (= ... the suggestion that he ...)

## 5 past participles that look like past tenses: *the children asked ... told the police*

Past participles (e.g. *arrested, accused*) are often used descriptively after nouns,
rather like reduced relative clauses (see 498.10). When these look the same as

past tenses, they can cause confusion. In the following examples from news reports, *arrested* means 'who was arrested', *accused* means 'who is accused', and *asked* means 'who were asked'.

> *A court has heard that a young civil servant **arrested** after shootings on Tyneside left one man dead is to be charged with murder.*
>
> *A Karnak separatist **accused** of leading an attack on a French police barracks in which four gendarmes died has been arrested.*
>
> *A number of the children **asked** for comments on the proposals to expel some immigrants told the police they disagreed.*

## 6 reporting expressions: *The man who Ann said will tell us*

Complicated structures can be produced when reporting expressions are included in sentences.

> *This is the man who **Ann said** will tell us all about the church.*
> *There are those people that **I thought** were going to buy our house.*
> *Who **did you say** (that) you wanted to invite for Christmas?*
> *What **do you suppose** will happen now?*

This can also happen with reported question structures.

> *He's gone **I don't know how far**.*
> *We spent **I can't remember how much** money on our holiday.*
> *Mary gave me **you'll never guess what** for my birthday.*

## 7 heavy subject: *Getting up very early ... makes ...*

When the subject of a sentence is a long phrase or clause, the structure can be difficult to follow.

> ***Getting up very early in the morning** makes you feel really superior.*
> (The first seven words are the subject.)
>
> ***Going on holiday out of season when everybody else is working** can save you a lot of money.* (11-word subject)
>
> ***What Ann's little sister wanted above everything else in the whole world** was a horse.* (12-word subject)

## 8 heavy indirect object: *I gave all the people who had helped me ...*

Similar problems can be caused by a long indirect object.

> *She gave **all the people who had helped her with her research** copies of her book.*
>
> *He brought **the village where he had grown up** unexpected fame and prosperity.*

## 9 more examples

Here are more examples of the above structures, some of them extreme, taken from news reports and fiction.

> *A 24-year-old labourer who was arrested in Trafalgar Square when he allegedly attempted to knife a traffic warden is said to have injured three policemen.*
>
> *The Consumers' Association study showed 75% of parents thought junk food advertising campaigns made it harder for them to insist their children ate healthy food.*

▶

> *The rebel leader found out that in spite of the precautions of the soldiers he*
> *had bought the guns from the police had planted an informer among*
> *them.*
> *The report will look into claims the design of the courthouse the men escaped*
> *from was at fault.*
> *Statements reassuring the public patients needing intensive care are getting it*
> *are total nonsense.*
> *What they say is surprising isn't.*
> *Pictures of the baby the judge ordered should not be identified by reporters*
> *appeared in a Sunday newspaper.*
> *Police hunting thieves who dumped a ten-month-old baby in an alley after*
> *finding him inside a car they stole have charged two teenage boys.*
> *The head doorman at a nightclub where the ecstacy pill which killed P. L.*
> *was sold has admitted he knew drugs were sold at the club.*
> *But what bothered him more than what the files that were in the drawer*
> *could mean was the feeling that something was certainly missing.*
> *Police called to a house in Hampshire after neighbours reported cries for help*
> *found 18-year-old M. F. stuck in a cat-flap after being locked out of his*
> *home.*
> *Millennium Dome chiefs have refused to discuss reports they ignored advice*
> *attendance figures at the attraction would be lower than hoped. The*
> *Sunday Times says the Millennium Commission warned Dome owners*
> *the New Millennium Experience Company its own estimate was between*
> *4.5m and 5m. NMEC reportedly insisted there would be at least 7m*
> *visitors this year.*

(The Millennium Dome was a tourist attraction built in London to celebrate the year 2000. It lost an enormous amount of money.)

## 516   shade and shadow

*Shade* is protection from the sun.

> *I'm hot. Let's find some **shade** to sit in.*
> *The temperature's 30 degrees in the **shade**.*

A *shadow* is the 'picture' made by something that blocks out light.

> *In the evening your **shadow** is longer than you are.*
> *There's an old story about a man without a **shadow**.*

## 517   short answers: Yes, he can etc

Answers are often grammatically incomplete, because they do not need to repeat words that have just been said. A common 'short answer' pattern is **subject + auxiliary verb**, together with whatever other words are really necessary.

> *Can he swim?* ~ *Yes, **he can**.* (More natural than *Yes, he can swim.*)
> *Has it stopped raining?* ~ *No, **it hasn't**.*
> *Are you enjoying yourself?* ~ *I certainly **am**.*
> *Don't forget to write.* ~ *I **won't**.*
> *You didn't phone Debbie last night.* ~ *No, but **I did** this morning.*

We use *do* if there is no other auxiliary.
>  *She likes cakes.* ~ *She really **does**.*
>  *That surprised you.* ~ *It certainly **did**.*

Non-auxiliary *be* and *have* are used in short answers.
>  *Is she happy?* ~ *I think **she is**.*
>  *Have you a light?* ~ *Yes, **I have**.*

Short answers can be followed by tags (see 487–488).
>  *Nice day.* ~ *Yes, it is, **isn't it**?*

Note that stressed, non-contracted affirmative forms are used in short answers.
>  *Yes, **I am**.* (NOT ~~Yes, I'm.~~)

For similar structures, see 484 (reply questions), 487–488 (question tags) and 181(ellipsis).
For *So am I* etc, see 541.1.
For *So I am* etc, see 541.2.

# 518 should (1): introduction

## 1 forms

*Should* is a modal auxiliary verb (see 353–354). It has no *-s* in the third person singular.
>  *The postman **should** be here soon.* (NOT ~~The postman shoulds~~ ...)

Questions and negatives are made without *do*.
>  ***Should** we tell Judy?* (NOT ~~Do we should~~ ...?)

*Should* is followed by an infinitive without *to*.
>  *Should I **go**?* (NOT ~~Should I to go?~~)
>  *She should **be** told the truth.*

There is a contracted negative *shouldn't*.
>  *The meeting **shouldn't** take long.*

*Should* has a weak pronunciation /ʃəd/, often used when it is not stressed (see 616).

## 2 obligation, probability

*Should* can be used to talk about obligation: things that it is good or important for people to do (see 519.1).
>  *Everybody **should** wear car seat belts.*

It can also be used to say what we think is probable, because it is logical or normal (see 519.2).
>  *She's away, but she **should** be back tomorrow.*

With these meanings, *should* is like a weaker form of *must*.

## 3 *It is important/surprising that ... should ...*

*Should* is used in *that*-clauses after certain adjectives and nouns, especially in British English (see 521).
>  *It's **important** that somebody **should** talk to the police.*
>  *It's **surprising** that she **should** say that to you.*

▶

### 4 *if, in case,* etc

*Should* can be used in *if*-clauses (see 261.1 for details), after *in case* (see 271.2), after *for fear that* and *lest* (see 321) and after *so that* and *in order that* (see 543).

> *If you should see Caroline, tell her I've got the tickets.*
> *I'll get a chicken out of the freezer in case Aunt Mary should come.*
> *He turned the radio down so that he shouldn't disturb the old lady.*

### 5 *I should/would; we should/would*

*Should* can be used instead of *would* after *I* and *we* in certain cases. This happens:

- in sentences with *if* (see 258.3)
  > *If I had more time I should/would learn Japanese.*
- in indirect speech (corresponding to *shall/will* in direct speech – see 275)
  > *I told her that we should/would be ready at 8.00.* ('We shall/will be ready . . . .')
- and in 'future in the past' sentences (see 221).
  > *I looked at the house where I should/would spend the next three years.*

## 519 should (2): obligation, deduction etc

### 1 obligation: *Everybody should wear seat belts*

We often use *should* to talk about obligation, duty and similar ideas. It is less strong than *must* (see 520).

> *Everybody should wear car seat belts.*
> *You shouldn't say things like that to Granny.*
> *Applications should be sent before December 30th.*
>   (More polite than *Applications must be sent . . .*)

In questions, *should* is used to ask for advice or instructions, like a less definite form of *shall* (see 217).

> *Should I go and see the police, do you think?*
> *What should we do?*

For the difference between *should* and *had better,* see 230.

### 2 probability: *She should be back tomorrow*

We can use *should* to say that we know something is probable (because it is logical or normal in the circumstances).

> *She's away, but she should be back tomorrow.* (= I have good reasons to believe that she will be back tomorrow.)
> *Henry should get here soon – he left home at six.*
> *We're spending the winter in Florida. ~ That should be nice.*

### 3 past use: *I knew that I should . . .; I was supposed to . . .*

*Should* is used unchanged in past indirect speech, if *should* was used in direct speech.

> *I thought 'I should write to Jane.'* → *I knew that I should write to Jane.*

In other cases, *should* + **infinitive** is not normally used to talk about the past. Instead, we can use for example *was/were supposed to . . .* (see 572).

*It was going to be a long day. I **was supposed to** clean up all the stables, and*
*then start on the garden.* (NOT *. . . ~~I should clean up~~. . .*)
*She **was supposed to** be in her office, but she wasn't.* (NOT *~~She should be in~~*
*~~her office, but she wasn't.~~*)

## 4 *should have . . .*

*Should have* + **past participle** can be used to talk about past events which did
not happen, or which may or may not have happened.
> *I **should have phoned** Ed this morning, but I forgot.*
> *Ten o'clock: she **should have arrived** in the office by now.*
> *You **shouldn't have called** him a fool – it really upset him.*

For *should* after *in case*, see 271.2.
For *should* after *so that* and *in order that*, see 543.
For *How should . . .?* and *Why should . . .?*, see 482.2.
For special uses of *should* in other subordinate clauses, see 521.

# 520 should (3): should, ought and must

## 1 *should* and *ought*

*Should* and *ought* (see 403) are very similar, and can often replace each other.
> *They **ought** to be more sensible, **shouldn't** they?*
They are both used to talk about obligation and duty, to give advice, and to say
what we think it is right for people to do or have done. *Should* is much more
frequent than *ought*.
> *You **should** / **ought to** see 'Daughter of the Moon' – it's a great film.*
> *You **should** / **ought to** have seen his face!*
*Should* and *ought* are not used in polite requests.
> ***Could you** move your head a bit? I can't see.* (NOT *~~You should / ought to move~~*
> *~~your head a bit . . .~~*)
*Should* and *ought* are both also used to talk about logical probability.
> *I've bought three loaves – that **should** / **ought to** be enough.*
> *That **should** / **ought to** be Janet coming upstairs now.*
*Ought*, unlike *should*, is followed by a *to*-infinitive.

## 2 *Must* is stronger than *should/ought*

*Must* has similar meanings to *should* and *ought*, but is stronger or more
definite. It expresses great confidence that something will happen, or that
something is true; *should* and *ought* express less confidence. Compare:
– *The doctor said I **must** give up smoking.*
  (an order which is likely to be obeyed)
*You really **ought to** give up smoking.*
  (a piece of advice which may or may not be followed)
– *Rob **must** be at home by now.* (= I'm sure he is at home.)
*Rob **should** be at home by now.* (= I think he is probably at home.)
*Should* can be used instead of *must* to make instructions sound more polite.
> *This form **should** be filled in in ink.*
> *Applications **should** be sent by 31 January.*
▶

### 3  *must* not used

*Should* and *ought* can be used for predictions – to say what people expect to happen. *Must* is not often used in this way.

> It **should** be fine tomorrow. (BUT NOT ~~It must be fine tomorrow.~~)
> Next week's exam **should** be easy. (BUT NOT ~~Next week's exam must be easy.~~)

**Should have** and **ought to have** + **past participle** can be used to talk about unfulfilled obligation in the past. *Must* is not used like this.

> You **should have been** nicer to Annie. (BUT NOT ~~You must have been nicer to Annie.~~)

For details of the use of *must*, see 358–361.
For the difference between *should/ought* and *had better*, see 230.

# 521  should (4): in subordinate clauses

### 1  importance: *It's important that ... should ...*

In formal British English, *should* can be used in *that*-clauses after adjectives and nouns expressing the importance of an action (e.g. *important, necessary, vital, essential, eager, anxious, concerned, wish*).

> It's **important** that somebody **should** talk to the police.
> Is it **necessary** that my uncle **should** be informed?
> I'm **anxious** that nobody **should** be hurt.
> It is his **wish** that the money **should** be given to charity.

This also happens after some verbs expressing similar ideas, especially in sentences about the past.

> He **insisted** that the contract **should** be read aloud.
> I **recommended** that she **should** reduce her expenditure.

In a less formal style, other structures are preferred.

> It's **important** that she **talks** to me when she gets here.
> Was it **necessary to tell** my uncle?

In American English, this use of *should* is unusual; subjunctives may be used (see 561).

> It's important that somebody **talk** to the police.
> Was it necessary that my uncle **be** informed?
> I recommend that she **reduce** her expenditure.

### 2  reactions: *It's surprising that she should ...*

*Should* is also used in subordinate clauses after words expressing personal judgements and reactions, especially to facts which are already known or have already been mentioned. (This use, too, is more common in British than American English. It is not particularly formal.)

> It's **surprising** that she **should** say that to you.
> I was **shocked** that she **shouldn't** have invited Phyllis.
> I'm **sorry** you **should** think I did it on purpose.
> Do you think it's **normal** that the child **should** be so tired?

In American English, *would* is more usual in this kind of sentence.

> It was **natural** that they **would** want him to go to a good school. (BrE ... that they should ...)

Sentences like these can also be constructed without *should*. Subjunctives cannot be used.

> It's **surprising** that she **says/said** that sort of thing to you. (BUT NOT ~~It's surprising that she say~~ ...)
>
> I was **shocked** that she **didn't** invite Phyllis.

For *should* in *if*-clauses, see 261.1; after *in case*, see 271.2; after *lest*, see 321; after *so that* and *in order that*, see 543.

# 522 since: tenses

## 1 main clause: *I've known her since ...*

In sentences with *since* (referring to time), we normally use present perfect and past perfect tenses in the main clause.

> **I've known** her since 1980. (NOT ~~I know her since~~ ...)
>
> We **haven't seen** Jamie since Christmas.
>
> I was sorry when Jacky moved to America; we **had been** good friends since university days.

However, present and past tenses are also occasionally found, especially in sentences about changes.

> You**'re looking** much better since your operation.
>
> She **doesn't come** round to see us so much **since** her marriage.
>
> **Since** last Sunday I **can't stop** thinking about you.
>
> Things **weren't going** so well since Father's illness.

## 2 *It's a long time since ...*

In British English, present and past tenses are common in the structure *It is/was ... since ...*

> **It's** a long time **since** the last meeting.
>
> **It was** ages **since** that wonderful holiday.

American English prefers perfect tenses in this structure.

> **It's been** a long time **since** the last meeting.
>
> **It had been** ages **since** that wonderful vacation.

## 3 *since*-clause: *since we were at school*

*Since* can be used as a conjunction of time, introducing its own clause. The tense in the *since*-clause can be perfect or past, depending on the meaning. Compare:

> – I've known her **since we were at school together**.
>   I've known her **since I've lived in this street**.
> – You've drunk about ten cups of tea **since you arrived**.
>   You've drunk about ten cups of tea **since you've been sitting here**.
> – We visit my parents every week **since we bought the car**.
>   We visit my parents every week **since we've had the car**.

For more about present perfect tenses, including American usage, see 455–460.
For past perfect tenses, see 423–425.
For the differences between *since*, *for* and *from*, see 208.
For *since* meaning 'as' or 'because', see 72.

# 523   **singular** and **plural** (1): regular plurals

The plural of most nouns is made by just adding -*s* to the singular. But there are some special cases.

## 1   plural of nouns ending in consonant + *y*

If the singular ends in **consonant** + *y* (for example -*by*, -*dy*, -*ry*, -*ty*), the plural is normally made by changing *y* to *i* and adding -*es*.

| Singular | Plural |
|---|---|
| ... consonant + *y* | ... consonant + *ies* |
| *baby* | *babies* |
| *lady* | *ladies* |
| *ferry* | *ferries* |
| *party* | *parties* |

If the singular ends in **vowel** + *y* (e.g. *day*, *boy*, *guy*, *donkey*), the plural is made by adding -*s* (*days*, *boys*, *guys*, *donkeys*).

Proper names ending in **consonant** + *y* usually have plurals in -*ys*.
> *Do you know the **Kennedys**?* (NOT ... ~~the Kennedies?~~)
> *I hate **Februarys**.*

## 2   plural of nouns ending in -*sh*, -*ch*, -*s*, -*x* or -*z*

If the singular ends in -*sh*, -*ch*, -*s*, -*x* or -*z*, the plural is made by adding -*es*.

| Singular | Plural |
|---|---|
| ... *ch*/*sh*/*s*/*x*/*z* | ... *ches*/*shes*/*ses*/*xes*/*zes* |
| *church* | *churches* |
| *crash* | *crashes* |
| *bus* | *buses* |
| *box* | *boxes* |
| *buzz* | *buzzes* |

Nouns ending in a single -*z* have plurals in -*zzes*: *quiz*/*quizzes*, *fez*/*fezzes*.

## 3   plural of nouns ending in -*o*

Some nouns ending in -*o* have plurals in -*es*. The most common:

| Singular | Plural | Singular | Plural |
|---|---|---|---|
| *echo* | *echoes* | *potato* | *potatoes* |
| *hero* | *heroes* | *tomato* | *tomatoes* |
| *negro* | *negroes* | | |

Nouns ending in **vowel + o** have plurals in *-s* (e.g. *radios, zoos*). So do the
following, and most new words ending in *-o* that come into the language:

| Singular | Plural | Singular | Plural |
|----------|--------|----------|--------|
| *commando* | *commandos* | *photo* | *photos* |
| *concerto* | *concertos* | *piano* | *pianos* |
| *Eskimo* | *Eskimos* | *solo* | *solos* |
| *kilo* | *kilos* | *soprano* | *sopranos* |
| *logo* | *logos* | | |

The following words can have plurals in *-s* or *-es*; *-es* is more common.

| Singular | Plural | Singular | Plural |
|----------|--------|----------|--------|
| *buffalo* | *buffalo(e)s* | *tornado* | *tornado(e)s* |
| *mosquito* | *mosquito(e)s* | *volcano* | *volcano(e)s* |

# 524 singular and plural (2): irregular and special plurals

## 1 irregular plurals in *-ves*

The following nouns ending in *-f(e)* have plurals in *-ves*.

| Singular | Plural | Singular | Plural |
|----------|--------|----------|--------|
| *calf* | *calves* | *self* | *selves* |
| *elf* | *elves* | *sheaf* | *sheaves* |
| *half* | *halves* | *shelf* | *shelves* |
| *knife* | *knives* | *thief* | *thieves* |
| *leaf* | *leaves* | *wife* | *wives* |
| *life* | *lives* | *wolf* | *wolves* |
| *loaf* | *loaves* | | |

*Dwarf, hoof, scarf* and *wharf* can have plurals in either *-fs* or *-ves. Hooves,
scarves* and *wharves* are more common than the plurals in *-fs*.
Other words ending in *-f(e)* are regular.

## 2 other irregular plurals

| Singular | Plural | Singular | Plural |
|----------|--------|----------|--------|
| *child* | *children* | *ox* | *oxen* |
| *foot* | *feet* | *penny* | *pence* |
| *goose* | *geese* | *person* | *people* |
| *louse* | *lice* | *tooth* | *teeth* |
| *man* | *men* | *woman* | *women* |
| *mouse* | *mice* | | |

The regular plural *pennies* can be used to talk about separate penny coins (and
one-cent coins in the USA); *pence* is used to talk about prices and sums of
money. Some British people now use *pence* as a singular (e.g. *That'll be three
pounds and one pence, please*).
*Persons* is sometimes used as a plural of *person* in official language. There is
also a singular noun *people* (plural *peoples*) meaning 'nation'. ▶

## 3   plural same as singular

Some words ending in -s do not change in the plural. Common examples:

| Singular | Plural | Singular | Plural |
|----------|--------|----------|--------|
| *barracks* | *barracks* | *headquarters* | *headquarters* |
| *series* | *series* | *works* (= factory) | *works* |
| *crossroads* | *crossroads* | *means* | *means* |
| *species* | *species* | *Swiss* | *Swiss* |

Note that some singular uncountable nouns end in -s. These have no plurals. Examples are *news, billiards, draughts* (and some other names of games ending in -s), *measles* (and some other illnesses).

Most words ending in -ics (e.g. *mathematics, physics, athletics*) are normally singular uncountable and have no plural use.

Too **much mathematics** is usually taught in schools. (NOT ~~Too many mathematics are~~ . . .)

Some words ending in -ics (e.g. *politics, statistics*) can also have plural uses.

**Politics is** a complicated business. (BUT *What* **are** *your* **politics?**)

**Statistics is** useful in language testing. (BUT *The unemployment* **statistics are** *disturbing.*)

Other nouns which do not change in the plural are *craft* (meaning 'vehicle'), *aircraft, hovercraft, spacecraft, Chinese, Japanese* (and other nationality nouns ending in -*ese*), *sheep, deer, fish,* and the names of some other living creatures, especially those that are hunted or used for food. *Fish* has a rare plural *fishes,* but the normal plural is *fish.*

*Dozen, hundred, thousand, million, stone* (= 14 pounds) and *foot* (= 12 inches) have plurals without -s in some kinds of expressions. For details, see 389.15.

*Dice* (used in board games) is originally the plural of *die,* which is not now often used in this sense; in modern English *dice* is generally used as both singular and plural.

*Data* is originally the plural of *datum,* which is not now used. In modern English *data* can be used either as an uncountable noun (*this data is* . . .) or as a plural (*these data are* . . .), with no difference of meaning.

*Media* is originally the plural of *medium.* The plural expression *the media* (meaning 'radio, TV, newspapers, the internet . . .') is now quite often used as an uncountable noun with a singular verb.

## 4   foreign plurals

Some words which come from foreign languages have special plurals. Examples:

| Singular | Plural |
|----------|--------|
| *analysis* | *analyses* (Latin) |
| *appendix* | *appendices* (Latin) |
| *bacterium* | *bacteria* (Latin) |
| *basis* | *bases* (Greek) |
| *cactus* | *cacti* (Latin) or *cactuses* (less common) |
| *corpus* | *corpora* (Latin) |
| *crisis* | *crises* (Greek) |

| | |
|---|---|
| *criterion* | *criteria* (Greek) |
| *diagnosis* | *diagnoses* (Greek) |
| *formula* | *formulae* (Latin) or *formulas* |
| *fungus* | *fungi* (Latin) or *funguses* |
| *hypothesis* | *hypotheses* (Greek) |
| *kibbutz* | *kibbutzim* (Hebrew) |
| *nucleus* | *nuclei* (Latin) |
| *oasis* | *oases* (Greek) |
| *phenomenon* | *phenomena* (Greek) |
| *radius* | *radii* (Latin) |
| *stimulus* | *stimuli* (Latin) |
| *vertebra* | *vertebrae* (Latin) |

Note that some foreign plurals (e.g. *agenda, spaghetti*) are singular in English (see 148.5).

## 5 plurals in 's

An apostrophe (') is used before the *-s* in the plurals of letters of the alphabet, and sometimes in the plurals of dates and abbreviations.
  *She spelt 'necessary' with two c's.*
  *I loved the 1960's.* (*the 1960s* is more common)
  *PC's are getting cheaper.* (*PCs* is more common)
It is not correct to use *-'s* in other plurals, e.g. ~~jean's~~.

## 6 compound nouns

In **noun + adverb** combinations, the plural *-s* is usually added to the noun.

| Singular | Plural |
|---|---|
| *passer-by* | *passers-by* |
| *runner-up* | *runners-up* |

The plural of *mother-in-law* and similar words is generally *mothers-in-law* etc, but some people use *mother-in-laws* etc; the plural of *court martial* (= military court or military trial) is either *courts martial* (more formal) or *court martials* (less formal).
In **noun + noun** combinations, the first noun is usually singular in form even if the meaning is plural (e.g. *shoe shop*). There are some exceptions. (see 531).

## 7 plurals with no singular forms

*Cattle* is a plural word used to talk collectively about bulls, cows and calves; it has no singular, and cannot be used for counting individual animals (one cannot say, for instance, *three cattle*).
  *Many cattle are suffering from a disease called BSE.* (NOT ~~Much cattle is~~ ...)
Police, staff and crew are generally used in the same way.
  *The police are looking for a fair-haired man in his twenties.* (NOT ~~The police is looking~~ ... OR ~~A police~~ ...)
  *The staff are on strike.* (BUT *A member of staff said* ..., NOT ~~A staff~~ ...)
However numbers are sometimes used before these three words (e.g. *four staff, six crew*).
The expressions *the British, the Dutch, the English, the French, the Irish, the Spanish* and *the Welsh* (see 17.2) are also plural, with no singular forms. ▶

*In 1581 **the Dutch** declared their independence from Spain.*
(BUT *A Dutchman came into the shop.* NOT *A ~~Dutch~~...*)
*Trousers, jeans, pyjamas* (AmE *pajamas*), *pants, scales, scissors, glasses, spectacles* (meaning 'glasses'), *binoculars, pliers,* and the names of many similar divided objects are plural, and have no singular forms. (The equivalent words in some other languages are singular.)
*Your **jeans are** too tight.* (NOT *~~Your jean is~~...*)
*Where **are** my **glasses**? ~ They're on your nose.*
To talk about individual items, we can use *a pair of* (see 430).
*Have you got **a pair of nail-scissors**?*
Other common words which are normally plural and uncountable include:
*arms, clothes* (see 133), *congratulations, contents, customs* (at a frontier), *funds* (= money), *goods, groceries, manners* (= social behaviour), *the Middle Ages* (a period in history), *oats* (but *corn, wheat, barley* and *rye* are singular uncountable), *odds* (= chances), *outskirts, premises* (= building), *regards, remains, savings, surroundings, thanks, troops.*
***Congratulations** on your new job.* (NOT *~~Congratulation~~...*)
*She lives on **the outskirts** of Cambridge.* (NOT *...~~the outskirt~~...*)

For cases where plural nouns are used with singular verbs and pronouns (and the opposite), see 526–527.

## 525 singular and plural (3): pronunciation of plurals

### 1 nouns ending in /s/, /z/ and other sibilants

After one of the sibilant sounds /s/, /z/, /ʃ/, /ʒ/, /tʃ/ and /dʒ/, the plural ending *-es* is pronounced /ɪz/.

| | | |
|---|---|---|
| *buses* /ˈbʌsɪz/ | *crashes* /ˈkræʃɪz/ | *watches* /ˈwɒtʃɪz/ |
| *quizzes* /ˈkwɪzɪz/ | *garages* /ˈgærɑːʒɪz/ | *bridges* /ˈbrɪdʒɪz/ |

### 2 nouns ending in other unvoiced sounds

After any other unvoiced sound (/p/, /f/, /θ/, /t/ or /k/), the plural ending *-(e)s* is pronounced /s/.

| | | |
|---|---|---|
| *cups* /kʌps/ | *cloths* /klɒθs/ | *books* /bʊks/ |
| *beliefs* /bɪˈliːfs/ | *plates* /pleɪts/ | |

### 3 nouns ending in other voiced sounds

After vowels, and all voiced consonants except /z/, /ʒ/ and /dʒ/, the plural ending *-(e)s* is pronounced /z/.

| | | |
|---|---|---|
| *days* /deɪz/ | *clothes*/kləʊðz/ | *legs* /legz/ |
| *boys* /bɔɪz/ | *ends* /endz/ | *dreams* /driːmz/ |
| *trees* /triːz/ | *hills* /hɪlz/ | *songs* /sɒŋz/ |
| *knives* /naɪvz/ | | |

### 4 plurals with irregular pronunciation

| Singular | Plural |
|---|---|
| *bath* /bɑːθ/ | *baths* /bɑːθs/ or /bɑːðz/ |
| *house* /haʊs/ | *houses* /ˈhaʊzɪz/ |
| *mouth* /maʊθ/ | *mouths* /maʊθs/ or /maʊðz/ |

| **Singular** | **Plural** |
|---|---|
| *path* /pɑːθ/ | *paths* /pɑːθs/ or /pɑːðz/ |
| *roof* /ruːf/ | *roofs* /ruːfs/ or /ruːvz/ |
| *truth* /truːθ/ | *truths* /truːθs/ or /truːðz/ |
| *wreath* /riːθ/ | *wreaths* /riːθs/ or /riːðz/ |
| *youth* /juːθ/ | *youths* /juːθs/ or /juːðz/ |

Third person singular forms (e.g. *catches, wants, runs*) and possessive forms (e.g. *George's, Mark's, Joe's*) follow the same pronunciation rules as regular plurals.

# 526 singular and plural (4): singular nouns with plural verbs

## 1 groups of people: *The team is/are ...*

In British English, singular words like *family, team, government*, which refer to groups of people, can have either singular or plural verbs and pronouns.
> *The team is/are going to lose.*

Plural forms are common when the group is seen as a collection of people doing personal things like deciding, hoping or wanting. Singular forms are more common when the group is seen as an impersonal unit. Compare:
- *My family have decided to move to York. They're going in April.*
  *The average family has 3.6 members. It is smaller than 50 years ago.*
- *My firm are wonderful. They do all they can for me.*
  *My firm was founded in the 18th century.*

We prefer *who* as a relative pronoun with plural forms, and *which* with singular forms. Compare:
> *The committee, who are hoping to announce important changes, ...*
> *The committee, which is elected at the annual meeting, ...*

When a group noun is used with a singular determiner (e.g. *a/an, each, every, this, that*), singular verbs and pronouns are normal. Compare:
> *The team are full of enthusiasm.*
> *A team which is full of enthusiasm has a better chance of winning.*
>    (More natural than *A team who are full ...*)

Sometimes singular and plural forms are mixed.
> *The group gave its first concert in June and they are now planning a tour.*

Examples of group nouns which can be used with both singular and plural verbs in British English:

| | | | |
|---|---|---|---|
| *bank* | *committee* | *government* | *public* |
| *the BBC* | *England (the* | *jury* | *school* |
| *choir* | *football team)* | *ministry* | *staff* |
| *class* | *family* | *orchestra* | *team* |
| *club* | *firm* | *party* | *union* |

In American English singular verbs are normal with most of these nouns in all cases (though *family* can have a plural verb). Plural pronouns can be used.
> *The team is in Detroit this weekend. They expect to win.*    ▶

## 2 *A number of people have ...*

Many singular quantifying expressions can be used with plural nouns and pronouns; plural verbs are normally used in this case.

*A **number of people have** tried to find the treasure, but **they** have all failed.*
(More natural than *A number of people has tried ...*)

*A **group of us are** going to take a boat through the French canals.*

*A **couple of my friends plan** to open a travel agency.* (NOT *A couple of my friends plans ...*)

*A **lot of social problems are** caused by unemployment.* (NOT *A lot of social problems is caused ...*)

*The **majority of criminals are** non-violent.*

*Some of these people are relations and **the rest are** old friends.*

*Half of **his students don't** understand a word he says.* (NOT *Half of his students doesn't ...*)

For more about *a lot* and *lots*, see 333. For *the rest*, see 501. For *(a) few*, see 329.
For singular and plural nouns with fractions, see 532.9.

# 527 **singular** and **plural** (5): plural expressions with singular verbs

## 1 amounts and quantities: *that five pounds*

When we talk about amounts and quantities we usually use singular determiners, verbs and pronouns, even if the noun is plural.

*Where **is that five pounds** I lent you?* (NOT *Where are those five pounds ...?*)

*Twenty **miles is** a long way to walk.*

*We've only got five litres of petrol left. ~ **That isn't** enough.*

## 2 calculations

Singular verbs are often possible after plural number subjects in spoken calculations.

*Two and two **is/are** four.*

*Ten times five **is** fifty.* (OR *Ten fives **are** fifty.*)

For more about spoken calculations, see 389.22–23.

## 3 *more than one*

*More than one* is generally used with a singular noun and verb.

*More than **one person is** going to have to find a new job.*

## 4 *one of ...*

Expressions beginning *one of* normally have a plural noun and a singular verb.

*One of **my friends is** getting married.* (NOT *One of my friends are ...*)

For singular and plural verbs in relative clauses after *one of ...*, see 529.1.

**5** *and*

Some expressions joined by *and* have singular determiners, verbs and pronouns. This happens when the two nouns are used together so often that we think of them as a single idea.

> This **gin and tonic isn't** very strong, is **it?**
> Your **toast and marmalade is** on the table.

**6 countries and organisations**

Plural names of countries usually have singular verbs and pronouns.

> **The United States is** anxious to improve **its** image in Latin America.

Plural names of organisations may also have singular verbs and pronouns.

> **Consolidated Fruitgrowers has** just taken over Universal Foodstores.

# 528 **singular** and **plural** (6): singular **they**

**1** *Somebody left their umbrella*

*They/them/their* is often used to refer to a singular indefinite person. This is common after *a person, anybody/one, somebody/one, nobody/one, whoever, each, every, either, neither* and *no*. *They* has a plural verb in this case.

> If a person doesn't want to go on living, **they are** often very difficult to help.
> If anybody calls, take **their** name and ask **them** to call again later.
> Somebody left **their** umbrella in the office. Would **they** please collect it?
> Nobody was late, **were they?**     Whoever comes, tell **them** I'm not in.
> Tell each person to help **themselves** to what they want.
> Every individual thinks **they're** different from everybody else.

This singular use of *they/them/their* is convenient when the person referred to could be either male or female (as in the examples above). *He or she, him or her* and *his or her* are clumsy, especially when repeated, and many people dislike the traditional use of *he/him/his* in this situation (see 222).

However, *they/them/their* can also be used when the person's sex is known. Two examples from interviews:

> I swear more when I'm talking to a boy, because I'm not afraid of shocking **them.**
> No girl should have to wear school uniform, because it makes **them** look like a sack of potatoes.

*They/them/their* is sometimes used for a definite person who is not identified.

> I had a friend in Paris, and **they** had to go to hospital for a month.

**2 correctness**

This use of *they/them/their* has existed for centuries, and is perfectly correct. It is most common in an informal style, but can also be found in formal written English. Here is an example from a British passport application form:

> Dual nationality: if the child possesses the nationality or citizenship of another country **they** may lose this when **they** get a British Passport.

# 529 **singular** and **plural** (7): mixed structures

In some complex structures, the same verb seems to belong with two different expressions, one singular and the other plural.    ▶

## 1 *one of the few women who have climbed Everest*

After expressions like *one of the . . .*, singular and plural verbs are both used in relative clauses beginning *who, which* or *that*.

> *She's **one of the few women** who **have/has** climbed Everest.*
> *This is **one of those books** that **are/is** read by everybody.*

Strictly speaking, a plural verb is correct (to agree with *the few women who* or *those books that*). However, singular verbs are also very common in these structures. More examples:

> **One of the things** that really **make/makes** me angry is people who don't answer letters.
> *We've got **one of those Japanese cars** that never **break/breaks** down.*

## 2 *A serious problem is wasps*

In English a verb normally agrees with the subject of a sentence, not with a following complement.

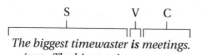

> *The biggest timewaster **is** meetings.*
> (NOT ~~The biggest timewaster **are** meetings.~~)

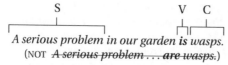

> *A serious problem in our garden **is** wasps.*
> (NOT ~~A serious problem . . . **are** wasps.~~)

However, if the subject is a long way from the verb, people sometimes make the verb agree with a complement.

> *The most interesting thing on radio and television last*

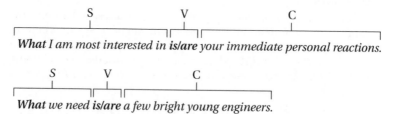

> *weekend, without any doubt, **was/were** the tennis championships.*

This often happens, too, when the subject is a relative *what*-clause, especially when the complement is long.

> *What I am most interested in **is/are** your immediate personal reactions.*

> *What we need **is/are** a few bright young engineers.*

For singular and plural verbs after interrogative *what* and *who*, see 532.3.

## 3 singular subject, plural continuation, plural verb

When a singular subject is modified by a following plural expression, people sometimes use a plural verb. This is not usually considered correct.

> ~~Nobody except his best friends like him.~~
> (More correct: *Nobody . . . likes him.*)
> ~~A good knowledge of three languages are necessary for this job.~~
> (More correct: *A good knowledge . . . is . . .*)

For singular or plural after *kind(s)*, *sort(s)*, *type(s)* etc, see 551.

# 530 singular and plural (8): distributive plural

## 1 people doing the same thing

To talk about several people each doing the same thing, English usually prefers a plural noun for the repeated idea.

> *Tell the kids to bring **raincoats** to school tomorrow.*
> (More natural than *Tell the kids to bring a raincoat . . .*)

Plural forms are almost always used in this case if there are possessives.

> *Tell the children to blow **their noses**.* (NOT *. . . ~~to blow their nose.~~*)
> *Six people lost **their lives** in the accident.*

Uncountable nouns cannot of course be used in the plural.

> *They were all anxious to increase their **knowledge**.* (NOT *. . . ~~their knowledges.~~*)

## 2 repeated events

In descriptions of repeated single events, singular and plural nouns are both possible. When no details are given, plural nouns are more natural.

> *I often get **headaches**.* (NOT *~~I often get a headache.~~*)
> *She sometimes goes for **rides** over the hills.*

When details of the time or situation are given, nouns are often singular.

> *I often get **a headache** when I've been working on the computer.*
> *She often goes for **a ride** over the hills before supper.*

Singular nouns may also be used to avoid misunderstanding.

> *I sometimes throw **a stone** into the river and wish for good luck.*
> (NOT *~~I sometimes throw stones~~ . . .* – only one stone is thrown each time.)

To refer to the time of repeated events, both singular and plural expressions are often possible with little difference of meaning.

> *We usually go and see my mother on **Saturday(s)**.*
> *He's not at his best in the **morning(s)**.*

## 3 generalisations and rules

In generalisations and rules, singular and plural nouns are both possible.

> *We use **a past participle** in **a perfect verb form**.* (OR *We use **past participles** in **perfect verb forms**.*)
> *All documents must be accompanied by **a translation** of the **original**.*
> (OR *All documents must be accompanied by **translations** of the **originals**.*)

Mixtures of singular and plural are possible.

> ***Subjects** agree with their **verb**.*

▶

*Children may resemble both their **father** and their **mother** in different ways.*
This often happens with fixed singular expressions like *at the beginning.*
*Discourse **markers** usually come **at the beginning** of sentences.*

## 531 singular and plural (9): noun + noun

### 1 first noun singular: *shoe shop*

In **noun + noun** structures (see 385–386), the first noun is normally singular in form even if it has a plural meaning.

> a ***shoe*** *shop* (= a shop that sells shoes)
> a ***toothbrush*** (= a brush for teeth)   ***trouser*** *pockets* (= pockets in trousers)
> a ***ticket*** *office* (= an office that sells tickets)

### 2 exceptions

Some nouns are plural in this structure. These include nouns which have no singular form (like *clothes*), nouns which are not used in the singular with the same meaning (like *customs*), and some nouns which are more often used in the plural than in the singular (like *savings*). In some cases, e.g. *antique(s)*, *drug(s)*, usage is divided, and both singular and plural forms are found. In general, plurals are becoming more common in this structure. Examples:

| | |
|---|---|
| a ***clothes*** shop | a ***drinks*** cabinet |
| a ***glasses*** case | a ***goods*** train (British English) |
| a ***customs*** officer | a ***sports*** car |
| ***arms*** control | a ***greeting(s)*** card |
| a ***savings*** account | an ***antique(s)*** dealer/shop |
| the ***accounts*** department | the ***drug(s)*** problem |
| the ***sales*** department | the ***arrival(s)*** hall (at an airport) |
| the ***outpatients*** department (of a hospital) | |

Note also that singular nouns ending in *-ics* can be used before other nouns.

> ***athletics*** *training*
> an ***economics*** *degree*

We use the plurals *men* and *women* to modify plural nouns when they have a 'subject' meaning; *man* and *woman* are used to express an 'object' meaning. Compare:

> – ***men*** *drivers* (= men who drive)
> ***women*** *pilots* (= women who fly planes)
> – ***man****-eaters* (= lions or tigers that eat people)
> ***woman****-haters* (= people who hate women)

## 532 singular and plural (10): other points

### 1 uncountable nouns: *hair, baggage* etc

Certain English singular uncountable nouns correspond to plural nouns in some other languages.

> *Your **hair** is very pretty.* (NOT *Your ~~hairs are~~ . . .*)
> *My **baggage** has been lost.* (NOT *My ~~baggages have~~ . . .*)

For a list of words of this kind, see 148.3.
For plural uncountables, see 149.5.

## 2 co-ordinated subjects: *A and B, A or B, A as well as B*, etc

When two singular subjects are joined by *and*, the verb is normally plural.

*Alice and Bob are going to be late.*

But note that some phrases with *and* are treated like single ideas, and used with singular verbs (see 527.5).

*Your **toast and marmalade is** on the table.*

When two subjects are joined by *as well as, together with* or a similar expression, the verb is usually singular if the first subject is singular.

*The **Prime Minister, as well as** several Cabinet Ministers, **believes** in a tough financial policy.*

*The **Managing Director, together with** his heads of department, **is** preparing a new budget.*

When two subjects are joined by *or* the verb is usually singular if the second subject is singular, and plural if it is plural. Compare:

*There's no room – either two chairs **or a table has** got to be moved.*

*There's no room – either a table **or two chairs have** got to be moved.*

When two singular subjects are joined by *neither . . . nor*, the verb is normally singular in a formal style, but can be plural in an informal style.

***Neither** she **nor** her husband **has** arrived.* (formal)

***Neither** she **nor** her husband **have** arrived.* (informal)

## 3 *who* and *what*

When *who* and *what* are used to ask for the subject of a clause, they most often have singular verbs, even if the question expects a plural answer.

***Who is** working tomorrow? ~ Phil, Lucy and Shareena (are working tomorrow).* (More natural than *Who are working tomorrow?*)

***Who was** at the party?* (More natural than *Who were at the party?*)

***What lives** in those little holes? ~ Rabbits (do).* (NOT ~~*What live . . .*~~)

When *who* and *what* are used to ask for the complement of a clause, they can have plural verbs.

***Who are** your closest friends? ~ (My closest friends are) Naomi and Bridget.*

***What are** your politics? ~ (My politics are) extreme left-wing.*

Relative *what*-clauses are normally the subject of a singular verb.

***What she needs is** friends.* (More natural than *What she needs are friends.*)

However, plural verbs are often used before longer plural complements, especially if *what* is a long way from the verb (see 529).

***What we need** most of all **are some really new ideas.***

## 4 *here's, there's* and *where's*

In an informal style, *here's, there's* and *where's* are common with plural nouns.

***Here's** your **keys.***          ***There's** some **children** at the door.*

***Where's** those **books** I lent you?*

## 5 *none, neither* and *either*

When *none, neither* and *either* are followed by *of* + **plural noun/pronoun**, they are normally used with singular verbs. Plural verbs are possible in an informal style.          ▶

*None* of the cures really **works**.
*None* of the cures really **work**. (informal)
*Neither* of my brothers **has/have** been outside England.
*Has/Have either* of them been seen recently?

## 6 another, a/an + adjective

Plural expressions of quantity can be used with *another* (see 54) and with
*a/an* + **adjective**.

> I want to stay for **another three weeks**.
> We'll need **an extra ten pounds**.
> He's been waiting for **a good two hours**.
> She spent **a happy ten minutes** looking through the photos.
> I've had **a very busy three days**.

Note also the expression **a good many/few** + **plural** (informal).

> I've lain awake **a good many nights** worrying about you.
> I bet that house could tell **a good few stories**.

## 7 kind, sort and type

In an informal style, we sometimes mix singular and plural forms when we use
demonstratives with *kind*, *sort* or *type*. For details, see 551.

> I don't like **those kind of boots**.

## 8 every (frequency)

*Every* (which is normally used with singular nouns) can be used before plural
expressions in measurements of frequency.

> I go to Ireland **every six weeks**.

## 9 fractions

Fractions between 1 and 2 are normally used with plural nouns (see 389.2).

> It weighs **one and a half tons**. (NOT . . . ~~one and a half ton.~~)
> The house has about **1.75 hectares** of land.

# 533 slang

## 1 What is slang?

'Slang' is a very informal kind of vocabulary, used mostly in speech by people
who know each other well. Examples:

> *Can you lend me some **cash**? (money)*       *My shoelace has **bust**. (broken)*
> *He's a real **prat**. (fool)*                        *Those boots are real **cool**. (fashionable)*
> *Let's **chill out**. (relax)*                         *How are the **kids**? (children)*

Slang expressions are not usually written, and not used in formal kinds
of communication.

## 2 strong feelings

Many English slang expressions relate to things that people feel strongly about
(e.g. sex, family and emotional relationships, drink, drugs, conflict between
social groups, work, physical and mental illness, death).

*She's got really nice **tits**. (breasts)*
*I spent the weekend at my **gran's**. (grandmother's)*
*God, we got **smashed** last night. (drunk)*
***Prods** out! (Protestants)*
*Can you get that **sitrep** to the MD by five? (situation report; Managing Director)*
*I've got some sort of **bug**. (illness)*
*He's **lost his marbles**. (gone mad)*
*When I **kick the bucket**, I want you all to have a big party. (die)*
Slang can be used in order to be offensive.
*Shut your **gob**! (mouth)*
For more about 'taboo' words for subjects that some people find shocking, see 575.

## 3 group membership; using slang

Many slang expressions (e.g. *cash*, *kids*) are widely used. However, some slang expressions are only used by members of particular social and professional groups, and nearly all slang is used between people who know each other well or share the same social background. So it is usually a mistake for 'outsiders' (including foreigners) to try deliberately to use slang. This can give the impression that they are claiming membership of a group that they do not belong to. There is also the danger that the slang may be out of date – some kinds of slang go out of fashion quickly, and when it gets into books it may already be dead. It is best for learners to avoid slang unless they are really sure of its use. If they start becoming accepted as part of an English-speaking community, they will learn to use the community's slang naturally and correctly along with the rest of their language.

# 534 small and little

*Small* simply refers to size. It is the opposite of *big* or *large* (see 106).
*Could I have a **small** brandy, please?*
*You're too **small** to be a policeman.*
The adjective *little* usually expresses some kind of emotion.
***Poor little** thing – come here and let me look after you.*
*What's he like? ~ Oh, he's a **funny little** man.*
*What's that **nasty little** boy doing in our garden?*
*They've bought a **pretty little** house in the country.*
In a few fixed expressions, *little* is used in the same way as *small* or *short*.
***little** finger*          *a **little** while*
*the **little** hand of a clock*     *a **little** way*
In British English *little* is unusual in 'predicative' position (after a verb), and comparative and superlative forms are not normally used.
*The puppy was so **small** and sweet.*
   (More natural than *The puppy was so little ...*)
*He's the **smallest** baby I've ever seen.*
   (More natural than *... the littlest baby ...*)

For *little* used as a determiner meaning 'not much' (e.g. *There's little hope*), see 329.

# 535 smell

## 1 British and American forms

In British English, regular and irregular past tenses and participles are both common: *smelled* and *smelt*. American forms are usually regular.

## 2 link verb

*Smell* can be used as a 'link verb' (see 328), followed by an adjective or noun, to say how something smells. Progressive forms are not used.

> *Those roses* **smell beautiful.** (NOT . . . ~~smell beautifully.~~)
> *The soup* **smells funny.** *What's in it?* (NOT . . . ~~is smelling funny~~ . . .)

Before a noun, *smell of* and *smell like* are used.

> *The railway carriage* **smelt of beer** *and old socks.*
> *His aftershave* **smelt like an explosion** *in a flower shop.*

*Smell* is sometimes used to mean 'smell bad'.

> *That dog* **smells.**

## 3 transitive verb: 'perceive'

*Smell* can be used with an object, to say what we perceive with our noses. Progressive forms are not used. We often use *can smell* (see 125).

> *As we walked into the house, we* **smelt something** *burning.*
> *I* **can smell supper.**

## 4 transitive verb: 'investigate'

Another transitive use is to say that we are using our noses to find out something. Progressive forms can be used.

> *What are you doing?* ~ *I'm* **smelling** *the meat to see if it's still OK.*

# 536 so: adverb meaning 'like this/that'

## 1 after *seem, appear* etc

*So* can be used in a formal style in a few cases to mean 'like this/that', 'in this/that way'. This happens, for example, after *seem, appear, remain, more* and *less*.

> *Will the business make a loss this year?* ~ *It* **appears so.**
> *The weather is stormy, and will* **remain so** *over the weekend.*
> *She was always nervous, and after her accident she became even* **more so.**
> *I read the front page very carefully, and the rest of the paper* **less so.**

## 2 not used in other cases

In other cases, *so* is not normally used adverbially to mean 'like this/that', 'in this/that way'.

> *Look – hold it up in the air* **like this.** (NOT . . . ~~hold it up in the air so.~~)
> *When he laughs* **like that** *I want to scream.* (NOT ~~When he laughs so~~ . . .)
> *I don't think we should do it* **in that way.** (NOT ~~do it so.~~)
> *He says he is ill and he looks it.* (NOT . . . ~~he looks so.~~)

For *so* with *say* and *tell*, see 540.  For *so am I* etc, see 541.
For *so* with *hope, believe* etc, see 539.  For *do so*, see 162.

# 537 **so** (conjunction) and **then**

*So* and *then* can both be used in replies, to mean 'since that is so', 'it follows from what you have said'.

> *It's more expensive to travel on Friday.* ~ ***Then/So*** *I'll leave on Thursday.*
> *I'll be needing the car.* ~ ***Then/So*** *I suppose I'll have to take a taxi.*

*So* (but not *then*) can also be used when the same speaker connects two ideas, to mean 'it follows from what I have said'.

> *It's more expensive to travel on Friday,* ***so*** *I'll leave on Thursday.*
> (NOT . . . ~~Then I'll leave on Thursday.~~)

For *so* used like *and*, see 157.14.

# 538 **so** (degree adverb): **so tired, so fast**

## 1 meaning

*So* means 'that much' or 'to that extent'. It is used when we are talking about a high degree of some quality – in situations where *very* is also a suitable word.

> *I'm sorry you're* ***so*** *tired.* (= I know you're very tired, and I'm sorry.)
> *It was* ***so*** *cold that we couldn't go out.* (= It was very cold weather, and because of that we couldn't go out.)
> *I wish she didn't drive* ***so*** *fast.*

## 2 *so* and *very*

*Very* (see 611) is used when we are giving new information. *So* is mainly used to refer to information which has already been given, which is already known, or which is obvious. Compare:

– *You're* ***very*** *late.* (giving new information)
*I'm sorry I'm* ***so*** *late.* (referring to information which is already known)
– *It was* ***very*** *warm in Scotland.* (giving new information)
*I didn't think it would be* ***so*** *warm.* (referring to information which is already known)

## 3 emphatic use

In an informal style, *so* can also be used like *very* to give new information, when the speaker wishes to emphasise what is said. This structure is rather like an exclamation (see 195).

> *He's* ***so*** *bad-tempered!* (= How bad-tempered he is!)
> *You're* ***so*** *right!*

## 4 *so . . . that*

We use *so*, not *very*, before *that*-clauses.

> *It was* ***so*** *cold* **that** *we stopped playing.* (NOT ~~It was very cold that we stopped playing.~~)
> *He spoke* ***so*** *fast* **that** *nobody could understand.* (NOT ~~He spoke very fast that . . .~~)

▶

## 5 before adjectives and adverbs

We can use *so* before an adjective alone (without a noun) or an adverb.
> *The milk was **so good** that we couldn't stop drinking it.*
> *Why are you driving **so fast**?*

*So* is not used with **adjective + noun**.
> *I didn't expect **such terrible weather**.* (NOT . . . ~~so terrible weather.~~)
> *I enjoyed my stay in your country, which is **so beautiful**.* (NOT ~~I enjoyed my stay in your so beautiful country.~~)

For *such*, see 569.

## 6 *so much*, etc

We can use *so much* and *so many* (see 542), *so few* and *so little* with or without nouns.
> *I've bought **so many** new books I don't know when I'll read them.*
> *There were **so few** interesting people there that we decided to go home.*
> *I've read **so much** and learnt **so little**.*

## 7 *so* and *so much*

We use *so*, not *so much*, before adjectives without nouns (see paragraph 5 above). Compare:
– *She had **so much heavy luggage** that she couldn't carry it.*
  *Her luggage was **so heavy** that she couldn't carry it.* (NOT ~~Her luggage was so much heavy . . .~~)
– *I've never seen **so much beautiful jewellery**.*
  *The jewellery is **so beautiful**!* (NOT . . . ~~so much beautiful!~~)

But we use *so much*, not *so*, before comparatives.
> *I'm glad you're feeling **so much better**.* (NOT . . . ~~so better.~~)

## 8 *so . . . as to . . .*

There is a structure with *so* followed by **adjective + *as to* + infinitive**. This is formal and not very common.
> *Would you be **so kind as to tell** me the time?* (= . . . kind enough to . . .)
>   (NOT ~~Would you be so kind and . . .~~ OR ~~Would you be so kind to . . .~~)

## 9 *so . . . a . . .*

There is another rather formal structure with ***so* + adjective + *a/an* + noun** (see 14).
> *I had never before met **so gentle a person**.* (= . . . such a gentle person.)

# 539 **so** and **not** with **hope, believe** etc

## 1 instead of *that*-clauses.

We often use *so* after *believe, hope, expect, imagine, suppose, guess, reckon, think, be afraid*, instead of repeating words in a *that*-clause.
> *Is Alex here? ~ I **think so**.* (NOT . . . ~~I think that Alex is here.~~)
> *Do you think we'll be in time? ~ I **hope so**.* (NOT ~~I hope.~~)
> *Did you lose? ~ I'm **afraid so**.*

We do not use *so* before a *that*-clause.

> *I hope **that** we'll have good weather.* (NOT ~~I hope so, that we'll have good weather.~~)

Note the special use of *I thought so* to mean 'my suspicions were correct'.

> *Empty your pockets. Ah, **I thought so**! You've been stealing biscuits again.*

*So* is not used after *know* (see 313).

> *You're late. ~ **I know**. OR I know that.* (NOT ~~I know so.~~)

## 2 negative structures

We can make these expressions negative in two ways.

> affirmative verb + *not*

> *Did you win? ~ **I'm afraid not**.*
> *We won't be in time for the train. ~ No, **I suppose not**.*

> negative verb + *so*

> *You won't be here tomorrow? ~ **I don't suppose so**.*
> *Will it rain? ~ **I don't expect so**.*

*Hope* and *be afraid* are always used in the first structure.

> *I **hope not**.* (NOT ~~I don't hope so.~~)

*Think* is more common in the second structure.

> *I **don't think so**.* (More common than *I think not*.)

## 3 *so* at the beginning of a clause

We can use *so* at the beginning of a clause with *say, hear, understand, tell, believe* and a number of other verbs. This structure is used to say how the speaker learnt something.

> *It's going to be a cold winter, or **so** the newspaper **says**.*
> *Mary's getting married. ~ Yes, **so** I **heard**.*
> *The Professor's ill. ~ **So** I **understand**.*

For *so* after *tell* and *say*, see 540.

# 540 *so* with **say** and **tell**

## 1 instead of *that*-clauses

*So* can be used after *say* and *tell* instead of repeating information in a *that*-clause.

> *She's going to be the next president. Everybody **says so**.* (= ... Everybody says that she's going to be the next president.)
> *You've got to clean the car. ~ Who **says so**?*
> *Taxes are going up. Bob **told** me **so**.*

Note that *so* is used in this way mostly when we are talking about the authority for statements, about reasons why we should believe them. When we simply want to identify the speaker, we prefer *that*. Compare:

> *Jane's crazy. ~ Who **says so**? ~ Dr Bannister.*
> *Jane's crazy. ~ Who **said that**? ~ I did.*

For *so* at the beginning of a clause (e.g. *so the newspaper says*), see 539.3.   ▶

## 2   *I told you so*

*I told you so* usually means 'I warned you, but you wouldn't listen to me'.
> *Mummy, I've broken my train.* ~ *I told you so. You shouldn't have tried to ride on it.*

## 3   other verbs

*So* cannot be used after all verbs of saying. We cannot say, for example, ~~She promised me so.~~

# 541   so have I, so am I etc

## 1   *so* + auxiliary + subject

We can use *so* to mean 'also', before **auxiliary verb + subject**. The structure is used to answer or add to what came before. Note the word order.
> *Louise can dance beautifully, and so can her sister.*
> *I've lost their address.* ~ *So have I.*

The same structure is possible with non-auxiliary *be* and *have*.
> *I was tired, and so were the others.*
> *I have a headache.* ~ *So have I.*

After a clause with no auxiliary verb, we use *do/does/did*.
> *He just wants the best for his country.* ~ *So did Hitler.*

We do not normally use a more complete verb phrase in this structure. We can say, for example, *So can her sister*, but not ~~So can her sister dance.~~

## 2   *so* + subject + auxiliary

*So* can also be followed by **subject + auxiliary verb** (note the word order) to express surprised agreement.
> *It's raining.* ~ *Why, so it is!*
> *You've just put the teapot in the fridge.* ~ *So I have!*

For *neither/nor am I* etc, see 374.

# 542   so much and so many

## 1   the difference

The difference between *so much* and *so many* is the same as between *much* and *many* (see 357). *So much* is used with singular (uncountable) nouns; *so many* is used with plurals.
> *I had never seen so much food in my life.*
> *She had so many children that she didn't know what to do.* (NOT ... ~~so much children~~ ...)

We use *so*, not *so much*, to modify adjectives and adverbs (see 538.5,6).
> *You're so beautiful.* (NOT ~~You're so much beautiful.~~)

But *so much* is used before comparatives (see 140).
> *She's so much more beautiful now.*

## 2 *so much/many* without a noun

We can drop a noun after *so much/many*, if the meaning is clear.
> *I can't eat all that meat – there's **so much**!*
> *I was expecting a few phone calls, but not **so many**.*

## 3 *so much* as an adverb

*So much* can be used as an adverb.
> *I wish you didn't smoke **so much**.*

## 4 special structures with *so much*

We can use *not so much . . . as* or *not so much . . . but* to make corrections and clarifications.
> *It **wasn't so much** his appearance I liked **as** his personality.*
> *It's **not so much** that I don't want to go, **but** I just haven't got time.*
In negative and *if*-clauses, *so much as* can be used to mean 'even'.
> *He **didn't so much as** say thank you, after all we'd done for him.*
> *If he **so much as** looks at another woman, I'll kill him.*

# 543 **so that** and **in order that**

## 1 purpose

These structures are used to talk about purpose. *So that* is more common than *in order that*, especially in an informal style. They are often followed by auxiliary verbs such as *can* or *will*; *may* is more formal.
> *She's staying here for six months **so that** she **can** perfect her English.*
> *I'm putting it in the oven now **so that** it'**ll** be ready by seven o'clock.*
> *We send monthly reports **in order that** they **may** have full information.*
In an informal style, *that* can be dropped after *so* (see 584).
> *I've come early **so** I can talk to you.*

## 2 present tenses for future

Present tenses are sometimes used for the future.
> *I'll send the letter express **so that** she **gets** / she'**ll get** it before Tuesday.*
> *I'm going to make an early start **so that** I **don't**/**won't** get stuck in the traffic.*
> *We must write to him, **in order that** he **does**/**will** not feel that we are hiding things.*

## 3 past structures

In sentences about the past, *would*, *could* or *should* are generally used with verbs after *so that* / *in order that*. *Might* is possible in a very formal style.
> *Mary talked to the shy girl **so that** she **wouldn't** feel left out.*
> *I took my golf clubs **so that** I **could** play at the weekend.*
> *They met on a Saturday **in order that** everybody **should** be free to attend.*
> *He built a chain of castles **so that** he **might** control the whole country.*

For the infinitive structures *in order to* and *so as to*, see 289.
For *so . . . that* expressing result, see 538.4.
For *lest* meaning 'so that . . . not', see 321.

# 544 so-and-so; so-so

## 1 *so-and-so*

This informal expression is used when one cannot remember a name.
*What's happened to old **so-and-so**?* (= ... what's his name?)
It can also replace a swearword or an insult.
*She's an old **so-and-so**.*

## 2 *so-so*

This informal expression means 'neither good nor bad.'
*How are you feeling? ~ **So-so**.* (NOT ... ~~*So-and-so.*~~)
*Was the concert any good? ~ **So-so**.*

# 545 'social' language

Every language has fixed expressions which are used on particular social
occasions – for example when people meet, leave each other, go on a journey,
sit down to meals and so on. Here are some of the most important English
expressions of this kind.

## 1 introductions

Common ways of introducing strangers to each other are:
*John, do you know Helen? Helen, this is my friend John.*
*Sally, I don't think you've met Elaine.*
*I don't think you two know each other, do you?*
*Can/May I introduce John Willis?* (more formal)
When people are introduced, they usually say *How do you do?* (formal), *Hello*,
or *Hi* (informal). Americans often say *How are you?* Note that *How do you do?*
is not a question, and the normal reply is *How do you do?* (It does not mean
the same, in British English, as *How are you?*) Another possible response is
*Glad/Pleased to meet you.*
People who are introduced often shake hands.

For the use of first names, surnames and titles, see 363.

## 2 greetings

When meeting people (formal):
*(Good) morning/afternoon/evening.*
When meeting people (informal):
*Hello.    Hi.* (very informal)
When leaving people:
*Good morning/afternoon/evening.* (very formal, unusual)
*Goodnight.    Goodbye.*
*Bye.* (informal)    *Bye-bye.* (often used to and by children)
*Cheers.* (informal – British only)    *Take care.* (informal)
*See you.* (informal)    *See you later / tomorrow / next week* etc. (informal)
*It was nice to meet / meeting you.*
Note that *Good day* is very unusual, and *Goodnight* is used only when leaving
people, not when meeting them.

## 3 asking about health etc

When we meet people we know, we often ask politely about their health or their general situation.

*How are you?*                             *How's it going?* (informal)
*How are things? / How's things?* (informal)   *How (are) you doing?*

Formal answers:

*Very well, thank you. And you?*     *Fine, thank you.*

Informal answers:

*Fine/Great, thanks.*     *All right.*      *(It) could be worse.*
*OK.*                     *Not too bad.*    *Mustn't grumble.*
*So-so.* (NOT ~~So and so.~~)

British people do not usually ask *How are you?* when they are introduced to people. And neither British nor American people begin letters to strangers by asking about health (see 146).

## 4 special greetings

Greetings for special occasions are:

*Happy birthday!* (OR *Many happy returns!*)
*Happy New Year / Easter!*
*Happy/Merry Christmas!*     *Happy anniversary!*
*Congratulations on your exam results / new job* etc (NOT ~~Congratulation on . . .~~)

## 5 small talk

British people often begin polite conversations by talking about the weather.

*Nice day, isn't it?* ~ *Lovely.*

## 6 getting people's attention

*Excuse me!* is commonly used to attract somebody's attention, or to call a waiter in a restaurant. We do not normally say *Excuse me, sir/madam* (see 363.2).

## 7 apologies

British people say *Excuse me* before interrupting or disturbing somebody, and *Sorry* after doing so. Compare:

*Excuse me. Could I get past? Oh, **sorry**, did I step on your foot?*
*Excuse me, could you tell me the way to the station?*

Americans also use *Excuse me* to apologise after disturbing somebody. *I beg your pardon* is a more formal way of saying 'Sorry'.

***I beg your pardon.** I didn't realise this was your seat.*

## 8 asking people to repeat

If people do not hear or understand what is said, they may say *Sorry?* (BrE), *What?* (informal), *(I beg your) pardon?* or *Pardon me?* (AmE).

*Mike's on the phone.* ~ *Sorry?* ~ *I said Mike's on the phone.*
*See you tomorrow.* ~ ***What?*** ~ *See you tomorrow.*
*You're going deaf.* ~ ***I beg your pardon?***                         ▶

## 9   journeys etc

Common ways of wishing people a good journey are:

> *Have a good trip.*        *Have a good journey.* (BrE)
> *Safe journey home.* (BrE)

After a journey (for example when we meet people at the airport or station), we may say:

> *Did you have a good journey/trip/flight?*
> *How was the journey/trip/flight?*

If somebody is leaving for an evening out or some kind of pleasant event, people might say *Have a good time!* or *Enjoy yourself!* (especially in American English sometimes just *Enjoy!*). *Good luck!* is used before examinations or other difficult or dangerous events.

When people return home, their friends or family may say

> *Welcome back/home.*

## 10   holidays

Before somebody starts a holiday, we may say:

> *Have a good holiday.* (AmE ... *vacation.*) OR *Have a good time.*

When the holiday is over, we may say:

> *Did you have a good holiday/vacation?*

## 11   meals

We do not have fixed expressions for the beginnings and ends of meals. It is common for guests or family members to say something complimentary about the food during the meal (for example *This is very nice*), and after (for example *That was lovely/delicious; thank you very much*). Some religious people say 'grace' (a short prayer) before and after meals. Waiters often say *Enjoy your meal* after serving a customer.

For the names of meals, see 347.

## 12   drinking

When people begin drinking alcoholic drinks socially, they often raise their glasses and say something. Common expressions are *Cheers!* (BrE) and *Your health!* When we drink to celebrate an occasion (such as a birthday, a wedding or a promotion), we often say *Here's to ...!*

> **Here's to** Betty!
> **Here's to** the new job!        **Here's to** the happy couple!

## 13   sending good wishes

Typical expressions are *Give my best wishes/regards/greetings/love to X*, *Remember me to X*, *Say hello to X for me*. When the wishes are passed on, common expressions are *X sends his/her best wishes/regards* etc, *X says hello*.

## 14   sympathy

Common formulae in letters of sympathy (for example on somebody's death) are *I was very/terribly/extremely sorry to hear about ...* and *Please accept my deepest sympathy*.

## 15 invitations and visits

Invitations often begin:
> *Would you like to . . .?*

Possible replies:
> *Thank you very much. That would be very nice/lovely.* (formal)
> *Thanks, that would be great.* (informal)
> *Sorry. I'm afraid I'm not free.*

It is normal to thank people for hospitality at the moment of leaving their houses.
> *Thank you very much. That was a wonderful evening.*

## 16 offers and replies

Offers often begin *Would you like . . .?* or *Can/May I get/offer you . . .?* (more formal). Offers to do things for people can begin *Would you like me to . . .?*, *Can/May I . . .?* or *Shall I . . .?* (mainly BrE). Typical replies are *Yes please*; *No thank you*; *Thanks, I'd love some*; *I'd love to*; *That's very nice/kind of you.* Note that *thank you* can be used for accepting as well as refusing.

## 17 asking for things

We normally ask for things by using *yes/no* questions. (see 435).
> *Could you lend me a pen?* (NOT *Please lend me a pen.*)

## 18 handing over things

We do not have an expression which is automatically used when we hand over things. We sometimes say *Here you are*, especially when we want to attract people's attention to the fact that we are passing something to them.
> *Have you got a map of London? ~ I think so. Yes, **here you are**. ~ Thanks.*

*There you go* is also possible in this situation, especially in AmE.

## 19 thanks

Common ways of thanking people are:

| | |
|---|---|
| *Thank you.* | *Thanks very much / a lot.* (NOT *Thank you a lot.*) |
| *Thank you very much.* | *Cheers.* (informal BrE) |
| *Thanks.* (informal) | |

Possible replies to thanks are:

| | |
|---|---|
| *Not at all.* | *You're welcome.* |
| *Don't mention it.* | *That's (quite) all right.* |
| *That's OK.* (informal) | *No problem.* (informal) |

But note that British people do not always reply to thanks, especially thanks for small things.

For more information about thanking and the use of *please*, see 433.

## 20 sleep

When somebody goes to bed, people often say *Sleep well*. In the morning, we may ask *Did you sleep well?* or *How did you sleep?*

For expressions used when telephoning, see 578.

# 546   some

## 1   meaning: indefinite quantity/number

*Some* is a determiner (see 154). It often suggests an indefinite quantity or number, and is used when it is not important to say exactly how much/many we are thinking of.

*I need **some** new clothes.*         *Would you like **some** tea?*

## 2   pronunciation

When *some* has this indefinite meaning, it usually has a 'weak' pronunciation /s(ə)m/ before (**adjective +**) **noun**.

*some* /s(ə)m/ *new clothes*     *some* /s(ə)m/ *tea*

For more about 'strong' and 'weak' pronunciations, see 616.

## 3   *some* and *any*

With this meaning, *some* is most common in affirmative clauses, and in questions which expect or encourage the answer 'Yes'. In other cases, *any* is generally used. For details, see 547. Compare:

– *There are **some** children at the front door.*
  *Do you mind if I put **some** music on?*
– *Did you meet **any** interesting people on holiday?*
  *She hasn't got **any** manners.*

## 4   *some* and *a/an*

*Some* (in this sense) is used in similar ways to the indefinite article *a/an* (see 65). However, it is not normally used with the same kind of nouns. Compare:

*I need **a** new **coat**.* (singular countable noun) (NOT *. . . ~~some new coat.~~*)
*I need **some** new shirts.* (plural countable noun)
*I need **some** help.* (uncountable noun)

## 5   when *some* is not used

With an uncountable or plural noun, *some* usually suggests the idea of an indefinite (but not very large) quantity or number. When there is no idea of a limited quantity or number, we do not usually use *some*. For details, see 67. Compare:

– *We've planted **some** roses in the garden.* (a limited number)
  *I like **roses**.* (no idea of number)
– *Bring **some** food in case we get hungry.*
  *The President has appealed for **food** for the earthquake victims.*

## 6   *some* and *some of; some* with no following noun

Before another determiner (article, demonstrative or possessive word) or a pronoun, we use *some of*. Compare:

– *I've got tickets for **some** concerts next month.* (NOT *. . . ~~some of concerts~~ . . .*)
  *Pete's coming to **some of the** concerts.* (NOT *. . . ~~some the concerts~~ . . .*)
– ***Some** people want to get to sleep.* (NOT *. . . ~~some of people~~ . . .*)
  ***Some of us** want to get to sleep.* (NOT *~~Some us~~ . . .*)

Nouns can be dropped after *some*, if the meaning is clear.

*I've got too many strawberries. Would you like **some**?*

Before *of*, or with no following noun, *some* is pronounced /sʌm/.
> *some* /sʌm/*of us*   *Would you like some* /sʌm/*?*

## 7  contrast with *others* etc

*Some* (pronounced /sʌm/) can have a more emphatic meaning, contrasting with *others*, *all* or *enough*.
> **Some** *people like the sea;* **others** *prefer the mountains.*
> **Some** *of us were late, but we were* **all** *there by ten o'clock.*
> *I've got* **some** *money, but not* **enough**.

## 8  an unknown person or thing

*Some* (/sʌm/) can refer to an unknown person or thing (usually with a singular countable noun).
> **Some** *idiot has taken the bath plug.*
> *There must be* **some** *job I could do.*
> *She's living in* **some** *village in Yorkshire.*

We can use this structure to suggest that we are not interested in somebody or something, or that we do not think much of him/her/it.
> *Mary's gone to America to marry* **some** *sheep farmer or other.*
> *I don't want to spend my life doing* **some** *boring little office job.*

## 9  *some party!*

In informal speech, *some* can show enthusiastic appreciation.
> *It was* **some** *party!*

## 10  with numbers

*Some* (/sʌm/) with a number suggests that the number is high or impressive.
> *We have exported* **some four thousand** *tons of bootlaces this year.*

For *somebody* and *anybody*, *something* and *anything* etc, see 548.
For *some time*, *sometime* and *sometimes*, see 549.

# 547  some and any

## 1  indefinite quantities

Both *some* (see 546) and *any* (see 55) can refer to an indefinite quantity or number. They are used when it is not easy, or not important, to say exactly how much/many we are thinking of.
> *I need to buy* **some** *new clothes.*     *Is there* **any** *milk left?*

## 2  the difference

*Some* is most common in affirmative clauses. *Any* (used in this sense) is a 'non-affirmative' word (see 381), and is common in questions and negatives. Compare:
> *I want* **some** *razor blades.* (NOT *I want any razor blades.*)
> *Have you got* **any** *razor blades?*
> *Sorry, I haven't got* **any** *razor blades.* (NOT *Sorry, I haven't got some* . . .)

For other uses of *any*, see 55.                                              ▶

### 3   *some* in questions

We use *some* in questions if we expect people to answer 'Yes', or want to encourage them to say 'Yes' – for example in offers and requests.

*Have you brought **some** paper and a pen?*
   (The hearer is expected to bring them.)
*Shouldn't there be **some** instructions with it?*
*Would you like **some** more meat?*
*Could I have **some** brown rice, please?*
*Have you got **some** glasses that I could borrow?*

### 4   *any* in affirmative clauses

We use *any* in affirmative clauses after words that have a negative or limiting meaning: for example *never, hardly, without, little*.

*You **never** give me **any** help.*      *I **forgot** to get **any** bread.*
*There's **hardly any** tea left.*      *We got there **without any** trouble.*
*There is **little** point in doing **any** more work now.*

For the 'free choice' use of *any* (e.g. ***Any** child could do this*), see 55.

### 5   *if*-clauses

Both *some* and *any* are common in *if*-clauses.
*If you want **some/any** help, let me know.*
Sometimes *any* is used to suggest 'if there is/are any'.
***Any** cars parked in this road will be towed away.*
   (= If there are any cars parked in this road, they will . . .)

## 548   somebody, someone, anybody, anyone etc

### 1   *-body* and *-one*

There is no significant difference between *somebody* and *someone*, *anybody* and *anyone*, *everybody* and *everyone* or *nobody* and *no one*. The *-one* forms are more common in writing; the *-body* forms are more frequent in speech in British English.

### 2   *some-* and *any-*

The differences between *somebody* and *anybody*, *something* and *anything*, *somewhere* and *anywhere* etc are the same as the differences between *some* and *any* (see 547 for details). Compare:

– *There's **somebody** at the door.*  – *Can I get you **something** to drink?*
   *Did **anybody** telephone?*      *If you need **something/anything**,*
                          *just shout.*

– *Let's go **somewhere** nice for dinner.*
   *I don't want to go **anywhere** too expensive.*

### 3   singular

When these words are subjects they are used with singular verbs.
***Everybody** likes her.* (NOT *Everybody like her.*)
*Is **everything** ready?* (NOT *Are everything ready?*)

*Somebody* normally refers to only one person. Compare:
> There's **somebody** outside who wants to talk to you.
> There are **some people** outside who want to talk to you.

## 4 use of *they*

*They*, *them* and *their* are often used with a singular meaning to refer back to *somebody* etc (see 528).
> If **anybody** wants a ticket for the concert, **they** can get it from my office.
> There's **somebody** at the door. ~ Tell **them** I'm busy.
> **Someone** left **their** umbrella on the bus.       **Nobody** phoned, did **they**?

## 5 complementation: *somebody nice*, etc

*Somebody* etc can be followed by adjectives or adverbial expressions.
> I hope he marries **somebody nice**.
> She's going to meet **someone in the Ministry**.
> I feel like eating **something hot**.
> Let's go **somewhere quiet** this weekend.

They can also be followed by *else* (see 183).
> Mary – are you in love with **somebody else**?
> I don't like this place – let's go **somewhere else**.

Note also the informal use of *much* after *any-* and *no-*.
> We didn't do **anything much** yesterday.
> There's **nothing much** on TV tonight.

## 6 *someplace*

*Someplace* is common in informal American English.
> Let's go **someplace** quiet.

## 7 *anyone* and *any one*; *everyone* and *every one*

*Anyone* means the same as *anybody*; *any one* means 'any single one (person or thing)'. Compare:
> Does **anyone** know where Celia lives?
> You can borrow **any one** book at a time.

There is a similar difference between *everyone* and *every one*. Compare:
> **Everyone** had a good time at the party.
> There aren't any cakes left – they've eaten **every one**.

For the difference between *no one* and *none*, see 380.
For question tags after *everything* and *nothing*, see 488.
For *some time*, *sometime* and *sometimes*, see 549.

# 549 some time, sometime and sometimes

*Some time* (with two stresses: /'sʌm 'taɪm/) means 'quite a long time'.
> I'm afraid it'll take **some time** to repair your car.
> She's lived in Italy for **some time**, so she speaks Italian quite well.

*Sometime* (/'sʌmtaɪm/) refers to an indefinite time, usually in the future; it often means 'one day'. It can also be written as two words: *some time*.
> Let's have dinner together **sometime** next week.
> When will I get married – this year, next year, **sometime**, never?       ▶

*Sometimes* (/ˈsʌmtaɪmz/) is an adverb of frequency (see 24). It means 'on some occasions', 'more than once' (past, present or future).

> I **sometimes** *went skiing when I lived in Germany.*
> **Sometimes**, *in the long winter evenings, I just sit and think about life.*

For *sometimes* and *once*, see 393

# 550 soon, early and quickly

## 1 soon

*Soon* means 'a short time after now' or 'a short time after then'.

> *Get well* **soon**. (NOT ~~Get well early.~~)
> *The work was hard at the beginning, but she* **soon** *got used to it.*

For *no sooner . . . than*, see 233.

## 2 early

The adverb *early* means 'near the beginning of the time-period that we are thinking about'. It does not usually mean 'a short time after now/then'.

> **Early** *that week, Luke was called to the police station.*
> *We usually take our holidays* **early** *in the year.* (NOT *. . . ~~soon in the year.~~*)
> *I usually get up* **early** *and go to bed* **early**. (NOT *~~I usually get up soon~~ . . .*)

Sometimes *early* means 'before the expected time'.

> *The plane arrived twenty minutes* **early**.

*Early* can also be used as an adjective.

> *I caught an* **early** *train.*     *You're very* **early**.

In a formal style, the adjective *early* can sometimes have the same kind of meaning as *soon*.

> *I should be grateful for an* **early** *reply.*
> *Best wishes for an* **early** *recovery.*

A watch or clock is *fast* or *slow*, not *early* or *late*.

> *My watch is five minutes* **fast**.

## 3 quickly

*Quickly* refers to the speed with which something is done. Compare:

> – *Come and see us* **quickly**. (= Hurry – make the arrangements fast.)
>   *Come and see us* **soon**. (= Come and see us before long.)
> – *He did the repair* **quickly** *but not very well.*
>   *I hope you can do the repair* **soon** *– I need the car.*

# 551 sort of, kind of and type of

## 1 articles

The article *a/an* is usually dropped after *sort of, kind of* and *type of*, but structures with articles are possible in an informal style.

> *That's a funny* **sort of** *(a) car.*     *What* **sort of** *(a) bird is that?*

## 2  singular and plural; *these sort of* etc

When we are talking about one sort of thing, we can use *sort of, kind of* or
*type of* followed by a singular noun.
> *This **sort of car** is enormously expensive to run.*
> *I'm interested in any new **type of development** in computer science.*
Singular *sort of, kind of* and *type of* can also be followed by plural nouns,
especially in an informal style.
> *I'm interested in any new **kind of developments** ...*
Plural demonstratives (*these* and *those*) can also be used.
> ***These sort of cars** are enormously expensive to run.*
> *Do you smoke **those kind of cigarettes**?*
This structure is often felt to be incorrect, and is usually avoided in a formal
style. This can be done by using a singular noun (see above), by using plural
*sorts/kinds/types*, or by using the structure ... *of this/that sort/kind/type.*
> *This sort of car is ...*
> *These kinds of car(s) are ...*    *Cars of that type are ...*

## 3  softeners

In an informal style, *sort of* and *kind of* can be used before almost any word or
expression, or at the end of a sentence, to show that we are not speaking very
exactly, or to make what we say less definite.
> *We **sort of thought** you might forget.*
> *Sometimes I **sort of wonder** whether I shouldn't **sort of get** a job.*
> *I've had **sort of an idea** about what we could do.*
> *She's **kind of strange**.*    *I've changed my mind, **kind of**.*

# 552  sound

*Sound* is a link verb (see 328). It is followed by adjectives, not adverbs.
> *You **sound unhappy**. What's the matter?*
Progressive forms are not very common.
> *Your idea **sounds** great.* (NOT *Your idea's sounding great.*)
However, progressive forms are possible when there is an idea of change.
> *The car **sounds** / **is sounding** a bit rough these days.*
*Sound* is often followed by *like* or *as if/though*.
> *That **sounds like** Bill coming up the stairs.*
> *It **sounds as if/though** he's had a hard day.*

# 553  speak and talk

## 1  little difference

There is litle difference between *speak* and *talk*. In certain situations one or the
other is preferred, but they are usually both possible.

## 2  formality

*Talk* is the more usual word for informal communication.
> *When she walked into the room everybody stopped **talking**.*
> *Could I **talk** to you about the football match for a few minutes?*    ▶

*Speak* is often used for communication in more serious or formal situations.
*I'll have to **speak** to that boy – he's getting very lazy.*
*They had a row last week, and now they're not **speaking** to one another.*
*After she had finished reading the letter, nobody **spoke**.*

## 3 lectures etc

*Talk* is often used for the act of giving an informal lecture (a *talk*); *speak* is preferred for more formal lectures, sermons etc. Compare:
*This is Patrick Allen, who's going to **talk** to us about gardening.*
*This is Professor Rosalind Bowen, who is going to **speak** to us on recent developments in low-temperature physics.*
*The Pope **spoke** to the crowd for seventy minutes about world peace.*

## 4 languages

*Speak* is the usual word to refer to knowledge and use of languages, and to the physical ability to speak.
*She **speaks** three languages fluently.*
*We **spoke** French so that the children wouldn't understand.*
*His throat operation has left him unable to **speak**.*

## 5 other cases

One usually asks to *speak to* somebody on the phone (AmE also *speak with*).
*Hello. Could I **speak to** Karen, please?*
*Talk* is used before *sense*, *nonsense* and other words with similar meanings.
*You're **talking** complete **nonsense**, as usual.* (NOT ~~You're speaking complete nonsense~~...)

# 554 speech (1): stress and rhythm

Stress and rhythm are important elements in English pronunciation. If learners pronounce all the syllables in a sentence too regularly, with the same force and at the same speed, they can be quite hard for English speakers to understand. And if learners are not sensitive to English stress and rhythm, they may not perceive unstressed syllables (especially 'weak forms' – see 616) at all, and this may make it difficult for them to follow natural English speech.

## 1 stress

*Stress* is the word for the 'strength' with which syllables are pronounced. In speech, some parts of English words and sentences sound louder than others. For example, the first syllable of CARpet, the second syllable of inSPECtion or the last syllable of conFUSE are usually stressed, while the other syllables in these words are not. In the sentence *Don't look at HIM – HE didn't do it*, the words *him* and *he* are stressed in order to emphasise them. Stressed syllables are not only louder; they may also have longer vowels, and they may be pronounced on a higher musical pitch.

## 2 word stress

English words with more than one syllable mostly have a fixed stress pattern. There are not many rules to show which syllable of a word will be stressed: one

usually has to learn the stress pattern of a word along with its meaning, spelling and pronunciation. Examples:
Stressed on first syllable:
AFter, CApital, HAPpen, EXercise, EAsy
Stressed on second syllable:
inSTEAD, proNOUNCE, aGREEment, parTIcularly
Stressed on third syllable:
enterTAIN, underSTAND, concenTRAtion
The stressed syllable of a word is the one that can carry an intonation movement (see 555 below).
Many short phrases also have a fixed stress pattern.
*front* DOOR *(not* FRONT *door)*
LIVing *room (not living* ROOM*)*
Related words can have different stress patterns.
*to* inCREASE      *an* INcrease
PHOtograph      phoTOgrapher      photoGRAphic
A good dictionary will show how words and common phrases are stressed.

## 3   variable stress

Some words have variable stress. In these, the stress is at or near the end when the word is spoken alone, but it can move to an earlier position when the word is in a sentence, especially if another stressed word follows. Compare:
– *afterNOON* (stress at the end)
*It's time for my* AFternoon SLEEP. (stress at the beginning)
– *JapanESE*
JApanese COOking
– *nineTEEN*
*The year* NINEteen TWENty
Many short phrases – for instance, two-word verbs – have variable stress.
– *Their marriage broke* UP.
*Money problems* BROKE *up their marriage.*
– *Do sit* DOWN.
*She* SAT *down and cried.*
– *It's dark* BLUE.
*a* DARK *blue* SUIT

## 4   stress and pronunciation

Unstressed syllables nearly always have one of two vowels: /ɪ/ (in unstressed prefixes written with *e*, like *de-*, *re-*, *pre-*, *ex-*) or /ə/ (in other cases).
Compare the first syllables in the following pairs of words:
– PREference (/'prefrəns/)          – CONfident (/'kɒnfɪdənt/)
preFER (/prɪ'fɜː(r)/)                 conFUSED (/kən'fjuːzd/)
– EXpert (/'ekspɜːt/)               – PARticle (/'pɑːtɪkl/)
exPERience (/ɪk'spɪərɪəns/)     parTIcular (/pə'tɪkjələ(r)/)
Many short words (mostly pronouns, prepositions, conjunctions and auxiliary verbs) have two quite different pronunciations: a normal 'weak' unstressed form, and a 'strong' form used when the word has special stress. (For details, see 616.)
*I was* (/wəz/) *here first.* ∼ *No you weren't.* ∼ *Yes I was* (/wɒz/).      ▶

## 5 emphatic and contrastive stress

*Stress* is often used to emphasise one part of a sentence, perhaps to make a contrast. Compare these three ways of saying the same words:
*Their ELDER daughter went to Cambridge.* (Not their younger daughter.)
*Their elder DAUGHTER went to Cambridge.* (Not their elder son.)
*Their elder daughter went to CAMBRIDGE.* (Not another university.)

For more about emphasis, see 184.

## 6 stress in sentences; rhythm

*Rhythm* is the word for the way stressed and unstressed syllables make patterns in speech. In sentences, we usually give more stress to nouns, ordinary verbs, adjectives and adverbs, and less stress to pronouns, determiners, prepositions, conjunctions and auxiliary verbs.
*She was SURE that the BACK of the CAR had been DAMaged.*
Stressed syllables are pronounced more slowly and clearly, and (in the opinion of some linguists) follow each other at roughly regular intervals. Unstressed syllables are pronounced more quickly and less clearly, and are fitted in between the stressed syllables. Compare the following two sentences. The second does not take much longer to say than the first: although it has three more unstressed syllables, it has the same number of stressed syllables.
*She KNEW the DOCtor.    She KNEW that there was a DOCtor.*

## 555 speech (2): intonation

Intonation is the word for the 'melody' of spoken language: the way the musical pitch of the voice rises and falls. Intonation systems in languages are very complicated and difficult to analyse, and linguists do not all agree about how English intonation works.

### 1 intonation in conversation

One use of intonation is to show how a piece of information fits in with what comes before and after. For instance, a speaker may raise his or her voice when taking over the conversation from somebody else, or to indicate a change of subject. A rise or fall on a particular word may show that this is the 'centre' of the message – the place where the new information is being given; or it may signal a contrast or a special emphasis. A rising tone at the end of a sentence may suggest that there is more to be said and perhaps invite another speaker to take over.

### 2 attitude

Intonation (together with speed, voice quality and loudness) can also say things about the speaker's attitude. For instance, when people are excited or angry they often raise and lower their voices more.

### 3 three patterns

There are three particularly common intonation patterns in English speech.

a   falling intonation

A falling intonation can suggest that we are saying something definite, complete. The voice falls on the last stressed syllable of a group of words.

*I'm tired.*     *Here's your dictionary.*     *Sally couldn't find him.*

A falling intonation is also common in *wh*-questions.

*What time's the last bus?*     *Where's the secretary?*

b   rising intonation

A rising intonation is common in *yes/no* questions. The voice rises at the end of a group of words, beginning on the last stressed syllable.

*Are you tired?*     *Is that the secretary?*     *Did he post it?*

In 'alternative questions' with *or*, the voice rises on the first part of the question and falls on the second part.

*Are you staying or going?*

c   fall-rise

A fall-rise intonation suggests that something is incomplete, or uncertain, or that there is more to be said.

*I'm tired.*     (perhaps suggesting *But maybe I'll go out with you anyway.*)

*I don't play tennis.*     (perhaps suggesting *But I do play other games.*)

*She's quite a good teacher.* (perhaps suggesting *But I'm not completely happy with her.*)

*The first week was good.* (perhaps suggesting *But not the second.*)

*Is this all you've written?* (perhaps suggesting *I was expecting more.*)

A fall-rise makes questions sound more interested or friendly. It is common in polite requests and invitations.

*Where's the secretary?*     *Please come in.*     *Is this your car?*

*What's your name?*     *Some more potatoes?*     ▶

## 4 intonation and misunderstandings

If a statement is made on a rising intonation, it may be misunderstood as a question.

> *That's our train.* ~ *I don't know.* ~ *Yes, it is, I'm telling you.*

If a declarative question (see 481) is made on a falling intonation, it may be misunderstood as a statement.

> *That's our train?* ~ *Is it?* ~ *No, I'm asking you.*

A falling intonation can also turn a polite request into an order.

> *Can I have some more coffee?* ~ *At once, Your Majesty.*

A fall-rise in the wrong place can be misunderstood as suggesting more than is said.

> *I'd like to play tennis.* ~ *So what's the problem?* ~ *There's no problem.*

For intonation in question tags, see 487.

# 556 spelling (1): capital letters

We use capital (big) letters at the beginning of the following kinds of words:

a  the names of days, months and public holidays (but not usually seasons)

| | | |
|---|---|---|
| *Sunday* | *March* | *Easter* |
| *Tuesday* | *September* | *Christmas* |

(BUT normally *summer, autumn*)

b  the names of people, institutions and places, including stars and planets

| | | |
|---|---|---|
| *John* | *Mary* | *the Smiths* |
| *the Foreign Office* | *North Africa* | *Canada* |
| *the United States* | *The Ritz Hotel* | *Oxford University* |
| *The Super Cinema* | *the Far East* | (compare *He teaches at* |
| *the Pole Star* | *Mars* | *a university*) |

(BUT normally *the earth, the sun, the moon*)

Words derived from people's names have capitals if they refer to the people.

> *Shakespearean drama* (BUT *to pasteurise:* this refers to a chemical process, not directly to the scientist Pasteur)

c  people's titles

| | | |
|---|---|---|
| *Mr Smith* | *Professor Blake* | |
| *Colonel Webb* | *the Managing Director* | *Dr Jones* |

*the Prime Minister is attending the summit*
   (Compare *How is the French prime minister elected?*)

d  nouns and adjectives referring to nationalities and regions, languages, ethnic groups and religions

| | | |
|---|---|---|
| *He's Russian.* | *I speak German.* | *Japanese history* |
| *Catalan cooking* | *She's Jewish.* | *He's a Sikh.* |

e the names of newspapers and magazines
*International Herald Tribune     New Scientist*

f the first word (and often other important words) in the titles of books, films and plays
*The Spy who Loved Me      Gone with the Wind*
*A Midsummer Night's Dream*

For the use of capitals with *East, North* etc, see 172.

# 557 spelling (2): -ly

## 1 adverb formation

We normally change an adjective into an adverb by adding *-ly*.

| | |
|---|---|
| *late → lately* | *real → really* (NOT ~~realy~~) |
| *right → rightly* | *definite → definitely* |
| *hopeful → hopefully* | *pale → palely* |
| *complete → completely* (NOT ~~completly~~) | |

Exceptions:

| | |
|---|---|
| *true → truly* | *whole → wholly* |
| *due → duly* | *full → fully* |

## 2 -y and -i-

*-y* usually changes to *-i-* (see 561).

| | |
|---|---|
| *happy → happily* | *dry → drily* or *dryly* |
| *easy → easily* | *gay → gaily* |

Exceptions:

*shy → shyly     sly → slyly     coy → coyly*

## 3 adjectives ending in consonant + *le*

*-le* changes to *-ly* after a consonant.

*idle → idly     noble → nobly     able → ably*

## 4 adjectives ending in -ic

If an adjective ends in *-ic*, the adverb ends in *-ically* (pronounced /ɪkli/),

*tragic → tragically     phonetic → phonetically*

Exception:

*public → publicly*

# 558 spelling (3): -ise and -ize

Many English verbs can be spelt with either *-ise* or *-ize*. In American English, *-ize* is preferred in these cases. Examples:

| | |
|---|---|
| *realise/realize* (BrE) | *realize* (AmE) |
| *mechanise/mechanize* (BrE) | *mechanize* (AmE) |
| *computerise/computerize* (BrE) | *computerize* (AmE) |
| *baptise/baptize* (BrE) | *baptize* (AmE) |

Most words of two syllables, and a few longer words, have -*ise* in both British and American English. Examples:

| | | |
|---|---|---|
| *surprise* (NOT ~~surprize~~) | *despise* | *supervise* |
| *revise* | *compromise* | *televise* |
| *advise* | *exercise* | *advertise* |
| *comprise* | *improvise* | |

*Capsize* has -*ize* in both British and American English.

Note also *analyse* (AmE *analyse/analyze*) and *paralyse* (AmE *paralyze*).

If in doubt, remember that in British English -*ise* is almost always acceptable. For American English, consult an American dictionary.

# 559 spelling (4): hyphens

## 1 What are hyphens?

Hyphens are the short lines (-) that we put between words in expressions like *ticket-office* or *ex-husband*.

## 2 When are hyphens used?

Hyphens are most common in the following cases:

a compound nouns

- compound nouns where the second part ends in -*er*
   *lorry-driver*   *bottle-opener*
- compound nouns where the first part ends in -*ing*
   *waiting-room*   *writing-paper*
- compound nouns made with prepositions and adverb particles
   *sister-in-law*   *make-up*   *in-joke*
- many compounds of two nouns, where the first noun has the main stress (but hyphens are becoming less common in these cases)
   '*water-bottle* OR '*water bottle*
   '*apple-tree* OR '*apple tree* BUT *apple* '*pie*

b compound adjectives

| | | |
|---|---|---|
| *red-hot* | *nice-looking* | *the London-Paris flight* |
| *blue-eyed* | *grey-green* | *the Scotland-France match* |
| *broken-hearted* | | |

When we use a longer phrase as an adjective before a noun, we often use hyphens. Compare:

– an **out-of-work** miner.      – a **shoot-to-kill** policy
   He's **out of work**.          They were ordered to **shoot to kill**.

c compound verbs beginning with a noun

   *baby-sit*   *house-hunt*

**d prefixes**

The prefixes *anti-, co-, ex-, mid-, non-, pre-, post-, pro-* and *self-* are often separated from what follows by hyphens.

| | | |
|---|---|---|
| *anti-war* | *mid-term* | *post-publication* |
| *co-producer* | *non-involvement* | *pro-hunting* |
| *ex-husband* | *pre-meeting* | *self-study* |

And other prefixes may be separated by hyphens in order to avoid unusual or misleading combinations of letters.

*un-American*    *re-examine*    *counter-revolution*

**e numbers 21-99; fractions**

*twenty-one*    *thirty-six*    *two-thirds*

## 3 word division

We also use hyphens to separate the parts of long words at the end of written or printed lines. (To see where to divide words, look in a good dictionary.)

*... is not completely in accordance with the policy of the present government, which was ...*

## 4 Are hyphens disappearing?

The rules about hyphens are complicated, and usage is not very clear. Perhaps because of this, people seem to be using hyphens less, especially in compound nouns. Many common short compounds are now often written 'solid', with no division between the words (e.g. *weekend, wideawake, takeover*); other less common or longer compounds are now more likely to be written as completely separate words (e.g. *train driver, living room*). The situation at present is rather confused, and it is not unusual to find the same expression spelt in three different ways (e.g. *bookshop, book-shop, book shop*). If one is not sure whether to use a hyphen between words or not, the best thing is to look in a dictionary, or to write the words without a hyphen.

# 560 spelling (5): final e

## 1 final -e dropped before vowels

When an ending that begins with a vowel (e.g. *-ing, -able, -ous*) is added to a word that ends in *-e*, we usually drop the *-e*.

| | | |
|---|---|---|
| *hope → hoping* | *note → notable* | *shade → shady* |
| *make → making* | *fame → famous* | |

Some words that end in *-e* have two possible forms before *-able* and *-age*. The form without *-e* is more common in most cases. Note:

*likeable* (usually with *e*)
*mov(e)able* (both forms common)
*mileage* (only with *e*)

Final *-e* is not dropped from words ending in *-ee, -oe* or *-ye*.

| | |
|---|---|
| *see → seeing* | *canoe → canoeist* |
| *agree → agreeable* | *dye → dyeing* |

▶

## 2 final -e not dropped before consonants

Before endings that begin with a consonant, final *-e* is not normally dropped.

*excite → excitement*     *complete → completeness*
*definite → definitely*

Exceptions: words ending in *-ue*

*due → duly*     *true → truly*     *argue → argument*

In words that end with *-ce* or *-ge*, we do not drop *-e* before *a* or *o*.

*replace → replaceable*     *courage → courageous*
(BUT *charge → charging, face → facing*)

*Judg(e)ment* and *acknowledg(e)ment* can be spelt with or without the *-e* after *g*.

For words ending in *-ie*, see 561.5. For adverbs ending in *-ly*, see 557.

# 561 spelling (6): y and i

## 1 changing y to i

When we add an ending to a word that ends in *-y*, we usually change *-y* to *-i-*.

*hurry → hurried*     *fury → furious*     *merry → merriment*
*marry → marriage*    *easy → easier*      *busy → business*
*happy → happily*

Generally, nouns and verbs that end in *-y* have plural or third person singular forms in *-ies*.

*story → stories*     *spy → spies*     *hurry → hurries*

## 2 exceptions

Two spellings are possible for the nouns *flyer/flier*.
A machine that dries things is a *dryer*.
Words formed from the adjective *dry*: normally *drier, driest, dryly/drily, dryness*.
Words formed from the adjective *sly*: *slyer, slyest, slyly, slyness*.

## 3 no change before i

We do not change *-y* to *-i-* before *i* (for example when we add *-ing, -ism, -ish, -ise*).

*try → trying*     *Tory → Toryism*     *baby → babyish*

## 4 no change after a vowel

We do not change *-y* to *-i-* after a vowel letter.

*buy → buying*         *play → played*
*enjoy → enjoyment*    *grey → greyish*

Exceptions:

*say → said*     *pay → paid*     *lay → laid*

## 5 changing ie to y

We change *-ie* to *-y-* before *-ing*.

*die → dying*     *lie → lying*
(but *dye → dyeing*)

# 562 spelling (7): doubling final consonants

## 1 doubling before vowels

We sometimes double the final consonant of a word before adding -*ed*, -*er*, -*est*, -*ing*, -*able*, -*y* (or any other ending that begins with a vowel).

*stop → stopped    sit → sitting    big → bigger*

## 2 Which consonants are doubled?

We double the following letters:

| | |
|---|---|
| *b*: *rub → rubbing* | *n*: *win → winnable* |
| *d*: *sad → sadder* | *p*: *stop → stopped* |
| *g*: *big → bigger* | *r*: *prefer → preferred* |
| *l*: *travel → travelling* | *t*: *sit → sitting* |
| *m*: *slim → slimming* | |

We double final -*s* in *gassing, gassed* (but not usually in other words), final -*z* in *quizzes, fezzes*, and final -*f* in *iffy* (a colloquial word for 'questionable', 'uncertain').

Final *w* (in words like *show, flow*) is part of a vowel sound, and is not doubled.

*show → showing; flow → flowed* (NOT ~~showwing, flowwed~~)

## 3 only at the end of a word

We only double consonants that come at the end of a word. Compare:

*hop → hopping* BUT *hope → hoping*
*fat → fatter* BUT *late → later*
*plan → planned* BUT *phone → phoned*

## 4 one consonant after one vowel letter

We only double when the word ends in one consonant after one vowel letter. Compare:

*fat → fatter* BUT *fast → faster* (NOT ~~fastter~~)
*bet → betting* BUT *beat → beating* (NOT ~~beatting~~)

## 5 only stressed syllables

We only double consonants in stressed syllables. We do not double in longer words that end in unstressed syllables. Compare:

*up'set → up'setting* BUT *'visit → 'visiting*
*be'gin → be'ginning* BUT *'open → 'opening*
*re'fer → re'ferring* BUT *'offer → 'offering*

Note the spelling of these words:

*'gallop → 'galloping → 'galloped* (NOT ~~gallopping, gallopped~~)
*de'velop → de'veloping → de'veloped* (NOT ~~developping, developped~~)

## 6 exception: final *l* in unstressed syllables

In British English, we double -*l* at the end of a word after one vowel letter, in most cases, even in unstressed syllables.

*'travel → 'travelling*
*'equal → 'equalled*

In American English, words like this are most often spelt with one *l*: *traveling*. ▶

## 7 other exceptions

Consonants are sometimes doubled at the end of final syllables that are pronounced with full vowels (e.g. /æ/), even when these do not carry the main stress.

'kidnap → 'kidnapped
'handicap → 'handicapped
'worship → 'worshippers (AmE also 'worshipers)
'combat → 'combating or 'combatting

Final -s is sometimes doubled in 'focus(s)ing and 'focus(s)ed

## 8 final c

Final -c changes to *ck* before -ed, -er, -ing etc.

picnic → picnickers
panic → panicking
mimic → mimicked

## 9 Why double?

The reason for doubling is to show that a vowel is pronounced short. This is because, in the middle of a word, a stressed vowel letter before one consonant is usually pronounced as a long vowel or as a diphthong (double vowel). Compare:

hoping /'həʊpɪŋ/           hopping /'hɒpɪŋ/
later /'leɪtə(r)/           latter /'lætə(r)/
diner /'daɪnə(r)/           dinner /'dɪnə(r)/

# 563 spelling (8): ch and tch, k and ck

After one vowel, at the end of a word, we usually write -ck and -tch for the sounds /k/ and /tʃ/.

back   neck   sick   lock   stuck
catch   fetch   stitch   botch   hutch

Exceptions:

yak   tic   public (and many other words ending in -ic)
rich   which   such   much   attach   detach

After a consonant or two vowels, we write -k and -ch.

bank   work   talk   march   bench
break   book   week   peach   coach

# 564 spelling (9): ie and ei

The sound /iː/ (as in *believe*) is often written *ie*, but not usually *ei*. However, we write *ei* after c for this sound. English-speaking children learn a rhyme: 'i before e, except after c'.

believe   chief   field   grief   piece   shield
ceiling   deceive   receive   receipt

Exceptions: *seize, Neil, Keith.*

# 565 spelling (10): spelling and pronunciation

In many English words, the spelling is different from the pronunciation. This is mainly because our pronunciation has changed a good deal over the last few hundred years, while our spelling system has stayed more or less the same. Here is a list of some difficult common words with their pronunciations.

## 1 usually two syllables, not three

The letters in brackets are usually not pronounced.

*asp(i)rin*          *ev(e)ry*          *om(e)lette*
*bus(i)ness*          *ev(e)ning*          *rest(au)rant*
*choc(o)late*          *marri(a)ge*          *sev(e)ral*
*diff(e)rent*          *med(i)cine* (AmE three syllables)

## 2 usually three syllables, not four

The letters in brackets are usually not pronounced.

*comf(or)table*          *temp(e)rature*
*int(e)resting*          *us(u)ally*
*secret(a)ry* (AmE four syllables)          *veg(e)table*

## 3 silent letters

The letters in brackets are not pronounced.

- *clim(b)   com(b)   dum(b)   dou(b)t   de(b)t*
- *mus(c)le*
- *han(d)kerchief   san(d)wich   We(d)nesday*
- *champa(g)ne   forei(g)n   si(g)n*
- *bou(gh)t   cau(gh)t   ou(gh)t   thou(gh)t   borou(gh)*
  *dau(gh)ter   hei(gh)t   hi(gh)   li(gh)t   mi(gh)t   nei(gh)bour   ni(gh)t*
  *ri(gh)t   strai(gh)t   throu(gh)   ti(gh)t   wei(gh)*
- *w(h)at   w(h)en   w(h)ere   w(h)ether   w(h)ich   w(h)ip   w(h)y*
  and similarly in other words beginning *wha, whe* or *whi*. (Some speakers use an unvoiced /w/ in these words.)
- *(h)onest   (h)onour   (h)our*
- *(k)nee   (k)nife   (k)nob   (k)nock   (k)now*
  and similarly in other words beginning *kn.*
- *ca(l)m   cou(l)d   ha(l)f   sa(l)mon   shou(l)d   ta(l)k   wa(l)k*
  *wou(l)d   autum(n)   hym(n)*
- *(p)neumatic   (p)sychiatrist   (p)sychology   (p)sychotherapy*
  *(p)terodactyl*     and similarly in other words beginning *pn, ps* or *pt.*
- *cu(p)board* /ˈkʌbəd/
- *i(r)on* (British pronunciation /aɪən/)
- *i(s)land   i(s)le*
- *cas(t)le   Chris(t)mas   fas(t)en   lis(t)en   of(t)en   whis(t)le*
  (*Often* can also be pronounced /ˈɒftən/.)
- *g(u)arantee   g(u)ard   g(u)errilla   g(u)ess   g(u)est   g(u)ide   g(u)ilt*
  *g(u)itar   g(u)y*
- *(w)rap   (w)rite   (w)rong*
- *(w)ho   (w)hom   (w)hore   (w)hose   (w)hole*

## 4   a = /e/

*any   many   Thames* /temz/

▶

**5**   *ch* = /k/

ache   archaeology   architect   chaos   character   chemist
Christmas   mechanical   Michael   stomach

**6**   *ea* = /e/

already   bread   breakfast   dead   death   dreadful   dreamt
head   health   heavy   instead   lead (the metal)   leant   leather
meant   measure   pleasant   pleasure   read (past)   ready   steady
sweater   threat   tread   weather

**7**   *ea* = /eɪ/

break   great   steak

**8**   *gh* = /f/

cough /kɒf/   draught /drɑːft/   enough /ɪˈnʌf/   laugh /lɑːf/
rough /rʌf/   tough /tʌf/

**9**   *o* = /ʌ/

above   brother   colour   come   comfortable   company   cover
done   front   glove   government   honey   London   love   lovely
Monday   money   month   mother   none   nothing   one   onion
other   oven   some   son   stomach   ton(ne)   tongue   once   won
wonder   worry

**10**   *o* = /uː/

lose   prove   to

**11**   *ou* = /ʌ/

country   couple   cousin   double   enough   rough   tough   trouble
young

**12**   *u* or *ou*= /ʊ/

bull   bullet   bush   butcher   could   cushion   full   pull   push
put   should   would

**13**   words pronounced with /aɪ/

biology   buy   dial   height   idea   iron   microphone   science
society   either (many British speakers)   neither (many British speakers)

**14**   other strange spellings

| | |
|---|---|
| area /ˈeərɪə/ | friend /frend/ |
| Australia /ɒsˈtreɪlɪə/ | fruit /fruːt/ |
| bicycle /ˈbaɪsɪkl/ | heard /hɜːd/ |
| biscuit /ˈbɪskɪt/ | heart /hɑːt/ |
| blood /blʌd/ | juice /dʒuːs/ |
| brooch /brəʊtʃ/ | minute /ˈmɪnɪt/ |
| business /ˈbɪznɪs/ | moustache /məˈstɑːʃ/ (AmE /ˈmʌstæʃ/) |
| busy /ˈbɪzi/ | once /wʌns/ |
| clothes /kləʊðz/ | one /wʌn/ |
| does /dʌz/ | theatre /ˈθɪətə(r)/ |

*doesn't* /'dʌz(ə)nt/    *two* /tuː/
*Edinburgh* /'edɪnbrə/    *woman* /'wʊmən/
*Europe* /'jʊərəp/    *women* /'wɪmɪn/
*foreign* /'fɒrən/

## 15   silent *r*

In standard southern British English, *r* is not normally pronounced before a consonant or at the end of a word.

*hard* /hɑːd/    *first* /fɜːst/    *order* /'ɔːdə/
*car* /kɑː/    *four* /fɔː/    *more* /mɔː/

But *r* is pronounced at the end of a word if a vowel follows immediately.

*four islands* /'fɔːr 'aɪləndz/    *more eggs* /'mɔːr 'egz/

Note the pronunciation of *iron*, and of words ending in *-ered* and *-re*.

*iron* /aɪən/ (AmE /'aɪrən/)    *wondered* /'wʌndəd/
*centre* /'sentə(r)/    *bothered* /'bɒðəd/
*theatre* /'θɪətə(r)/

We often add /r/ after words ending in the sound /ə/ even when this is not written with *r*, if another vowel follows immediately.

*India and Africa* /'ɪndɪər ənd 'æfrɪkə/

In most varieties of American English, and in many regional British accents, *r* is pronounced whenever it is written.

# 566   still, yet and already: time

## 1   meanings

*Still, yet* and *already* can all be used to talk about things which are going on, or expected, around the present. Briefly:
– *still* is used to say that something is continuing and has not stopped
– *yet* is used to talk about something that is expected
– *already* is used to say that something has happened early, or earlier than it might have happened.

## 2   still

*Still* is used to say that something has, perhaps surprisingly, not finished.

*She's **still** asleep.*    *Is it **still** raining?*
*I've been thinking for hours, but I **still** can't decide.*
*You're not **still** seeing that Jackson boy, are you?*

*Still* usually goes with the verb, in 'mid-position' (see 24).

## 3   yet

*Not yet* is used to say that something which is expected has not happened (but we think that it will).

*Is Sally here?* ~ ***Not yet.***
*The postman hasn't come **yet**.*

In questions, we use *yet* to ask whether something expected has happened.

*Is supper ready **yet**?*    *Has the postman come **yet**?*

*Yet* usually goes at the end of a clause, but it can go immediately after *not* in a formal style.    ▶

*Don't eat the pears – they aren't ripe **yet**.*
*The pears are **not yet** ripe.* (more formal)

## 4  already

*Already* is used to say that something has happened earlier than expected, or earlier than it might have happened.

*When's Sally going to come? ~ She's **already** here.*
*You must go to Scotland. ~ I've **already** been.*
*Have you **already** finished? That was quick!*

*Already* usually goes with the verb, in 'mid-position' (see 24.) It can also go at the end of a clause, for emphasis.

*Are you here **already**? You must have run all the way.*

We do not usually put *already* before time expressions.

*When I was fourteen I **already** knew that I wanted to be a doctor.* (NOT *Already when I was fourteen*...)

*In 1970 Britain's car industry was **already** in serious trouble.* (NOT *Already in 1970*...)

## 5  still not or not yet?

*Still not* looks back towards the past; *not yet* looks towards the future. Compare:

– *She **still** hasn't got a job.* (Looking back: she hasn't had a job since Christmas, and this situation is continuing.)
  *She hasn't got a job **yet**.* (Looking forward: she hasn't got a job now, but we're hoping that she will get one.)

– *I **still** can't speak French, after all these years of study.*
  *I can't speak French **yet**, but I hope I will be able to soon.*

## 6  yet or already in questions

Questions with *already* often suggest that something has happened. Compare:

– *Have you met Professor Hawkins **yet**?* (= I don't know whether you've met him.)
  *Have you **already** met Professor Hawkins?* (= I think you've probably met him.)

– *Is my coat dry **yet**?*
  *Is my coat dry **already**? That was quick!*

## 7  tenses

Various tenses are possible with all three words. In British English, perfect tenses are common with *already* and *yet*; Americans often use past tenses. Compare:

*Have you **paid** yet?* (BrE)  |  *Have you **paid** / Did you pay yet?* (AmE)
*She **has** already **left**.* (BrE)  |  *She (**has**) already **left**.* (AmE)

## 8  related to a past moment

All three words can be related to a past moment instead of to the present.

*I went to see if she had woken up **yet**, but she was **still** asleep. This was embarrassing, because her friends had **already** arrived.*

## 9 *yet* meaning 'still'

*Yet* is normally used in questions and negative sentences. But it is sometimes used in affirmative sentences in a formal style to mean 'still'.

*We have **yet** to hear from the bank.* (= We are still waiting to hear . . .)

## 10 *all ready*

*All ready* is not the same as *already*: it simply means the same as ***all + ready***. Compare:

*When's Jane coming?* ~ *She's **already** arrived.*
*Are you **all ready**?* ~ *No, Pete isn't.*

# 567 subjunctive

## 1 What is the subjunctive?

Some languages have special verb forms called 'subjunctive', which are used especially to talk about 'unreal' situations: things which are possible, desirable or imaginary. Older English had subjunctives, but in modern English they have mostly been replaced by uses of *should*, *would* and other modal verbs, by special uses of past tenses (see 426), and by ordinary verb forms. English only has a few subjunctive forms left: third-person singular present verbs without *-(e)s*, (e.g. *she see, he have*) and special forms of *be* (e.g. *I be, he were*). Except for *I/he/she/it were* after *if*, they are not very common.

## 2 *that she see*

Ordinary verbs only have one subjunctive form: a third person singular present with no *-(e)s* (e.g. *she see*). It is sometimes used in *that*-clauses in a formal style, especially in American English, after words which express the idea that something is important or desirable (e.g. *suggest, recommend, ask, insist, vital, essential, important, advice*). The same forms are used in both present and past sentences.

*It is essential that every child **have** the same educational opportunities.*
*It was important that James **contact** Arthur as soon as possible.*
*Our advice is that the company **invest** in new equipment.*
*The judge recommended that Simmons **remain** in prison for life.*

*Do* is not used in negative subjunctives. Note the word order.

*We felt it desirable that he **not leave** school before eighteen.*

With verbs that are not third-person singular, the forms are the same as ordinary present-tense verbs (but they may refer to the past).

*I recommended that you **move** to another office.*

## 3 *be*

*Be* has special subjunctive forms: *I be, you be* etc.

*It is important that Helen **be** present when we sign the papers.*
*The Director asked that he **be** allowed to advertise for more staff.*

*I were* and *he/she/it were*, used for example after *if* (see 258.4) and *wish* (see 630) in a formal style, are also subjunctives.

*If I **were** you I should stop smoking.*
*I wish it **were** Saturday.*

▶

### 4 fixed phrases

Subjunctives are also used in certain fixed phrases. Examples:

God **save** the Queen!    Long **live** the King!
God **bless** you.    Heaven **forbid**.
He's a sort of adopted uncle, as it **were**. (= ... in a way.)
**Be** that as it may ... (= Whether that is true or not ...)
If we have to pay £2,000, then so **be** it. (= We can't do anything to change it.)

### 5 other structures

Most subjunctive structures are formal and unusual in British English. In *that*-clauses, British people usually prefer **should** + **infinitive** (see 521), or ordinary present and past tenses.

It is essential that every child **should have** the same educational
    opportunities. (OR ... that every child has ...)
It was important that James **should contact** Arthur as soon as possible. (OR
    ... that James contacted ...)

## 568 such

### 1 word order

*Such* is used with nouns and noun phrases. It comes before *a/an*.
**such** people    **such** interesting ideas
**such a** decision (NOT ~~a such decision~~)

### 2 'of this/that kind'

*Such* can mean 'like this/that', 'of this/that kind'. This is most common in a formal style, with abstract nouns.

The committee wishes to raise fees. I would oppose **such** a decision.
There are various forms of secret writing. **Such** systems are called 'codes'.
In an informal style, and with concrete nouns, we prefer *like this/that* or *this/that kind of*.

... systems **like this** are called ...
He's got an old Rolls-Royce. I'd like a car **like that**. (NOT ~~I'd like such a car.~~)

### 3 high degree

Another use of *such* is to talk about a high degree of some quality. In this sense, *such* is common before **adjective** + **noun**.

I'm sorry you had **such a bad journey**.
    (= You had a very bad journey, and I'm sorry.)
It was a pleasure to meet **such interesting people**.
*Such* is also possible with this meaning before a noun alone, when the noun has an emphatic descriptive meaning.

I'm glad your concert was **such a success**.
Why did she make **such a fuss** about the dates?

### 4 *such* and *very, great* etc

*Very, great* and similar words are also used to talk about a high degree of some quality. The difference is that they give new information; *such* (= like this/that) normally refers to information that is already known. Compare:
- *I've had a **very** bad day.* (giving information)
  *Why did you have **such** a bad day?* (The information is already known.)
- *The weather was **very** cold.*
  *I wasn't expecting **such** cold weather.*
- *There was **great** confusion*
  *Why was there **such** confusion?*

However, in a very informal style *such* can also be used to mean 'very' or 'great', especially in exclamations.

> *She has **such** a marvellous voice!*      *He's **such** an idiot!*

### 5 *such . . . that; such . . . as to*

Structures with *very* cannot be followed directly by *that*-clauses. Instead, we can use *such . . . that.*

> *It was **such** a cold afternoon **that** we stopped playing.* (NOT ~~It was a very cold afternoon that . . .~~)

There is also a structure with *such* followed by *. . . + as to +* **infinitive**. This is formal and not very common.

> *It was **such** a loud noise **as to wake** everybody in the house.*
> (Less formal: *. . . **such** a loud noise **that it woke** . . .*)

### 6 *such as*

*Such as* is used to introduce examples.

> *My doctor told me to avoid fatty foods **such as** bacon or hamburgers.*

### 7 *such-and-such*

Note this informal expression.

> *She's always telling you that she's met **such-and-such** a famous person.*
> (= *. . .* one or other famous person.)

For the difference between *such* and *so*, see 569.

## 569 *such* and *so*

### 1 *such* before (adjective +) noun

We use *such* before a noun (with or without an adjective).

> *They're **such** fools.* (NOT ~~They're so fools.~~)
> *It was **such** good milk that we couldn't stop drinking it.* (NOT ~~It was so good milk that . . .~~)

*Such* comes before *a/an.*

> *She's **such** a baby.*
> *I've never met **such** a nice person.* (NOT *. . . ~~a such/so nice person.~~*)     ▶

## 2  *so* before adjective, adverb etc

We use *so* before an adjective alone (without a noun) or an adverb.
> *She's **so babyish**.* (NOT ~~She's such babyish.~~)
> *The milk was **so good** that we couldn't stop drinking it.*
> *Why do you talk **so slowly**?*

We can also use *so* before *much, many, few* and *little*.
> *We've got **so much** to do, and **so little** time.*

We use *so much*, not *so*, before comparatives.
> *I'm glad you're feeling **so much better**.* (NOT *...* ~~so better.~~)

For *so beautiful a day* etc, see 14.
For more about the meaning and use of *such*, see 568. For more about *so*, see 538.

# 570  suggest

## 1  infinitive not used

*Suggest* is not followed by **object + infinitive**. *That*-clauses and *-ing* structures are common.
> *Her uncle **suggested that** she (should) get a job in a bank.*
> *Her uncle **suggested getting** a job in a bank.* (NOT ~~Her uncle suggested her to get a job in a bank.~~)

## 2  indirect object not used

*Suggest* is not normally followed by an indirect object without a preposition.
> *Can you **suggest** a restaurant **to us**?* (NOT ~~Can you suggest us a restaurant?~~)

## 3  verb forms in *that*-clauses

In *that*-clauses after *suggest*, various verb forms are possible when we suggest what people should do.

a  Ordinary present and past tenses can be used.
> *Her uncle **suggests** that she **gets** a job in a bank.*
> *He **suggested** that she **got** a job in a bank.*

b  *Should* + infinitive without *to* is common.
> *He **suggests** that she **should get** a job in a bank.*
> *He **suggested** that she **should get** a job in a bank.*

c  Subjunctives (see 567) are also used, especially in American English.
> *He **suggests** that she **get** a job in a bank.*
> *He **suggested** that she **get** a job in a bank.*

## 4  direct suggestions

In direct suggestions ('I suggest ...'), *should* is not generally used.
> *I **suggest** (that) you **get** ...* (NOT ~~I suggest that you should get.~~)

## 571 suppose, supposing and what if

*Suppose, supposing* and *what if* can all be used with present tenses to make suggestions about things that might happen.

> *I haven't got a table cloth.* ~ *Suppose we use a sheet.*
> *Let's go swimming.* ~ *Supposing there are sharks.*
> *What if we invite your mother next weekend and go away the week after?*

A past tense makes the suggestion sound less definite.

> *Daddy, can I watch TV?* ~ *Suppose you did your homework first.*
> *I'm going to climb up there.* ~ *No! supposing you slipped!*
> *What if I came tomorrow instead of this afternoon?*

In sentences about the past, past perfect tenses are used to talk about situations that did not occur.

> *That was very clever, but supposing you had slipped?*

For more about past tenses with present or future meanings, see 426.

## 572 supposed to

*Be supposed* + **infinitive** is used to say what people have to do (or not do) according to the rules or the law, or about what is (not) expected to happen.

> *Catholics are supposed to go to church on Sundays.*
> *We're supposed to pay the Council Tax at the beginning of the month.*
> *You're not supposed to park on double yellow lines.*

There is often a suggestion that things do not happen as planned or expected.

> *This country is supposed to be a democracy.*
> *Lucy was supposed to come to lunch. What's happened?*
> *Cats are supposed to be afraid of dogs, but ours isn't.*

Questions with *supposed to* can suggest that there are problems.

> *The train's already left. What are we supposed to do now?*
> *How am I supposed to finish all this work by ten o'clock?*
> *That's a lovely picture, but what's it supposed to be?*

Another use of *supposed to* is to say what is generally believed.

> *He's supposed to be quite rich, you know.*
> *This stuff is supposed to kill flies. Let's try it.*

Note the pronunciation: /sə'pəʊst tə/, not /sə'pəʊzd tə/.

## 573 surely

### 1 not the same as *certainly*

*Surely* does not usually mean the same as *certainly*. We use *certainly* when we simply tell people that something is true. We use *surely* mostly to ask for people's agreement: to persuade them that something must be true, or that there are good reasons for believing it. Compare:

- *House prices are **certainly** rising fast at the moment.* ('I know this is so.')
  *House prices will **surely** stop rising soon.* ('I believe this must be so.')
- *I **certainly** posted the letter on Monday.* ('I know.')
  *She's **surely** got the letter by now.* ('It seems very probable.')

▶

**2 belief in spite of ...**

*Surely* can be used when we say that we think something is true in spite of reasons to believe the opposite, or in spite of suggestions to the contrary. These sentences are often like questions.

> *I'm going to marry Sonia. ~ **Surely** she's married already?*
> ***Surely** that's Henry over there? I thought he was in Scotland.*
> *Is it tonight we're going out? ~ No, tomorrow, **surely**?*

With *not, surely* can express difficulty in believing something.

> *Tim failed his exam. ~ Oh, **surely not**?*
> ***Surely** you're **not** going out in that hat?*
> *You **don't** think I'm going to pay for you, **surely**?*

## 574 sympathetic

*Sympathetic* usually means 'sharing somebody's feelings' or 'sorry for somebody who is in trouble'.

> *I'm **sympathetic** towards the strikers.*
> *She's always very **sympathetic** when people feel ill.*

*Sympathetic* is a 'false friend' for speakers of certain languages. It does not usually mean the same as, for example, *sympathique, sympathisch, sympatisk* or *simpático*.

> *The people in my class are all very **nice / pleasant / easy to get on with**.*
> (NOT ... ~~are all very sympathetic.~~)

## 575 taboo words and swearwords

### 1 introduction

Many languages have words which are considered dangerous, holy, magic or shocking, and which are only used in certain situations or by certain people. For instance, in some African tribes the names of dead chiefs must not be said; in many cultures, words associated with religious beliefs are used only on religious occasions, or only by priests. Words of this kind can be called 'taboo words'.

English has three main groups of taboo words and expressions:

a   A number of words connected with the Christian religion (e.g. the names *Christ, God*) are considered holy by some people. These people prefer to use such words only in formal and respectful contexts, and they may be upset or shocked by their 'careless' use.

b   Certain words relating to sexual activity and the associated parts of the body (e.g. *fuck, balls*) are regarded as shocking by many people. Thirty or forty years ago some of these words could not be printed or broadcast, and they are still comparatively unusual in public speech and writing. In polite or formal language these words are generally avoided, or replaced by other words and expressions (e.g. *make love* or *have sexual intercourse, testicles*).

c   Some words referring to the elimination of bodily wastes (what one does in the lavatory), and the associated parts of the body, are also regarded as 'dirty' or shocking (e.g. *piss, shit*). They are often replaced by more 'polite' words and expressions with the same meaning (e.g. *urinate, defecate*) or by substitutes (e.g. *go to the lavatory, wash one's hands*).

Because taboo words are shocking, they are common in situations where people want to express powerful emotions by using 'strong' language. This is called 'swearing'. When people swear, taboo words usually change their meanings completely. For example, *fuck off* and *piss off* have nothing to do with sex or urinating – they are simply violently rude ways of saying 'go away'. The strength of the original taboo word is borrowed for a different purpose.

Linguistic taboos in English-speaking countries are less strong than they used to be. Most taboo words and swearwords shock less than they did, say, twenty years ago. And increasingly, people are using informal taboo words which are felt to be amusingly 'naughty' rather than shocking, such as *bonk* or *shag* instead of *fuck*, or *willy* instead of *prick* (= penis).

None the less, students should be very careful about using taboo words and swearwords. There are two reasons for this. First of all, it is not easy to know the exact strength of these expressions in a foreign language, or to know what kind of people are shocked by them, and in what circumstances. One may easily say something that is meant as a joke, but which seriously upsets the people one is talking to. And secondly, using this sort of language generally indicates membership of a group: one most often swears in the company of people one knows well, who belong to one's own social circle, age group etc. (Children usually avoid swearing in front of adults so as not to annoy or shock them, and adults avoid swearing in front of children for similar reasons.) So a foreigner who uses swearwords may give the impression of claiming membership of a group that he or she does not belong to.

## 2  taboo words

The following are some of the most common English taboo words, with explanations of their literal meanings where necessary. Their approximate 'strength' is shown by stars: one-star words like *hell, damn* or *blast* (which are scarcely taboo in modern English) will not upset many people, while a three- or four-star word may be very shocking if it is used in the wrong situation. Note, however, that individual reactions to particular words (and to swearing in general) vary enormously, and that attitudes are changing rapidly (and generally becoming more tolerant of this kind of language). So people of different ages and backgrounds are likely to disagree a good deal about the strength of the words listed.

The words associated with religion are not considered shocking when used with their literal meaning, and the stars show their strength when used as swearwords. The strength of the other words is mostly the same whether they are used literally or for swearing.

▶

## Religion

| taboo word | meaning |
| --- | --- |
| damn * | condemn to hell (rare in literal sense; mainly used as swearword) |
| blast * (BrE) | strike with divine punishment (rare in literal sense; mainly used as swearword) |
| hell * | |

(*Damn, blast* and *hell* have lost most of their strength, and are scarcely regarded as swearwords by most people in modern English.)

God *
Jesus **
Christ **

## Parts of the body

| taboo word | meaning |
| --- | --- |
| arse *** | bottom, buttocks, anus |
| (AmE ass **) | |
| arsehole *** | anus |
| (AmE asshole **) | |
| balls *** | testicles |
| bollocks *** (BrE) | testicles |
| cock *** | penis |
| dick*** | penis |
| prick *** | penis |
| tits *** | breasts |
| cunt **** | woman's sex organs |
| twat *** | woman's sex organs (rare) |

## Sexual activity

| taboo word | meaning |
| --- | --- |
| fuck *** | have sex (with) |
| wank *** | masturbate (have sex with oneself) |
| (AmE jerk off ***) | |
| bugger *** (BrE) | have anal intercourse with a person or animal; person who does so (rare in literal sense) |
| come ** | reach a sexual climax (orgasm) |
| sod ** (BrE) | homosexual (abbreviation of *sodomite*; rare in literal sense) |
| bitch *** | female dog; earlier used for 'immoral' woman |
| whore ** | prostitute |
| bastard ** | child of unmarried parents |

## Lavatory

| taboo word | meaning |
| --- | --- |
| piss *** | urine; urinate |
| shit *** | excrement; defecate |
| crap ** | excrement; defecate |
| fart ** | let digestive gas out from the anus |

## 3   swearwords

All of the words listed above, and a few others, are used in swearing. The meaning of a swearword is always different from its literal (taboo) meaning (see introduction above). Compare:

*What are you doing **fucking** in my bed?*
　　　(= Why are you making love in my bed? – literal meaning of *fucking*)
*What are you **fucking** doing in my bed?*
　　　(= Why the hell are you in my bed? – *fucking* used as a swearword)

The meaning of a swearword can also change with its grammatical form. For instance, *piss off* is an aggressive way of saying *go away*; *pissed* is British slang for *drunk*; *pissed off* is British slang for *fed up*. Many swearwords are grammatically very flexible. *Fucking,* for example, can act both as an adjective (e.g. ***fucking** idiot*) and as an intensifying adverb (e.g. ***fucking** good, **fucking** soon, it's **fucking** raining, **fucking** well shut up*). It is even sometimes put into the middle of another word (*abso-**fucking**-lutely*). Swearwords are the only words in the language that have this grammatical range.

The following list shows some of the most common expressions used in swearing; they are grouped according to meaning.

a   **exclamation of annoyance**

| | | |
|---|---|---|
| *Damn (it)!* | *(My) God!* | *Bugger (it)!* (BrE) |
| *Blast (it)!* (BrE) | *Jesus!* | *Sod (it)!* (BrE) |
| *God damn it!* | *Christ!* | *Shit!* |
| *God damn!* (especially AmE) | *Jesus Christ!* | *Fuck (it)!* |
| *Hell!* | | |

Examples of use:
　　**Damn it!** *Can't you hurry up?*
　　**Christ!** *It's raining again!*
　　*Oh,* **fuck!** *I've lost the address!*

b   **exclamation of surprise**

| | |
|---|---|
| *(My) God!* | *Well, I'll be damned!* |
| *Jesus!* | *Son of a bitch!* (especially AmE) |
| *Christ!* | *Damn me!* |
| *Jesus Christ!* | *Bugger/Fuck me!* (BrE) |
| *God damn!* (especially AmE) | *Well, I'm damned/buggered!* (BrE) |

Examples of use:
　　**My God!** *Look at that!*
　　**Well, I'm damned!** *What are you doing here?*
　　**Bugger me!** *There's Mrs Smith. I thought she was on holiday.*

c   **surprised question**

*Who/What/Why etc the hell …?* (AmE also … *in hell …?*)
*Who/What/Why etc the fuck …?*

Examples of use:
　　**What the hell** *do you think you're doing?*
　　**Where the fuck** *are the car keys?*

▶

d　insult (noun)

Note that these nouns generally have no real meaning. They simply express a strong emotion such as hatred, anger, envy or contempt.

| | | | |
|---|---|---|---|
| *bastard* | *shit* | *bitch* (applied to women) | *(stupid) fuck* |
| *fart* | *sod* (BrE) | *son of a bitch* (AmE) | (esp AmE) |
| *prick* | *bugger* (BrE) | *arsehole* (AmE *asshole*) | *dickhead* (= idiot) |
| *fucker* | *wanker* (BrE) | *motherfucker* (AmE) | |
| *cunt* | *twat* (= idiot) | *cocksucker* (AmE) | |

Examples of use:
> *You **bastard**!*　*Lucky **sod**!*
> *Stupid old **fart**!*　*She's such a **bitch**!*
> *He's a real **prick**!*　*That guy's a real **asshole**!*
> *Stupid **fucker**!*　*Stupid **twat**!*

e　insult (imperative verb + object)

| | | |
|---|---|---|
| *Damn . . .!* | *Blast . . .!* (BrE) | *Sod . . .!* (BrE) |
| *Bugger . . .!* (BrE) | *Fuck . . .!* | *Screw . . .!* |

Examples of use:
> ***Damn** that child!*　***Fuck** you!*　***Screw** the government!*

f　insulting request to go away

| | |
|---|---|
| *Fuck off!* | *Bugger off!* (BrE) |
| *Piss off!* | *Sod off!* (BrE) |

Examples of use:
> *Can I have a word with you? ~ **Fuck off**!*
> *If Andy comes asking for money, tell him to **piss off**.*

g　expression of unconcern (= 'I don't care')

*I don't/couldn't give a damn/shit/fuck; . . . a bugger* (BrE).

Examples of use:
> *They can come and arrest me if they want to. **I don't give a fuck**.*
> *Mary's very angry with you. ~ **I don't give a bugger**.*

h　violent refusal/rejection/defiance

| | |
|---|---|
| *(I'll be) damned/fucked if I will!* | *Balls to . . .!* (BrE) |
| *. . . buggered if I will!* (BrE) | *Bollocks!* (BrE) |
| *Stuff it! (up your arse/ass)* | *Kiss my arse/ass!* |
| *Get stuffed!* (BrE) | *Suck my cock!* |
| *Balls!* | *Why don't you take a flying fuck?* |

Examples of use:
> *Mr Parsons wants you to clean out the lavatories. ~ **Fucked if I will!***
> *Management are offering another £8 a week. ~ They can **stuff it**.*
> *Give me a kiss. ~ **Get stuffed!***
> *You're afraid to fight. ~ **Balls!***
> ***Balls to** the lot of you! I'm going home.*

i   intensifying adjective/adverb (used to emphasise an emotion)

*damn(ed)*               *sodding* (BrE)
*bloody* (BrE)           *fucking*
*goddam* (AmE)
*Bloody* has no literal taboo equivalent in modern English.

Examples of use:

*That car's going **damn(ed)** fast.*   *She's a **fucking** marvellous singer.*
*Where's the **bloody** switch?*        *Put the **fucking** cat out!*
*It's **bloody** raining again.*

When these words are used before verbs, the word *well* is often added in British English.

*I **damn well hope** you never come back.*
*I'm not **fucking well paying** this time.*
*It's **bloody well raining** again.*

j   miscellaneous

*Fuck (up), screw (up)* and *bugger (up)* (BrE) can mean 'ruin', 'spoil' or 'destroy'.

*Somebody's **fucked up** the TV.*
*You've **buggered** my watch.*

*Fucked* and *buggered* can mean 'exhausted' (BrE).

*Want another game of tennis? ∼ No, I'm **fucked**.*

*Screw* (especially AmE) can mean 'cheat'.

*Don't buy a car from that garage – they'll **screw** you.*

*Cock up* (BrE), *balls up* (BrE), *fuck up* and *screw up* can be used as verbs or nouns to refer to mistakes of organisation. (When used as nouns, they are often written with hyphens.)

*That bloody secretary's **cocked up** my travel arrangements.*
*Sorry you didn't get your invitation – Mary made a **balls-up**.*
*The conference was a complete **fuck-up**.*
*Well, we really **screwed up** this time, didn't we?*

*Balls* (BrE), *bullshit* (AmE), *cock* and *crap* are used to mean 'nonsense'.

*What's his new book like? ∼ A load of **balls**.*
*Don't talk **crap**!*

In American English, *shit* can mean 'lies' or 'nothing'.

*Janie's getting married. ∼ No **shit**?*
*He don't know his ass from a hole in the ground. He don't know **shit**.*

*Bugger/fuck/damn/sod all* are used in British English to mean 'nothing'.

*There's **fuck** all in the fridge. We'll have to eat out.*

In British English, *pissed* means 'drunk' and *pissed off* means 'fed up'.

*Steve was **pissed** out of his mind again last night.*
*I'm getting **pissed off** with London.*

In American English, *pissed* is 'annoyed', 'angry'.

*I'm **pissed** at him because of what he's been saying about me.*

*A sod of a . . .* means 'a very bad . . .'

*It was **a sod of an exam**.*        *It's **a sod of a place** to get to.*

For information about slang, see 533.

## 576 take: time

We can use *take* to say how much time we need to do something. Five structures are common

### 1 The person is the subject:

> person + *take* + time + infinitive

*I took three hours to get home last night.*
*She takes all day to get out of the bathroom.*
*They took two hours to unload the ferry.*

### 2 The activity is the subject:

> activity + *take* (+ person) + time

*The journey took me three hours.*
*Gardening takes a lot of time.*
*Unloading the ferry took them two hours.*

### 3 The object of the activity is the subject:

> object of activity + *take* (+ person) + infinitive

*The ferry took them two hours to unload.*
*This house will take all week to clean.*

### 4 Preparatory *it* is the subject:

> *It* + *take* (+ person) + time + infinitive

*It took me three hours to get home last night.*
*It takes ages to do the shopping.*

### 5 *Before/until* is used:

> *It* + *take* (+ person) + time + *before/until*.

*It took us six weeks **before/until** we got the house clean.*
*It took a long time **before/until** she felt comfortable in her new school.*

## 577 taste

### 1 link verb

*Taste* can be used as a 'link verb' (see 328), followed by an adjective or noun, to say how something tastes. Progressive forms are not used.

> *This **tastes nice**. What's in it?* (NOT ... ~~tastes nicely.~~)
> *The wine **tastes funny**.* (NOT ... ~~is tasting funny~~ ...)

Before a noun, *taste of* and *taste like* are used.

> *The fish soup **tasted** mostly **of garlic**.*
> *Her lips **tasted like** wild strawberries.*

## 2 transitive verb: 'perceive'

*Taste* can be used with an object, to say what we perceive with our sense of taste. Progressive forms are not used. We often use *can taste* (see 125).

> *I **can taste** onion and mint in the sauce.* (NOT ~~I am tasting~~ . . .)

## 3 transitive verb: 'investigate'

Another transitive use is to say that we are using our sense of taste to find out something. Progressive forms can be used.

> *Stop eating the cake.* ~ *I'm just **tasting** it to see if it's OK.*

# 578 telephoning

## 1 answering a phone

People answering a private phone either say 'Hello' or give their name. People answering a business phone most often give their name.

> *'Hello'.*       *'Albert Packard.'*

## 2 asking for a person

> *Could I speak to Jane Horrabin?* (AmE also *Could I speak **with** . . .?*)

## 3 saying who you are

> *Hello, **this is** Corinne.* (NOT USUALLY . . . ~~I'm Corinne.~~)
> *Could I speak to Jane Horrabin?* ~ ***Speaking***. OR *This is Jane Horrabin (speaking).*

## 4 asking who somebody is

> *Who is **that**?* (AmE *Who is **this** / Who's there?*)
> *Who am I speaking to?*       *Who is that speaking?*

## 5 asking for a number

> ***Can/Could I have** extension two oh four six?*
> *What's the **(dialling) code** for Bristol?* (AmE . . . *area code* . . .?)
> *How do I get an **outside line**?*

## 6 if you want the other person to pay for the call

> *I'd like to make a **reversed** (OR **transferred**) **charge call** to Bristol 437878.* (AmE *I'd like to make a **collect call** . . .*)

## 7 if somebody is not there

> *I'm afraid she's not in at the moment.*
> *Can I **take a message**?*
> *Can I **leave a message**?*
> *Please **leave your message** after the tone.*
> *I'll **ring/call** again later.* (AmE *I'll call* . . .)
> *Could you ask her to **ring/call me back**?*
> *Could you ask her to ring/call me **at/on** Ardington 637022?*
> *Could you just tell her Jake called?*

▶

## 8 asking people to wait

*Just a moment.*        *Hold the line, please.*
*Hold on a moment, please.*    *Hang on.* (informal)

## 9 things a switchboard operator may say

*One moment, please.*      *(The number's) ringing for you.*
*(I'm) trying to connect you.*    *(I'm) putting you through now.*
*I'm afraid the number/line is engaged* (BrE) / *busy* (AmE). *Will you hold?*
*I'm afraid there's no reply from this number / from her extension.*

## 10 wrong number

*I think you've got the **wrong number**.*
*I'm sorry. I've got the **wrong number**.*

## 11 problems

*Could you speak louder? It's a **bad line** (BrE)/**bad connection**.*
*You're **breaking up**.*
*I'll call again.*         *I was/got **cut off**.*
*I rang/called you earlier but I **couldn't get through**.*

# 579 telling the time

## 1 saying what time it is

There are two common ways of saying what time it is.

| | |
|---|---|
| 8.05 | *eight (oh) five* OR *five past eight* |
| 8.10 | *eight ten* OR *ten past eight* |
| 8.15 | *eight fifteen* OR *a quarter past eight* |
| 8.25 | *eight twenty-five* OR *twenty-five past eight* |
| 8.30 | *eight thirty* OR *half past eight* |
| 8.35 | *eight thirty-five* OR *twenty-five to nine* |
| 8.45 | *eight forty-five* OR *a quarter to nine* |
| 8.50 | *eight fifty* OR *ten to nine* |
| 9.00 | *nine o'clock* |

Americans prefer to write a colon between the hours and the minutes: *8:50*.
People generally prefer to say *minutes past/ to* for times between the five-minute divisions.

     *seven **minutes** past eight* (More natural than *seven past eight*)
     *three **minutes** to nine* (More natural than *three to nine*)

The expression *o'clock* is only used at the hour. Compare:

     *Wake me at seven (o'clock).*
     *Wake me at ten past seven.* (NOT ... ~~ten past seven o'clock.~~)

*Past* is often dropped from *half past* in informal speech.

     *OK, see you at half two.* (= ... half past two.)

In American English *after* is often used instead of *past* (e.g. *ten **after** six*); but Americans do not say *half after*. And in American English *of, before* and *till* are possible instead of *to* (e.g. *twenty-five **of** three*).

## 2 asking what time it is

Common ways of asking about time are:

*What time is it?*     *Have you got the time?* (informal)
*What's the time?*     *Could you tell me the time?* (more formal)
*What time do you make it?* (OR *What do you make the time?*)
    (BrE, meaning 'What time is it by your watch?')

## 3 the twenty-four hour clock

The twenty-four hour clock is used mainly in timetables, programmes and official announcements. In ordinary speech, people usually use the twelve-hour clock. Compare:
– *Last check-in time is **20.15**.*
  *We have to check in by **a quarter past eight** in the evening.*
– *The next train from platform 5 is the **17.53** departure for Carlisle.*
  *What time does the next train leave? ~ **Five fifty-three**.*
– *The meeting will begin at **fourteen hundred**.*
  *We're meeting at **two o'clock**.*

If necessary, times can be distinguished by using *in the morning/afternoon/ evening*. In a more formal style, we can use *am* (= Latin *ante meridiem* – 'before midday') and *pm* (= *post meridiem* – 'after midday').

09.00 = *nine o'clock **in the morning*** (OR *nine **am***)
21.00 = *nine o'clock **in the evening*** (OR *nine **pm***)

# 580 tense simplification in subordinate clauses

## 1 reasons for tense simplification

If the main verb of a sentence makes it clear what kind of time the speaker is talking about, it is not always necessary for the same time to be indicated again in subordinate clauses. Compare:
– *This discovery **means** that we **will spend** less on food.*
  *This discovery **will mean** that we **spend** less on food.*
– *It **is** unlikely that he **will win**.*
  *I **will pray** that he **wins**.*

Verbs in subordinate clauses are often simpler in form than verbs in main clauses – for example present instead of future, simple past instead of *would* + infinitive, simple past instead of past perfect.

*You'll find Coca-Cola wherever you **go**.* (NOT *... wherever you will go.*)
*He would never do anything that **went** against his conscience.*
    (More natural than *... that would go against his conscience.*)
*I hadn't understood what she **said**.*
    (More natural than *... what she had said.*)

## 2 present instead of future: *I'll write when I have time*

Present tenses are often used instead of *will* + **infinitive** to refer to the future in subordinate clauses. This happens not only after conjunctions of time like *when, until, after, before, as soon as*, but in most other subordinate clauses –

▶

for instance after *if, whether* and *on condition that,* after question words and relatives, and in indirect speech.

*I'll write to her when I **have** time.* (NOT ... ~~when I will have time.~~)

*I'll think of you when I'm **lying** on the beach next week.* (NOT ... ~~when I will be lying~~ ...)

*Will you stay here until the plane **takes** off?*

*It will be interesting to see whether he **recognises** you.*

*I'll have a good time whether I **win** or **lose**.*

*I'll lend it to you on condition that you **bring** it back tomorrow.*

*I'll go where you **go**.*

*He says he'll give five pounds to anybody who **finds** his pen.*

*One day the government will really ask people what they **want**.*

*If she **asks** what I'm **doing** in her flat, I'll say I'm **checking** the gas.*

*I think you'll find the wind **slows** you down a bit.*

This can happen even if the main verb is not future in form, provided it refers to the future.

*Phone me when you **arrive**.*

*Make sure you **come** back soon.*

*You can tell who you **like** next week, but not until then.*

In comparisons with *as* and *than,* present and future verbs are both possible.

*She'll be on the same train as we **are/will** tomorrow.*

*We'll get there sooner than you **do/will**.*

## 3 present perfect: ... *when I've finished*

The present perfect is used instead of the future perfect, to express the idea of completion.

*I'll phone you when I've **finished**.* (NOT ... ~~when I will have finished.~~)

*At the end of the year there will be an exam on everything you've **studied**.* (NOT ... ~~everything you will have studied.~~)

## 4 future in subordinate clauses: ... *where she will be*

A future verb is necessary for future reference in a subordinate clause if the main verb does not refer to the future (or to the same time in the future).

*I don't know where she **will be** tomorrow.*

*I'm sure I **won't understand** a word of the lecture.*

*I'll hide it somewhere where he'll never **find** it.* (two different future times)

*If she rings, I'll tell her that I'll **ring** back later.* (two different future times)

For future verbs in *if*-clauses (e.g. *I'll give you £100 if it will help you to go on holiday*), see 260.

## 5 *in case, I hope, I bet, it doesn't matter* etc

A present tense is normally used with a future meaning after *in case* even if the main verb is present or past. For details, see 271.

*I've got my tennis things in case we **have** time for a game tomorrow.*

In an informal style, present verbs are often used with future meanings after *I hope* (see 250) and *I bet* (see 103).

*I hope you **sleep** well.*

*I bet he **gets** married before the end of the year.*

Present tenses are also used with future reference after *it doesn't matter, I don't care, I don't mind, it's not important* and similar expressions.

*It doesn't matter where we **go** on holiday.*
*I don't care what we **have** for dinner if I **don't have** to cook it.*

## 6 past instead of *would* ...

*Would*, like *will*, is avoided in subordinate clauses; instead, we generally use past verbs. This happens in *if*-clauses (see 258), and also after most other conjunctions.

> *If I **had** lots of money, I would give some to anybody who **asked** for it.*
> (NOT *~~If I would have~~... ~~who would ask for it.~~*)
> *Would you follow me wherever I **went**?* (NOT *... ~~wherever I would go?~~*)
> *In a perfect world, you would be able to say exactly what you **thought**.*
> (NOT *... ~~what you would think.~~*)
> *I would always try to help anybody who **was** in trouble, whether I **knew** them or not.*

For past tenses after *It's time*, see 306; for past tenses after *I'd rather*, see 491; for past tenses after *I wish*, see 630.

## 7 simplification of perfect and progressive verbs

Simple past verb forms are used quite often in subordinate clauses instead of present perfect and past perfect tenses, if the meaning is clear.

> *It's been a good time while it('s) **lasted**.*
> *I've usually liked the people I('ve) **worked** with.*
> *For thirty years, he had done no more than he **(had) needed** to.*
> *He probably crashed because he had gone to sleep while he **was** driving.*
> (More natural than *... while he had been driving.*)

Progressives are often replaced by simple forms in subordinate clauses.

> *He's working. But at the same time as he **works**, he's exercising.*
> (OR *... at the same time as he's working ...*)

## 8 exceptions

These rules do not usually apply to clauses beginning *because, although, since* or *as* (meaning 'because'), or to non-identifying relative clauses (see 495).

> *I won't mind the heat on holiday because I **won't move** about much.*
> *I'll come to the opera with you, although I probably **won't enjoy** it.*
> *You'll work with Mr Harris, who **will explain** everything to you.*

For tenses in indirect speech, see 275.

# 581 than and as
## as subjects, objects and complements

### 1 subjects: *more than is necessary; as happened*

*Than* and *as* can replace subjects in clauses (rather like relative pronouns).

> *He worries more **than** is necessary.* (NOT *... ~~more than it/what is necessary.~~*)
> *There were a lot of people at the exhibition – more **than** came last year.*
> (NOT *... ~~more than they came last year.~~*)
> *The train might be late, **as** happened yesterday.* (NOT *... ~~as it happened yesterday.~~*)

▶

*We've got food for as many people* ***as want*** *it.* (NOT . . . ~~as they want it.~~)
Common expressions with *as* in place of a subject: *as follows; as was expected; as was agreed; as is well known.*
> *I have prepared a new plan,* ***as follows.*** (NOT . . . ~~as it follows.~~)
> *They lost money,* ***as was expected.*** (NOT . . . ~~as it was expected.~~)
> *I am sending you the bill,* ***as was agreed.*** (NOT . . . ~~as it was agreed.~~)
> ***As is well known,*** *smoking is dangerous.* (NOT ~~As it is well known~~ . . .)

## 2  objects and complements: *as I did last year*

*Than* and *as* can also act as objects and complements.
> *They sent more vegetables* ***than I had ordered.*** (NOT . . . ~~than I had ordered them.~~)
> *Don't lose your passport,* ***as I did*** *last year.* (NOT . . . ~~as I did it last year.~~)
> *She was more frightened* ***than I was.*** (NOT . . . ~~than I was it.~~)
> *You're as tired* ***as I am.*** (NOT . . . ~~as I am it.~~)

Some English dialects use *what* after *as* and *than* in these cases.
> *They sent more paper* ***than what*** *I had ordered.* (non-standard)
> *You're as tired* ***as what*** *I am.* (non-standard)

# 582  thankful and grateful

*Grateful* is the normal word for people's reactions to kindness, favours etc.
> *I'm very* ***grateful*** *for all your help.* (NOT ~~I'm very thankful~~ . . .)
> *She wasn't a bit* ***grateful*** *to me for repairing her car.*

*Thankful* is used especially for feelings of relief at having avoided a danger, or at having come through an unpleasant experience.
> *I'm* ***thankful*** *that we got home before the storm started.*
> *We feel very* ***thankful*** *that she didn't marry him after all.*
> *Well, I'm* ***thankful*** *that's over.*

# 583  that-clauses

## 1  *that* as a connector

*That* is a conjunction with little real meaning. It is simply a connector – it shows that a clause forms part of a larger sentence. Compare:
> *I understood. He was innocent.* (two separate sentences)
> *I understood* ***that*** *he was innocent.* (The clause *he was innocent* has become the object of the verb in the larger sentence.)

## 2  *that*-clauses in sentences

A *that*-clause can be the subject of a sentence.
> ***That she should forget me so quickly*** *was rather a shock.*

It can be a complement after *be.*
> *The main thing is* ***that you're happy.***

Many verbs can have *that*-clauses as objects.
> *We* ***knew that*** *the next day would be difficult.*
> *I* ***regretted that*** *I was not going to be at the meeting.*

And many nouns and adjectives can be followed by *that*-clauses.
> *I admire your* ***belief that*** *you are always right.*
> *The Minister is* ***anxious that*** *nothing should get into the papers.*

## 3   the fact that . . .

It is unusual for *that*-clauses to stand alone as subjects. They are more often introduced by the expression *the fact*.

> **The fact that** *she was foreign made it difficult for her to get a job.*
> (NOT ~~That she was foreign made it difficult~~ . . .)
> **The fact that** *Simon had disappeared didn't seem to worry anybody.*
> (More natural than *That Simon had disappeared didn't* . . .)

*The fact* also introduces *that*-clauses after prepositions (*that*-clauses cannot follow prepositions directly).

> *The judge paid no attention **to the fact that** she had just lost her husband.*
> (NOT . . . ~~paid no attention to that she had just~~ . . .)
> *He held her completely responsible **for the fact that** she took food without paying for it.* (NOT . . . ~~responsible for that she took~~ . . .)
> *In spite **of the fact that** she had three small children, he sent her to prison for six months.* (NOT ~~In spite of that she had~~ . . .)

For cases when prepositions are dropped before *that*-clauses, see 453.

## 4   preparatory *it*

*It* is often used as a preparatory subject or object for a *that*-clause (see 446–447).

> **It** *surprised me **that he was still in bed.***
> (More natural than *That he was still in bed surprised me.*)
> *She made **it** clear **that she was not interested**.* (NOT ~~She made that she was not interested clear.~~)

For reasons why *that*-clauses are often moved to the ends of sentences, see 512.

## 5   *that*-clauses after verbs, nouns and adjectives

Some verbs, nouns or adjectives can be followed by *that*-clauses; some cannot. Compare:

> – *I **hope that** you'll have a wonderful time.*
>   *I want you to have a wonderful time.* (NOT ~~I want that you'll have~~ . . .)
> – *I understood his **wish that** we should be there.*
>   *I understood the importance of our being there.* (NOT . . . ~~the importance that we should be there.~~)
> – *It's **essential that** you visit the art museum.*
>   *It's worth your visiting the art museum.* (NOT ~~It's worth that you visit~~ . . .)

Unfortunately there is no easy way to decide which nouns, verbs or adjectives can be followed by *that*-clauses. It is best to check in a good dictionary.

## 6   verbs in *that*-clauses

In some kinds of *that*-clause, **should** + infinitive or subjunctives are often used instead of ordinary verb forms. For details, see 521, 567.

> *I insisted **that she should see** the doctor at once.* (OR . . . **that she see** . . .) ▶

## 7 compound conjunctions

Some conjunctions are made up of two or more words, including *that*.
Common examples: *so that, in order that, provided that, providing that, seeing that, given that, now that*.

> I got here early **so that** we could have a few minutes alone together.
> I'll come with you **providing that** Bill doesn't mind.
> OK, I'll help you, **seeing that** you asked so nicely.
> **Given that** Monday is a holiday, we could go to Scotland for the weekend.
> **Now that** the kids are at school, the house seems very quiet.

For *that*-clauses after reporting verbs ('indirect speech'), see 274–275.
For the relative pronoun *that*, see 494.

# 584 that: omission

We can often leave out the conjunction *that*, especially in an informal style.

## 1 indirect speech: *He said (that) . . .*

*That* can be left out informally after many common reporting verbs.

> James **said (that)** he was feeling better.
> I **thought (that)** you were in Ireland.
> The waiter **suggested (that)** we should go home.

*That* cannot be dropped after certain verbs, especially intransitive verbs – e.g.
*reply, email, shout*.

> James **replied that** he was feeling better. (NOT ~~James replied he was~~ . . .)
> She **shouted that** she was busy. (NOT ~~She shouted she was busy.~~)

For sentences like *Who do you think is outside?* see 486.

## 2 after adjectives: *I'm glad you're all right*

We can leave out *that* in clauses after some common adjectives.

> I'm **glad (that)** you're all right.
> It's **funny (that)** he hasn't written.    We were **surprised (that)** she came.

## 3 not dropped after nouns

*That* is not usually dropped after nouns.

> I did not believe his **claim that** he was ill. (More natural than . . . *his claim he was ill.*)
> He disagreed with Copernicus' **view that** the earth went round the sun.
> (NOT . . . ~~Copernicus' view the earth went~~ . . .)

## 4 conjunctions

*That* can be left out in an informal style in some common two-word
conjunctions, such as *so that, such . . . that, now that, providing that, provided that, supposing that, considering that, assuming that*.

> Come in quietly **so (that)** she doesn't hear you.
> I was having **such** a nice time **(that)** I didn't want to leave.
> The garden looks nice **now (that)** we've got some flowers out.
> You can borrow it **provided (that)** you bring it back tomorrow.
> **Assuming (that)** nobody gets lost, we'll all meet again here at six o'clock.

**5  relative structures**

We can usually leave out the relative pronoun *that* when it is the object in a relative clause (see 495).

> *Look! There are the people (**that**) we met in Brighton.*
> *Do it the way (**that**) I showed you.*

# 585  the matter (with)

We use *the matter (with)* after *something, anything, nothing* and *what*. It means 'wrong (with)'.

> *Something's **the matter with** my foot.*
> *Is anything **the matter**?*
> *Nothing's **the matter with** the car – you're just a bad driver.*
> *What's **the matter with** Frank today?*

*There* is often used as a 'preparatory subject' (see 587).

> ***There's** something **the matter with** the TV.*
> *Is **there** anything **the matter**?*

For *no matter what* etc, see 378.

# 586  there

The spelling *there* is used for two words with completely different pronunciations and uses.

**1  adverb of place**

*There* (pronounced /ðeə(r)/) is an adverb meaning 'in that place'.

> *What's that green thing over **there**?*
> ***There's** the book I was looking for.*

For the difference between *here* and *there*, see 245.

**2  introductory subject**

*There* (most often pronounced /ðə(r)/) is used as an introductory subject in sentences beginning *there is, there are, there might be* etc. For details, see 587.

> ***There's** a book under the piano.*

# 587  there is

**1  use**

In sentences which say that something exists (or does not exist) somewhere, we usually use *there* as a kind of preparatory subject, and put the real subject after the verb. Note the pronunciation of *there*: usually /ðə(r)/, not /ðeə(r)/.

> ***There's** a hole in my tights.* (More natural than *A hole is in my tights.*)
> ***There's** ice on the lake.* (More natural than *Ice is on the lake.*)

*It* cannot be used in this way.

> ***There** is a lot of noise in the street.* (NOT ~~It is a lot of noise in the street.~~)

*There are* is used with plural subjects. ▶

*I don't know how many people **there are** in the waiting room.* (NOT *...~~how many people there is~~...*)
However, *there's* can begin sentences with plural subjects in informal speech.
> ***There's** two policemen at the door, Dad.*
> ***There's** some grapes in the fridge, if you're still hungry.*

## 2 indefinite subjects

We use *there* in this way particularly with subjects that have indefinite articles, no article, or indefinite determiners like *some, any, no;* and with indefinite pronouns like *somebody, nothing.*
> *There are **some people** outside.*
> *There were **no footsteps** to be seen.*  *Is there **anybody** at home?*
> *There was **dancing** in the streets.*  *There's **something** worrying me.*

Note the use of *wrong* and *the matter* (see 585).
> *There's something **wrong**.*  *Is there anything **the matter**?*

Note also the structures with *sense, point, use* (see 57) and *need.*
> *There's **no sense** in making him angry.*
> *Is there **any point** in talking about it again?*
> *Do you think there's **any use** trying to explain?*
> *There's **no need** to hurry – we've got plenty of time.*

## 3 all tenses

*There* can be used in this way with all tenses of *be.*
> *Once upon a time **there were** three wicked brothers.*
> ***There has** never **been** anybody like you.*
> ***There will be** snow on high ground.*

And *there* can be used in question tags (see 488.4).
> ***There'll** be enough for everybody, **won't there?***

## 4 structures with auxiliary *be*

*There* can also be used in structures where *be* is a progressive or passive auxiliary. Note the word order.
> ***There was** a girl **water-skiing** on the lake.* (= A girl was water-skiing ...)
> (NOT *~~There was water-skiing a girl~~...*)
> ***There have been** more Americans **killed** in road accidents than in all the wars since 1900.* (= More Americans have been killed ...)
> (NOT *~~There have been killed more Americans~~...*)
> ***There'll be** somebody **meeting** you at the airport.*

## 5 more complex structures

*There* can be used with **modal verb + be**, and with some other verbs (e.g. *seem, appear, happen, tend*) before *to be.*
> ***There might be** drinks if you wait for a bit.*
> ***There must be** somebody at home – ring again.*
> *If the police hadn't closed the road **there could have been** a bad accident.*
> ***There seem to be** some problems.* (NOT *~~There seems to be~~...*)
> *Could you be quiet? **There happens to be** a lecture going on.*
> ***There tends to be** jealousy when a new little brother or sister comes along.*

Note also the structure *there is certain/sure/likely/bound to be.*

*There is sure to be trouble when she gets his letter.*
*Do you think there's likely to be snow?*
Infinitives (*there to be*) and *-ing* forms (*there being*) are also used.
*I don't want there to be any more trouble.*
*What's the chance of there being an election this year?*

## 6 other verbs

In a formal or literary style, some other verbs can be used with *there* besides *be*. These are mostly verbs which refer to states or arrivals.
*In a small town in Germany there once lived a poor shoemaker.*
*There remains nothing more to be done.*
*Suddenly there entered a strange figure dressed all in black.*
*There followed an uncomfortable silence.*

## 7 definite subjects

*There* is not normally used in a sentence with a definite subject (e.g. a noun with a definite article, or a proper name).
*The door was open.* (NOT ~~There was the door open.~~)
*James was at the party.* (NOT ~~There was James at the party.~~)
One exception to this is when we simply name people or things, in order to draw attention to a possible solution to a problem.
*Who could we ask? ~ Well, there's James, or Miranda, or Ann, or Sue, ...*
*Where can he sleep? ~ Well, there's always the attic.*
Another apparent exception is in stories that begin *There was this ...,* when *this* has an indefinite sense.
*There was this man, see, and he couldn't get up in the mornings. So he ...*

# 588 think

## 1 'have an opinion': not progressive

When *think* is used for opinions, progressive forms are unusual.
*I don't think much of his latest book.* (NOT ~~I'm not thinking much...~~)
*Who do you think will win the election?* (NOT ~~Who are you thinking...?~~)

## 2 other meanings: progressive possible

When *think* has other meanings (e.g. *consider* or *plan*) progressives are possible.
*You're looking worried. What are you thinking about?* (NOT ...~~What do you think about?~~)
*I'm thinking of changing my job.*

## 3 *-ing* forms

After *think*, *-ing* forms can be used, but infinitives are not usually possible unless there is an object (see paragraph 4 below).
*She's thinking of going to university next year.* (NOT ~~She's thinking to go...~~)
However, *think* + **infinitive** can be used when we talk about remembering to do something, or having the good sense to do something.
*Did you think to close the windows when it started raining?*  ▸

### 4   *think* + object (+ *to be*) + complement

In a very formal style, *think* is sometimes followed by an object and an adjective or noun complement.

> *They **thought her fascinating**.*     *We **thought him a fool**.*

*It* can be used as a preparatory object (see 442) for an infinitive or clause.

> *I **thought it better to pretend that I knew nothing**.*
> *We **thought it important that she should go home**.*

*To be* is occasionally used before the complement (suggesting objective judgement rather than subjective impression), but this is very unusual.

> *They **thought him to be a spy**.*

In more normal styles, *that*-clauses are preferred after *think*.

> *They **thought that** she was fascinating.*
> *We **thought that** he was a fool.*

However, the passive equivalent of the **object + complement** structure is reasonably common, usually with *to be*.

> *He **was thought to be** a spy.*

### 5   transferred negation: *I don't think . . .*

When *think* is used to introduce a negative clause, we most often put *not* with *think*, rather than with the following clause (see 369).

> *I **don't think** it will rain. (More natural than I think it won't rain.)*
> *Mary **doesn't think** she can come.*

However, we can express surprise with *I thought . . . not*.

> *Hello! I **thought** you **weren't** coming!*

### 6   indirect speech

*Think* does not usually introduce indirect questions.

> *I **was wondering** if I could do anything to help.*
> *(More natural than I was thinking if . . .)*

### 7   *I thought . . .*

Note the use of stressed *I thought . . .* to suggest that the speaker was right. Compare:

> *It isn't very nice. ~ Oh, dear. I thought you'd* LIKE *it. (But I was wrong.)*
> *It's beautiful! ~ Oh, I am glad. I* THOUGHT *you'd like it. (And I was right.)*

### 8   *I had thought . . ., I should think* etc

Past perfect forms can suggest that the speaker was mistaken, especially when *had* is stressed.

> *I **had thought** that we were going to be invited to dinner.*

*I should think* and *I should have thought* (also *I would / I'd . . .*) can introduce guesses.

> *I **should think** we'll need at least twelve bottles of wine.*
> *I **should (I would / I'd) have thought** we could expect at least forty people.*

This structure can also introduce criticisms.

> *I **should have thought** he could have washed his hands, at least.*

For *I (don't) think so* and *I thought so*, see 539.

# 589 this and that

## 1 people and things

*This/that/these/those* can be used as determiners with nouns that refer to either people or things.

> **this** child **that** house

But when they are used as pronouns without nouns, *this/that/these/those* normally only refer to things

> **This** costs more than **that**. (BUT NOT ~~This says he's tired.~~)
> Put **those** down – they're dirty. (BUT NOT ~~Tell those to go away.~~)

However, *this* etc can be used as pronouns when we say who people are.

> Hello. **This** is Elisabeth. Is **that** Ruth?     **That** looks like Mrs Walker.
> Who's **that**?                               **These** are the Smiths.

Note also *Those who* ... (see paragraph 6 below).

For a similar use of *it* to refer to people, see 428.9.

## 2 the difference

We use *this/these* for people and things which are close to the speaker.

> **This** is very nice – can I have some more?
> Get **this** cat off my shoulder.
> I don't know what I'm doing in **this** country. (NOT ... ~~in that country.~~)
> Do you like **these** ear-rings? Bob gave them to me.

We use *that/those* for people and things which are more distant from the speaker, or not present.

> **That** smells nice – is it for lunch?
> Get **that** cat off the piano.
> All the time I was in **that** country I hated it.
> I like **those** ear-rings. Where did you get them?

## 3 time

*This/these* can refer to situations and events which are going on or just about to start.

> I like **this** music. What is it?
> Listen to **this**. You'll like it. (NOT ~~Listen to that~~ ...)
> Watch **this**.     **This** is a police message.

*That/those* can refer to situations and events which have just finished, or which are more distant in the past.

> **That** was nice. What was it? (NOT ~~This was nice~~ ...)
> Did you see **that**?     Who said **that**?
> Have you ever heard from **that** Scottish boy you used to go out with?
>     (NOT ... ~~this Scottish boy you used to go out with.~~)

*That* can show that something has come to an end.

> ... and **that's** how it happened.
> Anything else? ~ No, **that's** all, thanks. (in a shop)
> OK. **That's** it. I'm leaving. It was nice knowing you.

## 4 acceptance and rejection

We sometimes use *this/these* to show acceptance or interest, and *that/those* to show dislike or rejection. Compare:

         ▶

*Now tell me about **this** new boyfriend of yours.*
*I don't like **that** new boyfriend of yours.*

## 5 on the telephone

On the telephone, British people use *this* to identify themselves, and *that* to ask about the hearer's identity.
*Hello. **This** is Elisabeth. Is **that** Ruth?*
Americans can also use *this* to ask about the hearer's identity.
*Who is **this**?*

## 6 *that, those* meaning 'the one(s)'

In a formal style, *that* and *those* can be used with a following description to mean 'the one(s)'. *Those who ...* means 'the people who ...'
*A dog's intelligence is much greater than **that** of a cat.*
***Those** who can, do. **Those** who can't, teach.*

## 7 *this* and *that* meaning 'so'

In an informal style, *this* and *that* are often used with adjectives and adverbs in the same way as *so*.
*I didn't realise it was going to be **this** hot.*
*If your boyfriend's **that** clever, why isn't he rich?*
In standard English, only *so* is used before a following clause.
*It was **so** cold that I couldn't feel my fingers.* (NOT ~~It was that cold that ...~~)
*Not all that* can be used to mean 'not very'.
*How was the play? ~ **Not all that** good.*

## 8 other uses

Note the special use of *this* (with no demonstrative meaning) in conversational story-telling.
*There was **this** travelling salesman, you see. And he wanted ...*
*That/those* can suggest that an experience is familiar to everybody.
*I can't stand **that** perfume of hers.*
This use is common in advertisements.
*When you get **that** empty feeling – break for a biscuit.*
*Earn more money during **those** long winter evenings. Telephone ...*

The differences between *this* and *that* are similar to the differences between *here* and *there* (see 245), *come* and *go* (see 134) and *bring* and *take* (see 112).
For *this one, that one* etc, see 395.
For *these* and *those* with singular *kind of, sort of,* see 551.
For *that which,* see 498.19.

# 590 this/that and it:
## things that have just been mentioned

## 1 referring back

*This, that* and *it* can all be used to refer back to things or situations that have just been talked or written about. *It* does not give any special emphasis.
*So she decided to paint her house pink. **It** upset the neighbours a bit.*

*This* and *that* are more emphatic; they 'shine a light', so to speak, on the things or situations, suggesting 'an interesting new fact has been mentioned'.

> *So she decided to paint her house pink. **This/That** really upset the neighbours, as you can imagine.*

*This* is preferred when there is more to say about the new subject of discussion.

> *So she decided to paint her house pink. **This** upset the neighbours so much that they took her to court, believe it or not. The case came up last week ...*
> *Then in 1917 he met Andrew Lewis. **This** was a turning point in his career: the two men entered into a partnership which lasted until 1946, and ...*
> (More natural than ... *That was a turning point ...*)

## 2 more than one thing

When more than one thing has been mentioned, *it* generally refers to the main subject of discussion; *this* and *that* generally refer to a new subject that has been introduced (often the last thing mentioned). Compare:

> – *We keep the ice-cream machine in the spare room. **It** is mainly used by the children, incidentally.* (The machine is used by the children.)
> *We keep the ice-cream machine in the spare room. **This/That** is mainly used by the children, incidentally.* (The spare room is used by the children.)
> – *I was carrying the computer to my office when I dropped it on the kitchen table. **It** was badly damaged.* (The computer was damaged.)
> *I was carrying the computer to my office when I dropped it on the kitchen table. **This** was badly damaged.* (The table was damaged.)

## 3 focus

*It* is only used to refer to things which are 'in focus' - which have already been talked about. *This* is preferred when we 'bring things into focus' before anything has been said about them. Compare:

> *I enjoyed 'Vampires' Picnic'. **It/This** is a film for all the family ...*
> *VAMPIRES' PICNIC: **This** is a film for all the family ...*
> (NOT *VAMPIRES' PICNIC: It is a film for all the family ...*)

## 4 referring forward

Only *this* can refer forward to something that has not yet been mentioned.

> *Now what do you think about **this**? I thought I'd get a job in Spain for six months, and then ...* (NOT *Now what do you think about that/it ...*)

For more about *this* and *that* and the differences between them, see 589.
For more about *it*, see 428.

# 591 This is the first/last ... etc

## 1 *This is the first time* etc

We use the present perfect in sentences constructed with *this/it/that is the first/second/third/only/best/worst* etc.

> *This is the first time that I've **heard** her sing.* (NOT *This is the first time that I hear her sing.*)

▶

*This is the fifth time you've **asked** me the same question* (NOT *~~This is the fifth time you ask~~...*)
*That's the third cake you've **eaten** this morning.*
*It's one of the most interesting books I've ever **read**.*
*I'm flying to New York tomorrow. It'll be the first time I've **travelled** by plane.*
When we talk about the past, we use the past perfect in these structures.
*It was the third time he **had been** in love that year.* (NOT *...~~the third time he was in love~~...*)

## 2 tenses with *This is the last ...* etc

Present (simple or progressive) and future tenses are both possible with *This is the last ...* and similar structures.
*This is the last time I **pay** / I'm **paying** for you.* (OR *This is the last time I'll pay for you.*)
*That's the last letter he **gets** / he's **getting** from me.* (OR *That's the last letter he'll get from me.*)
*This is the last thing I'm **going** to say to you.*

# 592 through: time

In American English, *through* can be used to mean 'up to and including'.
*The park is open from May **through** September.*
In British English, *through* is not normally used in this way. Instead, British people say, for example, *to ... inclusive*, or *until the end of ...*
*The park is open from May **to** September **inclusive**.* (OR *... from May **until the end of** September.*)

# 593 time

## 1 countability and article use

*Time* has various uses, some countable and some uncountable (for full details see a good dictionary). Most of these are straightforward, but there are problems in two areas:

### a measure of duration: how long

When we talk about the number of hours, days etc that are needed to complete something, *time* is generally uncountable (and therefore used without *a*).
*How **much time** do we need to load the van?*
*It took quite **some time** to persuade her to talk to us.*
*Don't worry – there's plenty of **time**.*
*This is a complete waste of **time**.*
However, *time* is countable in certain expressions like *a long/short time* and *quite a time*.
*I took **a long time** to get to sleep.*     *She was away for **quite a time**.*
*The time* can be used to mean 'enough time'; *the* is often dropped.
*Just come with me – I haven't got **(the) time** to explain.*

For the use of *take* with expressions of time, see 576.

b  clock times

When we talk about clock times, *time* is countable.

*Six o'clock would be **a** good **time** to meet.*
*She phoned me at various **times** yesterday.*

*The* is dropped in the expression *it's time.*

*It's **time** to stop.* (NOT ~~It's the time to stop.~~)

## 2  without preposition

Prepositions are often dropped before some common expressions with *time.*

*He's busy. Why don't you come **another time**?*
    (More natural than ... *at another time.*)
*What **time** does the match start?*
    (More natural than *At what time ...?*)
*You won't fool me **this time**.*

In relative structures after *time*, *that* is often used instead of *when* in an informal style (or dropped).

*Do you remember the time **(that)** Freddy pretended to be a ghost?*
*You can come up and see me any time **(that) you like**.*
*The first time **(that) I saw her**, my heart stopped.*

For similar structures with other time words, and with *place, way* and *reason*, see 498.6.

## 3  *on time* and *in time*

*On time* means 'at the planned time', 'neither late nor early'. The opposite is 'early' or 'late'. It is often used to refer to timetabled events.

*Only one of the last six trains has been **on time**.* (NOT ... ~~in time.~~)
*Peter wants the discussion to start exactly **on time**.* (NOT ... ~~in time.~~)

*In time* means 'with enough time to spare', 'before the last moment'. The opposite is *too late.*

*We arrived **in time** to get good seats.* (NOT ... ~~on time to get good seats.~~)
*He would have died if they hadn't got him to hospital **in time**.* (NOT ... ~~got him to hospital on time.~~)
*I nearly drove into the car in front, but I stopped just **in time**.*

For structures after *It's time*, see 306.
For ways of telling the time, see 579.
For *by the time*, see 117.
For tenses with *this is the first time ...*, *this is the last time ...* and similar structures, see 591.

# 594  tonight

*Tonight* refers to the present or coming night, not to the past night (*last night*). Compare:

*I had a terrible dream **last night**.* (NOT ~~I had a terrible dream tonight.~~)
*I hope I sleep better **tonight**.*

# 595 too

## 1 *too* and *very*

*Too* is different from *very* – *too* means 'more than enough', 'more than necessary' or 'more than is wanted'. Compare:
- *He's a **very** intelligent child.*
  *He's **too** intelligent for his class – he's not learning anything.*
- *It was **very** cold, but we went out.*
  *It was **too** cold to go out, so we stayed at home.*

## 2 *too* and *too much*

Before adjectives without nouns and before adverbs we use *too*, not *too much*.
  *You're **too** kind to me.* (NOT ~~You're too much kind to me.~~)
  *I arrived **too** early.* (NOT ~~I arrived too much early.~~)
*Too much* is used, for example, before nouns. For details see 596.
  *I've got **too much** work.*

## 3 modification: *much too, far too* etc

Expressions which modify comparatives (see 140) also modify *too*.
  **much** *too old* (NOT ~~very too old~~)     *a little too confident*
  *a lot too big*                          *a bit too soon*
  *far too young*                          *rather too often*

## 4 not used before adjective + noun

*Too* is not normally used before **adjective + noun**.
  *I put down the bag because it was too heavy.* (NOT ... *the too heavy bag.*)
  *She doesn't like men who are too tall.* (NOT *She doesn't like too tall men.*)
  *Let's forget this problem – it's too difficult.* (NOT ... *this too difficult problem.*)
In a rather formal style, *too* can be used before **adjective + a/an + noun** (see 14). Note the word order.
  *It's **too cold a day** for tennis.*

## 5 *too* ... + infinitive

We can use an infinitive structure after ***too* + adjective/adverb**.
  *He's **too old to work**.*     *It's far **too cold to go** out.*
We can also use an infinitive structure after *too much/many*.
  *There was **too much snow to go** walking.*
If the infinitive has its own subject, this is introduced by *for* (see 291).
  *It's too late **for the pubs** to be open.*
  *There was too much snow **for us** to go walking.*

## 6 *too salty to drink*, etc

The subject of a sentence with *too* can also be the object of a following infinitive. (For more about this structure, see 284.4.) Object pronouns are not normally used after the infinitive in this case.

*The water is too salty to drink.* (NOT ~~The water is too salty to drink it.~~)
However, object pronouns are possible in structures with *for*.
   *The water is too salty **for us** to drink (it).*
Note the two possible meanings of sentences like *He's too stupid to teach*:
1. *He's too stupid to be a teacher.*
2. *He's too stupid for anyone to teach – he can't be taught.*

### 7 That's really too kind of you

In informal speech *too* can sometimes be used to mean 'very'.
   *Oh, that's really **too** kind of you – thank you so much.*
   *I'm not feeling **too** well.*

### 8 only too ...

The expression *only too* is used to mean 'very', 'extremely'. It is common in formal offers and invitations.
   *We shall be **only too** pleased if you can spend a few days with us.*

For *too* meaning 'also', see 46.

## 596 too much and too many

### 1 the difference

The difference between *too much* and *too many* is the same as the difference between *much* and *many* (see 357). *Too much* is used with singular (uncountable) nouns; *too many* is used with plurals.
   *You put **too much** salt in the soup.*
   *I've had **too many** late nights recently.* (NOT ... ~~too much late nights~~ ...)

### 2 a bit too much, rather too many, etc

Expressions which modify comparatives and *too* (see 140) can also modify *too much* and *too many*.
   *She's wearing **a bit too much** make-up for my taste.*
   *I've been to **rather too many** parties recently.*
However, *much too many* is unusual.
   *You ask **far too many** questions.* (NOT ... ~~much too many questions.~~)

### 3 too much/many without a noun

We can drop a noun after *too much/many*, if the meaning is clear.
   *You've eaten **too much**.*
   *Did you get any answers to your advertisement? ~ **Too many**.*

For the difference between *too* and *too much*, see 595.2.

## 597 travel, journey, trip and voyage

*Travel* means 'travelling in general'. It is normally uncountable.
   *My interests are music and **travel**.*
The plural *travels* is sometimes used; it suggests a rather grand programme of travelling or exploration.

▶

*He wrote a wonderful book about his **travels** in the Himalayas.*
A *journey* is one 'piece' of travelling.
> *Did you have a good **journey**?* (NOT ~~Did you have a good travel?~~)
> *I met Jane on my last **journey** to England.* (NOT . . . ~~my last travel.~~)
A *trip* is a return journey together with the activity (business or pleasure)
which is the reason for the journey.
> *I'm going on a business **trip** next week.* (= I'm going on a journey and I'm
> going to do some business.)
> *Peter's school is organising a skiing **trip** to the Alps.*
Compare:
> *How was your **journey**?* ~ *The train broke down.*
> *How was your **trip**?* ~ *Successful.*
We do not so often use *trip* for expeditions which have a very serious purpose,
are very hard and/or take a very long time.
> *In 1863 the President **travelled** to Dakota to make peace with the Indians.*
> (NOT . . . ~~made a trip to Dakota to make peace~~ . . .)
> *Amundsen made his **journey** to the South Pole in 1911.*
> (NOT ~~Amundsen made his trip to the South Pole~~ . . .)
A long sea journey is often called a *voyage.*
Note the preposition: ***on** a journey/trip/voyage.*

# 598 turning verbs into nouns

## 1 using nouns for actions

It is very common to refer to an action by using a noun instead of a verb.
Nouns of this kind often have the same form as the related verbs. The structure
is especially common in an informal style.

> *There was a loud **crash**.*
> *Did I hear a **cough**?*
> *I need a **wash**.*
> *Let's have a **talk** about your plans.*
> *Let your sister have a **go** on the swing.* (BrE)

> *Just take a **look** at yourself.*
> *Would you like a **taste**?*
> *What about a **drink**?*
> *Come on – one more **try**!*

## 2 common structures

Nouns of this kind are often introduced by 'general-purpose' verbs such as
*have, take, give, make, go for.*
> *I'll **have a think** and let you know what I decide.* (informal BrE)
> *I like to **have/take a bath** before I go to bed.*
> *If it won't start, let's **give it a push**.*
> *I don't know the answer, but I'm going to **make a guess**.*
> *I try to **go for a run** every day.*
We can use *-ing* forms in a similar way after *do* (see 160.3).
> *She does a bit of **painting**, but she doesn't like to show people.*
These structures are very common when we talk about casual, unplanned or
unsystematic recreational activity. Compare:
> *Let's **have a swim**.* (More natural than *Let's swim.*)
> *Do you do any sport?* ~ *Yes, I **swim**.*

For details of 'action-nouns' with *have*, and a list of common expressions, see 236.
For *give*, see 226. For *go for*, see 227. For *go . . .ing*, see 228.

# 599 two-part verbs (1): phrasal verbs

## 1 verb + adverb particle: *get back, walk out*

Many English verbs can be followed by small adverbs ('adverb particles').
These two-part verbs are often called 'phrasal verbs'.

*Get back!*      *She **walked out**.*      *I **switched** the light **off**.*

Common adverb particles: *about, across, ahead, along, (a)round, aside, away, back, by, down, forward, in, home, off, on, out, over, past, through, up.*
Some of these words can also be used as prepositions. Compare:

*I switched the light **off**.* (adverb particle)
*I jumped **off** the wall.* (preposition)

For a detailed comparison, see 20.

## 2 idiomatic meanings: *break out; turn up*

The meaning of a two-word verb is often very different from the meanings of
the two parts taken separately.

*War **broke out** in 1939.* (*Broke out* is not the same as *broke + out*.)
*Joe **turned up** last night.* (= appeared – not the same as *turned + up*.)
*I **looked** the word **up** in the dictionary.* (*Look up* is not the same as *look + up*.)
*We had to **put off** the meeting till Tuesday.* (*Put off* is not the same as *put + off*.)

## 3 phrasal verbs with and without objects

Some phrasal verbs are intransitive (they do not have objects).

*I **got up** at 7.00 today.*      *That colour really **stands out**.*

Others are transitive.

*Could you **switch the light off**?*      *I helped Ann to **fill in the form**.*

## 4 word order with objects

Adverb particles can go either before or after noun objects (unlike most
adverbs – see 21.1).

*She switched **off the light**.* OR *She switched **the light off**.*

But they can only go after pronoun objects.

*She switched **it off**.* (NOT ~~She switched off it.~~)
*Is that the light **which** you switched **off**?* (NOT ... ~~the light off which you switched?~~)
*Give **me back** my watch.* OR *Give **me** my watch **back**.* (NOT ~~Give back me my watch.~~)

## 5 verbs with prepositions and particles together

A few verbs can be used with both an adverb particle and a preposition
(making them three-part verbs).

*I **get on with** her quite well.*
*Stop talking and **get on with** your work.*
*It's hard to **put up with** people who won't stop talking.*
*If you're on the road on Saturday night, **look out for** drunk drivers.*
*I'll think about it and **get back to** you.*
*She **went up to** the policeman and explained her problem.*

▶

*I'm **looking forward to** the party.*

For details of particular two-word verbs, see a good dictionary.

# 600 two-part verbs (2): prepositional verbs

## 1 verb + preposition: *listen to; look at*

Many English verbs are regularly followed by prepositions before objects.
> *You never **listen to** me.* (NOT ~~You never listen me.~~)
> *Alan walked down the road without **looking at** anybody.*

Prepositions are not used when there is no object.
> ***Listen!*** (NOT ~~Listen to!~~)

## 2 idiomatic meanings: *look after, get over*

The meaning of a two-word verb can be very different from the meanings of the two parts taken separately.
> *Could you **look after** the kids while I'm out?* (*Look after* is not the same as *look + after*.)
> *It took him six months to **get over** his illness.* (*Get over* is not the same as *get + over*.)

## 3 word order: *What are you thinking about?*

When an object comes at the beginning of a clause (e.g. in a question or relative clause), a two-word verb usually stays together, so that a preposition can be separated from its object and go at the end of the clause. For details of this and other preposition-final structures, see 452.
> ***What** are you thinking **about**?* (NOT ~~About what are you thinking?~~)
> *I've found the book **which** I was looking **for**.* (More natural in an informal style than ... *the book for which I was looking*.)

For the difference between prepositions and adverb particles, see 20.
For prepositional verbs in the passive, see 416.

# 601 unless

## 1 meaning

*Unless* has a similar meaning to *if ... not*, in the sense of 'except if'.
> *Come tomorrow **unless** I phone.* (= ... *if I don't* phone / **except if** I phone.)
> *I'll take the job **unless** the pay is too low.* (= ... **if** the pay **isn't** too low / **except if** the pay is too low.)
> *I'll be back tomorrow **unless** there's a plane strike.*
> *Let's have dinner out – **unless** you're too tired.*
> *I'm going to dig the garden this afternoon, **unless** it rains.*

## 2 when *unless* cannot be used

*Unless* means 'except if'. *Unless* is not used when the meaning is more like 'because ... not'. Compare:
> – *OK. So we'll meet this evening at 7.00 – **unless** my train's late.* (= ... except if my train's late.)

*My wife will be angry if I'm not home by 7.00.* (NOT ~~My wife will be angry unless I get home by 7.00.~~ – She will be angry because I'm not home.)
– *I'll drive over and see you, unless the car breaks down.* (= ... **except if** the car breaks down.)
*I'll be surprised if the car doesn't break down soon.* (NOT ~~I'll be surprised unless the car breaks down soon.~~ – I'll be surprised **because** it doesn't break down.)

## 3 tenses

In clauses with *unless*, we usually use present tenses to refer to the future (see 580).
*I'll be in all day unless the office phones.* (NOT ... ~~unless the office will phone.~~)

For more about sentences with *if*, see 256–264.

# 602 until

## 1 *until* and *till*

These two words can be used both as prepositions and conjunctions. They mean exactly the same. *Till* (AmE also *'til*) is informal.
*OK, then, I won't expect you until/till midnight.*
*I'll wait until/till I hear from you.*
*The new timetable will remain in operation until June 30.*

## 2 *until/till* and *to*

*To* can sometimes be used as a preposition of time with the same meaning as *until/till*. This happens after *from* ...
*I usually work from nine to five.* (OR ... *from nine until/till five.*)
We can also use *to* when counting the time until a future event.
*It's another three weeks to the holidays.* (OR ... *until/till the holidays.*)
In other cases, *to* is not generally used.
*I waited for her until six o'clock, but she didn't come.* (NOT ~~I waited for her to six o'clock ...~~)

For AmE *from ... through*, see 592.

## 3 distance and quantity: *until/till* not used

*Until/till* is used only to talk about time. To talk about distance, we use *to, as far as* or *up to; up to* is also used to talk about quantity.
*We walked as far as/up to the edge of the forest.* (NOT ... ~~till the edge ...~~)
*The minibus can hold up to thirteen people.* (NOT ... ~~until thirteen people.~~)
*You can earn up to £500 a week in this job.*

## 4 tenses with *until*

Present tenses are used to refer to the future after *until* (see 580).
*I'll wait until she gets here.* (NOT ... ~~until she will get here.~~)

▶

Present perfect and past perfect tenses can emphasise the idea of completion.
> *You're not going home **until** you've **finished** that report.*
> *I waited **until** the rain **had stopped**.*

## 5 structure with *Not until* ...

In a literary style it is possible to begin a sentence with *Not until* ... , using
inverted word order in the main clause (see 302).
> ***Not until** that evening **was she** able to recover her self-control.*
> ***Not until** I left home **did I** begin to understand how strange my family was.*

## 6 *until* and *by*: states and actions

We use *until* to talk about a situation or state that will continue up to a certain
moment. We use *by* (see 117) to say that an action or event will happen at or
before a future moment. Compare:
> – *Can I stay **until the weekend**?*
> *Yes, but you'll have to leave **by Monday midday** at the latest.* (= at twelve on
> Monday or before.)
> – *Can you repair my watch if I leave it **until Saturday**?*
> *No, but we can do it **by next Tuesday**.* (NOT ... ~~until next Tuesday.~~)

## 7 *until* and *before*

*Not until/till* can mean the same as *not before*.
> *I won't be seeing Judy **until/before** Tuesday.*
And both *until* and *before* can be used to say how far away a future event is.
> *It'll be ages **until/before** we meet again.*
> *There's only six weeks left **until/before** Christmas.*

# 603 up and down

## 1 'towards/away from the centre'

*Up* and *down* are not only used to refer to higher and lower positions. They
can also refer to more or less important or central places. (Trains to London
used to be called 'up trains', and trains from London 'down trains'.)
> *The ambassador walked slowly **up** the room towards the Queen's throne.*
> *She ran **down** the passage, out of the front door and **down** the garden.*
> *We'll be going **down** to the country for the weekend.*
But in the US *downtown* refers to the central business/entertainment area.

## 2 north and south

People often use *up* and *down* for movements towards the north and south
(perhaps because north is at the top of a map page).
> *I work in London, but I have to travel **up** to Glasgow every few weeks.*

## 3 'along'

Sometimes both *up* and *down* are used to mean 'along', 'further on', with little
or no difference of meaning.
> *The nearest post office is about half a mile **up/down** the road.*

# 604 used + infinitive

## 1 meaning

We use *used* + **infinitive** to talk about past habits and states which are now finished.

> *I used to smoke, but now I've stopped.* (NOT ~~I was used to smoke~~ ...)
> *That bingo hall used to be a cinema.*

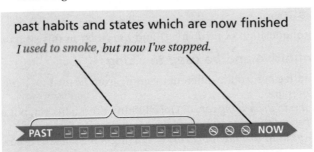

past habits and states which are now finished

*I used to smoke, but now I've stopped.*

PAST  NOW

## 2 only past

*Used to . . .* has no present form (and no progressive, perfect, infinitive or *-ing* forms). To talk about present habits and states, we usually just use the simple present tense (see 462).

> *He smokes.* (NOT ~~He uses to smoke.~~)
> *Her brother still collects stamps.*

## 3 questions and negatives

When questions and negatives are written, they often have *did . . . used* instead of *did . . . use.*

> *What did people use(d) to do in the evenings before TV?*
> *I didn't use(d) to like opera, but now I do.*

The contraction *usedn't* is also possible.

> *I usedn't to like opera.*

But the most common negative is *never used . . . .*

> *I never used to like opera.*

In a formal style, questions and negatives without *do* are possible, but these are not very common.

> *I used not to like opera, but now I do.* (OR *I used to not like opera . . .*)
> *Used you to play football at school?*

These forms are not used in tags.

> *You used not to like him, did you?* (NOT ~~. . . used you?~~)

## 4 when used to . . . is not used

*Used to* refers to things that happened at an earlier stage of one's life and are now finished: there is an idea that circumstances have changed. It is not used simply to say what happened at a past time, or how long it took, or how many times it happened.

> *I worked very hard last month.* (NOT ~~I used to work very hard last month.~~)
> *I lived in Chester for three years.* (NOT ~~I used to live in Chester for three years.~~)

▶

*I **went** to France seven times last year.* (NOT ~~I used to go to France seven times last year.~~)

## 5 word order

Mid-position adverbs (see 24) can go before or after *used*. The position before *used* is more common in an informal style.

*I **always used to** be afraid of dogs.* (informal)
*I **used always to** be afraid of dogs.* (formal)

## 6 pronunciation

Note the pronunciation of *used* /juːst/ and *use* /juːs/ in this structure.

## 7 *used + infinitive* and *be used to ...ing*

*Used* + **infinitive** has a quite different meaning from *be used to ...ing* (see next section). Compare:

*I **didn't use to drive** a big car.* (= Once I didn't drive a big car, but now I do.)
(NOT ~~I wasn't used to drive a big car.~~)
*I **wasn't used to driving** a big car.* (= Driving a big car was a new and difficult experience – I hadn't done it before.)

For the difference between *used to* and *would*, see 633.8.

# 605 [be] used to

## 1 meaning

If a person *is used to* something, it is familiar; he or she has experienced it so much that it is no longer strange or new.

*I've lived in Central London for six years now, so **I'm used to** the noise.*
*At the beginning I couldn't understand Londoners because I **wasn't used to** the accent.*

## 2 structures

*Be used to* can be followed by *-ing* forms, but not infinitives (see 298.2).

*I'm **used to driving** in London now, but it was hard at the beginning.*
(NOT ~~I'm used to drive in London...~~)
*It was a long time before she was **used to working** with old people.*

*Used* is an adjective in this structure, and can be modified by *quite* or *very*.

*I'm **quite used** to her little ways.*

## 3 *get used to ...ing* etc

*Get, become* and sometimes *grow* (see 128) can also be used before *used to* (*...ing*).

*You'll soon **get used** to living in the country.*
*Little by little, he **became used** to his new family.*
*It took them a long time to **grow used** to getting up in the night.*

## 4 pronunciation

Note that *used* is pronounced /juːst/ in this structure.

# 606 verb complementation: what can follow a verb?

## 1 different verbs, different structures

Different verbs can be followed by different kinds of word and structure. This is partly a matter of meaning: after a verb like *eat* or *break*, for instance, it is normal to expect a noun; after *try* or *stop*, it is natural to expect a verb. It is also partly a matter of grammatical rules that have nothing to do with meaning. Before an object, *wait* is followed by *for*; *expect* has no preposition. One can *tell somebody something*, but one cannot ~~explain somebody something~~. One *hopes to see somebody*, but one *looks forward to seeing somebody*. One *advises somebody to see the doctor*, but one does not ~~suggest somebody to see the doctor~~. Unfortunately there are no simple rules for this kind of problem; it is necessary to learn, for each verb, what kind of structures can follow it. A good dictionary will normally give this information.

## 2 verb + object; transitive and intransitive verbs

Some verbs are usually followed by nouns or pronouns that act as direct objects. In grammars these verbs are called 'transitive'. Examples are *invite*, *surprise*.

> *Let's invite Sally and Bruce.* (BUT NOT ~~Let's invite.~~)
> *You surprised me.* (BUT NOT ~~You surprised.~~)

Some verbs are not normally followed by direct objects. These are called 'intransitive'. Examples are *sit*, *sleep*.

> *Do sit down.* (BUT NOT ~~Do sit that chair.~~)
> *I usually sleep well.* (BUT NOT ~~She slept the baby.~~)

Many verbs can be both transitive and intransitive.

> *England lost the match.*      *Let's eat.*
> *England lost.*      *I can't eat this.*

Some transitive verbs can be followed by two objects (indirect and direct). For details, see 610.

> *I'll send you the form tomorrow.*
> *I'm going to buy Sarah some flowers.*

For verb structures used as objects, see paragraphs 8–10 below.
For structures with object complements, see paragraph 10 below.

## 3 *She opened the door / The door opened*

Some verbs are used transitively and intransitively with different kinds of subject; the intransitive use has a meaning rather like a passive (see 412) or reflexive (see 493) verb. Compare:

> – *She opened the door.*      – *The wind's moving the curtain.*
> *The door opened.*      *The curtain's moving.*

For more examples, see 609.

## 4 verbs with prepositions and particles

Many verbs need prepositions before their objects.

> *Why are you looking at me like that?* (NOT ~~Why are you looking me …?~~)
> *I'd like you to listen to this.* (NOT … ~~to listen this.~~)

▶

*Let's **talk about** your plans.* (NOT ~~Let's talk your plans.~~)
The preposition is dropped when there is no object.
   *Look!* (NOT ~~Look at!~~)
Other verbs can be used with adverb particles (see 20). Some of these
combinations are transitive; others are intransitive.
   *We'll have to **put off** our visit to Scotland.    It's time to **get up**.*

For more about two-part verbs like these, see 599–600.

## 5   complements of place

Usually, a preposition is necessary before an expression of place.
   *She **arrived at** the station last night.* (NOT ~~She arrived the station~~...)
   *Don't **walk on** the grass.* (NOT ~~Don't walk the grass.~~)
A few verbs can be used with direct objects referring to place.
   *I like **climbing mountains**.* (NOT ~~I like climbing on mountains.~~)
Some verbs are incomplete without an expression of place.
   *He **lives in York**.* (BUT NOT ~~He lives.~~)
   *She **got off the bus**.* (BUT NOT ~~She got.~~)

## 6   link verbs

Some verbs are followed not by an object, but by a subject complement – an
expression which describes the subject. These are called 'link verbs'. For
details, see 328.
   *Your room **is a mess**.*          *That **looks nice**.*
   *The toilets **are upstairs**.*     *I **felt a complete idiot**.*

## 7   verb + verb: auxiliaries

Many verbs can be followed by forms of other verbs. Auxiliary verbs are used
with other verbs to make questions and negatives, progressive forms, perfect
forms, and passives. For details, see 85.
   ***Do** you **want** some tea?*     *Where **have** you **been**?*
   *It **doesn't matter**.*            *These **are made** in France.*
Modal auxiliary verbs are used with other verbs to add ideas such as certainty,
probability, futurity, permission and obligation. For details, see 353–354.
   *You **must be** tired.*                    *The lecture **will start** at ten.*
   *The car **may need** a new engine.*        ***Can** I **borrow** your paper?*
   *We **ought to invite** the Maxwells this weekend.*

## 8   verb + verb: other verbs

Many verbs besides auxiliaries can be followed by forms of other verbs (or by
structures including other verbs). This can happen, for example, if we talk
about our attitude to an action: the first verb describes the attitude and the
second refers to the action. The second verb structure is often rather like the
direct object of the first verb.
   *I **enjoy playing** cards.*
   *I **saw** that she was crying.*        *I **hope to see** you soon.*
Different structures are possible, depending on the particular verb. Some verbs
can be followed by infinitives with or without *to* (see 282–283), some verbs can
be followed by *-ing* forms, with or without a preposition (see 296), and some
by clauses. Many verbs can be followed by more than one of these structures,

often with a difference of meaning or use. For each verb, it is necessary to know which structures are possible.

>We **seem to have** a problem. (NOT ~~We seem having a problem.~~)
>Can I **help wash up**?
>It's not very easy to **stop smoking**. (NOT . . . ~~to stop to smoke.~~)
>We're **thinking of moving**. (NOT ~~We're thinking to move.~~)
>I **suggest that you see** a solicitor. OR I **suggest seeing** a solicitor.
>    (NOT ~~I suggest you to see a solicitor.~~)

Sometimes the first verb does not give information about the subject – it says more about the action which the second verb refers to.

>I **happened to see** Alice the other day.
>We're **starting to get invited** to some of the neighbours' parties.
>My keys **seem to have disappeared**.

It is possible to have 'chains' of verbs following each other.

>I **keep forgetting to go** shopping.
>Don't **let** me **stop** you **working**.
>He **seems to be trying to sit** up.
>I don't **want to have to get** her **to start telling** lies.

## 9    verb + object + verb

Many verbs can be followed by an object as well as a verb structure.

>Can I **help you wash** up?
>I'd **like you to meet** Sally.
>We all **want you to be** happy. (NOT ~~We all want that you are happy.~~)
>We've got to **stop him making** a fool of himself.
>When are you going to **get the clock repaired**?
>Nobody **told me that you were** here.

For more about verb + object + infinitive, see 283.
For structures with object + -ing form, see 296.

## 10    verb + object + complement

Some transitive verbs can be followed by an object together with an object complement (an expression that gives more information about the object). For details, see 607.

>You **make me nervous**.      Let's **paint it blue**.

See the Index for problems with the structures after some common verbs.
For information about other verbs, see a good dictionary.


# 607    verb + object + complement

## 1    adjective and noun complements

Some transitive verbs can be followed by an object together with an object complement (an expression that gives more information about the object). This is often an adjective or noun phrase.

>You **make me nervous**.
>She's **driving us crazy**.        I **find her attitude strange**.
>Let's **cut it short**.            Don't **call me a liar**.      ▶

*I don't know why they elected **him President**.*
*Would you like to join the committee? ~ I would consider **it an honour**.*
A long and heavy object may come after the complement. Compare:
*He painted **the wall red**.* (NOT *He painted red the wall*.)
*He painted **red** all of the kitchen walls as well as the window frames
and ceiling.*

## 2   *see, describe* etc: structure with *as*

After some verbs, an object complement is introduced by *as*. This is common
when we say how we see or describe somebody/something.
*I **see** you **as** a basically kind person.*
*She **described** her attacker **as** a tall dark man with a beard.*
*His mother **regards** him **as** a genius.*
*After tests, they **identified** the metal **as** gold.*
The structure is also possible with *as being*.
*The police do not regard him **as (being)** dangerous.*

## 3   verbs of thinking and feeling: structure with *to be*

Some verbs that refer to thoughts, feelings and opinions (e.g. *believe, consider,
feel, know, find, understand*) can be followed by **object + infinitive** (usually *to
be*) in a formal style. In an informal style, *that*-clauses are more common.
*I **considered** him **to be** an excellent choice.*
(Less formal: *I considered that he was . . .*)
*We **supposed them to be** married.*
(Less formal: *We supposed that they were . . .*)
*They **believed** her **to be** reliable.*
(Less formal: *They believed that she was reliable.*)
This structure is very unusual with *think*.
*I **thought that** she was mistaken.*
(More natural than *I thought her to be mistaken*.)
*To be* can be dropped after *consider*.
*I **considered** him **(to be)** an excellent choice.*
Passive forms of these structures may be less formal than active forms (see
paragraph 6 below).

For more details of structures with *feel*, see 202; for *know*, see 313; for *think*, see 588.

## 4   *They found her (to be) . . .*

After *find* + **object**, *to be* suggests the result of a test or investigation. Compare:
– *Everybody **found** her very pleasant.*
  *The doctors **found** her **to be** perfectly fit.*
– *I **found** the bicycle very comfortable to ride.*
  *The testers **found** this bicycle **to be** the best value for money.*

## 5   structures with preparatory *it*

When the object of a verb is a clause, infinitive structure or *-ing* structure, and
there is an object complement, it is common to use *it* as a preparatory object.
Compare:
*She made **her views clear**.*
*She made **it clear** that she disagreed.* (NOT *She made that she disagreed
clear*.)

For details of this structure, see 447.

## 6 passive structures

Passive versions of these structures are common.

It *was painted* blue.
He *was elected* President.
Her attacker *was described* as a tall man with a beard.
The metal *was identified* as gold.
He *is not regarded* as being dangerous.
For a long time he *was thought* to be a spy.
She *was believed* to belong to a revolutionary organisation.
Seven people *are understood* to have been injured in the explosion.
It *was considered* impossible to change the date.

For the structures that are possible after a particular verb, see a good dictionary.

# 608 verbs of movement: she ran in etc

When we want to talk about a movement, its direction and its nature, there are several possibilities. We can use three separate words for the three ideas:

She *came in running*.

We can use a verb which includes the idea of direction, and describe the nature of the movement separately:

She *entered running*.

Or we can use a verb which makes clear the nature of the movement, and describe the direction separately:

She *ran in*.

In English, the third of these solutions is the most common.

She *danced across* the garden.
  (More natural than *She crossed the garden dancing.*)
I *jumped down* the stairs.
  (More natural than *I came down the stairs jumping.*)
They *crawled out* of the cellar.
We *flew past* Mont Blanc.

# 609 verbs with both active and passive meanings

## 1 She opened the door / The door opened

Some verbs are used transitively and intransitively with different kinds of subject. The intransitive use has a meaning rather like a passive (see 412) or reflexive (see 493) verb. Compare:

– She *opened* the door.
  The door *opened*.
– The wind's *moving* the curtain.
  The curtain's *moving*.
– Marriage has really *changed* her.
  She's *changed* a lot since she got married.
– We're *selling* a lot of copies of your book.
  Your book's *selling* well.

– Something *woke* her.
  Suddenly she *woke*.
– I can't *start* the car.
  The car won't *start*.

▶

## 2   *It scratches easily*

The intransitive structure is used with a lot of verbs that refer to things we can do to materials: for example *bend, break, crack, melt, polish, scratch, stain, tear, unscrew.*

> *Be careful what you put on the table – it **scratches** easily.* (= You can easily scratch it.)
> *These glasses are so fragile: they **break** if you look at them.*
> *The carpet's made of a special material that doesn't **stain**.*
> *The handle won't **unscrew** – can you help me?*

# 610   verbs with two objects

## 1   indirect and direct objects: *I gave John the keys*

Many verbs can have two objects – usually a person and a thing. This often happens with verbs that are used to talk about transferring or communicating things from one person to another, or doing things for somebody. A few other verbs are also used in this way. Common examples:

| | | | | | |
|---|---|---|---|---|---|
| *bet* | *get* | *make* | *play* | *sell* | *teach* |
| *bring* | *give* | *offer* | *post* | *send* | *tell* |
| *build* | *kick* | *owe* | *promise* | *show* | *throw* |
| *buy* | *leave* | *pass* | *read* | *sing* | *wish* |
| *cost* | *lend* | *pay* | *refuse* | *take* | *write* |

The thing that is given, sent, bought etc is called the 'direct object'; the person who gets it is the 'indirect object'. Most often, the indirect object comes first.

> *I bet **you ten dollars** you can't beat me at chess.*
> *He built **the children a tree-house**.*
> *Shall I buy **you some chocolate** while I'm out?*
> *Could you bring **me the paper**?*
> *The repair cost **me a lot**.*
> *I gave **John the keys**.*
> *If you're going upstairs, could you get **me my coat**?*
> *He left **his children nothing** when he died.*
> *Lend **me your bike**, can you?*
> *I'll make **you a cake** tomorrow.*
> *I owe **my sister a lot of money**.*
> *Can I play **you my new album**?*
> *I'll post **her the report** tomorrow.*
> *They promised **me all sorts of things**.*
> *Daddy, read **me a story**.*
> *He sent **his mother a postcard**.*
> *Let's take **her some flowers**.*
> *Will you teach **me poker**?*
> *We bought **the children pizzas**.*
> *Throw **me the ball**.*
> *We wish **you a Merry Christmas**.*

Not all verbs with this kind of meaning can be used like this – see paragraph 6.

## 2 indirect object last: *I gave the keys to John*

We can also put the indirect object after the direct object. In this case it normally has a preposition (usually *to* or *for*).

*I gave the keys **to John**.*
*I handed my licence **to the policeman**.*
*Mrs Norman sent some flowers **to the nurse**.*
*Mother bought the ice-cream **for you**, not **for me**.*

## 3 two pronouns: *Lend them to her*

When both objects are pronouns, it is common to put the indirect object last. *To* is occasionally dropped after *it* in informal British English.

*Lend them **to her**.*     *Send some **to him**.*     *Give it **(to)** me.*

It is also possible to put the indirect object first.

*Give **her** one.*     *Send **him** some.*

However, this structure is avoided in some cases: phrases ending with *it* or *them* (e.g. *He gave you it* or *Send them them*) are often felt to be unnatural.

## 4 *wh*-questions: *Who did you buy it for?*

Prepositions are used in *wh*-questions referring to the indirect object.

*Who did you buy it **for**?* (NOT ~~Who did you buy it?~~)
*Who was it sent **to**?* (NOT ~~Who was it sent?~~)

## 5 passives: *I've been given a picture*

When these verbs are used in passive structures, the subject is usually the person who receives something, not the thing which is sent, given etc.

*I've just been given a lovely picture.*
*We were all bought little presents.*

However, the thing which is given, sent etc can be the subject if necessary.

*What happened to the stuff he left behind?* ~ *Well, **the picture** was given to Mr Ferguson.*

For details of these passive structures, see 415.

## 6 structures with *donate, push, carry, explain, suggest, describe* and *take*

Not all verbs with this kind of meaning can be followed by **indirect object + direct object**. The structure is not possible, for example, with *donate, push, carry, explain, suggest* or *describe*.

*They donated **money to the museum**.* (BUT NOT ~~They donated the museum money.~~)
*I pushed **the plate to Ann**.* (BUT NOT ~~I pushed Ann the plate.~~)
*He carried **the baby to the doctor**.* (BUT NOT ~~He carried the doctor the baby.~~)
*I'd like him to explain **his decision to us**.* (BUT NOT ...~~to explain us his decision.~~)
*Can you suggest **a good dentist to me**?* (BUT NOT ~~Can you suggest me a good dentist?~~)
*Please describe **your wife to us**.* (BUT NOT ~~Please describe us your wife.~~)

*Take (to)* can be used with **indirect object + direct object**, but not *take (from)*.

*I **took her some money**.* (= I took some money to her, NOT ... from her.)

▶

**7 one object or two**

Some verbs can be followed by either a direct object, or an indirect object, or both.

*I asked **John**.*      *I asked **a question**.*      *I asked **John** a question.*

Other verbs like this include *teach, tell, pay, show, sing, play* and *write*. Note that when *sing, play* and *write* have no direct object, we put *to* before the indirect object. Compare:

– *Sing **her** a song.*
  *Sing **to her**.* (NOT *Sing her.*)
– *Write **me** a letter.*
  *Write **to me** when you get home.*
    (More common than *Write me ...* in standard British English.)

For structures with object complements (e.g. *They made him captain*), see 607.

# 611 **very** and **very much**

**1 adjectives and adverbs: *very kind, very quickly***

We use *very*, not *very much*, before adjectives and adverbs.
  *You're **very** kind.* (NOT *You're very much kind.*)
  *The situation is **very** serious.* (NOT *...very much serious.*)
  *I came **very** quickly.* (NOT *...very much quickly.*)
However, *very much* is used before comparatives.
  *I'm **very much** happier in my new job.* (NOT *... very happier ...*)

For *very* with superlatives (*very first, very best* etc), see 140.4.
For *the very same*, see 503.

**2 *not very***

*Not very* expresses quite a low degree.
  *It's **not very** warm – you'd better take a coat.*
  *That meal wasn't **very** expensive.* (= quite cheap.)
Note that *little* cannot be used in this way.
  *He's **not very** imaginative.* (NOT *He's little imaginative.*)

**3 past participles: *very much loved, very worried***

Before past participles we normally use *very much*.
  *She was **very much** loved by her grandchildren.* (NOT *She was very loved.*)
  *Journey times will be **very much** reduced by the new road.* (NOT *...very reduced ...*)
But we use *very* with some past participles that are used as adjectives. For details, see 410.4.
  *I'm **very** worried about Angela.* (NOT *...very much worried ...*)
  *We were **very** surprised when Pete passed his exam.* (More common than *... very much surprised ...*)

**4 *very much* (adverb)**

*Very much* can be an adverb.
  *We **very much** enjoyed the party.* (NOT *We very enjoyed.*)

We do not normally put *very much* between a verb and its object.

> *I **very much** like mountains.* (NOT ~~I like very much mountains.~~)

*Very much* can also be a determiner before a noun.

> *She didn't have **very much money**.*
> *Have you got **very much work** to do?*

*Very much* is not often used as a determiner in affirmative clauses (see 357.5).

> *There was **a lot of snow** on the road.* (NOT ~~There was very much snow.~~)

For *very . . . indeed*, see 273.

# 612 wait

*Wait* can be followed by an infinitive.

> *I'll **wait to hear** from you before I do anything.*

Before a direct object, *wait for* is used.

> *Please **wait for me** here.* (NOT ~~Please wait me here.~~)

*That*-clauses are not used, but an **object + infinitive** structure is possible.

> *We'll have to wait **for the photos to be** ready.* (NOT *. . . ~~wait that the photos are ready.~~*)

The time preposition *for* is often dropped after *wait*.

> *I **waited (for)** a very long time for her answer.*

The transitive verb *await* is formal, and is used mostly with abstract objects.

> *We're still **awaiting instructions**.*

For the difference between *wait for* and *expect*, see 196.

# 613 want

## 1 infinitive with *to*

After *want*, we normally use an infinitive with *to*.

> *I don't **want to come** back here ever again.* (NOT ~~I don't want come back~~ . . .)

*That*-clauses are not normally used after *want*, but an **object + infinitive** structure (see 283) is possible.

> *Do you **want me to make** you some coffee?* (NOT ~~Do you want (that) I make you some coffee?~~)
> *I don't **want that woman to come** here.*

## 2 structure with object complement

*Want* can be followed by an object together with a complement (adjective, adverb or past participle) to express ideas such as change or result.

> *They wanted **him dead**.*    *She doesn't want **him back**.*
> *I want **her out** of there now.*    *We want **the job finished** by Tuesday.*

*To be* or *as* is used before a noun complement.

> *I want you **to be my friend**.* (OR *. . . **as my friend**.* NOT ~~I want you my friend.~~)

## 3 *want* meaning 'need'

In informal British English, we can say that a thing 'wants' (= needs) something, particularly with reference to actions.

> *That car **wants** a clean.*    *Your hair **wants** a good brush.*

In this case, *want* can be followed by an *-ing* form (like *need* – see 366).

> *This coat **wants cleaning**.* (= . . . needs to be cleaned.)

▶

### 4 'I wanna hold your hand'

In informal speech, *want to* often sounds like 'wanna'. It is sometimes spelt like this in order to represent conversational pronunciation – for example in comic strips.

For *to* used instead of a whole infinitive (e.g. *I don't want to, thanks*), see 182.
For *want* and *will*, see 629.8.

## 614 -ward(s)

*Backward(s), forward(s), northward(s), outward(s)* and similar words can be used as adjectives or adverbs.

### 1 adjectives

When they are used as adjectives, they do not have *-s*.
> This country is very **backward** in some ways.
> You're not allowed to make a **forward** pass in rugby.
> He was last seen driving in a **northward** direction.

### 2 adverbs

When these words are adverbs, they can generally be used with or without *-s*. The forms with *-s* are generally a little more common in British English, and the forms without *-s* in American English.
> Why are you moving **backward(s)** and **forward(s)**?
> If we keep going **upward(s)** we must get to the top.
> Let's start driving **homeward(s)**.

In some figurative expressions such as *look forward to, bring forward, put forward*, the form without *-s* is always used.
> I **look forward to** hearing from you.
> She **put forward** a very interesting suggestion.

### 3 other words

*Towards* and *afterwards* are the usual forms in British English; in American English, *toward* and *afterward* are also common.

## 615 way

### 1 preposition dropped

In an informal style, we usually drop the prepositions *in* or *by* before *way*.
> You're doing it *(in)* **the wrong way**.     Come **this way**.
> Do it *(in)* **any way** you like.     We went there **the usual way**.

### 2 relative structures

In an informal style, we often say *the way (that)* instead of *the way in/by which*.
> I don't like **the way (that)** you talk to me.
> Let's go **the way (that)** we went yesterday.

### 3 infinitive or *-ing*

After *way* (meaning 'method'/'manner') we can use an infinitive structure or
*of . . . ing*. There is no important difference between the two structures.
> *There's no **way to prove** / **of proving** that he was stealing.*

### 4 *way of* and *means of*

*Way of* is unusual before a noun (except in the common expression *way of
life*). We use *means of* or *method of* instead.
> *The 19th century saw a revolution in **means of transport**.* (NOT *. . . ~~ways of
> transport.~~*)
> *They tried all possible **methods of instruction**, but the child learnt nothing.*

### 5 *in the way* and *on the way*

These expressions are quite different. *In the/my/etc way* is used for obstacles –
things that stop people getting where they want to.
> *I can't get the car out because those boxes are **in the way**.*
> *Please don't stand in the kitchen door – you're **in my way**.*

*On the/my etc way* means 'during the journey/movement' or 'coming'.
> *We'll have lunch **on our way**.*      *Spring is **on the way**.*

For *by the way*, see 157.8.

## 616 weak and strong forms

### 1 What are weak and strong forms?

Some English words – for example *at, for, have, and, us* – have two
pronunciations: one is used when they are not stressed, and the other when
they are. Compare:
> *I'm looking **at** /ət/ you.*      *What are you looking **at** /æt/?*

### 2 stressed or not?

Most of these words are prepositions, pronouns, conjunctions, articles and
auxiliary verbs. Such words are not usually stressed, because they are generally
found together with other more important words which carry the stress. So the
unstressed ('weak') pronunciation is the normal one. This usually has the
vowel /ə/ or no vowel; a few weak forms are pronounced with /ɪ/.
However, these words can be stressed when they are emphasised, or when
there is no other word to carry the stress. In these cases the 'strong'
pronunciation is used. This has the vowel that corresponds to the spelling.
Compare:
– *I **must** /məs/ go now.*
   *I really **must** /mʌst/ stop smoking.* (stressed for emphasis)
– *I **was** /wəz/ late.*
   *It **was** /wəz/ raining.*
   *Yes, it **was** /wɒz/.* (stressed at end of sentence: there is no other word to
      be stressed.)
– *Where **have** /əv/ you been?*
   *You might **have** /əv/ told me.*
   *What did you **have** /hæv/ for breakfast?* (non-auxiliary verb)      ▶

Contracted negatives always have a strong pronunciation.

*can't* /kɑ:nt/     *mustn't* /'mʌsnt/     *wasn't* /'wɒznt/

## 3  list of words with weak and strong forms

The most important words which have weak and strong forms are:

|  | **Weak form** | **Strong form** |
|---|---|---|
| a | /ə/ | /eɪ/ (unusual) |
| am | /(ə)m/ | /æm/ |
| an | /ən/ | /æn/ (unusual) |
| and | /(ə)n(d)/ | /ænd/ |
| are | /ə(r)/ | /ɑ:(r)/ |
| as | /əz/ | /æz/ |
| at | /ət/ | /æt/ |
| be | /bɪ/ | /bi:/ |
| been | /bɪn/ | /bi:n/ |
| but | /bət/ | /bʌt/ |
| can | /k(ə)n/ | /kæn/ |
| could | /kəd/ | /kʊd/ |
| do | /d(ə)/ | /du:/ |
| does | /dəz/ | /dʌz/ |
| for | /fə(r)/ | /fɔ:(r)/ |
| from | /frəm/ | /frɒm/ |
| had | /(h)əd/ | /hæd/ |
| has | /(h)əz/ | /hæz/ |
| have | /(h)əv/ | /hæv/ |
| he | /(h)ɪ/ | /hi:/ |
| her | /(h)ə(r)/ | /hɜ:(r)/ |
| him | /(h)ɪm/ | /hɪm/ |
| his | /(h)ɪz/ | /hɪz/ |
| is | /z, s/ | /ɪz/ |
| must | /m(ə)s(t)/ | /mʌst/ |
| not | /nt/ | /nɒt/ |
| of | /əv/ | /ɒv/ |
| our | /ɑ:(r)/ | /aʊə(r)/ |
| saint | /s(ə)nt/ (BrE only) | /seɪnt/ |
| shall | /ʃ(ə)l/ | /ʃæl/ |
| she | /ʃɪ/ | /ʃi:/ |
| should | /ʃ(ə)d/ | /ʃʊd/ |
| sir | /sə(r)/ | /sɜ:(r)/ |
| some (see 546) | /s(ə)m/ | /sʌm/ |
| than | /ð(ə)n/ | /ðæn/ (rare) |
| that (conj.) | /ð(ə)t/ | /ðæt/ |
| the | /ðə, ðɪ/ | /ði:/ |
| them | /ð(ə)m/ | /ðem/ |
| there (see 586) | /ðə(r)/ | /ðeə(r)/ |
| to | /tə/ | /tu:/ |
| us | /əs/ | /ʌs/ |
| was | /w(ə)z/ | /wɒz/ |
| we | /wɪ/ | /wi:/ |
| were | /wə(r)/ | /wɜ:(r)/ |

|        | Weak form    | Strong form |
|--------|--------------|-------------|
| who    | /hʊ/         | /huː/       |
| would  | /wəd, əd/    | /wʊd/       |
| will   | /w(ə)l/      | /wɪl/       |
| you    | /jʊ/         | /juː/       |
| your   | /jə(r)/      | /jɔː(r)/    |

## 617 well

### 1 *well* and *good*

*Well* and *good* can have similar meanings, but in this case *well* is an adverb, while *good* is an adjective. Compare:
- *The car runs **well**.* (adverb modifying *runs*) (NOT ~~The car runs good.~~)
  *It's a **well**-made car.* (adverb modifying *made*)
  *It's a **good** car.* (adjective modifying *car*)
- *He teaches very **well**.*
  *I like that teacher. He's **good**.* (NOT ~~He's well.~~)
- *She speaks English **well**.* (NOT ~~She speaks English good.~~)
  *She speaks **good** English.*
  *Her English is **good**.*

Note that we cannot say *She speaks well English.* (Adverbs cannot usually go between the verb and the object – see 21.1.)

### 2 *well* = 'in good health'

There is also an adjective *well*, meaning 'in good health'.
> *How are you? ~ Quite **well**, thanks.*
> *I don't feel very **well**.*

Note that the adjective *well* is only used to talk about health. Compare:
> *When I'm in the mountains I am always **well**.*
> *When I'm with you I'm **happy**.* (NOT ~~When I'm with you I'm well.~~)

*Well* is not common before a noun. We can say *She's well*, but it is less usual to say, for example, *She's a well girl*.

For *ill* and *sick*, see 266.  For *well* as a discourse marker, see 157.16,17,20.

## 618 when and if

A person who says *when* (referring to the future) is sure that something will happen. A person who says *if* is unsure whether it will happen. Compare:
- *I'll see you at Christmas **when** we're all at Sally's place.*
  (We are certain to be at Sally's place.)
  *I'll see you in August **if** I come to New York.*
  (Perhaps I'll come to New York, perhaps not.)

To talk about repeated, predictable situations and events (in the sense of 'whenever'), both *when* and *if* can be used with little difference of meaning.
> ***When/If** you heat ice it turns to water.*
> ***When/If** I'm in Liverpool I usually stay with my sister.*

## 619  where (to)

*To* is often dropped after *where*.
> **Where** *are you going (to)?*     **Where** *does this road lead (to)?*

*To* is not normally dropped in the short question *Where to?*
> *Could you send this off for me?* ~ **Where to?**

For *where* in relative clauses, see 494.10

## 620  whether ... or ...

We can use *whether ... or ...* as a double conjunction, with a similar meaning to *It doesn't matter whether ... or ...*
> *The ticket will cost the same,* **whether** *we buy it now* **or** *wait till later.*
> **Whether** *we go by bus* **or** *train, it'll take at least six hours.*

Several structures are possible with *whether ... or not*.
> *Whether you like it or not, ...*
> *Whether or not you like it, ...*
> *Whether you like it or whether you don't, ...*

For *whether* and *if,* see 621.

## 621  whether and if

### 1  indirect questions

*Whether* and *if* can both introduce indirect questions.
> *I'm not sure* **whether/if** *I'll have time.*
> *I asked* **whether/if** *she had any letters for me.*

After verbs that are more common in a formal style, *whether* is preferred.
> *We* **discussed whether** *we should close the shop.*
> (More normal than *We discussed if ...*)

In a formal style, *whether* is usually preferred in a two-part question with *or*.
> *The Directors have not decided* **whether** *they will recommend a dividend* **or** *reinvest the profits.*

If an indirect question is fronted (see 513), *whether* is used.
> **Whether I'll have time** *I'm not sure at the moment.*

### 2  prepositions

After prepositions, only *whether* is possible.
> *There was a big argument* **about whether** *we should move to a new house.*
> (NOT *... about if we should move ...*)
> *I haven't settled the question* **of whether** *I'll go back home.*

### 3  infinitives

*Whether,* but not *if,* is used before *to*-infinitives.
> *They can't decide* **whether to get** *married now or wait.* (NOT *They can't decide if to get married ...*)

## 4 subject, complement and adverbial clauses

When a question-word clause is a subject or complement, *whether* is normally preferred.

> ***Whether we can stay with my mother is another matter.*** (subject)
> *The question is **whether the man can be trusted**.* (complement)

*The question is if . . .* is also possible, but less common.

> ***The question is if the man can be trusted.***

## 5 not used in echo questions

*If* and *whether* are not normally used in 'echo questions' (see 483).

> *Are you happy? ~ Am I happy? No!* (NOT *. . . ~~If/Whether I'm happy?~~ . . .*)

# 622 which, what and who: question words

## 1 *which* and *what*: the difference

*Which* and *what* are often both possible, with little difference of meaning.

> ***Which/What** is the hottest city in the world?*
> ***Which/What** train did you come on?*
> ***Which/What** people have influenced you most in your life?*

We prefer *which* when we have a limited number of choices in mind.

> *We've got white or brown bread. **Which** will you have?*
> (More natural than . . . *What will you have?*)
> ***Which** size do you want – small, medium or large?*

When we are not thinking of a limited number of choices, *what* is preferred.

> ***What** language do they speak in Greenland?*
> (More natural than *Which language* . . .)
> ***What's** your phone number?* (NOT *~~Which is your phone number?~~*)

## 2 determiners: *which* and *what*

Before nouns, *which* and *what* can be used to ask questions about both things and people.

> ***Which** teacher do you like best?*
> ***Which** colour do you want - green, red, yellow or brown?*
> ***What** writers do you like?*　　　***What** colour are your baby's eyes?*

## 3 *which of*

Before another determiner (e.g. *the, my, these*) or a pronoun, we use *which of*. *Who* and *what* are not normally used with *of* like this in modern English.

> ***Which of** your teachers do you like best?* (NOT *~~Who/What of your teachers~~ . . .*)
> ***Which of** us is going to do the washing up?* (NOT *~~Who of us~~ . . .?*)
> ***Which of** these coats is yours?* (NOT *~~What of these~~ . . .?*)

## 4 without nouns: *who* for people

When these words are not followed by nouns or pronouns, we generally use *who*, not *which*, for people.

> ***Who** won – Smith or Fitzgibbon?* (NOT *~~Which won~~ . . .?*)
> ***Who** are you going out with – Lesley or Maria?*

▶

However, *which* can be used in questions about people's identity, and *what* can be used to ask about people's jobs and functions.

> **Which** *is your husband?* ~ *The one in jeans.*
> *So Janet's the Managing Director.* **What's** *Peter?*

For the difference between *who* and *whom*, see 623.
For relative *who* and *which* (e.g. *the man who* . . . ), see 494. For relative *what* (e.g. *what I need is* . . .), see 497.
For singular and plural verbs after *who* and *what*, see 532.3.

# 623 who and whom

*Whom* is unusual in informal modern English.

## 1 questions: *Who did they arrest?*

We normally use *who* as an object in questions.

> **Who** *did they arrest?*

Prepositions usually come at the end of *who*-questions (see 452).

> **Who** *did she go* **with?**

In a very formal style, *whom* is sometimes used.

> **Whom** *did they arrest?* (formal)

Prepositions normally come before *whom*.

> **With whom** *did she go?* (very formal)

## 2 relative clauses: *the man (who) we met*

In identifying relative clauses, (see 495), *whom* is unusual in an informal style. Either we leave out the object pronoun, or we use *that* or *who* (see 494–495 for details).

> *There's the man* **(that)/(who)** *we met in the pub last night.*

In a formal style *whom* is more common.

> *She married a man* **whom** *she met at a conference.*

In non-identifying relative clauses (see 495), we usually use *whom* as an object when necessary (but these clauses are uncommon in informal English).

> *This is John Perkins,* **whom** *you met at the sales conference.*
> *I have a number of American relatives, most of* **whom** *live in Texas.*

## 3 *who(m) he thought* etc

In a sentence like *He was trying to find an old school friend, who(m) he thought was living in New Zealand*, people are often unsure whether *whom* is possible (because it seems to be the object of the first following verb) or whether they should use *who* (because it is the subject of the second verb). *Who* is considered more correct, but *whom* is sometimes used. Another example:

> *There is a child in this class* **who(m)** *I believe is a musical genius.*

In cases with a following infinitive, usage is mixed, but *whom* is considered more correct.

> *There is a child in the class* **who(m)** *I believe to be a musical genius.*

# 624 who ever, what ever etc

These expressions show surprise or difficulty in understanding something.

*Who ever is that strange girl with Roger?*
*What ever are you doing?*
*How ever did you manage to start the car? I couldn't.*
*When ever will I have time to write some letters?*
*Why ever did I marry you?*

The expressions can also be written as single words: *whoever, whatever* etc.
Note that *whose* and *which* are not used with *ever* in this way.
In an informal style, *on earth*, *the hell* (AmE also *in hell*) or *the fuck* (taboo –
see 575) can be used instead of *ever*.

*Who on earth is that strange girl?*     *Why the hell did I marry you?*
*What the fuck is she talking about?*

For the conjunctions *whoever, whatever*, etc, see 625.

# 625 whoever, whatever etc

## 1 meaning and use

*Whoever* means 'it doesn't matter who', 'any person who', or 'the unknown
person who'. *Whatever, whichever, however, whenever* and *wherever* have
similar 'open' meanings.
A word of this kind has a double function, like a relative pronoun or adverb
(see 498.1). It acts as a subject, object or adverb in its own clause, but it also
acts as a conjunction, joining its clause to the rest of the sentence. Examples:

*Whoever phoned just now was very polite.*
*I'm not opening the door, whoever you are.*
*Send it to whoever pays the bills.*
*Whatever you do, I'll always love you.*
*Whatever is in that box is making a very funny noise.*
*Keep calm, whatever happens.*
*Spend the money on whatever you like.*
*Whichever of them you marry, you'll have problems.*
*We're free all next week. You'll be welcome whichever day you come.*
*However much he eats, he never gets fat.*
*People always want more, however rich they are.*
*However you travel, it'll take you at least three days.*
*Whenever I go to London I try to see Vicky.*
*You can come whenever you like.*
*Wherever you go, you'll find Coca-Cola.*

## 2 *whoever*, *whichever* and *whatever*: subjects and objects

*Whoever, whichever* and *whatever* can be the subjects or objects of the verbs in
their clauses. (Note that *whomever* is not used in modern English.)

*Whoever directed this film, it's no good.* (subject of *directed*)
*Whoever you marry, make sure he can cook.* (object of *marry*)
*Whatever you say, I don't think he's the right man.* (object of *say*)   ▶

*Whichever* and *whatever* can also go with nouns as determiners.
> **Whichever room** *you use, make sure you clean it up afterwards.*
> **Whatever problems** *you have, you can always come to me for help.*
> *If you change your mind for* **whatever reason**, *just let me know.*

## 3 clauses as subjects or objects

A clause with *whoever*, *whichever* and *whatever* can be the subject or object of the verb in the other clause.
> **Whoever told you that** *was lying.* (subject of *was lying*)
> *I'll marry* **whoever I like.** (object of *marry*)
> **Whichever climber gets to the top first** *will get a £5,000 prize.* (subject of *will get*)
> *I'll take* **whichever tent you're not using.** (object of *take*)
> **Whatever you want** *is fine with me.* (subject of *is*)
> *Prisoners have to eat* **whatever they're given.** (object of *eat*)

## 4 whenever = 'every time that'

*Whenever* can suggest repetition, in the sense of 'every time that'.
> **Whenever** *I see you I feel nervous.*
> *I stay with Monica* **whenever** *I go to London.*

## 5 whoever etc ... may

*May* can be used to suggest ignorance or uncertainty.
> *He's written a book on the philosopher Matilda Vidmi,* **whoever she may be.**
> *She's just written to me from Llandyfrdwy,* **wherever that may be.**

## 6 leaving out the verb: *whatever his problems*

In a clause like *whatever his problems are*, where *whatever* is the complement of the verb *be*, it is possible to leave out the verb.
> **Whatever his problems,** *he has no right to behave like that.*
> *A serious illness,* **whatever its nature,** *is almost always painful.*

After *however* + **adjective**, we can leave out a **pronoun** + *be*.
> *A grammar rule,* **however true** *(it is), is useless unless it can be understood.*

## 7 informal uses: short answers

In an informal style, these conjunctions are sometimes used as short answers.
> *When shall we start?* ~ **Whenever.** (= Whenever you like.)
> *Potatoes or rice?* ~ **Whichever.** (= I don't mind.)

*Whatever* is often used to mean 'I don't care' or 'I'm not interested'. This can sound rude.
> *What would you like to do? We could go and see a film, or go swimming.* ~ **Whatever.**

*Or whatever* can mean 'or anything else'.
> *Would you like some orange juice or a beer* **or whatever?**
> *If you play football or tennis* **or whatever,** *it does take up a lot of time.*

## 8 whatever meaning 'at all'

After *any* and *no*, *whatever* can be used to mean 'at all'.
> *Don't you have* **any** *regrets* **whatever?**
> *I can see* **no** *point* **whatever** *in buying it.*

In a formal style, *whatsoever* is sometimes used as an emphatic form of *whatever* in this structure.

For other uses of *whatever* and *however*, see a good dictionary.
For *who ever, what ever* etc, see 624.
For *no matter who/what/*etc, see 378.

# 626 whose: question word

## 1 with a noun or alone

The question word *whose* can be used with a noun as a determiner like *my*, *your* etc.
**Whose** *car is that outside?*
**Whose** *garden do you think looks the nicest?*
*Whose* can also be used alone, like *mine, yours* etc.
**Whose** *is that car outside?*     **Whose** *is this?* ~ *Mine.*

## 2 prepositions

Prepositions can normally come either before *whose* (more formal) or at the end of the clause (less formal). See 452 for details.
**For whose** *benefit were all these changes made?*
**Whose** *side are you* **on?**
In short questions with no verb, prepositions can only come before *whose*.
*I'm going to buy a car.* ~ **With whose** *money?* (NOT ~~Whose money with?~~)

For the relative pronoun *whose*, see 496.     For *whose* and *who's*, see 627.

# 627 whose and who's

*Whose* is a possessive word meaning 'of whom/which', used in questions and relative clauses. *Who's* is the contraction of *who is* or *who has*. Compare:
– **Whose** *is that coat?* (NOT ~~Who's is that coat?~~)
  *It was a decision* **whose** *importance was not realised at the time.*
    (NOT *...* ~~who's importance~~ *...*)
– *Do you know anybody* **who's** *going to France in the next few days?*
    (NOT *...* ~~anybody whose going~~ *...*)
  *I've got a cousin* **who's** *never been to London.* (NOT *...* ~~whose never been~~ *...*)
There is a similar confusion between *its* and *it's*: see 305.

# 628 why and why not

## 1 replies

We generally use *Why not?*, not *Why?*, in short replies to negative statements. Compare:
  *They've decided to move to Devon.* ~ **Why?**
  *I can't manage tomorrow evening.* ~ **Why not?**
    (More natural than *Why?*)
*Why not?* can also be used to agree to a suggestion.
  *Let's eat out this evening.* ~ *Yes,* **why not?**

## 2 Why should ...?

A structure with *why* followed by *should* can suggest surprise.

> *I wonder **why** she **should** want to go out with me.*

The structure can also suggest anger or refusal to do something.

> *I don't see **why** we **should** have to pay for your mistake.*
> *Give me a cigarette. ~ **Why should** I?*

For a similar structure with *how*, see 482.2.

## 3 infinitive structures

*Why* can be followed by an infinitive without *to*. This structure can suggest that an action is unnecessary or pointless.

> ***Why argue** with him? He'll never change his mind.* (NOT ~~Why arguing~~...? OR ~~Why to argue~~...?)
> ***Why pay** more at other shops? We have the best value.*

*Why not* + **infinitive without *to*** is used to make suggestions.

> *Sandy's in a bad mood. ~ **Why not give** her some flowers?*

*Why don't ...?* can be used in the same way.

> ***Why don't you give** her some flowers?*
> ***Why don't we go** and see Julie?*

# 629 will: various uses

## 1 forms

*Will* is a modal auxiliary verb (see 353–354). It has no -*s* in the third person singular; questions and negatives are made without *do*; after *will*, we use an infinitive without *to*.

> ***Will** the train be on time?*

Contractions are *'ll, won't*.

> *Do you think it**'ll** rain?*          *It **won't** rain.*

*Would* is used as a past or less definite form of *will* for some of its meanings; for details, see 633.

## 2 future auxiliary

We can use *will* as an auxiliary verb when we talk about the future. For details, see 212.

> *I **will be** happy when this is finished.*
> *This time tomorrow I**'ll be sitting** in the sun.*
> *He **will have finished** the whole job by this evening.*

## 3 certainty

*Will* can express certainty or confidence about present or future situations.

> *As I'm sure you **will** understand, we cannot wait any longer for our order.*
> *Don't phone them now – they**'ll** be having dinner.*
> *There's somebody coming up the stairs. ~ That**'ll** be Mary.*
> *Tomorrow **will** be cloudy, with some rain.*

*Will have* + **past participle** refers to the past.

> *Dear Sir, You **will** recently **have received** a form ...*
> *We can't go and see them now – they**'ll have gone** to bed.*

## 4 willingness and decisions

*Will* can express the speaker's willingness, or announce a decision.

> *Can somebody help me? ~ I **will**.*
> *There's the doorbell. ~ **I'll** go.*

*Will* can express a firm intention, a promise or a threat.

> *I really **will** stop smoking.*
> ***I'll** definitely pay you back next week.*
> ***I'll** kill her for this.*

We can use *will not* or *won't* to talk about unwillingness or refusal.

> *She **won't** open the door.*
> *Give me a kiss. ~ No, I **won't**.*
> *The car **won't** start.*

*Would not* can refer to past refusal.

> *She **wouldn't** open the door.*    *The car **wouldn't** start this morning.*

For details of these uses, see 217.

## 5 requests, orders and offers

We use *will you* to tell people what to do.

> ***Will you** send me the bill, please?*
> *Come this way, **will you**?*    ***Will you** be quiet!*

*Would you* is 'softer', more polite.

> ***Would you** send me the bill, please?*
> *Come this way, **would you**?*

*Will you ...?* can also be used to ask about people's wishes.

> ***Will you** have some more potatoes?*    *What **will you** drink?*

*Won't you ...?* expresses a pressing offer.

> ***Won't you** have some more wine?*

*Will* can be used in affirmative structures to give impersonal, military-type orders.

> *All staff **will** submit weekly progress reports.*

## 6 distancing: *I'll have to ask you ...*

Instructions and orders can be made less direct by 'distancing' (see 436) – for example by using *will* to displace them into the future.

> *I'm afraid you'll need to fill in this form.*
> *I'll have to ask you to wait a minute.*

And *will* is sometimes used to say how much money is owed.

> *That **will** be £1.65, please.*

## 7 typical behaviour

We can use *will* to talk about typical behaviour.

> *She'll sit talking to herself for hours.*
> *When you look at clouds they **will** often remind you of animals.*
> *If something breaks down and you kick it, it **will** often start working again.*
> *Sulphuric acid **will** dissolve most metals.*

Stressed *will* can be used to criticise people's typical behaviour.

> *She WILL fall in love with the wrong people.*
> *Well, if you WILL keep telling people what you think of them ...*

*Would* is used in a similar way to refer to the past. For details, see 633.7.    ▶

## 8 *will* and *want*

*Will* and *want* can both be used to talk about wishes, but they are rather different. *Will* is used mostly in 'interpersonal' ways, to express wishes that affect other people through orders, requests, offers, promises etc. *Want* simply refers to people's wishes – nothing more. *Will* is to do with actions, *want* is to do with thoughts. Compare:
- *Will you open the window?* (an order)
  *Do you **want** to open the window?* (a question about somebody's wishes)
- *She **won't** tell anybody.* (= She refuses to . . .)
  *She **doesn't want** to tell anybody.* (= She prefers not to . . .)

Note that *will* cannot be used with a direct object.
  *Do you **want** / Would you like an aspirin?* (NOT ~~Will you an aspirin?~~)

For a comparison between *will* and *going to*, see 216, 218.

# 630 wish

## 1 *wish* + infinitive

We can use **wish** + **infinitive** to mean *want. Wish* is very formal in this sense. Note that progressive forms are not used.
  *I **wish to see** the manager, please.* (NOT ~~I'm wishing to see~~ . . .)
  *If you **wish to reserve** a table, please telephone after five o'clock.*

An **object** + **infinitive** structure is also possible.
  *We do not **wish our names to appear** in the report.*

**Wish** + **direct object** is not normal without a following infinitive.
  *I **want** / **would like an appointment** with the manager.* (NOT ~~I wish an appointment with the manager.~~)

## 2 *I wish you* . . .

*Wish* is used with two objects in some fixed expressions of good wishes.
  *I **wish you a Merry Christmas**.*
  *We all **wish you a speedy recovery**.*
  *Here's **wishing you all the best** in your new job.*

## 3 *wish* + *that*-clause: meaning

We can also use *wish* with a *that*-clause (*that* can be dropped in an informal style). In this case, *wish* does not mean 'want' – it expresses regret that things are not different, and refers to situations that are unreal, impossible or unlikely. Tenses are similar to those used with *if* (see below).
  *I **wish** (that) I was better looking.*
  *Don't you **wish** (that) you could fly?*
  *We all **wish** (that) the snow would stay forever.*

**Wish** + **that**-clause is not generally used for wishes about things that seem possible in the future. We often use *hope* in this sense (see 250).
  *I **hope** you pass your exams.* (NOT ~~I wish you would pass your exams.~~)
  *I **hope** you feel better tomorrow.* (NOT ~~I wish you felt better tomorrow.~~)

## 4 *wish + that*-clause: tenses

In a *that*-clause after *wish*, we generally use the same tenses as we would use, for instance, after 'It would be nice if . . .' (see 258). Past tenses are used with a present or future meaning.

> *I wish I **spoke** French.* (= It would be nice if I spoke French.)
> *I wish I **had** a yacht.*     *I wish tomorrow **was** Sunday.*
> *All the staff wish you **weren't** leaving so soon.*
> *Do you ever wish you **lived** somewhere else?*

*Were* can be used instead of *was* in this structure, especially in a formal style.

> *I wish that I **were** better looking.*

Past perfect tenses are used for wishes about the past.

> *I wish you **hadn't said** that.* (= It would be nice if you hadn't said that.)
> *Now she wishes she **had gone** to university.*

In informal speech, sentences like *I wish you'd have seen it* sometimes occur. For similar structures with *if*, see 262.

## 5 *wish . . . would*

*Would* is very common in *that*-clauses after *wish* (much more common than it is in *if*-clauses). Sentences with *wish . . . would* express regret or annoyance that something will not happen.

> *Everybody wishes you **would** go home.* (= Why won't you go home?)
> *I wish you **would** stop smoking.* (= Why won't you stop smoking?)
> *I wish the postman **would** come soon.* (But it looks as if he won't.)
> *I wish it **would** stop raining.* (= It will keep on raining!)
> *Don't you wish that this moment **would** last for ever?*

Sentences with *wish . . . wouldn't* refer to things that do or will happen.

> *I wish you **wouldn't** keep making that stupid noise.*
> (= You will keep making . . .)

*Wish . . . would(n't)* can be like an order or a critical request. Compare:

> – *I wish you **wouldn't** drive so fast.* (Similar to *Please don't drive so fast.*)
>   *I wish you **didn't** drive so fast.* (More like *I'm sorry you drive so fast.*)
> – *I wish you **wouldn't** work on Sundays.* (= Why don't you stop?)
>   *I wish you **didn't** work on Sundays.* (= It's a pity.)

For similar structures with *if only*, see 265.
For other cases where past tenses have present or future meanings, see 426.

# 631 with

## 1 *trembling with rage, blue with cold* etc

*With* is used in a number of expressions which say how people are showing their emotions and sensations.

> *My father was trembling **with** rage.*
> *Annie was jumping up and down **with** excitement.*
> *When I found her she was blue **with** cold.*
> white **with** fear/rage                 green **with** envy
> red **with** anger/embarrassment         shivering **with** cold

▶

## 2   *angry with* etc

*With* is also used after a number of adjectives which say how people are feeling towards others.

> *I'm cross **with** you.*   *furious **with***      *upset **with***
> *angry **with***         *pleased **with***

After words which say how people act towards others (like *kind, nice, polite, rude, good*), we generally use *to*, not *with*.

> *She was very **nice to** me.* (NOT *... nice with me.*)

## 3   *with* meaning 'against'

After *fight, struggle, quarrel, argue, play* and words with similar meanings, *with* can be used with the same meaning as *against*.

> *Don't **fight with** him – he's bigger than you are.*
> *Will you **play** chess **with** me?*

## 4   accompanying circumstances and reasons

*With* can introduce accompanying circumstances or reasons (rather like *and there is/was* or *because there is/was*).

> *The runners started the race **with a light following wind.***
> ***With all this work to do,** I won't have time to go out.*
> ***With friends like you,** who needs enemies?*

*Without* can be used in similar ways.

> ***Without Sue and Jake,** we're going to have trouble finishing the repairs.*

## 5   possession

*With* is very often used, like *have*, to indicate possession and similar ideas.

> *There are so many people around **with no homes.***
>    *(= ... who have no homes.)*
> *They've bought a house **with a big garden.***

## 6   clothing, voices, transport etc

Note that *in* is often used instead of *with* to refer to articles of clothing.

> *Who's the man **in the funny hat**?*
> *Could you go and give this paper to the woman **in glasses**?*

We say *in a ... voice*, NOT *with a ... voice*.

> *Why are you talking **in such a loud voice**?*

Note also: *by car/train* etc (NOT *with the car* etc), and *write in pencil/ink*.

For the difference between *by* and *with*, see 119.

# 632   worth

## 1   *worth a lot,* etc

*Worth* can be followed by an expression describing the value of something.

> *That piano must be **worth a lot**.*
> *I don't think their pizzas are **worth the money**.*
> *Shall I talk to Rob? ~ It's not **worth the trouble**.*

In questions about value, either *what* or *how much* can be used.

> ***What / How much** is that painting worth?*

## 2 a million dollars' worth of . . .

A possessive can be used before *worth* in expressions with numbers.
> *They've ordered **a million dollars' worth** of computer software.*

## 3 It's worth talking to Joe; Joe's worth talking to

To talk about the value of an activity, we can use an *-ing* form with *worth*.
The *-ing* clause cannot be the subject; we often use preparatory *it*.
> ***It's worth talking** to Joe.* (NOT ~~Talking to Joe is worth.~~)
> ***It isn't worth repairing** the car.*
> ***Is it worth visiting** Leicester?*

We can also use a structure in which the object of the *-ing* form (*Joe, the car, Leicester*) is made the subject of the sentence.
> ***Joe's worth talking** to.*
> ***The car** isn't **worth repairing**.* (NOT ~~The car isn't worth repairing it.~~ OR
> ~~The car isn't worth to be repaired.~~)
> *Is **Leicester worth visiting**?*

For more about structures in which the object of a verb is the subject of the sentence (e.g. *She's easy to amuse*), see 284.4.

## 4 It's worth it

We often use *It's (not) worth it* to say whether something is worth doing.
> *If you pay a bit more you get a room to yourself. I think **it's worth it**.*
> *Shall we go and see the castle? ~ No, **it's not worth it**.*

## 5 worthwhile

*Worthwhile* (or *worth while*) is sometimes used instead of *worth*, particularly to express the idea 'worth spending time'.
> *Is it **worthwhile** visiting Leicester?*

Infinitives are also possible after *worthwhile*.
> *We thought it might be **worthwhile to compare** the two years' accounts.*

Note also the structure *worth somebody's while*.
> *Would you like to do some gardening for me? I'll make it **worth your while**.*
> (= . . . I'll pay you enough.)

## 6 well worth

*Worth* can be modified by *well*.
> *Leicester's **well worth** visiting.* (NOT . . . ~~very worth~~ . . .)

# 633 would: various uses

## 1 forms

*Would*, the past form of *will*, is a modal auxiliary verb (see 353–354).
Questions and negatives are made without *do*; after *would*, we use an infinitive without *to*.
> ***Would** your daughter like to play with my little girl?*

Contractions are *'d*, *wouldn't*.
> *I**'d** like some advice, please.*
> *I wish she **wouldn't** take things so seriously.*

▶

## 2 *would* and *will*

*Would* is used as a softer, less definite form of *will* (see 629), or in some cases as the past of *will*.

## 3 indirect speech

In indirect speech, *would* is used after past reporting verbs where *will* was used in direct speech. For details, see 275.

    DIRECT SPEECH:    *Tomorrow will be fine.*

    INDIRECT SPEECH: *The forecast said the next day **would** be fine.*

*Would* itself does not usually change in indirect speech (see 278).

    DIRECT SPEECH:    ***Would** you like some help?*

    INDIRECT SPEECH: *She asked if I **would** like some help.*

## 4 future in the past

*Would* is also used to express the idea of 'future in the past' – to talk about a past action which had not yet happened at the time we are talking about. For details, see 221.

    *In Berlin, he first met the woman whom he **would** one day marry.*

    *There was a chance that my letter **would** arrive in time.*

## 5 interpersonal uses

*Would* is used in polite requests and offers as a softer form of *will*.

    ***Would** you open the window, please?*

    *If you **would** come this way . . .*

    ***Would** you mind standing up for a moment?*

    ***Would** you like tea, or **would** you prefer coffee?*

## 6 past willingness and refusals

*Would* can refer to past willingness of a general kind, but not to willingness to do something on a particular past occasion. Compare:

    *She **would** hoover, dust and iron, but she didn't like doing windows.*

    *She **agreed** to come and see me.* (NOT *She would come and see me.*)

But *would not* can be used to refer to a refusal on a particular past occasion.

    *I asked him very politely, but he **wouldn't** tell me.*

    *The car **wouldn't** start again this morning.*

For present refusals with *will not / won't*, see 629.4.

## 7 typical behaviour

*Would* is used as the past of *will* (see 629.7) to talk about typical behaviour in the past.

    *When she was old, she **would** sit in the corner talking to herself for hours.*

    *Sometimes he **would** bring me little presents without saying why.*

    *On Sundays when I was a child we **would** all get up early and go fishing.*

Sentences with stressed *would* can be used to criticise people's behaviour.

    *He was a nice boy, but he **WOULD** talk about himself all the time.*

Stressed *would* can also be used to criticise a single past action – the meaning is 'that's typical of you'.

    *You **WOULD** tell Mary about the party – I didn't want to invite her.*

## 8    *would* and *used to*

*Used to* (see 604) can refer to repeated actions and events in the past, in the same way as *would*.

> *When she was old, she **used to** sit in the corner talking to herself for hours.*
> *Sometimes he **used to** bring me little presents without saying why.*

But only *used to* can refer to past states. Compare:

> *When we were children we **would** / **used to** go skating every winter.*
> *I **used to** have an old Rolls-Royce.* (BUT NOT ~~I would have an old Rolls-Royce.~~)

And we use *used to*, not *would*, to talk about regular and important habitual behaviour.

> *Robert **used to** play a lot of football.* (NOT ~~Robert would play~~ . . .)
> *I **used to** smoke.* (NOT ~~I would smoke.~~)

## 9    conditional auxiliary: *I would . . . if*

*Would* (first person also *I/we should* – see 258) is often used as an auxiliary with verbs that refer to unreal or uncertain situations – for example in sentences with *if*. (Compare the use of *will/shall* to refer to more definite situations.)

> *I **would/should** tell you if I knew.*
> *It **would have been** nice if he'd thanked you.*
> *We **would/should** like to talk to you for a minute.*

For *would* after *wish*, see 630.5.     For *would* after *if only*, see 265.

# 634    *yes* and *no*

## 1    answers to negatives

In English, *yes* is used with affirmative sentences and *no* with negative sentences. In answers to negative questions and statements, *yes* and *no* are chosen according to the form of the answer, not in order to show agreement or disagreement with the speaker.

> *Aren't you going out? ~ **No, I'm not**.* (NOT ~~Yes, I'm not.~~)
> *I have no money. ~ **No, I haven't** either.* (NOT ~~Yes, I haven't too.~~)
> *Haven't you got a raincoat? ~ **Yes, I have**.* (NOT ~~No, I have.~~)

## 2    contradicting

Some languages have a special word for contradicting negative statements or suggestions (e.g. French *si* or German *doch*). English does not have a word like this. We often use a short answer structure (see 517).

> *The phone isn't working. ~ **(Yes,) it is**.* (NOT ~~The phone isn't working. ~ Yes.~~)

Affirmative sentences are contradicted with negative short answers.

> *It's raining. ~ **(No,) it isn't**.*

For more about negative questions, see 368.
For *yes* and *no* in answers to *Do/Would you mind . . .?*, see 351.

# Index